Principles of Public Speaking

Principles of Public Speaking

Edited by Michael Youngs

Cover image by rawpixel Located at: https://unsplash.com/photos/2QjrfhS08ro

Published by SUNY OER Services
Milne Library
State University of New York at Geneseo
Geneseo, NY 14454

Distributed by State University of New York Press

Except where expressly noted otherwise, the contents of this course are based on materials originally published by Lumen Learning CC-BY-SA Creative Commons Attribution-ShareAlike License. The original version of the materials as published as Introduction to Psychology may be access for free at https://courses.lumenlearning.com/suny-fmcc-publicspeakingprinciples/.

ISBN: 978-1-64176-037-9

This book was produced using Pressbooks.com, and PDF rendering was done by PrinceXML.

Contents

About This Book

Your Principles of Public Speaking textbook is a compilation of articles written by instructors for universities around the country. The entire compilation is provided free of charge online through a Creative Commons license. You can access or even copy all the material here, for your own reference, even after the semester ends.

Different Versions
An electronic version is made available via your course in Blackboard, through the College Library, and at https://courses.lumenlearning.com/suny-fmcc-publicspeakingprinciples/. You may also purchase a physical copy at the College Bookstore. The electronic version has access to multimedia content including video, slideshows, and interactive activities. The print version will have all the same reading material, but not include the multimedia content.

About the Author
There are many different authors; look to the "Licenses and Attributions" section at the end of each chapter to identify contributors. This compilation was edited by Michael Youngs at Fulton-Montgomery Community College.

Chapter 1: The Origins of Public Speaking

Objectives and Introduction

Origins of Public Speaking

By: Peter A. DeCaro, Ph.D.
University of Alaska, Fairbanks, AK

Learning Objectives

After reading this chapter, you should be able to:

- Identify the historical events that led up to democracy and recognize persuasion and public speaking as art forms in Athens, Greece.

- Describe the nature of public speaking in Athens during the 5th century B.C. and the role it played in a democratic society.

- Apply Plato's approach to dialectics and logic.

- Explain Aristotle's descriptions of rhetoric and public speaking.

- Describe the Roman Republic's adoption of rhetoric to public speaking.

- Elucidate Cicero's influence on the Roman Republic and public speaking.

- Describe the relevance of Quintillion's influence on the Roman Empire, rhetoric, and public speaking.

- Recognize the impact that St. Augustine, Christianity, and the Middle Ages had on rhetoric and public speaking.

- Clarify the roles that the Renaissance, Rationalism, and the Humanists had on the rebirth of rhetoric and public speaking.

- Explain the role that Classical rhetoric and the advent of psychology in the 18th and 19th centuries, known as the Modern Period, had on public speaking.

- Describe the influence of the Elocutionary Movement on public speaking.

- Describe the restoration of public speaking in the United States.

Introduction

The art of public speaking was practiced long before the Greeks wrote about it in their treatises more than 2,500 years ago. For Greek men, it was a way of life, a way of being, just like football and baseball are to us today. We attribute today's field of communication to the ancient Greeks because they were the first to systematize the art of public speaking, which they called "rhetoric."

The art, or use of public speaking, is quite different today than when it was practiced by the Greeks, and then the Romans. Theirs was a time that didn't have multimedia—television, radio, internet, movies, newspapers, and the like—for getting their messages to the masses. Instead, the Greeks and Romans informed, praised, or persuaded people the old fashion way—through discourse—otherwise known as the oral tradition. That meant speaking face to face with their audience.

"Parthenon" by Lisa Schreiber. CC-BY-NC-ND.

What we know today as the art of public speaking has undergone a number of changes since the days of Pericles, Cicero, and Quintilian. Public speaking brought us through the Middle Ages, experienced a rebirth as a result of the Renaissance, redefined to conquer and explain the known and unknown, interpreted to perform theatrics, and finally, along this historical path from the ancient Greeks and Romans, the art of public speaking was reinvented to accommodate the electronic age of the twentieth and twenty-first centuries.

So what is public speaking? Has it really changed since the days of the Greeks and Romans, St. Augustine, and Descartes? No, the concept of public speaking hasn't changed; it has basically remained the same. However, as the field of communication transitioned from one era to another, so did the understanding of public speaking.

This chapter is meant to give you, the reader, an accurate and detailed history of how the art of public speaking came into existence beginning with the ancient Greeks and Romans. We will learn how the Greeks came to develop the art and then were followed by the Romans who codified and refined public speaking. After the fall of the Roman Empire, we will see how public speaking was kept alive by just a few individuals until the Renaissance, when documents, or extants (which are treatises and writings that survived history), were discovered in Italy, and the approaches, both scientific and Humanistic, that defined the art of public speaking came about. Finally, we visit the latter part of the 19th and 20th centuries to understand contemporary public speaking.

> God, that all-powerful Creator of nature and architect of the world, has impressed man with no character so proper to distinguish him from other animals, as by the faculty of speech. – Quintilian

Attributions

Ancient Greece

The Rise of Democracy

In order to understand what contemporary public speaking is, we first must understand the genesis of public speaking. We begin with the Greeks and rhetoric. **Rhetoric**, as defined by Aristotle, is the "faculty of discovering in the particular case all the available means of persuasion."[1] For the Greeks, rhetoric, or the art of public speaking, was first and foremost a means to persuade. Greek society relied on oral expression, which also included the ability to inform and give speeches of praise, known then as epideictic (to praise or blame someone) speeches. The ability to practice rhetoric in a public forum was a direct result of generations of change in the governing structures of Attica (a

"Biblioteca" by queulat00. CC-BY.

peninsula jutting into the Aegean Sea), with the city of Athens located at its center. The citizens of Athens were known as Athenians, and were among the most prosperous of people in the Mediterranean region.

> Speech is the mirror of action. – Solon

It was in the Homeric Period, also known as "The Age of Homer," between 850 B.C. and 650 B.C., that an evolution in forms of government from monarchy to oligarchy, and tyranny to eventual democracy, began in ancient Greece. Homer was the major figure of ancient Greek literature and the author of the earliest epic poems, the Iliad and the Odyssey. In the year 630 B.C., the last tyrant of Attica, Ceylon, seized the Acropolis, which was the seat of government in Athens, and established himself as the ruler of all Attica. He didn't rule for long. Ceylon was overthrown within weeks by farmers and heavily armed foot soldiers known as hoplites. Many of Ceylon's followers were killed, and the few that escaped death fled into the mountains. Thus, Athenian democracy was born.

---

1. Kennedy, G. (1963). *The Art of Persuasion in Greece*. Princeton: University Press. p. 19

In 621 B.C., the citizens of Athens commissioned **Draco**, who was an elder citizen considered to be the wisest of the Greeks, to sort their laws into an organized system known as codification, because until that time, they simply remained an oral form of custom and tradition and weren't written like the laws of today. Draco was concerned only with criminal offenses, which until this time had been settled through blood feud (an eye-for-an-eye type of revenge between families) or rulings by the King. Draco established courts, complete with juries, to hear cases of homicide, assault, and robbery. By conforming the codes for criminal offenses into standards of practice, Draco began the tradition of law, where cases were decided on clearly enunciated crimes and penalties determined by statute rather than by the whims of the nobility. His laws helped constitute a surge in Athenian democracy.

In 593 B.C. Draco's laws were reformed by Solon, an Athenian legislator, who introduced the first form of popular democracy into Athens. Solon's courts became the model for the Romans and centuries later for England and America. Murphy and Katula argued: "It is with Solon's reforms that we mark the unalterable impulse toward popular government in western civilization."[2] The Athenian period of democratization included legislative as well as judicial reform.

It was during the reign of **Pericles**, from 461 B.C. to 429 B.C., that Athens achieved its greatest glory. Some of these accomplishments included the installation of a pure democracy to maintain, a liberalized judicial system to include poor citizens so that they could serve on juries, and the establishment of a popular legislative assembly to review annually all laws. In addition, he established the right for any Athenian citizen to propose or oppose a law during assembly. Pericles' achievements far exceeded those mentioned. Because of his efforts, Athens became the crossroads of the world—the center of western civilization—and with it came the need for public speaking.

"Persuasion is the civilized substitute for harsh authority and ruthless force," wrote R.T. Oliver.[3] Oliver said that the recipients of any persuasive discourse must feel free to make a choice. In a free society it is persuasion that decides rules, determines behavior,and acts as the governing agent in human physical and mental activities. In every free society individuals are continuously attempting to change the thoughts and/or actions of others. It is a fundamental concept of a free society. Ian Harvey suggested that the technique of persuasion is the technique of persuading free people to a pattern of life; and persuasion is the only possible means of combining freedom and order.[4] That combination successfully achieved is the solution to the overriding problems of our time. Rhetoric (persuasion), public speaking and democracy are inextricable. As long as there is rhetoric, and public speaking to deliver that message, there will exist democracy; and as long as there is democracy, there will exist rhetoric and public speaking.

"Discurso Funebre Pericles" by Philipp Foltz. Public domain.

2. Murphy James J. and Katula, R.A. (1995). *A Synoptic History of Classical Rhetoric*. 2nd ed. Davis: Ca. Hermagoras Press.
3. Oliver, R.T. (1950). *Persuasive Speaking*. New York: Longmans, Green and Co. p.1
4. Harvey, I. (1951). *The Technique of Persuasion*. London: The Falcon Press.

I believe that the will of the people is resolved by a strong leadership. Even in a democratic society, events depend on a strong leadership with a strong power of persuasion, and not on the opinion of the masses. – Yitzhak Shamir

The Nature of Rhetoric

Pericles' democracy established the need for training in public speaking. Greek assemblies debated old and new laws on a yearly basis. The court-rooms that Solon reformed now bristled with litigation. Pericles' juries numbered between 500 and 2,000 people, so speaking at a public trial was similar to speaking at a public meeting. And to speak at a legislative assembly required serious, highly developed, and refined debate, because at stake generally were issues of peace and war. Murphy and Katula stated that the Athenian citizens realized that their very future often depended on their ability to speak persuasively.[5] Public speaking was an Olympic event where the winner received an olive wreath and was paraded through his town like a hero. Thus, Athens became a city of words, a city dominated by the orator. Athens witnessed the birth of what we know today as *rhetoric*.

"Socrates" by Coyau. Coyau / Wikimedia Commons / CC-BY-SA-3.0.

To say that rhetoric played an important role in Greek and Roman life would be an understatement. The significance of rhetoric and **oratory** was evident in Greek and Roman education. George Kennedy[6] noted that rhetoric played the central role in ancient education. At about the age of fourteen, (only) boys were sent to the school of the rhetorician for theoretical instruction in public speaking, which was an important part of the teaching of the sophists. Public speaking was basic to the educational system of Isocrates (the most famous of the sophists); and it was even taught by Aristotle."[7]

Dialectics and Logic

It is important to note that rhetoric and oratory are not the same, although we use rhetoric and oratory synonymously; nor are rhetoric and dialectic the same. Zeno of Elea (5th century B.C.), a Greek mathematician and philosopher of the Eleatic school, is considered to be the inventor of dialectical reasoning. However, it is Plato, another Greek philosopher and teacher of Aristotle, and not Socrates, that we attribute the popularity of dialectical reasoning. **Dialectic** can be defined as a debate intended to resolve a conflict between two contradictory (or polar opposites), or apparently contradictory ideas or elements logically, establishing truths on both sides rather than disproving one argument. Both rhetoric and dialectic are forms of critical analysis.

Among the most significant thinkers of the fifth century B.C. were the traveling lecturers known as **sophists**. They were primarily teachers of political excellence who dealt with practical and immediate issues of the day, and whose investigations led in many instances to a **philosophical relativism**. Unlike Socrates and Plato, the sophists believed that absolute truth was unknowable and perhaps nonexistent,

5. Murphy and Katula 1995
6. Kennedy, G. (1963). *The Art of Persuasion in Greece*. Princeton: University Press.
7. Kennedy 1963, p. 7

especially in the sphere of forensics and political life, where no universal principles could be accepted. Courses of action had to be presented in persuasive fashion. Unlike the sophists, Socrates taught that truth was absolute and knowable and that a clear distinction should be made between dialectic, the question and answer method of obtaining the one correct answer, and rhetoric, which does not seem interested in the universal validity of the answer but only in its persuasiveness for the moment. Plato developed this criticism of rhetoric to such an extent that he is the most famous and most thorough-going of the enemies of rhetoric. Plato preferred the philosophical method of formal inquiry known as *dialectic*.

> In making a speech one must study three points: first, the means of producing persuasion; second, the language; third, the proper arrangement of the various parts of the speech. – Aristotle

The Rhetorical Approach

Aristotle wrote that rhetoric is the faculty of discovering in the particular case all the available means of persuasion. He cited four uses of rhetoric: (1) by it truth and justice maintain their natural superiority; (2) it is suited to popular audiences, since they cannot follow scientific demonstration; (3) it teaches us to see both sides of an issue, and to refute unfair arguments; and (4) it is a means of self-defense. For Aristotle, rhetoric is the process of *developing* a persuasive argument, and oratory is the process of *delivering* that argument. He stated that the "authors of 'Arts of Speaking' have built up but a small portion of the art of rhetoric; because this art consists of proofs alone—all else is but accessory. Yet these writers say nothing of enthymemes, the very body and substance of persuasion."[8]

"The School of Athens" by Raphael. Public domain.

Aristotle said that rhetoric has no special subject-matter; that is, it isn't limited to particular topics and nothing else. He claimed that certain forms of persuasion come from outside and do not belong to the art itself. This refers to, for example, witnesses, forced confessions, and contracts that Aristotle said are external to the art of speaking. He considered these to be *non-artistic* proofs. Aristotle identified what he considered to be *artistic* proofs which must be supplied by the speaker's invention (the "faculty of discovering" that Aristotle used in his definition of rhetoric); and these artistic means of persuasion are threefold. They consist in (1) evincing through the speech a personal character that will win the confidence of the listener; (2) engaging the listener's emotions; and (3) proving a truth, real or apparent, by argument. Aristotle concluded that the *mastery* of the art, then, called for (1) the power of logical reasoning (logos); a knowledge of character (ethos); and a knowledge of the emotions (pathos).

In summary, Plato had opposed rhetoric to dialectic; Aristotle compared the two: both have to do with things which are within the field of knowledge of all men and are not part of any specialized science.

8. (Book 1, p. 1)

They do not differ in nature, but in subject and form: dialectic is primarily philosophical, rhetoric political; dialectic consists of question and answer, rhetoric of a set speech. Both can be reduced to a system and thus are properly called "art."

Rhetoric is the art of ruling the minds of men. – Plato

Aristotle became the primary source of all later rhetorical theory. Eventually, the dispute between rhetoric and philosophy in the time of Aristotle had ended in a compromise in which philosophy accepted rhetoric as a means to a goal. The rhetoric of not only Cicero and Quintilian, but of the Middle Ages, of the Renaissance, and of modern times, is basically Aristotelian.

Attributions

CC licensed content, Shared previously

- Chapter 2 Ancient Greece. **Authored by**: Peter A. DeCaro, Ph.D.. **Provided by**: University of Alaska, Fairbanks, AK. **Located at**: http://publicspeakingproject.org/psvirtualtext.html. **Project**: The Public Speaking Project. **License**: *CC BY-NC-ND: Attribution-NonCommercial-NoDerivatives*

- 475_efeso_biblioteca_celso. **Authored by**: queulat00. **Located at**: https://flic.kr/p/axRstZ. **License**: *CC BY: Attribution*

- Parc de Versailles, Rond-Point des Philosophes, Isocrate, Pierre Granier MR1870 04. **Authored by**: Coyau. **Located at**: http://commons.wikimedia.org/wiki/File:Parc_de_Versailles,_Rond-Point_des_Philosophes,_Isocrate,_Pierre_Granier_MR1870_04.jpg. **License**: *CC BY-SA: Attribution-ShareAlike*

Public domain content

- Discurso funebre pericles. **Authored by**: Philipp Foltz. **Located at**: http://commons.wikimedia.org/wiki/File:Discurso_funebre_pericles.PNG. **License**: *Public Domain: No Known Copyright*

- Sanzio 01 Plato Aristotle. **Authored by**: Raphael. **Provided by**: Web Gallery of Art. **Located at**: http://commons.wikimedia.org/wiki/File:Sanzio_01_Plato_Aristotle.jpg. **License**: *Public Domain: No Known Copyright*

The Roman Republic's Adoption of Rhetoric

As Athens declined in power, a new force emerged, the Roman Republic. The Senate was the only permanent governing body and the only body where debate was possible. In order to debate, one had to know the persuasive art of rhetoric and oratory, or public speaking.

Greek rhetoric appeared in republican Rome in the middle of the second century B.C. The teachers of rhetoric were Greek, and they taught in both Greek and Latin. Eventually Roman teachers were produced. The remarkable thing about Roman rhetorical theory, wrote Murphy and Katula,[1] is that it appeared for the first time in its fullest form around 90 B.C., with very little direct evidence as to how it developed into its completed form. Sometime after Aristotle, writers refined and identified the subject of rhetoric into five parts—Invention, Arrangement, Style, Memory, and Delivery. These five canons are still a part of public speaking in education today. Two Romans stand out as quintessential figures of Roman rhetoric, Cicero and Quintilian.

"Cicero Denounces Catiline" by Cesare Maccari. Public domain.

Cicero's Influence

Marcus Tullius Cicero was born on January 3, 106 BC and was murdered on December 7, 43 BC. His life coincided with the decline and fall of the Roman Republic, and he was an important participant in many of the significant political events of his time. He is considered to be the greatest of the Roman orators, and was, among other things, a lawyer, politician, and philosopher.

1. Murphy James J. and Katula, R.A. (1995). A Synoptic History of Classical Rhetoric. 2nd ed. Davis: Ca. Hermagoras Press.

In Cicero's Rome the government eventually came under the control of a well-trained ruling class. Legal training became an integral part of this ruling class. Roman rhetoric provided rules for all forms of oratory; however, legal speaking became the primary emphasis of textbooks.

Cicero is noted for writing the *De Inventione* when he was about twenty years old. It is important because it gives us insight into the general nature of rhetorical instruction in the first century B.C. And later in life, as a more mature individual, he wrote the *De Oratore*, which he compared and contrasted to the *De Inventione*. Cicero's contributions to the theory of oral discourse included the belief that the orator must have a firm foundation of general knowledge. Cicero believed that the perfect orator should be able to speak wisely and eloquently on any subject with a dignified, restrained delivery. Corbett wrote that "Cicero felt that the perfect orator had to be conversant with many subjects. In order to invent his arguments, the perfect orator must have a command of a wide range of knowledge."[2] Cicero despised the shallowness of orators who depended exclusively on perfect diction and elegant words that lacked substance. His ideal person was the philosopher-statesman-learned orator who used rhetoric to mold public opinion.

> It is not by muscle, speed, or physical dexterity that great things are achieved, but by reflection, force of character, and judgment. – Marcus Tullius Cicero

Cicero firmly held that oratory was more than legal pleadings or a school subject. Cicero considered oratory to be the highest form of intellectual activity and an instrument indispensable for the welfare of the state. In addition, he combined the three functions of the orator to the three levels of style. He was able to provide his colleagues with a broad interpretation of **Atticism,** and he revived the best of the Greek theoreticians and practitioners of oratory. It can be said that Cicero was an idealist. As a student of Greek rhetoric, he encouraged his contemporaries to practice the same ideals, ethics and standards of the past. His primary focus was to adapt Hellenic (ancient Greece) doctrine to the needs of Rome. During Cicero's time, Rome had become a place where the free expression of ideas was no longer tolerated. The government had been corrupted.

2. Corbett, E.P.J. (1965). Classical Rhetoric for the Modern Student. New York: Oxford University Press. p.542

Quintilian's Influence

Marcus Fabius Quintilianus (A.D. 35–95) was a cele-
brated orator, rhetorician, Latin teacher and writer who promoted rhetorical theory from ancient Greece and from the
height of Roman rhetoric. His work on rhetoric, the *Institutio Oratoria*, is an exhaustive volume of twelve books and
was a major contribution to educational theory and literary
criticism. Many later rhetoricians, especially from the
Renaissance, derived their rhetorical theory directly from
this text.

> The mind is exercised by the variety and multiplicity
> of the subject matter, while the character is molded by
> the contemplation of virtue and vice. – Quintilian

"Quintillian" by unknown. Public domain.

During the hundred years plus which elapsed between the
death of Cicero and the birth of Quintilian, education had
vastly spread all over the Roman Empire, with rhetoric as
the most important part of education. But by Quintilian's
time[3], the popular trend in oratory was not rhetoric in the traditional sense, rather it was called "silver
Latin," a style that favored ornate embellishment over clarity and precision. During this time rhetoric was
primarily composed of three aspects: the theoretical (contemplating new rhetorical methods), the educational (teaching students the five canons), and the practical (courtroom and political speeches).

Quintilian's *Institutio Oratoria* may be read as a reaction against this trend; it advocated a return to simpler
and clearer language. Gwynn wrote that Quintilian adopted Cicero's oratory prowess as the model for this
return to rhetorical tradition; because during the previous century, Cicero's far more concise style was
the standard.[4] Quintilian disliked the excessive ornamentation popular in the oratory style of his contemporaries (silver Latin). Quintilian believed that deviating from natural language and the natural order of
thought in pursuit of an over-elaborate style created confusion in both the orator and his audience.

Much of this work dealt with the technical aspects of rhetoric and the *Institutio Oratoria* stood—along
with Aristotle's *Rhetoric* and Cicero's writing—as one of the ancient world's greatest works on rhetoric.
According to Barrett,[5] he organized the practice of oratory into five canons: *inventio* (discovery of arguments), *dispositio* (arrangement of arguments), *elocutio* (expression or style), *memoria* (memorization),
and *pronuntiatio* (delivery). This thorough presentation reflects his extensive experience as an orator and
teacher, and in many ways the work can be seen as the culmination of Greek and Roman rhetorical theory.

Quintilian emphasized the value of rhetoric as a moral force in the community. "My aim," said Quintilian,
"is the education of the perfect orator."[6] Since the function of the orator is to advance the cause of truth and
good government, Quintilian said he must by definition be a good man morally and not just an effective

---

3. Gwynn, Aubrey. *Roman Education from Cicero to Quintilian.* Oxford: Clarendon Press, 1926.
4. Gwynn 1926
5. Barrett, H. (1987). *The Sophists: Rhetoric, Democracy, and Plato's Idea of Sophistry.* Novato, CA; Chandler & Sharp Publishers.
6. Quintilian. (1987). Carbondale: Illinois University Press. "Revised and enlarged version of On the early education of the citizen-
orator, published by Bobbs-Merrill Company, 1965." I. Pref. 8

speaker. According to Gwynn this was a revolutionary doctrine in the development of rhetoric: Aristotle saw rhetoric as morally neutral, a human tool whose moral character resided in the speaker not the art.[7] Quintilian saw rhetoric as a means for a better self- governing society; to make moral goodness integral to oratory.

How does Quintilian's perspective on rhetoric compare to Plato, Aristotle, and Cicero? Plato defined rhetoric as a philosophy rather than an art, an unnecessary tool. Plato was concerned more with the truth than Quintilian, while Aristotle believed that rhetoric was "finding the available means of persuasion." Quintilian challenged this definition because he felt that Aristotle had omitted the fact that anyone, not just the learned, can persuade. To Quintilian, rhetoric was "the good man speaking well."[8]

Quintilian's system of rhetorical education aimed at the creation of the ideal Roman orator: a virtuous, efficient, courageous, eloquent man. His goal was to prepare an orator-philosopher-statesman who could combine wisdom with persuasion for the sake of regulating the state. It was this insistence on the intellectual and moral training of the aspiring orator that made Cicero and Quintilian the two most potent classical influences on rhetorical education in England and America.

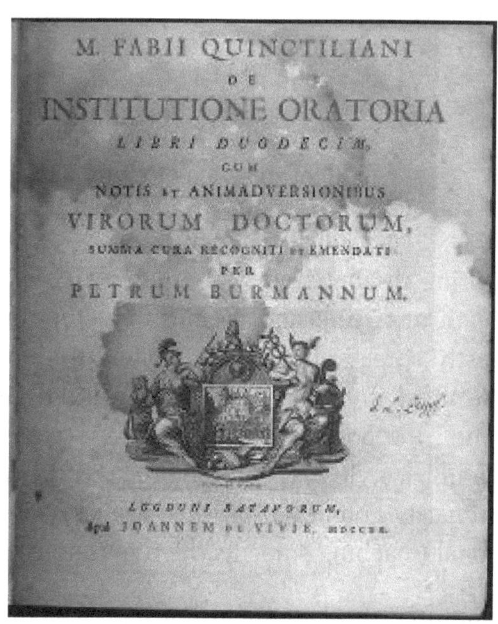

"Title page of Quintilian's Institutio oratoria" by Aristeas. Public domain.

From the death of Quintilian (about A.D. 100) until the fall of the Roman Empire (A.D. 410), very little was contributed to the rhetorical doctrine. A Greek cultural movement in the second and third centuries A.D. (although some sources place this movement during the fourth and fifth centuries A.D.) called the "Second Sophistic," was centered in Athens.[9] However, the art of oratory focused more on excessive performance (delivery) and professional speech making rather than the art of intellectual development. There isn't a total gap between Quintilian and medieval rhetoric. This period produced works by Victorinus, who wrote a systematic commentary on Cicero's rhetoric, Aquila Romanus, Fortunatianus, and Sulpitius Victor. They are mentioned because they reflect the type of rhetorical education common to the third and fourth centuries and provide a bridge between classical and medieval rhetoric.

Attributions

CC licensed content, Shared previously

- Chapter 2 The Roman Republic. **Authored by**: Peter A. DeCaro, Ph.D.. **Provided by**: University of Alaska, Fairbanks, AK. **Located at**: http://publicspeakingproject.org/psvirtualtext.html. **Project**: The Public Speaking Project. **License**: *CC BY-NC-ND: Attribution-NonCommercial-NoDerivatives*

Public domain content

- Cicero Denounces Catiline. **Authored by**: Cesare Maccari. **Located at**: http://commons.wikimedia.org/wiki/File:Maccari-Cicero.jpg. **License**: *Public Domain: No Known Copyright*. **License Terms**: This image (or other media file) is in the public domain because its copyright has expired.

- Quintillian. **Authored by**: Unknown. **Located at**: http://commons.wikimedia.org/wiki/File:Quintilian.jpg. **License**: *Public*

7. Gwynn 1926
8. Honeycutt, L. (2007). http://honeyl.public.iastate.edu/quintilian/index.html
9. Barrett, H. (1987). *The Sophists: Rhetoric, Democracy, and Plato's Idea of Sophistry*. Novato, CA; Chandler & Sharp Publishers.

Domain: No Known Copyright. **License Terms**: This image (or other media file) is in the public domain because its copyright has expired.

- Quintilian, Institutio oratoria ed. Burman Leiden 1720, title page. **Authored by**: Aristeas. **Located at**: http://commons.wikimedia.org/wiki/File:Quintilian,_Institutio_oratoria_ed._Burman_(Leiden_1720),_title_page,_detail.jpg#mediaviewer/File:Quintilian,_Institutio_oratoria_ed._Burman_(Leiden_1720),_title_page.jpg. **License**: *Public Domain: No Known Copyright*

The Middle Ages

A thing is not necessarily true because badly uttered, nor false because spoken magnificently. – Saint Augustine

St. Augustine

The Middle Ages (400–1400 A.D.) followed the Second Sophistic movement, wrote Foss,[1] and during this period, rhetoric became aligned with preaching, letter writing, and education. As Christianity grew in power, rhetoric was condemned as a pagan art; many Christians believed that the rhetorical ideas expressed by the pagans of classical Greece and Rome should not be studied and that one's belief in Christian truth brought with it the ability to communicate that truth effectively. St. Augustine had been a teacher of rhetoric before converting to Christianity in A.D. 386, and is considered to be the only major thinker on rhetoric associated with the Middle Ages. Rhetoric played a role in education in the Middle Ages as one of the three great liberal arts. Along with logic and grammar, rhetoric is considered part of the trivium of learning, similar in function to the West's three R's of reading, writing and arithmetic today.

Christianity

The clearest bridge to the Middle Ages, according to Murphy and Katula,[2] is found in the *De doctrina christiana* of Saint Augustine (354–430 A.D.). Augustine divided his work into four books. The first three deal with "sign," or "that which is used to signify something else."[3] For example, language was for Augustine a set of conventional signs which human beings agree to show each other to convey ideas and feelings. He posited that the world itself is a sign of God. Augustine argued that human beings needed to know the nature of signs in order to understand the language of the Bible, and then needed to understand rhetoric in

1. Foss, S.K.; Foss, K.A.; Trapp, R. (1991). *Contemporary Perspectives on Rhetoric*. Prospect Heights, IL: Waveland Press.
2. Murphy James J. and Katula, R.A. (1995). *A Synoptic History of Classical Rhetoric*. 2nd ed. Davis: Ca. Hermagoras Press.
3. Robertson, D.W. (1958). *Saint Augustine on Christian Doctrine*. New York: Library of Liberal Arts.

order to explain the Christian message, and then teach it to others. He believed every Christian was obligated to spread Christ's message (e.g. Matthew 18:20), thus, rhetoric became an obligation to every Christian.

His influence prevailed, and the Christian Church adopted the Ciceronian rhetoric as a guide to preachers. Saint Augustine is sometimes called "the last classical man and the first medieval man." With respect to rhetoric, Foss et al.,[4] stated that this is certainly true, and it is possible to see him an agent of communication from one age to another.

Attributions

CC licensed content, Shared previously

- Chapter 2 The Middle Ages. **Authored by**: Peter A. DeCaro, Ph.D.. **Provided by**: University of Alaska, Fairbanks, AK. **Located at**: http://publicspeakingproject.org/psvirtualtext.html. **Project**: The Public Speaking Project. **License**: *CC BY-NC-ND: Attribution-NonCommercial-NoDerivatives*

Public domain content

- Image of St. Augustine. **Provided by**: University of Texas at Austin. **Located at**: https://commons.wikimedia.org/wiki/File:Augustinus_1.jpg. **Project**: The Hundred Greatest Men. **License**: *Public Domain: No Known Copyright*

---

4. Foss et al. 1991

The Renaissance

The end of the Middle Ages was witnessed by the birth of the **Renaissance** (1400–1600), and with it the rise of Humanism, a movement that brought such thinkers and writers as Petrarch, Francis Bacon, Albertus Magnus, Joseph Webber, Ben Jonson, William Shakespeare, Thomas More, Descartes, Hobbes, Locke, Hume, and Kant. This emergence also produced the great discoveries of Copernicus, Galileo, Kepler, and Newton. In architecture it brought about the revival of the classical style. And in the fine arts it inspired new schools of painting in Italy, such as Raphael, Leonardo, Bellini, Michael Angelo, Giorgione, and the Flemish school in the Netherlands.

"Shakespeare" by National Portrait Gallery. Public domain.

The Renaissance is the name of the great intellectual and cultural movement of the revival of interest in classical culture that occurred in the 14th, 15th, and 16th centuries. The Renaissance began in Italy as a major revolt against an intellectually barren medieval spirit, and especially against scholasticism, in favor of intellectual freedom. A hunger developed for all things classical. Greek scholars were encouraged to travel to Italy. Florence became the cradle of classical revival. Latin classics were in demand. Libraries were built. And schools for the study of Greek and Latin in their classic forms were opened in Rome and other major cities.

The Humanists

The second period of the Renaissance produced a continued passion for classical study, which was later coined "Humanism" in 1808 by a German educator, F.J. Niethammer, to describe a program of study distinct from scientific and engineering educational programs. Of all the practices of Renaissance Europe, nothing is used to distinguish the Renaissance from the Middle Ages more than Humanism as both a program and a philosophy.

The Humanists began by rediscovering lost Latin texts, rather than searching for classical Greek extants. The two most important classical authors of the Renaissance were Cicero and Quintilian, not Aristotle or Plato. Petrarch spearheaded the rediscovery of Cicero; and one of the texts he found, the Brutus, a handbook on rhetoric, became one of the most important books in the Renaissance. Quintilian later became the basis of the Humanistic education curriculum. The most important influences on Petrarch were Cicero and Augustine. He took from Cicero the principles of composing Latin and much of his philosophy; and from Augustine he derived his ideas about the relationship of the human to the divine. Throughout the Renaissance, the single most important author, classical or otherwise, during the entire Humanist movement is Cicero.

"Friedrich Immanuel Niethammer" by DALIBRI. Public domain.

> Love is the crowning grace of humanity, the holiest right of the soul, the golden link which binds us to duty and truth, the redeeming principle that chiefly reconciles the heart to life, and is prophetic of eternal good. – Petrarch

Interested in the human world as constructed through language, rather than the natural world, the Humanists focused on the human epistemologically. They emphasized the world of human culture and language, believing in the power of the word not only because it gives those with a command of it special advantage in daily interactions, but because of its inherent capacity to disclose to the world of humans. The Italian Humanists believed rhetoric, not philosophy, to be the primary discipline because it is through language that humans gain access to the world.[1]

---

1. Foss, S.K.; Foss, K.A.; Trapp, R. (1991). *Contemporary Perspectives on Rhetoric*. Prospect Heights, IL: Waveland Press.

A second trend in rhetoric also began during the Renaissance — a trend that dominated the theories of rhetoric to follow. Rationalism, represented by the work of Peter Ramus (1515–1572) and René Descartes (1596–1650), sought objective, scientific truths that would exist for all time. Foss et al., wrote that, "Not surprisingly, the rationalists had little patience for rhetoric: while poetry and oratory might be aesthetically pleasing, they were seen as having no connection to science and truth."[2]

Howell (1956) claimed that Ramus was a French scholar who made rhetoric subordinate to logic by placing invention and organization under the rubric of logic and leaving rhetoric with only style and delivery. Ramus argued that invention should not be an intellectual process governed by contingencies, as Aristotle or Cicero would have it. He presented invention as a rhetorical procedure that must conform to the theory of logic. He successfully argued that rhetoric must be concerned with the canons of style and delivery only. Ramus' identification of rhetoric with style launched a denigration of invention that lasted for centuries.[3] (Virtualology.com, 2007).

"Portrait of René Descartes" by Frans Hals. Public domain.

René Descartes is one of the most important Western philosophers of the past few centuries. During his lifetime, Descartes was just as famous as an original physicist, physiologist and mathematician. But it is as a highly original philosopher that he is most frequently read today. He attempted to restart philosophy in a fresh direction. For example, his philosophy refused to accept the Aristotelian and Scholastic traditions that had dominated philosophical thought throughout the Medieval period; it attempted to fully integrate philosophy with the "new" sciences; and Descartes changed the relationship between philosophy and theology. Descartes believed that in order to reach certain knowledge, the foundations of thought provided by others had to be abandoned. He was willing to accept only that which would withstand all doubt. He rejected truths established in speech or in the course of social or political action. Language became only a means of communicating the truth once it was discovered, not a powerful sphere in which human life emerges.[4]

> I think; therefore I am. – Rene Descartes

Attributions

CC licensed content, Shared previously

- Chapter 2 The Renaissance. **Authored by**: Peter A. DeCaro, Ph.D.. **Provided by**: University of Alaska, Fairbanks, AK. **Located at**: http://publicspeakingproject.org/psvirtualtext.html. **Project**: The Public Speaking Project. **License**: *CC BY-NC-ND: Attribution-NonCommercial-NoDerivatives*

Public domain content

- Shakespeare. **Provided by**: The National Portrait Gallery. **Located at**: https://commons.wikimedia.org/wiki/File:Shakespeare.jpg.

2. Foss et al. 1991, p. 8
3. Virtualology.com (2007). Retrieve on January 26, 2007 from http://www.virtualology.com/rhetoricaltheory/peterramus.com/
4. Foss, et al., 1991

License: *Public Domain: No Known Copyright*

- Friedrich Immanuel Niethammer. **Authored by**: DALIBRI. **Located at**: https://commons.wikimedia.org/wiki/File:Friedrich_Immanuel_Niethammer.jpg. **License**: *Public Domain: No Known Copyright*

- Frans Hals - Portret van Renu00e9 Descartes. **Authored by**: Frans Hals. **Located at**: http://commons.wikimedia.org/wiki/File:Frans_Hals_-_Portret_van_Ren%C3%A9_Descartes.jpg. **License**: *Public Domain: No Known Copyright*

The Modern Period

Dominated by the rationalism instituted by Descartes and Ramus, modern rhetoric continued to promote the importance of science and philosophy over rhetoric. Francis Bacon (1561–1626) was a prominent figure of the modern period. He was concerned with the lack of scholarly progress during the Middle Ages and sought to promote a revival of secular knowledge through an empirical examination of the world. His definition of rhetoric suggests his effort to bring the power of language under rational control, ". . . the duty of rhetoric is to apply Reason to Imagination for the better moving of the will."[1] Bacon, then, advanced the scientific approach to the study of rhetoric that would support the three trends of modern rhetorical thought.

The three trends in rhetoric that characterized the modern period are—epistemological, belletristic, and elocutionist. **Epistemology** is the study of the origin, nature, methods, and limits of human knowledge. Epistemological thinkers, such as Bacon, sought to change classical approaches in terms of modern developments in psychology. They attempted to understand rhetoric in relation to the psychological process and contributed to the development of a rhetoric premised on human nature.

"Francis Bacon" by Drebbel. Public domain.

The Epistemological Tradition

George Campbell (1719–1796) and Richard Whately (1758–1859) exemplify the best of the epistemological tradition. Campbell authored *The Philosophy of Rhetoric* (1776). He drew on Aristotle, Cicero, and Quintilian as well as faculty psychology and empiricism (experience of the senses) of his times. Faculty psychology attempted to explain human behavior in terms of the five faculties of the mind—understanding, memory, imagination, passion, and will—and Campbell's definition of rhetoric was directed to these

1. Dick, H.C., ed. (1955). Selected Writings of Francis Bacon. New York: Modern Library. p.100).

faculties. Campbell distinguished three types of evidence—mathematical axioms, derived through reasoning; consciousness, or the result of sensory stimulation; and common sense, an intuitive sense shared by virtually all humans.[2]

> As one may bring himself to believe almost anything he is inclined to believe, it makes all the difference whether we begin or end with the inquiry, "What is truth?" – Richard Whately

Richard Whately published *Elements of Rhetoric* in 1828. His view of rhetoric was similar to Campbell's in its dependence on psychology, but he shifted from Campbell by making argumentation the focus of the art of rhetoric. He is also known for his analysis of presumption [of innocence] and burden of proof, which paved the way for modern argumentation and debate practices. The epistemologists combined their knowledge of classical rhetoric and contemporary psychology to create rhetorics based on an understanding of human nature. By doing this, they introduced audience- centered approaches to rhetoric and pioneered the way for contemporary investigations with audience analysis.

The Belles Lettres Movement

The second direction rhetoric took in the modern period is known as the belles lettre movement; the term, in French, literally means "fine or beautiful letters." This is a departure from both the rationalists and elocutionists because this form of literature valued the aesthetic qualities of writing rather than any informative value it may have. The scope of what was considered to be rhetoric broadened to include all of the fine arts of the period, poetry, music, drama, gardening and architecture, along with oral discourse, writing and criticism.

Hugh Blair is best known for his advocacy of the belletristic movement. He was a Presbyterian preacher and occupied the Chair of Rhetoric and Belles Lettres at the University of Edinburgh. He had a number of publications, but his most well-known was the *Lectures on Rhetoric and Belles Lettres*, which was based on his lectures. *Lectures* is important because it drew on the works of Cicero and Quintilian and combined them with the modern works of Addison and Burke to become one of the first whole language guides.

"Hugh Blair" by John Kay. Public domain.

Blair's theories were founded in the belief that the principles of rhetoric evolve from the principles of nature.

> Gentleness corrects whatever is offensive in our manner. – Hugh Blair

2. Foss, S.K.; Foss, K.A.; Trapp, R. (1991). *Contemporary Perspectives on Rhetoric*. Prospect Heights, IL: Waveland Press.

The Elocutionary Movement

The **elocutionary movement**, the third rhetorical trend of the modern period, reached its height in the mid- eighteenth century. Before the Elocutionary Movement most scholars of rhetoric quickly assimilated the Latin *elocutio* (style) with the English word elocution. However, by the eighteenth century scholars more accurately began to regard elocution as the Latin *pronunciato* (delivery). This change in association gave rise to the Elocutionary Movement, a movement that focused primarily on delivery. Although there are many theorists associated with the Elocutionary Movement, the most widely publicized is Thomas Sheridan. Sheridan was an Irish actor and educator of elocution. He wanted to reform the educational system of Britain to correct the serious neglect of rhetorical delivery-elocution. This belief not only involved the voice, but also incorporated the entire person with facial expressions, gesture, posture and movement.

"Thomas Sheridan" by Roger Ingpen. Public domain.

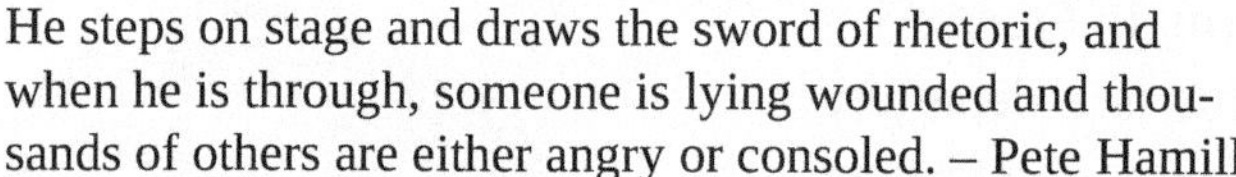

He steps on stage and draws the sword of rhetoric, and when he is through, someone is lying wounded and thousands of others are either angry or consoled. – Pete Hamill

However, the elocutionists of this period regarded themselves as rhetoricians and their work as rhetoric. There were a number of reasons why the movement flourished. During the eighteenth and nineteenth century an increasing number of professions required the skill of public speaking. As a result, a needed change from style to delivery developed in response to the poor delivery styles of contemporary preachers, lawyers, and other public figures.

Foss et al.[3] explain that like the epistemologists, the elocutionists were concerned about contributing to a more scientific understanding of the human being and believed that their observations on voice and gesture—characteristics unique to humans—constituted such contribution. The elocutionists also sought to determine the effects of delivery on the various faculties of the mind, thus continuing the link with modern psychology.

3. Foss et al. 1991

The practices the elocutionists promoted eventually led to their demise. Toward the end of their success the public began to see rhetoric as empty, insincere speaking that hid beneath the mask of sophistication. It declined as a subject matter of study and of teaching. As college curriculum became more diverse and specialized, new departments were formed that did not include rhetoric as a multidisciplinary art; rather, instruction was generally limited to departments of English—until a major shift again occurred in the development of rhetoric in the United States in 1910. In 1914 a new association, the Speech Communication Association, was formed in the United States by a small group of public speaking teachers who wanted to restore the rich qualities and scope that were once attributed to rhetoric. Today, this organization is called the National Communication Association.

"Cicero" by Tobiasnordmark. Public domain.

Conclusion, Review Questions, and Activities

Conclusion

We have explored a brief history of rhetoric, the basis for persuasion, from the time of Aristotle to the beginning of the twentieth century. This exploration is by no means complete, but it is intended to provide you with a particular understanding about rhetoric. From Aristotle to Saint Augustine, we see that rhetoric served a threefold purpose: first, it was a tool designed to develop and cultivate one's mental faculties in order to be a "good citizen" who could serve the state well. And serving the state well meant having the ability to think well and to discover and develop sound arguments. Second, it gave a person the oratorical skills necessary to convince a decision-maker or decision-making body, that they should adhere to a particular argument. And third, all of this could only be attained if one had moral fiber—ethos—in both thought and character. These conditions were seminal for the classists in their pursuit of advancing the art of

"Diogenes brings a plucked chicken to Plato" **by unknown.** *Public domain.*

rhetoric. Eventually, new thoughts and trends distorted, altered, and at times, removed these conditions. The Greeks and Romans held one's character to the highest degree, and no man could be rhetorically successful if they did not possess this quality.

Rhetoric brought us through the Middle Ages and St. Augustine as a unifying figure. The Renaissance gave us a rebirth of the Greek and Roman classical art of public speaking, a new breath for public discourse and education, and the emergence of *humanist* and *rational* thinkers. And we have learned that the art of public speaking was, for a short time in the late 19th and early 20th centuries, used as a means for entertainment.

Today, persuasion has taken many forms, with rhetoric being just one of these forms. We know that people will say and do most anything to get their way, whether that be in politics, sales, religion, or advertising, and whether what they attempt to do is ethical or not. As you continue to read this on-line text, remember one fundamental premise: that public speaking, ultimately, is all about affecting human behavior; about getting people to do something they normally would not want to do. The key to public speaking is effectively answering the question, "How do I create a message that will connect with my audience?"

> The design of Rhetoric is to remove those Prejudices that lie in the way of Truth, to Reduce the Passions to the Government of Reasons; to place our Subject in a Right Light, and excite our Hearers to a due consideration of it. – Mary Astell

Review Questions

1. What historical events gave rise to Athens establishing democracy for its citizens?
2. Who was Draco, and what did he do in Athens?
3. Under whose reign did Athens enjoy its greatest glory, and why?
4. Who was Plato, and what form of inquiry did he advocate?
5. Who was Aristotle, and what is he most noted for?
6. What did the Romans borrow from the Greeks and how did they improve upon it?
7. Why was Cicero considered to be the greatest Roman orator?
8. What did Quintilian contribute to the art of persuasion?
9. What role did rhetoric play in education in the Middle Ages?
10. The Renaissance gave birth to the Humanists and Rationalists. Can you describe the differences between the two and name two representatives from each and their contributions to persuasion?
11. What is the "epistemological tradition" and who best represent this movement?

Activities

1. Create two teams of at least three students per team. One team will represent the dialectical approach to problem solving and the other team will represent the Aristotelian rhetorical tradition. One team will attempt to explain how a problem is solved and conclusions arrived at through the dialectical approach, the other through the rhetorical approach. The problem to be solved will be created by student consensus.

2. The Humanists and Rationalists viewed persuasion from differing perspectives. Students should form teams that represent each perspective, choose an issue, then argue or advocate for their side using each perspective, and then compare the process of problem-solving to see how they arrived at their conclusions.

> 3. Review the approaches that Aristotle, Cicero, and Quintilian held toward rhetoric, then identify and compare and contrast the similarities and differences between them and how these differences advanced the art of public speaking.

Attributions

CC licensed content, Shared previously

- Chapter 2 Conclusion. **Authored by**: Peter A. DeCaro, Ph.D.. **Provided by**: University of Alaska, Fairbanks, AK. **Located at**: http://publicspeakingproject.org/psvirtualtext.html. **Project**: The Public Speaking Project. **License**: *CC BY-NC-ND: Attribution-NonCommercial-NoDerivatives*

Public domain content

- Diogenes brings a plucked chicken to Plato. **Provided by**: www.hampel-auctions.com and www.artvalue.com. **Located at**: http://commons.wikimedia.org/wiki/File:Anonymous_-_Diogenes_brings_a_plucked_chicken_to_Plato.jpg. **License**: *Public Domain: No Known Copyright*. **License Terms**: This image (or other media file) is in the public domain because its copyright has expired.

Glossary and References

Glossary

TERM	DEFINITION
Atticism	An expression characterized by conciseness and elegance.
Dialectic	Dialecticcan be defined as a debate intended to resolve a conflict between two contradictory (or polar opposites), or apparently contradictory ideas or elements logically, establishing truths on both sides rather than disproving one argument.
Draco	In 621 B.C., the citizens of Athens commissioned Draco, an elder citizen considered to be the wisest of the Greeks, to codify the laws, which had remained an oral form of custom and tradition. He began the tradition of law, where cases were decided on clearly enunciated crimes and penalties determined by statute rather than by the whims of the nobility. His laws helped constitute a surge in Athenian democracy.
Elocutionary Movement	Elocutionary Movement is a movement that focused primarily on delivery. It not only involved the voice, but also incorporated the entire person with facial expressions, gesture, posture and movement.
Epistemology	Epistemology is the study of the origin, nature, methods, and limits of human knowledge.
Marcus Fabius Quintilianus	Marcus Fabius Quintilianus, also referred to as Quintilian, was a celebrated orator, rhetorician, Latin teacher and writer who promoted rhetorical theory from ancient Greece and from the height of Roman rhetoric.
Marcus Tullius Cicero	Marcus Tullius Cicero is considered to be the greatest of the Roman orators, and was, among other things, a lawyer, politician, and philosopher.
Oratory	The ability to speak with rhetorical skill and eloquence.
Pericles	Responsible for the installation of a pure democracy to maintain popular support, a liberalized judicial system to include poor citizens so that they could serve on juries, and the establishment of a popular legislative assembly to review annually all laws. In addition, he established the right for any Athenian citizen to propose or oppose a law during assembly. Pericles' democracy established the need for training in public speaking.
Philosophical Relativism	Philosophical relativism is the concept that points of philosophical views have no absolute truth or validity, having only relative subjective value according to differences in perception and thought.
Renaissance	The Renaissance is the name of the great intellectual and cultural movement of the revival of interest in classical culture that occurred in the 14th, 15th, and 16th centuries.
René Descartes	René Descartes is one of the most important Western philosophers of the past few centuries. He was also an original physicist, physiologist and mathematician who attempted to restart philosophy in a fresh direction.
Rhetoric	Rhetoric is the faculty of discovering in the particular case all the available means of persuasion.
Sophists	5th century B.C. Greek philosophers and teachers who speculated on theology, metaphysics, and the sciences, and who were characterized by Plato as superficial manipulators of rhetoric and dialectic (thefreedictionary.com)
St. Augustine	St. Augustine had been a teacher of rhetoric before converting to Christianity in 386, and is considered to be the only major thinker on rhetoric associated with the Middle Ages.
Syllogism	A syllogism is a deductive form of argument, proceeding from a generalization to a specific application. It is a systematic arrangement of arguments consisting of a major premise, a minor premise, and a conclusion.

Zeno of Elea	Zeno of Elea was a 5th century B.C. Greek mathematician and philosopher of the Eleatic school who is considered to be the inventor of dialectical reasoning.

References

Atkins, J.W.H. (1952). Literary Criticism in Antiquity. London: Methuen.

Barrett, H. (1987). The Sophists: Rhetoric, Democracy, and Plato's Idea of Sophistry. Novato, CA; Chandler & Sharp Publishers.

Bowra, C.M. (1957). The Greek Experience. New York: The New American Library

Campbell, G. (1776). The Philosophy of Rhetoric. Bitzer, L., ed. (1963). Carbondale: Southern Illinois University Press.

Clark, D. L. (1957). Rhetoric in Greco- Roman Education. Westport, CT: Greenwood.

Cooper, L. (1952). The Greek Genius and Its Influence. Ithaca, N.Y.

Corbett, E.P.J. (1965). Classical Rhetoric for the Modern Student. New York: Oxford University Press.

Dick, H.C., ed. (1955). Selected Writings of Francis Bacon. New York: Modern Library.

Ehninger, D., ed. (1963). Richard Whately, *Elements of Rhetoric*. Carbondale: Southern Illinois University Press.

Fearnside, W.W. (1980). About Thinking. Englewood Cliffs, N.J.: Prenticed-Hall, Inc.

Freeley, A.J. & Steinberg, D.L. (2005). Argumentation and Debate, 11th ed. Belmont, CA: Wadsworth Publishing Co.

Freeman, K. (1963). The Murder of Herodes. New York: W.W. Norton, Inc.

Foss, S.K.; Foss, K.A.; Trapp, R. (1991). Contemporary Perspectives on Rhetoric. Prospect Heights, IL: Waveland Press.

Grimaldi, W.M.A. (1980). Aristotle, *Rhetoric I*: A Commentary: New York: Fordham University Press.

Guthrie, W.K.C. (1956). Plato, Protagoras and Meno. Baltimore, MD: Penguin Books.

Harvey, I. (1951). The Technique of Persuasion. London: The Falcon Press.

Honeycutt, L. (2007). http://honeyl.public.iastate.edu/qui ntilian/index.html

Howell, W.S. (1956). Logic and Rhetoric in England, 1500-1700. New York: Russell & Russell.

Ijsseling, S. (1976). Rhetoric and Philosophy in Conflict: An Historical Survey. The Hague: Martinus.

Golden, J.L.; Berquist, G.F.; Coleman, W.E. (1983). The Rhetoric of Western Thought, 3rd ed.. Dubuque: Kendall/Hunt.

Gwynn, Aubrey. Roman Education from Cicero to Quintilian. Oxford: Clarendon Press, 1926.

Inch, E.S.; Warnick, B.; Endres, D. (2006). Critical Thinking and Communication. New York: Pearson Education, Inc.

Kennedy, G. (1963). The Art of Persuasion in Greece. Princeton: University Press.

Larson, Charles, U. (1995). Persuasion: Reception and Responsibility. 7th ed. Belmont, CA: Wadsworth Publishing.

Murphy James J. and Katula, R.A. (1995). A Synoptic History of Classical Rhetoric. 2nd ed. Davis: Ca. Hermagoras Press.

Oliver, R.T. (1950). Persuasive Speaking. New York: Longmans, Green and Co.

Quintilian. (1987). Carbondale: Illinois University Press. "Revised and enlarged version of On the early education of the citizen-orator, published by Bobbs-Merrill Company, 1965."

Reike, R.D.; Sillars, M.O.; Peterson, T.R. (2005). Argumentation and Critical Thinking. New York: Pearson Education, Inc.

Robertson, D.W. (1958). Saint Augustine on Christian Doctrine. New York: Library of Liberal Arts.

Rolfe, J.C. (1963). Cicero and His Influence. New York: Cooper Square.

Virtualology.com (2007). Retrieved on January 26, 2007 from http://www.virtualology.com/rheto ricaltheory/peterramus.com/

photo credits

P. 1 The Parthenon by Lisa Schreiber

P. 2 Pericles' Funeral Oration by Phillip von Foltz http://commons.wikimedia.org/wiki/File:Discur so_funebre_pericles.PNG

P. 3 Parc de Versailles. Isocrates, Pierre Granier (1684-1688) ; Photo by Coyau http://commons.wiki-media.org/wiki/File:Parc_ de_Versailles,_Rond- Point_des_Philosophes,_Isocrate,_Pierre_Granier_ MR1870_04.jpg

P. 4 The School of Athens [Plato and Aristotle] by Raffaello http://commons.wikimedia.org/wiki/ File:Sanzi o_01_Plato_Aristotle.jpg

P. 4 Cicero Denounces Catiline by Cesare Maccari (1840 – 1919) http://upload.wikimedia.org/wikipedia/ commo ns/a/a3/Maccari-Cicero.jpg

P. 5 Quintillian by Unknown http://commons.wikimedia.org/wiki/File:Quinti lian.jpg

p. 6 Saint Augustine by Sandro Bottecelli http://commons.wikimedia.org/wiki/File:Saint_ Augustine_Por-trait.jpg

P. 7 Shakespeare by John Taylor ? http://commons.wikimedia.org/wiki/File:Shake speare.jpg

P. 7 Friedrich Immanuel Niethammer by Unknown http://upload.wikimedia.org/wikipedia/commo ns/5/5b/Friedrich_Immanuel_Niethammer.jpg P. 8 Francis Bacon by Unknown http://upload.wikimedia.org/wikipedia/commo ns/6/65/Francis_Bacon.jpg

P. 8 Renes Descartes by Frans Hals (1649 – 1700) http://commons.wikimedia.org/wiki/File:Frans_ Hals_-_Portret_van_Ren%C3%A9_Descartes.jpg P. 9 Hugh Blair by John Kay http://commons.wikimedia.org/wiki/File:Hugh_ Blair.jpg

P. 9 Thomas Sheridan by Roger Ingpen http://commons.wikimedia.org/wiki/File:Thom as_Sheridan.jpg

P. 10 Diogenes brings a plucked chicken to Plato by Anonymous http://commons.wikimedia.org/wiki/File:Anony mous_- _Diogenes_brings_a_plucked_chicken_to_Plato.jpg P. 10 Cicero by Unlnown http://commons.wikimedia.org/wiki/File:Cicero .jpg

Attributions

CC licensed content, Shared previously

Chapter 2: Introduction to 21st Century Public Speaking

Objectives and Introduction

Introduction to Public Speaking

By Lisa Schreiber, Ph.D. and Morgan Hartranft

Millersville University, Millersville, PA

Learning Objectives

After reading this chapter, you should be able to:

- Articulate at least three reasons why public speaking skills are important.
- Describe the difference between the linear and the transactional model of communication.
- List, define, and give an example of each of the components of communication.
- Differentiate between the major types of speeches.
- Identify the eleven core public speaking competencies.
- Apply chapter concepts in final questions and activities.

Introduction

Humans' ability to communicate using formalized systems of language sets us apart from other living creatures on the Earth. Whether these language conventions make us superior to other creatures is debatable, but there is no question that overall, the most successful and most powerful people over the centuries have mastered the ability to communicate effectively. In fact, the skill of speaking is so important that it has been formally taught for thousands of years.

The ironic feature of public speaking is that while we recognize that it is an important skill to have, many of us do not like or want to give speeches. You may be reading this book because it was assigned to you in a class, or you may be reading it because you have to give a speech in your personal or professional life. If you are reading this book because you like public speaking or you have a burning desire to learn more about it, you're in the minority.

The good news about public speaking is that although it may not be on the top of the list of our favorite activities, *anyone* can learn to give effective presentations. You don't have to look like a Hollywood star and you don't have to use fancy words to be a successful speaker. What is important is that the audience understands you and remembers what you have to say. By learning and using the techniques provided in this reading material, you will discover how to create engaging speeches and present them using your own delivery style.

"Europe for Tibet Solidarity Rally 200 His Holiness, the 14th Dalai Lama" by Wolfgang H. Wögerer. CC BY-SA.

Wherever I go meeting the public… spreading a message of human values, spreading a message of harmony, is the most important thing. – Dalai Lama

Attributions

CC licensed content, Shared previously

Welcome to Public Speaking

Given the demands for good communication skills in the civic realm and in the workplace, a course in public speaking is perhaps more important than ever. There is no quick path to a great speech. Good speaking is developed through practice and hard work.

The public speaking course is a unique course. Unlike, say, a course in the principles of law or the history of Central Asia, the public speaking course requires you to both know content and be able to perform a skill well. You will learn important principles of public speaking and argumentation, but simply knowing these principles is insufficient; you must also be able to apply them well. By the same token, you might be able to get through a speech without saying "um," but if the content of the speech is bad, it is not a good speech. The best public speakers not only speak smoothly, they also say important and interesting things.

HOW TO BE A STUDENT OF PUBLIC SPEAKING

The most successful model for teaching public speaking (and the one this class follows) relies on a mix of instruction, imitation, and practice.

- **Instruction** reinforces the lessons learned from the history of public speaking study. The instruction in this class draws most explicitly from the rhetorical tradition. We will study principles of argumentation, arrangement, and style.

- **Imitation** means that when studying a performance skill like speaking, we benefit by identifying and imitating the best practices of skilled speakers. I don't mean stealing or plagiarizing, I mean trying to link phrases together in a manner similar to a speaker we think sounds good. There are a number of speeches that you will watch this quarter (online and in class). The intent of these speeches is to show you some best practices. You shouldn't simply watch a speech like you would a television show; you should look to find some verbal or nonverbal behaviors that you would like to be able to imitate.

- **Practice** is the most obvious leg of public speaking study. If you are going to get better at public speaking, you must be able to apply the lessons of instruction and imitation by practicing your speeches. The nice thing about public speaking is that you can practice it almost anywhere. However, your practice time is best spent by speaking in situations where you have an attentive audience (as opposed to a curious dog or a sleeping roommate).

MISCONCEPTIONS ABOUT PUBLIC SPEAKING

1. **You can't learn to be a good public speaker; you have to be born a naturally good speaker.** Everyone can become a better public speaker through study and practice. I love to ski. I wasn't born being a good skier; rather, I grew up skiing. I skied as often as I could and I got better. The same is true of public speaking. You were born with the basic equipment needed for speaking in public—lungs and a mouth.

2. **I can only learn public speaking through practice alone.** This misconception often works in conjunction with the misconception #1 and #3. I see this as a hugely egoistic argument since it assumes that only you know what good public speaking is and only you know how to improve. Let me return to the skiing analogy (though you could substitute any sports or skills analogy, like playing a musical instrument). Most people develop their skiing ability by simply skiing a lot. But if you want to get better, you need to seek outside information about the principles of skiing. That's why people pay a lot of money for ski lessons. Ski instructors can both model good skiing behaviors and they can talk about the physics of metal on snow and the physiology of your muscles on skis.

3. **Public speaking is just delivery (speech content doesn't matter).** This is like saying that a good essay is simply one that has good grammar or punctuation. A good essay should have good grammar and punctuation, but it also needs good content. The same holds true of a speech. When we listen to a speech we judge the speaker according to what they say as well as how they say it. Think about presidential debates. After any presidential debate, pundits flood the airwaves and pick apart both content and delivery, but they spend far more time discussing what the candidates said.

4. **Reading a speech is the best way to ensure a good speech.** You will hear me talking a lot about the similarities between writing and speaking, but they also differ in many important respects. A speech is an act of communication with a specific audience. Reading a speech undermines this (and as we will see, can actually make you more nervous). If you were having a conversation with a friend about your classes and suddenly started reading a prepared set of comments, the conversation would sink. Why? A conversation is dynamic and relies on com-

municating with the other person. A speech is like a conversation in this way, you are engaging in a shared act of communication with the audience.

RHETORIC

A class on public speaking is essentially a rhetoric class. The word ***rhetoric*** is often used to indicate that the speaker is lying ("his record doesn't match his rhetoric") or that the speaker is filling air with meaningless talk ("let's move past all the rhetoric and get down to business"). It is true that term has gotten a lot of bad press over the past 2,000 years or so, but the study of rhetoric is the study of what is persuasive. We are certainly not the first group to study what goes into a dynamic and persuasive speech. The ancient Greeks and Romans spent a lot of time thinking and writing about good speaking. Throughout history, thinkers and charlatans alike have devoted a considerable amount of effort to figuring out what sounds good, looks good, and works to motivate various audiences.

DEFINITIONS OF RHETORIC

Since the study of rhetoric has been around for so many years, there are a number of different definitions for the word. Aristotle defined rhetoric as "the faculty of discovering in any particular case the available means of persuasion." Plato held that rhetoric is "the art of winning the soul by discourse." The Roman thinker Quintilian suggested simply that rhetoric is the art of speaking well. John Locke however held a dimmer view of the art and wrote that rhetoric is a "powerful instrument of error and deceit." The contemporary writer Gerard Hauser suggests, "Rhetoric is communication that attempts to coordinate social action. For this reason, rhetorical communication is explicitly pragmatic. Its goal is to influence human choices on specific matters that require immediate attention."

For the purposes of this class, we will define rhetoric as "the study and art of effective speaking." This doesn't begin to capture all the ways in which rhetoric could be (and has been) defined, but it does focus our study on the aspects of rhetoric most relevant to our present concern.

5 MAIN PARTS OF RHETORIC/PUBLIC SPEAKING

Earlier thinkers argued that the study and practice of rhetoric involved five main parts.

1. **INVENTION**: The first thing that must go into a good speech is good material. Invention means finding or thinking up good speech content. Basically, a good speaker knows what s/he is talking about. There are a number of different strategies that we will study to help prime the mental pump. Our focus in this class is on good arguments (solid claims supported with good evidence). Aristotle suggested that the speech content was either artistic (you had to think it up) or inartistic (it already existed). Proving your claims requires both inartistic and artistic proofs. We all know that good arguments require evidence, so let's look at the artistic proofs. Aristotle saw three main ways to make an argument

   - **LOGOS**: We convince people through our use of logic. So, I can argue that it rained last night by pointing to the puddles on the ground. I use the evidence of rain puddles to make a claim about something that I didn't see, relying on the basic logical premise that "puddles generally indicate recent rain." This isn't the most contentious of arguments, you say. Very true, but the principle is the same. We use appeals to logic to help support our arguments. Economists make logical arguments all the time. They have evidence about current trends, but they argue about where to invest money based on logic— they don't know 100% what the market will do, but they can try to figure out where to invest based on historical precedent, prevailing wisdom, and informal logic.

   - **PATHOS**: We persuade people by appealing to their emotions. Of course, we are not simply logical animals, we have emotions, and these often shape how we see and understand the world. Now an appeal to pathos doesn't mean that we simply tug at people's heart strings or we try to scare them into acting our way. Of course this happens, but you would be hard pressed to call it good argumentation. Aristotle saw pathos as putting the audience in the right frame of mind. So, if you are arguing for something that might seem unfamiliar to your audience, you would be well advised to tell some personal stories that helped people understand the human element. The commercials you see asking for help in funding starving populations rely a lot on pathos. They are trying to evoke your compassion by showing you what the living conditions are like for many in need.

   - **ETHOS**: We can persuade people by virtue of good character. Aristotle suggested that of the three artistic proofs, ethos was potentially the most persuasive. Do we trust the speaker's credibility as a person and her/his credibility on the topic? Do we trust that the speaker has our best interests at heart? We can gain ethos by doing all the research that a good speech needs and then demonstrating that ethos by being able to talk about the topic intelligently. We can "borrow" ethos by citing the best research available. Ultimately, though ethos must be earned by showing the audience that you are a credible source on this topic.

   - A good speech requires you to think about a host of different issues ranging from possible arguments, oppositional arguments, and all the different types of evidence you can use. A good speech also includes a mix of logos, pathos, and ethos. The process of sorting through all this material and deciding on the best for you case is the process of invention.

2. **ARRANGEMENT**: Once you determine what you speech will be about and what types of artistic and inartistic proofs you will use, then you need to think about the best possible way to

arrange your speech. How much background information do you need to give? How should you arrange your main points? How long or short should the introduction be? In many ways, arranging a speech is more difficult than arranging an essay because a reader can jump around in an essay (look at the section headings, jump back and revisit something s/he was unclear on, etc.), but an audience member must listen to the speaker's flow of information in chronological time. Given this, you must think about how your audience will hear and understand your speech.

3. **STYLE**: Once you know *what* you will say and the *order* in which you will say it, then you can begin to focus more on the details of exactly *how* you will say it. Some speeches are stylistically rich (Abraham Lincoln's Gettysburg Address is a famous example) while others are more stylistically plain (say, a business presentation), yet both have a type of style. The rhetorician Cicero talked about high, middle, and low styles in public speaking. We are probably familiar with the high style; many political orators use it for famous speeches. In the U.S. the State of the Union Address is usually delivered in a middle or high style. We are also probably familiar with the low style. If not, watch a television talk show; here the style is very casual. Ultimately, style is governed by the topic and the audience you are addressing. In this class, we are concerned most with the middle and middle-high style. You should think strategically about your style and how you audience will hear and understand your words. The three main speech assignments move from low-middle style (impromptu speech), to middle style (persuasive speech), to middle- high style (advocacy speech).

4. **MEMORY**: This part of rhetoric was really important for speakers in classical Greece and Rome because they delivered really long speeches (often in very high style). It remains important for us because a speech is spoken not read. If you don't practice your speech, you won't be familiar with it. If you aren't familiar with your speech, you will probably read it to us. This is not a class in public reading, but in public speaking. You should not try to memorize your speeches word for word. This will only exacerbate any fear you have of public speaking. However, you should know the main parts of your speech. This comes down to a matter of knowledge and practice. You need to know your material well enough so that you can talk about the topic intelligently (invention). You also need to practice enough so that you know how best to explain this topic to the audience (arrangement and style).

5. **DELIVERY**: The final part of a study of rhetoric is the one that people fear the most: standing up in front of an audience and actually delivering the speech. Of course, if you have the invention, arrangement, style, and memory parts down pat, the delivery part shouldn't give you too many headaches. That said, there are a number of delivery issues that can help or hurt your speech. We will study some of those delivery issues that are most distracting and those techniques that are most beneficial. However, the basic delivery approach we will focus on in this class is conversational delivery. This doesn't mean simply speaking as you would with your friends about any subject, but finding a style that looks good, sounds good, and helps your ethos.

Attributions

CC licensed content, Shared previously

- Image of Rhetorica. **Authored by**: falco. **Located at**: https://pixabay.com/en/hildesheim-germany-lower-saxony-711009/. **License**: *CC0: No Rights Reserved*
- Welcome to Public Speaking. **Authored by**: Matt McGarrity. **Provided by**: University of Washington. **License**: *CC BY: Attribution*
- Image of students. **Authored by**: Berklee Valencia Campus. **Located at**: https://flic.kr/p/oXLyzW. **License**: *CC BY-NC-ND: Attri-*

Benefits of Public Speaking

According to the Association of American Colleges and Universities, there are a core set of skills that are necessary "both for a globally engaged democracy and for a dynamic, innovation fueled economy."[1] In the category of "Intellectual and practical skills" **public speaking** is listed as one of these core skills. This is not particularly surprising given that communication skills are critical for intellectual development, career trajectory, and civic engagement. Public speaking is universally applicable to all types of majors and occupations and is seen by U.S. employers as a critical employability skill for job seekers.[2] No matter what your ambitions and interests are, developing speaking skills will benefit your personal, professional, and public life.

Personal

People don't just give presentations on the job and in classes. At times we are called upon to give speeches in our personal lives. It may be for a special event, such as a toast at a wedding. We may be asked to give a eulogy at a funeral for a friend or loved one. As a part of volunteer work, one may have to introduce a guest speaker at an event or present or accept an award for service. Developing the skill to give these types of speeches can help us to fulfill essential roles in our family and community. Another great personal benefit of public speaking is that it builds self- confidence. It's no surprise that speaking in public is scary, but by engaging in the activity you will build self-confidence through the experience.

1. Rhodes, T. (Ed.) (2010). Assessing outcomes and improving achievement: Tips and tools for using rubrics. Washington D. C.: Association of American Colleges and Universities.
2. Rockler-Gladen, N. (2009, March 21). *Job skills that every college student needs: Writing, speaking, professionalism, and other important knowledge.* Suite 101.com. Retrieved from http://studyskills.suite101.com/article.cfm/job_skills_that_every_college_student_needs

Professional

TV announcers, teachers, lawyers, and entertainers must be able to speak well, but most other professions require or at the very least can benefit from the skills found in public speaking. It is believed 70% of jobs today involve some form of public speaking.[3] With the recent economic shift from manufacturing to service careers, the ability to communicate with others has become crucial. Top CEOs advise that great leaders must be able to communicate ideas effectively, they must be able to persuade, build support, negotiate and speak effectively in public.[4] The chapters on "Informative Speaking" and "Persuasive Speaking" can help readers understand how to write presentations that enhance their leadership skills. But before you even start a career, you have to get a job. Effective speaking skills make you more attractive to employers, enhancing your chances of

"Alice Walker" by Virginia DeBolt. CC-BY-SA.

securing employment and later advancing within your career. Employers, career counselors, and the National Association of Colleges and Employers (NACE) all list good communication skills at the top of the list of qualities sought in potential employees. According to NACE's executive director, Marilyn Mackes, the Job Outlook 2013 Report found that employers are looking for people who can communicate effectively.[5] Monster.com advises, "articulating thoughts clearly and concisely will make a difference in both a job interview and subsequent job performance."[6]

> Action is a great restorer and builder of confidence. Inaction is not only the result, but the cause, of fear. Perhaps the action you take will be successful; perhaps different action or adjustments will have to follow. But any action is better than no action at all. – Norman Vincent Peale

Public

Learning about public speaking will allow you to participate in democracy at its most basic level. Public speaking is important in creating and sustaining a society, which includes informed, active participants. Even if you do not plan to run for office, learning about public speaking helps you to listen more carefully to and critically evaluate other's speeches. Listening and critical thinking allow you to understand public dilemmas, form an opinion about them, and participate in resolving them. The progress of the past century involving segregation, women's rights and environmental protection are the result of people advancing new ideas and speaking out to others to persuade them to adopt changes.

Attributions

CC licensed content, Shared previously

3. Aras, K. (2012). *The nuts and bolts of public speaking: Practical tools for powerful presentations*. Retrieved from http://www.thecommunicationfactory.com/seminars/skills/PublicSpeaking.php

4. Farrell, R. (2011). Soft skills all great leaders should have. CareerBuilder. http://www.careerbuilder.com/Article/CB-2335-Leadership-Management-Soft-skillsall-great-leaders-should-have/

5. Koncz, A. and Allen, C. (2012). *Employers look for communication skills, ability to work in a team in new college grads.* www.naceweb.org/pressreleases/.

6. McKay, J. (2005). Employers complain about communication skills. *Pittsburgh Post Gazette*. Retrieved from http://www.post-gazette.com/business/businessnews/2005/02/06/Employers-complain-about-communication-skills/stories/200502060145

Models of Communication

It should be clear by now that public speaking happens all around us in many segments of our lives. However, to truly understand what is happening within these presentations, we need to take a step back and look at some of the key components of the communication process.

Linear Model of Communication

The first theoretical model of communication was proposed in 1949 by Shannon and Weaver for Bell Laboratories.[1] This three-part model was intended to capture the radio and television transmission process. However it was later adapted to human communication and is now known as the linear model of communication. The first part of the model is the sender, and this is the person who is speaking. The second part of the model is the channel, which is the apparatus for carrying the message (i.e., the phone or TV). The third part of the model is the receiver, and this is the person who picks up the message. In this model, communication is seen as a one-way process of transmitting a message from one person to another person. This model can be found in Figure 1.1. If you think about situations when you communicate with another person face-to-face or when you give a speech, you probably realize that this model is inadequate—communication is much more complicated than firing off a message to others.

Figure 1.1
Linear Model of Communication

"Figure 1.1" by Public Speaking Project. CC-BY-NC-ND.

---

1. Shannon, C. E., & Weaver, W. (1949). *The mathematical theory of communication*. Urbana: University of Illinois Press.

Transactional Model of Communication

Models of communication have evolved significantly since Shannon and Weaver first proposed their well-known conceptual model over sixty years ago. One of the most useful models for understanding public speaking is Barnlund's transactional model of communication.[2] In the transactional model, communication is seen as an ongoing, circular process. We are constantly affecting and are affected by those we communicate with. The transactional model has a number of interdependent processes and components, including the encoding and decoding processes, the communicator, the message, the channel and noise. Although not directly addressed in Barnlund's (2008) original transactional model, participants' worldviews and the context also play an important role in the communication process. See Figure 1.2 for an illustration.

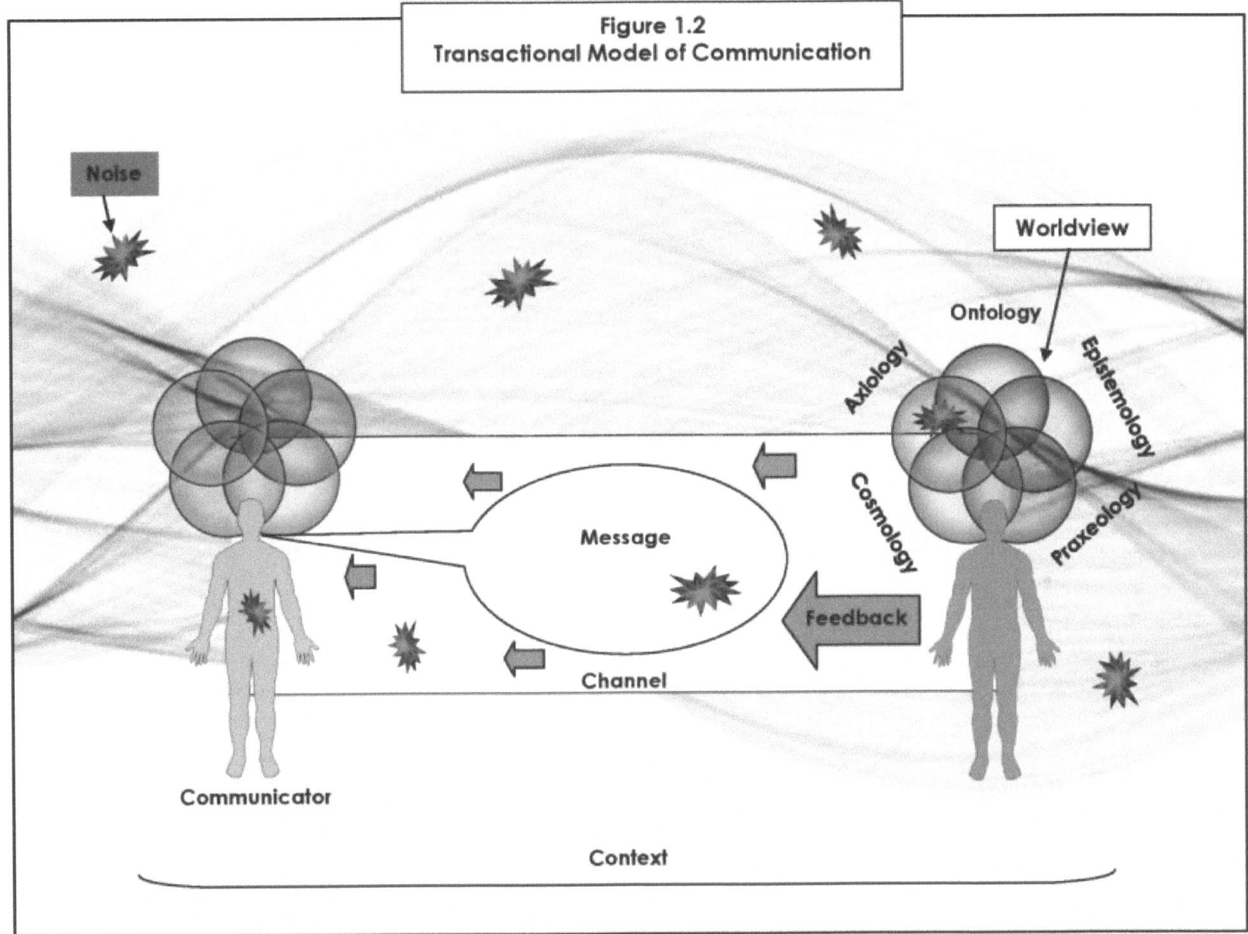

He who would learn to fly one day must first learn to stand and walk and run and climb and dance; one cannot fly into flying. ~ Friedrich Nietzsche

Attributions

CC licensed content, Shared previously

- Chapter 1 Models of Communication. **Authored by**: Lisa Schreiber, Ph.D. and Morgan Hartranft. **Provided by**: Millersville University, Millersville, PA. **Located at**: http://publicspeakingproject.org/psvirtualtext.html. **Project**: Public Speaking Project.

2. Barnlund, D. C. (2008). *A transactional model of communication*. In. C. D. Mortensen (Eds.), Communication theory (2nd Ed), pp. 47–57. New Brunswick, New Jersey: Transaction.

Elements of the Communication Process

Encoding and Decoding

Encoding refers to the process of taking an idea or mental image, associating that image with words, and then speaking those words in order to convey a message. So, if you wanted to explain to your aunt the directions to your new apartment, you would picture in your mind the landscape, streets and buildings, and then you would select the best words that describe the route so your aunt could find you.

Decoding is the reverse process of **listening** to words, thinking about them, and turning those words into mental images. If your aunt were trying to find her way to your apartment, she would listen to your words, associate these words with streets and landmarks that she knows, and then she would form a mental map of the way to get to you. Ramsey's "Using Language Well" (Chapter 10) provides additional insight into the encoding and decoding process.

Communicator

The term **communicator** refers to all of the people in the interaction or speech setting. It is used instead of sender and receiver, because when we are communicating with other people we are not only sending a message, we are receiving messages from others simultaneously. When we speak, we observe others' **nonverbal behavior** to see if they understand us and we gauge their emotional state. The information we gain from these observations is known as feedback. Over the telephone, we listen to paralinguistic cues, such as pitch, tone, volume and fillers (i.e., "um," "uh," "er," "like," and so on). This means that communication is not a one-way process. Even in a public speaking situation, we watch and listen to audience members' responses. If audience members are interested, agree, and understand us, they may lean forward in their seats, nod their heads, have positive or neutral facial expressions, and provide favorable vocal cues (such as laughter, "That's right," "Uh huh," or "Amen!"). If audience members are bored, disagree, or are confused by our message, they may be texting or looking away from us, shake their heads, have unhappy or confused expressions on their faces, or present oppositional vocal cues (like groans, "I don't think so," "That doesn't make sense," or "You're crazy!"). Thus, communication is always a transactional process—a give and take of messages.

Message

The **message** involves those verbal and nonverbal behaviors, enacted by communicators, that are interpreted with meaning by others. The verbal portion of the message refers to the words that we speak, while the nonverbal portion includes our tone of voice and other non-vocal components such as personal appearance, posture, gestures and body movements, eye behavior, the way we use space, and even the way that we smell. For instance, the person who gets up to speak wearing a nice suit will be interpreted more positively than a person giving the exact same speech wearing sweats and a graphic t-shirt. Or if a speaker tries to convince others to donate to a charity that builds wells in poor African villages using a monotone voice, she will not be as effective as the speaker who gives the same speech but speaks with a solemn tone of voice. If there is ever a conflict between the verbal and the non-verbal aspects of a message, people will generally believe the nonverbal portion of the message. To test this, tighten your muscles, clench your fists at your sides, pull your eye brows together, purse your lips, and tell someone in a harsh voice, "NO, I'm NOT angry!" See if they believe your words or your nonverbal behavior.

The message can also be intentional or unintentional. When the message is intentional, this means that we have an image in our mind that we wish to communicate to an audience or a person in a conversation, and we can successfully convey the image from our mind to others' minds with relative accuracy. An unintentional message is sent when the message that we wish to convey is not the same as the message the other person receives. Let's say you are returning from an outing with your significant other and she or he asks, "Did you have a good time?" You *did* have a good time but are distracted by a TV commercial when asked, so you reply in a neutral tone, "Sure, I had fun." Your significant other may interpret your apathetic tone of voice and lack of eye contact to mean that you did not enjoy the evening, when in fact you actually did. Thus as communicators, we cannot always be sure that the message we wish to communicate is interpreted as we intended.

Channel

The **channel** is very simply the means through which the message travels. In face-to-face communication the channel involves all of our senses, so the channel is what we see, hear, touch, smell and perhaps what we taste. When we're communicating with someone online, the channel is the computer; when texting the channel is the cell phone; and when watching a movie on cable, the channel is the TV. The channel can have a profound impact on the way a message is interpreted. Listening to a recording of a speaker does not have the same psychological impact as listening to the same speech in person or watching that person on television. One famous example of this is the 1960 televised presidential debate between John F. Kennedy and Richard Nixon. According to History.com (2012), on camera, Nixon looked away from the camera at the reporters asking him questions, he was sweating and pale, he had facial hair stubble, and he wore a grey suit that faded into the set background. "Chicago mayor Richard J. Daley reportedly said [of Nixon], 'My God, they've embalmed him before he even died.'"[1] Kennedy, on the other hand, looked into the camera, was tanned, wore a dark suit that made him stand out from the background, and appeared to be calm after spending the entire weekend with aides practicing in a hotel room. Most of those who listened to the radio broadcast of the debate felt that it was a tie or that Nixon had won, while 70% of those watching the televised debate felt that Kennedy was the winner.

---

1. History.com. (2012). The Kennedy-Nixon Debates. History.com. Retrieved from http://www.history.com/topics/us-presidents/kennedy-nixon-debates

"Kennedy Nixon Debate" by United Press International. Public domain.

Noise

The next aspect of the model of communication is noise. **Noise** refers to anything that interferes with message transmission or reception (i.e., getting the image from your head into others' heads). There are several different types of noise. The first type of noise is **physiological noise**, and this refers to bodily processes and states that interfere with a message. For instance, if a speaker has a headache or the flu, or if audience members are hot or they're hungry, these conditions may interfere with message accuracy. The second type of noise is psychological noise. **Psychological noise** refers to mental states or emotional states that impede message transmission or reception. For example, if someone has just broken up with a significant other, or if they're worried about their grandmother who is in the hospital, or if they are thinking about their shopping list, this may interfere with communication processes as well. The third type of noise is actual **physical noise,** and this would be simply the actual sound level in a room. Loud music playing at a party, a number of voices of people talking excitedly, a lawnmower right outside the window, or anything that is overly loud will interfere with communication. The last type of noise is cultural noise. **Cultural noise** refers to message interference that results from differences in peoples' worldviews. Worldview is discussed in more detail below, but suffice it to say that the greater the difference in worldview, the more difficult it is to understand one another and communicate effectively.

Worldview

Most people don't give a lot of thought to the communication process. In the majority of our interactions with others, we are operating on automatic
pilot. Although the encoding and decoding process
may appear to be fairly straightforward, it is actually much more complicated than it seems. The reason for this is because we all have different
worldviews. **Worldview** is the overall framework
through which an individual sees, thinks about, and
interprets the world and interacts with it. There are
five core components to our worldview.

"The 2nd most famous face in Pushkar" **by Shreyans Bhansali**. *CC-BY-NC-SA.*

1. Epistemology is the way that we
acquire knowledge and/or what counts as
knowledge. Think about the process of
conducting research. Thirty years ago, to find a series of facts one had to use a card catalogue
and scour the library stacks for books. Now researchers can access thousands of pages of information via their computer from the comfort of their own home. Epistemology is linked to public
speaking because it governs audience members' preferred learning styles and who or what they
consider to be credible sources.

2. Ontology refers to our belief system, how we see the nature of reality or what we see as true
or false. We may (or may not) believe in aliens from outer space, that butter is bad for you, that
the Steelers will win the Superbowl, or that humans will be extinct in 200 years. Speech writers should be careful not to presume that audience members share the same beliefs. If a speaker
claims that illness can be aided with prayer, but several people in the audience are atheists, at
best the speaker has lost credibility and at worst these audience members could be offended.

3. Axiology represents our value system, or what we see as right or wrong, good or bad, and fair
or unfair. One of the ways that you can tell what people value is to ask them what their goals are,
or to ask them what qualities they look for in a life partner. Our values represent the things that
we hope for—they do not represent reality. Values can have an impact on multiple levels of the
public speaking process, but in particular values impact speaker credibility and effectiveness in
persuasion. For instance, some cultures value modest dress in women, so a female speaker wearing a sleeveless blouse while speaking could cause her to lose credibility with some audience
members. Or if audience members value the freedom to bear arms over the benefits of government regulation, a speaker will have a difficult time convincing these audience members to vote
for stricter gun control legislation.

4. Cosmology signifies the way that we see our relationship to the universe and to other people.
Cosmology dictates our view of power relationships and may involve our religious or spiritual beliefs. Controversial speech topics (like universal health care and the death penalty) are
often related to this aspect of worldview as we must consider our responsibilities to other human
beings and our power to influence them. Interestingly, cosmology would also play a role in such

logistical points as who is allowed to speak, the order of speakers on a schedule (e.g., from most to least important), the amount of time a speaker has to speak, the seating arrangement on the dais, and who gets the front seats in the audience.

5. Praxeology denotes our preferred method of completing everyday tasks or our approach to solving problems. Some speech writers may begin working on their outlines as soon as they know they will need to give a speech, while others may wait until a few days before their speech to begin preparing (we do not recommend this approach). Praxeology may also have an impact on a speaker's preference of delivery style, methods of arranging main points, and choice of slideware (i.e., Power Point versus Prezi).

"NFL Superfans" by HMJD02. CC-BY-SA.

It is always good to explore the stuff you don't agree with, to try and understand a different lifestyle or foreign worldview. I like to be challenged in that way, and always end up learning something I didn't know. – Laura Linney

It is important to understand worldview because it has a profound impact on the encoding and decoding process, and consequently on our ability to be understood by others. Try this simple experiment. Ask two or three people to silently imagine a dog while you imagine a dog at the same time. "Dog" is a very **concrete word** (a word that describes a tangible object that can be perceived through the senses), and it is one of the first words children in the United States learn in school. Wait a few seconds and then ask each person what type of dog they were thinking of. Was it a Chihuahua? A greyhound? Golden retriever? Rottweiler? Or some other dog? Most likely each person you asked had a different image in his or her mind than you had in yours. This is our worldview at work.

To further illustrate, you may tell a co-worker, "I can't wait to go home this weekend—we are having lasagna!" Seems like a fairly clear-cut statement, doesn't it? Unfortunately, it is not. While "lasagna" is also a concrete word, our worldviews cause us to interpret each word in the statement differently. Where is "home?" Who is making the meal? What ingredients will be used in the lasagna? Is this dish eaten as a regular meal or for a special occasion? Will there be leftovers? Are friends invited? Since everyone who has eaten lasagna has had a different experience of the cuisine, we all acquire a different image in our mind when we hear the statement "…we are having lasagna!"

"Lasagna" by David K. CC-BY-SA.

Complicating matters is the fact that the more abstract the word becomes, the more room there is for interpretation. **Abstract words** (words that refer to ideas or concepts that are removed from material reality)

like "peace," "love," "immoral," "justice," "freedom," "success," and "honor" can have a number of different meanings; each of which is predicated on one's worldview. Communicators have their own unique worldviews that shape both the encoding and decoding processes, which means that we can never be completely understood by another person. People from the Midwest may call carbonated beverages "pop," while those from the East Coast may say "soda," and those from Georgia may say "coke." Even when simple terms are used like "oak tree" or "fire hydrant," each listener will form a different mental image when decoding the message. Never take communication for granted, and never assume your listener will understand you. It takes hard work to make yourself understood by an audience.

Context is worth 80 IQ points.- Alan Kay

Context

The last element of the communication process is the **context** in which the speech or interaction takes place. In the 1980's context was taught as the actual physical setting where communication occurred, such as in a place of worship, an apartment, a workplace, a noisy restaurant, or a grocery store. People communicate differently in each one of these places as there are unwritten rules of communication (called **norms**) that govern these settings. More recently the concept of context has evolved and expanded to include the type of relationships we have with others and the communicative rules that govern those relationships. So you do not

"Talking technique" **by The U.S. Army.** CC-BY.

speak the same way to your best friend as you do to a small child, your parent, your boss, your doctor or a police officer. And you may speak to your best friend differently in your apartment than you do in your parents' home, and your communication may also change when you are both out with friends on the weekend. In sum, the context refers to the norms that govern communication in different situations and relationships.

Attributions

CC licensed content, Shared previously

- Chapter 1 Elements of the Communication Process. **Authored by**: Lisa Schreiber, Ph.D. and Morgan Hartranft. **Provided by**: Millersville University, Millersville, PA. **Located at**: http://publicspeakingproject.org/psvirtualtext.html. **Project**: The Public Speaking Project. **License**: *CC BY-NC-ND: Attribution-NonCommercial-NoDerivatives*

- the 2nd most famous face in Pushkar. **Authored by**: Shreyans Bhansali. **Located at**: https://flic.kr/p/7mWPS6. **License**: *CC BY-NC-SA: Attribution-NonCommercial-ShareAlike*

- lasagna. **Authored by**: David K. **Located at**: https://flic.kr/p/9fmq9J. **License**: *CC BY-SA: Attribution-ShareAlike*

- NFL Superfans. **Authored by**: HMJD02. **Located at**: http://commons.wikimedia.org/wiki/File:NFL_Superfans.jpg. **License**: *CC BY-SA: Attribution-ShareAlike*

- The U.S. Army - Talking technique. **Provided by**: The U.S. Army. **Located at**: http://commons.wikimedia.org/wiki/File:Flickr_-_The_U.S._Army_-_Talking_technique.jpg. **License**: *CC BY: Attribution*

Public domain content

- Kennedy Nixon Debat 1960. **Authored by**: United Press International. **Provided by**: Wikimedia Commons. **Located at**: http://commons.wikimedia.org/wiki/File:Kennedy_Nixon_Debat_(1960).jpg. **License**: *Public Domain: No Known Copyright*

- Kennedy Nixon Debat 1960. **Authored by**: United Press International. **Provided by**: Wikimedia Commons. **Located at**: http://commons.wikimedia.org/wiki/File:Kennedy_Nixon_Debat_(1960).jpg. **License**: *Public Domain: No Known Copyright*

Types of Speeches and Speaking Occasions

There are three general purposes for speaking in public. The general purpose of a speech is usually determined by the occasion in which the speech will be presented. The first general purpose is to inform your audience. In an informative speech, the presenter will share information about a particular person, place, object, process, concept, or issue by defining, describing, or explaining. Occasions for which an informative speech would be presented include a report presented to coworkers, a teacher presenting information to his or her class, and a training session for a job. The second purpose for public speaking is to persuade. In a persuasive speech, the presenter will attempt to reinforce or change their audiences' beliefs, attitudes, feelings, or values. Several occasions where persuasion is used include a sales pitch to potential customers, a politician's campaign speech, or a debate during a public forum. The last general purpose is to commemorate or entertain. These types of speeches often strengthen the bonds between audience members from recalling a shared experience or intend to amuse audiences through humor, stories, or illustrations. Examples of this purpose include a toast, such as a best man's speech at a wedding reception; a eulogy to praise the dead; a commencement speech at graduation; or presenting an award. It is important to note that these general purposes may overlap one another. One might wish to use some forms of entertainment while informing or persuading his or her audience.

"Insider Secrets of Public Speaking" by Nadine Dereza. CC-BY.

> A desire presupposes the possibility of action to achieve it; action presupposes a goal which is worth achieving. – Ayn Rand

Speaking Competencies

We assume you are reading this book or chapter because you wish to improve your speaking skills – a worthy goal. As Ayn Rand alludes to in her quote, a desire to succeed is the first step in achieving this objective. Nevertheless, you cannot hit a target unless you know what it is. Thus, the final portion of this chapter is devoted to an overview of eleven speaking competencies which we consider to be the standards for evaluating a variety of presentations at every level of mastery. These are based on the *Public Speaking Competence Rubric* [PSCR].[1] A complete copy of the rubric can be found at Activities.

1. Useful topic. The first speaking competency is to *select a topic that is appropriate to the audience and the occasion*. An advanced speaker selects a worthwhile topic that engages the audience. His topic also presents the audience with new information that they did not know before the speech. A beginning speaker selects a topic that lacks originality or is out of date. His topic provides no new information to the audience. An ineffective speaker may give a speech in which a single topic cannot be deduced by the audience.

2. Engaging introduction. To *formulate an introduction that orients the audience to the topic and the speaker* is the second speaking competency. An advanced speaker writes an introduction that contains an excellent attention-getter. She firmly establishes her credibility. She provides a sound orientation to the topic, states her thesis clearly, and previews her points in a cogent and memorable way. For the beginning speaker, her attention-getter is mundane and she somewhat develops her credibility. Her thesis is awkwardly composed and she provides little direction for the audience. The ineffective speaker has no opening technique, no credibility statement and provides no background on the topic. In addition she has no thesis statement and no preview of her points.

"Untitled" by Krystle. CC-BY.

---

1. Schreiber, L., Paul, G. & Shibley, L. R. (2012). The development and test of the Public Speaking Competence Rubric. *Communication Education, 61*(3), 205–233

3. Clear organization. Competency three is to *use an effective organizational pattern*. An advanced speaker is very well organized and delivers a speech with clear main points. His points are mutually exclusive and directly related to the thesis. Further, he employs effective transitions and signposts to help the speech flow well. The beginning speaker has main points that are somewhat organized, but the content of these points may overlap. Transitions may also be present in his speech, but they are not particularly effective. In the ineffective speaker's speech, there is no clear organizational pattern, there are no transitions, and it sounds as if the information is randomly presented.

Don't leave inferences to be drawn when evidence can be presented. -Richard Wright

4. Well-supported ideas. Fourth on the list of speaking competencies is to *locate, synthesize, and employ compelling supporting materials*. In the advanced speaker's speech, her key points are well supported with a variety of credible materials, and her sources provide excellent support for her thesis. In addition, all of her sources are clearly cited. A beginning speaker has points that are generally supported with a fair mix of materials. Only some of her evidence supports her thesis, and her source citations need to be clarified. An ineffective speaker gives a speech with no supporting materials or no source citations.

5. Closure in conclusion. The fifth speaking competency is to *develop a conclusion that reinforces the thesis and provides psychological closure*. The advanced speaker provides a clear and memorable summary of his points, and he refers back to the thesis or big picture. His speech also ends with a strong clincher or call to action. A beginning speaker provides some summary of his points, but there is no clear reference back to his thesis. The closing technique of his speech can also be strengthened. In an ineffective speaker's speech, there is no conclusion. His speech ends abruptly and without closure.

"Speaking Out – Public speaking made easy" **by Christian Heilmann.** *CC-BY.*

6. Clear and vivid language. *To demonstrate a careful choice of words* is the sixth speaking competency. An advanced speaker's language is exceptionally clear, imaginative and vivid. Her language is also completely free from bias, grammatical errors and inappropriate usage. The beginning speaker selects language that is adequate to make her point. She has some errors in grammar and occasionally uses slang, jargon or awkward sentence structure. The ineffective speaker has many errors in her grammar and syntax. She also mispronounces words and extensively uses slang, jargon, and/or sexist or racist terms.

7. Suitable vocal expression. Competency number seven is to *effectively use vocal expression and paralanguage to engage the audience*. Excellent use of vocal variation, intensity and pacing are characteristics of the advanced speaker. His vocal expression is also natural and enthusiastic, and he avoids fillers. Some vocal variation is evident in the beginning speaker's speech. He also enunciates clearly, speaks audibly, and generally avoids fillers (e.g., "um," "uh," "like," etc.). An ineffective speaker is inaudible, enunciates poorly, and speaks in a monotone voice. His speech also has poor pacing, and he distracts listeners with fillers.

8. Corresponding nonverbals. Eighth on the list of competencies is to *demonstrate nonverbal behavior that supports the verbal message.* An advanced speaker has posture, gestures, facial expression and eye contact that are natural, well developed, and display high levels of poise and confidence. Some reliance on notes is seen with the beginning speaker, but she has adequate eye contact. She also generally avoids distracting mannerisms. The ineffective speaker usually looks down and avoids eye contact. She has nervous gestures and other nonverbal behaviors that distract from or contradict the message.

> Body language is a very powerful tool. We had body language before we had speech, and apparently, 80% of what you understand in a conversation is read through the body, not the words. – Deborah Bull

9. Adapted to the audience. The ninth speaking competency is to *successfully adapt the presentation to the audience.* The advanced speaker shows how information is important to audience members, and his speech is tailored to their beliefs, values and attitudes. He may also make allusions to culturally shared experiences. A beginning speaker assumes but does not articulate the importance of the topic. His presentation is minimally adapted to the audience, and some of the ideas presented in the speech are removed from the audience's frame of reference or experiences. An ineffective speaker's speech is contrary to the audience's beliefs, values and attitudes. His message may be generic or canned and no attempt is made to establish common ground.

10. Adept use of visual aids. To skillfully make use of visual aids is the tenth competency. Exceptional explanation and presentation of visual aids is characteristic of the advanced speaker. Her speech has visuals that provide powerful insight into the speech topic, and her visuals are of high professional quality. The beginning speaker's visual aids are generally well developed and explained, although there may be minor errors present in the visuals. An ineffective speaker uses visual aids that distract from her speech. Her visuals may not be relevant, or her visuals may be of poor professional quality.

"Space Apps NYC Hackathon-2014" by jonny goldstein. CC-BY.

11. Convincing persuasion. The eleventh and final speaking competency is to *construct an effectual persuasive message with credible evidence and sound reasoning.* An advanced speaker articulates the problem and solution in a clear, compelling manner. He supports his claims with powerful and credible evidence while completely avoiding reasoning fallacies. His speech also contains a memorable call to action. In the beginning speaker's speech, the problem and solution are evident, and most claims are supported with evidence. He also has generally sound reasoning and a recognizable call to action. For the ineffective speaker, the problem and/or solution are not defined. His claims are not supported with evidence, his speech contains poor reasoning, and there is no call to action. Readers should note that the competencies listed above are not all inclusive. Ultimately one must adjust, expand, and apply these competencies as best fits the requirements of the speaking situation. But they do provide a starting point for new or less experienced speakers to begin to understand all of the interrelated components of a speech.

Being ignorant is not so much a shame, as being unwilling to learn. – Benjamin Franklin

Attributions

CC licensed content, Shared previously

- Chapter 1 Speaking Competencies. **Authored by**: Lisa Schreiber, Ph.D. and Morgan Hartranft. **Provided by**: Millersville University, Millersville, PA. **Located at**: http://publicspeakingproject.org/psvirtualtext.html. **Project**: The Public Speaking Project. **License**: *CC BY-NC-ND: Attribution-NonCommercial-NoDerivatives*
- IMG_4278. **Authored by**: Krystle. **Located at**: https://flic.kr/p/8dfBHP. **License**: *CC BY: Attribution*
- Speaking Out - Public speaking made easy. **Authored by**: Christian Heilmann. **Located at**: https://flic.kr/p/7Ciem5. **License**: *CC BY: Attribution*
- Space Apps NYC Hackathon-2014. **Authored by**: jonny goldstein. **Located at**: https://flic.kr/p/ncwMTc. **License**: *CC BY: Attribution*

Conclusion, Review Questions, and Activities

Our capacity to communicate through systems of language differentiates us from other species, but the use of that language to communicate effectively is actually harder than anticipated, particularly in front of an audience. Fortunately, by reading this book, you can learn the skills required to communicate more effectively one-on-one and in a speaking situation.

The speeches you present will be given in a particular context. In your role as communicator, you will encode and deliver a message which will then be decoded by audience members (also communicators). At the same time you are speaking, you will be receiving verbal and nonverbal feedback from the audience. The way that the message is decoded will depend entirely on the amount of noise interfering with the message as well as the worldviews of audience members.

Every new speaker should work to become skilled at the eleven core public speaking competencies. These competencies include: selecting a useful topic, writing an engaging introduction, organizing the points of the speech, finding effective supporting materials for the points, adding a conclusion that provides closure, using clear and vivid language, making sure that one's vocal expression corresponds to the goals of the speech, using nonverbals that complement the message, adapting the message to one's audience, using visual aids effectively, and using credible evidence and sound reasoning in persuasive messages. Each one of the competencies just listed is covered in depth in one or more chapters in this book.

The authors of this textbook hope that readers will find the chapters useful in developing their own communication competence. Whether you are new to giving presentations, or a more experienced speaker, it is important to remember that the best way to improve your public speaking skills is through preparation and practice. Although it may take time to learn effective speaking skills, the effort is well worth the benefits you will reap in your personal, professional, and public life.

"Untitled" by clarita. morgueFile.

An effective speaker knows that the success or failure of his talk is not for him to decide—it will be decided in the minds and hearts of his hearers. – Dale Carnegie

Review Questions

1. What are the personal, professional and public benefits of enhancing your public speaking skills?

2. What is the difference between the linear and transactional model of communication?

3. Define and give an original example of each of the elements of the communication process.

4. Which of the elements of the communication process do you think has the greatest impact on the way a message is interpreted. Explain.

5. What are the three types of speeches? For each of the three types of speeches, give two examples of an occasion or situation in which that type of speech might be given.

6. List the eleven speaking competencies. For each competency listed, describe the differences between the advanced speaker and the inexperienced speaker.

Activities

1. Working in groups of 3–5, generate a list of the characteristics of ineffective speakers you have seen. Next, generate a list of the characteristics of the effective speakers you have seen. What three qualities do you believe are most important to be a successful speaker? Explain.

2. Locate a speech on YouTube. While watching the speech, identify the strengths and weaknesses of the speaker's content and delivery? What three things could the speaker

improve on? What three things did you like about the speaker? If you were to deliver the speech, how would you do things differently?

3. Locate a copy of the *Public Speaking Competence Rubric* (http://www.publicspeaking-project.org/activities.html). Read through each of the levels of each of the competencies, and try to determine what your level of skill is for each of the speaking competencies. If you are able, have a friend or colleague watch one of your speeches and ask him or her to evaluate your level of skill for each of the competencies. Compare your responses to see how much correspondence there is between your responses and the evaluator's responses. In what areas are you strongest? What do you need to improve upon?

Attributions

CC licensed content, Shared previously

- Chapter 1 Conclusion, Review Questions, and Activities. **Authored by**: Lisa Schreiber, Ph.D. and Morgan Hartranft. **Provided by**: Millersville University, Millersville, PA. **Located at**: http://publicspeakingproject.org/psvirtualtext.html. **Project**: The Public Speaking Project. **License**: *CC BY-NC-ND: Attribution-NonCommercial-NoDerivatives*

- medicalcongress68. **Authored by**: clarita. **Provided by**: MorgueFile. **Located at**: http://mrg.bz/ZwbstJ. **License**: *All Rights Reserved*. **License Terms**: Free to remix, commercial use, no attribution required. http://www.morguefile.com/license/morguefile

Glossary and References

Glossary

TERM	DEFINITION
Abstract Word	Words that refer to ideas or concepts that are removed from material reality.
Axiology	A part of worldview; refers to an individual or group's value system.
Channel	The means through which the message travels.
Communicator	The people in the interaction or speech setting who encode and decode messages simultaneously.
Concrete Word	A word that describes a tangible object that can be perceived through the senses.
Context	The communication rules that govern different physical settings and/or different types of relationships.
Cosmology	A part of worldview; refers to the way individuals and groups see themselves in relation to other people and their view of their place in the universe.
Cultural Noise	Differences in worldview that cause message interference.
Decoding	The process of listening to words and interpreting the words so they are associated with a mental image.
Encoding	The process of taking a mental image, associating the image with words, and then speaking those words.
Epistemology	A part of worldview; refers to the way an individual or group acquires knowledge or what counts as knowledge.
Listening	The psychological process of interpreting and making sense of the messages we receive.
Message	The words, nonverbal behavior, or other signals transmitted from one person to another.
Noise	Anything that interferes with the message transmission or the encoding and decoding process.
Nonverbal Behavior	All of the messages we send — except for the words we say. Can include appearance, eye behavior, kinesics (body movement), proxemics (use of space), touch, time, and smell.
Norms	The verbal and nonverbal rules (usually unspoken) that govern communicative behavior.
Ontology	A part of worldview; refers to an individual's or group's belief system.
Praxeology	A part of worldview; refers to the way an individual or group goes about tasks or solving problems.
Psychological Noise	Message interference that results from disturbed or excited mental states.
Physiological Noise	Message interference that results from bodily discomfort.
Physical Noise	Message interference that results when the noise level (as measured in decibels) makes it difficult to hear a message.
Public Speaking	The act of delivering a speech in front of a live audience.
Worldview	The overall framework through which an individual sees, thinks about, and interprets the world and interacts with it.

References

Aras, K. (2012). The nuts and bolts of public speaking: Practical tools for powerful presentations. Retrieved from http://www.thecommunicationfactory.com/seminars/skills/PublicSpeaking.php

Barnlund, D. C. (2008). A transactional model of communication. In. C. D. Mortensen (Eds.), *Communication theory* (2nd Ed), pp. 47-57. New Brunswick, New Jersey: Transaction.

Farrell, R. (2011). Soft skills all great leaders should have. CareerBuilder. http://www.careerbuilder.com/Article/CB-2335- Leadership-Management-Soft-skills-all-great-leaders-should-have/

History.com. (2012). The Kennedy- Nixon Debates. History.com. Retrieved from http://www.history.com/topics/kennedy-nixon-debates

Koncz, A. and Allen, C. (2012). Employers look for communication skills, ability to work in a team in new college grads. www.naceweb.org/pressreleases/.

McKay, J. (2005). Employers complain about communication skills. Pittsburgh Post Gazette.

Rhodes, T. (Ed.) (2010). Assessing outcomes and improving achievement: Tips and tools for using rubrics. Washington D. C.: Association of American Colleges and Universities.

Rockler-Gladen, N. (2009, March 21). Job skills that every college student needs: Writing, speaking, professionalism, and other important knowledge. Suite 101.com. Retrieved from http://studyskills.suite101.com/article.cfm/job_skills_that_every_college _student_needs

Schreiber, L., Paul, G. & Shibley, L. R. (2012). The development and test of the Public Speaking Competence Rubric. *Communication Education, 61 (3)*, 205 – 233.

Shannon, C. E., & Weaver, W. (1949). *The mathematical theory of communication.* Urbana: University of Illinois Press

U.S. Department of Labor (2000). Skills and tasks for jobs: A SCANS report for America 2000. The Secretary's Commission on Achieving Necessary Skills. Washington, D.C.

photo credits

p. 1 The Dali Lama http://commons.wikimedia.org/wiki/File: Dalai-Lama-talking-to-KD.jpg By Wakan Foundation for the Arts

p. 2 Ronsenbaum talking to woman http://commons.wikimedia.org/wiki/File: Michael_Rosenbaum_(4995506953).jpg By Vagueonthehow

p. 2 Alice Walker http://commons.wikimedia.org/wiki/File: Alice_Walker_(cropped)1.jpg By Virginia Debolt

p. 5 The Kennedy / Nixon Debate 1960 http://en.wikipedia.org/wiki/File:Kennedy_Nixon_Debat_(1960).jpg By the National Park Service

p. 6 FEMA worker talking to woman http://upload.wikimedia.org/wikipedia/co mmons/1/17/FEMA_-_32747_-_FEMA_Community_Relations_worker_talking_to_a_Ohio_resident.jpg Ficara / FEMA

p. 6 Superfans http://commons.wikimedia.org/wiki/File:NFL_Superfans.jpg By HMJD02

p. 7 Hand cyclists at Warrior Games http://commons.wikimedia.org/wiki/File: Flickr_-_The_U.S._Army_-

_Talking_technique.jpg By U.S. Army

p. 9 Reasons not to like public speaking http://www.flickr.com/photos/codepo8/4 348896264/by Christian Heilmann

p. 9 Woman drawing http://www.flickr.com/photos/jonnygoldstein/3958940167/sizes/m/in/photostream/ by Jonny Goldstein

Attributions

CC licensed content, Shared previously

- Chapter 1 Glossary and References. **Authored by**: Lisa Schreiber, Ph.D. and Morgan Hartranft. **Provided by**: Millersville University, Millersville, PA. **Located at**: http://publicspeakingproject.org/psvirtualtext.html. **Project**: The Public Speaking Project. **License**: *CC BY-NC-ND: Attribution-NonCommercial-NoDerivatives*

Chapter 3: Informative Speaking

Objectives and Introduction

Informative Speaking

By Lisa Schreiber, Ph.D.
Millersville University, Millersville, PA

Learning Objectives

After reading this chapter, you should be able to:

- Explain why informative speeches are important
- Recognize the functions of informative speeches
- Identify the main responsibilities of the informative speaker
- List and describe the four types of informative speeches
- Discuss techniques to make informative speeches interesting, coherent, and memorable
- Apply chapter concepts in review questions and activities

Introduction

Not only is there an art in knowing a thing, but also a certain art in teaching it. – Cicero

Every day you give others information in an informal way, whether you realize it or not. You give your grandparents driving directions to your college campus. You tell your professor about a breaking news story. You teach a friend how to ride a motorcycle. You explain to your significant other your spiritual philosophy. You show a co-worker how to operate the cash register. You help your younger brother build his first Facebook page. Or you share your summer travel experience with your roommate. Without a doubt, information plays a vital role in  our everyday lives. In the dictionary, the term "inform" has several meanings, including to impart knowledge; to animate or inspire; to give information or enlightenment; to furnish evidence; to make aware of something; to communicate something of interest or special importance; to give directions; and to provide intelligence, news, facts or data. When you deliver an **informative speech**, your primary purpose is to give your audience information that they did not already know, or to teach them more about a topic with which they are already familiar.

Your ability to give informative speeches is one of the most important skills you will ever master, and it will be used both during the course of your career, and in your personal life. A pharmaceutical sales representative who can't describe the products' chemical composition, uses and side effects, will have trouble making a sale. A high school math teacher who can't explain algebra in simple terms will have students who will not learn. A manager who can't teach workers how to assemble microchips will have a department with low productivity and quality. And a little league coach who is unable to instruct players on batting and catching techniques will have a disadvantaged team. It is easy to imagine how difficult it would be to go about the business of our daily lives without the ability to give and receive information. Speeches to inform are the most common types of speeches (Gladis, 1999), so speech writers should give priority to learning how to construct them.

A speaker hasn't taught until the audience has learned.

Attributions

CC licensed content, Shared previously

- Chapter 15 Objectives, Outline, and Introduction. **Authored by**: Lisa Schreiber, Ph.D.. **Provided by**: Millersville University, Millersville, PA. **Located at**: http://publicspeakingproject.org/psvirtualtext.html. **Project**: Public Speaking Project. **License**: *CC BY-NC-ND: Attribution-NonCommercial-NoDerivatives*
- Teacher. **Authored by**: JD Lasica. **Located at**: https://www.flickr.com/photos/jdlasica/2431624696/. **License**: *CC BY-NC: Attribution-NonCommercial*

Role of Speaker

Human history becomes more and more a race between education and catastrophe. – H. G. Wells

Now that you understand the importance of informing others, this next section will show you the speakers' responsibilities for preparing and presenting informative speeches.

Informative Speakers Are Objective

Most public speaking texts discuss three **general purposes** for speeches: to inform, to persuade, and to entertain. Although these general purposes are theoretically distinct, in practice, they tend to overlap. Even in situations when the occasion calls for an informative speech (one which enhances understanding), often persuasive and entertaining elements are present. First, all informative speeches have a persuasive component by virtue of the fact that the speaker tries to convince the audience that the facts presented are accurate (Harlan, 1993). Second, a well-written speech can make even the most dry, technical information entertaining through engaging illustrations, colorful language, unusual facts, and powerful visuals.

In spite of this caveat, when planning your informative speech your primary intent will be to increase listeners' knowledge in an impartial way. For instance, in a speech about urban legends (Craughwell, 2000), your specific purpose statement may be: *"At the end of my speech, my audience will understand what an urban legend is, how urban legends are spread, and common variations of urban legends."* The topic you choose is not as important as your approach to the material in determining whether your speech is informative or persuasive (Peterson, Stephan, & White, 1992). Can you imagine how speeches on witchcraft, stem cell research, the federal deficit, or hybrid cars could be written either to inform or persuade? Informative speeches need to be as objective, fair, and unbiased as possible. You are not asking your audience to take action or convincing them to change their mind. You are teaching them something and allowing them to decide for themselves what to do with the information. When writing your speech, present all sides of the story and try to remove all unrelated facts, personal opinions, and emotions (Westerfield, 2002).

Informative Speakers are Credible

An objective approach also enhances a speaker's **credibility**. Credibility, or ethos, refers to an audience's perception that the speaker is well prepared and qualified to speak on a topic (Fraleigh & Tuman, 2011). Peterson, Stephan, and White (1992) explain that there are two kinds of credibility; the reputation that precedes you before you give your speech (antecedent credibility) and the credibility you develop during the course of your speech (consequent credibility). In many cases, the audience has no prior knowledge of the speaker, so they make judgments about the quality of the evidence and arguments in the speech. In addition, they look at and listen to the speaker to determine if s/he is a reliable source of information.

Audience members have no motivation to listen to a speaker they perceive as lacking authority or credibility—except maybe to mock the speaker. To avoid this pitfall, there are at least three ways to boost your credibility as a speaker; by establishing your expertise, helping your audience identify with you, and showing you are telling the truth (see examples in Table 15.1). It seems to be common sense that we do not listen to speakers who do not know what they are talking about, who cannot relate to us, or who give the impression of being dishonest. However, in planning informative speeches, we can get so wrapped up in the topic that is easy to forget about the elements of credibility. Just remember that in order to teach, we first have to show that we are worthy of our audience's attention.

Table 15.1 Boost Your Credibility	
Establish Expertise By:	• Citing reputable sources • Making sure your facts are accurate • Covering your points in enough detail to demonstrate your knowledge • Revealing your personal expertise with the topic
Help the Audience Identify with You By:	• Wearing appropriate and attractive clothing • Mentioning what you have in common • Being friendly and enthusiastic • Relating to listeners' situations, feelings, and motives
Show You are Telling the Truth By:	• Presenting both sides of an issue • Sharing what motivated you to select your topic • Having open, natural nonverbals that correspond to what you say • Approaching the speech with ethics and positive intentions for your audience

In the end, you make your reputation and you have your success based upon credibility and being able to provide people who are really hungry for information what they want. – Brit Hume

Informative Speakers Are Knowledgeable

Good informative speeches contain a number of different source citations throughout the speech. To show that the information you present is accurate and complete, these sources should be up-to-date, reliable, unbiased, and directly relevant to your topic. Even if you plan to give a speech about an activity you have done all of your life, you will still need to seek out additional sources for your speech. By all means, you should cite and use your own experiences with the topic, but if you want to appear objective, you will need to show that your ideas and experiences correspond with others'. Using a variety of sound reference materials helps you appear well-informed and more trustworthy.

In our information age, people are fortunate to have unlimited and free access to information on virtually any topic they can imagine via the internet. Unfortunately, in addition to the credible information, the internet contains an abundance of garbage. Good speech writers know that it is important to avoid weak or questionable sources (e.g. Wikipedia, Britannica.com or Ask.com) when constructing their speeches. Start by asking what you know, find out what the experts know, and then move to find out what information other sources can provide (Gladis, 1999). You can search your library catalogue or Amazon.com to locate books (which provide details and depth), and then check out or order these books via interlibrary loan (often free) if they are not available in your library. Explain not only *how* something is done, but also why it is done for a great speech (MacInnis, 2006). This variety gives a speech depth and a level of interest that cannot be achieved merely by doing a Google search and using the first five websites that pop up. For additional ideas on locating sources, *"Sources of interesting information"* is provided at the end of this chapter.

The cure for boredom is curiosity. There is no cure for curiosity. – Dorothy Parker

Informative Speakers Make the Topic Relevant

When you are selecting your topic and thinking about what you want to accomplish in your informative speech, two factors should drive your decision. Foremost, you want to select a topic that holds a high degree of interest for you (i.e. the topic is meaningful to you). Students who feel at a loss for topic ideas should turn their attention to their own lives and activities. If you like to play video games, you might give a speech about how they are made. If you have a passion for ska reggae music, you might bring in MP3 cuts to help define the boundaries of this music genre. If you have to work three jobs to help pay for school, you could give a speech on effective time management. Genuine curiosity will make the research and preparation process easier. Further, when you have enthusiasm for a topic, it shows when you speak.

On the other hand, if you do not really care about your topic, your audience is not likely to care either.

In addition to having relevance for you, it is crucial that you tie your topic directly to your listeners. Early in the speech, give listeners at least one reason why they should care about your topic and the ways in which the information will be beneficial or entertaining (Morreale & Bovee, 1998). Establishing a motive for your audience to listen to you is commonly referred to by the acronym **WIIFM**—"What's in it for me?" This is what the audience consciously or unconsciously asks when you start speaking (Urech, 1998). To establish WIIFM, you clearly link the topic to the listeners' values, attitudes, beliefs and lifestyle. Consider not only what the audience *wants* to hear, but also what they *need* to hear (Gladis, 1999; Maxey & O'Connor, 2006). Take the topic of retirement planning as an example. Younger listeners may not perceive this as relevant to their lives when they are not yet making a steady salary. But, if you can demonstrate how investing even a small amount every month can grow to a considerable nest egg by retirement age, and that getting into the habit of saving early can lower the number of years they have to work, the topic becomes more interesting for them.

Making the topic relevant for your audience can also mean that you show them how to apply the information immediately. In a speech on relaxation techniques, a speaker can lead the audience through a simple stress reduction exercise they can use at home. For a speech on handwriting analysis, listeners can be given paper, asked to write a sample sentence and shown how to interpret some points on the sample. If the audience members have laptops, a speaker can show them how to improve one of their digital photos. If listeners can use the information they learn quickly, they tend to remember it longer, and they are more likely to try the action again later (Nelson, et al., 2010).

Attributions

CC licensed content, Shared previously

Functions of Informative Speeches

People encounter a number of formal and informal informative presentations throughout their day, and these presentations have several consequences. First, informative presentations *provide people with knowledge*. When others share facts or circumstances associated with some topic, our comprehension, awareness or familiarity is increased. The speaker imparts information, and this information is turned into knowledge. A music teacher describes the difference between a note and chord as an introduction to music. When issuing a warning to a teenager, a police officer explains the nature of the moving violation. A travel agent clarifies for customers the policies for airline ticket refunds. Participants at a cultural fair are enlightened by a shaman explaining her spiritual practices. Knowledge helps us to understand the world around us, enables us to make connections, and helps us to predict the future.

> All men by nature desire knowledge. – Aristotle

Second, informative presentations *shape our perceptions*. These presentations can affect how people see a subject by bringing it to light, or may influence what is seen as important by virtue of directing attention to the subject (Osborn & Osborn, 1991). Information helps us to interpret our experiences, it shapes our values and beliefs, it may alter our self-concept, and it gives meaning to situations. Imagine you meet your new boss, and she is very curt and pre-occupied during the first staff meeting. You may at first perceive her as being rude, unless later you

find out that just before your meeting with her she learned that her father had been hospitalized with a stroke. Learning this new information allowed you to see the situation from a different perspective. In the same way, informative presentations enable us to get a sense of "the big picture" and improve our ability to think and evaluate.

Some informative presentations may be aimed at helping listeners understand the number, variety, and quality of alternatives available to them (Hogan et al., 2010). Consequently, informative presentations also serve to *articulate alternatives*. A car sales associate might explain to you the features of one car in comparison to another car in order to help you differentiate between the models. A doctor might explain to your grandmother her treatment options for arthritis. A fitness trainer may demonstrate to you several types of exercises to help you strengthen your abdominal muscles and reduce your waistline. If you go to a temporary employment agency, a staff member may provide you will a range of job options that fit your qualifications. Successful informative presentations provide information which improves listeners' ability to make wise decisions, because they understand all of their options (Jaffe, 1998).

Finally, informative presentations *enhance our ability to survive and evolve*. Our existence and safety depend upon the successful communication of facts and knowledge. An informative speech "helps keep countries developing, communicates valuable and useful information in thousands of areas, and continues to change, improve or upgrade the lives of audiences" (Wilbur, 2000, p. 99). For thousands of years, cultural and technical knowledge was passed from generation to generation orally. Even today with the presence of the internet, you are still likely to get a good amount of information verbally. We have all seen "how to" YouTube videos, and although these have a significant visual components, the "experts" still have to give a verbal explanation. Through meetings, presentations and face-to-face interactions, we gain information about how to perform and improve in our jobs. To keep our children safe, we don't give them an instruction manual, we sit down with them and explain things. All of the knowledge we accumulate while we live will be passed down to (hopefully) improve on the lives of those who come after us. Much of this information will be passed down in the form of a presentation.

Attributions

CC licensed content, Shared previously

- Chapter 15 Functions of Informative Speeches. **Authored by**: Lisa Schreiber, Ph.D.. **Provided by**: Millersville University, Millersville, PA. **Located at**: http://publicspeakingproject.org/psvirtualtext.html. **Project**: Public Speaking Project. **License**: *CC BY-NC-ND: Attribution-NonCommercial-NoDerivatives*
- Home For Sale Sign. **Authored by**: Mark Moz. **Located at**: https://www.flickr.com/photos/106574022@N04/11415768915/. **License**: *CC BY: Attribution*

Types of Informative Speeches

In the last section we examined how informative speakers need to be objective, credible, knowledgeable, and how they need to make the topic relevant to their audience. This section discusses the four primary types of informative speeches. These include definitional speeches, descriptive speeches, explanatory speeches, and demonstration speeches.

Definitional Speeches

In definitional speeches the speaker attempts to set forth the meaning of concepts, theories, philosophies, or issues that may be unfamiliar to the audience. In these types of speeches, speakers may begin by giving the historical derivation, classification, or synonyms of terms or the background of the subject. In a speech on "How to identify a sociopath," the speaker may answer these questions: Where did the word 'sociopath' come from? What is a sociopath? How many sociopaths are there in the population? What are the symptoms? Carefully define your terminology to give shape to things the audience cannot directly sense. Describing the essential attributes of one concept compared to another (as through use of analogies) can increase understanding as well. For a speech on "Elderly Abuse," the speaker may compare this type of abuse to child or spousal abuse for contrast.

Regardless of the listeners' level of knowledge about the subject, it is very important in these types of speeches to show the relevance of the topic to their lives. Often the topics discussed in definitional speeches are abstract—distanced from reality. So provide explicit, real-life examples and applications of the subject matter. If you were going to give a speech about civil rights, you would need to go beyond commonly held meanings and show the topic in a new light. In this type of speech, the speaker points out the unique and distinguishing properties or boundaries of a concept *in a particular context* (Rinehart, 2002). The meaning of "civil rights" has changed significantly over time. What does it mean today compared to the 1960s? How will knowing this distinction help audience members? What are some specific incidents involving civil rights issues in current news? What changes in civil rights legislation might listeners see in their lifetimes?

Sample Definitional Speech Outline

Title: *"Life is suffering," and Other Buddhist Teachings* (Thompson, 1999)

Specific Purpose: At the end of my speech, my audience will understand the Four Noble Truths and the Eightfold Path in Buddhism

Central Idea: Regardless of your religious beliefs, Buddhist philosophy teaches a number of useful lessons you can apply to your own life.

I. Four Noble Truths

- All life involves *dukkha* (suffering)
- Suffering is caused by *tanha* (longing for things to be other than they are)
- If this longing stops (*nirodha*), suffering will cease
- The way to eliminate longing is to follow the Eightfold Path

II. The Noble Eightfold Path (the Middle Way)

- Right view
- Right intention
- Right speech
- Right action
- Right livelihood
- Right effort
- Right mindfulness
- Right contemplation

Descriptive Speeches

The purpose of **descriptive speeches** is to provide a detailed, vivid, word picture of a person, animal, place, or object. Audiences should carry away in their minds a clear vision of the subject (Osborn & Osborn, 1991). Consider this description of the Taj Mahal in Agra, India by Steve Cassidy (edited for length).

To gaze in wonder at that magnificent dome and elegant gardens will be a moment that you remember for the rest of your life. The Taj Mahal just takes your breath away. What is immediately striking is its graceful symmetry—geometric lines run through formal gardens ending in a white marble platform. Atop this platform is great white bulbous dome complemented by four towering minarets in each corner. The whole image shimmers in a reflecting pool flanked by beautiful gardens—the effect is magical. The first stretch by the reflecting pool is where most people pose for their photos. But we were impressed by the fresh, green gardens. As you approach through the gardens two mosques come into view flanking the Taj—both exquisitely carved and built of red sandstone.

In the descriptive speech, determine the characteristics, features, functions, or fine points of the topic. What makes the person unique? How did the person make you feel? What adjectives apply to the subject? What kind of material is the object made from? What shape is it? What color is it? What does it smell like? Is it part of a larger system? Can it be seen by the naked eye? What is its geography or location in space? How has it changed or evolved over time? How does it compare to a similar object? When preparing for the speech, try to think of ways to appeal to as many of the senses as possible. As an example, in a speech about different types of curried dishes, you could probably verbally describe the difference between yellow, red, and green curry, but the speech will have more impact if the audience can see, smell, and taste samples.

Sample Descriptive Speech Outline

Title: *Easter Island: The Navel of the World* (Fischer, 2006)

Specific Purpose: At the end of my speech, my audience will be able to visualize some of the main attractions on Easter Island.

Central Idea: Easter Island hosts a number of ancient, mysterious, and beautiful attractions that make it an ideal vacation destination.

  I. Stone Giants—"Moai"

- Average 13 feet high; 14 tons
- Play sacred role for Rapa Nui (native inhabitants)
- Central Ahu ceremonial sites

  II. Coastline activities

- Beaches
- Snorkeling & Scuba
- Surfing

  III. Rano Kau Chilean National Park

- Giant crater
- Sheer cliffs to ocean

> • Sea birds

Be able to describe anything visual, such as a street scene, in words that convey your meaning. ~ Marilyn vos Savant

Explanatory Speeches

An **explanatory speech** (also known as a briefing) is similar to the descriptive speech in that they both share the function of clarifying the topic. But explanatory speeches focus on reports of current and historical events, customs, transformations, inventions, policies, outcomes, and options. Whereas descriptive speeches attempt to paint a picture with words so that audiences can vicariously experience it, explanatory speeches focus on the *how* or *why* of a subject and its consequences. Thus, a speaker might give a *descriptive* speech on the daily life of Marie Antoinette, or an *explanatory* speech on how she came to her death. Recall that definitional speeches focus on delineating concepts or issues. In this case, a speaker might give a *definitional* speech about the Emergency Economic Stabilization Act of 2008, or an *explanatory* speech on why the financial bailout was necessary for U.S. financial stability.

If a manager wanted to inform employees about a new workplace internet use policy, s/he might cover questions like: Why was a policy implemented? How will it help? What happens if people do not follow established policies? Explanatory speeches are less concerned with appealing to the senses than connecting the topic to a series of related other subjects to enhance a deep understanding (McKerrow, Gronbeck, Ehninger, & Monroe, 2000). For example, to explain the custom of the Thai *wai* greeting (hands pressed together as in prayer), you also need to explain how it originated to show one had no weapons, and the ways it is tied to religion, gender, age, and status.

Sample Explanatory Speech Outline

Title: *Giant Waves, Death, and Devastation: The 2004 Indian Ocean Tsunami* (National Geographic, 2006)

Specific Purpose: At the end of my speech, my audience will be aware of the nature of the 2004 Tsunami and the destruction it caused.

Central Idea: The 2004 Asian Tsunami was one of the worst natural disasters in human history in terms of magnitude, loss of human life, and enduring impact.

    I. Geological event

- Earthquake epicenter and magnitude
- Tsunami forms (waves reach up to 100 feet)
- Tsunami strikes land of various countries with no warning

   II. Human casualties reach almost 230,000—top 10 of all natural disasters

- The countries and people involved
- Loss of food, water, hospitals, housing, electricity, and plumbing
- Threat of disease

III. Ongoing effects

- Environmental destruction
- Economic devastation
- Psychological trauma

I hear and I forget. I see and I remember. I do and I understand. – Confucious

Demonstration Speeches

The most practical of all informative speeches, a demonstration speech shows listeners how some process is accomplished or how to perform it themselves. The focus is on a chronological explanation of some process (how potato chips are made), procedure (how to fight fires on a submarine), application (how to use the calendar function in Outlook), or course of action (how court cases proceed to Supreme Court status). Speakers might focus on processes that have a series of steps with a specific beginning and end (how to sell a home by yourself) or the process may be continuous (how to maintain the hard drive on your computer to prevent crashes). Demonstration speeches can be challenging to write due to the fact that the process may involve several objects, a set of tools, materials, or a number of related relationships or events (Rinehart, 2002). Nevertheless, these types of speeches provide the greatest opportunity for audience members to get involved or apply the information later.

When preparing this speech, remember first to keep the safety of the audience in mind. One speaker severely burned his professor when he accidently spilled hot oil from a wok on her. Another student nearly took the heads off listeners when he was demonstrating how to swing a baseball bat. Keep in mind also that you may need to bring in examples or pictures of completed steps in order to make efficient use of your time. Just think of the way that cooking demonstrations are done on TV—the ingredients are pre-measured, the food is premixed, and the mixture magically goes from uncooked to cooked in a matter of seconds. Finally, if you are having your audience participate during your presentation (making an origami sculpture), know what their knowledge level is so that you don't make them feel unintelligent if they are not successful. Practice your speech with friends who know nothing about the topic to gauge if listeners can do what you are asking them to do in the time allotted.

Sample Demonstration Speech Outline

Title: *How to Survive if You Get Stranded in the Wilderness* (U.S. Department of Defense, 2006).

Specific Purpose: At the end of my speech my audience will understand what to do if they unexpectedly become stranded in the wilderness.

Central Idea: You can greatly improve your ability to stay alive and safe in the wilderness by learning a few simple survival techniques.

    I. Size up the situation

- Size up the surroundings
- Size up your physical and mental states
- Size up your equipment (handout "What to Include in a Survival Kit")

    II. Survival Basics

- Obtaining water
- Acquiring food
- Building a fire
- Locating shelter

    III. Finding help

- Call or signal rescue personnel
- Wilderness navigation
- Leaving "bread crumb" trail

Attributions

CC licensed content, Shared previously

- Chapter 15 Types of Informative Speeches. **Authored by**: Lisa Schreiber, Ph.D.. **Provided by**: Millersville University, Millersville, PA. **Located at**: http://publicspeakingproject.org/psvirtualtext.html. **Project**: Public Speaking Project. **License**: *CC BY-NC-ND: Attribution-NonCommercial-NoDerivatives*
- Taj Mahal, Agra, India. **Authored by**: Yann. **Located at**: https://commons.wikimedia.org/wiki/File:Taj_Mahal,_Agra,_India.jpg. **License**: *CC BY-SA: Attribution-ShareAlike*

Public domain content

- Maoi at Rano Raraku. **Authored by**: Aurbina. **Located at**: https://commons.wikimedia.org/wiki/File:Moai_Rano_raraku.jpg. **License**: *Public Domain: No Known Copyright*

Developing Informative Speeches

The first sections of this chapter explained the importance of informative speaking, the functions of informative speeches, the role of the informative speaker, and the four major types of informative speeches. This final section of the chapter discusses three goals in developing informative speeches and advice for increasing the effectiveness of your speech. These three goals include 1) arousing the interest of your audience, 2) presenting information in a way that can be understood, and 3) helping the audience remember what you have said (Fujishin, 2000).

Generate and Maintain Interest

Use Attention-Getting Elements

Before you capture the interest of an audience, you have to get their attention. As you know, attention getters are used in the introduction of a speech, but **attention getters** can also be used throughout your speech to maintain an audience's attention. There are a number of techniques you can use that will naturally draw listeners' attention (German, et al., 2010).

Intensity refers to something that has a high or extreme degree of emotion, color, volume, strength or other defining characteristic. In a speech about sharks' senses, showing how sharks smell 10,000 times better than humans would be an example of the intensity principle.

Novelty involves those things that are new or unusual. Discussing the recent invention of the flesh-eating mushroom death suit developed by Jae Rhim Lee would be novel. This suit is designed to help bodies decompose naturally above ground to avoid the use of dangerous embalming chemicals.

Contrast can also be used to draw attention through comparison to something that is different or opposite. This works best when the differences are significant. If you were showing the audience how to make hot sauce, and you showed a bar graph comparing the scoville units (level of hotness) of different chili peppers, this would be contrast. Jalapenos rate at 2500–8000 scoville units, habaneros rate at 100,000–350,000, and the naga jolokia rates at 855,000–1,041,241.

Audiences will also attend to movement or **Activity**. To employ this technique, the speaker can either use action words, well-chosen movements, an increased rate of speech, or s/he can show action with video. A speech describing or showing extreme sports with high levels of risk, a fast pace, or amazing stunts could be used to illustrate activity.

Finally, **Humor** can be used to draw attention to a subject or point, but be sure that it is relevant and in good taste. In a speech about the devotion of Trekkies (Star Trek fans), you could share the example of Tony Alleyne who designed and outfitted his flat in England as a replica of the deck of the Voyager. You could also direct the audience's attention to couples who have wedding ceremonies spoken in Klingon.

Tell a Story

Story telling is not only the basis for most of our entertainment; it is also one of the best ways to teach an audience (Carlson, 2005). Also known as narratives, stories typically have a beginning in which the characters and setting are introduced, a rise in action, some complication or problem, and a resolution. Stories with compelling characters can be used in a creative way to weave facts otherwise dry and technical facts together (Walters, 1995), as in a speech about preparing a space shuttle for take-off from a mouse's perspective. Jaffe (1998) differentiates between three types of narratives that can be used in informative speeches. The first type of story is a natural reality in which natural or scientific facts are brought together in chronological accounts, as in the formation of the Grand Canyon. The second narrative involves social realities which detail historic events, and the development of cultures and institutions. The last kind of story, the ultimate reality, is focused on profound philosophical and spiritual questions like "Where do we come from?" and "What happens to us when we die?"

Nursery rhymes and song lyrics familiar to the audience can also be used in an interactive way to get listeners interested in the topic (Maxey & O'Connor, 2006). In a speech about the global population explosion, you could ask audience to finish the phrase "There was an old woman who lived in a shoe…" Common commercials, lyrics to Beatles songs, holiday songs, and children's games are universal.

The wisest mind has something yet to learn. – George Santayna

Commercial jingles and song lyrics also work to get the audience involved. You could start a speech on boating safety with these lyrics: Just sit right back / And you'll hear a tale / A tale of a fateful trip / That started from this tropic port / Aboard this tiny ship (from *Gilligan's Island*). Depending on the make-up of your audience, you might use lyrics from Johnny Cash, Billy Holiday, The Doors, The Beatles, JayZ, The Judds or the Arctic Monkeys. Just remember you probably can't read all of the lyrics, you need to make sure the lyrics are directly linked to your topic, and you should be sure to cite the artist and song title.

Just for fun, can you name the artist who sang the lyrics below? Can you think of a speech topic that would correspond to the lyrics? (Answer at the end of the chapter)

Lyric	Artist	Speech Topic
Money, get away. Get a good job with good pay and you're okay. Money, it's a gas. Grab that cash with both hands and make a stash. New car, caviar, four star daydream Think I'll buy me a football team.		

Be Creative

Speakers who are different are memorable (Maxey & O'Connor, 2006). To give your speech impact, be imaginative and dare to push the envelope of conformity. When you have spent time researching a topic, you may be able to envision ways to incorporate surprising facts, props or visuals that make your presentation different from others, and therefore more memorable. You could dress like a Shakespearian actor for a speech about the famous playwright. You could have the audience move their chairs and take part in a yoga demonstration. Or you might use your own audience plants to help with a speech entitled "Behind the Scenes of TV Talk Shows." When one student got up to speak, he drew a row of houses on the blackboard and then began to drink a glass of water and speak about the life giving properties of water. After making a few comments, he threw the glass of water on the blackboard—erasing most of the houses. Then he began his speech on the devastating effects of a flood (be sure to get your professor's permission before you do something like this!). Another student giving a speech about "Clowning" had two actual clowns wait in the hall until she was ready to bring them in and show off their make-up and costumes. The speaker was wise to have her cohorts in the room just long enough to make the point (but not the entire time which would distract from the speaker), and the audience was attentive and grateful for the variety. Hanks and Parry (1991) explain that anyone can be creative, if s/he wants to be and is willing to make the effort. For some tips on how to foster your creativity, see Table 16.2. However, you need to remember that creativity is just a tool to help you teach your audience. Do not overlook the requirements of the occasion, the content of your research, or the needs of your audience in your zeal to be creative.

Table 16.2 Tips for Jump Starting Your Creativity From Everyday Creativity by Carlin Flora (2009)
<ul><li>Take a different way to work</li><li>Collaborate with others with complementary skills</li><li>Seek inspiration in beautiful surroundings</li><li>Start working on the problem right away</li><li>Work in a blue room (it boosts creativity)</li><li>Get a hobby or play music</li><li>Think about your problem right before falling asleep</li></ul>

The worst enemy to creativity is self-doubt. – Sylvia Plath

Stimulate Audience Intellect

Most people have a genuine desire to understand the world around them, to seek out the truth, and learn how to solve problems. The role of the informative speaker is to satisfy this desire to learn and know. To illustrate our quest for knowledge, consider the success of the Discovery Channel, the Learning Channel, the History Channel, the Food Network and other educational broadcasts. So how do we appeal to the minds of listeners? Think about all of the information we encounter every day but do not have time to pursue. Think about subjects that you would like to know more about. Ask what information would be universally interesting and useful for listeners. Many people fly on airplanes, but do they know how to survive a plane crash? People also share many ordinary illnesses, so what are some common home remedies? All of the people on earth originated someplace, so who were our ancient ancestors?

In addition to finding topics that relate to listeners, the information we supply should be up to date. For instance, Egypt recently had a revolution, and if you are giving a speech on traveling to the Pyramids, you should be aware of this. When you are talking about a topic that your audience is familiar with, you should share little known facts or paint the subject in a new light. In a speech about a famous person, you might depict what they are like behind the scenes, or what they were like growing up. In a speech about a new technology, you might also talk about the inventors. In a speech about a famous city, you could discuss the more infamous landmarks and attractions.

Create Coherence

Organize Logically

Several types of organizational patterns are discussed in the *Selecting and Arranging Main Points* chapter. Using these as a starting point, you should make sure the overall logic of the speech is well thought out. If you were giving speech best suited to chronological order, but presented the steps out of order, it would be very difficult to follow. Those of you who have seen the movie *Memento* (which presented the sequence of events backwards), may have noticed how difficult it was to explain the plot to others. In a logical speech, the points you are trying to draw are obvious, the supporting materials are coherent and correspond exactly to the thesis, and the main points are mutually exclusive and flow naturally from start to finish. Clarity of thought is critical in presenting information. As Peggy Noonan (1998, p. 64) argues:

> *The most moving thing in a speech is always the logic. It's never the flowery words and flourishes, it's not sentimental exhortations, it's never the faux poetry we're all subjected to these days. It's the logic; it's the thinking behind your case. A good case well argued and well said is inherently moving. It shows respect for the brains of the listeners. There is an implicit compliment in it. It shows that you are a serious person and that you are talking to other serious persons.*

When planning your speech, ask questions like: What information needs to come first? What organizational pattern best suits the topic? What information must be shared or omitted to aid in audience understanding? What points or sub-points should be grouped together to aid listeners' understanding?

Use Simple Language

One common mistake that speech writers make when they are writing their speech is to use the same language that they would use in a written document. Experienced speech writers know that simple language and ideas are easier to understand than complex ones. "Clear speaking is not an alternative to intelligent discourse, but rather an enabler of intelligent discourse" (Carlson, 2005, p. 79). Did you know that Lincoln's Gettysburg address contains only 271 words, and 251 of these words only have one or two syllables (Hughes & Phillips, 2000)? Another benefit of using simple language is that you are less likely to trip over or mispronounce simple words.

Table 16.3 Simplify Your Language	
Low Impact	**High Impact**
Under the present circumstances	Currently
At the present time	Now
Are in agreement with	Agree

Table 16.3 Simplify Your Language	
Low Impact	**High Impact**
Due to the fact that	Because
Is fully operational	Works
In close proximity to	Near
Of sufficient magnitude	Big enough
In the event of	If
Each and everyone	Each
In the course of	During
Never before or since	Never
Deciduous trees (jargon)	Trees that lose their leaves
Somnolent (jargon)	Drowsy
Awesome (slang)	Impressive
Put the bit on (slang)	Borrow
No brainer (cliché)	Easy decision
An arm and a leg	Expensive
Vertically challenged (euphemism)	Short
Gone to the great beyond (euphemism)	Dead

Instead of "protracted," say "drawn out." Instead of "conundrum," say "puzzle." And instead of "loquacious," say "talkative." As you are writing your speech you also want to avoid technical jargon, slang, clichés, and euphemisms. This type of language is difficult to understand and tends to be low impact. Compare the *Low Impact* language column with the *High Impact* column in Table 16.3 above to see examples of ways to make your language more powerful.

Avoid Information Overload

No one is given an unlimited amount of time to speak. You can't cover everything that there is to know about your topic. And even if you could speak forever about everything there was to know about a subject, your listeners would never be able to take it all in. **Information overload** occurs when a person feels that they are faced with an overwhelming amount of information, with the effect that they are unable to process it all or unable to make decision. So whether you have five minutes to give a presentation or three eight-hour days, you will need to narrow and focus your speech topic and objectives. If you know that you have ten minutes to speak, you will not be able to cover "Car Maintenance for Dummies," but you probably could give a good speech entitled "How to Change the Oil in Your Car." When planning your speech, be sure to determine the amount of information that can reasonably be covered in the time allowed. In fact, rather than taking the entire allotted speaking time, you should get into the practice of speaking only for 90—95% of the time that you are given (Reynolds, 2008). More is not always better—and your audience will appreciate it if you can skillfully make your point with time to spare.

Today knowledge has power. It controls access to opportunity and advancement. – Peter Drucker

Make Your Speech Memorable

Build in Repetition

Audience retention is determined by a number of factors including listeners' interest, knowledge, physical and emotional state, level of stress, background, and other competing demands (Fujishin, 2000). One way to help your audience remember the content of your speech is by repetition (Hughes & Phillips, 2000). There are three ways to incorporate repetition into your speech. The first form repetition involves restating your main points in your introduction, body and conclusion. When you do this, you will restate your points using different language—not repeat the points word for word.

The second form of repetition is where a word or a phrase is repeated in a poetic way, either throughout the speech or at a critical point in the speech. One example of this would be Abraham Lincoln's "government of the people, by the people, for the people." Another example can be found in Sojourner Truth's speech, delivered in 1851 at a women's rights convention.

> *… That man over there says that women need to be helped into carriages, and lifted over ditches, and to have the best place everywhere. Nobody ever helps me into carriages, or over mud-puddles, or gives me any best place! And ain't I a woman? Look at me! Look at my arm! I have ploughed and planted, and gathered into barns, and no man could head me! And ain't I a woman? I could work as much and eat as much as a man—when I could get it—and bear the lash as well! And ain't I a woman? I have borne thirteen children, and seen most all sold off to slavery, and when I cried out with my mother's grief, none but Jesus heard me! And ain't I a woman?*

The final way to use repetition in your speech is through nonverbal communication. When you say the word "four" and you hold up four fingers, or when you verbally agree with a point and nod your head at the same time, you are reinforcing the idea verbally and nonverbally.

Appeal to Different Ways of Learning

Individuals have different learning styles, so some people are visual [V] learners, some are aural [A] learners, some learn by reading [R] and writing, and some learn kinesthetically [K] (Fleming, 2001). You can test your own learning style at www.varklearn.com. Understanding your own and others' learning styles is useful for two reasons. First, you will find that you tend to teach others using your own learning style. Second, regardless of your own learning styles, you need to appeal to as many different learning styles as possible in your informative speech. To see how each learning style prefers to be taught, see the table below.

Unfortunately, since the ear alone is a very poor information gathering device, steps must be taken to improve retention. Typically listeners only retain only a small fraction of what is explained to them verbally. The first way to enhance retention is to appeal to as many of the senses as possible. Studies show that audiences retain 20 percent of what they hear, 30 percent of what they see, and 50 percent of what they hear *and* see (Westerfield, 2002). When the audience has an opportunity to *do* something (adding the kinesthetic sense), their retention increases to 80 percent (Walters, 1995). Or, if participation is not possible, a handout will raise retention to an impressive 85 percent—if the audience can review the handout at least once (Slutsky & Aun, 1997).

Table 16.4 The VARK Model of Learning	
Learning Style	**Approach the Learner With…**
Visual Learners	Maps, charts, graphs, diagrams, brochures, flow charts, highlighters, different colors, pictures, word pictures, and different spatial arrangements
Aural Learners	Explanations of new ideas, large and small group discussions, lectures, audio recordings, stories, and jokes
Read/Write Learners	Lists, essays, reports, textbooks, definitions, printed handouts, readings, manuals, and web pages
Kinesthetic Learners	Field trips, hands-on projects, sensory stimulations, laboratories, recipes and solutions to problems, and collections of samples
From Hawk and Shaw (2007, p. 7) and Fleming (2001).	

Another way to help your listeners remember is by the use of techniques like *association*, linking the new topic to things that the audience knows about or already understands. If you were giving a speech about rugby, you might compare it to soccer and football to help the audience understand the rules. The use of *acronyms* also aids retention. On the *"Krusty Krab Training Video"* episode of Spongebob Squarepants (a spoof on corporate training videos), they use the acronym "POOP." When I asked my then eight-year-old son if he remembered (several weeks after watching the episode) what "POOP" stood for, he immediately and correctly answered "People Order Our Patties." The final technique to help audiences remember information is the *simplicity criterion*. Information is best retained when it is explained from top to bottom (rather than bottom to top), when events are presented from first to last (rather than last to first), and when information is presented in the positive voice (rather than in the negative voice) (Devito, 1981).

Use Visuals

Visual aids can be a very powerful and efficient way to present facts that might otherwise be difficult to convey verbally. The benefits of visuals used for informative speeches include increasing interest, understanding, retention, and the speed at which your audience can understand complex facts. We live in a mediated culture, where people are visually oriented. This means that they expect to be visually stimulated with pictures, graphs, maps, video images and objects. Speakers who do not make use of visuals may be at a disadvantage

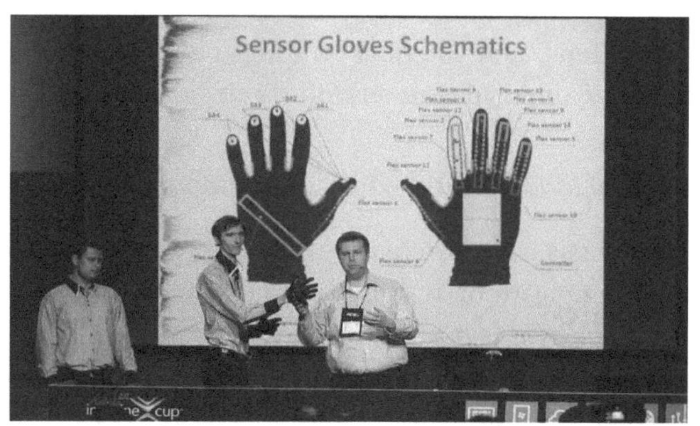

when compared to speakers who use them. This is assuming of course that the visuals enhance what you are saying and that you use them well. As you know, plenty of people use Power Point, and it does not necessarily make their speech better or more memorable.

Perhaps the best reason to use visuals aids during an informative speech is to help your audience understand a concept that may be difficult to understand just by explaining it. In a speech about heart bypass surgery, would it be better to verbally describe the parts of the human heart, or to show a picture of it? How about a model of the heart? How about an actual human heart? Be sure to consider your audience! What if your speech is about an abstract concept that does not lend itself well to slick graphic representations? One way trainers get their audiences involved and make their presentations memorable is to provide handouts which the listeners complete (in part) themselves. You could use fill-in-the blank statements (where you provide the answer), open-ended questions where listeners can write their thoughts, and activities like matching or crossword puzzles. Regardless of the type of visual media you select for your speech, just make sure that it does not overpower you or the subject. Work to keep the audience's attention on you and what you are saying, and use the visual to complement what *you* have to say.

Attributions

CC licensed content, Shared previously

Conclusion, Review Questions, and Activities

Conclusion

Only one person in a million becomes enlightened without a teacher's help. – Bodhidharma

The primary goal of informative speaking is to increase listeners' knowledge so they can better understand the world around them and can make more informed decisions. Discussing the impact a speaker can have on an audience, Perry Wilbur (2000, p. 99) explains:

> *Always keep in mind that if your talk helps just one listener in your audience, it has been successful. It is far more likely to have an impact on a number of listeners in your audiences. That is one of the real powers of spoken communication. Develop skill for getting the material across to audiences, and you can and will change lives for the better and make a worthy contribution as a speaker.*

Informative speaking is a crucial skill that, if developed, will help you be more successful in both your personal life and your professional career.

When constructing an informative speech, you should strive to be objective, spend time developing your credibility, demonstrate that you have done your research, and link your subject to the lives of the listeners.

There are four main types of informative speeches. Definitional speeches present the meanings of concepts, theories, philosophies, or issues. Descriptive speeches provide detailed word pictures of people, animals, places, or objects. Explanatory speeches report events, customs, transformations, inventions,, policies, outcomes or options. Demonstration speeches show listeners how some process is done or how to do it themselves.

Several techniques can be used by speakers to increase the effectiveness of their informative speech. Speakers can arouse interest by using attention getting elements, telling a story, adding creative features, and stimulating the intellect of the audience. Speakers can create coherence through logical organization, the use of simple language, and by avoiding information overload. Finally, a speaker can make a speech more memorable via repetition, appealing to different ways of learning, and by using visuals appropriately.

If you have knowledge, let others light their candles at it. – Margaret Fuller

Review Questions

1. For each of the characters described below, what types of informative speeches might each person be called upon to give in her or his personal and professional life? List as many as you can think of for each.

   - Stacy is an emergency room physician and medical school professor. She also serves on the board of directors for a local college. For recreation she enjoys rock climbing.

   - Rick is an animal control officer who volunteers his time at both the animal shelter and the local Habitat for Humanity group. He is in a bowling league with other city employees.

   - Akiko is in insurance sales and volunteers in the math classroom at her children's middle school. As a hobby, she collects and sells antiques.

2. Early in the module, the importance of credibility was discussed. Can you think of any presentations you heard where you DID NOT feel that the speaker had credibility? What did the speakers do and/or say to make you think they lacked credibility? If you were to give these speakers advice on how to improve their credibility, what would you say?

3. The chapter states that speakers need to be objective, credible, knowledgeable and that they need to make the topic relevant to the audience. Rank these responsibilities in order from most to least important, and then explain your ranking.

4. Imagine you are giving an informative speech on _______________ [you fill in the blank]. How would you apply each of the five attention getting techniques—intensity, novelty, contrast, activity and humor—in your speech? Make note of at least one idea for each technique.

5. After you have selected a topic for your informative speech, answer the questions below to help determine ways to orient your topic to your audience. Questions adapted from Ulloth and Alderfer, (1998b, pp. 61–62).

   - How much information does your audience already have about your topic?

   - What social or cultural influences of audience members might affect their reaction to your topic?

   - How can your topic be made interesting if the audience has no knowledge or apparent interest in it?

   - Are there any mental, physical, or emotional factors in the audience that may affect their response to your speech?

   - What do you want your audience to understand after you have delivered your speech?

Answers to song lyrics question in Developing Informative Speeches:
Mystery Artist: Pink Floyd "Money" from Dark Side of the Moon

Activities

1. The list directly below includes a number of potential sources for your informative speech (Walters, 1995; Ulloth & Alderfer, 1998; Slutsky & Aun, 1997). Using this list for ideas, which of these potential sources could be used in the research process for each of the following speech topics?

Speech Topics

Tattoos	Action figure collecting	Free local activities
Making great BBQ	Music piracy	Auctions
Bruce Lee	Decorating on a budget	Creating a web site

Source of Interesting Materials

- Libraries
- Bookstores
- Used book stores
- Video stores
- Music stores
- Reference books
- Phone books (use for experts and specialized businesses)
- Schools and colleges (where your topic is taught or researched)
- Magazines and newsletters
- Trade associations and publications
- Special interest clubs and groups
- People selling products and services
- Research departments of television stations and newspapers
- Objects related to the subject
- Museums
- Computer search engines and data bases (on and off campus)
- Other sources (e.g. specialized stores, friends, colleagues, educational videos)

2. Use the list of potential informative speech topics below to complete the steps of this activity.

   A. Which of the topics listed below might also be used for a persuasive speech?

   B. For each of the four different types of informative speeches (Definitional, Descriptive, Explanatory, Demonstration), identify three topics that would be appropriate to use for each type of speech.

   C. At this point, you should have twelve topics listed—three each under each type of speech. Now, take one topic from each of the four groups and generate a specific purpose statement and three potential main points. You will have four different speeches, each with their own specific purpose and main points.

Potential Speech Topics

- Adventure vacations
- The Alamo
- Alternatives to chemotherapy
- Boating safety
- Building a pond
- Changing the oil in your car
- Characteristics of successful managers
- Cultural changes resulting from 9/11

- Diamond selection
- Ghandi's achievements
- Hospice care
- Hot air balloons
- How a meteor killed the dinosaurs
- How to set up a wireless network
- Illicit drug policy
- Matching dog breeds with owners

- Orchids
- Ramadan
- Robots for the home
- Space vacations
- Using Power Point effectively
- Unemployment and the economy
- What to do when your identity is stolen

Attributions

CC licensed content, Shared previously

- Chapter 15 Conclusion, Review Questions, and Activities. **Authored by**: Lisa Schreiber, Ph.D.. **Provided by**: Millersville University, Millersville, PA. **Located at**: http://publicspeakingproject.org/psvirtualtext.html. **Project**: Public Speaking Project. **License**: *CC BY-NC-ND: Attribution-NonCommercial-NoDerivatives*

Glossary and References

Glossary

TERM	DEFINITION
Activity	The use of action words, physical or visual movement, or faster rate of speech to draw the audience's attention.
Attention Getter	A device or technique used to gain the audience's attention in the introduction or keep the audience's attention during the course of a speech.
Contrast	An attention getting technique whereby supporting ideas are compared to emphasize difference.
Credibility	Refers to the audience's perception of the speaker's expertise, authenticity, and trustworthiness.
Definitional Speech	A type of speech in which the speaker attempts to explain or identify the essential qualities or components of concepts, theories, philosophies, or issues.
Demonstration Speech	A speech that shows listeners how some process is accomplished or how to perform it themselves.
Descriptive Speech	A speech that provides a detailed, vivid, word picture of a person, animal, place, or object.
Explanatory Speech	Also known as a briefing, the focus of this speech is on reports of current and historical events, customs, transformations, inventions, policies, outcomes, and options.
General Purpose	The speaker's overall goal, objective, or intent: to inform, to persuade, or to entertain.
Humor	The use of amusing or comical facts, stories, or forms of expression to maintain an audience's attention.
Information Overload	An overwhelming feeling of being faced with so much information one cannot completely process it.
Informative Speech	A speech in which the primary purpose is to provide the audience with information that they did not already know, or to teach them more about a topic with which they are already familiar.
Intensity	Supporting material that is characterized by a high degree of emotion, color, volume, strength, or other defining characteristic.
Novelty	Very recent or unusual supporting ideas.

WIIFM	An acronym that stands for "What's in it for me?" This is the question that listeners ask themselves when they begin to listen to a speech. Listeners want to know; What does this speech have to do with my life? Is this information useful to me? Is the speaker talking about something I already know? Is the subject interesting? Why should I pay attention?

References

Beebe, S. A., & Beebe, S. J. (1991). *Public speaking: An audience-centered approach*. Englewood Cliffs, NJ: Prentice Hall.

Brydon, S. R., & Scott, M. D. (2006). *Between one and many: The art and science of public speaking*, (5th ed). Boston: McGraw Hill.

Carlson, T. (2005). *The how of wow: A guide to giving a speech that will positively blow 'em away*. New York: American Management Association.

Cassidy, S. (2011). *The Taj Mahal: The most beautiful building in the world*. Retrieved from http://www.epinions.com/review/trvlDest-Asia-IndiaAgra_and_the_Taj_Mahal/content_7472 7001732

Craughwell, T. J. (2000). *The baby on the car roof: And 222 more urban legends*. New York: Black Dog & Leventhal Publishers.

U. S. Department of Defense. (2006). *Army field manual FM 21-76, survival, evasion and recovery*. Retrieved from http://www.survivalebooks.com/survivalf m3-0570.html

Devito, J. A. (1981). *The elements of public speaking*. New York: Harper & Row, Publishers.

Fischer, S. R. (2006). *The island at the end of the world*. London, UK: Reaktion Books.

Fleming, N. D. (2001). *Teaching and learning styles: VARK strategies*. Christchurch, New Zealand: N.D. Fleming.

Flora, C. (2009, NovemberDecember). Everyday creativity. *Psychology Today*, 62–73.

Fujishin, R. (2000). *The natural speaker*. Boston: Allyn & Bacon.

George, A. (2011, July 20). Designing a mushroom death suit. *New Scientist*. Retrieved from http://www.newscientist.com/blogs/cultu relab/2011/07/designing-a-mushroomdeath-suit.html?DCMP=OTCrss&nsref=online-news

Gladis, S. (1999). *The manager's pocket guide to public presentations*. Amherst, MA: HRD Press.

Hanks, K. & Parry, J. (1991). *Wake up your creative genius*. Menlo Park, CA: Crisp Publications.

Harlan, R. (1993). *The confident speaker: How to master fear and persuade an audience*. Bradenton, FL: McGuinn & McGuire Publishing.

Hawk, T. F. & Shah, A. J. (2007). Using learning style instruments to enhance student learning. *Decision Sciences Journal of Innovative Education,* 5 (1),1–19.

Hughes, D., & Phillips, B. (2000). *The Oxford Union guide to successful public speaking.* London: Virgin Books Ltd.

Jaffe, C. (1998). *Public speaking: Concepts and skills for a diverse society* (2nd Ed.). Belmont, CA: Wadsworth Publishing Company.

Lucas, S. E. (2007). *The art of public speaking* (9th Ed.). New York: McGraw Hill.

MacInnis, J. L. (2006). *The elements of great public speaking: How to be calm, confident, and compelling.* Berkeley, CA: Ten Speed Press.

Maxey, C., & O'Connor, K. E. (2006). *Present like a pro: The field guide to mastering the art of business, professional, and public speaking.* New York: St. Martin's Press.

McKerrow, R. E., Gronbeck, B. E., Ehninger, D., & Monroe, A. H. (2000). *Principles and types of speech communication* (14th Ed.). New York: Longman.

Morreale, S. P., & Bovee, C. L. (1998). *Excellence in public speaking.* Fort Worth: Harcourt Brace College Publishers.

National Geographic. (2006). *Tsunami: Killer wave* [Motion Picture].

Noonan, P. (1998). *Simply speaking: How to communicate your ideas with style, substance, and clarity.* New York: Regan Books.

Osborn, M., & Osborn, S. (1991). *Public Speaking,* (2nd ed). Boston: Houghton Mifflin.

Peterson, B. D., Stephan, E. G., & White, N. D. (1992). *The complete speaker: An introduction to public speaking,* (3rd ed). St. Paul, MN: West Publishing Company.

Pincus, M. (2006). *Boost your presentation IQ.* New York: McGraw-Hill.

Reynolds, G. (2008). *Presentation Zen: Simple ideas on presentation design and delivery.* Berkeley, CA: New Riders.

Rinehart, S. M. (2002). *Giving academic presentations.* Ann Arbor, MI: The University of Michigan Press.

Slutsky, J., & Aun, M. (1997). *The Toastmasters International guide to successful speaking.* Chicago: Dearborn Financial Publishing, Inc.

Sprague, J., & Stuart, D. (1984). *The speaker's handbook.* San Diego, CA: Harcourt Brace Jovanovich, Publishers.

Thompson, M. (1999). *Eastern philosophy.* Chicago: Hodder & Stoughton, Ltd.

Ulloth, D., & Alderfer, R. (1998a). *Public speaking: An experiential approach.* Belmont, CA: Wadsworth Publishing Company.

Ulloth, D., & Alderfer, R. (1998b). *Student workbook for public speaking: An experiential approach.* Belmont, CA: Wadsworth Publishing Company.

Urech, E. (1998). *Speaking globally: Effective presentations across international and cultural boundaries.* Dover, NH: Kogan Page Limited.

Verderber, R. F. (1994). *The challenge of effective speaking,* (9th Ed.). Bemont, CA: Wadsworth Publishing Company.

Walters, L. (1995). *What to say when: A complete resource for speakers, trainers, and executives.* New York: McGraw Hill, Inc.

Westerfield, J. (2002). *I have to give a presentation, now what?* New York: Silver Lining Books.

Wilbur, L. P. (2000). *Holding audience attention: How to speak with confidence, substance and power.* Colorado Springs, CO: Piccadilly Books, Ltd.

photo credits

P. 3 Aztec Speaker by Orin Zebest http://www.flickr.com/photos/orinrobertjohn/ 1796533234/

P. 12 Beauty Undressed by Shannon Cutts http://www.flickr.com/photos/40940503@N0 5/4982554199/in/ photostream/ http://www.key-to-life.com/programs

Attributions

CC licensed content, Shared previously

Chapter 4: Listening Effectively

Objectives and Introduction

Listening Effectively

By Jenn Q. Goddu, M.A.
Queens University of Charlotte, Charlotte, NC

Learning Objectives

After reading this chapter, you should be able to:

- explain the difference between listening and hearing
- understand the value of listening
- identify the three attributes of active listeners
- recognize barriers to effective listening
- employ strategies to engage listeners
- provide constructive ?feedback as a listener

"You're not listening!" An unhappy teen shouts this at a concerned parent. A frustrated parent yells this as a toddler runs through a parking lot. A teacher says it while flicking the overheard lights on and off, trying to get her unruly students to heed her. A woman offers these three words as a parting shot before hanging up on her significant other. A man complains of this to his spouse during a couple's counseling session. We can imagine all these scenarios and more; all of them rooted in a speaker wondering if his or her audience is truly listening.

Public speaking requires an audience to hear. Otherwise it's private speaking, and anyone overhearing you might wonder if you've lost your wits. What makes public speaking truly effective is when the audience hears and listens. You might think the two are synonymous. But they aren't, as you will soon understand. In a classic listening text, Adler notes, "How utterly amazing is the general assumption that the ability to listen well is a natural gift for which no training is required."[1] Since listening requires great effort, this chapter offers the skills needed to listen effectively.

Developing your listening skills can have applications throughout your educational, personal, and professional lives. You will begin by examining the difference between hearing and listening. This module will also help you understand your role as a listener, not only in a public speaking class, but also in the world. You'll read about attributes of an active listener, barriers to listening, and strategies to listen better. Finally, building on valuable lessons regarding listening, this chapter concludes with suggestions public speakers can use to encourage audiences to listen more attentively.

"Listen to your kids" **by Bindaas Madhavi.** *CC-BY-NC-ND.*

We have two ears and one tongue so that we would listen more and talk less. – Diogenes

Attributions

CC licensed content, Shared previously

- Chapter 4 Objectives, Outline, and Introduction. **Authored by**: Jenn Q. Goddu, M.A.. **Provided by**: Queens University of Charlotte, Charlotte, NC. **Located at**: http://publicspeakingproject.org/psvirtualtext.html. **Project**: The Public Speaking Project. **License**: *CC BY-NC-ND: Attribution-NonCommercial-NoDerivatives*
- Listen to your kids. **Authored by**: Bindaas Madhavi. **Located at**: https://flic.kr/p/a5Lczv. **License**: *CC BY-NC-ND: Attribution-NonCommercial-NoDerivatives*

1. Adler, M. J. (1983). *How to speak, how to listen*. New York: Macmillan.

Video: Selecting a Topic

To help you select topics for your first speech, watch the following video:

- https://youtu.be/Cy4uu3w91xg

Attributions

All rights reserved content

- Finding a Purpose and Selecting a Topic for Public Speaking Tools. **Authored by**: Christie Fierro. **Located at**: https://youtu.be/Cy4uu3w91xg. **License**: *All Rights Reserved*. **License Terms**: Standard YouTube License

Hearing Versus Listening

A mother takes her four-year-old to the pediatrician reporting she's worried about the girl's hearing. The doctor runs through a battery of tests, checks in the girl's ears to be sure everything looks good, and makes notes in the child's folder. Then, she takes the mother by the arm. They move together to the far end of the room, behind the girl. The doctor whispers in a low voice to the concerned parent: "Everything looks fine. But, she's been through a lot of tests today. You might want to take her for ice cream after this as a reward." The daughter jerks her head around, a huge grin on her face, "Oh, please, Mommy! I love ice cream!" The doctor, speaking now at a regular volume, reports, "As I said, I don't think there's any problem with her hearing, but she may not always be choosing to listen."

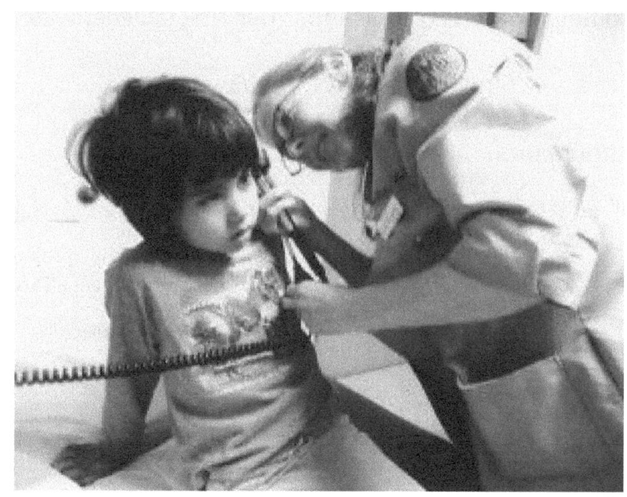

Hearing is something most everyone does without even trying. It is a physiological response to sound waves moving through the air at up to 760 miles per hour. First, we receive the sound in our ears. The wave of sound causes our eardrums to vibrate, which engages our brain to begin processing. The sound is then transformed into nerve impulses so that we can perceive the sound in our brains. Our auditory cortex recognizes a sound has been heard and begins to process the sound by matching it to previously encountered sounds in a process known as **auditory association**.[1] Hearing has kept our species alive for centuries. When you are asleep but wake in a panic having heard a noise downstairs, an age-old self-preservation response is kicking in. You were asleep. You weren't listening for the noise—unless perhaps you are a parent of a teenager out past curfew—but you hear it. Hearing is unintentional, whereas **listening** (by contrast) requires you to pay conscious attention. Our bodies hear, but we need to employ intentional effort to actually listen.

1. Brownell, J. (1996). *Listening: Attitudes, principles, and skills*. Boston: Allyn and Bacon.

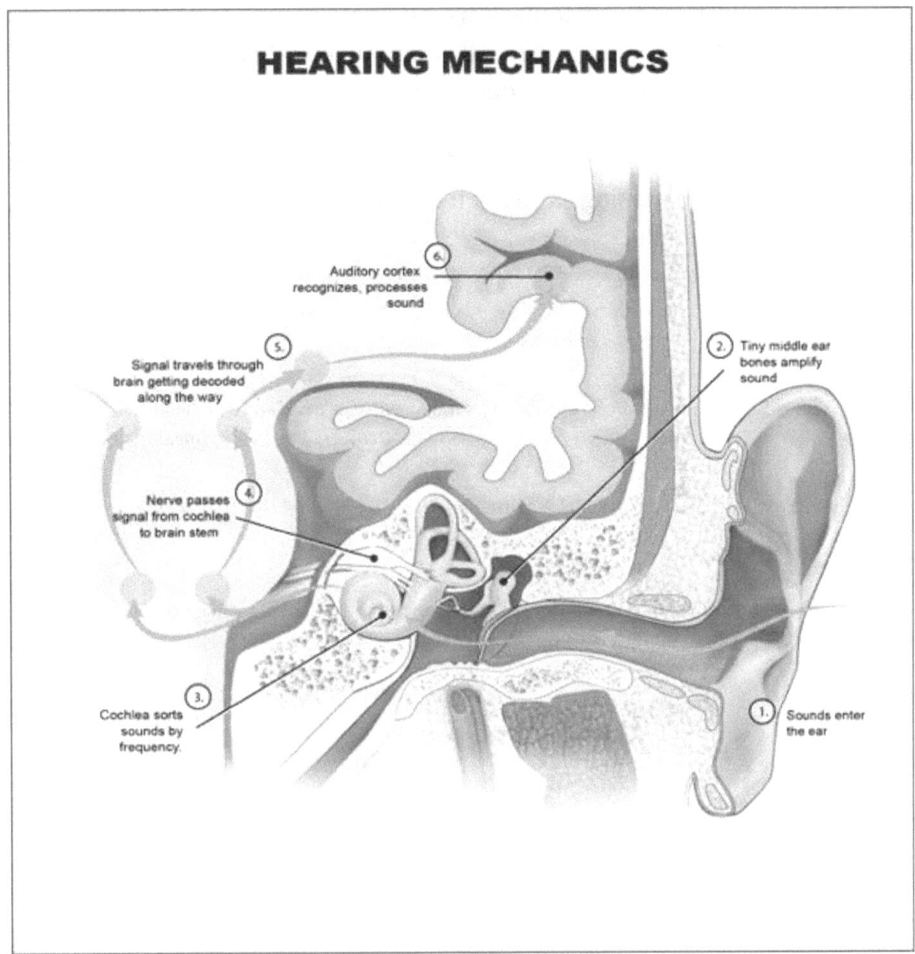

We regularly engage in several different types of listening. When we are tuning our attention to a song we like, or a poetry reading, or actors in a play, or sitcom antics on television, we are listening for pleasure, also known as **appreciative listening**. When we are listening to a friend or family member, building our relationship with another through offering support and showing empathy for her feelings in the situation she is discussing, we are engaged in **relational listening**. Therapists, counselors, and conflict mediators are trained in another level known as **empathetic or therapeutic listening**. When we are at a political event, attending a debate, or enduring a salesperson touting the benefits of various brands of a product, we engage in critical listening. This requires us to be attentive to key points that influence or confirm our judgments. When we are focused on gaining information whether from a teacher in a classroom setting, or a pastor at church, we are engaging in **informational listening**.[2]

Yet, despite all these variations, Nichols called listening a "lost art."[3] The ease of sitting passively without really listening is well known to anyone who has sat in a boring class with a professor droning on about the Napoleonic wars or proper pain medication regimens for patients allergic to painkillers. You hear the words the professor is saying, while you check Facebook on your phone under the desk. Yet, when the

2. Ireland, J. (2011, May 4). *The kinds of listening skills*. Livestrong.com. Retrieved from http://www.livestrong.com/article/82419-kinds-listening-skills/

3. Nichols, R. G. (1957). *Listening is a 10 part skill*. Chicago, IL: Enterprise Publications. Retrieved from http://d1025403.site.my hosting.com/files.listen.org/Nichol sTenPartSkill/Mr39Enf4.html

exam question features an analysis of Napoleon's downfall or a screaming patient fatally allergic to codeine you realize you didn't actually listen. Trying to recall what you heard is a challenge, because without your attention and intention to remember, the information is lost in the caverns of your cranium.

Listening is one of the first skills infants gain, using it to acquire language and learn to communicate with their parents. Bommelje suggests listening is the activity we do most in life, second only to breathing.[4] Nevertheless, the skill is seldom taught.

Attributions

CC licensed content, Shared previously

- Chapter 4 Hearing Versus Listening. **Authored by**: Jenn Q. Goddu, M.A.. **Provided by**: Queens University of Charlotte, Charlotte, NC. **Located at**: http://publicspeakingproject.org/psvirtualtext.html. **Project**: The Public Speaking Project. **License**: *CC BY-NC-ND: Attribution-NonCommercial-NoDerivatives*
- Doctor Aunt. **Authored by**: Eden, Janine and Jim. **Located at**: https://flic.kr/p/5M3xBP. **License**: *CC BY: Attribution*

Public domain content

- Image of hearing mechanics. **Authored by**: Zina Deretsky. **Provided by**: National Science Foundation. **Located at**: http://commons.wikimedia.org/wiki/File:Hearing_mechanics.jpg. **License**: *Public Domain: No Known Copyright*

---

4. Bommelje, R. (2011). LISTEN, LISTEN, LISTEN. In The top 10 ways to strengthen your selfleadership. International Listening Leadership Institute. Retrieved from http://www.listeningleaders.com/Articles.html

The Value of Listening

Listening is a critical skill. The strategies endorsed in this chapter can help you to be a more attentive listener in any situation.

Academic Benefits

Bommelje, Houston, and Smither studied effective listening among 125 college students and found a strong link between effective listening and school success, supporting previous research in the field linking listening skills to grade point average.[1] This finding is unsurprising as the better you listen while in class, the better prepared you will be for your assignments and exams. It is quite simple really. When students listen, they catch the instructions, pointers, feedback, and hints they can use to make the assignment better or get a better score on the test.

> Learning is a result of listening, which in turn leads to even better listening and attentiveness to the other person. – Alice Miller

1. Bommelje, R., Houston, J. M., & Smither, R. (2003). *Personality characteristics of effective listening: A five factor perspective. International Journal of Listening, 17*, 32–46.

Professional Benefits

Connecting listening skills to better leadership, Hoppe lists many professional advantages of active listening, indicating that it helps us: better understand and make connections between ideas and information; change perspectives and challenge assumptions; empathize and show respect or appreciation, which can enhance our relationships; and build self-esteem.[2] When people aren't listening, it becomes much more difficult to get things done effectively and trust is broken while fostering resentments. Bell and Mejer, identifying poor listening as a "silent killer of productivity and profit," state change becomes extremely difficult to implement in a work environment when people are not listening.[3]

"The SEIU family listens to Sen. Joe Biden" by SEIU Walk a Day in My Shoes 2008. CC-BY.

Effective listening can also help you to make a better impression on employers. This can begin at the interview. You really want the job, but you are really nervous. As a result, you are having trouble paying attention to what the CEO of the company is saying in your final interview. She asks you if you have any questions, and you ask something you were wondering about in the elevator on the way up to this penthouse office. You're unlikely to get the job if you ask something she's just talked about. Even if you, somehow, convince her to hire you, you will make little progress at the firm if your supervisors often have to tell you things again, or you make decisions that cost the company in lost profits because you weren't listening effectively in a team meeting.

Ferrari identifies listening as the "most critical business skill of all." He notes, "listening can well be the difference between profit and loss, between success and failure, between a long career and a short one."[4]

Personal Benefits

If listening is done well, the **communication loop** is effectively completed between speaker and receiver. The speaker shares a message with the receiver, having selected a particular method to communicate that message. The receiver aims to interpret the message and share understanding of the message with the speaker. Communication effectiveness is determined by the level of shared interpretation of the message reached through listener response and feedback. When done successfully, the loop is complete, and both sender and receiver feel connected. The active listener who employs the positive attributes detailed in this chapter is more likely to be better liked, in turn increasing her self-esteem. She is also likely to be better able to reduce tension in situations and resolve conflict.[5] After all, the symbols for ears, eyes, undivided

2. Hoppe, M. H. (2006). *Active listening: Improve your ability to listen and lead* [ebook]. Greensboro, NC: Center for Creative Leadership.
3. Bell, C. & Mejer, C. (2011, February 13). *The silent killers of productivity and profit*. ASTD.com. Retrieved from https://www.td.org/Publications/Magazines/TD/TD-Archive/2011/02/The-Silent-Killers-of-Productivity-and-Profit
4. Ferrari, B. (2012). *Power listening: Mastering the most critical business skill of all*. New York: Penguin.
5. Wobser, A. (2004). Developing positive listening skills: How to really listen. Huntsville, TX. Educational Video Network.

attention, and heart comprise the Chinese character for "to listen."[6] Truly listening to the words of a speaker is sure to make a positive difference in your interactions whether they are academic, professional, or personal.

"To Listen" by U.S. Department of State. Public domain.

Attributions

CC licensed content, Shared previously

- Chapter 4 The Value of Listening. **Authored by**: Jenn Q. Goddu, M.A.. **Provided by**: Queens University of Charlotte, Charlotte, NC. **Located at**: http://publicspeakingproject.org/psvirtualtext.html. **Project**: The Public Speaking Project. **License**: *CC BY-NC-ND: Attribution-NonCommercial-NoDerivatives*
- The SEIU family listens to Sen. Joe Biden. **Authored by**: SEIU Walk a Day in My Shoes 2008. **Located at**: http://commons.wikimedia.org/wiki/File:The_SEIU_family_listens_to_Sen._Joe_Biden.jpg. **License**: *CC BY: Attribution*

Public domain content

- Chinese symbol ting1 to listen. **Provided by**: US State Department. **Located at**: http://www.state.gov/m/a/os/65759.htm. **License**: *Public Domain: No Known Copyright*

6. McFerran, J. (2009, August 29). Open-door policy not enough to be a leader who can listen. Winnipeg Free Press. doi:7BS2732928311 p. G1

Three A's of Active Listening

Effective listening is about self-awareness. You must pay attention to whether or not you are only hearing, *passively* listening, or *actively* engaging. Effective listening requires concentration and a focused effort that is known as active listening. Active listening can be broken down into three main elements.

> Know how to listen, and you will profit even from those who talk badly. – Plutarch

Attention

We know now that attention is the fundamental difference between hearing and listening. Paying attention to what a speaker is saying requires intentional effort on your part. Nichols, credited with first researching the field of listening, observed, "listening is hard work. It is characterized by faster heart action, quicker circulation of the blood, a small rise in bodily temperature."[1] Consider that we can process information four times faster than a person speaks. Yet, tests of listening comprehension show the average person listening at only 25% efficiency. A typical person can speak 125 words-per-minute, yet we can process up to three times faster, reaching as much as 500 words-per-minute. The poor listener grows impatient, while the effective listener uses the extra processing time to process the speaker's words, distinguish key points, and mentally summarize them.[2]

Hoppe[3] advises active listening is really a state of mind requiring us to choose to focus on the moment, being present and attentive while disregarding any of our anxieties of the day. He suggests listeners prepare themselves for active attention by creating a **listening reminder**. This might be to write "Listen" at the top of a page in front of you in a meeting.

1. Nichols, R. G. (1957). *Listening is a 10 part skill*. Chicago, IL: Enterprise Publications. Retrieved from http://d1025403.site.myhosting.com/files.listen.org/NicholsTenPartSkill/Mr39Enf4.html
2. Nichols 1957
3. Hoppe, M. H. (2006). Active listening: *Improve your ability to listen and lead* [ebook]. Greensboro, NC: Center for Creative Leadership.

While reading a book, or having a discussion with an individual, you can go back and reread or ask a question to clarify a point. This is not always true when listening. Listening is of the moment, and we often only get to hear the speaker's words once. The key then is for the listener to quickly ascertain the speaker's central premise or controlling idea. Once this is done, it becomes easier for the listener to discern what is most important. Of course, distinguishing the speaker's primary goal, his main points, and the structure of the speech are all easier when the listener is able to listen with an open mind.

Attitude

Even if you are paying attention, you could be doing so with the wrong attitude, the second A. Telling yourself this is all a waste of time is not going to help you to listen effectively. You'll be better off determining an internal motivation to be attentive to the person speaking. Approaching the task of listening with a positive attitude and an open-mind will make the act of listening much easier. Bad listeners make snap judgments that justify the decision to be inattentive. Yet, since you're already there, why not listen to see what you can learn? Kaponya warns against psychological **deaf spots** which impair our ability to perceive and understand things counter to our convictions. It can be as little as a word or phrase that might cause "an emotional eruption" causing communication efficiency to drop rapidly.[4] For instance, someone who resolutely supports military action as the best response to a terrorist action may be unable to listen objectively to a speaker endorsing negotiation as a better tool. Even if the speaker is effectively employing logic, drawing on credible sources, and appealing to emotion with a heartrending tale of the civilian casualties caused by bombings, this listener would be unable to keep an open mind. Failing to acknowledge your deaf spots will leave you at a deficit when listening.

You will always need to make up your own mind about where you stand—whether you agree or disagree with the speaker—but it is critical to do so *after* listening. Adler proposes having four questions in mind while listening: "What is the whole speech about?" "What are the main or pivotal ideas, conclusions, and arguments?" "Are the speaker's conclusions sound or mistaken?" and "What of it?" Once you have an overall idea of the speech, determine the key points, and gauge your agreement, you can decide why it

4. Kaponya, P. J. (1991). *The human resource professional: Tactics and strategies for career success.* New York: Praeger Publishers.

matters, how it affects you, or what you might do as a result of what you have heard. Yet, he notes it is "impossible" to answer all these questions at the same time as you are listening.[5] Instead, you have to be ready and willing to pay attention to the speaker's point of view and changes in direction, patiently waiting to see where she is leading you.

> There are things I can't force. I must adjust. There are times when the greatest change needed is a change of my viewpoint. ~ Denis Diderot

Adjustment

To do this well, you need the final of the three A's: adjustment. Often when we hear someone speak, we don't know in advance what he is going to be saying. So, we need to be flexible, willing to follow a speaker along what seems like a verbal detour down a rabbit hole, until we are rewarded by the speaker reaching his final destination while his audience marvels at the creative means by which he reached his important point. If the audience members are more intent on reacting to or anticipating what is said, they will be poor listeners indeed.

Take time now to think about your own listening habits by completing the listening profile, adapted from Brownell.[6] The next section will consider ways to address the challenges of listening effectively.

Listening Profile
The questions below correspond to each of the six listening components in HURIER: Hearing, Understanding, Remembering, Interpreting, Evaluating, and Responding. Before answering the questions, first guess which of the six you will do best at. In which area will you likely score lowest? Now respond to the following prompts gauging your listening behavior on a five-point scale (1 = almost never, 2 = infrequently, 3 = sometimes, 4 = often, 5 = almost always).
_______ 1. I am constantly aware that people and circumstances change over time.
_______ 2. I take into account the speaker's personal and cultural perspective when listening to him or her.
_______ 3. I pay attention to the important things going on around me.
_______ 4. I accurately hear what is said to me.
_______ 5. I understand the speaker's vocabulary and recognize that my understanding of a work is likely to be somewhat different from the speaker's.
_______ 6. I adapt my response according to the needs of the particular situation.
_______ 7. I weigh all evidence before making a decision.
_______ 8. I take time to analyze the validity of my partner's reasoning before arriving at my own conclusion.
_______ 9. I can recall what I have heard, even when in stressful situations.
_______ 10. I enter communication situations with a positive attitude.
_______ 11. I ask relevant questions and restate my perceptions to make sure I have understood the speaker correctly.
_______ 12. I provide clear and direct feedback to others.
_______ 13. I do not let my emotions interfere with my listening or decision-making.
_______ 14. I remember how the speaker's facial expressions, body posture, and other nonverbal behaviors relate to the verbal message.
_______ 15. I overcome distractions such as the conversation of others, background noises, and telephones, when someone is speaking.
_______ 16. I distinguish between main ideas and supporting evidence when I listen.

5. Adler, M. J. (1983). *How to speak, how to listen.* New York: Macmillan.
6. Brownell, J. (1996). *Listening: Attitudes, principles, and skills.* Boston: Allyn and Bacon.

Listening Profile
_______ 17. I am sensitive to the speaker's tone in communication situations.
_______ 18. I listen to and accurately remember what is said, even when I strongly disagree with the speaker's viewpoint.
Add your scores for 4 + 10 + 15. This is your hearing total. Add your scores for 5 + 11 + 16. This is your understanding total. Add your scores for 1 + 7 + 8. This is your evaluating total. Add your scores for 3 + 9 + 18. This is your remembering total. Add your scores for 2 + 14 + 17. This is your interpreting total. Add your scores for 6 + 12 + 13. This is your responding total.
In which skill area do you score highest? Which is your lowest? How would these listening behaviors affect your interactions with peers, parents, instructors, or professional coworkers?

Attributions

CC licensed content, Shared previously

- Chapter 4 Three A's of Active Listening. **Authored by**: Jenn Q. Goddu, M.A.. **Provided by**: Queens University of Charlotte, Charlotte, NC. **Located at**: http://publicspeakingproject.org/psvirtualtext.html. **Project**: The Public Speaking Project. **License**: *CC BY-NC-ND: Attribution-NonCommercial-NoDerivatives*

- conversation. **Authored by**: Daniel. **Located at**: https://www.flickr.com/photos/danielcoy/4175199668/. **License**: *CC BY-ND: Attribution-NoDerivatives*

Public domain content

- US Navy 061007-N-4399G-029 Sailors aboard the dock landing ship USS Harpers Ferry (LSD 49) listen attentively to Wayne Guillory give an American Government class lecture. **Authored by**: United States Navy. **Located at**: http://commons.wikimedia.org/wiki/File:US_Navy_061007-N-4399G-029_Sailors_aboard_the_dock_landing_ship_USS_Harpers_Ferry_(LSD_49)_listen_attentively_to_Wayne_Guillory_give_an_American_Government_class_lecture.jpg. **License**: *Public Domain: No Known Copyright*

Barriers to Effective Listening

We get in our own way when it comes to effective listening. While listening may be the communication skill we use foremost in formal education environments, it is taught the least (behind, in order, writing, reading, and speaking).[1] To better learn to listen it is first important to acknowledge strengths and weaknesses as listeners. We routinely ignore the barriers to our effective listening; yet anticipating, judging, or reacting emotionally can all hinder our ability to listen attentively.

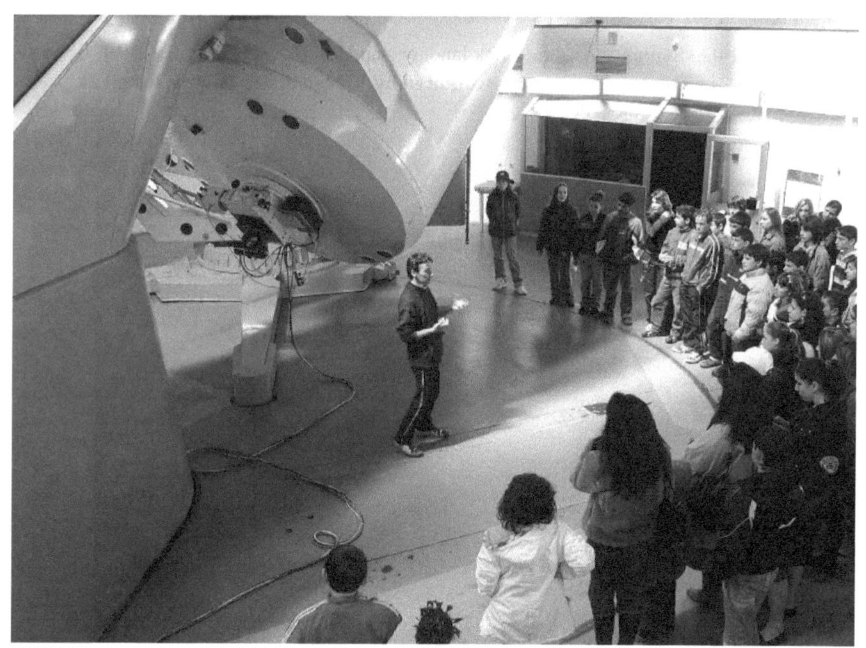

Anticipating

Anticipating, or thinking about what the listener is likely to say, can detract from listening in several ways. On one hand, the listener might find the speaker is taking too long to make a point and try to anticipate what the final conclusion is going to be. While doing this, the listener has stopped actively listening to the speaker. A listener who knows too much, or thinks they do, listens poorly. The only answer is humility, and recognizing there is always something new to be learned.

1. Brownell, J. (1996). *Listening: Attitudes, principles, and skills*. Boston: Allyn and Bacon.

Anticipating what we will say in response to the speaker is another detractor to effective listening. Imagine your roommate comes to discuss your demand for quiet from noon to 4 p.m. every day so that you can nap in complete silence and utter darkness. She begins by saying, "I wonder if we could try to find a way that you could nap with the lights on, so that I could use our room in the afternoon, too." She might go on to offer some perfectly good ideas as to how this might be accomplished, but you're no longer listening because you are too busy anticipating what you will say in response to her complaint. Once she's done speaking, you are ready to enumerate all of the things she's done wrong since you moved in together. Enter the Resident Assistant to mediate a conflict that gets out of hand quickly. This communication would have gone differently if you had actually listened instead of jumping ahead to plan a response.

> An expert is someone who has succeeded in making decisions and judgments simpler through knowing what to pay attention to and what to ignore. – Edward de Bono

Judging

Jumping to conclusions about the speaker is another barrier to effective listening. Perhaps you've been in the audience when a speaker makes a small mistake; maybe it's mispronouncing a word or misstating the hometown of your favorite athlete. An effective listener will overlook this minor gaffe and continue to give the speaker the benefit of the doubt. A listener looking for an excuse not to give their full attention to the speaker will instead take this momentary lapse as proof of flaws in all the person has said and will go on to say.

This same listener might also judge the speaker based on superficialities. Focusing on delivery or personal appearance—a squeaky voice, a ketchup stain on a white shirt, mismatched socks, a bad haircut, or a proclaimed love for a band that no one of any worth could ever profess to like—might help the ineffective listener justify a choice to stop listening. Still, this is always a choice. The effective listener will instead accept that people may have their own individual foibles, but they can still be good speakers and valuable sources of insight or information.

Reacting Emotionally

When the speaker says an **emotional trigger**, it can be even more difficult to listen effectively. A guest speaker on campus begins with a personal story about the loss of a parent, and instead of listening you become caught up grieving a family member of your own. Or, a presenter takes a stance on drug use, abortion, euthanasia, religion, or even the best topping for a pizza that you simply can't agree with. You begin formulating a heated response to the speaker's perspective, or searing questions you might ask to show the holes in the speaker's argument. Yet, you've allowed your emotional response to the speaker interfere with your ability to listen effectively. Once emotion is involved, effective listening stops.

> Bore, n. A person who talks when you wish him to listen. – Ambrose Bierce

Attributions

- Chapter 4 Barriers to Effective Listening. **Authored by**: Jenn Q. Goddu, M.A.. **Provided by**: Queens University of Charlotte, Charlotte, NC. **Located at**: http://publicspeakingproject.org/psvirtualtext.html. **Project**: The Public Speaking Project. **License**: *CC BY-NC-ND: Attribution-NonCommercial-NoDerivatives*

- Visitors NAO Rozhen Telescope. **Authored by**: Daniel. **Located at**: https://flic.kr/p/GDDKD. **License**: *CC BY-SA: Attribution-ShareAlike*

Strategies to Enhance Listening

Keep an Open Mind

Thinking about listening might make you feel tense in the moment. The effective listener is instead calm with a focused and alert mind. You are not waiting to hear what you want to hear, but listening to "what is said as it is said."[1] Effective listeners keep an open mind. Remember that listening to a point of view is not the same as accepting that point of view. Recognizing this can help you to cultivate a more open perspective, helping you to better adjust as you listen actively to a speaker. Also, it might help you to curtail your emotions. If you do encounter a point that incenses you, write it down to return to later. For now, you should keep on listening.

Identify Distractions

In any setting where you are expected to listen, you encounter numerous distractions. For instance, the father sitting in the living room watching television, might want to turn off the television to better enable him to listen to his son when he comes into the room saying, "Dad, I have a problem." In the classroom setting, you might be distracted sitting beside friends who make sarcastic comments throughout the class. In a new product meeting with the sales team, you could be unnerved by the constant beep of your phone identifying another text, email, or phone message has arrived. Identifying the things that will interrupt your attention, and making a conscious choice to move to a different seat or turn off your phone, can help position you to listen more effectively.

"Esther Brimmer Listens to Debate at HRC emergency session on Syria" **by United States Mission Geneva.** *CC-BY.*

---

1. Ramsland, K. M. (1992). *The art of learning: A self-help manual for students*. Albany: SUNY UP.

Come Prepared

Another useful strategy is to come prepared when you can. Any time you enter a listening situation with some advance working knowledge of the speaker and what might be expected of you as a listener, you will be better able to adjust and engage more deeply in what is being said. For instance, you might read the assigned readings for class, do the lab work before the lecture writing up the results, read a biography of a guest speaker before you go to an event, review the agenda from the previous staff meeting, or consult with a colleague about a client before going on-site to make a sale.

Take Notes

Taking notes can also advance your ability to be actively engaged in the speaker's words. You need not write down everything the speaker is saying. First, this is quite likely to be impossible. Second, once you are caught up in recording a speaker's every word, you are no longer listening. Use a tape recorder instead—having asked the speaker's permission first—if you feel you really must capture every word the speaker utters. You want to focus your efforts on really listening with an active mind. Learning to focus your attention on main points, key concepts, and gaining the overall gist of the speaker's talk is another skill to develop. You might endeavor to do this by jotting down a few notes or even drawing visuals that help you to recall the main ideas. The manner in which you take the notes is up to you; what is important is the fact that you are listening and working to process what is being said. Writing down questions that come to mind and asking questions of the speaker when it is possible, are two more ways to guarantee effective listening as you have found an internal motivation to listen attentively.

> Education is the ability to listen to almost anything without losing your temper or your self-confidence. – Robert Frost

Attributions

CC licensed content, Shared previously

- Chapter 4 Strategies to Enhance Listening. **Authored by**: Jenn Q. Goddu, M.A.. **Provided by**: Queens University of Charlotte, Charlotte, NC. **Located at**: http://publicspeakingproject.org/psvirtualtext.html. **Project**: The Public Speaking Project. **License**: *CC BY-NC-ND: Attribution-NonCommercial-NoDerivatives*
- Esther Brimmer Listens to Debate at HRC emergency session on Syria. **Authored by**: United States Mission Geneva. **Located at**: http://commons.wikimedia.org/wiki/File:Esther_Brimmer_Listens_to_Debate_at_HRC_emergency_session_on_Syria.jpg. **License**: *CC BY: Attribution*

Providing Feedback to Speakers

There are many ways in which a listener can offer feedback to a speaker, sometimes even wordlessly. Keeping an open mind is something you do internally, but you can also demonstrate openness to a speaker through your **nonverbal communication**.

Nonverbal Feedback

Boothman recommends listening with your whole body, not just your ears.[1] Consider how confident you would feel speaking to a room full of people with their eyes closed, arms and legs crossed, and bodies bent in slouches. These listeners are presenting nonverbal cues that they are uninterested and unimpressed. Meanwhile, a listener sitting up straight, facing you with an intent look on his face is more likely to offer reassurance that your words are being understood.

Eye contact is another nonverbal cue to the speaker that you are paying attention. You don't want to be bug-eyed and unblinking; the speaker might assume there is a tiger behind her and begin to panic as you seem to be doing. However, attentive eye contact can indicate you are listening, and help you to stay focused too. There are some cultures where maintaining eye contact would cause discomfort, so keep that in mind. Also, you may be someone who listens better with eyes closed to visualize what is being said. This can be difficult for a speaker to recognize, so if this is you consider incorporating one of the following nonverbals while you listen with eyes closed.

Nodding your head affirmatively, making back-channel responses such as "Yes," "Umhum," or "OK" can help the speaker gauge your interest. Even the speed of your head nod can signal your level of patience

1. Boothman, N. (2008). *How to make people like you in 90 seconds or less*. NY: Workman Publishing.

or understanding.[2] Leaning in as a listener is far more encouraging than slumping in your seat. Miller suggests the "**listener's lean**" demonstrates "ultimate interest. This joyous feedback is reflexive. It physically endorses our communiqué."[3] Nevertheless, sending too many nonverbal responses to the speaker can go wrong too. After all, a conference room full of people shifting in their seats and nodding their heads may translate as a restless audience that the speaker needs to recapture.

The only way to entertain some folks is to listen to them. ~ Kin Hubbard

Verbal Feedback

While speakers sometimes want all questions held until the end of a presentation, asking questions when the opportunity presents itself can help you as a listener. For one, you have to listen in order to be able to ask a question. Your goal should be to ask open-ended questions ("What do you think about….?" rather than "We should do …., right?"). You can use questions to confirm your understanding of the speaker's message. If you're not entirely sure of a significant point, you might ask a clarifying question. These are questions such as "What did you mean?" "Can you be more specific?" or "What is a concrete example of your point?" These can help your comprehension, while also offering the speaker feedback. When asking questions, approach the speaker in a positive, non-threatening way. A good listener doesn't seek to put the speaker on the defensive. You want to demonstrate your objectivity and willingness to listen to the speaker's response.

Finally, paraphrasing what has been said in your interactions with the speaker can be another useful tool for a good listener. Imagine the difference if, before you respond to an upset colleague, you take a moment to say, "I understand you are disappointed we didn't consult you before moving forward with the product release…" before you say, "we didn't have time to get everyone's input." Reflecting back the speaker's point of view before you respond allows the speaker to know you were listening and helps foster trust that everyone's voice is being heard.

Attributions

2. Pease, A., & Pease, B. (2006). *The definitive book of body language.* New York: Bantam Books.
3. Miller, C. (1994). *The empowered communicator: Keys to unlocking an audience.* Nashville: Broadman & Holman Publishers.

CC licensed content, Shared previously

- Chapter 4 Providing Feedback to Speakers. **Authored by**: Jenn Q. Goddu, M.A.. **Provided by**: Queens University of Charlotte, Charlotte, NC. **Located at**: http://publicspeakingproject.org/psvirtualtext.html. **Project**: The Public Speaking Project. **License**: *CC BY-NC-ND: Attribution-NonCommercial-NoDerivatives*

- Visitors Listen to Lecture in Reconstructed Barracks - Dachau Concentration Camp Site - Dachau - Bavaria - Germany. **Authored by**: Adam Jones, Ph.D.. **Located at**: http://commons.wikimedia.org/wiki/File:Visitors_Listen_to_Lecture_in_Reconstructed_Barracks_-_Dachau_Concentration_Camp_Site_-_Dachau_-_Bavaria_-_Germany.jpg. **License**: *CC BY-SA: Attribution-ShareAlike*

- Conversation In The Park. **Authored by**: sswj. **Located at**: http://Conversation%20In%20The%20Park. **License**: *CC BY-NC-ND: Attribution-NonCommercial-NoDerivatives*

Encouraging Effective Listening

William Henry Harrison was the ninth President of the United States. He's also recognized for giving the worst State of the Union address—ever. His two-hour speech delivered in a snowstorm in 1841 proves that a long speech can kill (and not in the colloquial "it was so good" sense). Perhaps it was karma, but after the President gave his meandering speech discussing ancient Roman history more than campaign issues, he died from a cold caught while blathering on standing outside without a hat or coat.[1]

Now, when asked what you know about Abraham Lincoln, you're likely to have more answers to offer. Let's focus on his Gettysburg Address. The speech is a model of brevity. His "of the people, by the people, for the people" is always employed as an example of parallelism, and he kept his words simple. In short, Lincoln considered his listening audience when writing his speech.

"William Henry Harrison" by James Reid Lambdin. Public domain.

> The habit of common and continuous speech is a symptom of mental deficiency. It proceeds from not knowing what is going on in other people's minds. – Walter Bagehot

When you sit down to compose a speech, keep in mind that you are **writing for the ear** rather than the eye. Listeners cannot go back and reread what you have just said. They need to grasp your message in the amount of time it takes you to speak the words. To help them accomplish this, you need to give listeners a clear idea of your overarching aim, reasons to care, and cues about what is important. You need to inspire them to want to not just hear but engage in what you are saying.

Make Your Listeners Care

Humans are motivated by ego; they always want to know "what's in it for me?" So, when you want to want to get an audience's attention, it is imperative to establish a reason for your listeners to care about what you are saying.

---

1. William Henry Harrison: Inaugural Address. (1989). U. S. Inaugural Addresses. Bartleby.com. Accessed Sept. 2, 2012.

Some might say Oprah did this by giving away cars at the end of an episode. But, that only explains why people waited in line for hours to get a chance to sit in the audience as her shows were taped. As long as they were in the stands, they didn't need to listen to get the car at the end of the show. Yet Oprah had audiences listening to her for 25 years before she launched her own network. She made listeners care about what she was saying. She told them what was in that episode for them. She made her audience members feel like she was talking to them about their problems, and offering solutions that they could use—even if they weren't multibillionaires known worldwide by first name alone.

Audiences are also more responsive when you find a means to tap their **intrinsic motivation**, by appealing to curiosity, challenging them, or providing contextualization.[2] You might appeal to the audience's curiosity if you are giving an informative speech about a topic they might not be familiar with already. Even in a narrative speech, you can touch on curiosity by cueing the audience to the significant thing they will learn about you or your topic from the story. A speech can present a challenge too. Persuasive speeches challenge the audience to think in a new way. Special Occasion speeches might challenge the listeners to reflect or prompt action. Providing a listener with contextualization comes back to the what's in it for me motivation. A student giving an informative speech about the steps in creating a mosaic could simply offer a step-by-step outline of the process, or she can frame it by saying to her listener, "by the end of my speech, you'll have all the tools you need to make a mosaic on your own." This promise prompts the audience to sit further forward in their seats for what might otherwise be a dry how-to recitation.

Cue Your Listeners

Audiences also lean in further when you employ active voice. We do this in speaking without hesitation. Imagine you were walking across campus and saw the contents of someone's room dumped out on the lawn in front of your dorm. You'd probably tell a friend: "The contents of Jane's room were thrown out the window by Julie." Wait, that doesn't sound right. You're more likely to say: "Julie threw Jane's stuff out the window!" The latter is an example of active voice. You put the actor (Julie) and the action (throwing Jane's stuff) at the beginning. When we try to speak formally, we can fall into passive voice. Yet, it sounds stuffy, and so unfamiliar to your listener's ear that he will struggle to process the point while you've already moved on to the next thing you wanted to say.

"Make way for ducklings" **by lee.** *CC-BY-NC-ND.*

> Twice and thrice over, as they say, good is it to repeat and review what is good. – Plato

Knowing that your audience only hears what you are saying the one time you say it, invites you to employ repetition. Listeners are more likely to absorb a sound when it is repeated. We are often unconsciously

2. VanDeVelde Luskin, C. (2003, September). Mark Lepper: Intrinsic motivation, extrinsic motivation and the process of learning. In Bing Times Online, Stanford University, retrieved from http://web.stanford.edu/dept/bingschool/cgi-bin/bt/sep2003/mark-lepper-intrinsic-motivation-extrinsic-motivation-and-the-process-of-learning/

waiting for a repetition to occur so we can confirm what we thought we heard.[3] As a result, employing repetition can emphasize an idea for the listener. Employing repetition of a word, words, or sentence can create a rhythm for the listener's ear. Employing repetition too often, though, can be tiresome.

If you don't want to repeat things so often you remind your listener of a sound clip on endless loop, you can also cue your listener through vocal emphasis. Volume is a tool speakers can employ to gain attention. Certainly parents use it all of the time. Yet, you probably don't want to spend your entire speech shouting at your audience. Instead, you can modulate your voice so that you say something important slightly louder. Or, you say something more softly, although still audible, before echoing it again with greater volume to emphasize the repetition. Changing your pitch or volume can help secure audience attention for a longer period of time, as we welcome the variety.

Pace is another speaker's friend. This is not to be confused with the moving back and forth throughout a speech that someone might do nervously (inadvertently inducing motion sickness in his audience). Instead it refers to planning to pause after an important point or question to allow your audience the opportunity to think about what you have just said. Or, you might speak more quickly (although still clearly) to emphasize your fear or build humor in a long list of concerns while sharing an anecdote. Alternately, you could slow down for more solemn topics or to emphasize the words in a critical statement. For instance, a persuasive speaker lobbying for an audience to stop cutting down trees in her neighborhood might say, "this can't continue. It's up to you to do something." But imagine her saying these words with attention paid to pacing and each period representing a pause. She could instead say, "This. Can't. Continue. It's up to you. Do something."

Convince Them to Engage

Listeners respond to people. Consider this introduction to a speech about a passion for college football:

> *It's college football season! Across the nation, the season begins in late summer. Teams play in several different divisions including the SEC, the ACC, and Big Ten. Schools make a lot of money playing in the different divisions, because people love to watch football on TV. College football is great for the fans, the players, and the schools.*

Now, compare it to this introduction to another speech about the same passion:

> *When I was a little boy, starting as early as four, my father would wake me up on Fall Saturdays with the same three words: "It's Game Day!" My dad was a big Clemson Tigers fan, so we might drive to Death Valley to see a game. Everyone would come: my mom, my grandparents, and friends who went to Clemson too. We would all tailgate before the game—playing corn hole, tossing a foam football, and watching the satellite TV. Even though we loved*

"Clemson Tigers football running down the hill" by Jim Ferguson. CC-BY.

3. Brownell, J. (1996). *Listening: Attitudes, principles, and skills*. Boston: Allyn and Bacon.

Clemson football best, all college football was worth watching. You never knew when there would be an upset. You could count on seeing pre-professional athletes performing amazing feats. But, best of all, it was a way to bond with my family, and later my friends.

Both introductions set up the topic and even give an idea of how the speech will be organized. Yet, the second one is made more interesting by the human element. The speech is personalized.

The college football enthusiast speaker might continue to make the speech interesting to his listeners by appealing to commonalities. He might acknowledge that not everyone in his class is a Clemson fan, but all of them can agree that their school's football team is fun to watch. Connecting with the audience through referencing things the speaker has in common with the listeners can function as an appeal to **ethos**. The speaker is credible to the audience because he is like them. Or, it can work as an appeal to **pathos**. A speaker might employ this emotional appeal in a persuasive speech about Habitat for Humanity by asking her audience to think first about the comforts of home or dorm living that they all take for granted.

> If you engage people on a vital, important level, they will respond. – Edward Bond

In speaking to the audience about the comforts of dorm living, the speaker is unlikely to refer to the "dormitories where we each reside." More likely, she might say, "the dorms we live in." As with electing to use active voice, speakers can choose to be more conversational than they might be in writing an essay on the same topic.

The speaker might use contractions, or colloquialisms, or make comparisons to popular television shows, music, or movies. This will help the listeners feel like the speaker is in conversation with them—admittedly a one-sided one—rather than talking at them. It can be off-putting to feel the speaker is simply reciting facts and figures and rushing to get through to the end of their speech, whereas listeners respond to someone talking to them calmly and confidently. Being conversational can help to convey this attitude even when on the inside the speaker is far from calm or confident. Nevertheless, employ this strategy with caution. Being too colloquial, for instance using "Dude" throughout the speech, could undermine your credibility. Or a popular culture example that you think is going to be widely recognized might not be the common knowledge you think it is, and could confuse audiences with non-native listeners.

> Choice of attention—to pay attention to this and ignore that—is to the inner life what choice of action is to the outer. In both cases, a man is responsible for his choice and must accept the consequences, whatever they may be. – W. H. Auden

Attributions

CC licensed content, Shared previously

- Chapter 4 Encouraging Effective Listening. **Authored by**: Jenn Q. Goddu, M.A.. **Provided by**: Queens University of Charlotte, Charlotte, NC. **Located at**: http://publicspeakingproject.org/psvirtualtext.html. **Project**: The Public Speaking Project. **License**: *CC BY-NC-ND: Attribution-NonCommercial-NoDerivatives*

- make way for ducklings. **Authored by**: lee. **Located at**: https://flic.kr/p/yvJUP. **License**: *CC BY-NC-ND: Attribution-NonCommercial-NoDerivatives*

- Clemson Tigers football running down the hill. **Authored by**: Jim Ferguson. **Located at**: http://commons.wikimedia.org/wiki/File:Clemson_Tigers_football_running_down_the_hill.jpg. **License**: *CC BY: Attribution*

Public domain content

- William Henry Harrison. **Authored by**: James Reid Lambdin. **Located at**: https://commons.wikimedia.org/wiki/ File:James_Reid_Lambdin_-_William_Henry_Harrison_-_Google_Art_Project.jpg. **License**: *Public Domain: No Known Copyright*

Conclusion, Review Questions, and Activities

Admittedly, this discussion of listening may add a layer of intimidation for public speakers. After all, it can be daunting to think of having to get an audience to not only hear, but also truly listen.

Nevertheless, once we recognize the difference and become aware of active listening and its barriers, we can better tailor our spoken words to captivate and engage an audience. A broader awareness of the importance of effective listening is another weapon in your arsenal as a public speaker. At the same time, building up your own effective listening skills can enhance your academic, professional, and personal success. Being heard is one thing, but speakers need listeners to complete the communication loop. Reap the rewards: Instead of saying "I hear you," try out "I'm listening."

"Defense.gov photo essay" by Elaine Wilson. Public domain.

Review Questions

1. What distinguishes listening from hearing?

2. What are some benefits for you personally from effective listening?

3. Name and give an example of each of the three A's of active listening.

4. Identify the three main barriers to listening. Which of these barriers is most problematic for you? What ?can you do about it?

5. What does an effective listener do with the extra thought process time while a speaker is speaking only ?150 words-per-minute?

6. How can you communicate non-verbally that you are listening?

7. What are some considerations in offering constructive feedback?

8. What are strategies that help hold your listeners' attention during your speech?

Activities

1. Discuss the following in small groups. How do your listening behaviors change in the following situations: A) At a concert, B) In class, C) At the dinner table with your parents, D) In a doctor's office? What are the distractions and other barriers to listening you might encounter in each setting? What might you do to overcome the barriers to effective listening in each situation?

2. Listen to someone you disagree with (maybe a politician from the opposing party) and work to listen actively with an open mind. Try to pay attention to the person's argument and the reasons he offers in support of his point of view. Your goal is to identify why the speaker believes what he does and how he proves it. You need not be converted by this person's argument.

3. Reflect on a situation in your personal life where poor listening skills created a problem. Briefly describe the situation, then spend the bulk of your reflection analyzing what went wrong in terms of listening and how, specifically, effective listening would have made a difference. Share your observations in small group class discussion.

4. Spend a few minutes brainstorming your trigger words. What are the words that would provoke a strong emotional response in you? List three concrete strategies you might use to combat this while being an effective listener.

Attributions

CC licensed content, Shared previously

- Chapter 4 Conclusion, Review Questions, and Activities. **Authored by**: Jenn Q. Goddu, M.A.. **Provided by**: Queens University of Charlotte, Charlotte, NC. **Located at**: http://publicspeakingproject.org/psvirtualtext.html. **Project**: The Public Speaking Project. **License**: *CC BY-NC-ND: Attribution-NonCommercial-NoDerivatives*

Public domain content

- Defense.gov photo essay 090902-D-4894W-008. **Authored by**: Elaine Wilson. **Provided by**: United States Department of Defense. **Located at**: http://commons.wikimedia.org/wiki/File:Defense.gov_photo_essay_090902-D-4894W-008.jpg. **License**: *Public Domain: No Known Copyright*

Glossary and References

Glossary

TERM	DEFINITION
Appreciative Listening	Listening for entertainment or pleasure purposes. This is the type of listening we might employ listening to music, watching television, or viewing a movie.
Auditory Association	The process by which the mind sorts the perceived sound into a category so that heard information is recognized. New stimuli is differentiated by comparing and contrasting with previously heard sounds.
Communication Loop	A traditional communication model that has both sender and receiver sharing responsibility for communicating a message, listening, and offering feedback. The sender encodes a message for the receiver to decode. Effectiveness of the communication depends on the two sharing a similar interpretation of the message and feedback (which can be verbal or nonverbal).
Constructive Feedback	Focuses on being specific, applicable, immediate, and intends to help the speaker to improve. The feedback should be phrased as "The story you told about you and your sister in Disneyland really helped me to understand your relationship…" rather than "that was great, Jane."
Critical Listening	When we are listening, aiming to gain information with which we will evaluate a speaker, or the product or proposal the speaker is endorsing. This is often employed when we are looking to make choices, or find points of disagreement with a speaker.
"Deaf Spots"	The preconceived notions or beliefs a listener might hold dear that can interfere with listening effectively. These are barriers to having an open mind to receive the sender's message.
Emotional Trigger	A word, concept, or idea that causes the listener to react emotionally. When listeners react to a speaker from an emotional perspective, their ability to listen effectively is compromised.
Empathetic (Therapeutic) Listening	A level of relationship listening that aims to help the speaker feel heard and understand, also appreciated. This is also known as therapeutic listening as it is employed most often by counselors, conflict mediators, or religious representatives.
Ethos	A speaker aims to establish credibility on the topic at hand with her audience by appealing to ethos. This reflects the speaker's character, her ability to speak to the values of the listener, and her competence to discuss the topic.
Hearing	Hearing is a three-step process. It involves receiving sound in the ear, perceiving sound in the brain, and processing the information offered by the sound to associate and distinguish it.
Informational Listening	Listening to learn information. For instance, this is the kind of listening students employ in classroom settings to gain knowledge about a topic.
Intrinsic Motivation	Effective listeners will find a reason within themselves to want to hear, understand, interpret, and remember the speaker's message. Wanting to pass a possible quiz is an extrinsic motivation, while wanting to learn the material out of curiosity about the topic is intrinsic motivation.
"Listener's Lean"	Audience members who are intent on what is being said will lean forward. This is a nonverbal endorsement of the listener's attention and the effect of the speaker's message.
Listening	This is the conscious act of focusing on the words or sounds to make meaning of a message. Listening requires more intentional effort than the physiological act of hearing.

Listening Reminder	A note made by a listener acknowledging intent to focus on the speaker's message and tune out distractions. A reminder might also encourage a listener to keep an open mind, or to provide open and encouraging body language.
Nonverbal Communication	Physical behaviors that communicate the message or the feedback from the listener. These include leaning in, nodding one's head, maintaining eye contact, crossing arms in front of the body, and offering sounds of agreement or dissent.
Pathos	An appeal to the audience's emotions, trying to trigger sympathy, pity, guilt, or sorrow. Pathos, along with ethos, and logos, make up the rhetorical triangle of appeals, according to Aristotle. An effective speaker will appeal to all three.
Relational Listening	The active and involved listening we do with people we love and care about. This is listening where we acknowledge our sympathy for the speaker, encourage them to tell more, and build trust with friends or family members by showing interest in their concerns.
Writing for the Ear	Keeping in mind, when writing a speech, that you must use language, pace, repetition, and other elements to help your audience to hear and see what you are speaking about. Remember, the listener must hear and understand your message as you speak it.

References

Adler, M. J. (1983). *How to speak, how to listen*. New York: Macmillan.

Bell, C. & Mejer, C. (2011, February 13). The silent killers of productivity and profit. ASTD.com. Retrieved from http://www.astd.org/Publications/ Magazines/TD/TD- Archive/2011/02/The-Silent-Killers-of-Productivity-and-Profit

Bommelje, R. (2011). LISTEN, LISTEN, LISTEN. In The top 10 ways to strengthen your self- leadership. International Listening Leadership Institute. Retrieved from http://www.listening leaders.com/Articles.html

Bommelje, R., Houston, J. M., & Smither, R. (2003). Personality characteristics of effective listening: A five factor perspective. *International Journal of Listening*, 17, 32- 46.

Boothman, N. (2008). *How to make people like you in 90 seconds or less*. NY: Workman Publishing.

Brownell, J. (1996). *Listening: Attitudes, principles, and skills*. Boston: Allyn and Bacon.

Ellis, D. (1998). *Becoming a master student*. New York: Houghton Mifflin Company.

Ferrari, B. (2012). *Power listening: Mastering the most critical business skill of all*. New York: Penguin.

Hoppe, M. H. (2006). *Active listening: Improve your ability to listen and lead* [ebook]. Greensboro, NC: Center for Creative Leadership.

Ireland, J. (2011, May 4). The kinds of listening skills. Livestrong.com. Retrieved from http://www.livestrong.com/article/ 82419-kinds-listening-skills/

Kaponya, P. J. (1991). *The human resource professional: Tactics and strategies for career success*. New York: Praeger Publishers.

McFerran, J. (2009, August 29). Open-door policy not enough to be a leader who can listen. Winnipeg Free Press. doi:7BS2732928311

Miller, C. (1994). *The empowered communicator: Keys to unlocking an audience*. Nashville: Broadman & Holman Publishers.

Nichols, R. G. (1957). Listening is a 10 part skill. Chicago, IL: Enterprise Publications. Retrieved from http://d1025403.site.my hosting.com/files.listen.org/Nichol sTenPartSkill/Mr39Enf4.html

Nichols, M. P. (1995). *The lost art of listening*. New York: Guilford.

Pease, A., & Pease, B. (2006). *The definitive book of body language*. New York: Bantam Books.

Ramsland, K. M. (1992). *The art of learning: A self-help manual for students*. Albany: SUNY UP.

VanDeVelde Luskin, C. (2003, September). Mark Lepper: Intrinsic motivation, extrinsic motivation and the process of learning. In Bing Times Online, Stanford University, retrieved from http://www.stanford.edu/ dept/bings chool/cgi-bin/bt/sep2003/mark- lepper-intrinsic-motivation- extrinsic-motivation-and-the-process-of-learning/

William Henry Harrison: Inaugural Address. (1989). U. S. Inaugural Addresses. Bartleby.com. Accessed Sept. 2, 2012.

Wobser, A. (2004). *Developing positive listening skills: How to really listen*. Huntsville, TX. Educational Video Network

photo credits

p. 2 Hearing mechanics http://commons.wikimedia.org/wiki/File:Hearing_mechanics.jpg By Zina Deretsky

P. 3 Senator Joe Biden http://commons.wikimedia.org/wiki/File:The_SEIU_family_listens_to_ Sen._Joe_Biden.jpg by SEIU Walk a Day in My Shoes

p. 3 Chinese symbol for listening http://www.state.gov/m/a/os/65759.htm

p. 4 Navy class http://commons.wikimedia.org/wiki/File:US_Navy_061007-N-4399G-029_Sailors_aboard_the_dock_landing_ship_USS_Harpers_Ferry_(LS   D_49)_listen_atten-tively_to_Wayne_Guillory_give_an_American_Government_class_lecture.jpg By U.S. Navy photo by Mass Communication Specialist Seaman Charles Thomas Green

p. 5 A public lecture at NAO Rozhen http://commons.wikimedia.org/wiki/File:Lecture_Rozhen.jpg by Daniel Chanliev

p. 6 Esther Brimmer http://commons.wikimedia.org/wiki/File:Esther_Brimmer_Listens_to_ Debate_at_HRC_emergency_session_on_Syria.jpg by United States Mission Geneva

p. 7 Dachau concentration camp lecture http://commons.wikimedia.org/wiki/File:Visitors_Listen_to_Lec-ture_in _Reconstructed_Barracks_-_Dachau_Concentration_Camp_Site_- _Dachau_-_Bavaria_-_Ger-many.jpg by Adam Jones, Ph.D.

p. 8 William Henry Harrison http://commons.wikimedia.org/wiki/File:William_Henry_Harri-son_by_James_Reid_Lambdin,_1835.jpg by The White House Historical Association

p. 9 Clemson Tigers http://commons.wikimedia.org/wiki/File:Clemson_Tigers_football_running_down_the_hill.jpg by Jim Ferguson

p. 10 Audience members listen to Trevor Romain, http://commons.wikimedia.org/wiki/File:Defense.gov_photo_essay_090 902-D-4894W-008.jpg by Elaine Wilson

Attributions

CC licensed content, Shared previously

Appendix A: Listening Profile

The questions below correspond to each of the six listening components in HURIER: Hearing, Understanding, Remembering, Interpreting, Evaluating, and Responding.

Before answering the questions, first guess which of the six you will do best at. In which area will you likely score lowest?

Now, respond to the following prompts gauging your listening behavior on a five-point scale (1= almost never, 2=infrequently, 3= sometimes, 4= often, 5= almost always).

_____ 1. I am constantly aware that people and circumstances change over time.

_____ 2. I take into account the speaker's personal and cultural perspective when listening to him or her.

_____ 3. I pay attention to the important things going on around me.

_____ 4. I accurately hear what is said to me.

_____ 5. I understand the speaker's vocabulary and recognize that my understanding of a work is likely to be somewhat different from the speaker's.

_____ 6. I adapt my response according to the needs of the particular situation.

_____ 7. I weigh all evidence before making a decision.

_____ 8. I take time to analyze the validity of my partner's reasoning before arriving at my own conclusion.

_____ 9. I can recall what I have heard, even when in stressful situations.

_____ 10. I enter communication situations with a positive attitude.

_____ 11. I ask relevant questions and restate my perceptions to make sure I have understood the speaker correctly.

_____ 12. I provide clear and direct feedback to others.

_____ 13. I do not let my emotions interfere with my listening or decision-making.

_____ 14. I remember how the speaker's facial expressions, body posture, and other nonverbal behaviors relate to the verbal message.

_____ 15. I overcome distractions such as the conversation of others, background noises, and telephones, when someone is speaking.

_____ 16. I distinguish between main ideas and supporting evidence when I listen.

_____ 17. I am sensitive to the speaker's tone in communication situations.

_____ 18. I listen to and accurately remember what is said, even when I strongly disagree with the speaker's viewpoint.

Add your scores for 4 + 10 + 15. This is your hearing total.

Add your scores for 5 + 11 + 16. This is your understanding total.

Add your scores for 1 + 7 + 8. This is your evaluating total.

Add your scores for 3 + 9 + 18. This is your remembering total.

Add your scores for 2 + 14 + 17. This is your interpreting total.

Add your scores for 6 + 12 + 13. This is your responding total.

In which skill area do you score highest? Which is your lowest? How would these listening behaviors affect your interactions with peers, parents, instructors, or professional co-workers?

Source: Adapted from J. Brownell, (1996), Listening: Attitudes, Principles and Skills, pp. 29 – 31, Boston: Allyn & Bacon.

Attributions

CC licensed content, Shared previously

- Chapter 4 Appendix A Listening Profile. **Authored by**: Jenn Q. Goddu, M.A.. **Provided by**: Queens University of Charlotte, Charlotte, NC. **Located at**: http://publicspeakingproject.org/psvirtualtext.html. **Project**: The Public Speaking Project. **License**: *CC BY-NC-ND: Attribution-NonCommercial-NoDerivatives*

Chapter 5: Organizing and Outlining

Objectives and Introduction

Organizing and Outlining

By Joshua Trey Barnett
University of Indiana, Bloomington, IN

Learning Objectives

After reading this chapter, you should be able to:

- Select a topic appropriate to the audience and occasion.
- Formulate a specific purpose statement that identifies precisely what you will do in your speech.
- Craft a thesis statement that clearly and succinctly summarizes the argument you will make in your speech.
- Identify and arrange the main points of your speech according to one of many organizational styles discussed in this chapter.
- ?Connect the points of your speech to one another.
- Create a preparation and speaking outline for your speech.

Meg jaunted to the front of the classroom—her trusty index cards in one hand and her water bottle in the other. It was the mid-term presentation in her entomology class, a course she enjoyed more than her other classes. The night before, Meg had spent hours scouring the web for information on the Woody Adelgid, an insect that has ravaged hemlock tree populations in the United States in recent years. But when she made it to the podium and finished her well- written and captivating introduction, her speech began to fall apart. Her index cards were a jumble of unorganized infor-mation, not linked together by any unifying theme or purpose. As she stumbled through lists of facts, Meg—along with her peers and instructor—quickly realized that her presentation had all the necessary parts to be compelling, but that those parts were not organized into a coherent and convincing speech.

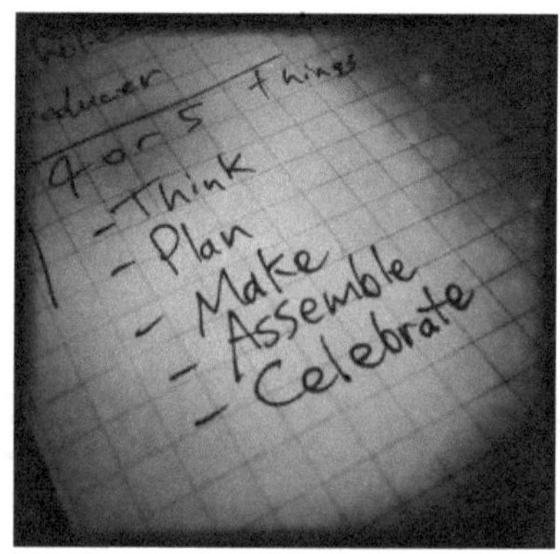

"Rough Outline For A Course" by Chris Campbell. CC-BY-NC.

Giving a speech or presentation can be a daunting task for anyone, especially inexperienced public speakers or students in introductory speech courses. Speaking to an audience can also be a rewarding experience for speakers who are willing to put in the extra effort needed to craft rhetorical masterpieces. Indeed, speeches and presentations must be crafted. Such a design requires that speakers do a great deal of preparatory work, like selecting a specific topic and deciding on a particular purpose for their speech. Once the topic and pur-pose have been decided on, a thesis statement can be prepared. After these things are established, speak-ers must select the main points of their speech, which should be organized in a way that illuminates the speaker's perspective, research agenda, or solution to a problem. In a nutshell, effective public speeches are focused on particular topics and contain one or more main points that are relevant to both the topic and the audience. For all of these components to come together convincingly, organizing and outlining must be done prior to giving a speech.

This chapter addresses a variety of strategies needed to craft the body of public speeches. The chapter begins at the initial stages of speechwriting— selecting an important and relevant topic for your audience. The more difficult task of formulating a purpose statement is discussed next. A purpose statement drives the organization of the speech since different purposes (e.g., informational or persuasive) necessitate dif-ferent types of evidence and presentation styles. Next, the chapter offers a variety of organizational strate-gies for the body of your speech. Not every strategy will be appropriate for every speech, so the strengths and weaknesses of the organizational styles are also addressed. The chapter then discusses ways to connect your main points and to draw links between your main points and the purpose you have chosen. In the final section of this chapter, one of the most important steps in speechwriting, outlining your speech, is discussed. The chapter provides the correct format for outlines as well as information on how to write a preparation outline and a speaking outline.

Chaos is inherent in all compounded things. Strive on with diligence. – Buddha

Attributions

CC licensed content, Shared previously

- Chapter 8 Objectives, Outline, and Introduction. **Authored by**: Joshua Trey Barnett. **Provided by**: University of Indiana, Bloom-ington, IN. **Located at**: http://publicspeakingproject.org/psvirtualtext.html. **Project**: The Public Speaking Project. **License**: *CC BY-NC-ND: Attribution-NonCommercial-NoDerivatives*

- Rough Outline For A Course. **Authored by**: Chris Campbell. **Located at**: https://www.flickr.com/photos/cgc/5057298847/in/photolist-8GTYKH-3ZuCKv-aYAeTK-KyPrf-e9Md1-LtwZr-6NwxoZ-2Cji3-ZpYcW-4ex5St-KXoxk-9x6rJP-aYBj8F-KtgVG-p4HuF-4o92dW-5oX72p-68yv6i-49eaDj-7kzGSp-52sD2h-7Qq7tu-NWth6--7tQDV-fsA8zq-ePFL6-91kboN-91msXM-91m1Tv-4HNTCB-87nuT6-91mfQt-91usiH-9LgZfQ-91xwbj-91nq4v-5t2yNu-fMvjLK-2V2uSq-7XMo7g-8WnoZh-91vi1q-7JorFk-79Xgdc-7a245b-7a2453-79XgbD-7a244Y-agDbc5. **License**: *CC BY-NC: Attribution-NonCommercial*

The Topic, Purpose, and Thesis

Before any work can be done on crafting the body of your speech or presentation, you must first do some prep work—selecting a topic, formulating a purpose statement, and crafting a thesis statement. In doing so, you lay the foundation for your speech by making important decisions about what you will speak about and for what purpose you will speak. These decisions will influence and guide the entire speechwriting process, so it is wise to think carefully and critically during these beginning stages.

> I think reading is important in any form. I think a person who's trying to learn to like reading should start off reading about a topic they are interested in, or a person they are interested in. – Ice Cube

Questions for Selecting a Topic

- What important events are occurring locally, nationally and internationally?
- What do I care about most?
- Is there someone or something I can advocate for?
- What makes me angry/happy?
- What beliefs/attitudes do I want to share?
- Is there some information the audience needs to know?

Selecting a Topic

Generally, speakers focus on one or more interrelated topics—relatively broad concepts, ideas, or problems that are relevant for particular audiences. The most common way that speakers discover topics is by simply observing what is happening around them—at their school, in their local government, or around the world. This is because all speeches are brought into existence as a result of circumstances, the multiplicity of activities going on at any one given moment in a particular place. For instance, presidential candidates craft short policy speeches that can be employed during debates, interviews, or town hall meetings during campaign seasons. When one of the candidates realizes he or she will not be successful, the particular circumstances change and the person must craft different kinds of speeches—a concession speech, for example. In other words, their campaign for presidency, and its many related events, necessitates the creation of various speeches. Rhetorical theorist Lloyd Bitzer[1] describes this as the rhetorical situation. Put simply, the **rhetorical situation** is the combination of factors that make speeches and other discourse meaningful and a useful way to change the way something is. Student government leaders,

"The Reader" by Shakespearesmonkey. CC-BY-NC.

for example, speak or write to other students when their campus is facing tuition or fee increases, or when students have achieved something spectacular, like lobbying campus administrators for lower student fees and succeeding. In either case, it is the situation that makes their speeches appropriate and useful for their audience of students and university employees. More importantly, they speak when there is an opportunity to change a university policy or to alter the way students think or behave in relation to a particular event on campus.

But you need not run for president or student government in order to give a meaningful speech. On the contrary, opportunities abound for those interested in engaging speech as a tool for change. Perhaps the simplest way to find a topic is to ask yourself a few questions. See the textbox entitled "Questions for Selecting a Topic" for a few questions that will help you choose a topic.

There are other questions you might ask yourself, too, but these should lead you to at least a few topical choices. The most important work that these questions do is to locate topics within your pre-existing sphere of knowledge and interest. David Zarefsky[2] also identifies brainstorming as a way to develop speech topics, a strategy that can be helpful if the questions listed in the textbox did not yield an appropriate or interesting topic.

Starting with a topic you are already interested in will likely make writing and presenting your speech a more enjoyable and meaningful experience. It means that your entire speechwriting process will focus on something you find important and that you can present this information to people who stand to benefit from your speech.

<hr>

1. Bitzer, L. (1968). The rhetorical situation. *Philosophy & Rhetoric*, *1*(1), 1–14.
2. Zarefsky, D. (2010). *Public speaking: Strategies for success* (6th edition). Boston: Allyn & Bacon.

Once you have answered these questions and narrowed your responses, you are still not done selecting your topic. For instance, you might have decided that you really care about conserving habitat for bog turtles. This is a very broad topic and could easily lead to a dozen different speeches. To resolve this problem, speakers must also consider the audience to whom they will speak, the scope of their presentation, and the outcome they wish to achieve. If the bog turtle enthusiast knows that she will be talking to a local zoning board and that she hopes to stop them from allowing businesses to locate on important bog turtle habitat, her topic can easily morph into something more specific. Now, her speech topic is two-pronged: bog turtle habitat and zoning rules.

Formulating the Purpose Statements

By honing in on a very specific topic, you begin the work of formulating your **purpose statement**. In short, a purpose statement clearly states what it is you would like to achieve. Purpose statements are especially helpful for guiding you as you prepare your speech. When deciding which main points, facts, and examples to include, you should simply ask yourself whether they are relevant not only to the topic you have selected, but also whether they support the goal you outlined in your purpose statement. The **general purpose statement** of a speech may be to inform, to persuade, to inspire, to celebrate, to mourn, or to entertain. Thus, it is common to frame a **specific purpose statement** around one of these goals. According to O'Hair, Stewart, and

"Bog turtle sunning" by U.S. Fish and Wildlife Service. *Public domain.*

Rubenstein, a specific purpose statement "expresses both the topic and the general speech purpose in action form and in terms of the specific objectives you hope to achieve."[3] For instance, the bog turtle habitat activist might write the following specific purpose statement: *At the end of my speech, the Clarke County Zoning Commission will understand that locating businesses in bog turtle habitat is a poor choice with a range of negative consequences.* In short, the general purpose statement lays out the broader goal of the speech while the specific purpose statement describes precisely what the speech is intended to do.

Success demands singleness of purpose. – Vince Lombardi

Writing the Thesis Statement

The specific purpose statement is a tool that you will use as you write your talk, but it is unlikely that it will appear verbatim in your speech. Instead, you will want to convert the specific purpose statement into a **thesis statement** that you will share with your audience. A thesis statement encapsulates the main points of a speech in just a sentence or two, and it is designed to give audiences a quick preview of what the entire speech will be about. The thesis statement for a speech, like the thesis of a research- based essay, should be

3. O'Hair, D., Stewart, R., Rubenstein, H. (2004). *A speaker's guidebook: Text and reference* (2nd edition). Boston: Bedford/St. Martin's.

easily identifiable and ought to very succinctly sum up the main points you will present. Moreover, the thesis statement should reflect the general purpose of your speech; if your purpose is to persuade or educate, for instance, the thesis should alert audience members to this goal. The bog turtle enthusiast might prepare the following thesis statement based on her specific purpose statement: Bog turtle habitats are sensitive to a variety of activities, but land development is particularly harmful to unstable habitats. The Clarke County Zoning Commission should protect bog turtle habitats by choosing to prohibit business from locating in these habitats. In this example, the thesis statement outlines the main points and implies that the speaker will be arguing for certain zoning practices.

Attributions

CC licensed content, Shared previously

- Chapter 8 The Topic, Purpose, and Thesis. **Authored by**: Joshua Trey Barnett. **Provided by**: University of Indiana, Bloomington, IN. **Located at**: http://publicspeakingproject.org/psvirtualtext.html. **Project**: The Public Speaking Project. **License**: *CC BY-NC-ND: Attribution-NonCommercial-NoDerivatives*
- The Reader. **Authored by**: Shakespearesmonkey. **Located at**: https://www.flickr.com/photos/shakespearesmonkey/4939289974/. **License**: *CC BY-NC: Attribution-NonCommercial*

Public domain content

- Image of a bog turtle . **Authored by**: R. G. Tucker, Jr.. **Provided by**: United States Fish and Wildlife Service. **Located at**: http://commons.wikimedia.org/wiki/File:Bog_turtle_sunning.jpg. **License**: *Public Domain: No Known Copyright*

Writing the Body of Your Speech

Once you have finished the important work of deciding what your speech will be about, as well as formulating the purpose statement and crafting the thesis, you should turn your attention to writing the body of your speech. All of your main points are contained in the body, and normally this section is prepared well before you ever write the introduction or conclusion. The body of your speech will consume the largest amount of time to present; and it is the opportunity for you to elaborate on facts, evidence, examples, and opinions that support your thesis statement and do the work you have outlined in the specific purpose statement. Combining these various elements into a cohesive and compelling speech, however, is not without its difficulties, the first of which is deciding which elements to include and how they ought to be organized to best suit your purpose.

> Good design is making something intelligible and memorable. Great design is making something memorable and meaningful. – Dieter Rams

The **main points** of any speech are the key pieces of information or arguments contained within the talk or presentation. In other words, the main points are what your audience should remember from your talk. Unlike facts or examples, main points are broad and can be encapsulated in just a sentence or two and represent the big ideas you want to convey to your audience. In general, speeches contain two to seven main points[1] that collectively lead to some understanding by the end of the speech. For informative speeches, main points might include historical details that advance a particular understanding of an event. For a persuasive speech, however, your main points may be your separate arguments that, when combined, help to make your case. When writing your main points, you may want to do so in **parallel structure**. Parallel structure refers to main points that are worded using the same structure, perhaps by starting

---

1. Bower, G. H. (1990). Organizational factors in memory. *Cognitive Psychology*, *1*, 18–46.

with a common introductory clause.[2] Main points do not stand alone; instead, speakers must substantiate their main points by offering up examples, statistics, facts, anecdotes, or other information that contribute to the audience's understanding of the main points. All of these things make up the **sub-points**, which are used to help prove the main points. This is where all of your research and supporting information comes into play.

Attributions

CC licensed content, Shared previously

- Chapter 8 Writing the Body of Your Speech. **Authored by**: Joshua Trey Barnett. **Provided by**: University of Indiana, Blooming-ton, IN. **Located at**: http://publicspeakingproject.org/psvirtualtext.html. **Project**: The Public Speaking Project. **License**: *CC BY-NC-ND: Attribution-NonCommercial-NoDerivatives*

- Writing. **Authored by**: Rubin Starset. **Located at**: https://www.flickr.com/photos/rubin110/4130157287/. **License**: *CC BY-NC-SA: Attribution-NonCommercial-ShareAlike*

2. Verderber, R. F., Verderber, K. S., & Sellnow, D. D. (2008). *The challenge of effective speaking* (14th edition). Belmont, CA: Thomson Learning.

Organizational Styles

After deciding which main points and sub-points you must include, you can get to work writing up the speech. Before you do so, however, it is helpful to consider how you will organize the ideas. From presenting historical information in chronological order as part of an informative speech to drawing a comparison between two ideas in a persuasive speech to offering up problems and solutions, there are many ways in which speakers can craft effective speeches. These are referred to as organizational styles, or templates for organizing the main points of a speech.

Chronological

When you speak about events that are linked together by time, it is sensible to engage the chronological organization style. In a **chronological speech**, main points are delivered according to when they happened and could be traced on a calendar or clock. Arranging main points in chronological order can be helpful when describing historical events to an audience as well as when the order of events is necessary to understand what you wish to convey. Informative speeches about a series of events most commonly engage the chronological style, as do many demonstrative speeches (e.g., how to bake a cake or build an airplane). Another time when the chronological style makes sense is when you tell the story of someone's life or career. For instance, a speech about Oprah Winfrey might be arranged chronologically (see

"Vintage alarm clock" by peter-rabbit. CC-BY-NC.

textbox). In this case, the main points are arranged by following Winfrey's life from birth to the present time. Life events (e.g., birth, her early career, her life after ending the Oprah Winfrey Show) are connected together according to when they happened and highlight the progression of Winfrey's career. Organizing the speech in this way illustrates the interconnectedness of life events.

Oprah Winfrey (Chronological Arrangement)

Thesis: Oprah's career can be understood by four key, interconnected life stages.

I. Oprah's childhood was spent in rural Mississippi, where she endured sexual abuse from family members.

II. Oprah's early career was characterized by stints on local radio and television networks in Nashville and Chicago.

III. Oprah's tenure as host of the *Oprah Winfrey Show* began in 1986 and lasted until 2011, a period of time marked by much success.

IV. Oprah's most recent media venture is OWN: The Oprah Winfrey Network, which plays host to a variety of television shows including *Oprah's Next Chapter*.

Doing the best at this moment puts you in the best place for the next moment. – Oprah Winfrey

Topical

When the main points of your speech center on ideas that are more distinct from one another, a topical organization style may be engaged. In a **topical speech**, main points are developed separately and are generally connected together within the introduction and conclusion. In other words, the topical style is crafted around main points and sub-points that are mutually exclusive but related to one another by virtue of the thesis. It makes sense to use the topical style when elements are connected to one another because of their relationship to the whole. A topical speech about the composition of a newspaper company can be seen in the following textbox. The main points are linked together by the fact that they are all a part of the same business. Although they are related in that way, the topical style illustrates the ways in which the four different departments function apart from one another. In this example, the topical style is a good fit because the four departments are equally important to the function of the newspaper company.

Composition of a Newspaper Company (Topical Arrangement)

Thesis: The newspaper has four primary departments.

I. The advertising department sells display advertisements to local and national businesses.

II. The editorial department produces the written content of the newspaper, including feature stories.

III. The production department lays out the pages and manages pre- press work such as distilling the pages and processing colors.

IV. The business department processes payments from advertisers, employee paperwork, and the bi-weekly payroll.

Spatial

Another way to organize the points of a speech is through a **spatial speech**, which arranges main points according to their physical and geographic relationships. The spatial style is an especially useful organization style when the main point's importance is derived from its location or directional focus. In other words, when the scene or the composition is a central aspect of the main points, the spatial style is an appropriate way to deliver key ideas. Things can be described from top to bottom, inside to outside, left to right, north to south, and so on. Importantly, speakers using a spatial style should offer commentary about the placement of the main points as they move through the speech, alerting audience members to the location changes. For instance, a speech about The University of Georgia might be arranged spatially; in this example, the spatial organization frames the discussion in terms of the campus layout. The spatial style is fitting since the differences in architecture and uses of space are related to particular geographic areas, making location a central organizing factor. As such, the spatial style highlights these location differences.

University of Georgia (Spatial Arrangement)

Thesis: The University of Georgia is arranged into four distinct sections, which are characterized by architectural and disciplinary differences.

I. In North Campus, one will find the University's oldest building, a sprawling tree- lined quad, and the famous Arches, all of which are nestled against Athens' downtown district.

II. In West Campus, dozens of dormitories provide housing for the University's large undergraduate population and students can regularly be found lounging outside or at one of the dining halls.

III. In East Campus, students delight in newly constructed, modern buildings and enjoy the benefits of the University's health center, recreational facilities, and science research buildings.

IV. In South Campus, pharmacy, veterinary, and biomedical science students traverse newly constructed parts of campus featuring well-kept landscaping and modern architecture.

Comparative

When you need to discuss the similarities and differences between two or more things, a comparative organizational pattern can be employed. In **comparative speeches**, speakers may choose to compare things a couple different ways. First, you could compare two or more things as whole (e.g., discuss all traits of an apple and then all traits of an orange). Second, you could compare these things element by element (e.g., color of each, smell of each, AND taste of each). Some topics that are routinely spoken about comparatively include different cultures, different types of transportation, and even different types of coffee. A comparative speech outline about eastern and western cultures could look like this.

"Let's compare apples to oranges" by frankieleon. CC-BY.

Eastern vs. Western Culture (Comparison Arrangement)

Thesis: There are a variety of differences between Eastern and Western cultures.

I. Eastern cultures tend to be more collectivistic.

II. Western cultures tend to be more individualistic.

III. Eastern cultures tend to treat health issues ?holistically.

IV. Western cultures tend to ?treat health issues more acutely.

In this type of speech, the list of comparisons, which should be substantiated with further evidence, could go on for any number of main points. The speech could also compare how two or more things are more alike than one might think. For instance, a speaker could discuss how singers Madonna and Lady Gaga share many similarities both in aesthetic style and in their music.

Problem-Solution

Sometimes it is necessary to share a problem and a solution with an audience. In cases like these, the **problem-solution speech** is an appropriate way to arrange the main points of a speech. One familiar example of speeches organized in this way is the political speeches that presidential hopefuls give in the United States. Often, candidates will begin their speech by describing a problem created by or, at the very least, left unresolved by the incumbent. Once they have established their view of the problem, they then go on to flesh out their proposed solution. The problem- solution style is especially useful when the speaker wants to convince the audience that they should take action in solving some problem. A political candidate seeking office might frame a speech using the problem-solution style (see textbox).

"FEMA" by Dave Gatley. Public domain.

Presidential Candidate's Speech (Problem-Solution Arrangement)

Thesis: The US energy crisis can be solved by electing me as president since I will devote resources to the production of renewable forms of energy.

I. The United States is facing an energy crisis because we cannot produce enough energy ourselves to sustain the levels of activity needed to run the country. (problem)

II. The current administration has failed to invest enough resources in renewable energy practices. (problem)

III. We can help create a more stable situation if we work to produce renewable forms of energy within the United States. (solution)

IV. If you vote for me, I will ensure that renewable energy creation is a priority. (solution)

The difference between what we do and what we are capable of doing would suffice to solve most of the world's problems. – Mahatma Gandhi

This example illustrates the way in which a problem-solution oriented speech can be used to identify both a general problem (energy crisis) and a specific problem (incumbent's lack of action). Moreover, this example highlights two kinds of solutions: a general solution and a solution that is dependent on the speaker's involvement. The problem-solution speech is especially appropriate when the speaker desires to promote a particular solution as this offers audience members a way to become involved. Whether you are able to offer a specific solution or not, key to the problem-solution speech is a clear description of both the problem and the solution with clear links drawn between the two. In other words, the speech should make specific connections between the problem and how the solution can be engaged to solve it.

Causal

Similar to a problem-solution speech, a **causal** speech informs audience members about causes and effects that have already happened. In other words, a causal organization style first addresses some cause and then shares what effects resulted. A causal speech can be particularly effective when the speaker wants to share the relationship between two things, like the creation of a vaccine to help deter disease. An example of how a causal speech about a shingles vaccine might be designed follows:

"Domino" by Bro. Jeffrey Pioquinto, SJ. CC-BY.

As the example illustrates, the basic components of the causal speech are the cause and the effect. Such an organizational style is useful when a speaker needs to share the results of a new program, discuss how one act led to another, or discuss the positive/negative outcomes of taking some action.

Shingles Speech (Cause-Effect Arrangement)

Thesis: The prevalence of the disease shingles led to the invention of a vaccine.

1. Shingles is a disease that causes painful, blistering rashes in up to one million Americans every year. (cause)

2. In 2006, a vaccine for shingles was licensed in the United States and has been shown to reduce the likelihood that people over 60 years old will get shingles. (effect)

Every choice you make has an end result. – Zig Ziglar

Choosing an organizational style is an important step in the speechwriting process. As you formulate the purpose of your speech and generate the main points that you will need to include, selecting an appropriate organizational style will likely become easier. The topical, spatial, causal, comparative and chronological methods of arrangement may be better suited to informative speeches, whereas the refutation pattern may work well for a persuasive speech. Additionally, Chapter 16 offers additional organization styles suited for persuasive speeches, such as the refutation speech and Monroe's Motivated Sequence.[1] Next, we will look at statements that help tie all of your points together and the formal mode of organizing a speech by using outlines.

1. Monroe, A. H. (1949). *Principles and types of speech.* Glenview, IL: Scott, Foresman and Company.

Attributions

CC licensed content, Shared previously

- Chapter 8 Organizational Styles. **Authored by**: Joshua Trey Barnett. **Provided by**: University of Indiana, Bloomington, IN. **Located at**: http://publicspeakingproject.org/psvirtualtext.html. **Project**: The Public Speaking Project. **License**: *CC BY-NC-ND: Attribution-NonCommercial-NoDerivatives*

- vintage alarm clock. **Authored by**: peter-rabbit. **Located at**: https://flic.kr/p/drEszC. **License**: *CC BY-NC: Attribution-NonCommercial*

- let's compare apples to oranges. **Authored by**: frankieleon. **Located at**: https://flic.kr/p/bscqLn. **License**: *CC BY: Attribution*

- Domino. **Authored by**: Bro. Jeffrey Pioquinto, SJ. **Located at**: https://flic.kr/p/pA9ftS. **License**: *CC BY: Attribution*

Public domain content

- FEMA - 1337 - Photograph by Dave Gatley taken on 03-01-1998 in California. **Authored by**: Dave Gatley. **Provided by**: Federal Emergency Management Agency. **Located at**: http://commons.wikimedia.org/wiki/File:FEMA_-_1337_-_Photograph_by_Dave_Gatley_taken_on_03-01-1998_in_California.jpg. **License**: *Public Domain: No Known Copyright*

Connecting Your Main Points

Since main points are discrete and interconnected ideas, and since every speech contains more than one main point, it is necessary to strategically make connections between one point and another. To link the ideas of your speech, you will need to develop **signposts**, "words and gestures that allow you to move smoothly from one idea to the next throughout your speech, showing relationships between ideas and emphasizing important points."[1] There are several ways to incorporate signposts into your speech, and it is important to do so since these small signals keep listeners engaged and informed about where you are in the speech. Transitional statements, internal previews, and summaries are all signposts that can help keep your speech moving along.

If you cry "forward," you must without fail make plain in what direction to go. – Anton Chekhov

---

Transitional Statements to Show Similarity and Difference

To Show Similarity Between Points:

- "Similarly"
- "In the same way"
- "Also"
- "Likewise"
- "In other words"

To Show Difference Between Points:

---

1. Beebe, S. A. & Beebe, S. J. (2003). *The public speaking handbook* (5th edition). Boston: Pearson.

- "However"
- "Unlike the last point"
- "On the other hand"
- "Conversely"
- "In opposition"
- "Another view is that"

One way to connect points is to include **transitional statements**. Transitional statements are phrases or sentences that lead from one distinct- but-connected idea to another. They are used to alert audiences to the fact that you are getting ready to discuss something else. When moving from one point to another, your transition may just be a word or short phrase. For instance, you might say "next," "also," or "moreover." You can also enumerate your speech points and signal transitions by starting each point with "First," "Second," "Third," et cetera. The textbox above offers a short list of transitional statements that are helpful when you need to show similarity or difference between the points. You might also incorporate non-verbal transitions, such as brief pauses or a movement across the stage. Pausing to look at your audience, stepping out from behind a podium, or even raising or lowering the rate of your voice can signal to audience members that you are transitioning.

Another way to incorporate signposts into your speech is by offering **internal previews** within your speech. Internal previews, like the name implies, lay out what will occur during your speech. They tell the audience what to expect. Because audience members cannot flip back and forth between pages, internal previews help keep them on track and aware of what to be listening for and what to remember. Internal previews are similar to the preview statements you will learn about in the chapter on introductions and conclusions (Chapter 9), except that they appear within the body of your speech and are more small-scale than the broad preview you should provide at the beginning of your speech. In general, internal previews are longer than transitional statements. If you were giving a problem-solution speech, you might include a variation of this internal preview: "Now that I have described the problems, let's now discuss some ways that we can solve these issues." The internal preview offers a natural segue from problems to solutions and makes audience members aware that another point is about to be made.

When speeches are longer than a few minutes and include complex ideas and information, speakers often include **summaries** within the body of their speech. Summaries provide a recap of what has already been said, making it more likely that audiences will remember the points that they hear again. Additionally, summaries can be combined with internal previews to alert audience members that the next point builds on those that they have already heard.

The speaker below has just finished discussing several reasons trout habitats need federal protection, and next he will discuss some ways that audience members can agitate for government action on these issues. His combined internal preview and summary would look something like this:

"Trout" by Jonathunder. CC-BY-SA.

> *So, in review, trout habitats need federal protection because they bear a large pollution burden, they mostly exist on private property, and they are indicators of other environmental health issues. Next, I will discuss some ways that you can encourage the federal government to protect these habitats.*

In this example, the speaker first reminds audience members of what he has already addressed and then tells them what he will talk about next. By repeating the main points in summary fashion, the speaker gives audience members another opportunity to consider his main ideas.

> Good communication does not mean that you have to speak in perfectly formed sentences and paragraphs. It isn't about slickness. Simple and clear go a long way. – John Kotter

Attributions

CC licensed content, Shared previously

- Chapter 8 Connecting Your Main Points. **Authored by**: Joshua Trey Barnett. **Provided by**: University of Indiana, Bloomington, IN. **Located at**: http://publicspeakingproject.org/psvirtualtext.html. **Project**: The Public Speaking Project. **License**: *CC BY-NC-ND: Attribution-NonCommercial-NoDerivatives*

- Trout. **Authored by**: Jonathunder. **Located at**: http://commons.wikimedia.org/wiki/File:Trout.jpg. **License**: *CC BY-SA: Attribution-ShareAlike*

- Golden Gate Bridge 0002. **Authored by**: RyanJWilmot. **Located at**: https://commons.wikimedia.org/wiki/File:Golden_Gate_Bridge_0002.jpg. **License**: *CC BY-SA: Attribution-ShareAlike*

Outlining Your Speech

Most speakers and audience members would agree that an organized speech is both easier to present as well as more persuasive. Public speaking teachers especially believe in the power of organizing your speech, which is why they encourage (and often require) that you create an outline for your speech. **Outlines**, or textual arrangements of all the various elements of a speech, are a very common way of organizing a speech before it is delivered. Most extemporaneous speakers keep their outlines with them during the speech as a way to ensure that they do not leave out any important elements and to keep them on track. Writing an outline is also important to the speechwriting process since doing so forces the speakers to think about the main points and sub-points, the examples they wish to include, and the ways in which these elements correspond to one another. In short, the outline functions both as an organization tool and as a reference for delivering a speech.

Outline Types

There are two types of outlines. The first outline you will write is called the **preparation outline**. Also called a working, practice, or rough outline, the preparation outline is used to work through the various components of your speech in an inventive format. Stephen E. Lucas[1] put it simply: "The preparation outline is just what its name implies—an outline that helps you prepare the speech" (p. 248). When writing the preparation outline, you should focus on finalizing the purpose and thesis statements, logically ordering your main points, deciding where supporting material should be included, and refining the overall organizational pattern of your speech. As you write the preparation outline, you may find it necessary to rearrange

*"Alpena Mayor Carol Shafto Speaks at 2011 Michigan Municipal League Convention" **by Michigan Municipal League.** CC-BY-ND.*

your points or to add or subtract supporting material. You may also realize that some of your main points are sufficiently supported while others are lacking. The final draft of your preparation outline should

1. Lucas, Stephen E. (2004). *The art of public speaking* (8th edition). New York: McGraw-Hill.

include full sentences, making up a complete script of your entire speech. In most cases, however, the preparation outline is reserved for planning purposes only and is translated into a speaking outline before you deliver the speech.

A **speaking outline** is the outline you will prepare for use when delivering the speech. The speaking outline is much more succinct than the preparation outline and includes brief phrases or words that remind the speakers of the points they need to make, plus supporting material and signposts.[2] The words or phrases used on the speaking outline should briefly encapsulate all of the information needed to prompt the speaker to accurately deliver the speech. Although some cases call for reading a speech verbatim from the full-sentence outline, in most cases speakers will simply refer to their speaking outline for quick reminders and to ensure that they do not omit any important information. Because it uses just words or short phrases, and not full sentences, the speaking outline can easily be transferred to index cards that can be referenced during a speech.

Outline Structure

Because an outline is used to arrange all of the elements of your speech, it makes sense that the outline itself has an organizational hierarchy and a common format. Although there are a variety of outline styles, generally they follow the same pattern. Main ideas are preceded by Roman numerals (I, II, III, etc.). Sub-points are preceded by capital letters (A, B, C, etc.), then Arabic numerals (1, 2, 3, etc.), and finally lowercase letters (a, b, c, etc.). Each level of subordination is also differentiated from its predecessor by indenting a few spaces. Indenting makes it easy to find your main points, sub-points, and the supporting points and examples below them. Since there are three sections to your speech— introduction, body, and conclusion— your outline needs to include all of them. Each of these sections is titled and the main points start with Roman numeral I.

Outline Formatting Guide

Title: Organizing Your Public Speech

Topic: Organizing public speeches

Specific Purpose Statement: To inform listeners about the various ways in which they can organize their public speeches.

Thesis Statement: A variety of organizational styles can used to organize public speeches.

Introduction
Paragraph that gets the attention of the audience, establishes goodwill with the audience, states the purpose of the speech, and previews the speech and its structure.

(Transition)

Body

I. Main point

---

2. Beebe, S. A. & Beebe, S. J. (2003). *The public speaking handbook* (5th edition). Boston: Pearson.

> A. Sub-point
> B. Sub-point
> C. Sub-point
>
>> 1. Supporting point
>> 2. Supporting point
>
> (Transition)
>
> **Conclusion**
> Paragraph that prepares the audience for the end of the speech, presents any final appeals, and summarizes and wraps up the speech.
>
> **Bibliography**

In addition to these formatting suggestions, there are some additional elements that should be included at the beginning of your outline: the title, topic, specific purpose statement, and thesis statement. These elements are helpful to you, the speechwriter, since they remind you what, specifically, you are trying to accomplish in your speech. They are also helpful to anyone reading and assessing your outline since knowing what you want to accomplish will determine how they perceive the elements included in your outline. Additionally, you should write out the transitional statements that you will use to alert audiences that you are moving from one point to another. These are included in parentheses between main points. At the end of the outlines, you should include bibliographic information for any outside resources you mention during the speech. These should be cited using whatever citations style your professor requires. The textbox entitled "Outline Formatting Guide" provides an example of the appropriate outline format.

> If you do not change direction, you may end up where you are heading. – Lao Tzu

Preparation Outline

This chapter contains the preparation and speaking outlines for a short speech the author of this chapter gave about how small organizations can work on issues related to climate change (see appendices). In this example, the title, specific purpose, thesis, and list of visual aids precedes the speech. Depending on your instructor's requirements, you may need to include these details plus additional information. It is also a good idea to keep these details at the top of your document as you write the speech since they will help keep you on track to developing an organized speech that is in line with your specific purpose and helps prove your thesis. At the end of the chapter, in Appendix A, you can find a full length example of a Preparation (Full Sentence) Outline.

Speaking Outline

In Appendix B, the Preparation Outline is condensed into just a few short key words or phrases that will remind speakers to include all of their main points and supporting information. The introduction and conclusion are not included since they will simply be inserted from the Preparation Outline. It is easy to forget your catchy attention-getter or final thoughts you have prepared for your audience, so it is best to include the full sentence versions even in your speaking outline.

Using the Speaking Outline

Once you have prepared the outline and are almost ready to give your speech, you should decide how you want to format your outline for presentation. Many speakers like to carry a stack of papers with them when they speak, but others are more comfortable with a smaller stack of index cards with the outline copied onto them. Moreover, speaking instructors often have requirements for how you should format the speaking outline. Whether you decide to use index cards or the printed outline, here are a few tips. First, write large enough so that you do not have to bring the cards or pages close to your eyes to read them. Second, make sure you have the cards/pages in the correct order and bound together in some way so that they do not get out of order. Third, just in case the cards/pages do get out of order (this happens too often!), be sure that you number each in the top right corner so you can quickly and easily get things organized. Fourth, try not to fiddle with the cards/pages when you are speaking. It is best to lay them down if you have a podium or table in front of you. If not, practice reading from them in front of a mirror. You should be able to look down quickly, read the text, and then return to your gaze to the audience.

"TAG speaks of others first" by Texas Military Forces. CC-BY-ND.

Any intelligent fool can make things bigger and more complex… It takes a touch of genius – and a lot of courage to move in the opposite direction. – Albert Einstein

Attributions

CC licensed content, Shared previously

- Chapter 8 Outlining Your Speech. **Authored by**: Joshua Trey Barnett. **Provided by**: University of Indiana, Bloomington, IN. **Located at**: http://publicspeakingproject.org/psvirtualtext.html. **Project**: The Public Speaking Project. **License**: *CC BY-NC-ND: Attribution-NonCommercial-NoDerivatives*

- Alpena Mayor Carol Shafto Speaks at 2011 Michigan Municipal League Convention. **Authored by**: Michigan Municipal League. **Located at**: https://flic.kr/p/aunJMR. **License**: *CC BY-ND: Attribution-NoDerivatives*

- TAG speaks of others first. **Authored by**: Texas Military Forces. **Located at**: https://www.flickr.com/photos/texasmilitaryforces/5560449970/. **License**: *CC BY-ND: Attribution-NoDerivatives*

Conclusion and Module Activities

If you have been using this chapter to guide you through the organizational stages of writing your speech, you have likely discovered that getting organized is very challenging but also very rewarding. Like cleaning up a messy kitchen or organizing your closet, doing the more tedious work of organizing your speech is an activity you will appreciate most once it is done. From the very beginning stages of organization, like choosing a topic and writing a thesis statement, to deciding how best to arrange the main points of your speech and outlining, getting organized is one step toward an effective and engaging speech or presentation.

Had Meg, the student mentioned in the opening anecdote, taken some time to work through the organizational process, it is likely her speech would have gone much more smoothly when she finished her introduction. It is very common for beginning speakers to spend a great deal of their time preparing catchy introductions, fancy PowerPoint presentations, and nice conclusions, which are all very important. However, the body of any speech is where the speaker must make effective arguments, provide helpful information, entertain, and the like, so it makes sense that speakers should devote a proportionate amount of time to these areas as well. By following this chapter, as well as studying the other chapters in this text, you should be prepared to craft interesting, compelling, and organized speeches.

"Alt-Disney $11" by Jeff Carson. CC-BY-NC-SA.

Review Questions

1. Name three questions you should ask yourself when selecting a topic.

2. What is the difference between a general and specific purpose statement? Write examples of each for each of these topics: dog training, baking a cake, climate change.

3. How does the thesis statement differ from the specific purpose statement?

4. Which speech organization style arranges points by time? Which one arranges points by direction? Which one arranges points according to a five-step sequence?

5. Which speech organization styles are best suited for persuasive speeches?

6. Define signpost. What are three types of signposts?

7. What is the correct format for a speech outline?

Activities

1. **Reverse outlining**. During a classmate's speech, pay special attention to the organization style that he or she employs. As they give their speech, try to construct an outline based on what you hear. If your classmate has followed many of the suggestions provided in this and other chapters, you should be able to identify and replicate the structure of the speech. Compare your "reverse" outline with the speaking outline. Discuss any areas of discrepancy.

2. **Topic Proposal Workshop**. Often, selecting a topic can be one of the most challenging steps in developing a speech for your class. Prior to class, review the textbox "Questions for selecting a topic" on page 8-2. Answer these questions and choose a tentative topic. Write up a short paragraph about your topic that describes its importance, why it interests you, and what you would like to convey to an audience about your proposed topic. In class, meet with two or three additional students to discuss and workshop each of your topics. As you discuss your topic with others, jot down what questions they had, what aspects they seemed to find most interesting, and any suggestions your peers might have. Once the workshop is complete, proceed with narrowing your topic to something manageable.

Attributions

CC licensed content, Shared previously

Glossary and References

Glossary

TERM	DEFINITION
Chronological Speech	A speech in which the main points are delivered according to when they happened and could be traced on a calendar or clock.
Comparative Speech	A speech in which two or more objects, ideas, beliefs, events, places, or things are compared or contrasted with one another.
Causal Speech	A speech that informs audience members about causes and effects that have already happened.
General Purpose Statement	The overarching goal of a speech; for instance, to inform, to persuade, to inspire, to celebrate, to mourn, or to entertain.
Internal Previews	Short descriptions of what a speaker will do and say during a speech; may be at the beginning and within the body of a speech.
Main Points	The key pieces of information or arguments contained within a talk or presentation.
Monroe's Motivated Sequence	An organization style that is designed to motivate the audience to take a particular action and is characterized by a five-step sequence: (1) attention, (2) need, (3) satisfaction, (4), visualization, and (5) action appeal.
Organizational Styles	Templates for organizing the main points of a speech that are rooted in traditions of public discourse and can jumpstart the speechwriting process.
Outline	Hierarchal textual arrangement of all the various elements of a speech.
Parallel Structure	Main points that are worded using the same structure.
Preparation Outline	A full-sentence outline that is used during the planning stages to flesh out ideas, arrange main points, and to rehearse the speech; could be used as a script if presenting a manuscript style speech.
Problem-Solution Speech	A speech in which problems and solutions are presented alongside one another with a clear link between a problem and its solution.
Refutation Speech	A speech that anticipates the audience's opposition, then brings attention to the tensions between the two sides, and finally refutes them using evidential support.
Rhetorical Situation	According to Lloyd Bitzer, "a complex of persons, events, objects, and relations presenting an actual or potential exigence which can be completely or partially removed if discourse, introduced into the situation, can so constrain human decision or action as to bring about the significant modification of the exigence" (1968, p. 6).
Signposts	According to Beebe and Beebe, "words and gestures that allow you to move smoothly from one idea to the next throughout your speech, showing relationships between ideas and emphasizing important points" (2005, p. 204).
Spatial Speech	A speech in which the main points are arranged according to their physical and geographic relationships.
Speaking Outline	A succinct outline that uses words or short phrases to represent the components of a speech and that is used during speech delivery.

Specific Purpose Statement	A sentence or two that describe precisely what the speech is intended to do.
Sub-Points	Information that is used to support the main points of a speech.
Summaries	Short recaps of what has already been said; used to remind the audience of the points already addressed.
Thesis Statement	A one- or two-sentence encapsulation of the main points of a speech, also called the central idea.
Topical Speech	A speech in which main points are developed separately and are generally connected together within the introduction and conclusion.
Transitional Statements	Phrases or sentences that lead from one distinct-but-connected idea to another.

References

Beebe, S. A. & Beebe, S. J. (2003). *The public speaking handbook (5th edition)*. Boston: Pearson.

Bower, G. H. (1990). Organizational factors in memory. *Cognitive Psychology*, 1, 18-46.

Bitzer, L. (1968). The rhetorical situation. *Philosophy & Rhetoric,* 1(1), 1-14.

Lucas, Stephen E. (2004). *The art of public speaking (8th edition).* New York: McGraw-Hill.

Monroe, A. H. (1949). *Principles and types of speech.* Glenview, IL: Scott, Foresman and Company.

O'Hair, D., Stewart, R., Rubenstein, H. (2004). *A speaker's guidebook: Text and reference* (2nd edition). Boston: Bedford/St. Martin's.

Verderber, R. F., Verderber, K. S., & Sellnow, D. D. (2008). *The challenge of effective speaking (14th edition)*. Belmont, CA: Thomson Learning.

Zarefsky, D. (2010). *Public speaking: Strategies for success (6th edition).* Boston: Allyn & Bacon.

photo credits

p. 3 Bog Turtle by R.G. Tucker

http://commons.wikimedia.org/wiki/File:Bog_turtle_sun ning.jpg

p. 4 Oscar Mayer Wienermobile byJalopnik

http://jalopnik.com/5310348/ten+pack-of-dogs-history- of-the-wienermobile/gallery/1

p. 4 Mac vs PC http://i2.cdn.turner.com/cnn/2011/TECH/web/04/22/ma c.pc.users/t1larg.mac.pc.2.jpg

p. 5 Rio Nido Mudslide by Dave Gately

http://commons.wikimedia.org/wiki/File:FEMA_- _1337_-_Photograph_by_Dave_Gat-ley_taken_on_03-01- 1998_in_California.jpg

p. 8 Rainbow Trout by Jonathunder http://commons.wikimedia.org/wiki/File:Trout.jpg

p. 8 Mayor Carol Shafto by Michigan Municipal League

http://www.flickr.com/photos/michigancommunities/62 28314099/

p. 10 Maj. Gen John Nichols by Texas Military Forces

http://www.flickr.com/photos/texasmilitaryforces/55604 49970/

Attributions

CC licensed content, Shared previously

- Chapter 8 Glossary. **Authored by**: Joshua Trey Barnett. **Provided by**: University of Indiana, Bloomington, IN. **Located at**: http://publicspeakingproject.org/psvirtualtext.html. **Project**: The Public Speaking Project. **License**: *CC BY-NC-ND: Attribution-NonCommercial-NoDerivatives*

Appendix A: Full Sentence Outline

Example Preparation (Full Sentence) Outline

Title: For the Fish: Climate Work By and For Fishers

Specific Purpose: To persuade trout fishers that climate change is a threat to coldwater fisheries and that they should organize to create collective change to the environmental issues surrounding climate change.

Thesis: Trout fisheries are endangered by climate change, but fishers can (and should) work to mitigate these issues.

Visual Aids: PowerPoint presentation

Introduction

Most of you have heard about climate change and have wondered whether or how it might be affecting trout fisheries. Unfortunately, climate scientists' predictions about climate change seem to indicate that trout fisheries may bear a number of consequences if climate change continues to go unbridled. However, we also know that many of the worst effects of climate change can be mitigated if we engage in collective action now. In this speech, I will begin by offering a brief history of climate science, then describe how these issues affect trout fisheries, and finally offer some examples of how we can personally and collectively work to mitigate these issues.

Body

I. Climate change is not a recent invention of a few liberal scientists. On the contrary, scientists have been talking about climate change since the mid-1800s (Weart, 2009).

    A. In 1859, Tyndall discovers some gases block infrared radiation. He believes this may cause a change in climate.

    B. In 1896, Arrhenius publishes the first calculation of global warming from human CO_2 emissions.

C. From 1870-1920, the Second Industrial Revolution takes place.

D. In 1938, Callendar argues that CO2 greenhouse global warming is under way.
[*… history lesson proceeds …*]

(*Summary*: In short, this history lesson teaches us that Earth has been getting warmer.)

(*Preview*: Next, let's look at how climate change may be affecting trout fisheries.)

II. Climate change appears to have some serious consequences for trout fisheries. I will discuss four ways in which climate change may be said to negatively influence trout fisheries.

A. First, changing weather patterns brings more or less water to some parts of Earth.

1. Trout fisheries rely on a steady flow of clean, cold water. Too much or too little can quickly destroy trout habitats.

2. Some areas may experience severe droughts, another threat to trout fisheries.

B. Second, warming land and aquatic temperatures lead to a reduction in available trout habitat.

1. Changing temperatures influence predator/prey patterns.

2. Habitat reduction due to warmer temperatures may increase competition between cold- and warm-water fishes.

C. Third, stream flow patterns may change, affecting availability of aquatic insects.

And fourth, brook trout may be especially vulnerable.

1. Previous brook trout decimation has been related to habitat loss.

2. Climate change could exacerbate this by causing further habitat destruction.

(*Summary*: Although these challenges are large scale, there is some hope that we can mitigate these issues.)

(*Preview*: Next, I will discuss some ways that individuals and collectives can help reverse some of the issues caused by climate change.)

III. There are two key areas in which we can mitigate climate change: personal actions and collective actions.

A. Personally, individuals can make changes in their everyday lives (Sorenen, 2008).

1. Individuals can reduce CO2 emissions by driving less or not at all. Instead they could ride a bike or take public transit.

2. Individuals can also reduce energy consumption by changing usage patterns, like drying their clothes outside instead of using an electric dryer.

3. Individuals could help alleviate one of the largest contributors to climate change, overpopulation, by preventing unwanted births.

B. Collectively, there are several actions we can take to mitigate climate change (Cuomo, 2010).

1. Collectives should lobby policy makers to make serious changes:

a. Reduce fossil fuel consumption.

b. Create caps on industrial emissions.

c. Encourage and support renewable and sustainable energy.

2. U.S. should support Kyoto Treaty, which was passed in 2005.

Conclusion

It should be clear at this point that climate change is an issue that trout fishers will have to deal with in the future. Although the issues are large and daunting, I have provided some clear examples of how we can both personally and collectively mitigate these issues. I hope you will consider taking at least some of my advice today. I will leave you with something that Henrik Tikkanen once said: "Because we don't think about future generations, they will never forget us."

Attributions

CC licensed content, Shared previously

Appendix B: Speaking Outline

Example Speaking Outline (Excluding Introduction and Conclusion)

I. Climate science is not new (Weart, 2009).

    A. 1859 – Tyndall

    B. 1896 – Arrhenius

    C. 1870-1920 – Second Industrial Revolution

    D. 1938 – Callendar

    [… *history lesson proceeds* …]

(*Summary*: In short, this history lesson teaches us that Earth has been getting warmer.)

(*Preview*: Next, let's look at how climate change may be affecting trout fisheries.)

II. Climate change is bad for trout in four ways.

    A. Weather patterns

        1. Too much/little rain is bad

        2. Droughts

    B. Warming leads to habitat reduction

        1. Predator/prey patterns.

        2. Competition between cold- and warm-water fishes.

    C. Stream flow patterns may change

    D. Brook trout vulnerable

        1. Population decimated by habitat loss

2. Exacerbated by climate change

(Summary: Although these challenges are large scale, there is some hope that we can mitigate these issues.)

(Preview: Next, I will discuss some ways that individuals and collectives can help reverse some of the issues caused by climate change.)

III. Personal and collective mitigation

A. Personal (Sorenen, 2008)

1. Reduce CO2 emissions

2. Reduce energy consumption

3. Birth control

B. Collective (Cuomo, 2010)

1. Lobby for:

a. Reduce fossil fuel consumption

b. Create caps on industrial emissions

c. Encourage and support renewable and sustainable energy

2. Support Kyoto

Attributions

CC licensed content, Shared previously

- Chapter 8 Appendix B. **Authored by**: Joshua Trey Barnett. **Provided by**: University of Indiana, Bloomington, IN. **Located at**: http://publicspeakingproject.org/psvirtualtext.html. **Project**: The Public Speaking Project. **License**: *CC BY-NC-ND: Attribution-NonCommercial-NoDerivatives*

Chapter 6: Delivering Your Speech

Objectives and Introduction

Delivering Your Speech

By Victor Capecce, M.F.A.
Millersville University, Millersville, PA

Learning Objectives

After reading this chapter, you should be able to:

- Identify, define and give an example of each of ?the four main types of ?delivery
- Determine the best ?speaking style for different types of speaking occasions
- Identify and utilize voice aspects of speaking
- Recognize and utilize the key "ingredients" of a ?well-performed speech
- Adapt to the physical aspects of a speaking ?venue
- Plan the speech in ?preparation for delivery/performance of a speech.

Introduction

Imagine this. A speech topic is perfectly chosen; the content is nicely organized and flawlessly researched; a great deal of work was invested in preparing the "text" or "script" of the speech, but the speech is poorly delivered. Will the speech be effective? Will the audience stay alert and follow it? Will the audience properly interpret the speaker's intended message? These last questions contribute to the universal fear of public speaking. It is not the preparation of a speech that strikes terror in the hearts of so many, but the performance of a speech!

"Allida Black Speaking at Courage to Lead Summit" **by United States Mission Geneva.** *CC-BY-ND.*

> Don't lower your expectations to meet your performance. Raise your level of performance to meet your expectations. Expect the best of yourself, and then do what is necessary to make it a reality. – Ralph Marston

Since an audience does not usually read the text of a speech, but simply listens to it, all the preparation of the content by the speaker must be encoded into a complex combination of communication channels (words, sounds, visual elements, etc.) ready to be performed. The purpose of this chapter is to offer guidance to transfer the speech from the page to the stage.

There is an old Burlesque joke:

> *One man on a New York street comes up to another and asks,*
> *"How can I get to Carnegie Hall?"*
>
> *The second man answers, "PRACTICE."*

Practice is the key to excellent performance. Trite as it might sound (or obvious), the basic foundation for a good speech delivery involves the two "P's": Preparation and Practice. There is not an actor, athlete, or musician worth his/her salary who does not prepare and practice. Even when a performance is given with spontaneity, the "P's" are crucial.

Stand-up comedy is everywhere; and those who are successful comedians do not make up their monologues on the spot. The phrasing, the pauses, the timing, is all rehearsed to assure the laughs will happen on cue. Good stand up comics are skilled in making it look as though they are making up their routine on the spot, which is part of the success of a good comedy performance. New speakers should think of themselves as performers facing an audience; actors ascending to stage; athletes stepping up to bat.

This chapter will describe the basic methods of delivery, and offer guidance in the aspects of presentation (such as voice, inflection, eye contact, and body and facial language). Some basic strategies for in setting up the room and podium for speaking will also be covered.

> It is delivery that makes the orator's success. – Johann Wolfgang Von Goethe

Attributions

CC licensed content, Shared previously

Video: Storytelling

Storytelling is very powerful. **Do not** begin your speech with "Today, I am going to talk to you about _____". Hook your audience with a story.

- https://youtu.be/QINv6rebyTU

The best speeches involve someone's story:

NPPA 2011 TV BOP Photography: Feature 1st Place from NPPA video contests (https://vimeo.com/nppa-contests) on Vimeo.

- https://vimeo.com/21139974

Don't be afraid of humor or controversy. It's o.k. to joke around even when your message is powerful. Humor can be a very effective way to tell the story.

- https://youtu.be/-KhMj6p21dU
- https://youtu.be/3iIkOi3srLo

Tip: Words we are saying wrong:

- https://youtu.be/zcThN1dZMe4

When planning live or video presentations, you need to be very mindful of color contrast. Read this very helpful article that will guide you in making better decisions when choosing color and brightness: "10 colour contrast checking tools to improve the accessibility of your design" from *456 Berea St*.

- http://www.456bereastreet.com/archive/200709/10_colour_contrast_checking_tools_to_improve_the_accessibility_of_your_design/

- Top 27 Mispronounced Words. **Authored by**: Good Mythical Morning. **Located at**: http://youtu.be/zcThN1dZMe4. **License**: *All Rights Reserved*. **License Terms**: Standard YouTube License

- Follow the Frog. **Authored by**: Rainforest Alliance. **Located at**: http://youtu.be/3iIkOi3srLo. **License**: *All Rights Reserved*. **License Terms**: Standard YouTube License

- What Has Aid Ever Done For Anyone? Apart From.... **Authored by**: SaveTheChildren. **Located at**: http://youtu.be/-KhMj6p21dU?list=PLGmeFIOjhJzfwXQ1ICi7u9yJ-oBW273cF. **License**: *All Rights Reserved*. **License Terms**: Standard YouTube License

- Proud Fathers. **Authored by**: kauflust. **Located at**: http://youtu.be/QINv6rebyTU. **License**: *All Rights Reserved*. **License Terms**: Standard YouTube License

Methods of Delivery

There are four basic **methods** (sometimes called styles) of presenting a speech: manuscript, memorized, extemporaneous, and impromptu. Each has a variety of uses in various forums of communication.

Manuscript Style

The word **manuscript** is the clue to the style. The speech is written and the speaker reads it word for word to the audience. Originally, it was done from the hand-written paper manuscript. Today the **manuscript style** is common, but the paper is gone. Who reads the speech to the audience? Answer: Newscasters and television personalities. In the old days, the manuscript was hand-lettered on cue cards, which were held next to the camera lens. Then paper scrolls, like printed piano rolls were used, especially in Soap Operas. Today, a special teleprompter (working like a periscope) is attached to the camera so the newscaster is looking at the lens while reading.

"Marketing Mix" by Matthew Hurst. CC-BY-SA.

Why is the manuscript important and in use? Precision. In the news- reporting industry, every fraction of a second counts because broadcast time is costly. Also, the facts and names must be exact and accurate so there is no room for error. Errors in reporting decrease the credibility of the news organization and the newscaster.

The most regular use of the teleprompter for **manuscript** delivery is by the U.S. President. In fact, the teleprompter, used by every President since Reagan, is called a "Presidential Teleprompter." It is made of two pieces of glass, each flanking the podium. They reflect the text from a monitor on the floor like a periscope. The glass on both sides has the same text, and the speaker looks alternately from one glass to the other as though looking at the audience through the glass. The audience cannot see the projected text. The speeches a President gives will often reflect national policy, define international relationships, and the press will scrutinize every syllable. It has to be more than brilliantly accurate; it has to be impeccably phased.

Professional writers and policy experts compose the speech; and the President delivers it as though he not only wrote it, but made it up on the spot. That is the skill of a good politician, actor, or speaker. Those who are not skilled using a teleprompter or manuscript will sound stilted and boring.

> **Try This! Manuscript Delivery**
>
> Watch the local or national 6 p.m., 11 p.m. and 6 a.m. newscasts on the same T.V. station. Make notes on which news items repeat and how closely, or exactly, the phrasing is, even if different personalities are presenting the same item.

Memorized Style

The **memorized style** of speaking is when the manuscript is committed to memory and recited to the audience verbatim (word for word). In the days when **elocution** was taught, this was a typical approach. A speech was a recitation. The Optimists Club (a national organization) used to have a "Oratory" contest for high school students. Contestants wrote essays on a given theme, to create a speech at a specific time length (e.g.: three minutes). The essay was memorized and the delivery was judged by 1) the quality of the writing, 2) the accuracy with which it was recited; and 3) the precise length of time. Such contests seem archaic by today's more casual and somewhat less formal standards.

Where is a memorized delivery style still common? Due to copyright laws and licensing contract agreements (other than scripts that are in the public domain), actors on stage are obligated to memorize the script of the play and perform it **verbatim** exactly as written. It is typical for speakers on high school and university speech and debate teams to memorize their competitive speeches. Corporate conventions often use large LCD monitors on the front of the stage as teleprompters. This allows the speaker to move more freely across the stage while sticking to his or her script. Some monologists (such as the stand-up comics mentioned at the start of the chapter) also use a memorized delivery style. In all cases, they create the impression that the speech is spontaneous. You might consider using the memorized delivery style if your speech is relatively short, or you know you will have to deliver your speech repeatedly such as a tour operator would.

Impromptu Style

Theoretically, an "impromptu" speech is "made up on the spot." It is unprepared and unrehearsed. Often ceremonial toasts, grace before meals, an acknowledgement, an introduction, offering thanks and so on, fall into this category. While there are some occasions when a speech in those categories is actually prepared (prepare your acceptance for the Academy Award BEFORE you are called!), there are many occasions when there is little or no opportunity to prepare.

Impromptu speeches are generally short and are often given with little or no notice. Notes are rare and the speaker generally looks directly at the audience. It would be presumptuous and arrogant to declare rules for Impromptu Speaking. It is fair to explain that "impromptu" describes a range from absolutely no preparation, to a modest amount of preparation (mostly thought) and rarely incorporates research or the formalities of outlines and citations that more formal speeches would include.

> Be still when you have nothing to say; when genuine passion moves you, say what you've got to say, and say it hot. – D. H. Lawrence

An indelibly memorable example occurred to me when my siblings threw a surprise 10th anniversary party for my Mom (Margaret) and our stepdad (Lidio). It was the third marriage for both of them, and they were in their 60's. As soon as the yells of "surprise" subsided, Lidio picked up his wine glass and proposed a toast:

"*Apr. 3 – Cheers!*" *by KimManleyOrt.*
CC-BY-NC-ND.

> "I can't believe this surprise! I don't know what to say… um, Dino [his brother] when was that Yankee game Dad took us to when we were kids? It was 4th of July, wasn't it? 1939? And it was like it was yesterday; and today reminds me of that day, when Lou Gehrig came out to the mound. He was slow, but we were all cheering the 'Pride of the Yankees.' He wasn't playing anymore, he was too sick, but he looked around the crowd, and said 'I'm the luckiest man alive.' That's how I feel with you all here today; to celebrate our 10th anniversary. I'm here with you and with Margaret; and I'm the luckiest man alive."

The speech was short, emotionally charged, wonderfully articulate, and absolutely unprepared. The speech had one central emotionally charged message; simple, in words and phrasing, but complex by bringing an image of great sentimentality to the occasion. He was able to react to the moment, and speak "from the heart."

In contrast, legendary magician Harry Houdini was often asked to perform for the amusement of his fellow passengers when sailing to Europe. I always associate "impromptu" with the stories of Houdini's shipboard conjuring. Nothing was further from "impromptu." The skill of the great magician was in making his illusions seem spontaneous with what appeared to be ordinary items that "happened" to be on hand. Houdini spent endless hours planning and rehearsing. The true illusion was that they "appeared" to be impromptu.

> Take advantage of every opportunity to practice your communication skills so that when important occasions arise, you will have the gift, the style, the sharpness, the clarity, and the emotions to affect other people. – Jim Rohn

Extemporaneous Style

Sandwiched between the *memorized* and *impromptu* delivery styles you find the extemporaneous speech style. For this style, the speech is not completely written out. It is usually delivered with keynotes for reference. Most public speaking courses and books describe **extemporaneous** speeches as carefully prepared and rehearsed, but delivered using notes of key words and phrases to support the speaker. Phrasing is pre-rehearsed, words are pre-chosen, and the organization is fluid and well constructed. There should be no fumbling for words, no rambling, and length of time should be carefully monitored. The style does offer the speaker flexibility to include references to the immediate surroundings, previous speeches, news of the day, and so on.

The trouble with talking too fast is you may say something you haven't thought of yet." – Ann Landers

How you develops the notes and what they look like are up to the individual, but a natural extemporaneous delivery is difficult if you are relying on a manuscript. Under no circumstances should the speaker be spending more than 20% of the speaking time looking at the notes. It would be ideal to practice so you only glance at your notes approximately 5% of the time of the speech.

Those who have limited experience in formal speaking find it helpful to write out the speech as though it were an essay, then read it, edit it, then create speaking notes from the text. This helps with editing and with thinking through the phrases. This process of public speaking was taught decades ago to my contemporaries and me and has fallen out of fashion. But it is a useful way of thoroughly thinking through the speech. If this procedure is used, it is advisable to rehearse the speech with the notes without the essay prior to delivering the speech. But be warned: having the fully written essay at the podium might detract from the delivery.

"Speech Notes" by Jess J. CC-BY-NC-ND.

The extemporaneous style is the method most often recommended (and often required) in today's public speaking courses, and is generally the best method in other settings as well. While it is not the only method of delivering a speech, it is the most useful for presentations in other courses, in the corporate world and in pursuing future careers.

Attributions

CC licensed content, Shared previously

- Chapter 12 Methods of Delivery. **Authored by**: Victor Capecce, M.F.A.. **Provided by**: Millersville University, Millersville, PA. **Located at**: http://publicspeakingproject.org/psvirtualtext.html. **Project**: The Public Speaking Project. **License**: *CC BY-NC-ND: Attribution-NonCommercial-NoDerivatives*

- marketing mix. **Authored by**: Matthew Hurst. **Located at**: https://www.flickr.com/photos/skewgee/3911933434/. **License**: *CC BY-SA: Attribution-ShareAlike*

- Apr. 3 - Cheers!. **Authored by**: KimManleyOrt. **Located at**: https://www.flickr.com/photos/kimmanleyort/6897547042/. **License**: *CC BY-NC-ND: Attribution-NonCommercial-NoDerivatives*

- speech notes. **Authored by**: Jess J. **Located at**: https://www.flickr.com/photos/jessicajuriga/3988478147/. **License**: *CC BY-NC-ND: Attribution-NonCommercial-NoDerivatives*

Vocal Aspects of Delivery

Though we speak frequently during the course of a day, a formal speech requires extra attention to detail in preparation of a more formal speech presentation. What can one do in advance to prepare for a speech? The challenge is partly determined by the speaker's experience, background and sometimes cultural influence and existing habits of speaking. Articulation, Pronunciation, Dialect, Tone, Pitch, and Projection each depends on long-term practice for success. These aspects are like signatures, and should be developed and used by each speaker according to his own persona.

Voice, or vocal sound, is made when controlled air being exhaled from the lungs, passes over the vocal cords causing a controlled vibration. The vibrating air resonates in the body, chest cavity, mouth, and nasal passages. The vibrating air causes a chain reaction with the air in the room. The room's air, set in motion by the voice, is captured by the listener's ear. The vibration of the air against the eardrum is transferred to electrical impulses that are interpreted by the listener's brain. Thus, the sounds we can make are predicated on the breaths that we take.

Try This! Breathing

Talk without breathing. It cannot be done. So if you are screaming (like a baby), you are also breathing!

The first word of advice on speaking to an audience: BREATHE!

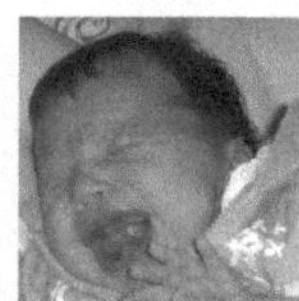

*"Crying baby"
by Brazzouk.
CC-BY-SA.*

Articulation

We are often judged by how well we speak in general. A measure of perceived intellect or education is how well we **articulate**. That is: how well and correctly we form our vowels and consonants using our lips, jaw, tongue, and palate to form the sounds that are identified as speech. **Diction** and **enunciation** are other terms that refer to the same idea. For instance, saying "going to" instead of "gonna" or "did not" instead of "dint" are examples of good versus poor articulation. Consonant and vowels are spoken with standard accepted precision, and serious students and speakers will strive to practice the clarity of their sounds. Proper diction is as integral to the English language as proper spelling, but it takes practice.

Pronunciation

Proper **articulation** applied to a given word is that word's **pronunciation**. The pronunciation includes how the vowels and consonants are produced as well as which syllable is emphasized. For generations, speakers depended on "markings (such as the International Phonetics Alphabet or similar Dictionary Symbols) to discover or decide how words were officially pronounced. With online dictionaries now readily available, one needs only to "look up" a word and select "play" to hear an audible recording of the official and precise way a word should be pronounced. Now there is no excuse for mispronouncing a word in a speech. A mispronounced word will obliterate a speaker's credibility, and the audience's attention will be focused on the fault rather than the message.

Try This! Pronunciation

1. Flip though a book, article or scholarly work until you come to a word that is unfamiliar and you can only guess its pronunciation.

2. Go to the Merriam-Webster Dictionary website, and look up the word.

3. When the definition appears, click the icon of the loudspeaker. The word is audibly pronounced for you.

The online dictionary is useful in both articulation as well as pronunciation.

Accent, Dialect, and Regionalisms

Subtleties in the way we pronounce words and phrase our speech within a given language are evident in **accents**, **regionalisms**, and **dialects**. An accent refers to the degree of prominence of the way syllables are spoken in words, as when someone from Australia says "undah" whereas we say "under." A **regionalism** is a type of expression, as when someone says "The dog wants walked," instead of "the dog wants to go for a walk." Dialect is a variety of language where one is distinguished from others by grammar and vocabulary. In Pennsylvania you might hear people say that they are going to "red up the room," which means "to clean the room."

"Iraqi speaker" by Office of United States Rep. Ellen Tauscher. Public domain.

Those who depend on speaking for a career (broadcasters, politicians, and entertainers) will often strive for unaccented General or Standard English. Listen to most major network newscasters for examples of **regionalism-free** speech. A given audience may be prejudiced towards or against a speaker with an identifiable accent or dialect. Though we would wish prejudice were not the case, the way we speak implies so much about our education, cultural background, and economic status, that prejudice is inevitable. Any speaker should be aware of how accent, **dialect**, and regionalisms can be perceived by a given audience. If you speak in a way that the audience might find difficult to understand, make an extra effort to pay attention to the accent and phrasing of your speech. Ask a sympathetic and objective listener to help you when you practice.

> We often refuse to accept an idea merely because the tone of voice in which it has been expressed is unsympathetic to us. – Friedrich Nietzsche

Vocal Quality

The quality of the voice, its **timbre** (distinctive sound) and texture, affects audibility and can affect the articulation. Our voices are unique to each of us. It is a result of our physical vocal instrument, including diaphragm, vocal cords, lungs and body mass. Some examples of vocal quality include warm, clear, soft, scratchy, mellow and breathy. Each speaker should practice at maximizing the vocal effect of his instrument, which can be developed with vocal exercises. There are numerous books, recordings and trainers available to develop one's vocal quality when needed. The quality of one's voice is related to its range of pitch.

Try This! Inflection

Your voice goes UP, and then your voice goes d o w n.

Pitch and Inflection

Identical to musical parlance, the **pitch** is the "highness" or "lowness" of the voice. Each of us has a range of **tone**. Vocal sounds are actually vibrations sent out from the vocal cords resonating through chambers in the body. The vibrations can literally be measured in terms of audio frequency in the same way music is measured. When the **pitch** is altered to convey a meaning (like raising the pitch at the end of a sentence that is a question), it is the inflection. **Inflections** are variations, turns and slides in pitch to achieve the meaning.

In his writing "Poetics," Aristotle lists "Music" as an element of the Drama. Some scholars interpret that to include the musicalization of the spoken word with **dramatic inflection**. The meaning and effectiveness of a spoken line is greatly dependent on the "melody" of its inflection.

Though archaic, the study of **elocution** formalizes the conventions of inflection. In some contemporary cultures, inflection has been minimized because it sounds too "melodramatic" for the taste of the demographic group. It would be sensible to be aware of and avoid both extremes. With good animated inflection, a speaker is more interesting, and the inflection conveys energy and "aliveness" that compels the audience to listen.

When public speaking was known as elocution, sentences were "scored" like music, and spoken using formal rules. Sentences ending as a question went UP at the end. Sentences ending in a period, ended with a base note. And everyone had fun with exclamation points!

For most of music in history, including Opera, Broadway, and early Rock and Roll, songs were written so that the melody (raising and lowering the pitch) was consistent with what would be spoken. Many of today's songs, notably Rap songs, depend solely on rhythm. There is little if any inflection (melody) to enhance a lyric's meaning. Certain languages differ in their dependence on inflection. Japanese and German seem monotonic compared to Italian and French, which offer great variety of inflection.

The human voice is the most beautiful instrument of all, but it is the most difficult to play. – Richard Strauss

"Ice-T" by Tino Jacobs. CC-BY.

Even someone one who is not a singer can be expressive with inflection and pitch. Like the "Think System" of Professor Harold Hill in the musical The Music Man. If you THINK varied pitch, you can SPEAK varied pitch. Think of pitch inflections as seasoning spices that can make the speech more interesting. Sing "Happy Birthday." You do not have to concentrate or analyze how to create the melody in your voice. Your memory and instinct take over. Notice how the pitch also provides an audible version of punctuation, letting the audience know if your sentence has ended, if it is a question, and so on. The melody lets the audience know that there is more to come (a comma) and when the phrase is ended (a period). Remember that in a speech, the audience does not have the written punctuation to follow, so you have to provide the punctuation with your inflection.

Try This! Vocal Variation

Find a listening partner. Using only the sounds of "la" ha," and "oh," covey the meaning of the following:1. It's the biggest thing I've ever seen!

2. I've fallen and can't get up!

3. I've got a crush on him/her.

4. That soup is disgusting and spoiled.

5. I got an "A" in my Speech Final!

If you cannot relay the meaning with just sounds, try a second time (each) with gestures and facial expressions until the listener understands. Then say the lines with the expressive inflections you have developed using only the sounds.

Those who do not use inflection, or use a range of pitch, are speaking in monotone. And, as the word implies, it can be monotonous, boring, and dull. A balance between melodramatic and monotonous would be preferred. The inflection should have a meaningful and interesting variety. Be careful not to turn a pattern of inflection into a repetitious sound. Think through each phrase and its musicalization separately.

Many speakers have developed the habit of ending each sentence as though it is a question. It may be becoming increasingly common. In the wake of the Valley Girl syndrome of the 1980's, a bad inflection habit has entered the speech pattern: Some speakers end a declarative sentence with the inflection of a question.

Do you know what I mean?

A word of caution: Inflection and varied pitch must be "organic," that is to say, natural for the speaker. You cannot fake it, or it sounds artificial and disingenuous. It is a skill that needs to develop over a period of time.

Rate of Speaking

Table 12.1: Finding the Right Pace for Your Speech	
If you speak too quickly…	**If you speak too slowly…**
the audience might get the impression you have nothing important to say.	the audience might think you are too tired to be presenting.
the audience has a difficult time catching up and comprehending what you are saying. They need time to digest the information. So plan on periodic pauses.	the audience can forget the first part of your sentence by the time you get to the last! (It happens!) And they lose interest.
the audience might think you really do not want to be there.	the audience might think you are wasting their time by taking longer than necessary to relay your message.
As a speaker, you cannot race with the audience, nor drag their attention down. Like Goldilocks, look for the pace that is "just right."	

In order to retain clarity of the speech with articulation and inflection, the speaker must be aware that there is a range of appropriate **tempo** for speaking. If the tempo is too slow, the speech might resemble a monotonous peal. If it is too fast, the articulation could suffer if consonants or vowels are dropped or rushed to keep up the speed. An audience could become frustrated with either extreme. The tempo needs to be appropriate to the speaker's style, but neither paced like a Gilbertian Lyric (as in "Gilbert and Sullivan") patter nor a funereal dirge. A comfortable and clear pace is the best. An ideal speaking rate will allow you to comfortably increase your pace to create a sense of excitement, or slow down to emphasize the seriousness of a topic.

> It is simple nonsense to speak of the fixed tempo of any particular vocal phrase. Each voice has its peculiarities. – Anton Seidl

Pauses Versus Vocalized Pauses

A text that is read has punctuation that the reader can see…miniature landmarks to define the text. When spoken, similar punctuation is needed for comprehension, and the speaker's responsibility is to offer the text with pauses. Space between phrases, properly planted, gives the audience the opportunity to understand the structure of the speaker's sentences and paragraphs. It also gives time for the audience to "digest" crucial phrases.

Generally, spoken sentences and paragraphs need to be simpler and shorter than what can be comprehended by reading. Pauses can help increase comprehension.

However, pauses that are filled with "uh's, "um's," etc., are called **vocalized pauses**, or **fillers**, and should be avoided. They can be distracting and annoying, and give the impression of a lack of preparation if used excessively. Even worse is the use of vernacular phrases like, "y'know" (a contraction of "Do You Know") which gives the impression of lack of education or lack of concern for the audience. The use of vocalized pauses may be the result of a habit that deserves an effort to be overcome. Avoid using phrases such as "Uh," "OK?", "y'know", "like…, I mean," "right?"

Vocal Projection

The volume produced by the vocal instrument is **projection**. Supporting the voice volume with good breathing and energy can be practiced, and helping a speaker develop the correct volume is a main task of a vocal trainer, teacher or coach. Good vocal support with good posture, breathing, and energy should be practiced regularly, long before a speech is delivered. There are numerous exercises devoted to developing projection capabilities.

While there is no need to shout, a speaker should project to be easily heard from the furthest part of the audience. Even if the speech is amplified with a microphone/sound system, one must speak with projection and energy. As with your rate of speech, you should speak at a volume that comfortably allows you to increase the volume of your voice without seeming to shout or decrease the volume of your voice and still be heard by all audience members.

Do not expect to walk up to the podium and have a full voice. Actors spend about a half-hour doing vocal warm-ups, and singers warm up much more. You might not have an opportunity to warm up immediately before your speech, but when you can, warm up with humming, yawning (loudly) or singing scales: all while breathing deeply and efficiently. It will loosen your voice, prevent irritation, and fire up your vocal energy.

Try This! Projection

Go to the room in which you are to speak. Have a friend sit as far away from the podium is possible. Rehearse your speech, talking loudly enough so your friend can hear you comfortably. That is the projection you will need. When you mentally focus on the distant listener, you will tend to project better.

One final note: If public speaking is or will be an important part of your career, it would be sensible to have an evaluation of your voice, articulation and projection done by an objective professional so you can take any remedial action that might be recommended. There are courses of study, private lessons, and professional voice coaches to work with your voice projection, tone, and pitch.

Words mean more than what is set down on paper. It takes the human voice to infuse them with deeper meaning. – Maya Angelou

Attributions

CC licensed content, Shared previously

- Chapter 12 Vocal Aspects of Delivery. **Authored by**: Victor Capecce, M.F.A.. **Provided by**: Millersville University, Millersville, PA. **Located at**: http://publicspeakingproject.org/psvirtualtext.html. **Project**: The Public Speaking Project. **License**: *CC BY-NC-ND: Attribution-NonCommercial-NoDerivatives*
- Crying baby. **Authored by**: Brazzouk. **Provided by**: MorgueFile. **Located at**: https://commons.wikimedia.org/wiki/File:Crying_baby.jpg. **License**: *CC BY-SA: Attribution-ShareAlike*
- Ice-T. **Authored by**: Tino Jacobs. **Located at**: http://commons.wikimedia.org/wiki/File:Ice-T_(2).jpg. **License**: *CC BY: Attribution*

Public domain content

- Iraqi Speaker. **Authored by**: Office of United States Rep. Ellen Tauscher (D - California). **Located at**: http://commons.wikimedia.org/wiki/File:Iraqi_Speaker.jpg. **License**: *Public Domain: No Known Copyright*

Nonverbal Aspects of Delivery

Personal Appearance

Women in Business Leadership Conf. **by UCLA Anderson.**
CC-BY-NC-SA.

Here is the golden rule: Dress appropriately for the situation. You don't need to sport a power tie (the predictable red tie politicians wore in the 1980s), but you should be comfortable and confident knowing that you look good.

Table 12.2: Dressing Appropriately

What to Wear:	What NOT to wear:
• A button-down shirt or blouse • Trousers (khaki or dark) or a skirt • A dress appropriate for a business setting • A nice sweater • Limited, tasteful jewelry • A suit or jacket may be appropriate • A tie or scarf (optional)	• T-shirts, sweatshirts, or sweatsuits • Sleeveless tops • Printed logos or sayings (unless appropriate to the speech) • Caps or hats • Torn jeans • Visible underwear • Noisy or dangling jewelry • Flip flops • Provocative clothing • Pockets full of keys or change

With the exception of wearing formal black-tie tuxedo to a hockey game, it is good practice to dress a bit more formal than less. Err on the side of formal. Most class speeches would be best in business casual (which can vary from place to place and in time). The culture or standards of the audience should be considered. For men, it is usually a button-down shirt and casual dress pants. For women, it may be skirt or slacks and blouse/shirt.

There are exceptions depending on the speech. A student once arrived in pajamas to deliver his 9 a.m. speech. At first, I thought he got up too late to dress for class. However, his speech was on Sleep Deprivation, and his costume was deliberate. What he wore contributed to his speech.

If you have long hair, be sure it is out of the way so it won't cover your face. Flipping hair out of your face is very distracting, so it is wise to secure it with clips, gel, or some other method. Be sure you can be seen, especially your eyes and your mouth, even as you glance down to the podium.

Think of it as an interview…just like in an interview, you will want to make a good first impression. The corporate culture of the business will determine the dress. Always dress at the level of the person conducting the interview. For example, a construction foreman (or project manager) will conduct an interview to hire you as a carpenter. Do not dress like a carpenter; dress like the project manager.

Actors know when they audition, the role is won by the time they step into the room. A speaker can launch success by stepping confidently to the podium.

Be tidy and clean. If you appear as though you took time to prepare because your speech is important, then your audience will recognize and respect what you have to say.

Movement and Gestures

Overall movement and specific gestures are integral to a speech. Body stance, gestures and facial expressions can be generally categorized as **body language**. Movement should be relaxed and natural, and not excessive. How you move takes practice. Actors usually have the advantage of directors helping to make decisions about movement, but a good objective listener or a rehearsal in front of a large mirror can yield productive observations.

Moving around the performance space can be a very powerful component of a speech; however, it should be rehearsed as part of the presentation. Too much movement can be distracting. This is particularly true if the movement appears to be a result of nervousness. Avoid fidgeting, stroking your hair, and any other nervousness-related movement.

Among the traditional common fears of novice speakers is not knowing what to do with one's hands. Sometimes the speaker relies on clutching to the podium or keeping hands in pockets. Neither is a good pose. From my own observation, hand gestures are very common in Italy. We Italians can be seen in conversation from across the street, and

"Barack Obama at Las Vegas Presidential Forum" by Center for American Progress Action Fund. CC-BY-SA.

an observer can often tell what is being said. There is no need to imitate an Italian in delivering a speech, but hand movement and the energy that the movement represents, can help hold attention as well as help express the message.

An actor practices using his whole body for expression, and regularly practices physical exercises to keep the body and hands and arms relaxed and in motion. An actor's hand gestures are developed in rehearsal. A speaker's gestures should also be considered during practice.

During the period when elocution was taught, hand gestures were regimented like a sign language. This is nonsense. Like inflections, gestures and movement should be organic and spontaneous, not contrived. If there is a hint of artificiality in your presentation, you will sacrifice your credibility.

Try This! Gestures

Using only your hands, convey the following:

1. "It's OK."
2. "I give up."
3. "He's crazy."
4. "We will be victorious."

Facial Expressions

Most readers are very familiar with emoticons like these:

? ? :p ? ? :/

Emoticons were not casual inventions, but graphic depictions of facial expressions that convey various meanings of emotions. They are based on a nearly universal language of expression that we begin learning soon after birth. We smile, we frown, we roll our eyes, and we wink. We open eyes wide with astonishment. We raise our eyebrows…occasionally one at a time, in suspicion; both, in astonishment. Sometimes we pucker our lips, either to offer a kiss or express disapproval, disappointment, or grave concern.

"Castefest 2011, Gothic" **by Qsimple.** *CC-BY-NC-SA.*

> I pretty much try to stay in a constant state of confusion just because of the expression it leaves on my face. – Johnny Depp

Since facial expression is a valid form of communication, it is integral to delivering a speech. The face supports the text, and the speaker's commitment to the material is validated. The press scrutinizes a politician for every twitch of insincerity. Detectives have created a science of facial communication for interviewing suspects. Like inflections, gestures and movement: facial expressions should be organic and spontaneous, not contrived. If there is a hint of artificiality in your expression, you will sacrifice your credibility.

Try This! Facial Expressions

While looking in a mirror, try to express these thoughts without words:

1. "I am thrilled that I am getting a raise."
2. "I am worried about tomorrow."
3. "Lemons are too sour for me."
4. "I am suspicious about what he did."

After you have determined a facial expression for each, say the phrase. And see how well the verbal expression goes with the nonverbal expression.

Eye Contact

Next to clearly speaking an organized text, eye contact is another very important element of speaking. An audience must feel interested in the speaker, and know the speaker cares about them.

Whether addressing an audience of 1000 or speaking across a "deuce" (table for two), eye contact solidifies the relationship between the speaker and audience. Good eye contact takes practice. The best practice is to be able to scan the audience making each member believe the speaker is speaking to him or her.

However, there are some eye contact failures.

Head Bobber

This is a person who bobs his or her head looking down on the notes and up to the audience in an almost rhythmic pattern.

Balcony Gazer

A person who looks over the heads of his or her audience to avoid looking at any individual.

The Obsessor

A person who looks at one or two audience members or who only looks in one direction.

The best way to develop good eye contact is to have an objective listener watch and comment on the eye contact.

The eyes are called the windows to the soul, and the importance of eye contact in communication cannot be overemphasized. Ideally, a speaker should include 80% to 90% of the delivery time with eye contact.

Eye contact is so important that modern teleprompters are designed to allow the speaker to look at the audience while actually reading the speech. The Presidential Teleprompter (two angled pieces of glass functioning like a periscope) is used so the politician can "connect" to the audience without missing a single syllable. Audience members will be much more attentive and responsive if they believe the speech is directed to them.

With good eye contact, the speaker can also observe and gauge the attention and response of the audience. This is actually part of the feedback process of communication. The ideal is that the audience is not overly aware of the speaker using notes.

How do you develop good eye contact? First, practice the speech with a generous amount of eye contact. Second, know the speech well enough to only periodically (and quickly) glance at your notes. Third, prepare your notes so they can be easily read and followed without hesitation.

> There are no secrets to success. It is the result of preparation, hard work, and learning from failure. – Colin Powell

Attributions

CC licensed content, Shared previously

- Chapter 12 Nonverbal Aspects of Delivery. **Authored by**: Victor Capecce, M.F.A.. **Provided by**: Millersville University, Millersville, PA. **Located at**: http://publicspeakingproject.org/psvirtualtext.html. **Project**: The Public Speaking Project. **License**: *CC BY-NC-ND: Attribution-NonCommercial-NoDerivatives*
- Barack Obama at Las Vegas Presidential Forum. **Provided by**: Center for American Progress Action Fund. **Located at**: http://commons.wikimedia.org/wiki/File:Barack_Obama_at_Las_Vegas_Presidential_Forum.jpg. **License**: *CC BY-SA: Attribution-ShareAlike*
- Women in Business Leadership Conf.. **Authored by**: UCLA Anderson. **Located at**: https://flic.kr/p/kvxbXN. **License**: *CC BY-NC-SA: Attribution-NonCommercial-ShareAlike*
- Castlefest 2011, Gothic. **Authored by**: Qsimple, Memories For The Future Photography. **Located at**: https://www.flickr.com/photos/qsimple/6029566567/. **License**: *CC BY-NC-SA: Attribution-NonCommercial-ShareAlike*

Mastering the Location

The Room

Do not wait until the moment you step up to speak to see what it will be like. Check out the room (venue) and the podium before you need to speak.

Check the width of the room and where the audience will be seated. Rehearse giving the imaginary audience eye contact.

Will you be lighted brighter than the audience? Will they be able to see your face? Can you easily project your voice to the back row? Will you have a microphone?

*"Phoenix Auditorium" **by Basil Jradeh.** CC-BY-SA.*

The Podium

Check the podium. Approach it with the confidence you should exhibit when speaking. Touch it. Lean on it. Is it the right height? (It should be about the height of your elbow.) Is it sturdy? Are your feet visible? Is there enough light to see your notes placed on top? Will you be well lit? Is the podium easily visible to the entire audience? How far left and right do you need to look to see the whole audience?

If you are using note cards, try placing them on the podium to be sure they will work, and you can maneuver them easily.

Plan where you will stand. It does not have to be behind the **lectern**. Practice standing with good posture; know where you will keep your hands and be sure your gestures are not hidden by the podium.

You might be a speaker who does not stay behind the podium, but you should still check it out. Every morsel of familiarity will contribute to your confidence in speaking.

The Equipment

If you are using any multi-media such as PowerPoint, slides, video, or music, try it long before the speech. Of course, you would have practiced the speech with the media on your own, but if at all possible, run it in the venue in which you will speak.

Check the controls, slide clicker, and the relationship between the screen and the podium. Be sure the audience can see you as well as the screen. The screen should be positioned so you can glance at it without turning away from the audience. You should not be reading from the screen.

Check your own files to be sure the equipment in the room can play it correctly. Do not assume that every file can be played. Always be prepared by having multiple versions of your audio/video. If you have only one version, and it does not play, you will be very frustrated.

Check all PowerPoint slides. Give a last look at the spelling, content, and watch for some typical issues such as changes of formatting and inserted video or audio files not playing.

Even seasoned presenters break into a cold sweat over equipment failures or unpleasant surprises, so avoid the stress by checking the equipment.

Using a Microphone

In some cases, rather than merely using live voice projection, there will be a microphone for amplification. If at all possible, test it before the performance. Be sure the amplification is suitable for your projection. Be sure how near or far you should be for proper audio pick-up.

It is important to note that amplification cannot make up for poor articulation or weak inflections, but it can compensate for a room that is large or acoustically insufficient for speech.

If you are prone to move away from the podium, or plan any movement, be aware that the microphone must be considered.

"Andrea Dernbach und Hoda Salah" **by Heinrich Böll** *Stiftung. CC-BY-SA.*

If it is a stationary microphone, be careful to maintain a consistent distance, or the volume of your speaking will pop from louder to softer. Changes in volume or position can result in distortion or feedback (an escalating humming sound). Be careful that consonants do not "ring" with amplification.

In some venues, the time delay with the reverberation can cause an overlap of vocal sounds. You may have to slow down or use more pauses to prevent syllables from overlapping.

I drank some boiling water because I wanted to whistle. – Mitch Hedberg

Water Rules

Water is the only liquid that should be provided for a speaker. It should be cool, but not ice cold to prevent temperature shock to the throat and vocal cords. If it is poured into a glass, the glass should not be too full so the quantity does not overwhelm the speaker. Under no circumstances should there be ice in the glass or in the pitcher at the podium. Pieces of ice can be a choking hazard to a speaker who is focused on speaking rather than drinking. The current trend is to provide bottled water for a guest speaker. It should be opened, but the cap kept on assuring sanitation. The water should be placed on an absorbent tray that prevents suction from making raising the glass difficult to pick up.

Drinking water is necessary for the hydration of the vocal chords. The act of taking a sip is sometimes used to achieve a pause in a speech for effect.

"Glass of water" **by Jin Choi. CC-BY-SA.**

Attributions

CC licensed content, Shared previously

- Chapter 12 Mastering the Location. **Authored by**: Victor Capecce, M.F.A.. **Provided by**: Millersville University, Millersville, PA. **Located at**: http://publicspeakingproject.org/psvirtualtext.html. **Project**: The Public Speaking Project. **License**: *CC BY-NC-ND: Attribution-NonCommercial-NoDerivatives*

- Phoenix Auditorium. **Authored by**: Basil Jradeh. **Located at**: http://commons.wikimedia.org/wiki/File:Phoenix_Auditorium.jpg. **License**: *CC BY-SA: Attribution-ShareAlike*

- Andrea Dernbach und Hoda Salah. **Authored by**: Heinrich Boll Stiftung. **Located at**: http://commons.wikimedia.org/wiki/File:Flickr_-_boellstiftung_-_Andrea_Dernbach_und_Hoda_Salah_(1).jpg. **License**: *CC BY-SA: Attribution-ShareAlike*

- Glass of water?. **Authored by**: Jin Choi. **Located at**: https://www.flickr.com/photos/openuser/5621037010/. **License**: *CC BY-SA: Attribution-ShareAlike*

Preparation, Practice, and Delivery

Preparing Notes

Once you have created a comprehensive outline and have thought through your speech, you should be able to create your note cards or whatever you might be using (notes or an iPad for instance). Every speaker is a bit different, and different speech topics and organizational patterns may require different notation techniques.

"Best man's speech notes" **by stacey shintani.** *CC-BY-NC-SA.*

Your note cards (or cue sheets) must have enough information on them to be able to deliver the speech without missing details and organized in the precise order that you have planned. A common technique is to print the outline in a font that is large enough to be read from a distance.

You should be able to glance at the cards, get your bearings, and look back at the audience. If you are reading the cards word-for-word, there are too many words on them, unless it is an extended exact quote, or group of statistics that must be delivered precisely.

Be sure your notes or cards are numbered (e.g., boldly in the upper right hand corner), so you can keep them organized. Color-coding is often done to easily distinguish the cards at a glance. Losing your place can be very stressful to you and distracting to the audience.

Avoid writing or printing on two sides; flipping a page or card is distracting to the audience. The audience should not be aware of the notes. It is best to simply slide the cards aside to advance to the next card.

Rehearse your speech using the notes that you will bring to the podium. Be sure you can glance at the notes, get your information, and look up to have eye contact with the audience.

All the real work is done in the rehearsal period. – Donald Pleasence

Figure 12.1: Rehearsal Checklist

- Rehearse a few days before you are to deliver your speech
- Use the note sheets or cards you will be using or delivery
- Practice with the presentation aids you will be using for delivery
- Practice with the presentation aids you will be using
- Time your speech and cut or expand it if needed
- Rehearse with a colleague or an audience if possible
- If you can, rehearse in the room with the podium you will use
- Plan what you will do with your hands
- Plan and practice your opening and closing carefully, so you can deliver them exactly

Rehearsing the Speech

Remember how to get to Carnegie Hall. Rehearse your speech—aloud and ideally with a colleague or fellow student as an audience. Rehearse in front of a mirror if needed. There are some students who record a rehearsal speech so they can get a real sense of what the audience will hear. If you are using presentation aids, rehearse with them for timing and familiarity so you only have to glance at the screen or easel. Time the speech to be sure it within the assigned time. Phrase the speech as you will phrase it in the actual delivery (and listen for the verbal fillers, awkward pauses, and other non- fluencies). Plan what to do with your hands.

You should also know exactly how your speech will begin and end. Regardless of how dependent on notes the speaker may be, here is one constant word of advice: know exactly how you are going to begin your speech. Not just an idea, but verbatim, with every inflection, every gesture, every eye contact with the audience. The first few sentences should be so ingrained, that you could perform it during an earthquake without batting an eye.

A memorized introduction accomplishes several goals. First, it gives you the opportunity to breathe, and realize it's not so bad to be up there after all! Second, it lets the audience know you are prepared. Third, it signals to the audience that what you are about to say is important. Finally, it gives you the opportunity for direct eye contact (because you are not reading) and commands the audience's attention. Eye contact is a signal to the audience that you care about them!

The conclusion of your speech is equally important. In show business parlance, the end of a song or a scene is called a "button." It is a "TAH-DAH" moment that lets the audience know you are finished, and that it is their turn to applaud. The ending impression your speech leaves with the audience is greatly affected by how effective the ending is. The content and structure notwithstanding, you should also know exactly how you will end (verbatim), so there is no hesitation, no stumbling, no tentative "I guess that's all" feeling. A confident and decisive beginning will draw the audience to you; a confident logical ending will be very effective in preserving a lasting impression on the audience.

Stress is an important dragon to slay — or at least tame — in your life. – Marilu Henner

Managing Stress

As William Ball noted in his book for actors and directors, *A Sense of Direction*, getting in front of a group and speaking is people's greatest fear (greater than fear of death). Fear and stress result in psychological and physical manifestations that can affect a speech.

Stress physically causes muscles to tighten, often including vocal cords. This raises, and often limits, the vocal pitch of the speaker under stress. The tempo of the speech may also be affected. Novice speakers tend to rush as though to be anxious to "get it over with." It is a factor to remember in a corporate or business meeting: the speaker should speak slowly enough because what he has to say is important, and the audience should listen. Remember, as noted above, rushing gives the impression that the speaker thinks the message is not worth the time.

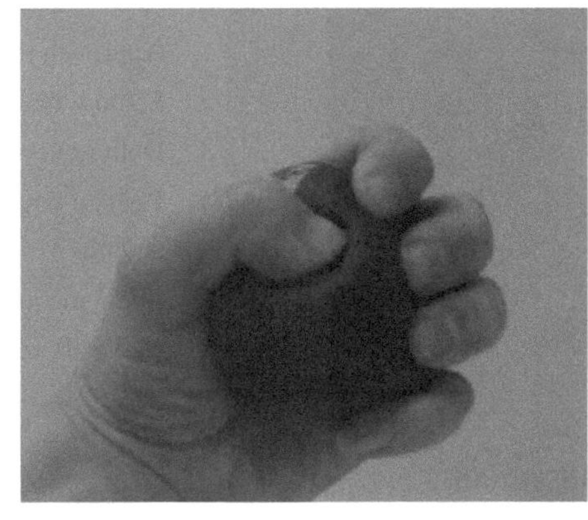

"Is it a bad sign when work starts handing these out?" **by skittledog.** *CC-BY-NC-SA.*

Stress can accelerate perspiration. It is wise to have a facial tissue or small towel handy for dabbing for comfort. Stress can also make the mouth and throat feel dry. Sipping water is a simple solution.

There are a myriad of solutions to relieving a speaker's stress: from hypnosis to imagining the audience to be naked. Among the simplest and most effective is to do a moderate amount of exercise prior to the speech, even as basic as walking. Exercising helps to naturally chemically relieve the tension; and helps deepen the breathing that supports the voice.

Simultaneously while exercising the body, it is a good idea to warm up the voice. The vocal cords are muscles, which should not be jump-started.

Physical exercises will likely help relaxing for better posture and hand and body gestures. As part of the relaxation process, actors "warm up" physically before performances and often do relaxation exercises to help concentration and relieve stress.

The best antidote for stress is to be well prepared and confident.

Delivering the Speech

You have taken all of the right steps before stepping up to the podium or lectern. You have selected a good topic. You have researched the topic. You have organized the best information in a compelling way. You have rehearsed your speech. You have received feedback on your rehearsal from an objective listener. You have carefully constructed your notes and practiced with them. You have planned and practiced your speech introduction and conclusion verbatim. You have checked out the room and the equipment. You did something to reduce your stress before your speech. You did vocal warm-ups. You chose the perfect outfit to wear. You made sure your gum was discarded and your hair pulled back. You arrived at least 15 minutes before your speech. You leapt to the podium with great enthusiasm when introduced.

Now you must deliver. If you look up the word "deliver," you will find it means more than to just "give." To "give" is a willingness to offer something without obligation or the expectation of something in return. To "give" also implies a pre-determined responsibility. You have a responsibility as a speaker to "deliver" information that will help your audience or enlighten them in some way. Speeches are delivered.

Figure 12.2: Steps for Effective Delivery

1. Approach the podium as you rehearsed.
2. Stand with confident posture.
3. Deliver your brilliant opening.
4. Realize you are a hit with the audience.
5. Breathe.
6. Spontaneously interject a humorous observation related to your topic.
7. Make all your points without hesitation, "*ums*," "*likes*," or "*uhs*."

Attributions

CC licensed content, Shared previously

Conclusion, Review Questions, and Activities

The true test for this chapter is in the actual presentation of the speech. Like voice and diction, understanding what makes a speech effective without practice is insufficient. Merely knowing the best form for a golf swing is useless unless put into practice; and practice reinforces the knowledge. Comprehending the rules for driving on the road is moot (and/or dangerous) if the rules are not obeyed in practice. The same is true for this chapter. Practice speaking will make you a more effective speaker!

A speech is poetry: cadence, rhythm, imagery, sweep! A speech reminds us that words, like children, have the power to make dance the dullest beanbag of a heart. – Peggy Noonan

"Lhadon Speaks" by SFT HQ. CC-BY.

Review Questions

1. Develop a list of ten potential speech topics. For each topic, think of a setting in which a speech on that topic might be delivered. Next, determine what type(s) of delivery (manuscript, memorized, impromptu, extemporaneous) would be most appropriate for the topic and setting.

2. What three aspects of vocal delivery do you believe are most important to a speaker's credibility? Explain.

3. How might a speaker's accent affect the audience's perception of him or her? Illustrate your answer with an example.

4. What guidelines did you find most useful in the section about what to wear for your speech?

5. How do you perceive speakers who do not make eye contact with their audience? What suggestions would you give these speakers to improve their eye contact?

6. What type of equipment is available in the space(s) where you plan to give your speeches? What kinds of presentations can be used with this type of equipment?

7. List three methods you would personally use to reduce your anxiety before your speeches.

8. What piece of advice from the chapter did you find most useful?

Activities

1. **Practice Inflection:** Gather some children's books (aimed at ages 6-10) and read them aloud in class. Practice the use of inflection to indicate the punctuation, the energy, and the characters. Do not be afraid to seem foolish. Remember that this is how most children learn to read and speak.

2. **Pronunciation:** Bring in several books or publications of a variety of types and disciplines. Scan through the text and find words that are unusual. Look them up in an online dictionary and see how they are pronounced. This could be turned into a game of "stump the speaker" guessing how each word is pronounced. It can also be used to point out some simple yet often mispronounced words.

3. **Projection:** Stand in as large a circle as possible. Each person has a partner across the room. Partners introduce each other and carry a conversation over the noise of others doing the same thing. Do not shout. Keep it going for a few minutes (it will be loud), then quiz the partners about the conversation they had.

4. Find a partner and work on any of the "Try This" activities in the chapter.

Attributions

CC licensed content, Shared previously

- Chapter 12 Conclusion, Review Questions, and Activities. **Authored by**: Victor Capecce, M.F.A.. **Provided by**: Millersville University, Millersville, PA. **Located at**: http://publicspeakingproject.org/psvirtualtext.html. **Project**: The Public Speaking Project. **License**: *CC BY-NC-ND: Attribution-NonCommercial-NoDerivatives*

- Lhadon Speaks. **Authored by**: SFT HQ. **Located at**: http://commons.wikimedia.org/wiki/File:Lhadon_Speaks.jpg. **License**: *CC BY: Attribution*

Glossary and References

Glossary

TERM	DEFINITION
Accent	The prominence of a syllable in terms of loudness, pitch, and/or length.
Articulation	The act of producing clear, precise and distinct speech.
Body Language	Body stance, gestures and facial expressions.
Dialect	A variety of language, cant or jargon that is set apart from other varieties of the same language by grammar, vocabulary or patterns of speech sounds.
Diction	The accent, inflection, intonation and sound quality of a speaker's voice. Also known as enunciation.
Elocution	The formal study and practice of oral delivery, especially as it relates to the performance of voice and gestures.
Extemporaneous Delivery	Learning your speech well enough so that you can deliver it from a key word outline.
Impromptu Speeches	A speech delivered without previous preparation.
Inflections	Variations, turns and slides in pitch to achieve meaning.
Manuscript Delivery	Reading the text of a speech word for word.
Memorized Delivery	Learning a speech by heart and then delivering it without notes.
Performance	The execution of a speech in front of an audience.
Pitch	The highness or lowness of one's voice or of sound.
Pronunciation	Saying words correctly, with the accurate articulation, stress and intonation, according to conventional or cultural standards.
Regionalism	A speech form, expression or custom that is characteristic to a particular geographic area.
Tempo	The rate, pace, or rhythm of speech.
Timbre	The characteristic quality of the sound of one's voice.
Tone	The particular sound quality (e.g. nasal or breathy) or emotional expression of the voice.
Verbatim	To say with exactly the same words.
Vocalized Pauses	Verbal fillers in speech such as "um," "uh," "like," "and," or "you know."

References

Ball, W. (1984). *A sense of direction: Some observations on the art of directing*. New York: Drama Book.

Brydon, S. R., & Scott, M. D. (2006). *Between one and many: The art and science of public speaking.* Boston, MA: McGraw-Hill.

DeVito, J. A. (2003). *The essential elements of public speaking.* Boston: Allyn and Bacon.

Giffin, K., & Patton, B. R. (1971). *Fundamentals of interpersonal communication.* New York: Harper & Row.

Gregory, H. (2010). Selected chapters from *Public speaking for college and career,* ninth edition. Boston: McGraw-Hill Learning Solutions.

Monroe, A. H., & Ehninger, D. (1974). *Principles and types of speech communication.* Glenview, Ill.,: Scott, Foresman.

A Research Guide for Students. (n.d.). A Research Guide for Students. Retrieved February 26, 2012, from http://www.aresearchguide.com/

Sprague, J., & Stuart, D. (1984). *The speaker's handbook.* San Diego: Harcourt Brace Jovanovich.

Welcome to Mirror Image. (n.d.). Mirror Image Teleprompters. Retrieved February 26, 2012, from http://www.teleprompters.com/mirrorimage/ind ex.php

photo credits

p. 1 Allida Black Speaking at the Courage to Lead Conference by U.S. Mission Geneva http://www.every-stockphoto.com/photo.php?imageId=752   7414&searchId=488e81758eb12a809a21e316d0f1ab1b&npos=230

p. 5 Iraqi speaker by Scanlan http://commons.wikimedia.org/wiki/File:Iraqi_Speaker.jpg

p. 6 Ice-T by Tino Jacobs http://commons.wikimedia.org/wiki/File:Ice-T_(2).jpg

p.9 [President] Barack Obama at Las Vegas Presidential Forum by Center for American Progress Action Fund http://commons.wikimedia.org/wiki/File:Barack_Obama_at_Las_Vegas_Presidential_Forum.jpg

p. 10 Chris Coons as the 2010 Democrat nominee for U.S. Senate in Delaware by Chris Coons http://commons.wikimedia.org/wiki/File:Chris_Coons.jpg

p. 10 Phoenix Auditorium by Basil Jradeh http://commons.wikimedia.org/wiki/File:Phoenix_Auditorium.jpg

p. 11 Lhandon Speaks by STF HQ http://upload.wikimedia.org/wikipedia/commons/8/88/Lhadon_Speaks.jpg

p. 11 Andrea Dernbach and Hoda Salah by Heinrich Boell Stiftung http://commons.wikimedia.org/wiki/File:Flickr_-_boellstiftung_ _Andrea_Dernbach_und_Hoda_Salah.jpg

p. 14 Anthony Pico by Dale Frost http://commons.wikimedia.org/wiki/File:Anthonypico.jpg

Attributions

Chapter 7: Introductions and Conclusions

Objectives and Introduction

Introductions and Conclusions

By Warren Sandmann, Ph.D.
Minnesota State University, Mankato, MN

Learning Objectives

After reading this chapter, you should be able to:

- List and describe the four functions of an introduction
- List and describe the common types of attention getters
- Describe and implement strategies for preparing introductions
- List and describe the four functions of a conclusion
- List and describe common types of conclusions
- Describe and implement strategies for preparing conclusions
- Apply chapter concepts in review questions and activities

Introduction

First impressions count. Carlin Flora, writing in *Psychology Today*, recounts an experiment in which people with no special training were shown 20- to 32-second video clips of job applicants in the initial stages of a job interview. After watching the short clips, the viewers were asked to rate the applicants on characteristics including self-assurance and likability—important considerations in a job interview. These ratings were then compared with the findings from the trained interviewers who spent 20 minutes or more with the job applicants. The result: The 20- to 32-second ratings were basically the same as the ratings from the trained interviewers.[1]

When we stand in front of an audience, we have very little time to set the stage for a successful speech. As seen from the example above, audience members begin evaluating us immediately. What we sometimes forget since we are so focused on the words we have to say is that we are being evaluated even before we open our mouths.

"Imagine Cup 2012" by ImagineCup. CC-BY.

He has the deed half done who has made a beginning. – Horace

Attributions

CC licensed content, Shared previously

- Chapter 9 Objectives, Outline, and Introduction. **Authored by**: Warren Sandmann, Ph.D.. **Provided by**: Minnesota State University, Mankato, MN. **Located at**: http://publicspeakingproject.org/psvirtualtext.html. **Project**: The Public Speaking Project. **License**: *CC BY-NC-ND: Attribution-NonCommercial-NoDerivatives*

---

1. Flora, C. (May-June 2004). The onceover you can trust: First impressions. *Psychology Today*, *37*(3), 60–64.

Functions of Introductions

Speech introductions are an essential element of an effective public speech. Introductions have four specific functions that need to be met in a very short period of time. Introductions must gain the audience's attention and their goodwill, they must state the purpose of the speech and they must preview the main points.

These first two functions of the introduction, gaining the attention of the audience and the good will of the audience, have most to do with getting the audience to want to listen to you. The other two functions of the introduction, stating the purpose of the speech and previewing the structure of the speech, have to do with helping the audience understand you.

The secret of successful speakers? Passion and compassion with a purpose. – Lily Walters

Gain Attention and Interest

The first function of the introduction is to the get the attention AND the interest of the audience. The "and" here is important. Anyone can walk into a room full of people sitting quietly, and YELL AT THE TOP OF THEIR LUNGS. That will get attention. However, it will probably not garner much interest—at least not much positive interest.

Gaining attention and interest is essential if you want the audience to listen to what you have to say, and audiences will decide fairly quickly if they want to pay attention. Standing in front of an audience, slouched, hands in pockets, cap pulled low over your head, and mumbling, "my name is… and I am going to tell you about…" is an

"Yell" by Vetustense Photorogue. CC-BY-NC.

effective method of NOT getting attention and interest. Before you even open your mouth, your attire, stance, and physical presence are all sending out loud signals that you have no interest in the speech, so why should the audience.

Gain the Goodwill of the Audience

Over 2000 years ago, probably the pre-eminent speech teacher of all time, Aristotle noted the importance of gaining the goodwill of the audience:

> *...it is not only necessary to consider how to make the speech itself demonstrative and convincing, but also that the speaker should show himself to be of a certain character...and that his hearers should think that he is disposed in a certain way toward them; and further, that they themselves should be disposed in a certain way towards him.*[1]

When an audience has decided to listen to you—when you have gained their attention and interest—you still need them to think favorably of you. The most effective way of doing this is by establishing your credibility to speak. Credibility is your believability. You are credible when the audience thinks you know what you are talking about. There are a number of methods for developing credibility, and you will use them throughout the speech. In the introduction, however, since you have comparatively little time to develop this credibility, your options are a bit more limited.

> To be persuasive, we must be believable. To be believable, we must be credible. To be credible, we must be truthful. – Hellmut Walters

Essentially, credibility has two elements: external credibility and internal credibility. **External credibility** is the type of credibility you as a speaker gain by association: use of sources that the audience finds credible, for example. In an introduction, you may be able to develop external credibility by this means, as we will see later in this section.

More importantly, given the immediate nature of an introduction, is **internal credibility**. You develop internal credibility as the speaker through specific actions. First, be appropriately attired for a public presentation. Second, make eye contact with the audience *before* you speak. Third, speak clearly, fluently and confidently.

You can also demonstrate internal credibility by demonstrating personal experience with or knowledge of the topic of your speech. Audiences are more positively disposed toward a speaker who has had experience with the topic of his or her speech. You can also demonstrate credibility and goodwill by showing a connection to your audience, demonstrating shared experiences or shared values.

"Captive Audience" by J J. CC-BY-NC-ND.

A student giving a speech to a class about a month before spring break, right in the middle of an extended cold spell of a long Midwestern winter, offered this introduction as a way to show shared values and experiences:

1. Aristotle (1982). The art of rhetoric. (J.H. Freese, Trans.). Cambridge, MA: Harvard University Press.

I need everyone to close his or her eyes. All right, now I need everyone to picture how he or she got to school today. Did you bundle up with a hat, some mittens, boots, and two jackets because it's so cold outside before you left for class? While walking to class, was it cold? Did your ears burn from the icy wind blowing through the air? Were your hands cold and chapped? Now I want you all to think about the sun beating down on your body. Picture yourself lying on the beach with sand between your toes and the sound of the ocean in the background. Or picture yourself poolside, with a Pina Coloda perhaps, with tropical music playing in the background. Picture yourself in Mazatlan, Mexico.[2]

"Pueblo Bonito Emerald Bay" **by Bryce Edwards.** CC-BY.

When speakers can identify with the audience and can show how the audience and the speaker share experiences, then the audience is more receptive to what the speaker has to say. The speaker is both more credible and more attractive to the audience.

The secret of success is constancy of purpose. – Benjamin Disraeli

Clearly State the Purpose

This seems like such a basic step, yet it is one too often missed; and without this step, it is difficult for the audience to follow, much less evaluate and comprehend, a speech. In both basic composition classes and basic public speaking classes, this function is much the same: State the **thesis** of your speech. In all speeches, there should be that one sentence, that one statement that succinctly and accurately lets the audience know what the speech will be about and what the speaker plans to accomplish in the speech. Speakers, especially novice speakers but also experienced ones, are so concerned with the content of the speech that they forget to let us know about the purpose. A good thesis statement clearly announces the topic and purpose of the speech.

For example, a standard problem- solution speech should have a thesis statement that clearly states the problem and the need for a solution.

So right now let's see how dependence on fossil fuels costs you money and how use of ethanol as a supplement will save you money and save the world from energy dependence.

2. Townsend, C. (2007, February 5). Spring break in Mexico. Speech posted at http://msustr0.campus.mnsu.edu:8080/cah/gorgias/333/MMS/Cassie.wmv

We know the topic and we know what the speaker will be attempting to prove. Once a thesis statement is clearly announced, the final function of the introduction is ready.

Preview and Structure the Speech

The thesis statement lets the audience know what the speech is about and what you as speaker want to accomplish. The **preview** statement lets the audience know HOW you will develop the speech. A preview can be understood as a roadmap—a direction for the speech that leads to a successful conclusion. A preview lets the audience know what will come first, what comes next, and so on, to the end of the speech.

The preview is essentially an outline—an oral outline—of the basic organizational pattern of the speech. Previews help the audience follow the content because they already know the structure. Remember, though, that the basic structure of a speech is not linear, it is circular. Organizational patterns for speeches have a conclusion which, as we will see later, brings the audience back to the beginning.

Taking as an example the thesis statement from above, a sample preview for that speech could appear as the following:

> *To see how we can end our dependence on fossil fuels, we will first take a look at why we as a society are so dependent upon fossil fuels; secondly, find out what continues to cause this dependence; and finally, see how ethanol as a fuel supplement will help end this dependence and make the world a better place for all of us.*

"Oil Well" by joshuadelaughter. CC-BY-NC.

Attributions

CC licensed content, Shared previously

Attention-Getting Strategies

Now that we have discussed the four basic functions of the introduction, let's look at ten potential attention-getting strategies. This is not an exhaustive list, and many of these attention getters can be combined or adapted to fit the needs of the speaker, the occasion and the audience. Regardless of the specific strategy used for the introduction, all introductions still need to meet the four basic functions of an introduction.

> You will get good attention and people will be more inclined to listen to you if you can make a statement whereby their response is… "No kidding!" – Gael Boardman

Tell a Story

Human beings love stories. In all cultures, stories are used to communicate and share values, traditions and knowledge. Rhetorician Walter Fisher[1] argues that human beings are best understood as *homo narrans*, as people who tell stories. As an introductory device, stories (and anecdotes and illustrations) are very effective attention getters.

First, stories have a built-in structure that everyone recognizes and expects. Stories have a beginning, middle and end, and this built-in structure allows the audience and the speaker to immediately share this experience.

Secondly, because this built-in structure, stories as attention getters lend themselves readily to a well- structured speech. You as speaker can start the story, get right to the climax, and then stop. You have the attention of the audience; you have shared experiences with them; and now you also have the conclusion of the speech all set to go—the end of the story.

> Speakers who talk about what life has taught them never fail to keep the attention of their listeners. – Dale Carnegie

---

1. Fisher, W. (1987). *Human communication as narration: Toward a philosophy of reason, value, and action.* Columbia: University of South Carolina Press.

Refer to the Occasion

You are presenting this speech for a reason. The audience is present at this speech for a reason. These reasons can provide you with an effective attention getter. Referring to the occasion is often used as an introduction to tribute speeches, toasts, dedication ceremonies and historical events. Speech scholar Lloyd Bitzer[2] argues that all speeches are made at least in part in response to specific occasions, so referring to the occasion seems a good idea.

Bono, lead singer of the rock group U2 and an activist for a number of humanitarian issues, addressed the 54th annual National Prayer Breakfast, and started his speech with these words:

> *Well, thank you. Thank you Mr. President, First Lady, King Abdullah of Jordan, Norm [Coleman], distinguished guests. Please join me in praying that I don't say something we'll all regret.*[3]

"National Prayer Breakfast" **by Paul Morse. Public domain.**

Refer to Recent or Historical Events

In addition to referring to the occasion, another effective attention- getting device is to refer to current events or to historical events. This style of reference again helps to create a shared experience for the speaker and the audience, as the speaker reminds all present that they have these events in common. Additionally, referring to current or historical events can also help establish goodwill and personal credibility by demonstrating that the speaker is aware of the relationship between this particular speech and what is going on in the world at that time, or what has occurred in the past.

2. Bitzer, L. (1968). The rhetorical situation. *Philosophy and Rhetoric*, 1, 1–14.
3. Bono. (2006, February 2). Keynote address at the 54th national prayer breakfast. Speech posted at http://www.american-rhetoric.com/speeches/bononationalprayerbreakfast. htm

Abraham Lincoln (1863), in one of the most well-known speeches in American history, refers both to historical events and current events in the beginning of the *Gettysburg Address*:

> *Fourscore and seven years ago our fathers brought forth on this continent a new nation, conceived in liberty and dedicated to the proposition that all men are created equal. Now we are engaged in a great civil war, testing whether that nation or any nation so conceived and so dedicated can long endure.*

History, despite its wrenching pain, cannot be unlived, but if faced with courage, need not be lived again. – Maya Angelou

"Abraham Lincoln" by Alexander Gardner. Public domain.

Refer to Previous Speeches

Most of you reading this material are doing so because you are in a public speaking or introductory communication class of some kind. And that means that most of you will be presenting your speeches right after someone else has presented his or her speech. Even if you are not in a classroom situation, many other speaking situations (such as presenting at a city council or other government meeting, or taking part in a forum or lecture series) result in speakers presenting right after another person has spoken.

In these situations, speakers before you may have already addressed some of the information you were planning to discuss, or perhaps have given a speech on the same topic you are now planning to address. By referring to the previous speeches, you enhance your credibility by showing your knowledge of the previous speech, and you have the opportunity to either compare or contrast your speech to the previous speeches.

Edward Kennedy, at the 1980 Democratic National Convention, began his speech with a short tribute and acknowledgement to the previous speaker, member of Congress Barbara Mikulski:

> *Thanks very much, Barbara Mikulski, for your very eloquent, your eloquent introduction. Distinguished legislator, great spokeswoman for economic democracy and social justice in this country, I thank you for your eloquent introduction.*

"Ted Kennedy, Senator from Massachusetts" by United States Senate. Public domain.

Refer to Personal Interest

One of the key considerations in choosing an appropriate topic for your speech is that you have a personal interest in that topic. An effective attention getter then, can be your description of that personal interest. By noting your personal interest, you will demonstrate your credibility by showing your knowledge and experience with this topic, and because you have a personal interest, you are more likely to present this information in a lively and clear manner—again, enhancing your credibility. Referring to your personal interest in this topic in the introduction also helps you set the stage for additional anecdotes or examples from your personal experience later in the speech.

In speaking at the 1992 Democratic National Convention, Elizabeth Glaser began her speech by acknowledging her very personal interest in the topic:

> *I'm Elizabeth Glaser. Eleven years ago, while giving birth to my first child, I hemorrhaged and was transfused with seven pints of blood. Four years later, I found out that I had been infected with the AIDS virus and had unknowingly passed it to my daughter, Ariel, through my breast milk, and my son, Jake, in utero.*[4]

Use Startling Statistics

Startling statistics startle an audience and catch its attention, and encourage that audience to listen further as you present the context of the surprising statistic. Long-time radio announcer Paul Harvey is well known for the catch phrase "And now, the rest of the story." The same function should be at work here. When you startle the audience, you set them up to want to hear the "rest of the story."

Be careful, though. Use of startling statistics requires that you do a number of things. First, make sure the statistic is accurate. Second, make sure the statistic is relevant to the topic of the speech. Startling an audience with an irrelevant statistic diminishes the speech and decreases your credibility. Third, make sure you then present "the rest of the story." You need to place this startling statistic in the context of your speech so that everything fits together.

"Happy Pi Day" by Mykl Roventine. CC-BY-NC-SA.

One speaker used an effective startling statistic to help introduce a speech on the dangers of heart disease:

> *According to the Center for Disease Control, in the United States 26.6 million adults have heart disease. This would be about 12% of adults, or three people in this room.*

Use an Analogy

Analogies compare something that your audience knows and understands with something new and different. For your speech, then, you can use an **analogy** to show a connection between your speech topic (something new and different for the audience) and something that is known by your audience.

---

4. Glaser, E. (1992, July 14). 1992 Democratic national convention address. Speech posted at http://www.americanrhetoric.com/speeches/elizabethglaser1992dnc.htm

Analogies can be effective because they use ideas, information and values of the audience to draw a connection to your speech topic—and to you as a speaker. Analogies create connections between you and the audience.

One very common (and often misquoted) analogy comes from the 1919 Supreme Court case of *Schenck v United States*. Justice Oliver Wendell Holmes used this analogy to support his reasoning that some forms of expression can be suppressed because they present a "clear and present danger." Holmes noted that "[t]he most stringent protection of free speech would not protect a man falsely shouting fire in a theater and causing a panic."[5]

> One good analogy is worth three hours discussion. – Dudley Field Malone

"Justice Oliver Wendell Holmes" by National Photo Company. Public domain.

Use a Quotation

Using a quotation from a well- known figure, or using a quotation from a lesser-known figure if the quotation is particularly suitable for your speech topic, is a common attention-getting technique. When you quote that well-known figure, you are in a sense, borrowing some of that person's credibility for your speech, enhancing your credibility with the audience. Even when you use a less than well-known figure, the quotation can be effective if it nicely sets up your speech topic and is something to which your audience can relate.

Be careful with quotations, however. First, just using the quotation is not sufficient. You need to place the quotation in the context of your speech (as well as meet the other required functions of an introduction, of course). Second, it is easy to fall into a bad (and somewhat lazy) habit of simply finding a quotation and using it to start every speech. Third, simply using a quotation is no guarantee that your audience will find that quotation interesting or apt for the speech, and may also find the author of the quotation to be lacking in credibility—or your audience may simply not like the author of the quotation. Finally, beware of overly-long quotations (three or more sentences): Remember, this is just part of the introduction, not a main point of the speech.

5. Schenck v. United States, 249 US 47 (1919).

In his farewell address, former President Ronald Reagan (1989) utilized a very short quotation to emphasize his feelings upon leaving office.

> *People ask how I feel about leaving. And the fact is, "parting is such sweet sorrow." The sweet part is California and the ranch and freedom. The sorrow — the goodbyes, of course, and leaving this beautiful place.*

"Reagan farewell salute" by White House Photographic Office. Public domain.

> *Using rhetorical questions in speeches is a great way to keep the audience involved. Don't you think those kinds of questions would keep your attention? – Bo Bennett*

Ask a Question

The use of questions can be a very effective way to get attention, whether those questions are rhetorical in nature, and are only meant to be considered and pondered by the audience, or are meant to be answered by the audience (generally a good technique to get audience involvement and interest).

Rhetorical questions are designed to allow you as speaker to get the audience to think about your topic without actually speaking the answer to the question. Rhetorical questions allow you as speaker to maintain the most control over a speech situation, and allow you to guard against an inappropriate or even offensive response.

Using questions that ask for real responses, however, has additional benefits, if a speaker feels comfortable with his or her audience, and is able to handle some impromptu situations. Getting the audience to physically and verbally involve themselves in your topic guarantees that they're paying attention. Using questions that lead to positive answers can also enhance your connection to and credibility with the audience.

Starting a speech with a question whether rhetorical or actual does require thought and practice on your part. You need to carefully consider the question and possible answers. Remember—even if you think the question is rhetorical, your audience may not know this and may answer the question. You also need to carefully deliver the question. Too often, speakers will use a question as an introduction—but then give the audience no time to either think about the answer or answer the question. You need to use timing and pause when starting with a question. You also need to be careful to use eye contact in asking questions, since you are above all asking for audience involvement, and your eye contact requests that involvement.

> It is not enough for me to ask questions; I want to know how to answer the one question that seems to encompass everything I face: What am I here for? – Abraham Joshua Heschel

In 1992, Ross Perot selected a little-known retired military figure, Admiral James Stockdale, as his Vice Presidential running mate. In the fall debates, Stockdale began his opening statement with two questions: "Who am I? Why am I here?" (Stockdale, 1992). The questions received applause and also laughter, though the later reaction to these questions was mixed at best. Some saw this as confusion on the part of Stockdale.[6] Stockdale considered these two questions to illustrate his difference from the other two "mainstream" candidates, Al Gore and then Vice President Dan Quayle. Traditional politicians, Gore and Quayle were readily recognized as compared to Stockdale.

Humor is the affectionate communication of insight. – Leo Rosten

Use Humor

The use of humor in an introduction can be one of the most effective types of introductions—if done well. Humor can create a connection between the speaker and audience, can get an audience relaxed and in a receptive frame of mind, and can allow an audience to perceive the speaker (and the topic) in a positive light.

Humor done badly can destroy the speech and ruin a speaker's credibility.

"Audience enjoy Stallman's jokes" by *Wikimania2009 and Damiu00e1n Buonamico.* CC-BY.

So first, a word of warning: None of us (those reading this, those teaching this class, and those writing this) are as funny as we think we are. If we were that funny, we would be making our living that way. Humor is hard. Humor can backfire. Humor is to a large extent situation-bound. Most likely, there will be a number of members of your audience who do not use English as a first language (there are plenty of people reading this who are English as a Second Language learners). Much humor requires a native understanding of English. Most likely, there will be a number of people in your audience who do not share your cultural upbringing—and humor is often culture-bound. Be careful with humor.

In general, there is basically only one safe and suitable style of humor: light and subtle self-deprecation. In other words, you as speaker are the only really safe subject for humor.

6. Lehrer, J. (Interviewer) & Stockdale, J. (Interviewee). (1999). Debating our Destiny: Admiral James Stockdale. Retrieved from http://www.pbs.org/newshour/debati ngourdestiny/interviews/stockdale.html

Using humor to tell stories about other people, other groups, and even other situations, may work—but it is just as likely to offend those people, members of those groups, and people in that situation. Using self-deprecating humor will not offend others, but unless you can do this with a light and subtle touch, you may be harming your credibility rather than creating a connection between yourself and the audience.

Now, with all these warnings, you may want to stay far away from humor as an introduction. Humor can work, however.

Ann Richards, at the 1988 Democratic National Convention, used humor in the introduction to her Keynote Address. Knowing the audience, Richards was able to use partisan humor to establish a connection to the audience and score points against the political opposition.

> *I'm delighted to be here with you this evening, because after listening to George Bush all these years, I figured you needed to know what a real Texas accent sounds like.*

"Ann Richards" by Kenneth C. Zirkel. CC-BY-SA.

Attributions

CC licensed content, Shared previously

- Chapter 9 Attention Getting Strategies. **Authored by**: Warren Sandmann, Ph.D.. **Provided by**: Minnesota State University, Mankato, MN. **Located at**: http://publicspeakingproject.org/psvirtualtext.html. **Project**: The Public Speaking Project. **License**: *CC BY-NC-ND: Attribution-NonCommercial-NoDerivatives*

- Happy Pi Day (to the 69th digit)!. **Authored by**: Mykl Roventine. **Located at**: https://flic.kr/p/67tNgs. **License**: *CC BY-NC-SA: Attribution-NonCommercial-ShareAlike*

- Ann Richards. **Authored by**: Kenneth C. Zirkel. **Located at**: http://commons.wikimedia.org/wiki/File:Ann_Richards.jpg. **License**: *CC BY-SA: Attribution-ShareAlike*

- Audience enjoy Stallman's jokes. **Authored by**: Wikimania2009 and Damiu00e1n Buonamico. **Located at**: http://commons.wikimedia.org/wiki/File:Audience_enjoy_Stallman%27s_jokes.jpg. **License**: *CC BY: Attribution*

Public domain content

- Image of Abraham Lincoln. **Authored by**: Alexander Gardner . **Located at**: http://commons.wikimedia.org/wiki/File:Abraham_Lincoln_head_on_shoulders_photo_portrait.jpg. **License**: *Public Domain: No Known Copyright*

- National prayer breakfast 2006. **Authored by**: Paul Morse. **Located at**: http://commons.wikimedia.org/wiki/File:National_prayer_breakfast_2006.jpg%20. **License**: *Public Domain: No Known Copyright*

- Ted Kennedy, official photo portrait crop. **Provided by**: United States Senate. **Located at**: http://commons.wikimedia.org/wiki/File:Ted_Kennedy,_official_photo_portrait_crop.jpg. **License**: *Public Domain: No Known Copyright*

- Justice Oliver Wendell Holmes standing. **Authored by**: National Photo Company. **Located at**: http://commons.wikimedia.org/wiki/File:Justice_Oliver_Wendell_Holmes_standing.jpg. **License**: *Public Domain: No Known Copyright*

- Reagan farewell salute. **Authored by**: White House Photographic Office. **Located at**: http://commons.wikimedia.org/wiki/File:Reagan_farewell_salute.jpg. **License**: *Public Domain: No Known Copyright*

Preparing the Introduction

Construct the Introduction Last

While this may seem both counter-intuitive and somewhat strange, you really do want to leave the development of the introduction for the last part of your speech preparation. Think of it this way: You can't introduce the ideas in your speech until you have determined these ideas.

The introduction is prepared last because you want to make sure that the body of the speech drives the introduction, not the other way around. The body of the speech contains most of your content, your arguments, your evidence, and your source material: The introduction sets up the body, but it should not overwhelm the body of the speech, nor should it dictate the content or structure of the speech.

Once you have the body of the speech complete, then you consider the introduction. With the body of the speech complete, it is relatively simple to complete two of the four functions of the introduction. You already know the purpose of the speech, so now you need to put it in a one-sentence statement. And you already know the structure and main points of the speech, so you can put that structure into the preview.

"A woman typing on a laptop" by Matthew Bowden via **Wikipedia Commons.** *Permitted use.*

With the structural functions of the introduction complete, you can carefully choose and craft the type of introduction you wish to use, and concentrate on making sure that the introduction also fulfills the other two necessary functions: gaining the attention and interest of the audience, and gaining the goodwill of the audience.

Make It Relevant

Another reason why your introduction should be the last part of your speech you prepare is so that the introduction can relate to the speech. If you prepare the introduction before you prepare the body of the speech, your introduction may be wonderful—but completely disconnected from the rest of the speech.

When you consider the type of introduction you wish to use, you might note that many of the types could easily lend themselves to disconnection from the speech. A startling statistic may shock and get an audience's attention—but if it is not relevant to the speech itself, the introduction is at best wasted and more likely distracting to the audience. A quotation may be both profound and catchy—but if the quotation has little to do with the speech itself, the introduction is once again wasted or distracting.

Now, because your introduction will contain the thesis statement and preview, at least part of the introduction will be relevant to the rest of the speech. However, the entire introduction needs to be relevant. If your audience hears an introduction that they perceive to lack connection to the rest of the speech, they will have difficulty following your main ideas, any attention and interest you may have gained will be more than offset by the loss of goodwill and personal credibility, and your speech will not make the positive impression you desire.

> The wise ones fashioned speech with their thought, sifting it as grain is sifted through a sieve. – Buddha

Be Succinct

In most classroom speeches, and in most speech situations outside the classroom, the speaker will be on a time limit. Even if you are giving a speech in a setting where there is no stated time limit, most people will simply not pay attention to a speech that goes on and on and on.

Since you are on a time limit, and since, as noted above, the body of the speech is the heart of your speech, the introduction of your speech needs to be concise and succinct. There is no magic formula for the length of an introduction, and you do need to meet all four functions in your introduction. Many authors suggest that the introduction be no more than 10-15% of the total speaking time.

Most audiences expect you to introduce your speech and then move quickly into the body of the speech. While the expectations vary from culture to culture, most of the speaking situations in which you will find yourself will involve audiences that have been taught to listen for an introduction with a main thesis statement of some type. This is the standard speech format with which the majority of your audience will be familiar and comfortable. Failing to meet that expectation of your audience is in a sense a violation, and communication scholars Burgoon and Hale[1] have shown that **expectancy violations** create difficulties in communication situations.

"Ed Milliband with banner" by allispossible.org.uk. CC-BY.

---

1. Burgoon, J. K. & and Hale, J. L. (1988). Nonverbal expectancy violations: Model elaboration and application to immediacy behaviors. *Communication Monographs, 55*(1), 58–79.

Write It Out Word for Word

In another chapter, you may have read and studied speech delivery techniques, and in your class, you may be encouraged to use an extemporaneous style of delivery for your speeches. That is good advice. However, introductions are best written out word for word and then delivered as memorized.

Introductions are succinct (as we learned above), and introductions have to do a lot of work in a short period of time. Because of this, you as a speaker need to carefully consider every word of your introduction. The best method for doing so is to write your introduction out word for word. Then you can more easily see if you have met all four functions, and can also have a very good idea just how long the introduction will be. Just as importantly, memorizing and then delivering the introduction word for word gives you the most control over this important (yet short) part of your speech.

Attributions

CC licensed content, Shared previously

- Chapter 9 Preparing the Introduction. **Authored by**: Warren Sandmann, Ph.D.. **Provided by**: Minnesota State University, Mankato, MN. **Located at**: http://publicspeakingproject.org/psvirtualtext.html. **Project**: The Public Speaking Project. **License**: *CC BY-NC-ND: Attribution-NonCommercial-NoDerivatives*
- Ed Miliband with banner. **Authored by**: allispossible.org.uk. **Located at**: https://www.flickr.com/photos/wheatfields/1812763231/. **License**: *CC BY: Attribution*
- Woman typing on a laptop. **Authored by**: Matthew Bowden. **Located at**: http://commons.wikimedia.org/wiki/File:Woman-typing-on-laptop.jpg. **License**: *CC BY: Attribution*. **License Terms**: The copyright holder of this file allows anyone to use it for any purpose, provided that the copyright holder is properly attributed. Redistribution, derivative work, commercial use, and all other use is permitted.

Functions of Conclusions

So: You are at the end of your speech, and you can't wait to sit down and be done! You start speeding up your rate of delivery, but your volume goes down a bit because you are rushing and running out of breath. You finish the last main point of your speech and race off to your seat: That is not the best way to conclude a speech.

Just as with introductions, conclusions have specific functions to fulfill within a speech. And just as with introductions, there are a number of types of conclusions. In this section of this chapter, we will look at these functions, discuss the relationship between introductions and conclusions, and offer some strategies for preparing and delivering an effective conclusion.

"Cool Park Architecture / Tianjin, China" **by SamHakes.** *morgueFile license.*

The basic structure of a speech is not linear but circular. Speeches should not take you on a straight line from A to Z. Speeches should take you in a circle from A to Z. Speeches start at the top of the circle with the introduction, work their way all around the circle, and end up back at the top with the conclusion. All the parts fit together and flow together in this circle, and the conclusion takes you right back to the introduction—with an enhanced understanding of the topic.

Prepare the Audience for the End of the Speech

A speech does not just stop—or, to be more precise, a speech should not just stop. A speech, effectively structured and delivered, should move smoothly from point to point and then to the conclusion. One of the most important functions of the conclusion is to prepare the audience for the end of the speech.

Throughout the speech, you have been providing the audience with verbal and nonverbal cues to where you are going in the speech. As you move to the conclusion, you need to continue to provide these cues. You can use language cues ("now that we have seen that we can solve this problem effectively, we can review the entire situation"), movement cues (physically moving back to the center of the room where you began the speech), and paralinguistic cues (slow the rate of the speech, use more pauses) to help prepare your audience for the end of the speech.

When you prepare the audience for the end of the speech, you let them know that they need to be ready for any final comments or appeals from you, and that they should be prepared to acknowledge you as a speaker.

Present any Final Appeals

Depending on the type of speech you are presenting, you will be asking the audience for something. You may be asking them to act in a certain way, or to change their attitude toward a certain person or topic. You may be asking them to simply understand what you have had to say in your presentation. Regardless, one of the tasks of the conclusion is to leave the audience motivated positively toward you and the topic you have been presenting.

Psychologists and sociologists (as well as communication scholars) know that there is both a **primacy** and **recency** effect in presenting information.[1] Essentially, people tend to better remember information presented first or last—they remember what they hear at the beginning of the speech or at the end. In presenting your appeals to the audience, you can take advantage of the recency effect to increase the likelihood of your audience acting on your appeals.

Former President Lyndon Johnson, in a speech announcing a major policy initiative known as the Great Society, concluded his speech with a series of challenges and appeals to his audience.

> *For better or for worse, your generation has been appointed by history to deal with those problems and to lead America toward a new age. You have the chance never before afforded to any people in any age. You can help build a society where the demands of morality, and the needs of the spirit, can be realized in the life of the Nation.*

"LBJ at the University of Michigan" by Cecil W. Stoughton. Public domain.

1. Garlick, R. (1993). Verbal descriptions, communicative encounters and impressions. *Communication Quarterly, 41,* 394–404.

So, will you join in the battle to give every citizen the full equality which God enjoins and the law requires, whatever his belief, or race, or the color of his skin?

Will you join in the battle to give every citizen an escape from the crushing weight of poverty?

Will you join in the battle to make it possible for all nations to live in enduring peace — as neighbors and not as mortal enemies?

Will you join in the battle to build the Great Society, to prove that our material progress is only the foundation on which we will build a richer life of mind and spirit?

There are those timid souls that say this battle cannot be won; that we are condemned to a soulless wealth. I do not agree. We have the power to shape the civilization that we want. But we need your will and your labor and your hearts, if we are to build that kind of society.[2]

The appeals were significant in that the speech was delivered as a commencement address at the University of Michigan, at a time in American society when college and university students were protesting many government actions.

When Demosthenes was asked what were the three most important aspects of oratory, he answered, Action, Action, Action. – Plutarch

"President Johnson poverty tour" **by Cecil W. Stoughton. Public domain.**

Summarize and Close

A conclusion is structural in function. Just as the introduction must include a statement of the purpose of the speech, as well as a preview of the main ideas of the speech, the conclusion must include a restatement of the thesis and a review of the main ideas of the speech. The review and restatement are mirror images of the preview statement in the introduction. Structurally, the restatement and review bring the speech back to the top of the circle and remind the audience where we started. Functionally, they help cue the audience that the end of the speech is coming up.

Let's go back to the thesis and preview example. The example was from a speech on ethanol, and the sample thesis was "So right now let's see how dependence on fossil fuels costs you money and how use of ethanol as a supplement will save you money and save the world from energy obsolescence."

In the conclusion of this speech, one effective method to summarize and wrap-up is to simply restate the thesis and preview—but in the past tense, since we have now heard the speech.

Today we have seen how dependence on fossil fuels costs you money and how use of ethanol as a supplement will save you money and save the world from energy obsolescence. We learned first why

2. Johnson, L. (1964, May 22). The great society. Speech posted at
http://www.americanrhetoric.com/sp eeches/lbjthegreatsociety.htm

we as a society are so dependent upon fossil fuels in the first place, and then secondly we found out what causes this dependence, and third, we saw how ethanol as a fuel supplement will help end this dependence, and finally we discovered how simple it is to implement this solution and make the world a better place for all of us.

By restating the thesis and reviewing the main ideas, you once again take advantage of both the primacy and recency effect, and you create a complete and coherent structure to your speech.

End with a Clincher

With conclusions, however, there are some additional forms you may wish to use, and there are some variations and adaptations of the introductions that you will want to use as you prepare your conclusions.

Earlier in this section when we discussed introductions, it was argued that stories are quite possibly the most effective form of introduction: Stories appear to be almost "hard-wired" into our individual and cultural make-up; and stories have a built-in structure. Stories, then, also make excellent conclusions, and can be used as conclusions in at least two ways. First, you can complete the story that you started in the introduction. Remember: You stopped right before the climax or denouement, and now, you can finish the story. Alternatively, you can retell the story, and this time the story will reflect what the audience has learned from your speech. Either method provides coherence and closure to the story and the speech.

Humor also remains an effective type of conclusion, but the same dangers with the use of humor discussed in the section on introductions applies to the conclusion. Still, effective use of humor leaves the audience in a receptive frame of mind, and, so long as the humor is relevant to the speech, provides a positive reminder to the audience of the main purpose of the speech.

Because of the functions of conclusions, there are two additional types of conclusions you may wish to consider: Appeals and Challenges.

> I appeal to you, my friends, as mothers: are you willing to enslave your children? You stare back with horror and indignation at such questions. But why, if slavery is not wrong to those upon whom it is imposed? – Angelina Grimke

Appeals and Challenges

Since the conclusion comes at the end of the speech, it is appropriate to leave the audience with an appeal or a challenge (or a combination of the two). Similar in nature, appeals and challenges primarily divide by tone. Appeals are generally phrased more as requests, while challenges can take on a more forceful tone, almost ordering or daring audiences to engage in thought or action.

One of the most historically memorable and effective conclusions that utilized appeal and challenge was Dr. Martin Luther King Jr.'s I Have a Dream speech.

"Martin Luther King Jr." Public domain.

> *And so let freedom ring from the prodigious hill-tops of New Hampshire. Let freedom ring from the mighty mountains of New York. Let freedom ring from the heightening Alleghenies of Pennsylvania. Let freedom ring from the snow-capped Rockies of Colorado. Let freedom ring from the curvaceous slopes of California. But not only that: Let freedom ring from Stone Mountain of Georgia. Let freedom ring from Lookout Mountain of Tennessee. Let freedom ring from every hill and molehill of Mississippi. From every mountainside, let freedom ring. And when this happens, when we allow freedom to ring, when we let it ring from every village and every hamlet, from every state and every city, we will be able to speed up that day when all of God's children, black men and white men, Jews and Gentiles, Protestants and Catholics, will be able to join hands and sing in the words of the old Negro spiritual: Free at last! Free at last! Thank God Almighty, we are free at last![3]*

Attributions

CC licensed content, Shared previously

- Chapter 9 Functions of Conclusions. **Authored by**: Warren Sandmann, Ph.D.. **Provided by**: Minnesota State University, Mankato, MN. **Located at**: http://publicspeakingproject.org/psvirtualtext.html. **Project**: The Public Speaking Project. **License**: *CC BY-NC-ND: Attribution-NonCommercial-NoDerivatives*
- Cool Park Architecture. **Authored by**: SamHakes. **Provided by**: MorgueFiles. **Located at**: http://mrg.bz/dbrQuL. **License**: *Other*. **License Terms**: Free to remix, commercial use, no attribution required. http://www.morguefile.com/license/morguefile
- BP Oil Flood Protest in New Orleans 30. **Authored by**: Derek Bridges. **Located at**: http://commons.wikimedia.org/wiki/File:BP_Oil_Flood_Protest_in_New_Orleans_30.jpg. **License**: *CC BY: Attribution*

3. King, Jr., M. L. (1963, August 28). I have a dream." Speech posted at http://www.americanrhetoric.com/sp eeches/mlkihaveadream.htm

Composing the Conclusion

Just as with introductions, there are two important points to remember from the start. First, regardless of the form of conclusion, all summary remarks must meet certain required functions. Second, most conclusions will be a combination of two or more forms. There is a third point to remember about conclusions as well: Conclusions need to provide a match to the introduction, so that there is symmetry and completeness to the speech structure. Because of this, very often, the conclusion will be of the same form as the introduction. At the very least, the conclusion must refer to the introduction so there is a sense of completeness. Naturally enough, the forms of conclusions you can use and develop are similar to the forms of introductions you can use and develop.

Eloquent speech is not from lip to ear, but rather from heart to heart. – William Jennings Bryan

Prepare the Conclusion

The conclusion is the last part of the speech to prepare.

What is common writing practice for the introduction is also true of the conclusion. As previously discussed, introductions and conclusions are similar in nature, they provide mirror images of one another other, and they are often of the same type. So you complete the introduction and conclusion at the same time. You do so to make sure that both elements work together.

As you prepare the conclusion, make sure as well that there are no false conclusions. You need to prepare the audience for the end of the speech—but you can only prepare them one time, and there can be only one end to the speech. By the same token,

"Kyung-wha Kang" by United States Mission Geneva. CC-BY-ND.

you need to make sure that the conclusion is not so abrupt or sudden that no one in the audience is aware you have completed your speech. Keep in mind as well that conclusions should comprise no more than 10% of the total speaking time.

Just as with the introduction, write out the conclusion word for word. This is your last chance to impress your audience and to make sure that they understand what you have said. Do not leave the conclusion to chance: write it out.

> Success depends upon previous preparation, and without such preparation there is sure to be failure.
> – Confucius

Do Not Include Any New Information

While it is important to present your appeal and any call to action in the conclusion, it is also important to NOT present new information in your conclusion. Remember: one of the functions of the conclusion is to prepare the audience for the end of the speech. If all of the sudden you present a new argument, new information, or a new point, you will confuse your audience.

If you present new information in the conclusion, you will also lose the ability to integrate this information with the rest of the speech. Remember that all elements of the speech need to flow together. New ideas at the very end of the speech will not enhance the flow of the speech. Additionally, because you are just now bringing in this information at the end of the speech, you will have no or very little time to develop these ideas, or to provide supporting information and documentation for these ideas.

Follow the Structure

The approach of using the built-in structure of the specific introduction/conclusion technique is as equally effective with quotations, questions and startling statistics as it is with stories.

You can use the same quotation at the end as at the beginning, but because of what we have learned in the speech, the quotation has a new and more developed meaning. You can also use a new quotation that draws a comparison and contrast to the beginning quotation, and also highlights what we have learned in the speech.

You can use the same question at the conclusion as you did at the beginning, and regardless of whether you ask for a response or pose it as a rhetorical question (and allow the audience to consider the answer), the answer will be different because of your speech. The audience will be able to see what you have accomplished in the speech. You can also pose a new question, one that again points out what the audience has learned from your speech.

Startling statistics, as quotations and questions, now take on new meaning because of all that you have told the audience in your speech. Reminding the audience of startling statistics should provide them with a key reminder of the main point of your speech.

Attributions

- Chapter 9 Composing the Conclusion. **Authored by**: Warren Sandmann, Ph.D.. **Provided by**: Minnesota State University, Mankato, MN. **Located at**: http://publicspeakingproject.org/psvirtualtext.html. **Project**: The Public Speaking Project. **License**: *CC BY-NC-ND: Attribution-NonCommercial-NoDerivatives*

- Kyung-wha Khang, Deputy High Commissioner for Human Rights. **Authored by**: United States Mission Geneva. **Located at**: https://www.flickr.com/photos/us-mission/4174523290/. **License**: *CC BY-ND: Attribution-NoDerivatives*

Conclusion, Review Questions, and Activities

This chapter first shows how to structure and develop introductions and conclusions. Second, it argues that introductions function to gain audience attention and goodwill, and that introductions help structure the speech with a thesis statement and preview. Third, the chapter explains that conclusions help audiences remember the key ideas of a speech. Finally, the chapter reveals that there are a variety of different techniques for introductions and conclusions, and that many of the techniques for introductions apply to conclusions as well.

"Classic Raux" by Tim Samoff. CC-BY-ND.

Introductions set the stage for the speech that is to come; conclusions make sure that the audience goes away changed in a positive manner. Short in time, they require careful thought and precise language to be effective. Done well, introductions prepare an audience to learn, and conclusions help to insure that an audience has understood the purpose of the speech.

> When you can do the common things of life in an uncommon way, you will command the attention of the world. – George Washington Carver

Review Questions

1. What are the four basic functions of introductions, and why are these functions important?

2. List and give one original example of each of the ten attention-getting devices.

3. What are three reasons why stories are effective as introductions?

4. Why is humor both useful and dangerous at the same time?

5. What is a preview statement, and why is it important as part of an introduction?

6. What are the four basic functions of conclusions, and why are these functions important?

7. Compare and contrast an appeal and a challenge. When would you use each technique?

8. What does it mean to "follow the structure" in a conclusion?

9. Why are introductions and conclusions prepared last?

Activities

1. Review the following speech and then write a brief (150-200 words) analysis on how the speaker used (or did not use) effective introduction and conclusion techniques. ?http://msustr0.campus.mnsu.edu:8080/cah/gorgias/333/CollieSampPersSpeech.wmv

2. Read Lincoln's Gettysburg Address (http://americanrhetoric.com/speeches/gettysburgaddress.htm) and then rewrite the introduction to use:

   - Humor

   - Rhetorical Question

   - A story

     - Each introduction should be relevant to the topic and no more than 100 words in length.

3. Working with a partner, create at least five analogies that could be used as part of an effective introduction for any of the topics listed below.

   - Commonalities of the world's major religions

   - Dealing with gaming addiction

   - Selecting a college

   - Why the penny should be eliminated

   - My worst first date

   - Protecting your identity online and offline

   - Making the perfect lasagna

   - The three most important factors in choosing an automobile

   - The dangers of radon

   - Traveling through Europe on a budget

4. Locate an informative or a persuasive speech on Youtube. Watch the speech once in its entirety, and then watching it a second time, answer these questions.

- What attention-getting technique was used? Was it effective?

- Did the speaker establish his / her credibility effectively?

- Was the thesis or purpose of the speech clear?

- Did the speaker preview the main points of the speech?

- Did the main points of the speech correspond with the preview?

- Did the speaker prepare the audience for the end of the speech?

- Did the speaker present any final appeals? Was this effective?

- What type of clincher (closing technique) was used? Was it effective?

Attributions

CC licensed content, Shared previously

Glossary and References

Glossary

TERM	DEFINITION
Analogy	A figure of speech that essentially compares something that your audience knows and understands with something new and different.
Preview	Sometimes called a road map, a preview is a brief oral outline in which the speaker clearly and concisely states the main points of the speech.
Internal Credibility	This is a form of credibility based on attributes that are largely controlled by a speaker, such as appearance, confidence, charisma, trustworthiness, and speaking ability.
Expectancy Violation	Expectancy violations occur when people engage in behavior that is unexpected or inappropriate for the situation.
External Credibility	This is a form of credibility based on attributes that a speaker can "borrow," such as using credible sources and referring to credible and popular people and events.
Primacy Effect	According to this principle, audiences are likely to remember what they hear or read first.
Recency Effect	According to this principle, audiences are likely to remember what they hear or read last.
Rhetorical Question	When a speaker asks a question that is not meant to be answered outloud, or a question for which the audience already knows the answer. This is often used as a way to get an audience to think about the topic.
Thesis	One sentence or statement that succinctly and accurately lets the audience know what the speech will be about and what the speaker plans to accomplish in the speech.

References

Aristotle (1982). *The art of rhetoric.* (J.H. Freese, Trans.). Cambridge, MA: Harvard University Press.

Bitzer, L. (1968). The rhetorical situation. *Philosophy and Rhetoric, 1,* 1-14.

Bono. (2006, February 2). Keynote address at the 54th national prayer breakfast. Speech posted at http://www.americanrhetoric.com/speeches/bononationalprayerbreakfast.htm

Burgoon, J. K. & and Hale, J. L. (1988). Nonverbal expectancy violations: Model elaboration and application to immediacy behaviors. *Communication Monographs, 55,* (1), 58-79.

Flora, C. (May-June 2004). The once- over you can trust: First impressions. *Psychology Today, 37* (3), 60-64.

Fisher, W. (1987). *Human communication as narration: Toward a philosophy of reason, value, and action*. Columbia: University of South Carolina Press.

Garlick, R. (1993). Verbal descriptions, communicative encounters and impressions. *Communication Quarterly*, 41, 394-404.

Glaser, E. (1992, July 14). 1992 Democratic national convention address. Speech posted at http://www.americanrhetoric.com/speeches/elizabethglaser1992dnc.htm

Johnson, L. (1964, May 22). The great society. Speech posted at http://www.americanrhetoric.com/speeches/lbjthegreatsociety.htm

Kennedy, T. (1980, August 12). 1980 democratic national convention address. Speech posted at http://www.americanrhetoric.com/speeches/tedkennedy1980dnc.htm

King, Jr., M. L. (1963, August 28). I have a dream." Speech posted at http://www.americanrhetoric.com/speeches/mlkihaveadream.htm

Lehrer, J. (Interviewer) & Stockdale, J. (Interviewee). (1999). Debating our Destiny: Admiral James Stockdale. Retrieved from http://www.pbs.org/newshour/spc/debatingourdestiny/interviews/stockdale.html

Lincoln. A. (1863, November 19). The Gettysburg address. Speech posted at http://www.americanrhetoric.com/speeches/gettysburgaddress.htm

Reagan, R. (1989, January 11). Farewell address to the nation. Speech posted at http://www.americanrhetoric.com/speeches/ronaldreaganfarewelladdress.html

Richards, A. (1998, July 19). Democratic national convention keynote address. Speech posted at http://www.americanrhetoric.com/speeches/annrichards1988dnc.htm

Schenck v. United States, 249 US 47 (1919).

Stockdale, J. (1992, October 19). The 1992 vice presidential debate. Speech posted at http://www.debates.org/index.php?page=october-13-1992-debate-transcript

Townsend, C. (2007, February 5). Spring break in Mexico. Speech posted at http://msustr0.campus.mnsu.edu:8080/cah/gorgias/333/MMS/Cassie.wmv

photo credits

p. 4 Bono at the National Prayer Breakfast by Paul Morse http://commons.wikimedia.org/wiki/File:National_prayer_breakfast_2006.jpg

p. 5 Kelly McCann by schipulites http://www.everystockphoto.com/photo.php?imageId=2101671&searchId=117192ced800c1f4d61c5a6c55f6ee64&npos=4

p. 5 Justice Oliver Wendell Holmes by National Photo Company http://commons.wikimedia.org/wiki/File:Justice_Oliver_Wendell_Holmes_standing.jpg

p. 6 President Ronald Reagan by White House Photographic Office http://upload.wikimedia.org/wikipedia/commons/7/73/Reagan_farewell_salute.jpg

p. 7 Laughing Audience by Damian Buonamico http://commons.wikimedia.org/wiki/File:Audience_enjoy_Stallman%27s_jokes.jpg

p. 7 Governor Ann Richards by Kenneth Zirkel http://commons.wikimedia.org/wiki/File:Ann_Richards.jpg

p. 8 Ed Miliband by net_efekt http://www.everystockphoto.com/photo.php?imageId=2282400&searchId=d1715ef c5a67ac1c988152b8136e3dfa&npos=37

p. 8 Woman with Laptop by Matthew Bowden http://commons.wikimedia.org/wiki/File: Woman-typing-on-laptop.jpg

p. 9 LBJ at the University of Michigan Commencement by LBJ Library and Museum http://commons.wikimedia.org/wiki/File:LBJ_at_the_University_of_Michigan.jpg

p. 10 President Johnson's Poverty Tour 1964 by Cecil Saughton http://commons.wikimedia.org/wiki/File:225-9-wh64_small.jpg

p. 10 Woman speaks at BP Oil Flood Protest New Orleans by Derek Bridges http://commons.wikimedia.org/wiki/File:BP_Oil_Flood_Protest_in_New_Orleans_30.jpg

p. 11 Martin Luther King March on Washington by National Archives and Records Administration http://commons.wikimedia.org/wiki/File:Martin_Luther_King_-_March_on_Washington.jpg

p. 11 Kyung-wha Khang Deputy High Commissioner for Human Rights by U.S. Mission Geneva http://www.everystockphoto.com/photo.php?imageId=7527423&searchId=488e81758eb12a809a21e316d0f1ab1b&npos=205

* All other photos from Microsoft Clipart

Attributions

CC licensed content, Shared previously

- Chapter 9 Glossary and References. **Authored by**: Warren Sandmann, Ph.D.. **Provided by**: Minnesota State University, Mankato, MN. **Located at**: http://publicspeakingproject.org/psvirtualtext.html. **Project**: The Public Speaking Project. **License**: *CC BY-NC-ND: Attribution-NonCommercial-NoDerivatives*

Chapter 8: Visual Aids

Objectives and Introduction

Visual Aids

By Sheila Kasperek, MLIS, MSIT
Mansfield University, Mansfield, PA

Learning Objectives
After reading this chapter, you should be able to: • Identify when and how visual aids will enhance a presentation • Identify the different types of visual aids • Identify effective and ineffective use of visual aids • Apply basic design principles to slide design • Identify best practices to incorporating visual aids in a presentation

Introduction

"I know you can't read this from the back there," the presenter apologizes to a screen so full of words you would think the entire speech had been crammed into one slide. This is just the first of a seemingly endless string of slides I can't read, charts so full of numbers I can't decipher the meaning, and clip art so clichéd I can't help but roll my eyes and sigh. It is not long before I'm presented with an incredibly dense graph I can't make any sense of since he keeps interrupting my concentration with actual talking. "When is he going to come to the point already?" I think to myself as I start to doodle in the margins of the handout of the PowerPoint slides for the very talk I'm cur-

rently sitting through. Why did he even bother with a presentation? He could have just emailed us all of the handout and saved us from this painful, dull spectacle. As he reads from his slides and belabors his statistics, my mind drifts to grocery lists and the upcoming weekend. I can think of a hundred better uses for an hour.

It seems nearly impossible to see a presentation that doesn't revolve around a lengthy PowerPoint, so much so that you might think it was a requirement for giving a speech. The phrase "death by PowerPoint" was coined in response to the ubiquitous, wordy, and intellectually deadening presentations that focus on the slides rather than the content or the presenter. With the speaker reading directly from the slides, or worse, showing slides with text so small that it can't be read, viewers are often left wondering what the need for the presentation is at all. A simple handout would convey the message and save everyone's time. PowerPoint, however, is just one of the visual aids available to you as a speaker. Your ability to incorporate the right visual aid at the right time and in the right format can have a powerful effect on your audience. Because your message is the central focus of your speech, you only want to add visual aids that enhance your message, clarify the meaning of your words, target the emotions of your audience, and/or show what words fail to clearly describe.

A visual image is a simple thing, a picture that enters the eyes. – Roy H. Williams

Learning how to create effective visuals that resonate with your audience is important for a quality presentation. Understanding basic principles of how visual information is processed alone and in combination with audio information can make or break your visuals' effectiveness and impact. Incorporating visuals into your speech that complement your words rather than stand in place of them or distract from them, will set you apart from other presenters, increase your credibility, and make a bigger and more memorable impact on your audience.

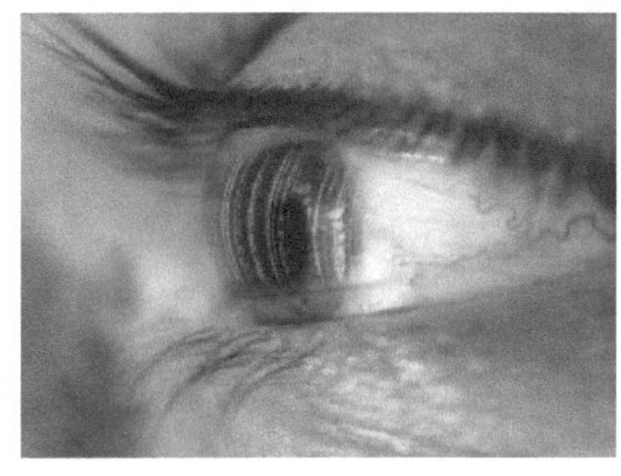

"mwdCyborgLenses" by em den. CC-BY-NC-SA.

Attributions

CC licensed content, Shared previously

- Chapter 13 Objectives, Outline, and Introduction. **Authored by**: Sheila Kasperek, MLIS, MSIT. **Provided by**: Mansfield University, Mansfield, PA. **Located at**: http://publicspeakingproject.org/psvirtualtext.html. **Project**: The Public Speaking Project. **License**: *CC BY-NC-ND: Attribution-NonCommercial-NoDerivatives*

- Grifo mu00e1gico. **Authored by**: emijrp. **Located at**: http://commons.wikimedia.org/wiki/File:Grifo_m%C3%A1gico.JPG. **License**: *CC BY-SA: Attribution-ShareAlike*

- mwdCyborgLenses. **Authored by**: emden09. **Located at**: https://www.flickr.com/photos/emden09/16356102352/. **License**: *CC BY-NC-SA: Attribution-NonCommercial-ShareAlike*

Effective Visual Aids

Before you just open up PowerPoint and begin creating slides, you should stop for a moment and consider what type of visual aid will best serve your purpose and if you even need an aid at all. Select a visual aid that adds to your presentation in a meaningful way, not merely something pretty to look at or a substitute for thorough preparation. Visuals are not there for you to hide behind when you are in front of your audience. Because of the tendency for novice speakers to use visuals as a crutch in their speeches, it has even been suggested that beginner speakers be forbidden from using visual aids while they are learning to present.[1]

"Cake depicting a cheeseburger" **by Michael Prudhomme.** *CC-BY-SA.*

Visual aids serve a unique role in a presentation, and you should consider the specific purpose and desired outcome of your speech when determining if, when, to what extent, and in what format you use visual aids.

Visuals can spark interest, build emotional connections, clarify your words, explain abstract ideas, help draw conclusions, or increase understanding. For instance, a speaker may show a stacks of books to represent the amount of data storage in a speech about the evolution of computers; or demonstrate the proper use of ear plugs by distributing ear plugs, showing how to insert them, and then blasting an air horn in a speech about preventing hearing loss in order to make the value of ear protection more memorable and concrete. Done well—simple, visible, relevant, memorable, and audience-focused— visual aids can have a profound impact on your audience and your overall message.

Visual aids can be an important part of conveying your message effectively since people learn far more by hearing and seeing than through hearing or seeing alone.[2] The brain processes verbal and visual information separately. By helping the audience build visual and verbal memories, they are more likely to be

1. Palmer, E. (2011). *Well spoken: Teaching speaking to all students.* Portland, ME: Stenhouse Publishers.
2. Vasile, A. J. (2004). *Speak with confidence: A practical guide* (9th ed.). Boston, MA: Pearson.

able to remember the information at a later time.[3] If you can find a visual aid to complement what you are saying, you will help your audience understand the information you are presenting and remember your message. For example, a speaker might show the proper and improper ways to bow when being introduced in Japan while at the same time talking about the movements and also displaying a slide with the appropriate angles and postures for bowing. By using multiple modes in concert with each other, the message is strengthened by the pairing of words, images, and movement.

Not just any visual will do, however. Each visual should be relevant to your message, convey an important point, be clearly understandable, and be visible by your entire audience. Visuals should be used to make concepts easier to understand and to reinforce your message. They should illustrate important points that are otherwise hard to understand.[4]

Use visuals for speeches about processes, products, or demonstrations of how to do something, such as a diagram of how email is delivered in a speech about computer security. Use visuals when you need to explain things you cannot see because they are hidden or abstract, like a model of your internal organs in a speech about gastric bypass surgery. Use them when you need to grab your audience's attention or stir their emotions. A speaker could use a photo of a starving child and a bag of rice that represents the daily calorie intake of a poor child in a speech about food insecurity to create a visceral reaction in the audience. As they say, a picture is worth a thousand words, so use images to tell a story or create a visual metaphor. Visual metaphors are useful when trying to evoke an emotion, such as showing an image of someone running or diving into a pool when you want to evoke action on the part of your audience. The images convey the message to "get going" or "dive in." When talking about numbers or statistics, use visuals to provide context, comparison, and to help your audience understand the meaning of data. Done well, graphs can convey data.[5] While there are many possible reasons to use visuals in your presentation, your guiding principle should be: does this make the message clearer or more memorable? If you cannot answer with a resounding "YES!" then re-think the plan for your visuals and begin again.

"Diving in the Adriatic" by melschmitz. morgueFile license.

Attributions

CC licensed content, Shared previously

- Chapter 13 Effective Visual Aids. **Authored by**: Sheila Kasperek, MLIS, MSIT. **Provided by**: Mansfield University, Mansfield, PA. **Located at**: http://publicspeakingproject.org/psvirtualtext.html. **Project**: The Public Speaking Project. **License**: *CC BY-NC-ND: Attribution-NonCommercial-NoDerivatives*

3. Malamed, C. (2009). *Visual language for designers: Principles for creating graphics that people understand.* Beverly, MA: Rockport Publishers.
4. Detz, J. (2000). *It's not what you say, it's how you say it.* New York, NY: St. Martin's Griffen; Palmer, E. (2011). *Well spoken: Teaching speaking to all students.* Portland, ME: Stenhouse Publishers; Young, K. S., & Travis, H. P. (2008). *Oral communication: Skills, choices, and consequences* (2nd ed.). Long Grove, IL: Waveland Press.
5. Malamed, C. (2009). *Visual language for designers: Principles for creating graphics that people understand.* Beverly, MA: Rockport Publishers; Palmer, E. (2011). *Well spoken: Teaching speaking to all students.* Portland, ME: Stenhouse Publishers; Tufte, E. R. (2003). *The cognitive style of PowerPoint.* Cheshire, CT: Graphics Press; Vasile, A. J. (2004). *Speak with confidence: A practical guide* (9th ed.). Boston, MA: Pearson.

- Cake depicting a cheeseburger. **Authored by**: Michael Prudhomme. **Located at**: http://commons.wikimedia.org/wiki/File:Cake_depicting_a_cheeseburger.jpg. **License**: *CC BY-SA: Attribution-ShareAlike*

- Diving in the Adriatic. **Authored by**: melschmitz. **Provided by**: MorgueFile. **Located at**: http://mrg.bz/SMkUNQ. **License**: *Other*. **License Terms**: You are allowed to copy, distribute, transmit the work and to adapt the work. Attribution is not required. You are prohibited from using this work in a stand alone manner.

Types of Visual Aids

In the past, transparencies displayed with overhead projectors, posters, and flip charts were common visual aids, but these have mostly been replaced with computer technology. For many people, the term "visual aids" for presentations or speeches is synonymous with PowerPoint (often long, dry, painful PowerPoint at that), but this is just one type of visual aid. You should consider all the available options to determine what will be most effective and appropriate for your presentation.

> If you wear clothes that don't suit you, you're a fashion victim. You have to wear clothes that make you look better. – Vivienne Westwood

Personal Appearance

Some people chose to dress up as part of their presentation, and this can help set the tone of the speech or reinforce a specific point. A speaker may choose to wear a handmade sweater in a talk about knitting in order to inspire others to begin the hobby. Another speaker may opt for a firefighter's uniform in a speech about joining the local volunteer fire department in an effort to appeal to the respect most people have for people in uniform.

If you aren't dressing in relation to your topic, you should dress appropriately for your audience and venue. A presentation to a professional audience or at a professional conference would lend itself to appropriate business attire. If you are giving a presentation to your local Girl Scout troop, more casual clothing may be the best choice. Any time you are doing a demonstration, make sure you are dressed appropriately to give the demonstration. It is difficult for a speaker to show how to correctly put on a rock climbing harness if she is wearing a skirt the day of the presentation.

"Firefighters Onboard Royal Navy Destroyer HMS Edinburgh" **by UK Ministry of Defence.** *CC-BY-NC.*

Beyond dressing appropriately for your audience and topic, the audience will make judgments about you even before your presentation begins. Your dress, mannerisms, the way you greet the audience when they are arriving, how you are introduced, and the first words out of your mouth all impact your credibility and ability to connect with your audience. Make sure you are calm and welcoming to your audience when they arrive and greet them in a professional manner. Your credibility and professionalism suffer when the audience arrives and you are busy scrambling around attempting to finish your preparations.[1]

Objects and Props

Objects and props, such as a bicycle helmet for a speech on bike safety or an actual sample of the product you are trying to sell, can greatly enhance your presentation. Seeing the actual item will often make it easier for your audience to understand your meaning and will help you connect with your audience on an emotional level. Props can be used as part of demonstrations (discussed below) or as a stand-alone item that you refer to in your speech.

"Honestly I Don't Remember Much from This Lecture" **by Daniel Lu.**

There are several important considerations for using props in your presentation. If you have a large audience, showing the prop at the front of the venue may mean that audience members can't see the item. The alternative to this is to pass the item around, though Young and Travis[2] advise caution in passing objects around during your speech, as most people will be seeing the object after you have moved on with your talk. Having your prop out of sync with your presentation, either as it is passed around disrupting your audience's attention or by having your prop visible when you aren't talking about it, is distracting to your audience and message. To make the most effective use of props in your presentation, carefully consider how the object will be visible to your entire audience when you are speaking about it, and make sure it is out of sight when you are not.

1. Duarte, N. (2010). *Resonate: Present visual stories that transform audiences.* Hoboken, NJ: John Wiley & Sons.
2. Young, K. S., & Travis, H. P. (2008). *Oral communication: Skills, choices, and consequences* (2nd ed.). Long Grove, IL: Waveland Press.

Demonstration

A demonstration can serve two different purposes in a speech. First, it can be used to "wow" the audience. Showing off the features of your new product, illustrating the catastrophic failure of a poorly tied climbing knot, or launching a cork across the room during a chemistry experiment are all ways of capturing the audience's attention. Demonstration should not be gimmicky, but should add value to your presentation. When done well, it can be the memorable moment from your speech, so make sure it reinforces the central message of your talk.

"A dad teaches his daughter the hula hoop at the 2011 Downton Cuckoo Fair" by Anguskirk. CC-BY-NC-ND.

Demonstration can also be used to show how something is done. People have different learning styles, and a process demonstration can help visual learners better understand the concept being taught. Consider for a moment the difference between reading the instructions on how to perform CPR, watching someone perform CPR, and trying CPR on the training dummy. As evidenced by the huge number of online videos illustrating how to do something, there is great value in watching while you learn a new task.

If your presentation includes a process where seeing will improve understanding, consider including a demonstration.

Because you have a limited time to present, make sure your demonstrations are succinct, well rehearsed, and visible to the entire audience. Be prepared for the demonstration to fail and have a back-up plan in place. It is better to move forward with your presentation than to fret with trying to get your demonstration perfect or fixed. However, if you are providing a demonstration of your new product, make sure it is as error free as possible. If you can't be positive the product will perform as expected, it is better to skip the demonstration.

Posters and Flip Charts

If you are presenting to a small audience, around a dozen people, you may choose to use a poster rather than PowerPoint. The focus of your poster should be to support your core message and can be left behind to remind those in attendance of your presentation after you have left. Posters should look professional (e.g., not handwritten), be visible to everyone in the room, and follow design rules covered later in this chapter. Before your presentation, you should ask whether posters must be hung or be free standing. For posters that will be hung from a wall, sturdy poster or matte boards will suffice. If your poster is going to be free standing or if you are going to use the same poster for multiple presentations, you should consider using a tri-fold display board.

Other text-based visual aids include white boards and flip charts. Both can be used to write or draw on during the presentation and should be used with several caveats. Writing during your presentation actually takes away from your speaking time, so make sure to factor this into your speaking time. Speaking and writing at the same time can be tricky because the audience will have a difficult time processing what they are hearing when they are also trying to read what you write. Additionally, if you are writing, you need to be careful not to turn your back on your audience, which is makes it harder for them to hear you and for you to connect with your audience. Legible handwriting that can be seen at a distance is of prime importance, so using these

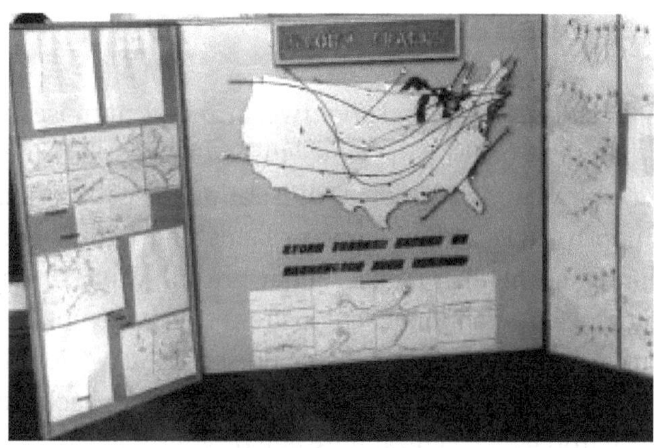

"Dad's Jr. Year Science Fair Project" **by Rev. Xanatos Satanicos Bombasticos.** CC-BY-NC-SA.

kinds of visual aids should be limited to small audiences. While some speakers write and draw to highlight important points, this takes an enormous amount of skill and practice. For those with less developed skills, flip charts are best limited to situations where audience input is necessary for the direction or continuation of the presentation.[3]

The soul never thinks without a picture. – Aristotle

Audio and Video

A large amount of digitized audio and video is now available to be included and embedded in your presentation. Select short clips; Young and Travis[4] recommend only 10–20 seconds, but this will depend in part on the length of the presentation, the purpose of the presentation, and clip content and relevance. You should not have a presentation primarily composed of audio/video clips. Select only clips that reinforce the message or serve as an appropriate segue into your next topic.

When including audio or video in your speech, there are several technical considerations. It is important that the clip be properly cued to start at exactly where you want it to begin playing. It distracts from both your audience's attention and your credibility when you are fumbling with technology during a speech. It is also important that your file format can be played on the computer you are using. Since not all computers will play all file formats, be sure to test playability and audio volume before your presentation. Again, going back to providing a professional appearance from your first interaction with your audience, you should iron out the technical details before they enter the room. As with a demonstration, if your clip isn't playing properly, move on rather than attempt to correct the issue. Fumbling with technology is a waste of your audience's valuable time.

3. Duarte, N. (2008). *Slide:ology: The art and science of creating great presentations.* Sebastopol, CA : O'Reilly Media.
4. Young, K. S., & Travis, H. P. (2008). *Oral communication: Skills, choices, and consequences* (2nd ed.). Long Grove, IL: Waveland Press.

Handouts

There are many schools of thought on the use of handouts during a presentation. The most common current practice is that the presenters provide a copy of their PowerPoint slides to the participants before or after the presentation. This is so common that some academic and professional conferences require presenters to submit their slides prior to the event, so copies of the slides can be made for each attendee. Despite this prevailing trend, you should avoid using your slides as handouts because they serve different purposes. Using your presentation slides as the handout both shortchanges your slides and fails as a handout.

Handouts are best used to supplement the content of your talk. If you are providing statistical data, your slide may only show the relevant statistic focusing on the conclusion you want your audience to draw. Your handout, on the other hand, can contain the full table of data. If you need to show a complex diagram or chart, a handout will be more legible than trying to cram all that information on a slide. Since you need to simplify the data to make it understandable on a slide, the handout can contain the evidence for your message in a way that is legible, detailed, complex, and shows respect for the audience's time and intelligence.[5]

"Lt. Lydia Battey distributes handouts" **by Kerryl Cacho. Public domain.**

You don't need to include everything in your talk, and you don't need to pack all your information into your slides. Write a handout document with as much detail as you want and keep the slides simple. Presenters often feel the need to display all the data and information they have so they will appear knowledgeable, informed, and thoroughly prepared. You can help ease this feeling by creating a handout with all of the detailed data you wish, which leaves your slides open to focus on your key message.[6]

> There are many true statements about complex topics that are too long to fit on a PowerPoint slide. – Edward Tufte

Crafting an appropriate handout will take additional time for the presenter, but doing so will result in a take-away document that will stand on its own and a slide show that focuses on effective visual content. Duarte (2008) and Tufte (2003) recommend handouts only for dense, detailed information. Reynolds[7] expands on this idea, noting that your handout needs to be complete enough to stand in your place since you won't be there to present the information or answer questions.

When to distribute handouts is also heavily debated. So common is the practice of providing handouts at the beginning of a presentation that it may seem wrong to break the convention. It is important to understand, however, that if people have paper in front of them while you are speaking, their attention will be split between the handout, your other visual aids, and your words. To counter this, you might consider distributing handouts as they are needed during the presentation and allowing time for people to review them

5. Tufte, E. R. (2003). *The cognitive style of PowerPoint*. Cheshire, CT: Graphics Press.
6. Reynolds, G. (2008). *Presentation Zen: Simple ideas on presentation design and delivery*. Berkeley, CA: New Riders.
7. Reynolds, G. (2008). *Presentation Zen: Simple ideas on presentation design and delivery*. Berkeley, CA: New Riders.

before continuing on.[8] This may not be a viable option for shorter presentations, and the interruption in the flow of the presentation may be hard to recover from. Unless having the documents in front of your audience is absolutely critical to the success of the presentation, handouts should be distributed at the end of the presentation.

Slideware

Slideware is a generic term for the software used create and display slide shows such as *Microsoft PowerPoint, Apple iWorks Keynote, Google Drive Presentation, Zoho Show* and others. Composed of individual slides, collectively known as the **slide deck**, slideware is a de facto standard for presentation visual aids despite criticisms and complaints about the format. In truth, the problem is not with the software but in the use of the program. The focus of much of the remainder of this chapter will be suggestions and best practices for creating effective slide decks that will be high impact and avoid many of the complaints of slideware detractors. Before this discussion, there are two distinct slideware presentation styles that should be mentioned.

"Steve Jobs Presentation" by *Ken.gz.* CC-BY.

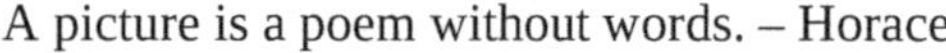
A picture is a poem without words. – Horace

Pecha Kucha

Pecha Kucha is a method of presenting using a slide deck of 20 slides that display for 20 seconds per slide, advance automatically, and generally contain no text.[9] This method began in 2003 as a way to contain the length of presentations of architects and continues to grow in popularity, but is still reserved mostly for people in creative industries.[10] Because of the restrictive format, Pecha Kucha-style presentations help the speaker practice editing, pacing, connecting with the audience, focusing on the message, and using images in place of words.[11]

Prezi

While not quite slideware, **Prezi** is digital presentation software that breaks away from the standard slide deck presentation. It requires users to plot out their themes before adding primarily image-focused content.[12] Instead of flipping through the slide deck, the presenter zooms in and out of the presentation to

8. Vasile, A. J. (2004). *Speak with confidence: A practical guide* (9th ed.). Boston, MA: Pearson.
9. Duarte, N. (2008). *Slide:ology: The art and science of creating great presentations.* Sebastopol, CA : O'Reilly Media.
10. Lehtonen, M. (2011). Communicating competence through PechaKucha presentations. *Journal of Business Communication, 48*(4), 464–481.
11. Beyer, A. (2011). Improving student presentations: Pecha Kucha and just plain PowerPoint. *Teaching of Psychology, 38*(2), 122–126.
12. Panag, S. (2010). A Web 2.0 Toolkit for Educators. *Youth Media Reporter*, 489–91.

visually demonstrate connections not available in other slideware. The design of the software lends itself toward more rapidly changing visuals. This helps to keep the viewer engaged but also lends itself to over-populating the blank canvas with images.[13]

Prezi's fast moving images and, at times, unusual movement can make users dizzy or disoriented. Careful work is needed during planning and practice so that the point of the talk isn't the wow factor of the Prezi software, but that your visuals enhance your presentation. The best way to learn more about this emerging tool is to visit the Prezi website to view examples.

If opting to use Prezi in a corporate environment, you should strongly consider one of the paid options for the sole purpose of removing the Prezi logo from the presentation.

Attributions

CC licensed content, Shared previously

Public domain content

---

13. Yee, K., & Hargis, J. (2010). PREZI: A different way to present. *Turkish Online Journal of Distance Education (TOJDE)*, *11*(4), 9–11.

Design Principles

Slide and slide show design have a major impact on your ability to get your message across to your audience. Numerous books address various design fundamentals and slide design, but there isn't always consensus on what is "best." What research has shown, though, is that people have trouble grasping information when it comes at them simultaneously. "They will either listen to you or read your slides; they cannot do both."[1] This leaves you, the presenter, with a lot of power to direct or scatter your audience's attention. This section will serve as an overview of basic design considerations that even novices can use to improve their slides.

First and foremost, design with your audience in mind. Your slide show is not your outline. The show is also not your handout. As discussed earlier, you can make a significantly more meaningful, content-rich handout that complements your presentation if you do not try to save time by making a slide show that serves as both. Keep your slides short, create a separate handout if needed, and write as many notes for yourself as you need.

All decisions, from the images you use to their placement, should be done with a focus on your message, your medium, and your audience. Each slide should reinforce or enhance your message, so

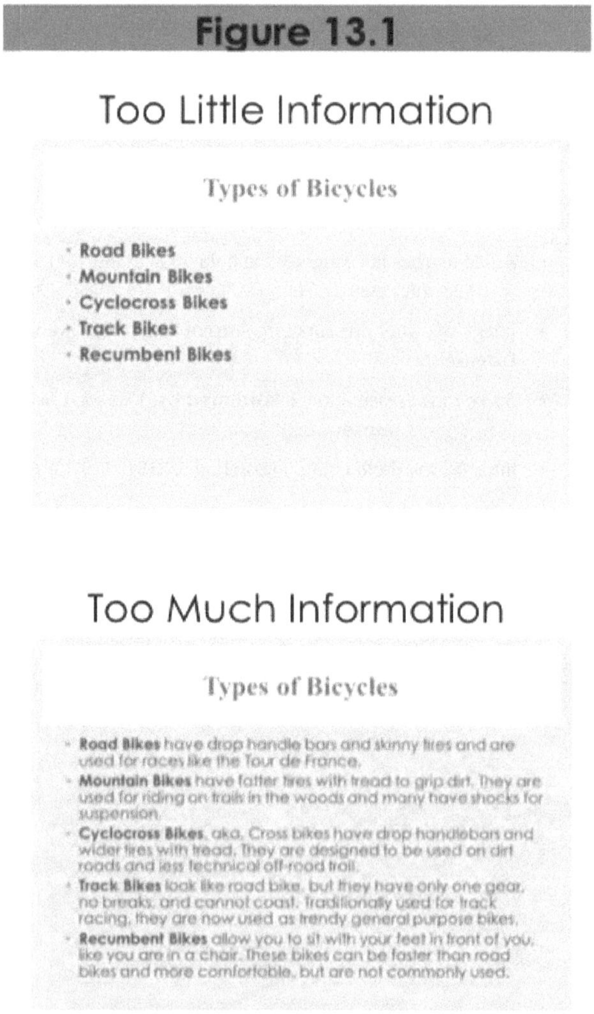

Figure 13.1

Too Little Information

Types of Bicycles

- Road Bikes
- Mountain Bikes
- Cyclocross Bikes
- Track Bikes
- Recumbent Bikes

Too Much Information

Types of Bicycles

- **Road Bikes** have drop handle bars and skinny tires and are used for races like the Tour de France.
- **Mountain Bikes** have fatter tires with tread to grip dirt. They are used for riding on trails in the woods and many have shocks for suspension.
- **Cyclocross Bikes**, aka. Cross bikes have drop handlebars and wider tires with tread. They are designed to be used on dirt roads and less technical off-road trail.
- **Track Bikes** look like road bike, but they have only one gear, no breaks, and cannot coast. Traditionally used for track racing, they are now used as trendy general purpose bikes.
- **Recumbent Bikes** allow you to sit with your feet in front of you, like you are in a chair. These bikes can be faster than road bikes and more comfortable, but are not commonly used.

Figure 13.1 by the Public Speaking Project. *CC-BY-NC-ND*.

1. Duarte, N. (2008). *Slide:ology: The art and science of creating great presentations.* Sebastopol, CA : O'Reilly Media.

make conscious decisions about each element and concept you include[2] and edit mercilessly. Taken a step further, graphic designer Robin Williams[3] suggests each element be placed on the slide deliberately in relation to every other element on the slide.

Providing the right amount of information, neither too much nor too little, is one of the key aspects in effective communication.[4] See Figure 13.1 as an example of slides with too little or too much information. The foundation of this idea is that if the viewers have too little information, they must struggle to put the pieces of the presentation together. Most people, however, include too much information (e.g., slides full of text, meaningless images, overly complicated charts), which taxes the audience's ability to process the message. "There is simply a limit to a person's ability to process new information efficiently and effectively."[5] As a presenter, reducing the amount of information directed at your audience (words, images, sounds, etc.) will help them to better remember your message.[6] In this case, less is actually more.

The first strategy to keeping it simple is to include only one concept or idea per slide. If you need more than one slide, use it, but don't cram more than one idea on a slide. While many have tried to proscribe the number of slides you need based on the length of your talk, there is no formula that works for every presentation. Use only the number of slides necessary to communicate your message, and make sure the number of slides corresponds to the amount of time allotted for your speech. Practice with more and fewer slides and more and less content on each slide to find the balance between too much information and too little.

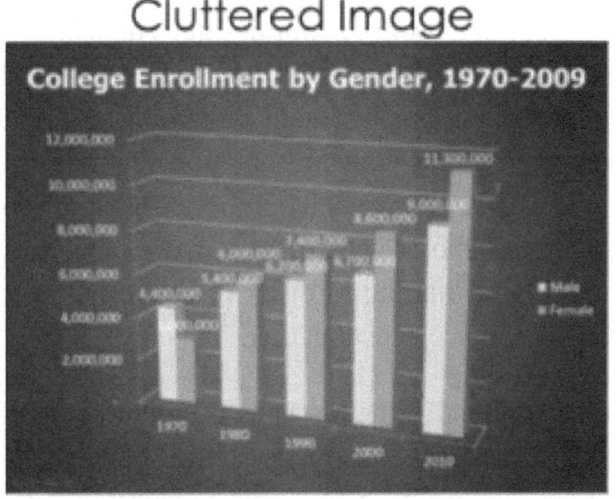

Figure 13.2 by the Public Speaking Project. CC-BY-NC-ND.

With simplicity in mind, the goal is to have a slide that can be understood in 3 seconds. Think of it like a billboard you are passing on the highway.[7] You can achieve this by reducing the amount of irrelevant information, also known as **noise**, in your slide as much as possible. This might include eliminating background images, using clear icons and images, or creating simplified graphs. Your approach should be to remove as much from your slide as possible until it no longer makes any sense if you remove more.[8]

2. Reynolds, G. (2008). *Presentation Zen: Simple ideas on presentation design and delivery.* Berkeley, CA: New Riders.
3. Williams, R. (2004). *The nondesigner's design book: Design and typographic principles for the visual novice* (2nd ed.). Berkeley, CA: Peachpit Press.
4. Kosslyn, S. M. (2007). *Clear and to the point: 8 psychological principles for compelling PowerPoint presentations.* New York, NY: Oxford University Press.
5. Reynolds 2008
6. Mayer, R. E. (2001). *Multimedia learning.* Cambridge, UK: Cambridge University Press.
7. Duarte, N. (2010). *Resonate: Present visual stories that transform audiences.* Hoboken, NJ: John Wiley & Sons.
8. Reynolds 2008

Slide Layout

It is easy to simply open up your slideware and start typing in the bullet points that outline your talk. If you do this, you will likely fall into the traps for which PowerPoint is infamous. Presentation design experts Reynolds[9] and Duarte[10] both recommend starting with paper and pen. This will help you break away from the text-based, bullet-filled slide shows we all dread. Instead, consider how you can turn your words and concepts into images. Don't let the software lead you into making a mediocre slide show.

Regarding slide design, focus on simplicity. Don't over-crowd your slide with text and images. Cluttered slides are hard to understand (see Figure 13.2). Leaving empty space, also known as **white space**, gives breathing room to your design. The white space actually draws attention to your focus point and makes your slide appear more elegant and professional. Using repetition of color, font, images, and layout throughout your presentation will help tie all of your slides together. This is especially important if a group is putting visuals together collaboratively. If you have handouts, they should also match this formatting in order to convey a more professional look and tie all your pieces together.[11]

Another general principle is to use contrast to highlight your message. Contrast should not be subtle. Make type sizes significantly different. Make contrasting image placements, such as horizontal and vertical, glaringly obvious. A general principle to follow: if things are not the same, then make them very, very different,[12] as in Figure 13.3.

A common layout design is called the **rule of thirds**. If you divide the screen using two imaginary lines horizontally and two vertically, you end up with nine sections. The most visually interesting and pleasing portions of the screen will be at the points where the lines intersect.

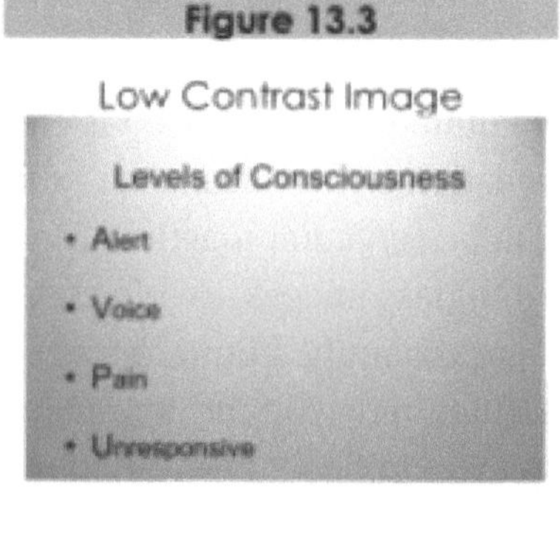

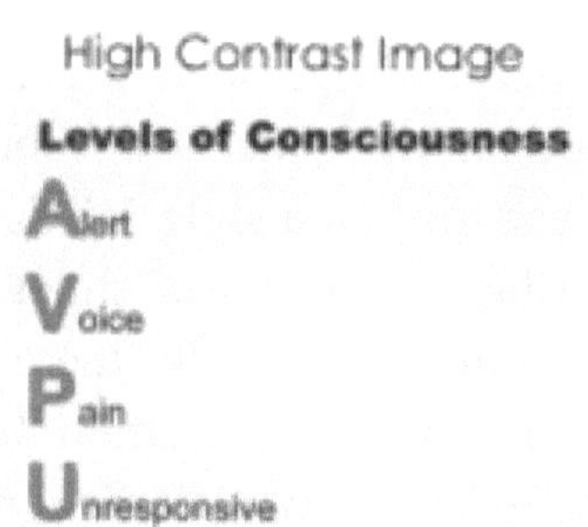

Figure 13.3 by the Public Speaking Project. CC-BY-NC-ND.

9. Reynolds 2008
10. Duarte 2010
11. Reynolds 2008
12. Williams 2004

Figure 13.4 by the Public Speaking Project. CC-BY-NC-ND.

Figure 13.5 by the Public Speaking Project. CC-BY-NC-ND.

Figure 13.6 by the Public Speaking Project. CC-BY-NC-ND.

Aligning your text and images with these points is preferred to centering everything on the screen.[13][14] See Figure 13.4. Feel free to experiment with the right and left aligned content for contrast and interest. Sticking with a centered layout means more work trying to make the slide interesting.[15]

Understanding how people view images (and thus slides) can help you direct the viewer's attention to the main point of your slide. In countries that read text from left to right and top to bottom, like English-speaking countries, people tend to also read images and slides the same way. Starting in the upper left of the screen, they read in a **Z pattern**, exiting the page in the bottom right corner unless their vision is sidetracked by the objects they are looking at (as in Figure 13.5).

Viewers' eyes are scanning from focus point to focus point in an image, so you need to consciously create visual cues to direct them to the relevant information. Cues can be created subtly by the placement of objects in the slide, by showing movement, or more obviously by using a simple arrow.[16] Make sure all people and pets are facing into your slide and preferably at your main point, as in Figure 13.6. If your slide contains a road, path, car, plane, etc., have them also facing into your slide. When the natural motion or gaze of your images points away from your slide, your viewers look that way too. Being aware of this and addressing the natural tendencies of people when viewing images can help you select images and design slides that keep the viewer engaged in your message.[17]

13. Kadavy, D. (2011). *Design for hackers: Reverse-engineering beauty.* West Sussex, UK : John Wiley & Sons
14. Reynolds 2008
15. Williams 2004
16. Malamed, C. (2009). *Visual language for designers: Principles for creating graphics that people understand.* Beverly, MA: Rockport Publishers.
17. Duarte 2008

Backgrounds and Effects

PowerPoint and other slideware has a variety of templates containing backgrounds that are easy to implement for a consistent slide show. Most of them, however, contain distracting graphics that are counter to the simplicity you are aiming for in order to produce a clear message. It is best to use solid colors, if you even need a background at all. For some slide shows, you can make the slides with full-screen images, thus eliminating the need for a background color.

> Graphic design is the paradise of individuality, eccentricity, heresy, abnormality, hobbies and humors.
> – George Santayana

Should you choose to use a background color, make sure you are consistent throughout your presentation. Different colors portray different meanings, but much of this is cultural and contextual, so there are few hard and fast rules about the meaning of colors. One universal recommendation is to avoid the color red because it has been shown to reduce your ability to think clearly. Bright colors, such as yellow, pink, and orange, should also be avoided as background colors, as they are too distracting. Black, on the other hand, is generally associated with sophistication and can be a very effective background as long as there is sufficient contrast with the other elements on your slide.[18]

When designing your presentation, it is tempting to show off your tech skills with glitzy transitions, wipes, fades, moving text, sounds, and a variety of other actions. These are distracting to your audience and should be avoided. They draw attention away from you and your message, instead focusing the audience's attention on the screen. Since people naturally look at what is moving and expect it to mean something, meaningless effects, no matter how subtle, distract your audience, and affect their ability to grasp the content. Make sure that all your changes are meaningful and reinforce your message[19].

Colors

There are complicated and fascinating biological and psychological processes associated with color and color perception that are beyond the scope of this chapter. Because color can have such a huge impact on the ability to see and understand your visuals, this section will explore basic rules and recommendations for working with color.

> Color does not add a pleasant quality to design—it reinforces it. – Pierre Bonnard

Much of what we perceive in terms of a color is based on what color is next to it. Be sure to use colors that contrast so they can be easily distinguished from each other (think yellow and dark blue

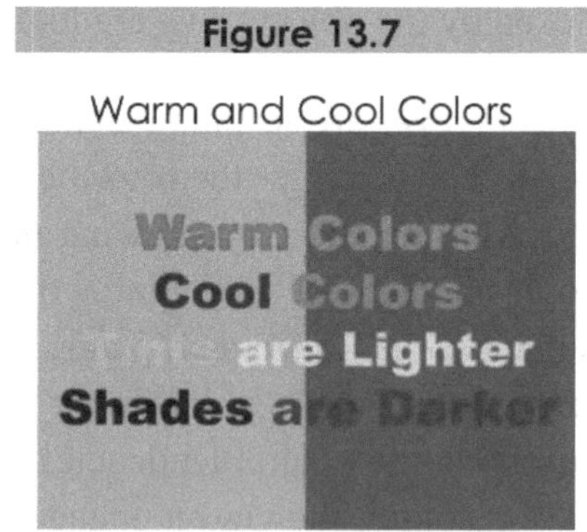

Figure 13.7 by the Public Speaking Project. CC-BY-NC-ND.

18. Kadavy 2011
19. Duarte 2008; Kosslyn 2007

for high contrast, not dark blue and purple).High contrast improves visibility, particularly at a distance. To ensure you have sufficient contrast, you can view your presentation in **greyscale** either in the software if available or by printing out your slides on a black and white printer.[20]

As seen in Figure 13.7, warm colors (reds, oranges, yellows) appear to come to the foreground when set next to a cool color (blues, grays, purples) which recede into the background. Tints (pure color mixed with white, think pink) stand out against a darker background. Shades (pure color mixed with black, think maroon) recede into a light background.[21] If you want something to stand out, these color combination rules can act as a guide.

Avoid using red and green closely together. Red-green color blindness is the predominate form of color blindness, meaning that the person cannot distinguish between those two colors (Vorick, 2011). There are other forms of color blindness, and you can easily check to see if your visuals will be understandable to everyone using an online tool such as the Coblis Color Blindness Simulator to preview images as a color-blindperson would see it. Certain red-blue pairings can be difficult to look at for the non-color blind. These colors appear to vibrate when adjacent to each other and are distracting and sometimes unpleasant to view.[22]

With all these rules in place, selecting a **color palette**, the group of colors to use throughout your presentation, can be daunting. Some color pairs, like **complementary colors** or **analogous colors** as in Figure 13.8, are naturally pleasing to the eye and can be easy options for the color novice. There are also online tools for selecting pleasing color palettes using standard color pairings including Kuler and Color Scheme Designer. You can also use websites like Colorbrewer to help identify an appropriate palette of colors that are visually distinct, appropriate for the colorblind, and that will photocopy well, should you decide to also include this information in a handout.

Follow this link to see the color examples discussed above:

- https://courses.lumenlearning.com/suny-fmcc-publicspeaking-principles/chapter/chapter-13-design-principles/

Figure 13.8 by the Public Speaking Project. CC-BY-NC-ND.

I'm a visual thinker, not a language-based thinker. My brain is like Google Images. – Temple Grandin

Fonts

There are thousands of fonts available today. One might even say there has been a renaissance in font design with the onset of the digital age. Despite many beautiful options, it is best to stick to standard fonts that are considered screen-friendly. These include the **serif fonts** Times New Roman, Georgia, and

20. Bajaj, G. (2007). *Cutting edge PowerPoint 2007 for dummies*. Hoboken, NJ: Wiley Publishing.
21. Kadavy 2011
22. Kosslyn 2007

Palatino, and the **sans serif** fonts Ariel, Helvetica, Tahoma, and Veranda.[23] These fonts work well with the limitations of computer screens and are legible from a distance if sized appropriately. Other non-standard fonts, while attractive and eye-catching, may not display properly on all computers. If the font isn't installed on the computer you are presenting from, the default font will be used which alters the text and design of the slide.

Readability is a top concern with font use, particularly for those at the back of your audience, furthest from the screen. After you have selected a font (see previous paragraph), make sure that the font size is large enough for everyone to read clearly. If you have the opportunity to use the presentation room before the event, view your slides from the back of the room. They should be clearly visible. This is not always possible and should not be done immediately preceding your talk, as you won't have time to effectively edit your entire presentation. Presentation guru Duarte[24] describes an ingenious way to test visibility from your own computer. Measure your monitor diagonally in inches, display your slides, then step back the same number of feet as you measured on your monitor in inches. If you have a 17 inch screen, step back 17 feet to see what is legible.

Figure 13.9

Bad Font Effects

Script Fonts

𝕯ecoratibe 𝔉onts

UPPER CASE

All Bold

SMALL CAPS

Shadows

Outlines

Word Art

Stretched

Figure 13.9 **by the Public Speaking Project.** *CC-BY-NC-ND.*

Create your own visual style… let it be unique for yourself and yet identifiable for others. – Orson Welles

In addition to font style and size, there are other font "rules" to improve your slides. Don't use decorative, script, or visually complex fonts. Never use the Comic Sans font if you want to retain any credibility with your audience. If you must use more than one font, use one serif font and one sansserif font. Use the same font(s) and size(s) consistently throughout your presentation. Don't use all upper case or all bold. Avoid small caps and all word art, shadows, outlines, stretching text, and other visual effects. Use italics and underlines only for their intended purposes, not for design. While there are many rules listed here, they can be summarized as" keep it as simple as possible."[25] See Figure 13.9 for examples of poor font choices.

Text

Nothing is more hotly debated in slide design than the amount of text that should be on a slide. Godin says "no more than six words on a slide. EVER."[26] Other common approaches include the 5×5 rule—5 lines

---

23. Kadavy 2011
24. Duarte 2008
25. Kadavy 2011; Kosslyn 2007
26. Reynolds 2008

of text, 5 words per line—and similar 6×6 and 7×7 rules.[27] Even with these recommendations, it is still painfully common to see slides with so much text on them that they can't be read by the audience. The type has to be so small to fit all the words on the slide that no one can read it. Duarte[28] keenly points out that if you have too many words, you no longer have a visual aid. You have either a paper or a teleprompter, and she recommends opting for a small number of words.

Once you understand that the words on the screen are competing for your audience's attention, it will be easier to edit your slide text down to a minimum. The next time you are watching a presentation and the slide changes, notice how you aren't really grasping what the speaker is saying, and you also aren't really understanding what you are reading. Studies have proved this split-attention affects our ability to retain information;[29] so when presenting, you need to give your audience silent reading time when you display a new slide. That is: talk, advance to your next slide, wait for them to read the slide, and resume talking. If you consider how much time your audience is reading rather than listening, hopefully you will decide to reduce the text on your slide and return the focus back to you, the speaker, and your message.

There are several ways to reduce the number of words on your page, but don't do it haphazardly. Tufte[30] warns against abbreviating your message just to make it fit. He says this dumbs down your message, which does a disservice to your purpose and insults your audience's intelligence. Instead, Duarte[31] and Reynolds[32] recommend turning as many concepts as possible into images. Studies have shown that people retain more information when they see images that relate to the words they are hearing.[33] And when people are presented information for a very short time, they remember images better than words.[34]

Tip

An easy way to judge how much time your audience needs to read your slide silently, is to read the slide text to yourself in reverse order.

The ubiquitous use of bulleted lists is also hotly debated. PowerPoint is practically designed around the bulleted-list format, even though is it regularly blamed for dull, tedious presentations with either overly dense or overly superficial content.[35] Mostly this format is used (incorrectly) as a presenter's outline. *"No one can do a good presentation with slide after slide of bullet points. No One."*[36] Reserve bulleted lists for specifications or explaining the order of processes. In all other cases, look for ways to use images, a short phrase, or even no visual at all.

27. Weaver, M. (1999). Reach out through technology: Make your point with effective A/V. *Computers in Libraries, 19*(4), 62.
28. Duarte 2008
29. Mayer 2001
30. Tufte, E. R. (2003). *The cognitive style of PowerPoint.* Cheshire, CT: Graphics Press.
31. Duarte 2008
32. Reynolds 2008
33. Mayer 2001
34. Reynolds 2008
35. Tufte 2003
36. Reynolds 2008

*Figure 13.10 by the Public Speaking Project.
CC-BY-NC-ND.*

Quotes, on the other hand, are not as offensive to design when they are short, legible, and infrequently used. They can be a very powerful way to hammer a point home or to launch into your next topic.[37] See Figure 13.10 for an example. If you do use a quote in your slide show, immediately stop and read it out loud or allow time for it to be read silently. If the quote is important enough for you to include it in the talk, the quote deserves the audience's time to read and think about it. Alternately, use a photo of the speaker or of the subject with a phrase from the quote you will be reading them, making the slide enhance the point of the quote.

Images

Images can be powerful and efficient ways to tap into your audience's emotions. Use photographs to introduce an abstract idea, to evoke emotion, to present evidence, or to direct the audience attention, just make sure it is compatible with your message.[38] Photos aren't the only images available. You might consider using simplified images like **silhouettes**, **line art**, diagrams, enlargements, or **exploded views**, but these should be high quality and relevant. Simplified can be easier to understand, particularly if you are showing something that has a lot of detail. Simple images also translate better than words to a multicultural audience.[39] In all cases, choose only images that enhance your spoken words and are professional-quality. This generally rules out the clip art that comes with slideware, whose use is a sign of amateurism. Select high-quality images and don't be afraid to use your entire slide to display the image. Boldness with images often adds impact.

When using images, do not enlarge them to the point that the image becomes blurry, also known as **pixelation**. Pixelation, (Figure 13.11) is caused when the resolution of your image is too low for your output device (e.g. printer, monitor, projector). When selecting images, look for clear ones that can be placed in

37. Reynolds 2008
38. Kosslyn 2007
39. Malamad 2009

your presentation without enlarging them. A good rule of thumb is to use images over 1,000 pixels wide for filling an entire slide. If your images begin to pixelate, either reduce the size of the image or select a different image.

Figure 13.11 **by the Public Speaking Project.** *CC-BY-NC-ND.*

Figure 13.12 **by the Public Speaking Project.** *CC-BY-NC-ND.*

Never use an image that has a **watermark** on it, as in Figure 13.2. A watermark is text or a logo that is placed in a digital image to prevent people from re-using it. It is common for companies that sell images to have a preview available that has a watermark on it. This allows you, the potential customer, to see the image, but prevents you from using the image until you have paid for it. Using a watermarked image in your presentation is unprofessional. Select another image without a watermark, take a similar photo yourself, or pay to get the watermark-free version.

You can create images yourself, use free images, or pay for images from companies like iStockphoto for your presentations. Purchasing images can get expensive quickly, and searching for free images is time consuming. Be sure to only use images that you have permission or rights to use and give proper credit for their use. If you are looking for free images, try searching the Creative Commons database for images from places like Flickr, Google, and others. The creators of images with a **Creative Commons License** allow others to use their work, but with specific restrictions. What is and isn't allowed is described in the license for each image. Generally, images can be used in educational or non-commercial settings at no cost as long as you give the photographer credit. Also, images created by the U.S. government and its agencies are copyright free and can be used at no cost.

One final consideration with using images: having the same image on every page, be it part of the slide background or your company logo, can be distracting and should be removed or minimized. As mentioned earlier, the more you can simplify your slide, the easier it will be for your message to be understood.

Graphs and Charts

If you have numerical data that you want to present, consider using a graph or chart. You are trying to make a specific point with the data on the slide, so make sure that the point—the conclusion you want your audience to draw—is clear. This may mean that you reduce the amount of data you present, even though it is tempting to include all of your data on your slide.

It is best to minimize the amount of information and focus instead on the simple and clear conclusion.[40] You can include the complete data set in your handout if you feel it is necessary.[41] Particularly when it comes to numerical data, identify the meaning in the numbers and exclude the rest. "Audiences are screaming 'make it clear,' not 'cram more in.' You won't often hear an audience member say, 'That presentation would have been so much better if it were longer.'"[42] In some cases you can even ditch the graph altogether and display the one relevant fact that is your conclusion.

40. Duarte 2008
41. Reynolds 2008
42. Duarte 2008

Figure 13.13

Complex Chart

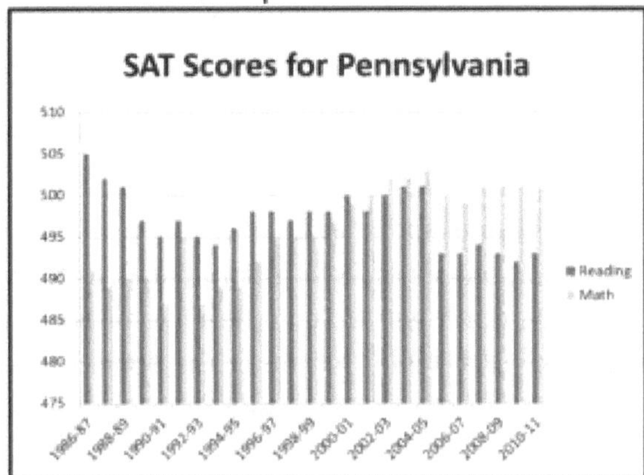

Chart

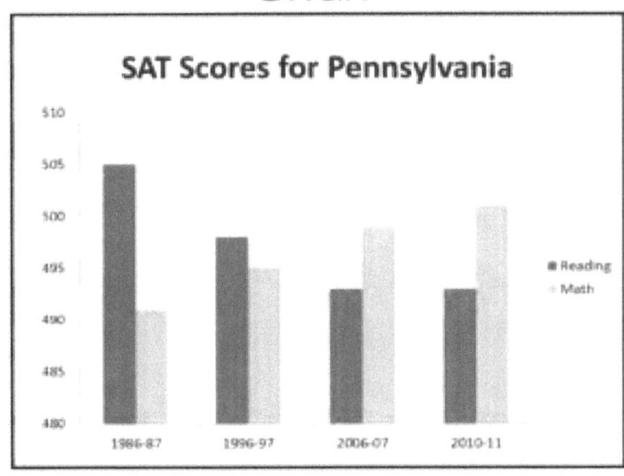

Simple Graphic

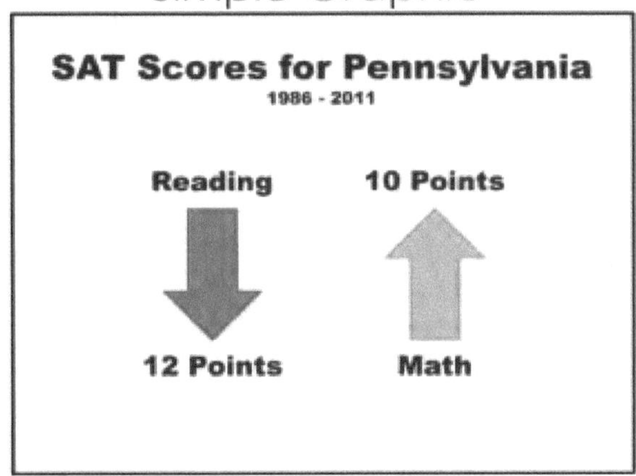

Figure 13.14

Pie Chart

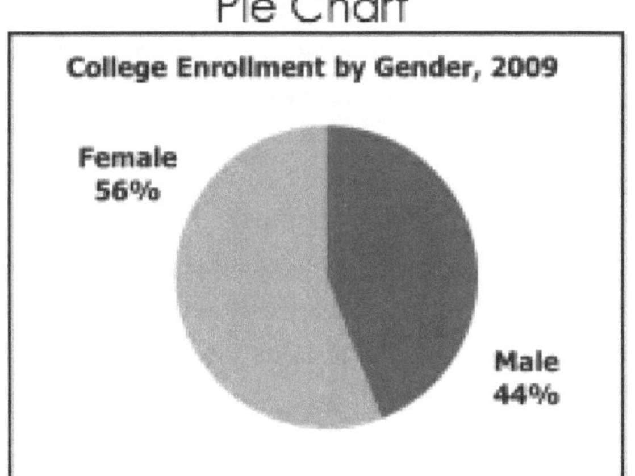

Line Graph

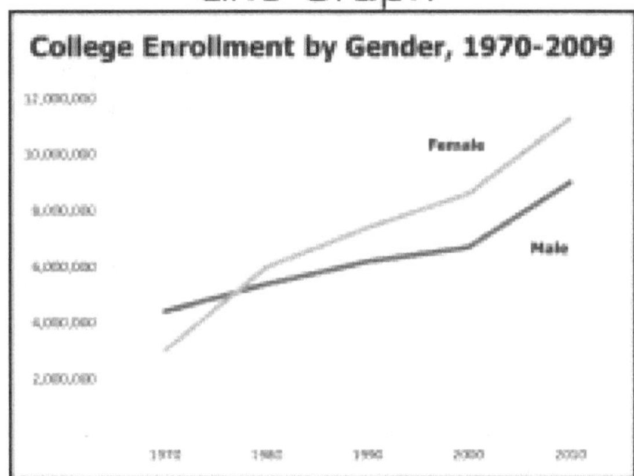

Bar Chart

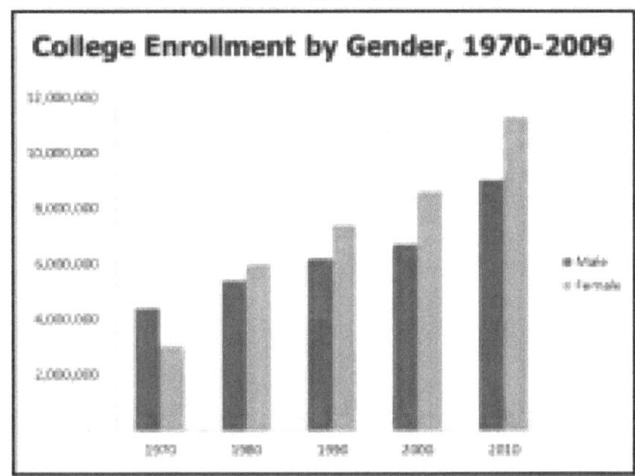

Different charts have different purposes, and it is important to select the one that puts your data in the appropriate context to be clearly understood.[43] Pie charts show how the parts relate to the whole and are suitable for up to eight segments, as long as they remain visually distinct.[44] Start your first slice of the pie at 12:00 with your smallest portion and continue around the circle clockwise as the sections increase in size. Usea line graph to show trends over time or how data relates or interacts. Bar charts are good for showing comparisons of size or magnitude[45] and for showing precise comparisons.[46] There are other types of charts and graphs available, but these are the most common.

When designing charts, one should use easily distinguishable colors with clear labels. Be consistent with your colors and data groupings.[47] For clarity, avoid using 3-D graphs and charts, and remove as much of the background noise (lines, shading, etc.) as possible.[48] All components of your graph, once the clutter is removed, should be distinct from any background color. Finally, don't get too complex in any one graph, make sure your message is as clear as possible, and make sure to visually highlight the conclusion you want the audience to draw.

Attributions

CC licensed content, Shared previously

- Chapter 13 Design Principles. **Authored by**: Sheila Kasperek, MLIS, MSIT. **Provided by**: Mansfield University, Mansfield, PA. **Located at**: http://publicspeakingproject.org/psvirtualtext.html. **Project**: The Public Speaking Project. **License**: *CC BY-NC-ND: Attribution-NonCommercial-NoDerivatives*

- Figures 13.1-13.14. **Authored by**: Sheila Kasperek and Tom Oswald . **Located at**: http://publicspeakingproject.org/psvirtual-text.html. **Project**: The Public Speaking Project. **License**: *CC BY-NC-ND: Attribution-NonCommercial-NoDerivatives*

43. Tufte 2003
44. Duarte 2008
45. Kosslyn 2007
46. Duarte 2008
47. Kosslyn 2007
48. Reynolds 2008

Implementation

If you have chosen to use visual aids in your presentation, it is important to give credit where credit is due. Make sure to mention the source of your props if you borrowed them from a person or organization. You should cite the source of all data and images used in your presentation. There are conflicting opinions about whether the source citations should be on the individual slides or at the end of the presentation on a final slide. Including citations throughout the slide deck places the source information adjacent to the relevant text, but it is often so small as to be unreadable. Placing citations at the end of your presentation reduces clutter on the slides and allows the citation information to be larger and more legible. In all cases, refer to your sources when speaking and be able to provide exact citations for anyone interested in your sources. Citing your sources provides credibility to your content and shows you are a professional.

"Astronomy Picture of the Day 2008 May 18" by NASA. Public domain.

Once you have decided on which visual aids to use and have prepared them for your presentation, you should practice with them repeatedly. Through practice you will be able to seamlessly incorporate them into your presentation, which will reduce distractions, increase your credibility, and keep the audience's attention focused on your message. Practice will also help determine the time required for your presentation so you can edit before you speak if necessary. No audience benefits from the speaker looking at the time, admitting how off schedule they are, or rushing through their remaining slides.

No matter which visual aid(s) you have chosen, they should be displayed only when you are ready to talk about them. Otherwise, the audience will spend time reading any text or guessing the meaning of the visual instead of focusing on the presenter's words. Once used, visuals should also be removed from sight so as not to continue to distract the audience.[1]

> A picture is the expression of an impression. If the beautiful were not in us, how would we ever recognize it? – Ernst Haas

Attributions

CC licensed content, Shared previously

- Chapter 13 Implementation. **Authored by**: Sheila Kasperek, MLIS, MSIT. **Provided by**: Mansfield University, Mansfield, PA. **Located at**: http://publicspeakingproject.org/psvirtualtext.html. **Project**: The Public Speaking Project. **License**: *CC BY-NC-ND: Attribution-NonCommercial-NoDerivatives*

Public domain content

- Astronomy Picture of the Day 2008 May 18. **Authored by**: Dana Berry. **Provided by**: NASA. **Located at**: http://commons.wikimedia.org/wiki/File:NASA_Astronomy_Picture_of_the_Day_2008_May_18_-_clip_01.jpg%20. **License**: *Public Domain: No Known Copyright*

1. Palmer, E. (2011). *Well spoken: Teaching speaking to all students*. Portland, ME: Stenhouse Publishers.

Visual Aid Tips

Table 13.1: Visual Aid Tips
Select only visual aids that enhance or clarify your message.
Select visual aids that will have the greatest impact on your audience.
Speak to your audience not to your visual aid or the screen.
Reveal your visuals only when they are relevant to your current point, and take them away when they are no longer being talked about.
Practice with your visual aids and make sure all demonstrations work smoothly.
Design visuals so they can be understood within three seconds.
Keep your visuals as simple as possible while still conveying your message.
When presenting text to your audience, give them time to read before you begin speaking again.
Be prepared to move on with your presentation should any of the visual aids falter or fail. No matter how great your visuals are, you need to be prepared to speak without them.

Attributions

CC licensed content, Shared previously

Conclusion, Review Questions, and Activities

Conclusion

This chapter addresses both the role and value of using visual aids, including slideware, objects, audio and video clips, and demonstrations. They should be used only when they help to clarify or enhance your spoken words or will help your audience remember your message.

Be sure that any visual aid you use adds to what you are saying. Slides should be brief, easy to understand, and complement your message. Objects and slides should not be revealed before you begin talking about them, lest your audience become distracted from your point. Remember that people cannot read your slides or handouts at the same time as they are listening to you.

When designing slides make sure they are clear and visible to the entire audience. Contrasting colors with consideration for common color blindness should be used. Screen- friendly fonts of sufficient size to be read from the back of the room are extremely important. Avoid clutter on your slides and leverage the power of white space, aiming always for simplicity and impact.

Practice your presentation with your visual aids, remembering to allow time for your audience to read any new text you present. Be prepared to continue in a professional manner should your visuals falter or fail. The ease with which you implement your visuals and move past any problems demonstrates your professionalism and bolsters your credibility.

Effective selection, design, and implementation of visual aids will increase your audience's attention and help to vanquish "death by PowerPoint." It will make you and your message clearer and more memorable, which will help you to achieve your primary goal: an audience that understands and connects with your message.

Review Questions

1. Other than slides, list three types of visual aids that can be used in a presentation and give an example of each.

2. What are the ways that visual aids can benefit a presentation? Harm a presentation?

3. Describe the benefits of white space in design.

4. Explain the different purposes and content of handouts as compared to slide shows.

5. List and explain two considerations when using color in your slides.

6. Discuss the pros and cons of having a large amount of text on a slide.

Activities

1. Using the data below, design 3 different types of charts/graphs to effectively display data from this table. Which is most effective and why?

City	Median Home Cost	Median Household Income	Unemployment Rate
Richmond, Virginia	$218,900	$38,266	6.90%
Asheville, North Carolina	$201,300	$39,408	8.50%
Durango, Colorado	$302,400	$53,882	7.00%

2. Design 6 different slides that express the following "The USDA study indicated that in 2010, 17.2 million households in America had difficulty providing enough food due to a lack of resources." (From http://www.fns.usda.gov/cga/pressreleases/2011/0391.htm) Which slide most clearly gets your point across and why?

3. Identify as many problems as you can in the slide on the right. Then re-design the slide to more effectively communicate the message.

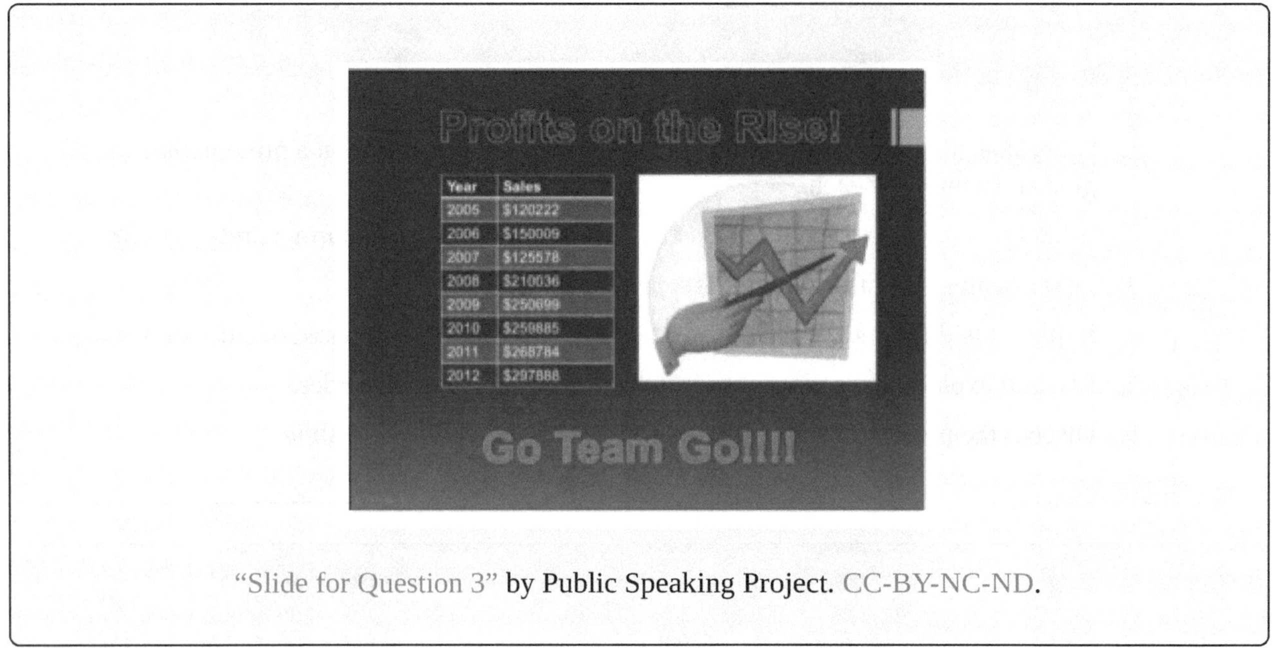

"Slide for Question 3" by Public Speaking Project. CC-BY-NC-ND.

Attributions

CC licensed content, Shared previously

- Chapter 13 Conclusion, Review Questions, and Activities. **Authored by**: Sheila Kasperek, MLIS, MSIT. **Provided by**: Mansfield University, Mansfield, PA. **Located at**: http://publicspeakingproject.org/psvirtualtext.html. **Project**: The Public Speaking Project. **License**: *CC BY-NC-ND: Attribution-NonCommercial-NoDerivatives*

Glossary and References

Glossary

TERM	DEFINITION
Analogous Colors	Colors that are next to each other on the color wheel, such as yellow and orange.
Color Palette	The selection of colors that are used throughout a single project.
Complementary Colors	Colors on opposite sides of the color wheel, such as red and green.
Creative Commons License	A designation by the copyright holder of an image or other work that it can be reused. The license identifies what specifically is allowed under what conditions and what credit must be given.
Exploded View	A picture or diagram where an object appears disassembled so the viewer can see the component parts in proper relationship to each other. They are used to show how things fit together and how parts interact to make a whole.
Greyscale	An image that has all the color information removed and replaced with appropriate shades of grey. These images are sometimes referred to as black- and-white.
Line Art	Simplified drawings made only of solid lines without color or shading. They are useful for showing the basic shape and construction of complicated objects.
Noise	In design, it refers to excess information on a slide or image or a cluttered image.
Pecha Kucha	A presentation format that uses exactly 20 slides, and each slide is only viewed for 20 seconds. This format focuses on timing, brevity, and practice.
Pixelation	The blurry appearance of images which are enlarged on a computer beyond their resolution. This often occurs when a small image is stretched to cover an entire slide.
Prezi	A newer type presentation software that allows for non- linear presentations and is more graphically oriented rather than text oriented.
Rule of Thirds	A layout design grid that divides a page into nine equal squares. Placing or aligning content along the grid lines creates a more powerful image.
Sans Serif Font	A type face whose characters do not have the small lines or flourishes at the end points of letters. Sans serif fonts include Arial, Helevetica, and Tahoma.
Serif Font	A type face whose characters have small lines or flourishes at the end points of letters. Serif fonts include Times New Roman, Georgia, and Palatino.
Silhouette	A simplified image of a person or object created from the outline of the image and filled in with a solid color, usually black.
Slide Deck	A term that refers to all the slides in a slideware presentation. It is a more generic term for PowerPoint slides.
Slideware	The software used to display digital slide shows. Examples of slideware include Microsoft PowerPoint, Apple iWork, Keynote, Google Drive Presentation, OpenOffice Impress.

Watermark	A noticeable image or graphic in an image that is placed there primarily to prevent reuse of that image by identifying the owner of the copyright. Often found on online images, it is designed to let you preview the image before you purchase it, at which time, the watermark is removed.
White Space	Empty space in your design that helps direct the viewers' attention to the parts of the slide that really matter. Use of white space can help reduce clutter on your slide.
Z Pattern	The natural tendency of people from English-speaking countries, among others, to view images in the same way that they read text, that is, left to right, top to bottom. This results in the eye tracking along a Z-shaped path through the image.

References

Bajaj, G. (2007). *Cutting edge PowerPoint 2007 for dummies*. Hoboken, NJ: Wiley Publishing.

Beyer, A. (2011). *Improving student presentations: Pecha Kucha and just plain PowerPoint*. Teaching of Psychology, 38(2), 122-126.

Detz, J. (2000). *It's not what you say, it's how you say it*. New York, NY: St. Martin's Griffen.

Duarte, N. (2008). *Slide:ology: The art and science of creating great presentations*. Sebastopol, CA : O'Reilly Media.

Duarte, N. (2010). *Resonate: Present visual stories that transform audiences*. Hoboken, NJ: John Wiley & Sons.

Gries, L. E., & Brooke, C. (2010). An inconvenient tool: Rethinking the role of slideware in the writing classroom. *Composition Studies*, 38(1), 11-28.

Kadavy, D. (2011). *Design for hackers: Reverse-engineering beauty*. West Sussex, UK : John Wiley & Sons

Kosslyn, S. M. (2007). *Clear and to the point: 8 psychological principles for compelling PowerPoint presentations*. New York, NY: Oxford University Press.

Lehtonen, M. (2011). Communicating competence through PechaKucha presentations. *Journal of Business Communication*, 48(4), 464-481.

Malamed, C. (2009). *Visual language for designers: Principles for creating graphics that people understand*. Beverly, MA: Rockport Publishers.

Mayer, R. E. (2001). *Multimedia learning*. Cambridge, UK: Cambridge University Press.

Palmer, E. (2011). *Well spoken: Teaching speaking to all students*. Portland, ME: Stenhouse Publishers.

Panag, S. (2010). *A Web 2.0 Toolkit for Educators*. Youth Media Reporter, 489-91.

Reynolds, G. (2008). *Presentation Zen: Simple ideas on presentation design and delivery*. Berkeley, CA: New Riders.

Tufte, E. R. (2003). *The cognitive style of PowerPoint*. Cheshire, CT: Graphics Press.

Tufte, E. R. (1997). *Visual and statistical thinking: Displays of evidence for making decisions.* Cheshire, CT: Graphics Press.

Vasile, A. J. (2004). Speak with confidence: A practical guide (9th ed.). Boston, MA: Pearson.

Vorvick, L. J. (2011). Color blindness. In MedlinePlus Medical Encyclopedia. Retrieved from http://www.nlm.nih.gov/medlinepl us/ency/article/001002.htm

Weaver, M. (1999). Reach out through technology: Make your point with effective A/V. Computers in Libraries, 19(4), 62.

Williams, R. (2004). *The non-designer's design book: Design and typographic principles for the visual novice* (2nd ed.). Berkeley, CA: Peachpit Press.

Yee, K., & Hargis, J. (2010). PREZI: A different way to present. *Turkish Online Journal of Distance Education* (TOJDE), 11(4), 9-11.

Young, K. S., & Travis, H. P. (2008). *Oral communication: Skills, choices, and consequences* (2nd ed.). Long Grove, IL: Waveland Press.

photo credits

p. 1 Magic Tap http://upload.wikimedia.org/wikipedia/commons/4/4b/Grifo_m%C3%A 1gico.JPG By emijrp

p. 2 Cheeseburger Cake http://commons.wikimedia.org/wiki/File:CakeBurgerSupreme.JPG by Michael Prudhomme

p. 5 Steve Jobs Presentation http://commons.wikimedia.org/wiki/File:Steve_Jobs_Presentation_2.jpg By Ken.gz

p. 5 Handouts http://commons.wikimedia.org/wiki/File:US_Navy_070808-N-9421C-143_Lt._Lydia_Battey_distributes_handouts_explaining_the_symptoms_of_tuberculosis_to_local_residents_at_Bunabun_Health_Center_in_M adang,_Papua_New_Guinea.jpg By U.S. Navy photo by Mass Communication Specialist 2nd Class Kerryl Cacho

p. 6 Dahlia http://commons.wikimedia.org/wiki/File:Dalia.jpg By Wirtual24

p. 6 – 12 Figures 13.1 – 13.14
Slide Graphics by Sheila Kasperek and Tom Oswald

p. 7 Beach leaping (In Figure 13.4): http://www.flickr.com/photos/foxtongue/4466028696/
By Foxtongue

P. 11 Roosevelt and Muir on Glacier Point (In Figure 13.10) http://memory.loc.gov/cgi- bin/query/D?consrvbib:4:./temp/~ammem_BRht: By Library of Congress

p. 13 Planets http://commons.wikimedia.org/wiki/File:NASA_Astronomy_Picture_of_the_Day_2008_May_18_-_clip_01.jpg By Dana Berry

Attributions

CC licensed content, Shared previously

Chapter 9: Critical Thinking and Reasoning

Objectives and Introduction

Chapter 6: Critical Thinking & Reasoning

By Terri Russ, J.D., Ph.D.
Saint Mary's College, Notre Dame, IN

Learning Objectives

After reading this chapter, you should be able to:

- Understand and explain the importance of critical thinking
- Identify the core skills associated with critical thinking
- Demonstrate the difference between deductive and inductive reasoning
- Construct a logically sound and well-reasoned argument
- Avoid the various fallacies that can arise through the misuse of logic
- Apply chapter concepts in final questions and activities

Introduction

As we meander through our daily routines, we are surrounded by numerous messages and people trying to get our attention and convince us to do something. We sign into our e-mail accounts and are bombarded with sales pitches to help us get rich quick or promise to fix all of our embarrassing physical problems. We drive to school and see billboards touting tantalizing restaurants or pitching local political candidates. We converse with our friends and family about current events like the crazy car thief who tried to avoid the police by driving down train tracks right into an oncoming train. Throughout all of these exchanges, we must constantly strive to make sense of the messages and determine which are true and which are not true, which are probably and which are improbable, which are intended and which are unintended. When we do this we practice **critical thinking**. We evaluate the **arguments** presented and determine if their **logic** is sound or if they rely on **fallacies** to build their case. In this chapter you will learn how to use critical thinking in all areas of your life, including preparing and presenting speeches. You will also learn how to construct a logical argument that avoids the pitfalls of fallacious thinking.

"Filos segundo logo" by *Filosofias filosoficas. CC-BY.*

Attributions

CC licensed content, Shared previously

- Chapter 6 Objectives, Outline, and Introduction. **Authored by**: Terri Russ, J.D., Ph.D.. **Provided by**: Saint Mary's College, Notre Dame, IN. **Located at**: http://publicspeakingproject.org/psvirtualtext.html. **Project**: The Public Speaking Project. **License**: *CC BY-NC-ND: Attribution-NonCommercial-NoDerivatives*

- Filos Segundo Logo. **Authored by**: Filosofias filosoficas. **Located at**: http://commons.wikimedia.org/wiki/File:Filos_segundo_logo.JPG%20. **License**: *CC BY: Attribution*

Video: Sample Student Demonstration Speeches

Demonstration Speech by Heather Pederson: "How to Make Kimbap"

- https://youtu.be/PY4rqJnnFy0

Demonstration Speech by Joanne Eller: "Chocolate covered strawberries with Grand Marnier"

- https://youtu.be/qmly4i3sFS8

Attributions

CC licensed content, Original

- Public Speaking. **Authored by**: Christie Fierro and Brent Adrian. **Provided by**: Lumen Learning. **Located at**: http://lumenlearning.com/. **Project**: Kaleidoscope Open Course Initiative. **License**: *CC BY: Attribution*

CC licensed content, Shared previously

- How to Make Kimbap. **Authored by**: Jasmine Pedersen. **Located at**: https://www.youtube.com/watch?v=PY4rqJnnFy0. **License**: *CC BY-NC-ND: Attribution-NonCommercial-NoDerivatives*

All rights reserved content

- Chocolate covered strawberries with Grand Marnier. **Authored by**: Joanne Moore. **Located at**: http://youtu.be/qmly4i3sFS8. **License**: *All Rights Reserved*. **License Terms**: Standard YouTube License

Thou Shalt Not Commit Logical Fallacies Poster

Here's a helpful poster that reviews many of the most common Logical Fallacies.

https://s3-us-west-2.amazonaws.com/oerfiles/Public+Speaking/FallaciesPoster24x36.pdf

Attributions

CC licensed content, Original

- Public Speaking. **Authored by**: Christie Fierro and Brent Adrian. **Provided by**: Lumen Learning. **Located at**: http://lumenlearning.com/. **Project**: Kaleidoscope Open Course Initiative. **License**: *CC BY: Attribution*

CC licensed content, Shared previously

- Thou Shalt Not Commit Logical Fallacies. **Authored by**: Jesse Richardson. **Located at**: https://yourlogicalfallacyis.com/pdf/FallaciesPoster24x36.pdf. **License**: *CC BY-ND: Attribution-NoDerivatives*

Critical Thinking

> We are approaching a new age of synthesis. Knowledge cannot be merely a degree or a skill…it demands a broader vision, capabilities in critical thinking and logical deduction, without which we cannot have constructive progress. – Li Ka Shing

Critical thinking has been defined in numerous ways. At its most basic, we can think of critical thinking as active thinking in which we evaluate and analyze information in order to determine the best course of action. We will look at more expansive definitions of critical thinking and its components in the following pages.

Before we get there, though, let's consider a hypothetical example of critical thinking in action.

> *Shonda was researching information for her upcoming persuasive speech. Her goal with the speech was to persuade her classmates to drink a glass of red wine every day. Her argument revolved around the health benefits one can derive from the antioxidants found in red wine. Shonda found an article reporting the results of a study conducted by a Dr. Gray. According to Dr. Gray's study, drinking four or more glasses of wine a day will help reduce the chances of heart attack, increase levels of good cholesterol, and help in reducing unwanted fat. Without conducting further research, Shonda changed her speech to persuade her classmates to drink four or more glasses of red wine per day. She used Dr. Gray's study as her primary support. Shonda presented her speech in class to waves of applause and support from her classmates. She was shocked when, a few weeks later, she received a grade of "D". Shonda's teacher had also found Dr. Gray's study and learned it was sponsored by a multi-national distributor of wine. In fact, the study in question was published in a trade journal targeted to wine and alcohol retailers. If Shonda had taken a few extra minutes to critically examine the study, she may have been able to avoid the dreaded "D."*

Shonda's story is just one of many ways that critical thinking impacts our lives. Throughout this chapter we will consider the importance of critical thinking in all areas of communication, especially public speaking. We will first take a more in-depth look at what critical thinking is—and isn't.

Before we get too far into the specifics of what critical thinking is and how we can do it, it's important to clear up a common misconception. Even though the phrase critical thinking uses the word "critical," it is not a negative thing. Being critical is not the same thing as criticizing. When we criticize something, we point out the flaws and errors in it, exercising a negative value judgment on it. Our goal with criticizing is less about understanding than about negatively evaluating. It's important to remember that critical thinking is not just criticizing. While the process may involve examining flaws and errors, it is much more.

Critical Thinking Defined

Just what is critical thinking then? To help us understand, let's consider a common definition of critical thinking. The philosopher John Dewey, often considered the father of modern day critical thinking, defines critical thinking as:

"John Dewey" by Eva Watson-Schütze. Public domain.

> *"Active, persistent, careful consideration of a belief or supposed form of knowledge in light of the grounds that support it and the further conclusions to which it tends."*[1]

The first key component of Dewey's definition is that critical thinking is active. Critical thinking must be done by choice. As we continue to delve deeper into the various facets of critical thinking, we will learn how to engage as critical thinkers.

Probably one of the most concise and easiest to understand definitions is that offered by Barry Beyer: "Critical thinking… means making reasoned judgments."[2] In other words, we don't just jump to a conclusion or a judgment. We rationalize and justify our conclusions. A second primary component of critical thinking, then, involves questioning. As critical thinkers, we need to question everything that confronts us. Equally important, we need to question ourselves and ask how our own biases or assumptions influence how we judge something.

In the following sections we will explore how to do critical thinking more in depth. As you read through this material, reflect back on Dewey's and Beyer's definitions of critical thinking.

Attributions

CC licensed content, Shared previously

Public domain content

1. Dewey, J. (1933). *Experience and education*. New York: Macmillan, 1933.
2. Beyer, B. K. (1995) Critical thinking. Bloomington, IN: Phi Delta Kappa Educational Foundation.

Logic and the Role of Arguments

Critical thinkers tend to exhibit certain traits that are common to them. These traits are summarized in Table 6.1:[1]

Table 6.1 Traits of Critical Thinkers	
Open-mindedness	Critical thinkers are open and receptive to all ideas and arguments, even those with which they may disagree. Critical thinkers reserve judgment on a message until they have examined the claims, logic, reasoning, and evidence used. Critical thinkers are fair-minded and understand that a message is not inherently wrong or flawed if it differs from their own thoughts. Critical thinkers remain open to the possibility of changing their view on an issue when logic and evidence supports doing so.
Analytic Nature	Critical thinkers are interested in understanding what is happening in a message. Critical thinkers ask questions of the message, breaking it into its individual components and examining each in turn. Critical thinkers dissect these components looking for sound logic and reasoning.
Systematic by Method	Critical thinkers avoid jumping to conclusions. Critical thinkers take the time to systematically examine a message. Critical thinkers apply accepted criteria or conditions to their analyses.
Inquisitive	Critical thinkers are curious by nature. Critical thinkers ask questions of what is going on around them and in a message. Critical thinkers want to know more and take action to learn more.
Judicious	Critical thinkers are prudent in acting and making judgments. Critical thinkers are sensible in their actions. That is, they don't just jump on the bandwagon of common thought because it looks good or everyone else is doing it.
Truth-Seeking Ethos	Critical thinkers exercise an ethical foundation based in searching for the truth. Critical thinkers understand that even the wisest people may be wrong at times.
Confident in Reasoning	Critical thinkers have faith in the power of logic and sound reasoning. Critical thinkers understand that it is in everyone's best interest to encourage and develop sound logic. More importantly, critical thinkers value the power of letting others draw their own conclusions.

Recall that critical thinking is an active mode of thinking. Instead of just receiving messages and accepting them as is, we consider what they are saying. We ask if messages are well-supported. We determine if their logic is sound or slightly flawed. In other words, we act on the messages before we take action based on them. When we enact critical thinking on a message, we engage a variety of skills including: listening, analysis, evaluation, inference and interpretation or explanation, and self-regulation[2]

1. Adapted from Facione, P. A. (1990). *Critical Thinking: A Statement of Expert Consensus for Purposes of Educational Assessment and Instruction, The Delphi Report (Executive Summary)*. Millbrae, CA: California Academic Press.
2. Adapted from Facione, P. A. (1990).

Next, we will examine each of these skills and their role in critical thinking in greater detail. As you read through the explanation of and examples for each skill, think about how it works in conjunction with the others. It's important to note that while our discussion of the skills is presented in a linear manner, in practice our use of each skill is not so straightforward. We may exercise different skills simultaneously or jump forward and backward.

Without an open-minded mind, you can never be a great success. – Martha Stewart

"Martha Stewart" **by nrkbeta.** CC-BY-SA.

Listening

In order to understand listening, we must first understand the difference between **listening** and **hearing**. At its most basic, hearing refers to the *physiological* process of receiving sounds, while listening refers to the *psychological* process of interpreting or making sense of those sounds.

Every minute of every day we are surrounded by hundreds of different noises and sounds. If we were to try to make sense of each different sound we would probably spend our day just doing this. While we may hear all of the noises, we filter out many of them. They pass through our lives without further notice. Certain noises, however, jump to the forefront of our consciousness. As we listen to them, we make sense of these sounds. We do this every day without necessarily thinking about the process. Like many other bodily functions, it happens without our willing it to happen.

Critical thinking requires that we consciously listen to messages. We must focus on what is being said – and not said. We must strive not to be distracted by other outside noises or the internal noise of our own preconceived ideas. For the moment we only need to take in the message.

Listening becomes especially difficult when the message contains highly charged information. Think about what happens when you try to discuss a controversial issue such as abortion. As the other person speaks, you may have every good intention of listening to the entire argument.

However, when the person says something you feel strongly about you start formulating a counter-argument in your head. The end result is that both sides end up talking past each other without ever really listening to what the other says.

Analysis

Once we have listened to a message, we can begin to analyze it. In practice we often begin analyzing messages while still listening to them. When we analyze something, we consider it in greater detail, separating out the main components of the message. In a sense, we are acting like a surgeon on the message, carving out all of the different elements and laying them out for further consideration and possible action.

Let's return to Shonda's persuasive speech to see analysis in action. As part of the needs section of her speech, Shonda makes the following remarks:

> *Americans today are some of the unhealthiest people on Earth. It seems like not a week goes by without some news story relating how we are the fattest country in the world. In addition to being overweight, we suffer from a number of other health problems. When I was conducting research for my speech, I read somewhere that heart attacks are the number one killer of men and the number two killer of women. Think about that. My uncle had a heart attack and had to be rushed to the hospital. They hooked him up to a bunch of different machines to keep him alive. We all thought he was going to die. He's ok now, but he has to take a bunch of pills every day and eat a special diet. Plus he had to pay thousands of dollars in medical bills. Wouldn't you like to know how to prevent this from happening to you?*

If we were to analyze this part of Shonda's speech (see Table 6.2), we could begin by looking at the claims she makes. We could then look at the evidence she presents in support of these claims. Having parsed out the various elements, we are then ready to evaluate them and by extension the message as a whole.

Evaluation

When we evaluate something we continue the process of analysis by assessing the various claims and arguments for validity. One way we evaluate a message is to ask questions about what is being said and who is saying it. The following is a list of typical questions we may ask, along with an evaluation of the ideas in Shonda's speech.

Is the speaker credible?

Yes. While Shonda may not be an expert per se on the issue of health benefits related to wine, she has made herself a mini-expert through conducting research.

Does the statement ring true or false based on common sense?

It sounds kind of fishy. Four or more glasses of wine in one sitting doesn't seem right. In fact, it seems like it might be bordering on binge drinking.

Does the logic employed hold up to scrutiny?

Based on the little bit of Shonda's speech we see here, her logic does seem to be sound. As we will see later on, she actually commits a few fallacies.

What questions or objections are raised by the message?

In addition to the possibility of Shonda's proposal being binge drinking, it also raises the possibility of creating alcoholism or causing other long term health problems.

How will further information affect the message?

More information will probably contradict her claims. In fact, most medical research in this area contradicts the claim that drinking 4 or more glasses of wine a day is a good thing.

Will further information strengthen or weaken the claims?

Most likely Shonda's claims will be weakened.

What questions or objections are raised by the claims?

In addition to the objections we've already discussed, there is also the problem of the credibility of Shonda's expert "doctor."

<table>
<tr><td colspan="2" align="center">Table 6.2 Analysis of Shonda's Speech</td></tr>
<tr><td align="center">Claims</td><td align="center">Evidence</td></tr>
<tr><td>
<ul>
<li>Americans are unhealthy</li>
<li>American is the fattest country</li>
<li>Americans suffer from many health problems</li>
<li>Heart attacks are the number one killer of men</li>
<li>Heart attacks are the number-two killer of women</li>
</ul>
</td><td>
<ul>
<li>Some news stories about America as the fattest country</li>
<li>Research about heart attacks</li>
<li>Story of her uncle's heart attack</li>
</ul>
</td></tr>
</table>

A wise man proportions his belief to the evidence. – David Hume

Inference and Interpretation or Explanation

"Imply" or "Infer"?

For two relatively small words, imply and infer seem to generate an inordinately large amount of confusion. Understanding the difference between the two and knowing when to use the right one is not only a useful skill, but it also makes you sound a lot smarter!

Let's begin with imply. Imply means to suggest or convey an idea. A speaker or a piece of writing implies things. For example, in Shonda's speech, she implies it is better to drink more red wine. In other words, she never directly says that we need to drink more red wine, but she clearly hints at it when she suggests that drinking four or more glasses a day will provide us with health benefits.

Now let's consider infer. Infer means that something in a speaker's words or a piece of writing helps us to draw a conclusion outside of his/her words. We infer a conclusion. Returning to Shonda's speech, we can infer she would want us to drink more red wine rather than less. She never comes right out and says this. However, by considering her overall message, we can draw this conclusion.

Another way to think of the difference between imply and infer is: A speaker (or writer for that matter) implies. The audience infers.

Therefore, it would be incorrect to say that Shonda infers we should drink more rather than less wine. She implies this. To help you differentiate between the two, remember that an inference is something that comes from outside the spoken or written text.

The next step in critically examining a message is to interpret or explain the conclusions that we draw from it. At this phase we consider the evidence and the claims together. In effect we are reassembling the components that we parsed out during analysis. We are continuing our evaluation by looking at the evidence, alternatives, and possible conclusions.

Before we draw any inferences or attempt any explanations, we should look at the evidence provided. When we consider evidence we must first determine what, if any, kind of support is provided. Of the evidence we then ask:

1. Is the evidence sound?

2. Does the evidence say what thespeaker says it does?

3. Does contradictory evidenceexist?

4. Is the evidence from a validcredible source?

Even though these are set up as yes or no questions, you'll probably find in practice that your answers are a bit more complex. For example, let's say you're writing a speech on why we should wear our seatbelts at all times while driving. You've researched the topic and found solid, credible information setting forth the numerous reasons why wearing a seatbelt can help save your life and decrease the number of injuries experienced during a motor vehicle accident. Certainly, there exists contradictory evidence arguing seat belts can cause more injuries. For example, if you're in an accident where your car is partially submerged in water, wearing a seatbelt may impede your ability to quickly exit the vehicle. Does the fact that this evidence exists negate your claims? Probably not, but you need to be thorough in evaluating and considering how you use your evidence.

Seatbelt by M.Minderhoud, CC-BY-SA.

A man who does not think for himself does not think at all. – Oscar Wilde

Self-Regulation

The final step in critically examining a message is actually a skill we should exercise throughout the entire process. With self-regulation, we consider our pre-existing thoughts on the subject and any biases we may have. We examine how what we think on an issue may have influenced the way we understand (or think we understand) the message and any conclusions we have drawn. Just as contradictory evidence doesn't automatically negate our claims or invalidate our arguments, our biases don't necessarily make our conclusions wrong. The goal of practicing self-regulation is not to disavow or deny our opinions. The goal is to create distance between our opinions and the messages we evaluate.

The Value of Critical Thinking

In public speaking, the value of being a critical thinker cannot be overstressed. Critical thinking helps us to determine the truth or validity of arguments. However, it also helps us to formulate strong arguments for our speeches. Exercising critical thinking at all steps of the speech writing and delivering process can help us avoid situations like Shonda found herself in. Critical thinking is not a magical panacea that will make us super speakers. However, it is another tool that we can add to our speech toolbox.

> When the mind is thinking, it is talking to itself. – Plato

As we will learn in the following pages, we construct arguments based on logic. Understanding the ways logic can be used and possibly misused is a vital skill. To help stress the importance of it, the Foundation for Critical Thinking has set forth universal standards of reasoning. These standards can be found in Table 6.3.

Table 6.3
Universal Standards of Reasoning
All reasoning has a purpose.
All reasoning is an attempt to figure something out, to settle some question, to solve some problem.
All reasoning is based on assumptions.
All reasoning is done from some point of view.
All reasoning is based on data, information, and evidence.
All reasoning is expressed through, and shaped by, concepts and ideas.
All reasoning contains inferences or interpretations by which we draw conclusions and give meaning to data.
All reasoning leads somewhere or has implications and consequences.

Logic and the Role of Arguments

We use logic every day. Even if we have never formally studied logical reasoning and fallacies, we can often tell when a person's statement doesn't sound right. Think about the claims we see in many advertisements today—Buy product X, and you will be beautiful/thin/happy or have the carefree life depicted in the advertisement. With very little critical thought, we know intuitively that simply buying a product will not magically change our lives. Even if we can't identify the specific fallacy at work in the argument (non causa in this case), we know there is some flaw in the argument.

"Sharia Law Billboard" by Matt57. Public domain.

By studying logic and fallacies we can learn to formulate stronger and more cohesive arguments, avoiding problems like that mentioned above. The study of logic has a long history. We can trace the roots of modern logical study back to Aristotle in ancient Greece. Aristotle's simple definition of logic as the means by which we come to know anything still provides a concise understanding of logic.[3]

Of the classical pillars of a core liberal arts education of logic, grammar, and rhetoric, logic has developed as a fairly independent branch of philosophical studies. We use logic everyday when we construct statements, argue our point of view, and in myriad other ways. Understanding how logic is used will help us communicate more efficiently and effectively.

Defining Arguments

When we think and speak logically, we pull together statements that combine reasoning with evidence to support an assertion, arguments. A logical argument should not be confused with the type of argument you have with your sister or brother or any other person. When you argue with your sibling, you participate in a conflict in which you disagree about something. You may, however, use a logical argument in the midst of the argument with your sibling. Consider this example:

"Man and Woman Arguing" by mzacha. morgueFile.

> *Brother and sister, Sydney and Harrison are arguing about whose turn it is to clean their bathroom. Harrison tells Sydney she should do it because she is a girl and girls are better at cleaning. Sydney responds that being a girl has nothing to do with whose turn it is. She reminds Harrison that according to their work chart, they are responsible for cleaning the bathroom on alternate weeks. She tells him she cleaned the bathroom last week; therefore, it is his turn this week. Harrison, still unconvinced, refuses to take responsibility for the chore. Sydney then points to the work chart and shows him where it specifically says it is his turn this week. Defeated, Harrison digs out the cleaning supplies.*

Throughout their bathroom argument, both Harrison and Sydney use logical arguments to advance their point. You may ask why Sydney is successful and Harrison is not. This is a good question. Let's critically think about each of their arguments to see why one fails and one succeeds.

Let's start with Harrison's argument. We can summarize it into three points:

1. Girls are better at cleaning bathrooms than boys.

2. Sydney is a girl.

3. Therefore, Sydney should clean the bathroom.

Harrison's argument here is a form of deductive reasoning, specifically a syllogism. We will consider syllogisms in a few minutes. For our purposes here, let's just focus on why Harrison's argument fails to persuade Sydney. Assuming for the moment that we agree with Harrison's first two premises, then it would seem that his argument makes sense. We know that Sydney is a girl, so the second premise is true. This leaves

3. Aristotle. (1989). Prior Analytics (Trans. Robin Smith). Cambridge, MA: Hackett Publishing.

the first premise that girls are better at cleaning bathrooms than boys. This is the exact point where Harrison's argument goes astray. The only way his entire argument will work is if we agree with the assumption girls are better at cleaning bathrooms than boys.

Let's now look at Sydney's argument and why it works. Her argument can be summarized as follows:

1. The bathroom responsibilities alternate weekly according to the work chart.

2. Sydney cleaned the bathroom last week.

3. The chart indicates it is Harrison's turn to clean the bathroom this week.

4. Therefore, Harrison should clean the bathroom.

Sydney's argument here is a form of inductive reasoning. We will look at inductive reasoning in depth below. For now, let's look at why Sydney's argument succeeds where Harrison's fails. Unlike Harrison's argument, which rests on assumption for its truth claims, Sydney's argument rests on evidence. We can define evidence as anything used to support the validity of an assertion. Evidence includes: testimony, scientific findings, statistics, physical objects, and many others. Sydney uses two primary pieces of evidence: the work chart and her statement that she cleaned the bathroom last week. Because Harrison has no contradictory evidence, he can't logically refute Sydney's assertion and is therefore stuck with scrubbing the toilet.

"Decorative toilet seat" **by Bartux~commonswikiv. Public domain.**

Defining Deduction

Deductive reasoning refers to an argument in which the truth of its premises guarantees the truth of its conclusions. Think back to Harrison's argument for Sydney cleaning the bathroom. In order for his final claim to be valid, we must accept the truth of his claims that girls are better at cleaning bathrooms than boys. The key focus in deductive arguments is that it must be impossible for the premises to be true and the conclusion to be false. The classic example is:

All men are mortal.
Socrates is a man.
Therefore, Socrates is mortal.

We can look at each of these statements individually and see each is true in its own right. It is virtually impossible for the first two propositions to be true and the conclusion to be false. Any argument which fails to meet this standard commits a logical error or fallacy. Even if we might accept the arguments as good and the conclusion as possible, the argument fails as a form of deductive reasoning.

> A few observations and much reasoning lead to error; many observations and a little reasoning to truth. – Alexis Carrel

Another way to think of deductive reasoning is to think of it as moving from a general premise to a specific premise. The basic line of reasoning looks like this:

"Deductive Reasoning"
CC-BY-NC-ND.

This form of deductive reasoning is called a syllogism. A syllogism need not have only three components to its argument, but it must have at least three. We have Aristotle to thank for identifying the syllogism and making the study of logic much easier. The focus on syllogisms dominated the field of philosophy for thousands of years. In fact, it wasn't until the early nineteenth century that we began to see the discussion of other types of logic and other forms of logical reasoning.

> Logic: the art of thinking and reasoning in strict accordance with the limitations and incapacities of the human misunderstanding. – Ambrose Bierce

It is easy to fall prey to missteps in reasoning when we focus on syllogisms and deductive reasoning. Let's return to Harrison's argument and see what happens.

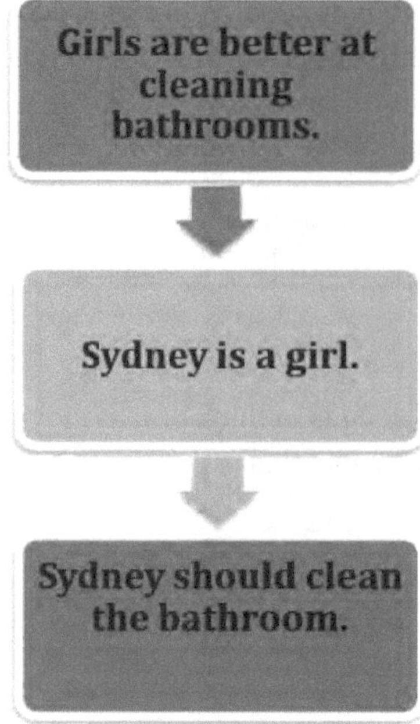

"Applied Deductive Reasoning"
CC-BY-NC-ND.

Considered in this manner, it should be clear how the strength of the conclusion depends upon us accepting as true the first two statements. This need for truth sets up deductive reasoning as a very rigid form of reasoning. If either one of the first two premises isn't true, then the entire argument fails.

Let's turn to recent world events for another example.

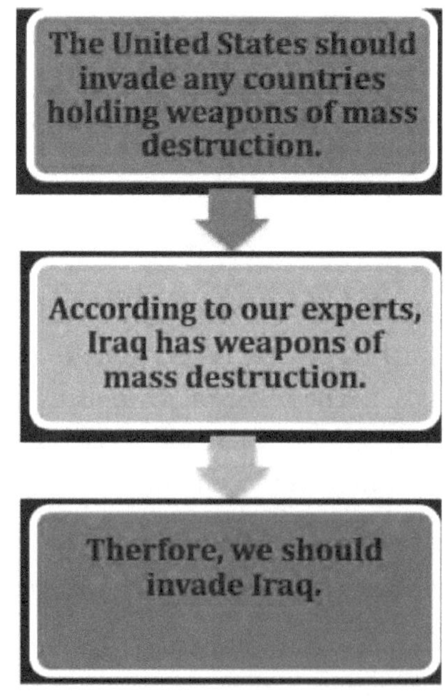

"US Invasion Deductive Reasoning Example" CC-BY-NC-ND.

In the debates over whether the United States should take military action in Iraq, this was the basic line of reasoning used to justify an invasion. This logic was sufficient for the United States to invade Iraq; however, as we have since learned, this line of reasoning also shows how quickly logic can go bad. We subsequently learned that the "experts" weren't quite so confident, and their "evidence" wasn't quite as concrete as originally represented.

Defining Induction

Inductive reasoning is often though of as the opposite of deductive reasoning; however, this approach is not wholly accurate. Inductive reasoning does move from the specific to the general. However, this fact alone does not make it the opposite of deductive reasoning. An argument which fails in its deductive reasoning may still stand inductively.

Unlike deductive reasoning, there is no standard format inductive arguments must take, making them more flexible. We can define an inductive argument as one in which the truth of its propositions lends support to the conclusion. The difference here in deduction is the truth of the propositions establishes with absolute certainty the truth of the conclusion. When we analyze an inductive argument, we do not focus on the truth of its premises. Instead we analyze inductive arguments for their strength or soundness.

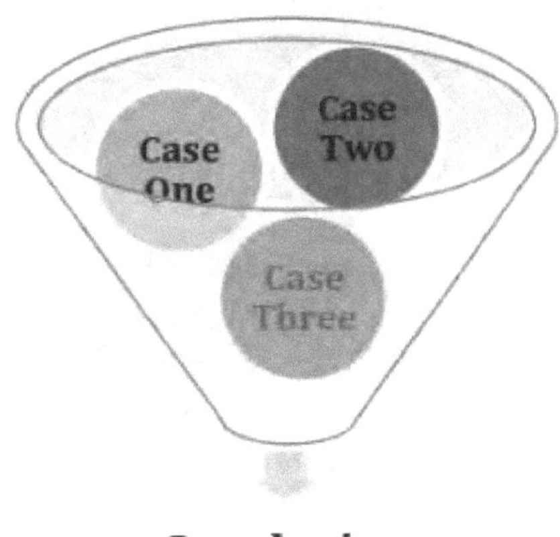

Another significant difference between deduction and induction is inductive arguments do not have a standard format. Let's return to Sydney's argument to see how induction develops in action:

1. Bathroom cleaning responsibilities alternate weekly according to the work chart.
2. Sydney cleaned the bathroom last week.
3. The chart indicates it is Harrison's turn to clean the bathroom this week.
4. Therefore, Harrison should clean the bathroom.

What Sydney does here is build to her conclusion that Harrison should clean the bathroom. She begins by stating the general house rule of alternate weeks for cleaning. She then adds in evidence before concluding her argument. While her argument is strong, we don't know if it is true. There could be other factors Sydney has left out. Sydney may have agreed to take Harrison's week of bathroom cleaning in exchange for him doing another one of her chores. Or there may be some extenuating circumstances preventing Harrison from bathroom cleaning this week.

> You should carefully study the Art of Reasoning, as it is what most people are very deficient in, and I know few things more disagreeable than to argue, or even converse with a man who has no idea of inductive and deductive philosophy. – William John Wills

Let's return to the world stage for another example. After the 9/11 attacks on the World Trade Center, we heard variations of the following arguments:

1. The terrorists were Muslim (or Arab or Middle Eastern)

2. The terrorists hated America.

3. Therefore, all Muslims (or Arabs or Middle Easterners) hate America.

"1993 Word Trade Center bombing" by Bureau of ATF 1993 Explosives Incident Report. Public domain.

Clearly, we can see the problem in this line of reasoning. Beyond being a scary example of hyperbolic rhetoric, we can all probably think of at least one counter example to disprove the conclusion. However, individual passions and biases caused many otherwise rational people to say these things in the weeks following the attacks. This example also clearly illustrates how easy it is to get tripped up in your use of logic and the importance of practicing self-regulation.

Attributions

CC licensed content, Original

- Image of man and woman arguing. **Authored by**: mzacha. **Provided by**: MorgueFile. **Located at**: http://mrg.bz/ynkIUa. **License**: *All Rights Reserved*. **License Terms**: Free to remix, commercial use, no attribution required. http://www.morguefile.com/license/morguefile

CC licensed content, Shared previously

- Chapter 6 Logic and the Role of Arguments. **Authored by**: Terri Russ, J.D., Ph.D.. **Provided by**: Saint Mary's College, Notre Dame, IN. **Located at**: http://publicspeakingproject.org/psvirtualtext.html. **Project**: The Public Speaking Project. **License**: *CC BY-NC-ND: Attribution-NonCommercial-NoDerivatives*

- Martha Stewart nrkbeta. **Authored by**: nrkbeta. **Located at**: http://commons.wikimedia.org/wiki/File:Martha_Stewart_nrkbeta.jpg. **License**: *CC BY-SA: Attribution-ShareAlike*

- Seat belt BX. **Authored by**: M.Minderhoud. **Located at**: http://commons.wikimedia.org/wiki/File:Seat_belt_BX.jpg. **License**: *CC BY-SA: Attribution-ShareAlike*

Public domain content

- Sharia-Law-Billboard. **Authored by**: Matt57. **Located at**: http://commons.wikimedia.org/wiki/File:Sharia-law-Billboard.jpg. **License**: *Public Domain: No Known Copyright*

- Decorative toilet seat. **Authored by**: Bartux. **Located at**: http://commons.wikimedia.org/wiki/File:Decorative_toilet_seat.jpg%20. **License**: *Public Domain: No Known Copyright*

- Image of 1993 World Trade Center bombing. **Provided by**: Bureau of ATF 1993 Explosives Incident Report. **Located at**: http://commons.wikimedia.org/wiki/File:WTC_1993_ATF_Commons.jpg. **License**: *Public Domain: No Known Copyright*

Understanding Fallacies

When we form arguments or examine others' arguments, we need to be cognizant of possible fallacies. A fallacy can be defined as a flaw or error in reasoning. At its most basic, a logical fallacy refers to a defect in the reasoning of an argument that causes the conclusion(s) to be invalid, unsound, or weak. The existence of a fallacy in a deductive argument makes the entire argument invalid. The existence of a fallacy in an inductive argument weakens the argument but does not invalidate it.

It is important to study fallacies so you can avoid them in the arguments you make. Studying fallacies also provides you with a foundation for evaluating and critiquing other arguments as well. Once you start studying and thinking about fallacies, you'll find they are everywhere. You could say that we live in a fallacious world!

The study of fallacies can be dated back to the start of the study of logic. In ancient Greece, Aristotle classified fallacies into two categories—linguistic and non-linguistic. Within these two categories, he identified 13 individual fallacies. Through time we have reclassified fallacies using various typologies and criteria. For our purposes, we will focus on formal and informal fallacies.

"Exclamation in a circle" by Orikrin1998. CC-BY.

Attributions

CC licensed content, Shared previously

Formal Fallacies

A formal fallacy exists because of an error in the structure of the argument. In other words, the conclusion doesn't follow from the premises. All formal fallacies are specific types of non sequiturs, or arguments in which the conclusions do not follow from the premises. Formal fallacies are identified by critically examining the structure of the argument exclusive of the individual statements. As you read through the following types of formal fallacies and examples, this definition will become more clear.

Bad Reasons Fallacy (Argumentum ad Logicam)

In this fallacy, the conclusion is assumed to be bad because the arguments are bad. In practice, a premise of the argument is bad and therefore the conclusion is bad or invalid. This fallacy is seen often in debate or argumentation. We summarize the fallacy as: He gave bad reasons for his argument; therefore, his argument is bad. Consider the following claim:

The new employee is too quiet and has no sense of style. We should fire him.

The problem here should be obvious. To be a good employee does not require a certain look or the ability to put together interesting outfits. (Just look around your campus or workplace and you'll probably see how true this is.) As such, the reasons for concluding the new faculty member should be fired are bad. We commit a fallacy if the conclusion to fire him is also bad or wrong. While the given reasons don't necessarily support the conclusion, there may be others that do.

"Bow Tie" by ambimb. CC-BY-NC-SA.

Bad reasoning as well as good reasoning is possible; and this fact is the foundation of the practical side of logic. – Charles Sanders Peirce

Masked Man Fallacy (Intentional Fallacy)

The masked man fallacy involves a substitution of parties. If the two things we substitute are identical, then the argument is valid:

> *Rosamond Smith wrote the book <u>Nemesis</u>.*
> *Rosamond Smith is an alias for Joyce Carol Oates.*
>
> *Joyce Carol Oates wrote the book <u>Nemesis</u>.*

This argument is valid because Rosamond Smith is in fact an alias for Joyce Carol Oates, so there is no flaw in the structure of the argument.

Consider the following example:

> *Chris told police that a red-haired woman stole her car. Ginny is a red-haired woman. Therefore, Chris told police that Ginny stole her car.*

The fallacy in this example occurs between the second premise and the conclusion. Looking at each premise individually, we can see that each is true. However, simply because each premise is true doesn't mean the conclusion is necessarily true. Even if Ginny did steal Chris's car, this fact doesn't make the conclusion true. The existence of this fact cannot be presumed to change what Chris told the police.

Fallacy of Quantitative Logic

Fallacies of quantitative logic revolve around the grammatical structure of the proposition. The focus is on the use of some sort of quantifying word such as "all" or "some." Consider this example:

"Callan" by Kristy Davies. CC-BY-NC.

> *All philosophers are wise.*

We can show the flaw in this statement by simply finding a counter-example. And since the fact of being wise is abstract, how do we truly know if one is wise or not? Consider how the statement changes with the use of a different quantifier:

> *Some philosophers are wise.*

This statement is stronger because it allows for the possibility there are counter-examples. However, the error arises from the fact that it is not a known quantity. We must infer from the statement that some philosophers are not wise.

Let's look at another example:

> *All conservatives are Republicans.*
> *Therefore, all Republicans are conservatives.*

Without thinking too hard you can probably think of one counter-example. Let's try one more:

> *Some doctors are not MDs. Therefore, some MDs are not doctors.*

While the first premise is true (there are other types of doctors), the second is clearly not true.

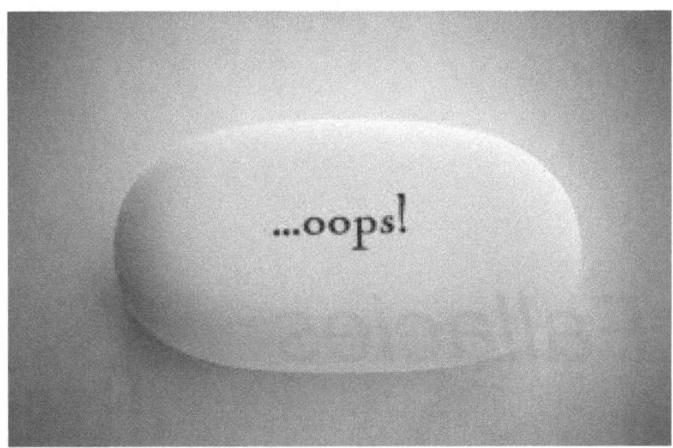

"…oops?" by jasmeet. CC-BY-NC-ND.

Attributions

CC licensed content, Shared previously

- Chapter 6 Formal Fallacies. **Authored by**: Terri Russ, J.D., Ph.D.. **Provided by**: Saint Mary's College, Notre Dame, IN. **Located at**: http://publicspeakingproject.org/psvirtualtext.html. **Project**: The Public Speaking Project. **License**: *CC BY-NC-ND: Attribution-NonCommercial-NoDerivatives*

- Bow Tie. **Authored by**: ambimb. **Located at**: https://www.flickr.com/photos/ambimb/5273713759/. **License**: *CC BY-NC-SA: Attribution-NonCommercial-ShareAlike*

- Callan. **Authored by**: Kristy Davies. **Located at**: https://www.flickr.com/photos/kristykristydavies/4149080530/. **License**: *CC BY-NC: Attribution-NonCommercial*

- ...oops. **Authored by**: jasmeet. **Located at**: https://www.flickr.com/photos/jasmeet/2439640057/. **License**: *CC BY-NC-ND: Attribution-NonCommercial-NoDerivatives*

Informal Fallacies

An informal fallacy occurs because of an error in reasoning. Unlike formal fallacies which are identified through examining the structure of the argument, informal fallacies are identified through analysis of the content of the premises. In this group of fallacies, the premises fail to provide adequate reasons for believing the truth of the conclusion. There are numerous different types of informal fallacies. In the following, we consider some of the more common types.

accident (sweeping generalization)

A fallacy by accident occurs when a generally true statement is applied to a specific case that is somehow unusual or exceptional. The fallacy looks like this:

Xs are normally Ys. Z is an (ab- normal) X. Therefore, Z is an Y.

Let's look at a specific example to see how this fallacy can easily occur:

Dogs are good pets.
Coyotes are dogs.
Therefore, coyotes are good pets.

The fallacy here should be clear. I love dogs and coyotes, but I don't know that I would want a coyote for a pet. The fallacy in this case could be easily fixed with the use of a simple qualifier such as the word "some." If we changed the first premise to read "Some dogs make good pets," then we can see how even if the second premise is true it doesn't automatically lead to the stated conclusion. The basic problem here is that a sometimes true statement is assumed to be universally true.

I do personal attacks only on people who specialize in personal attacks. – Al Franken

genetic fallacy (ad hominem)

If we examine this exchange we can see that Bill's arguments are sound and supported by what appears to be good evidence. However, Jane ignores these and focuses on Bill's supposed character – he's a big jerk. The fallacy happens when we connect the truth of a proposition to the person asserting it.

The ad hominem fallacy occurs when we shift our focus from the premises and conclusions of the argument and focus instead on the individual making the argument. An easy way to remember this fallacy is to think of it as the personal attack fallacy. It is the weak form of arguing that many of us employed on our elementary school playgrounds such as this exchange:

> *Bill: I think we should go back to class now.*

> *Jane: I don't think we need to worry about it.*

> *Bill: Well, the bell rang a few minutes ago. We're going to be late.*

> *Jane: Well, you're a big jerk and don't know anything, so we don't have to go back to class.*

If we examine this exchange we can see that Bill's arguments are sound and supported by what appears to be good evidence. However, Jane ignores these and focuses on Bill's supposed character – he's a big jerk. The fallacy happens when we connect the truth of a proposition to the person asserting it.

Let's consider a more serious example that we see in many political campaigns. We can map out the fallacy as follows:

> *My opponent has trait X. Therefore, she is not qualified to do the job.*

The focus here is on the individual's trait, even when the trait in question has nothing to do with the job. We saw this fallacy in play in the early days of the 2012 U.S. presidential campaign:

> *We will never get out of debt if we allow a Democrat to remain as president.*

The focus here has nothing to do with any individual candidate's skills, experience, or abilities. The focus is solely on their political affiliation.

> There is no greater impediment to the advancement of knowledge than the ambiguity of words. –
> Thomas Reid

ambiguity (equivocation)

Fallacies caused by ambiguity occur, not surprisingly, when some ambiguous term is used in the argument. An ambiguous term is one that has more than one meaning. The structure of the argument may be clear, and there may be solid evidence supporting the propositions. The problem arises from having nothing solid on which to base our conclusion. We saw this fallacy in play during the Clinton/Lewinsky investigations.

If you recall, when questioned about his relationship with Monica Lewinsky, President Clinton responded that he never had "sexual relations" with that woman. The phrase "sexual relations" can include a whole range of sexual behaviors.

Let's look at a more recent example:

We won't be safe until we win the war on terrorism.

Can you spot the ambiguity? Actually there are two: safe and terrorism. What is safe to one person is much less so to another. Likewise, behaviors that appear terrorist-like to one person are simply impassioned acts to another.

An appeal to the reason of the people has never been known to fail in the long run. – James Russell Lowell

fallacies of appeal

This type of fallacy is actually a group of fallacies. At its most basic, the truth of the argument rests on reference to some outside source or force. We will consider four of the most popular appeal fallacies – appeals to authority, emotion, ignorance, and pity.

appeal to authority (ad vericundiam)

When we appeal to authority we claim the truth of a proposition is guaranteed because of the opinion of a famous person. Appeals to authority look like this:

Authority figure X says Y. Therefore, Y is true.

We see this fallacy in play regularly in commercials or other advertisements featuring a doctor, lawyer, or other professional. Think about, for example, ads for the latest weight loss supplement. A doctor will discuss the science of the supplement. At times she will mention that she used the supplement and successfully lost weight. Even though we do learn something about the specifics of the supplement, the focus is on the doctor and her implied authoritative knowledge. We are to infer that the supplement will work because the doctor says it will work.

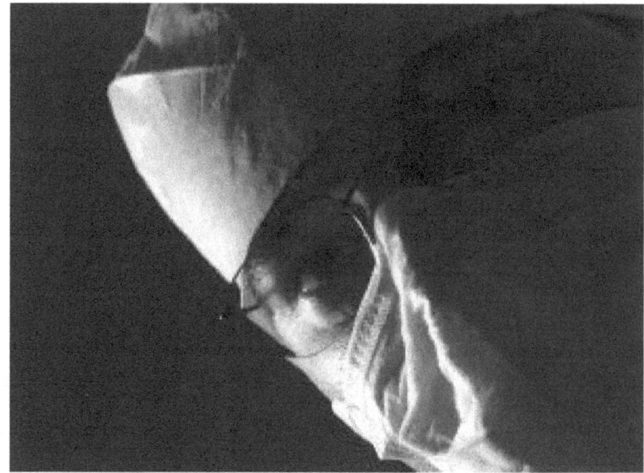

The fallacy in this type of reasoning occurs when we confuse the truth of the proposition with the person stating it. Instead of considering the strength of the argument and any evidence associated with it, we focus solely on the individual.

It can be easy to fall into the trap of this fallacy. For many of your speeches, you will be asked to research the issue at hand and present supporting evidence. This is a prime place for the fallacy to occur. While it is important to support your arguments with outside research, it is also important to critically evaluate all aspects of the information. Remember the example of Shonda's speech that opened this chapter? Her blind reliance on the research of Dr. Gray is an example of the appeal to authority fallacy.

> Anyone who conducts an argument by appealing to authority is not using his intelligence; he is just using his memory. – Leonardo da Vinci

appeal to emotion

This fallacy occurs with the use of highly emotive or charged language. The force of the fallacy lies in its ability to motivate the audience to accept the truth of the proposition based solely on their visceral response to the words used. In a sense, the audience is manipulated or forced into accepting the truth of the stated conclusions. Consider the following example:

> *Any campus member who thinks clearly should agree that Dr. Lenick is a flaming, radical, feminist, liberal. Dr. Lenick has made it clear she believes that equal rights should be granted to everyone without regard to the traditions and history of this campus or this country. Therefore, Dr. Lenick is a bad teacher and should be fired immediately.*

The thrust of this argument revolves around two interrelated components – Dr. Lenick's advocacy of equal rights for all and her alleged disregard for tradition and history. The emotional appeal rests in the phrase "flaming, radical, feminist, liberal" – words that indicate ideological beliefs, usually beliefs that are strongly held by both sides. Additionally, hot button words like these tend to evoke a visceral response rather than a logical, reasoned response.

> The highest form of ignorance is when you reject something you don't know anything about. – Wayne Dyer

appeal to Ignorance (argumentum ad ignorantiam)

When we appeal to ignorance, we argue that the proposition must be accepted unless someone can prove otherwise. The argument rests not on any evidence but on a lack of evidence. We are to believe the truth of the argument because no one has disproven it. Let's look at an example to see how appeals to ignorance can develop:

> *People have been seeing ghosts for hundreds of years. No one has been able to prove definitively that ghosts don't exist. Therefore, ghosts are real.*

Though rather simplistic, this example makes clear the thrust of this fallacy. The focus is not on supporting evidence, but on a blatant lack of evidence. While ghosts may exist, we don't know for sure they do – or don't for that matter. As such, we could also argue that because we can't prove that ghosts are real they must not exist.

appeal to pity (argumentium ad misericordium)

Appeals to pity are another form of pulling on the emotions of the audience. In the appeal to pity, the argument attempts to win acceptance by pointing out the unfortunate consequences that will fall upon the speaker. In effect, the goal is to make us feel sorry for the speaker and ignore contradictory evidence. This form of fallacy is used often by students. Consider this message a professor recently received at the end of the semester:

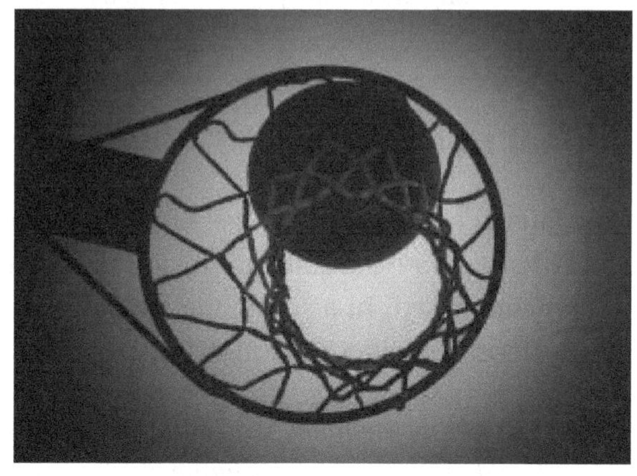

I know I have not done all the work for the semester and have been absent a lot. However, I am the key point guard for the basketball team. If I get any grade lower than a C, I will not be able to play basketball next semester. If I don't play, the team will lose. Will you please make sure that you give me at least a C for my final grade?

The student here acknowledges he does not deserve a grade of C or higher. He has missed assignments, failed the midterm, and accrued a number of absences. His argument asks the professor to ignore these facts, though, and focus on the fact that without him the team would lose. In other words, he hopes the professor will feel sorry for him and ignore the evidence.

begging the question (petitio principii)

A begging the question fallacy is a form of circular reasoning that occurs when the conclusion of the argument is used as one of the premises of the argument. Arguments composed in this way will only be considered sound or strong by those who already accept their conclusion.

Dilbert: And we know mass creates gravity because more dense planets have more gravity.

Dogbert: How do we know which planets are more dense?

Dilbert: They have more gravity.

To see how begging the question develops as a fallacy, let's turn to standard arguments in the abortion debate. One of the common arguments made by those who oppose legalized abortion is the following:

Murder is morally wrong. Abortion is murder. Therefore, abortion is morally wrong.

Most people would agree with the first premise that murder is morally wrong. The problem, then rests in the second premise. Not all individuals would agree that abortion is murder. However, as presented, the premise creates a presumption it is valid in all cases.

Those who advocate for legalized abortion are not immune from this fallacy. One of their standard arguments is:

The Constitution guarantees Americans the right to control their bodies.
Abortion is a choice affecting women's bodies.

Therefore, abortion is a constitutional right.

Like the previous example, the second premise generates a potential stopping point. While the choice to have or not have an abortion does clearly impact a woman's body, many individuals would argue this impact is not a deciding issue.

black-or-white Fallacy (bifurcation)

This fallacy is also known as an Either/or fallacy or False Dichotomy. The thrust of the fallacy occurs when we are only given the choice between two possible alternatives, when in fact more than two exist.

Returning to the abortion debates, we can see a form of this fallacy in play by simply looking at the way each side refers to itself. Those who oppose legalized abortion are Pro-Life. The implication here is that if you are for abortion then you are against life. The fallacy in this case is easy to figure out – there are many facets of life, not just abortion. Those who favor legalized abortion are Pro-Choice. The implication here is that if you are against abortion, then you are against choices. Again, the reasoning is faulty.

There is no black-and-white situation. It's all part of life. Highs, lows, middles. – Van Morrison

Let's look at another hot button topic to see how this fallacy develops in action. In recent years many family advocacy groups have argued that, what they call, the "liberal media" has caused the rapid moral decline of America. They usually ask questions like: Do you support families or moral depravity? This question ignores the whole range of choices between the two extremes.

composition

This fallacy occurs when we assume that if all the parts have a given quality, then the whole of the parts will have it as well. We jump to a conclusion without concrete evidence. We see this fallacy at work in the following example:

All of the basketball team's players are fast runners, high jumpers, and winners. Therefore, the team is a winner.

The problem here is the individuals must work together to make the team a winner. This might very well happen, but it might not.

To make this fallacy more clear, let's look at a humorous, though not so appetizing example:

I like smoothies for breakfast because I can drink them on the run. My favorite breakfast foods are scrambled eggs, fresh fruit, bagels with cream cheese, soy sausage links, cottage cheese, oatmeal, cold pizza, and triple espressos. Therefore, I would like a breakfast smoothie made of scrambled eggs, fresh fruit, bagels with cream cheese, soy sausage links, cottage cheese, oatmeal, cold pizza, and triple espressos.

If you're not feeling too nauseated to keep reading, you should be able to see the composition fallacy here. While each of these breakfast items may be appetizing individually, they become much less so when dropped into a blender and pureed together.

division

The opposite of the composition fallacy, a division fallacy occurs when we think the parts of the whole contain the same quality as the whole. Let's turn to another food-based example to see how this fallacy occurs:

Blueberry muffins taste good. Therefore, the individual ingredients comprising blueberry muffins also taste good.

On the surface, this argument may not appear to be problematic. However, think about the individual ingredients: blueberries, raw eggs, flour, sugar, salt, baking soda, oil, and vanilla. Of these, blueberries are the only items that generally taste good on their own. I don't know about you, but sitting down to a bowl of baking soda doesn't sound too appetizing.

Here's one more example to make the fallacy clearer:

Women in general make less money than men. Therefore, Brenda Barnes, CEO of the Sara Lee company, makes less money than the male delivery drivers who work for the company.

Common sense will tell you the CEO of a company makes more money than the hourly delivery drivers. Additionally, a few quick minutes of research will confirm this inference.

false cause (non causa, pro causa)

Sometimes called a Questionable Cause fallacy, this occurs when there exists a flawed causal connection between events. The fallacy is not just a bad inference about connection between cause and effect, but one that violates the cannons of reasoning about causation. We see two primary types of this fallacy.

Accidental or coincidental connection occurs when we assume a connection where one might or might not exist. We say event C caused event E when we have no clear proof. Here's an example:

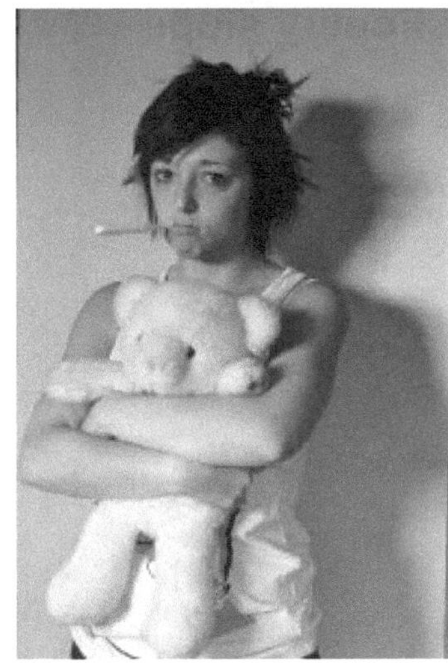

> *Yesterday Jen went out in the rain and got soaked. The next day she was in bed with the flu. Therefore, the rain caused her to get sick.*

Most of us probably grew up hearing statements like this without ever realizing we were being exposed to a logical fallacy in action. Flu is caused by exposure to a virus, not to bad weather.

The other type of causal fallacy occurs with a general causation between types of events. For example, we know that drinking excessive amounts of alcohol leads to alcoholism and cirrhosis of the liver. However, not every individual who drinks excessively develops either of these diseases. In other words, there is a possibility the disease will occur as a result of excessive drinking, but it is not an absolute.

red herring (irrelevant thesis)

This fallacy occurs when we introduce an irrelevant issue into the argument. The phrase "red herring" comes from the supposed fox hunting practice of dragging a dried smoke herring across the trail so as to throw off the hound from the scent. In logical reasoning, the red herring fallacy works in much the same way. No, this doesn't mean you make the argument while smelling like an old fish. What it does mean is that we attempt to distract the audience by introducing some irrelevant point, such as this:

> *Each year thousands of people die in car accident across the country. Why should we worry about endangered animals?*

This argument is trying to get us to focus on dead people instead of animals. While car accidents and the deaths resulting from them are a serious issue, this fact does not lessen the importance of worrying about endangered animals. The two issues are not equated with each other.

Political campaigns are a fertile ground for growing red herring fallacies. If you think back to the 2004 Presidential campaign you will find a number of red herrings. For example, at one point we were inundated with ads reminding us that John Kerry's wife was heir to the Heinz ketchup fortune. The implication was that by extension John Kerry was a rich elitist incapable of understanding the plight of working class and middle class individuals.

slippery slope

This fallacy occurs when we assume one action will initiate a chain of events culminating in an undesirable event later. It makes it seem like the final event, the bottom of the slope, is an inevitability. Arguments falling prey to the slippery slope fallacy ignore the fact there are probably a number of other things that can happen between the initial event and the bottom of the slope.

We hear examples of the slippery slope fallacy all around us:

> *If we teach sex education in school, then students will have more sex. If students have more sex, we will have a rash of unplanned pregnancies and sexually transmitted diseases. Students will be forced to drop out of school and will never have the chance to succeed in life.*

Clearly, just learning about sex doesn't automatically mean that you will engage in sex. Even more unlikely is the fact that merely learning about sex will force you to drop out of school.

strawman

This fallacy occurs when the actual argument appears to be refuted, but in reality a related point is addressed. The individual using a strawman argument will appear to be refuting the original point made but will actually be arguing a point not made in the original. The best strawman arguments will argue the new point to a conclusion that appears solid; however, because their point is not the original point, it is still a fallacy.

Examples of the strawman fallacy are everywhere and can appear to be quite persuasive:

> *President Obama cannot truly have American interests in mind because he's not truly American but Muslim.*

Statements similar to this were quite prevalent during the 2008 Presidential election and still appear on occasion. The assumption here is that if a person follows Islam and identifies as Muslim they clearly can't be American or interested in America. While there are many potential flaws in this argument as presented, for our purpose the most obvious is that there are many Americans who are Muslim and who are quite interested and concerned about America.

false analogy

When we use analogies in our reasoning, we are comparing things. A fallacy of weak analogy occurs when there exists a poor connection between examples. Structurally, the fallacy looks like this:

A and B are similar.
A has characteristic X. Therefore, B has characteristic X.

This fallacy often occurs when we try to compare two things that on the surface appear similar. For example:

Humans and animals are both living, breathing beings. Humans have civil rights. Therefore, animals have civil rights.

The problem in this argument is that while humans and animals are alike in their living and breathing status, there are numerous other ways they differ. We commit a fallacy when we infer that based on this initial similarity, they are similar in all other ways as well.

The other day while looking at houses, I heard another version of this argument from a real estate agent. The house I was looking at was an older house needing some TLC. I asked how old the roof was and the real estate agent responded:

I don't know for sure, but it's either 10 or 20 years old. You know, though, I put a roof on a house similar to this when I was younger and we haven't had to worry about it. It's been over 20 years now.

Ignoring for the moment that there's a big difference between a 10-year-old roof and a 20-year-old roof, the real estate agent mistakenly assumes that his roof and the roof of the TLC house are the same. They both provide a covering for the home, but that's about where their similarities end.

Attributions

CC licensed content, Shared previously

- Chapter 6 Informal Fallacies. **Authored by**: Terri Russ, J.D., Ph.D.. **Provided by**: Saint Mary's College, Notre Dame, IN. **Located at**: http://publicspeakingproject.org/psvirtualtext.html. **Project**: The Public Speaking Project. **License**: *CC BY-NC-ND: Attribution-NonCommercial-NoDerivatives*

- Image of coyote. **Authored by**: g'pa bill. **Located at**: https://flic.kr/p/89wB9C. **License**: *CC BY-NC-ND: Attribution-NonCommercial-NoDerivatives*

- Image of sick woman. **Authored by**: Courtney Carmody. **Located at**: https://flic.kr/p/8hrFDY. **License**: *CC BY: Attribution*

- Image of climbing on slippery slope. **Authored by**: Tony Roberts. **Located at**: https://flic.kr/p/9vhshy. **License**: *CC BY-NC-SA: Attribution-NonCommercial-ShareAlike*

- Image of comparing apple and orange. **Authored by**: Mike. **Located at**: https://flic.kr/p/ccmWs. **License**: *CC BY-NC-ND: Attribution-NonCommercial-NoDerivatives*

All rights reserved content

- Image of doctor in surgical mask. **Authored by**: wax115. **Provided by**: MorgueFile. **Located at**: http://mrg.bz/jwkCdC. **Project**: Free to remix, commercial use, no attribution required. http://www.morguefile.com/license/morguefile. **License**: *All Rights Reserved*

- Image of basketball hoop. **Authored by**: Annika. **Provided by**: MorgueFile. **Located at**: http://mrg.bz/XluBMB. **License**: *All Rights Reserved*. **License Terms**: Free to remix, commercial use, no attribution required. http://www.morguefile.com/license/morguefile

- Still image of bifurcated man. **Authored by**: gregorija1. **Located at**: http://youtu.be/vi7QQ5pO7_A. **License**: *All Rights Reserved.* **License Terms**: Standard YouTube License

Public domain content

- Image of US Soldiers. **Authored by**: Mass Communication Specialist 1st Class Jackey Bratt. **Provided by**: US Navy. **Located at**: http://commons.wikimedia.org/wiki/File:US_Navy_060920-N-4097B-026_Soldiers_from_the_U.S._Army%5Ersquo,s_Apache_Troop,_2nd_Squadron,_9th_Cavalry_Regiment_exit_a_home_in_Muqdadiyah,_Iraq,_after_searching_it.jpg. **License**: *Public Domain: No Known Copyright*
- Image of blueberry muffin. **Authored by**: Renee Comet. **Provided by**: National Cancer Institute. **Located at**: http://commons.wikimedia.org/wiki/File:Muffin_NIH.jpg. **License**: *Public Domain: No Known Copyright*

Conclusion, Review Questions, and Activities

In this chapter we have examined what critical thinking is and how it involves more than simply being critical. Understanding critical thinking helps in formulating and studying arguments. We see arguments every day in advertising, use arguments to persuade others, and we use them to benefit us. The overview of fallacies showed not all arguments are valid or even logical. Always critically think and examine any argument you confront, and remember that if it sounds too good to be true, it probably is a fallacious argument.

"Quiet Moment" **by anitapeppers.** *morgueFile.*

We practice critical thinking on a daily basis, often without any extra effort. Now that you know a bit more about how to do these things better, you should find that you can put together more persuasive arguments that avoid the pitfalls of fallacious thinking. More importantly, when you hear a statement such as, "You should drink at least four glasses of wine per day," you'll know that something isn't right. And if you do hear a statement like this, you will be prepared to think critically about the statement, and will be in a position to make a more educated decision about the information.

Review Questions
1. Explain the difference between critical thinking and being critical. Why should we care?
2. Explain how listening differs from hearing and why listening is the first component of practicing critical thinking.
3. List and discuss at least three ways that we use logic and argumentation in our daily

lives.

4. If I say, "There is plenty of pasta, so you should have some more," am I implying or inferring that you have not eaten enough?

5. What are a fallacies and why is it important that we study them?

6. Television commercials that use pictures of starving children and sad music as a way to get you to donate money are an example of what type of fallacy?

7. Name, define, and give examples of three different fallacies you have heard recently.

Exercises

1. Throughout this chapter, we have turned to the abortion debates for examples. In order to practice critical thinking in action, spend some time researching the major arguments each side uses. Because the debates in this area are so complex, you might want to narrow your focus just a bit. For example, you could focus on the issue of minors consenting to abortion or abortion in the case of rape or other sexual assault. Compile a list of the most common arguments used by each side. Your list should include: any evidence used to support claims, a list of the major claims, any conclusions. Return to the core critical thinking skills and critically evaluate how each side forms arguments and uses evidence. How do your own biases and thoughts on the issue of abortion influence your evaluation? If you were an advisor, what advisee would you give to each side to make their arguments stronger and more logically sound?

2. Your local newspaper's Letters to the Editor section is a prime spot to find logical fallacies in action. For several days, read the Letters to the Editor and identify all of the fallacies you find. Keep a log of the specific fallacies you find, dividing them by type. Once you have compiled a variety of example, take a step back and evaluate them. Questions that you might want to ask include: what fallacy or fallacies seem to be most popular? Why do you think this is? Pick a few of the most egregious fallacies and rewrite them correcting for the flaw in reasoning.

3. Throughout this chapter, we have studied arguments by looking at their various parts. In practice, arguments occur as part of larger statements or speeches making their analysis a bit more complicated. To understand the ways arguments occur in daily life, visit the American Rhetoric page (www.americanrhetoric.com). On this page you will find a number of political, activist, movie, and other speeches. Pick one and try to identify the major arguments that are set forth. What are the main claims? What are the sub-claims? What sorts of evidence or support are provided? Are there any fallacies present in the argument? If you were a speech writer, what advice would you give to improve the argument?

Attributions

CC licensed content, Shared previously

lege, Notre Dame, IN. **Located at**: http://publicspeakingproject.org/psvirtualtext.html. **Project**: The Public Speaking Project. **License**: *CC BY-NC-ND: Attribution-NonCommercial-NoDerivatives*

- quietmoment. **Authored by**: anitapeppers. **Provided by**: MorgueFile. **Located at**: http://www.morguefile.com/archive/display/39148. **License**: *Other*. **License Terms**: You are allowed to copy, distribute, transmit the work and to adapt the work. Attribution is not required. You are prohibited from using this work in a stand alone manner.

Glossary and References

Glossary

TERM	DEFINITION
Accident Fallacy	A fallacy that occurs when a generally true statement is applied to a specific case that is unusual.
Ambiguity Fallacy	A fallacy that occurs when a word having more than one meaning appears in the argument.
Analysis	The process of asking what is happening in a message through breaking it into its individual components and asking questions of each section.
Appeal to Authority	A fallacy that occurs when the truth of a proposition is thought to rest in the opinion of a famous other or authority.
Appeal to Ignorance	A fallacy that occurs when we argue something must be accepted because it cannot be proven otherwise.
Appeal to Pity	A fallacy that occurs when an argument attempts to win acceptance by focusing on the unfortunate consequences that will occur if it is not accepted.
Argument	Statements that combine reasoning with evidence to support an assertion.
Bad Reasons Fallacy	A fallacy that occurs when then we assume the conclusion of an argument to be bad because a part of the argument is bad.
Begging the Question	A fallacy that occurs when the conclusion of the argument is also used as one of the premises.
Black and White Fallacy	A fallacy that occurs when the audience is only given two choices.
Composition Fallacy	A fallacy that occurs when we assume that traits inherent in the parts are also present when the parts are combined into a whole.
Critical Thinking	Active thinking in which we evaluate and analyze information in order to determine the best course of action.
Deduction	An argument in which the truth of the premises of the argument guarantee the truth of its conclusion.
Division	A fallacy that occurs when we assume that the trait of a whole occurs when the whole is divided into its parts.
Evaluation	The process of assessing the various claims and premises of an argument to determine their validity.
Evidence	Research, claims, or anything else that is used to support the validity of an assertion.
Fallacy	A flaw or error in reasoning.
Fallacy of Quantitative Logic	A fallacy that occurs when we misuse quantifying words such as "all" or "some."
False Analogy	A fallacy that occurs when there exists a poor connection between two examples used in an argument.
False Cause	A fallacy that occurs when there exists a flawed connection between two events.
Genetic Fallacy	A fallacy that occurs when the individual is attacked.
Hearing	The physiological process of receiving noise and sounds.

Imply	To suggest or convey an idea.
Induction	An argument in which the truth of its propositions lend support to the conclusion.
Infer	To draw a conclusion that rests outside the message.
Interpretation	Explaining and extrapolating the conclusions that we draw from a statement.
Listening	The psychological process of attaching meaning to the sounds and noises we hear.
Masked Man Fallacy	A fallacy that occurs when we substitute parties that are not identical within an argument.
Non sequitor	An argument where the conclusion may be true or false, but in which there exists a disconnect within the argument itself.
Premise	A proposition (statement) supporting or helping to support a conclusion; an assumption that something is true.
Red Herring Fallacy	A fallacy that occurs when an irrelevant issue is introduced into the argument.
Self-regulation	The process of reflecting on our pre-existing thoughts and biases and how they may influence what we think about an assertion.
Slippery Slope Fallacy	A fallacy that occurs when we assume one action will initiate a chain of events that culminate in an undesirable event.
Strawman Fallacy	A fallacy that occurs when the actual argument appears to be refuted, but in reality a related point is addressed.
Syllogism	A form of deductive argument in which the conclusion is inferred from the premises. Most syllogisms contain a major premise, a minor premise, and a conclusion.

References

Aristotle. (1989). *Prior Analytics* (Trans. Robin Smith). Cambridge, MA: Hackett Publishing.

Beyer, B. K. (1995) *Critical thinking.* Bloomington, IN: Phi Delta Kappa Educational Foundation.

Dewey, J. (1933). *Experience and education.* New York: Macmillan, 1933.

Elder, L. & Richard, P. (1996). *Universal Intellectual Standards.* Dillon Beach, CA: Foundation for Critical Thinking. Retrieved from: http://www.criticalthinking.org/page.cfm?Pag eID=527&CategoryID=68

Facione, P. A. (1990). *Critical Thinking: A Statement of Expert Consensus for Purposes of Educational Assessment and Instruction, The Delphi Report* (Executive Summary). Millbrae, CA: California Academic Press.

photo credits

p. 1 Gears in head http://commons.wikimedia.org/wiki/File: Filos_segundo_logo.JPG By Filosofias Filosoficas

p. 2 John Dewey http://upload.wikimedia.org/wikipedia/co mmons/9/91/John_Dewey_in_1902.jpg By Postdlf

p. 3 Martha Stewart http://commons.wikimedia.org/wiki/File: Martha_Stewart_nrkbeta.jpg By Alĥemiisto

p. 5 Seat belt http://commons.wikimedia.org/wiki/File: Seat_belt_BX.jpg By Michiel 1972

p. 6 Sharia Law Billboard http://commons.wikimedia.org/wiki/File: Sharia-law-Billboard.jpg By Matt57

p. 7 Toilet http://commons.wikimedia.org/wiki/File: Decorative_toilet_seat.jpg By Bartux

p. 9 World Trade Center Bombing 1993 http://commons.wikimedia.org/wiki/File: WTC_1993_ATF_Commons.jpg By Smurfy

p. 12 U.S. Soldiers http://commons.wikimedia.org/wiki/File: US_Navy_060920-N-4097B- 026_Soldiers_from_the_U.S._Army%5E rsquo,s_Apache_Troop,_2nd_Squadron,_ 9th_Cavalry_Regiment_exit_a_home_in_ Muqdadiyah,_Iraq,_after_searching_it.jp g By The United States Navy

p. 13 Julianne Moore http://commons.wikimedia.org/wiki/File: Julianne_Moore_March_for_Women%27 s_Lives_2004.jpg By Pattymooney

p. 14 Ghost http://commons.wikimedia.org/wiki/File: Radiovector_-_ghost.jpg By Musilupa

p. 14 Star Trek "Let that be your last battlefield." Posted on YouTube by gregorija1

http://www.youtube.com/watch?v=vi7Q Q5pO7_A

p. 15 Blueberry muffin http://commons.wikimedia.org/wiki/File: Muffin_NIH.jpg By 17 Drew

Attributions

CC licensed content, Shared previously

Chapter 10: Audience Analysis

Objectives and Introduction

Audience Analysis

By Lisa Schreiber, Ph.D. and Morgan Hartranft
Millersville University, Millersville, PA

Learning Objectives

After reading this chapter, you should be able to:

- List techniques for analyzing a specific target ?audience.
- Explain audience analysis ?by direct observation.
- Describe audience analysis ?by inference.
- Identify the purpose of a ?basic questionnaire.
- Recognize and apply data ?sampling.
- Determine when to use a ?Likert-type test.
- Define the five categories ?of audience analysis.
- Summarize the purpose of the situational analysis.
- Explain audience analysis by demography.
- Recognize the difference between beliefs, attitudes and values.
- Identify reasons for sampling a multicultural audience.
- Apply the chapter concepts in final questions and activities.

Introduction

"RZA Audience Shankbone 2009 Tao of Wu" by David Shankbone.

Robert E. Mullins, a well-known local bank officer, was preparing a speech for the Rotary Club in Dallas, Texas on the topic of "finding the right loan" for a rather diverse audience. He knew his topic extremely well, had put a lot of hard work into his research, and had his visual aids completely in order. One of the things he had not fully considered, however, was the audience to which he would be speaking. On the day of the presentation, Mr. Mullins delivered a flawless speech on "secured" car and home loans, but the speech was not received particularly well. You see, on this particular week, a major segment of the audience consisted of the "Junior Rotarians" who wanted to hear about "personal savings accounts" and "college savings plans." It was a critical error. Had Mr. Mullins considered the full nature and demographic makeup of his audience prior to the event, he might not have been received so poorly.

In contemporary public speaking, the audience that you are addressing is the entire reason you are giving the speech; accordingly, the audience is therefore the most important component of all speechmaking. It cannot be said often or more forcefully enough: know your audience! Knowing your audience—their beliefs, attitudes, age, education level, job functions, language, and culture—is the single most important aspect of developing your speech strategy and execution plan. Your audience isn't just a passive group of people who come together by happenstance to listen to you. Your audience is assembled for a very real and significant reason: they want to hear what you have to say. So, be prepared.

> Spectacular achievement is always preceded by unspectacular preparation. – Robert H. Schuller

We analyze our audience because we want to discover information that will help create a bond between the speaker and the audience. We call this bond "identification." Aristotle loosely called it "finding a common ground." This isn't a one-way process between the speaker and the audience; rather, it is a two-way transactional process. When you ask an audience to listen to your ideas, you are inviting them to come partway into your personal and professional experience as an expert speaker. And, in return, it is your responsibility and obligation to go partway into their experience as an audience. The more you know and understand about your audience and their psychological needs, the better you can prepare your speech and your enhanced confidence will reduce your own speaker anxiety.[1]

This chapter is dedicated to understanding how a speaker connects with an audience through **audience analysis** by direct observation, analysis by inference, and data collection.[2] In addition, this chapter explores

---

1. Dwyer, K.K. (2005) *Conquer your speech anxiety:* Second Edition. Belmont, CA: Wadsworth.
2. Clevenger, T. (1966). *Audience analysis.* Indianapolis: Bobbs-Merrill.

the five categories of audience analysis: (1) the situational analysis, (2) the demographic analysis, (3) the psychological analysis, (4) the multicultural analysis, and (5) the topic interest and prior knowledge analysis.

Attributions

CC licensed content, Shared previously

- Chapter 5 Objectives, Outline, and Introduction. **Authored by**: Peter DeCaro, Ph.D., Tyrone Adams, Ph.D., and Bonnie Jefferis, Ph.D.. **Provided by**: University of Alaska - Fairbanks, University of Louisiana - Lafayette, and St. Petersburg College. **Located at**: http://publicspeakingproject.org/psvirtualtext.html. **Project**: The Public Speaking Project. **License**: *CC BY-NC-ND: Attribution-NonCommercial-NoDerivatives*

- RZA Audience Shankbone 2009 Tao of Wu. **Authored by**: David Shankbone. **Located at**: http://commons.wikimedia.org/wiki/File:RZA_Audience_Shankbone_2009_Tao_of_Wu.jpg. **License**: *CC BY: Attribution*

Video: Monroe's Motivated Sequence

An introduction to MMS:

- https://youtu.be/k0ED3PckYaM

Example of a powerful persuasive speech:

- https://youtu.be/EzZzZ_qpZ4w

Attributions

CC licensed content, Original

- Public Speaking. **Authored by**: Christie Fierro and Brent Adrian. **Provided by**: Lumen Learning. **Located at**: http://lumenlearning.com/. **Project**: Kaleidoscope Open Course Initiative. **License**: *CC BY: Attribution*

All rights reserved content

- KP's Speech Class Monroe's Motivated Sequence. **Authored by**: Krista Price. **Located at**: http://youtu.be/k0ED3PckYaM. **License**: *All Rights Reserved*. **License Terms**: Standard YouTube License
- Ron Finley A guerilla gardener in South Central LA. **Authored by**: TED. **Located at**: http://youtu.be/EzZzZ_qpZ4w. **License**: *All Rights Reserved*. **License Terms**: Standard YouTube License

Outline for Monroe's Motivated Sequence

Note: The verbiage here is only meant to trigger the direction for each particular step of Monroe's Sequence. You should not use this exact wording in your outline. Your content should simply cover each area shown here.

I. Attention Step

    Thesis/Preview

II. Need-

1. The problem
2. Here's proof that this is a serious problem
3. Here's how this problem impacts your life, audience
4. Some people say this isn't really a problem.
5. I say they're wrong, and here's why

Transition-

III. Satisfaction-

1. Here's the solution to this problem:
2. Here's how the solution works:
3. Here's proof that this solution does work to solve the problem:
4. Some say this kind of a solution won't work.
5. I say they're wrong, and here's why:

Transition-

IV. Visualization-

    1. Picture how much worse off we'll be if we don't move to use my solution

    2. Picture how much better the world will be once we put my solution into place

V. Action-

    1. Restate thesis:

    2. Call to action:

    3. Because if you don't:

    4. But if you do

    5. Tie Down

Sources:

Attributions

CC licensed content, Shared previously

- Outline for Monroe's Motivated Sequence. **Authored by**: Ellen Bremen. **Provided by**: Highline College. **Located at**: https://www.highline.edu/. **License**: *CC BY: Attribution*

Approaches to Audience Analysis

Whenever thinking about your speech, it is always a good idea to begin with a thorough awareness of your audience and the many factors comprising that particular audience. In speech communication, we simply call this "doing an audience analysis." An audience analysis is when you consider all of the pertinent elements defining the makeup and **demographic characteristics** (also known as **demographics**) of your audience.[1] From the Greek prefix *demo* (of the people), we come to understand that there are detailed accounts of human population characteristics, such as age, gender, education, occupation, language, ethnicity, culture, background knowledge, needs and interests, and previously held attitudes, beliefs, and values. Demographics are widely used by advertising and public relations professionals to analyze specific audiences so that their products or ideas will carry influence. However, all good public speakers consider the demographic characteristics of their audience, as well. It is the fundamental stage of preparing for your speech. Table 5.1 shows some examples of demographics and how they may be used when developing your speech. Of course, this is not an all-inclusive list. But, it does help you get a good general understanding of the demographics of the audience you will be addressing.

Table 5.1: Tailoring a Speech to Demographic Characteristics	
Demographic Characteristics	**Do's and Don'ts**
Ethnicity	Don't try to use words or phrases to "cuddle up" to one race or another. You would lose some credibility if you made a point in your speech and then said, "So get jiggy with it" or "You could enjoy that with your afternoon tea ceremony."[2]
Age	Stay away from jargon from one age range or another, like "OMG" or "the cat's pajamas"[3]
Sex/Gender	Use words that are not sex/gender-specific. Instead of policeman, fireman, and stewardess, use police officer, firefighter, and flight attendant. Do not use one sex/gender pronouns, like assuming a teacher is a "she" and a dentist is a "he."[4]
Income	Some people in your audience will have more money than others. So if you keep fit by maintaining membership in a prominent gym and you take classes there also, don't assume everyone else can afford to do so. You can tell your audience what you do, but give them options like parking far from the store and working out with a yoga or pilates CD at home.

1. McQuail, D. (1997). *Audience analysis*. Thousand Oaks, CA: Sage Publications.
2. Pearson, J.C., Nelson, P.E., Titsworth, S. & Harter, L. (2011). *Human communication* (4th Ed.). Boston: McGraw-Hill.
3. Gamble, T.K. & Gamble, M. (2013). *Communication works*. New York: McGrawHill.
4. Eisenberg, I. & Wynn, D. (2013) *Think communication*. Boston: Pearson.

Table 5.1: Tailoring a Speech to Demographic Characteristics	
Demographic Characteristics	**Do's and Don'ts**
Occupation	Unless you are speaking at a convention where everyone in your audience works in the same field, make your speech more explanatory. Your audience has not had extensive training in medical terms nor legal terms. So you need to explain what you are talking about, without using the big words which would make your audience feel confused, stupid, and put down.
Religion	Realize that your audience will likely have a wide variety of religions represented, an some people may have no religious or spiritual beliefs. So you can say that you read the Bible every night for 10 minutes, but that you are suggesting that everyone choose a religious or inspirational reading for presleep relaxation.[5]
Education Level	Even if you are speaking to an audience of college freshmen, not everyone has had the same educational experiences. For example, some of the people in your class may have completed a high school equivalency program like the GED, some may be high school students who are taking a college class, some may have gone to secondary school in another country, some may have been homeschooled, and some may have gone to a private honors-based prep school. You need to be careful not to talk down to your audience and not to use fancy sentences and words to try to impress your audience. Gauging the right level of communication for your speech is an important challenge.

So now you may be saying to yourself: "Gee, that's great! How do I go about analyzing my particular audience?" First, you need to know that there are three overarching methods (or "**paradigms**") for doing an audience analysis: audience analysis by direct observation, audience analysis by inference, and audience analysis through data collection. Once you get to know how these methods work, you should be able to select which one (or even combination of these methods) is right for your circumstances.

> Nothing has such power to broaden the mind as the ability to investigate systematically and truly all that comes under thy observation in life. – Marcus Aurelius

Direct Observation

Audience analysis by direct observation, or direct experience, is, by far, the most simple of the three paradigms for "getting the feel" of a particular audience. It is a form of qualitative data gathering. We perceive it through one or more of our five natural senses—hearing, seeing, touching, tasting, and smelling. Knowledge that we acquire through personal experience has more impact on us than does knowledge that we learn indirectly. Knowledge acquired from personal experience is also more likely to affect our thinking and will be retained for a longer period of time.
We are more likely to trust what we hear, see, feel, taste, and smell rather than what we learn from secondary sources of information.[6]

All you really need to do for this method of observation is to examine your audience. If you are lucky enough to be able to do this before speaking to your audience, you will be able to gather some basic reflective data (How old are they? What racial mix does this audience have? Does their non-verbal behavior indicate that they are excited to hear this speech?) that will help you arrange your thoughts and arguments for your speech.[7]

5. Gamble & Gamble 2013
6. Pressat, R. (1972). *Demographic analysis; methods, results, applications*. Chicago: Aldine-Atherton.
7. Nierenberg, G.I. & Calero, H.H. (1994) *How to read a person like a book*. New York: Barnes and Noble Books.

One excellent way to become informed about your audience is to ask them about themselves. In its most basic form, this is data collection. Whenever possible, have conversations with them—interact with members of your audience—get to know them on a personal level (Where did you go to school? Do you have siblings/pets? What kind of car do you drive?) Through these types of conversations, you will be able to get to know and appreciate each audience member as both a human being and as an audience member. You will come to understand what interests them, convinces them, or even makes them laugh. You might arouse interest and curiosity in your topic while you also gain valuable data.

"MobileHCI 2008 Audience" **by Nhenze.** *CC-BY-SA.*

For example, you want to deliver a persuasive speech about boycotting farm-raised fish. You could conduct a short attitudinal survey to discover what your audience thinks about the topic, if they eat farm-raised fish, and if they believe it is healthy for them. This information will help you when you construct your speech because you will know their attitudes about the subject. You would be able to avoid constructing a speech that potentially could do the opposite of what you intended.

Another example would be that you want to deliver an informative speech about your town's recreational activities and facilities. Your focus can be aligned with your audience if, before you begin working on your speech, you find out if your audience has senior citizens and/or high school students and/or new parents.

Clearly this cannot be done in every speaking situation, however. Often, we are required to give an **unacquainted-audience presentation**. Unacquainted-audience presentations are speeches when you are completely unfamiliar with the audience and its demographics. In these cases, it is always best to try and find some time to sit down and talk with someone you trust (or even several people) who might be familiar with the given audience. These conversations can be very constructive in helping you understand the context in which you will be speaking.

Not understanding the basic demographic characteristics of an audience, or further, that audience's beliefs, values, or attitudes about a given topic makes your presentation goals haphazard, at best. Look around the room at the people who will be listening to your speech. What types of gender, age, ethnicity, and educational- level characteristics are represented? What are their expectations for your presentation? This is all-important information you should know before you begin your research and drafting your outline. Who is it that I am going to be talking to?

> If we knew what it was we were doing, it would not be called research, would it? – Albert Einstein

Inference

Audience analysis by inference is merely a logical extension of your observations drawn in the method above. It is a form of critical thinking known as inductive reasoning, and another form of qualitative data gathering. An inference is when you make a reasoned tentative conclusion or logical judgment on the basis of available evidence. It is best used when you can identify patterns in your evidence that indicate something is expected to happen again or should hold true based upon previous experiences. A good speaker knows how to interpret information and draw conclusions from that information. As individuals we make inferences—or reasonable assumptions—all the time. For example, when we hear someone speaking Arabic, we infer that they are from the Middle East. When we see this person carrying a copy of The Koran, we infer that they are also a follower of the Muslim faith. These are reasoned conclusions that we make based upon the evidence available to us and our general knowledge about people and their traits.

When we reason, we make connections, distinctions, and predictions; we use what is known or familiar to us to reach a conclusion about something that is unknown or unfamiliar for it to make sense. Granted, of course, inferences are sometimes wrong. Here's a familiar example: You reach into a jar full of jelly beans, and they turn out to be all black. You love black jelly beans. You reach back into the jar and take another hand full, which turn out to be, again, all black. Since you can't see the jelly beans inside the jar you make an assumption based on empirical evidence (two handfuls of jelly beans) that all of the jelly beans are black. You reach into the jar a third time and take a hand full of jelly beans out, but this time they aren't any black jelly beans, but white, pink, and yellow. Your conclusion that all of the jelly beans were black turned out to be fallacious.

Data Sampling

Unlike audience analysis by direct observation and analysis by inference, audience analysis by data sampling uses statistical evidence to quantify and clarify the characteristics of your audience. These characteristics are also known as variables,[8] and are assigned a numerical value so we can systematically collect and classify them. They are reported as statistics, also known as quantitative analysis or quantitative data collection. Statistics are numerical summaries of facts, figures, and research findings. Audience analysis by data sampling requires you to survey your audience before you give your speech. You need to know the basics of doing a survey before you actually collect and interpret your data.

"Here's a Jellybean for You" by KaCey97078. CC-BY.

> If you make listening and observation your occupation, you will gain much more than you can by talk. – Robert Baden-Powell

Basic Questionnaire

There are a great number of survey methods available to the speaker. However, we will cover three primary types in this section because they are utilized the most. The first type of survey method you should know about is the basic questionnaire, which is a series of questions advanced to produce demographic and attitudinal data from your audience.

8. Tucker, K.T.; Weaver, II, R.L.; Berryman-Fink, C. (1981). *Research in speech communication.* Englewood Cliffs, N.J.: Prentice-Hall.

Clearly, audience members should not be required to identify themselves by name on the basic questionnaire. Anonymous questionnaires are more likely to produce truthful information. Remember, all you are looking for is a general read of your audience; you should not be looking for specific information about any respondent concerning your questionnaire in particular. It is a bulk sampling tool, only.

While you can easily gather basic demographic data (examples of demographic questions are shown in the chart following this section), we need to adjust our questions a bit more tightly, or ask more focused questions, in order to understand the audience's "predispositions" to think or act in certain ways. For example, you can put an attitudinal extension on the basic questionnaire (examples of attitudinal questions are shown in Figure 5.1).

These questions probe more deeply into the psyche of your audience members, and will help you see where they stand on certain issues. Of course, you may need to tighten these questions to get to the heart of your specific topic. But, once you do, you'll have a wealth of data at your disposal that, ultimately, will tell you how to work with your target audience.

"Man With a Clipboard" by Elizabeth M. CC-BY.

Ordered Categories

Another method of finding out your audience's value set is to survey them according to their value hierarchy. A value hierarchy is a person's value structure placed in relationship to a given value set.[9] The way to determine a person's value hierarchy is to use the ordered categories sampling method. Here, each audience member is given a list of values on a piece of paper, and each audience member writes these values on another piece of paper in order according to their importance to him/her. Each response is different, of course, because each audience member is different, but when analyzed by the speaker, common themes will present themselves in the overall data. Accordingly, the speaker can then identify with those common value themes. (Examples of an Ordered Value Set appear in Figure 5.1).

9. Rokeach, M. (1968). *Beliefs, attitudes, and values; a theory of organization and change* (1st ed.). San Francisco: Jossey-Bass.

Likert-type Testing

<table>
<tr><td colspan="2" align="center">Figure 5.1: Examples of Survey Questions</td></tr>
<tr valign="top"><td>

Demographic Questions

1. Academic level in college
    - freshman
    - sophomore
    - junior
    - senior
2. Marital status
    - single
    - married
    - divorced
    - widowed
3. Age
    - less than 18 years old
    - 18–30 years old
    - 31–45 years old
    - over 46 years of age

</td><td>

Attitudinal Questions

1. I regard myself as
    - conservative
    - liberal
    - socialist
    - independent
2. I believe that abortion
    - should be illegal
    - should remain legal
    - should be legal only in cases of rape
    - not sure
3. I think that prayer should be permitted in public schools
    - yes
    - no
    - undecided

</td></tr>
<tr valign="top"><td>

Value Ordered Questions

Place the following list of values in order of importance, from most important (1) to least important (5).

Freedom
Liberty
Justice
Democracy
Safety

1. __________
2. __________
3. __________
4. __________
5. __________

</td><td>

Likert-Type Questions

Indicate the degree to which you agree or disagree with each question.

1. Unsolicited email should be illegal.
    Strongly Agree   1   2   3   4   5   Strongly Disagree
2. Making unsolicited email illegal would be fundamentally unfair to businesses.
    Strongly Agree 1 2 3 4 5 Strongly Disagree
3. I usually delete unsolicited email before even opening it.
    Strongly Agree 1 2 3 4 5 Strongly Disagree

</td></tr>
</table>

The final method of asserting your audience's attitudes deals with Likert-type testing. Likert-type testing is when you make a statement, and ask the respondent to gauge the depth of their sentiments toward that statement either positively, negatively, or neutrally. Typically, each scale will have 5 weighted response categories, being +2, +1, 0, -1, and -2. What the Likert-type test does, that other tests do not do, is measure the extent to which attitudes are held. See how the Likert-type test does this in the example on "unsolicited email" in Figure 5.1.

A small Likert-type test will tell you where your audience, generally speaking, stands on issues. As well, it will inform you as to the degree of the audience's beliefs on these issues. The Likert-type test should be used when attempting to assess a highly charged or polarizing issue, because it will tell you, in rough numbers, whether or not your audience agrees or disagrees with your topic.

No matter what kind of data sampling you choose, you need to allow time to collect the information and then analyze it. For example, if you create a survey of five questions, and you have your audience of 20 people complete the survey, you will need to deal with 100 survey forms. At high levels such as political polling, the audience members quickly click on their answers on a webpage or on a hand-held "clicker," and the specific survey software instantly collects and collates the information for researchers. If you are in a small community group or college class, it is more likely that you will be doing your survey "the old-fashioned way"–so you will need some time to mark each individual response on a "master sheet" and then average or summarize the results in an effective way to use in your speech-writing and speech-giving.

Attributions

CC licensed content, Shared previously

- Chapter 5 Approaches to Audience Analysis. **Authored by**: Peter DeCaro, Ph.D., Tyrone Adams, Ph.D., and Bonnie Jefferis, Ph.D.. **Provided by**: University of Alaska - Fairbanks, University of Louisiana - Lafayette, and St. Petersburg College. **Located at**: http://publicspeakingproject.org/psvirtualtext.html. **Project**: The Public Speaking Project. **License**: *CC BY-NC-ND: Attribution-NonCommercial-NoDerivatives*
- MobileHCI 2008 Audience. **Authored by**: Nhenze. **Located at**: http://commons.wikimedia.org/wiki/File:MobileHCI_2008_Audience.jpg. **License**: *CC BY-SA: Attribution-ShareAlike*
- Here's a Jellybean for You. **Authored by**: KaCey97078. **Located at**: https://flic.kr/p/q1m9u. **License**: *CC BY: Attribution*
- Man With a Clipboard. **Authored by**: Elizabeth M. **Located at**: https://flic.kr/p/74U8kN. **License**: *CC BY: Attribution*

Categories of Audience Analysis

No matter which of the above inquiry methods you choose to do your audience analysis, you will, at some point, need to direct your attention to the five "categories" of audience analysis. These are the five categories through which you will learn to better appreciate your audience. Let's now examine these categories and understand the variables and constraints you should use to estimate your audience's information requirements.

Situational Analysis

The situational audience analysis category considers the situation for which your audience is gathered. This category is primarily concerned with why your audience is assembled in the first place.[1] Are they willingly gathered to hear you speak? Have your audience members paid to hear you? Or, are your audience members literally "speech captives" who have somehow been socially or systematically coerced into hearing you? These factors are decisively important because they place a major responsibility upon you as a speaker, whichever is the case. The entire tone and agenda of your speech rests largely upon whether or not your audience even wants to hear from you.

Untitled by *Konrad-Adenauer-Gemeinschaftshauptschule Wenden.* CC-BY-NC-SA.

Many audiences are considered captive audiences in that they have no real choice regarding the matter of hearing a given speech. In general, these are some of the most difficult audiences to address because these members are being forced to listen to a message, and do not have the full exercise of their own free will. Consider for a moment when you have been called to a mandatory work meeting. Were you truly happy to listen to the speaker, in all honesty? Some might

1. Caernarven-Smith, P. (1983). *Audience analysis & response* (1st Ed.). Pembroke, MA: Firman Technical Publications.

say "yes," but usually most would rather be doing something else with their time. This is an important factor to keep in mind when preparing your speech: some people simply do not want to listen to a speech they believe is compulsory.

The voluntary audience situation, in stark contrast, is completely different. A voluntary audience is willingly assembled to listen to a given message. As a rule, these audiences are much easier to address because they are interested in hearing the speech. To visualize how this works, reflect upon the last speech, concert, or show you've chosen to attend. While the event may or may not have lived up to your overall expectations, the very fact that you freely went to the occasion speaks volumes about your predisposition to listen to—and perhaps even be persuaded by—the information being presented.

Sometimes audiences are mixed in their situational settings, too. Take the everyday classroom situation, for instance. While students choose to attend higher education, many people in the college classroom environment sadly feel as if they are still "trapped" in school and would rather be elsewhere. On the other hand, some students in college are truly there by choice, and attentively seek out knowledge from their teacher-mentors. What results from this mixed audience situation is a hybrid captive-voluntary audience, with those who are only partially interested in what is going on in the classroom and those who are genuinely involved. You literally get to hone your speech skills on both types of audiences, thereby learning a skill set that many never get to exercise. You should begin this wonderful opportunity by considering ways to inform, persuade, and humor a mixed situation audience. Think of it as a learning occasion, and you'll do just fine.

Being popular with an audience is a very rickety ladder to be on. – Louis C. K.

Demographic Analysis

The second category of audience analysis is **demography**. As mentioned before, demographics are literally a classification of the characteristics of the people. Whenever addressing an audience, it is generally a good idea to know about its age, gender, major, year in school, race, ethnicity, religious affiliation, et cetera. There are two steps in doing an accurate demographic analysis: gathering demographic data and interpreting this data.[2]

Sometimes, this information is gathered by the questionnaire sampling method, and is done formally. On other occasions, this information is already available in a database and is made available to the speaker. Some noteworthy speakers even have "scouts" who do demographic research on an audience prior to a speaking event, and make interpretations on that audience based upon key visual cues. For example, congresspersons and senators frequently make public appearances where they use stock speeches to appeal to certain audiences with specific demographic uniqueness. In order to know what type of audience he or she will be addressing, these politicians dispatch staff aides to an event to see how many persons of color, hecklers, and supporters will be in attendance. Of course, studying demographic characteristics is, indeed, more an art form than a science. Still, it is a common practice among many professional speakers.

---

2. Benjamin, B. (1969). *Demographic analysis*. New York: Praeger.

Consider for a moment how valuable it would be to you as a public speaker to know that your audience will be mostly female, between the ages of 25 and 40, mostly married, and Caucasian. Would you change your message to fit this demographic? Or, would you keep your message the same, no matter the audience you were addressing? Chances are you would be more inclined to talk to issues bearing upon those gender, age, and race qualities. Frankly, the smart speaker would shift his or her message to adapt to the audience. And, simply, that's the purpose of doing demographics: to embed within your message the acceptable parameters of your audience's range of needs.

"Wiki Conference 2011" **by Sucheta Ghoshal.** CC-BY-SA.

This, of course, raises an extremely important ethical issue for the modern speaker. Given the ability to study demographic data and therefore to study your audience, does a speaker shift his or her message to play to the audience entirely? Ethically, a speaker should not shift his or her message and should remain true to his or her motives. Only you will be able to alleviate the tension between a speaker's need to adapt to an audience and his or her need to remain true to form.[3]

> My greatest challenge has been to change the mindset of people. Mindsets play strange tricks on us. We see things the way our minds have instructed our eyes to see. – Muhammad Yunus

Psychological Analysis

Unless your selected speech topic is a complete mystery to your audience, your listeners will already hold "attitudes, beliefs, and values" toward the ideas you will inevitably present. As a result, it is always important to know where your audience stands on the issues you plan to address ahead of time. The best way to accomplish this is to sample your audience with a quick questionnaire or survey prior to the event. This is known as the third category of audience analysis, or **psychological description**. When performing a description you seek to identify the audience's attitudes, beliefs, and values.[4] They are your keys to understanding how your audience thinks.

Attitudes

In basic terms, an **attitude** is a learned disposition to respond in a consistently favorable or unfavorable manner with respect to a person, an object, an idea, or an event.[5] Attitudes come in different forms. You are very likely to see an attitude present itself when someone says that they are "pro" or "anti" something. But, above all else, attitudes are learned and not necessarily enduring. Attitudes can change, and sometimes do, whereas beliefs and values do not shift as easily. A sample list of attitudes can be found in Table 5.2.

3. Natalle, E.J. & Bodenheimer, F.R. (2004) *The woman's public speaking handbook.* Belmont, CA: Wadsworth.
4. Campbell, K.K. & Huxman, S.S. *The Rhetorical Act: Thinking, Speaking, and Writing Critically* (3rd Ed.). Belmont, CA: Wadsworth.
5. Jastrow, J. (1918). The psychology of conviction: A study of beliefs and attitudes. New York: Houghton Mifflin.

Table 5.2: Examples of Attitudes
Pro-/Anti-war
Pro-diversity
Anti-affirmative action
Pro-choice
Pro-life
Pro-/Anti-gambling
Pro-/Anti-prostitution
Pro-/Anti-capital punishment
Pro-/Anti-free trade
Pro-/Anti-outsourcing
Pro-/Anti-welfare
Pro-/Anti-corporate tax cuts
Pro-/Anti-censorship

These are just a small range of issues that one can either be "for" or "against." And, while we are simplifying the social scientific idea of an attitude considerably here, these examples serve our purposes well. Remember, attitudes are not as durable as beliefs and values. But, they are good indicators of how people view the persons, objects, ideas, or events that shape their world.

> Other people's beliefs may be myths, but not mine. – Mason Cooley

Beliefs

Beliefs are principles[6] or assumptions about the universe.

Beliefs are more durable than attitudes because beliefs are hinged to ideals and not issues. For example, you may believe in the principle: "what goes around comes around." If you do, you believe in the notion of karma. And so, you may align your behaviors to be consistent with this belief philosophy. You do not engage in unethical or negative behavior because you believe that it will "come back" to you. Likewise, you may try to exude behaviors that are ethical and positive because you wish for this behavior to return, in kind. You may not think this at all, and believe quite the opposite. Either way, there is a belief in operation driving what you think. Some examples of beliefs are located in Table 5.3.

Table 5.3: Examples of Beliefs
The world was created by God.
Marijuana is an addictive gateway drug.
Ghosts are all around us.
Smoking causes cancer.
Anyone can acquire HIV.
Evolution is fact, not fiction.
Marijuana is neither addictive or harmful.
Ghosts are products of our imagination.

6. Bem, D. J. (1970). *Beliefs, attitudes, and human affairs.* Belmont, CA: Brooks/Cole Pub. Co.

<table>
<tr><td colspan="2" align="center">Table 5.3: Examples of Beliefs</td></tr>
<tr><td>Smoking does not cause cancer.</td></tr>
<tr><td>Only high-risk groups acquire HIV.</td></tr>
</table>

Values

A value, on the other hand, is a guiding belief that regulates our attitudes.[7] Values are the core principles driving our attitudes. If you probe into someone's attitudes and beliefs far enough, you will inevitably find an underlying value. Importantly, you should also know that we structure our values in accordance to our own value hierarchy, or mental schema of values placed in order of their relative individual importance. Each of us has our own values that we subscribe to and a value hierarchy that we use to navigate the issues of the world. But we really aren't even aware that we have a value hierarchy until some of our values come in direct conflict with each other. Then, we have to negotiate something called **cognitive dissonance**, or the mental stress caused by the choice we are forced to make between two considerable alternatives.

For example, let's assume that you value "having fun" a great deal. You like to party with your friends and truly enjoy yourself. And, in this day and age, who doesn't? However, now that you are experiencing a significant amount of independence and personal freedom, you have many life options at your disposal. Let's also say that some of your close personal friends are doing drugs. You are torn. Part of you wants to experience the "fun" that your close friends may be experiencing; but, the more sane part of you wants to responsibly decline. In honesty, you are juxtaposed between two of your own values—having "fun" and being responsible. This real life example is somewhat exaggerated for your benefit. Realize that we make decisions small and grand, based on our value hierarchies. Some basic values common to people around the world can be found in Table 5.4.

Table 5.4: Examples of Values		
Inner harmony	Enjoyment	Belonging
Friendship	Trust	Equality
Control	Family	Security
Peace	Wisdom	Tradition
Unity	Achievement	Power
Generosity	Conformity	Intelligence
Leadership	Creativity	Responsibility
Health	Independence	Loyalty

Values aren't buses… They're not supposed to get you anywhere. They're supposed to define who you are. – Jennifer Crusie

Multicultural Analysis

Demography looks at issues of race and ethnicity in a basic sense. However, in our increasingly diverse society, it is worthy to pay particular attention to the issue of speaking to a multicultural audience (as discussed in Chapter 14 *Speaking to a Global Audience*). Odds are that any real world audience that you

---

7. Rokeach, M. (1968). *Beliefs, attitudes, and values; a theory of organization and change* (1st ed.). San Francisco: Jossey-Bass.

encounter will have an underlying multicultural dimension. As a speaker, you need to recognize that the perspective you have on any given topic may not necessarily be shared by all of the members of your audience.[8] Therefore, it is imperative that you become a culturally effective speaker. Culturally effective speakers develop the capacity to appreciate other cultures and acquire the necessary skills to speak effectively to people with diverse ethnic backgrounds. Keep these factors in mind when writing a speech for a diverse audience.

Language

Many people speak different languages, so if you are translating words, do not use slang or jargon, which can be confusing. You could add a visual aid (a poster, a picture, a PowerPoint slide or two) which would show your audience what you mean – which instantly translates into the audience member's mind.[9]

Cognition

Realize that different cultures have different cultural-cognitive processes, or ways of looking at the very concept of logic itself. Accordingly, gauge your audience as to their diverse ways of thinking and be sensitive to these differing logics.

Ethnocentricity

Remember that in many cases you will be appealing to people from other cultures. Do not assume that your culture is dominant or better than other cultures. That assumption is called ethnocentrism, and ethnocentric viewpoints have the tendency to drive a wedge between you and your audience.[10]

"Audience Applause at MIT meeting in Beijing" by Philip McMaster. CC-BY-NC.

> Christian, Jew, Muslim, shaman, Zoroastrian, stone, ground, mountain, river, each has a secret way of being with the mystery, unique and not to be judged. – Rumi

Values

Not only do individuals have value systems of their own, but societies promote value systems, as well. Keep in mind the fact that you will be appealing to value hierarchies that are socially-laden, as well as those that are individually-borne.

8. Ting-Toomey. S & Chung, L.C. (2005). *Understanding intercultural communication.* Los Angeles: Roxbury Publishing.
9. Klopf, D.W. & Cambra, R.E. (1991) *Speaking skills for prospective teachers* (2nd Ed.). Englewood, CO: Morton Publishing Company. Tauber, R.T. & Mester, C.S. *Acting Lessons for Teachers, Using Performance Skills in the Classroom.* Westport, CT: Praeger Publishers.
10. Pearson, J.C., Nelson, P.E., Titsworth, S. & Harter, L. (2011). *Human communication* (4th Ed.). Boston: McGraw-Hill.

Communication Styles

While you are trying to balance these language, cognition, cultural, and value issues, you should also recognize that some cultures prefer a more animated delivery style than do others. The intelligent speaker will understand this, and adapt his or her verbal and nonverbal delivery accordingly.

Interest and Knowledge Analysis

Finally, if the goal of your speech is to deliver a unique and stirring presentation (and it should be), you need to know ahead of time if your audience is interested in what you have to say, and has any prior knowledge about your topic. You do not want to give a boring or trite speech. Instead, you want to put your best work forward, and let your audience see your confidence and preparation shine through. And, you don't want to make a speech that your audience already knows a lot about. So, your job here is to "test" your topic by sampling your audience for their topic interest and topic knowledge. Defined, topic interest is the significance of the topic to a given audience; often related to the

"25th March 2011" by Grace Flora. CC-BY-NC-ND.

uniqueness of a speaker's topic. Likewise, topic knowledge is the general amount of information that the audience possesses on a given topic. These are not mere definitions listed for the sake of argument; these are essential analytical components of effective speech construction.

Anyone who teaches me deserves my respect, honoring and attention. – Sonia Rumzi

Unlike multicultural audience analysis, evaluating your audience's topic interest and topic knowledge is a fairly simple task. One can do this through informal question and answer dialogue, or through an actual survey. Either way, it is best to have some information, rather than none at all. Imagine the long list of topics that people have heard over and over and over. You can probably name some yourself, right now, without giving it much thought. If you started listing some topics to yourself, please realize that this is the point of this section of this module; your audience is literally thinking the same exact thing you are. Given that, topic preparation is strategically important to your overall speech success.

Again, do not underestimate the power of asking your audience whether or not your topic actually interests them. If you find that many people are not interested in your topic, or already know a lot about it, you have just saved yourself from a potentially mind- numbing exercise. After all, do you really want to give a speech where your audience could care less about your topic—or even worse— they know more about the topic than you do yourself? Not at all! The purpose of this section is to help you search for the highly sought-after public speaking concept called **uniqueness**, which is when a topic rises to the level of being singularly exceptional in interest and knowledge to a given audience.

We know that you wish to excel in giving your speech, and indeed you shall. But first, let's make sure that your audience is engaged by your topic and hasn't already heard the subject matter so much that they, themselves, could give the speech without much (if any) preparation.

One final note: There's an old adage in communication studies that reasons: "know what you know; know what you don't know; and, know the difference between the two." In other words, don't use puffery to blind your audience about your alleged knowledge on a particular subject. Remember, there is likely to be someone in your audience who knows as much about your topic, if not more, than you do. If you get caught trying to field an embarrassing question, you might just lose the most important thing you have as a speaker: your credibility. If you know the answer, respond accordingly. If you do not know the answer, respond accordingly. But, above all, try and be a resource for your audience. They expect you to be something of an expert on the topic you choose to address.

> Given the choice between trivial material brilliantly told versus profound material badly told, an audience will always choose the trivial told brilliantly. – Robert McKee

Attributions

CC licensed content, Shared previously

- Chapter 5 Categories of Audience Analysis. **Authored by**: Peter DeCaro, Ph.D., Tyrone Adams, Ph.D., and Bonnie Jefferis, Ph.D.. **Provided by**: University of Alaska - Fairbanks, University of Louisiana - Lafayette, and St. Petersburg College. **Located at**: http://publicspeakingproject.org/psvirtualtext.html. **Project**: The Public Speaking Project. **License**: *CC BY-NC-ND: Attribution-NonCommercial-NoDerivatives*

- Untitled. **Authored by**: Konrad-Adenauer-Gemeinschaftshauptschule Wenden. **Located at**: https://flic.kr/p/bjyxL. **License**: *CC BY-NC-SA: Attribution-NonCommercial-ShareAlike*

- Wiki Conference 2011. **Authored by**: Sucheta Ghoshal. **Located at**: http://commons.wikimedia.org/wiki/File:Wiki_Conference_2011.JPG. **License**: *CC BY-SA: Attribution-ShareAlike*

- Audience Applause at MIT meeting in Beijing 00071. **Authored by**: Philip McMaster. **Located at**: https://www.flickr.com/photos/dragonpreneur/5932580803/. **License**: *CC BY-NC: Attribution-NonCommercial*

- 25th March 2011. **Authored by**: Grace Flora. **Located at**: https://www.flickr.com/photos/graceflora/5910320075/. **License**: *CC BY-NC-ND: Attribution-NonCommercial-NoDerivatives*

Conclusion, Review Questions, and Activities

When considering topics for your speech, it is critical for you to keep your audience in mind. Not doing so will put your speech at risk of not corresponding with the information needs of your audience, and further jeopardize your credibility as a speaker. This chapter examined methods of conducting an audience analysis and five categories of audience analysis. In sum, this information equips you with the foundational knowledge and skill-set required to ensure that your topic complements your audience. And, after all, if we are not adapting to meet the needs of our audience, we are not going to be informative or convincing speakers.

"Philip Levy spoke at the U.S. Embassy" by US Embassy. CC-BY-ND.

Winston Churchill is credited with the origin of the saying: "Fail to plan, plan to fail."[1] We, your authors, believe that if you have failed to fully consider the nature, make-up, and characteristics of your audience, you are—for all intents and purposes—neglecting the spirit of the public speaking exercise. Confidently speaking to audiences can be somewhat addictive. The experience, when properly executed, can be empowering and help you succeed personally and professionally throughout your life. But, you must first consider the audience you will be addressing and take their every requirement into account.[2] We are linked to, joined with, if not bound by, our audiences. Your main speaking ambition should be to seek identification with them, and for them to seek identification with you.

1. Lakein, A. (1989) *How to get control of your time and your life.* New York: Signet.
2. Lewis, D. (1989) The secret language of success. New York: Galahad Books.

Review Questions

1. Why is it important to conduct an audience analysis prior to developing your speech?

2. What is the purpose of performing a demographics survey?

3. Why is audience analysis by direct observation the most simple of the three paradigms?

4. What are some the problems a speaker faces when delivering an unacquainted-audience presentation?

5. Under what circumstances would a speaker make inferences about an audience during the course of an audience analysis??

6. What is a variable, and how is it used in data sampling?

7. Why are statistics considered to be a form of quantitative analysis and not qualitative analysis?

8. How does conducting a value hierarchy help the speaker when developing a speech?

9. What value does performing a Likert-type testing of attitudes give the speaker?

10. Which of the Five Categories of Audience Analysis is the most effective, and why do you think that?

11. What are the differences between beliefs, attitudes, and values?

12. What challenges does a speaker face when delivering a speech to a multicultural audience?

Activities

1. If you know who your audience will be prior to speaking, try performing a demographic analysis. You may want to find out data, such as age, group affiliation, sex, socio-economic status, marital status, etc. Once you've done that, see if any of that information can impact any aspects of your speech. If it does, then determine how and why it impacts your speech.

2. Another survey to conduct is an attitudinal survey. If you are delivering a persuasive speech, you'll want to know what your audience thinks about your topic. Audience members who have opinions about things generally have a self-interest in it; that is why they are interested in what you have to say. Perform a Likert-type survey analysis to help you determine how best to create your speech.

3. As you know, a person's values are the most difficult for any speaker to change. You can perform a values survey to determine how difficult it will be to change the minds of your audience. Every persuasive speech addresses some value or values. Take a position, such as "consuming horse meat as an alternative to beef," and ask potential audience members how they feel about eating horse meat—why and why not. By conducting a hypothetical survey you begin to understand how to create an effective survey and why it is so important to the speaker to conduct.

Attributions

CC licensed content, Shared previously

Glossary and References

Glossary

TERM	DEFINITION
Attitude	An attitude is a learned disposition to respond in a consistently favorable or unfavorable manner with respect to a person, an object, an idea, or an event.
Audience Analysis	A speaker analyzes an audience for demographics, dispositions and knowledge of the topic.
Beliefs	Beliefs are principles and are more durable than attitudes because beliefs are hinged to ideals and not issues.
Cognitive Dissonance	The psychological discomfort felt when a person is presented with two competing ideas or pieces of evidence.
Demographics	Demographics are the most recent statistical characteristics of a population.
Demographic Characteristics	Demographic characteristics are facts about the make-up of a population.
Demography	Demographics are literally a classification of the characteristics of the people.
Inference	Making an inference is the act or process of deriving logical conclusions from premises known or assumed to be true.
Ordered category	An ordered category is a condition of logical or comprehensible arrangement among the separate elements of a group.
Paradigm	A paradigm is a pattern that describes distinct concepts or thoughts in any scientific discipline or other epistemological context.
Psychological Description	A psychological description is a description of the audience's attitudes, beliefs, and values.
Quantitative Analysis	A quantitative analysis is the process of determining the value of a variable by examining its numerical, measurable characteristics.
Statistics	Statistics is the study of the collection, organization, analysis, and interpretation of data.
Unacquainted-Audience Presentation	An unacquainted-audience presentation is a speech when you are completely unaware of your audience's characteristics.
Uniqueness	Uniqueness occurs when a topic rises to the level of being exceptional in interest and knowledge to a given audience.
Variable	A variable is a characteristic of a unit being observed that may assume more than one of a set of values to which a numerical measure or a category from a classification can be assigned.
Value	A value is a guiding belief that regulates our attitudes.
Value Hierarchy	A value hierarchy is a person's value structure placed in relationship to a given value set.

References

Bem, D. J. (1970). *Beliefs, attitudes, and human affairs*. Belmont, CA: Brooks/Cole Pub. Co.

Benjamin, B. (1969). *Demographic analysis.* New York: Praeger.

Caernarven-Smith, P. (1983). *Audience analysis & response (1st Ed.).* Pembroke, MA: Firman Technical Publications.

Campbell, K.K. & Huxman, S.S. The Rhetorical Act: Thinking, Speaking, and Writing Critically (3rd Ed.). Belmont, CA: Wadsworth.

Clevenger, T. (1966). *Audience analysis*. Indianapolis: Bobbs- Merrill.

Dwyer, K.K. (2005) *Conquer your speech anxiety:* Second Edition. Belmont, CA: Wadsworth.

Eisenberg, I. & Wynn, D. (2013) *Think communication.*

Boston: Pearson. Gamble, T.K. & Gamble, M. (2013). *Communication works.* New York: McGraw- Hill.

Jastrow, J. (1918). The psychology of conviction: A study of beliefs and attitudes. New York: Houghton Mifflin.

Klopf, D.W. & Cambra, R.E. (1991) *Speaking skills for prospective teachers (2nd Ed.).* Englewood, CO: Morton Publishing Company.

Lakein, A. (1989) How to get control of your time and your life. New York: Signet.

Lewis, D. (1989) *The secret language of success*. New York: Galahad Books.

McQuail, D. (1997). *Audience analysis*. Thousand Oaks, CA: Sage Publications.

Natalle, E.J. & Bodenheimer, F.R. (2004) *The woman's public speaking handbook.* Belmont, CA: Wadsworth.

Nierenberg, G.I. & Calero, H.H. (1994) *How to read a person like a book*. New York: Barnes and Noble Books.

Pearson, J.C., Nelson, P.E., Titsworth, S. & Harter, L. (2011). Human communication (4th Ed.). Boston: McGraw-Hill.

Pressat, R. (1972). Demographic analysis; methods, results, applications. Chicago: Aldine- Atherton.

Rokeach, M. (1968). Beliefs, attitudes, and values; a theory of organization and change (1st ed.). San Francisco: Jossey-Bass.

Tauber, R.T. & Mester, C.S. Acting Lessons for Teachers, Using Performance Skills in the Classroom. Westport, CT: Praeger Publishers.

Ting-Toomey. S & Chung, L.C. (2005). *Understanding intercultural communicatio*n. Los Angeles: Roxbury Publishing.

Tucker, K.T.; Weaver, II, R.L.; Berryman-Fink, C. (1981). *Research in speech communication*. Englewood Cliffs, N.J.: Prentice-Hall.

photo credits

p. 1 Audience at RZA book reading http://commons.wikimedia.org/wiki/File:RZA_Audience_Shankbone_2009_Tao_of_Wu.jpg By David Shankbone

p. 3 Mobile HCI 2008 Audience http://commons.wikimedia.org/wiki/File:MobileHCI_ 2008_Audience.jpg By Nhenze

p. 6 Speakers at Wiki Conference 2011 http://commons.wikimedia.org/wiki/File:Wiki_Conference_2011.JPG By Sucheta Ghoshal

p. 9 Audience enjoys Stallman's jokes http://upload.wikimedia.org/wikipedia/commons/6/63/Audience_enjoy_Stallman%27s_jokes By Damian Buonamico

p. 9 Side shot audience http://www.flickr.com/photos/us_embassy_newzealan d/4747176345/ By U.S. Embassy New Zealand

Attributions

CC licensed content, Shared previously

Chapter 11: Persuasive Speaking

Objectives and Introduction

Persuasive Speaking

By Sarah Stone Watt, Ph.D., Pepperdine University Malibu, CA
& Joshua Trey Barnett, Indiana University Bloomington, IN

Learning Objectives

After reading this chapter, you should be able to:

- Explain what a persuasive speech is.
- Describe the functions of persuasive speeches.
- List the different types of persuasive speeches.
- Identify persuasive strategies that make a speech more effective.
- Apply the appropriate organizational pattern based on your persuasive goals.
- Distinguish between ethical and unethical forms of persuasion.
- Apply module concepts in final questions and activities.

Introduction

At the gas pump, on eggs in the grocery store, in the examination room of your doctor's office, everywhere you go, advertisers are trying to persuade you to buy their product. This form of persuasion used to be reserved for magazines and television commercials, but now it is unavoidable. One marketing research firm estimates that a person living in a large city today sees approximately 5,000 ads per day.[1] It is easy to assume that our over-exposure to persuasion makes us immune to its effect, but research demonstrates that we are more susceptible than ever. In fact, advertisers have gotten even better at learning exactly the right times and places to reach us by studying different audiences and techniques.[234]

I do not read advertisements. I would spend all of my time wanting things. – Franz Kafka

"Judi Chamberlin" by Tom Olin. CC-BY-SA.

We also encounter persuasion in our daily interactions. Imagine you stop at a café on your way to school, and the barista persuades you to try something new. While enjoying your espresso, a sales person attempts to persuade you to upgrade your home Internet package. Later, while walking across campus, you observe students who are enthusiastically inviting others to join their organizations. Within thirty minutes, you have encountered at least three instances of persuasion, and there were likely others emanating in the background unbeknownst to you. Amidst being persuaded, you were also actively persuading others. You may have tried to convince the Internet sales person to give you a better deal and an extended contract, and later persuaded a group of friends to enjoy a night on the town. Persuasion is everywhere.

Attributions

CC licensed content, Shared previously

1. Story, L. (2007, January 15). Anywhere the eye can see, it's likely to see an ad. *The New York Times*. Retrieved from: http://www.nytimes.com/2007/01/15/business/media/15everywhere.html? pagewanted=all

2. Aral, S. & Walker, D. (2012, 20 July). Identifying influential and susceptible members of social networks. *Science, 327*(6092), 337–341. Retrieved from: http://www.sciencemag.org/content/337/6092/337.abstract

3. Blackman, S. (2009, September 3). Tired consumers more susceptible to advertising. *CBS Money Watch*. Retrieved from: http://www.cbsnews.com/news/tired-consumers-more-susceptible-to-advertising/

4. Rosendaal, E., Lapierre, M.A., vanReijmersdal, E.A., & Buijzen, M. (2011). Reconsidering advertising literacy as a defense against advertising effects. *Media Psychology, 14*(4), 333–354.

What is Persuasive Speaking?

You are used to experiencing persuasion in many forms, and may have an easy time identifying examples of persuasion, but can you explain how persuasion works? Osborn and Osborn define **persuasion** this way: "the art of convincing others to give favorable attention to our point of view."[1] There are two components that make this definition a useful one. First, it acknowledges the artfulness, or skill, required to persuade others. Whether you are challenged with convincing an auditorium of 500 that they should sell their cars and opt for a pedestrian lifestyle or with convincing your friends to eat pizza instead of hamburgers, persuasion does not normally just happen. Rather it is planned and executed in a thoughtful manner. Second, this definition delineates the ends of persuasion—to convince others to think favorably of our point of view. Persuasion "encompasses a wide range of communication activities, including advertising, marketing, sales, political campaigns, and interpersonal relations."[2] Because of its widespread utility, persuasion is a pervasive part of our everyday lives.

Although persuasion occurs in nearly every facet of our day-to-day lives, there are occasions when more formal acts of persuasion—persuasive speeches—are appropriate. **Persuasive speeches** "intend to influence the beliefs, attitudes, values, and acts of others."[3] Unlike an informative speech, where the speaker is charged with making some information known to an audience, in a persuasive speech the speaker attempts to influence people to think or behave in a particular way. This art of convincing others is propelled by reasoned argument, the cornerstone of persuasive speeches. Reasoned arguments, which might consist of facts, statistics, personal testimonies, or narratives, are employed to motivate audiences to think or behave differently than before they heard the speech.

"Michael Bruno" by U.S. Fish and Wildlife Service Northeast Region. CC-BY.

There are particular circumstances that warrant a persuasive approach. As O'Hair and Stewart point out, it makes sense to engage strategies of persuasion when your end goal is to influence any of these

1. Osborn, M., & Osborn, S. (1997). *Public speaking* (4th ed.). Boston: Houghton Mifflin Company.
2. German, K. M., Gronbeck, B. E., Ehninger, D., & Monroe, A. H. (2004). *Principles of public speaking* (15th ed.). Boston: Pearson.
3. O'Hair, D., & Stewart, R. (1999). *Public speaking: Challenges and choices*. Boston: Bedford/St. Martin's.

things—"beliefs, attitudes, values, and acts"—or to reinforce something that already exists. For instance, safe sex advocates often present messages of reinforcement to already safe sexual actors, reminding them that wearing condoms and asking for consent are solid practices with desirable outcomes. By the same token, safer sex advocates also routinely spread the message to populations who might be likely to engage in unsafe or nonconsensual sexual behavior.

In a nutshell, persuasive speeches must confront the complex challenge of influencing or reinforcing peoples' beliefs, attitudes, values, or actions, all characteristics that may seem natural, ingrained, or unchangeable to an audience. Because of this, rhetors (or speakers) must motivate their audiences to think or behave differently by presenting reasoned arguments.

The triumph of persuasion over force is the sign of a civilized society. – Mark Skousen

Attributions

CC licensed content, Shared previously

- Chapter 16 What is Persuasive Speaking? . **Authored by**: Sarah Stone Watt, Ph.D. and Joshua Trey Barnett. **Provided by**: Pepperdine University, Malibu, CA and Indiana University, Bloomington, IN. **Located at**: http://publicspeakingproject.org/psvirtual-text.html. **Project**: The Public Speaking Project. **License**: *CC BY-NC-ND: Attribution-NonCommercial-NoDerivatives*
- Michael Bruno. **Provided by**: U.S. Fish and Wildlife Service Northeast Region. **Located at**: https://www.flickr.com/photos/usfws-northeast/10579077044/. **License**: *CC BY: Attribution*

Functions of Persuasive Speeches

So far, we have discussed the functions of persuasive speeches—to influence or reinforce—only peripherally as they relate to our working definition. Next, we turn to an in-depth discussion about how persuasive speeches function.

Speeches to Convince

Some persuasive speeches attempt to influence or reinforce particular beliefs, attitudes, or values. In these speeches, called **speeches to convince**, the speaker seeks to establish agreement about a particular topic. For instance, a climatologist who believes that global warming is caused by human behavior might try to convince an audience of government officials to adopt this belief. She might end her speech by saying, "In recent years, humans have been producing machines that expel CO_2 either in their production, their consumption, or in both. At the same time, the level of CO_2 in the atmosphere increased dramatically. The connection is clear to many of us that humans have caused this damage and that it is up to us to similarly intervene." Throughout her speech, the scientist would likely recite a number of statistics linking human productivity with global warming in her effort to convince the government officials that both the causes and solutions to the climatic changes were a distinctly human problem.

"AirPollutionSource" by US Environmental Protection Agency. Public domain.

Speeches to Actuate

Other times, persuasive speeches attempt to influence or reinforce actions. **Speeches to actuate** are designed to motivate particular behaviors. Think of a time when you found yourself up at 2 a.m. watching infomercials. Someone on the television screen was trying very hard to sell you a $20 spatula that morphed into a spoon with the click of a button. The salesperson described its utility and innovation for your kitchen, and he described why it would be a good purchase for you—after all, how does a busy person like you have time to use two different utensils? "But wait," he would say, "there's more!" In case he had not already convinced you that you needed this kitchen tool, he ended his spiel with a final plea—an extra Spoonatula for free. In this infomercial, the salesperson attempted to convince you that you needed to buy the kitchen tool—it will save you time and money. Thus, not only was the commercial an attempt to convince you to change how you felt about spoons and spatulas, but also an effort to incite you to action—to actually purchase the Spoonatula. This illustrates a function of persuasive speeches, to motivate behavior.

Attributions

CC licensed content, Shared previously

- Chapter 16 Functions of Persuasive Speeches. **Authored by**: Sarah Stone Watt, Ph.D. and Joshua Trey Barnett. **Provided by**: Pepperdine University, Malibu, CA and Indiana University, Bloomington, IN. **Located at**: http://publicspeakingproject.org/psvirtualtext.html. **Project**: The Public Speaking Project. **License**: *CC BY-NC-ND: Attribution-NonCommercial-NoDerivatives*

Public domain content

- AirPollutionSource. **Provided by**: US Environmental Protection Agency. **Located at**: http://commons.wikimedia.org/wiki/File:AirPollutionSource.jpg. **License**: *Public Domain: No Known Copyright*

Types of Persuasive Speeches

Persuasive speeches revolve around propositions that can be defended through the use of data and reasoning. Persuasive propositions respond to one of three types of questions: questions of fact, questions of value, and questions of policy. These questions can help the speaker determine what forms of argument and reasoning are necessary to support a specific purpose statement.

> Everything we hear is an opinion, not a fact. Everything we see is a perspective, not the truth. – Marcus Aurelius

Propositions of Fact

Questions of fact ask whether something "can potentially be verified as either true or false."[1] These questions can seem very straightforward—something is or it is not—but in reality, the search for truth is a complex endeavor. Questions of fact rarely address simple issues such as, "is the sky blue?" They tend to deal with deep-seated controversies such as the existence of global warming, the cause of a major disaster, or someone's guilt or innocence in a court of law. To answer these questions, a **proposition of fact** may focus on whether or not something exists. For example, in the U.S. there is a debate over the prevalence of racial profiling, the practice of law enforcement officers targeting people for investigation and arrest based on skin color. On one hand, the American Civil Liberties Union advances the proposition: "Racial profiling continues to be a prevalent and egregious form of discrimination in the United States."[2] They verify this claim using data from government studies, crime statistics, and personal narratives. However, journalist Heather MacDonald proposes that studies confirming racial profiling are often based in "junk science"; in fact she says, "there's no credible evidence that racial profiling exists."[3] To substantiate her proposition, MacDonald relies on a study of traffic stops on the New Jersey turnpike along with personal narratives, policy analysis, and testimony from a criminologist. The claim that racial profiling exists is either true or false, but there is evidence for and against both propositions; therefore no consensus exists.

While some propositions of fact deal with the existence of a particular phenomenon or the accuracy of a theory, others focus on causality. For example, the U.S. government appointed a commission to evaluate

1. Herrick, J.A. (2011). *Argumentation: Understanding and Shaping Arguments*. State College, PA: Strata Publishing.
2. American Civil Liberties Union (ACLU). (2012). Racial Profiling. Retrieved from: http://www.aclu.org/racialjustice/racial-profiling
3. MacDonald, H. (2002, March 27). The racial profiling myth debunked. *City Journal*. Retrieved from: http://www.city-journal.org/html/eon_3_27_02hm.html

the causes of the nation's recent economic crisis. In their report the commission concluded by proposing that recklessness in the financial industry and failures on the part of government regulators caused the economic crisis. However, Congressman Paul Ryan has proposed that Medicare is to blame, and the chief investment officer at JP Morgan has proposed that U.S. housing policy is the root cause of the problem.[4] Each of these three propositions of fact is backed by its own set of historical and economic analysis.

Propositions of fact may also be used to make predictions concerning what will happen in the future. In the summer of 2011, ten miles of a popular Southern California freeway were closed for an entire weekend. Motorists, news outlets, and government officials called the closure "Carmageddon" because they proposed there would be an "inevitable and likely epic traffic tie-up."[5] As a result of the predictions motorists stayed off the roads and made alternative plans that weekend resulting in much lighter traffic than expected. The proposition may have been true, but the prediction was not fulfilled because people were persuaded to stay off the freeway.

"Interstate 10 looking east from Crenshaw Boulevard" by Downtowngal. CC-BY-SA.

When advancing propositions of fact, you should focus on the evidence you can offer in support of your proposition. First, make sure that your speech contains sufficient evidence to back up your proposition. Next, take the time to interpret that evidence so that it makes sense to your audience. Last, emphasize the relationship between your evidence and your proposition as well as its relevance to the audience.[6]

> Bitter experience has taught us how fundamental our values are and how great the mission they represent. – Jan Peter Balkenende

Propositions of Value

Persuasive speakers may also be called to address questions of value, which call for a proposition judging the (relative) worth of something. These propositions make an evaluative claim regarding morality, aesthetics, wisdom, or desirability. For example, some vegetarians propose that eating meat is immoral because of the way that animals are slaughtered. Vegetarians may base this claim in a philosophy of utilitarianism or animal rights.[7]

4. Angelides, P. (2011, June 28). The real causes of the economic crisis? They're history. *The Washington Post*. Retrieved from: http://www.washingtonpost.com/opinions/the-real-causes-of-theeconomic-crisis-theyrehistory/2011/06/27/AG2nK4pH_story.html
5. Kandel, J. (2011, July 14). Los Angeles braces for weekend of "Carmageddon." Reuters. Retrieved from: http://www.reuters.com/article/2011/07/15/us-carmageddon-losangeles-idUSTRE76D2D720110715
6. Herrick 2011
7. DeGrazia, D. (2009). Moral vegetarianism from a very broad basis. *Journal of Moral Philosophy, 6*. Retrieved from: https://philosophy.columbian.gwu.edu/sites/philosophy.columbian.gwu.edu/files/image/DeGraziaMoral.pdf

Sometimes a **proposition of value** compares multiple options to determine which is best. Consumers call for these comparisons regularly to determine which products to buy. Car buyers may look to the most recent Car and Driver "10 Best Cars" list to determine their next purchase. In labeling a car one of the best on the market for a given year, Car and Driver says that the cars "don't have to be the newest, and they don't have to be expensive . . . They just have to meet our abundant needs while satisfying our every want."[8]

"McLarenF1" by Jagvar. Public domain.

Both the vegetarian and car examples offer standards for evaluating the proposition. Since propositions of value tend to be more subjective, speakers need to establish **evaluation criteria** by which the audience can judge and choose to align with their position. When advancing a proposition of value, offer a clear set of criteria, offer evidence for your evaluation, and apply the evidence to demonstrate that you have satisfied the evaluation criteria.[9]

> An inner process stands in need of outward criteria. – Ludwig Wittgenstein

The 2005 disagreement between family members over removing a woman's feeding tube after she had been in a coma for 15 years sparked a national debate over the value of life that highlights the importance of evaluation criteria. After years of failed medical treatments and rehabilitation attempts, Terri Schiavo's husband petitioned the court to remove her feeding tube, initiating a legal battle with her parents that went all the way to the President of the United States.[10] Opposing sides in the debate both claimed to value life. To support his proposition that his wife had a right to die, Mr. Schaivo applied the evaluation criteria of quality of life and argued that she would not want to continue to live in a vegetative state.[11] Ms. Schiavo's parents vehemently disagreed with his argument. They also claimed to value life and, with the support of religious groups, relied on the evaluation criteria of the sanctity of life to contend that she should be kept alive.[12] Both sides gained widespread support based on people's agreement or disagreement with their evaluation criteria. Despite intervention on behalf of both state and federal legislators, the courts eventually ruled that Mr. Schiavo had the right to have his wife's feeding tube removed and allow her to die.

> A policy is a temporary creed liable to be changed, but while it holds good, it has got to be pursued with apostolic zeal. – Mahatma Gandhi

8. Car and Driver (2011, December). 2012 10Best Cars. Car and Driver. Retrieved from: http://www.caranddriver.com/features/2012-10best-cars-feature

9. Herrick 2011

10. Cerminara, K. & Goodman, K. (2012). Schiavo Timeline. Retrieved from University of Miami Ethics Program: http://www.miami.edu/index.php/ethics/projects/schiavo/schiavo_timeline/

11. Caplan, A. (2005). The time has come to let Terri Schiavo die: Politicians, courts must allow husband to make final decision. *NBC News*. Retrieved from: http://www.nbcnews.com/id/7231440/ns/health-health_care/t/time-has-come-let-terri-schiavo-die/

12. Catholic Culture. (2005). The death of Terri Schiavo. *Catholic World News*. Retrieved from: https://www.catholicculture.org/news/features/index.cfm?recnum=37860

Propositions of Policy

Although the Schiavo case was rooted in a question of value, the debate resulted in a question of policy. **Questions of policy** ask the speaker to advocate for an appropriate course of action. This form of persuasive speech is used every day in Congress to determine laws, but it is also used interpersonally to determine how we ought to behave. A proposition of policy may call for people to stop a particular behavior, or to start one. For example, some U.S. cities have started banning single use plastic bags in grocery stores. Long before official public policy on this issue was established, organizations such as The Surfrider Foundation and the Earth Resource Foundation advocated that people stop using these bags because of the damage plastic bags cause to marine life. In this case local governments and private organizations attempted to persuade people to stop engaging in a damaging behavior— shopping with single use plastic bags. However, the organizations also attempted to persuade people to start a new behavior—shopping with reusable bags.

When answering a question of policy, speakers will typically begin by describing the status quo. If you are arguing that a change must be made, you must first identify the problem inherent in the current behavior, and then demonstrate that the problem is significant enough to warrant immediate consideration. Once you have established that there is a problem which the audience ought to consider, you can then offer your proposal for a preferable course of action.[13] Then, it is up to you to demonstrate that your proposed policy will have more benefits than costs.

In 2011 the U.S. Postal Service, the nation's second-largest employer, told Congress it was facing an $8.3 billion budget shortfall.[14] To solve the problem, the Postal Service proposed that be permitted to end Saturday mail delivery and close some post offices. To make their argument, they first described the status quo saying that the demand for their service had dramatically decreased with the popularity of email and online bill-pay services. They explained that in preceding years they laid off workers and cut spending to help with the shortfall of revenue, but now another plan was necessary to avoid defaulting on their financial obligations. They offered evidence that people preferred ending Saturday mail to alternatives such as paying more for stamps or allocating more tax money to post offices.[15] Although they made a compelling case, the USPS still needed to over-

"USPS mailboxes" **by EraserGirl.** *CC-BY.*

13. Herrick 2011
14. Bingham, A. (2011, July 22). Postal Service pushes to end Saturday delivery. *ABC News.* Retrieved from: http://abcnewsradioonline.com/business-news/postal-service-pushes-to-end-saturday-delivery.html
15. Bingham 2011

come perceived disadvantages to their proposition such as the negative impact on businesses and rural towns.[16][17] A full year later, the policy proposition passed the U.S. Senate but continues to await approval in the House.[18]

Attributions

CC licensed content, Shared previously

- Chapter 16 Types of Persuasive Speeches. **Authored by**: Sarah Stone Watt, Ph.D. and Joshua Trey Barnett. **Provided by**: Pepperdine University, Malibu, CA and Indiana University, Bloomington, IN. **Located at**: http://publicspeakingproject.org/psvirtualtext.html. **Project**: The Public Speaking Project. **License**: *CC BY-NC-ND: Attribution-NonCommercial-NoDerivatives*

- Interstate 10 looking east from Crenshaw Boulevard. **Authored by**: Downtowngal. **Located at**: http://commons.wikimedia.org/wiki/File:Interstate_10_looking_east_from_Crenshaw_Boulevard.jpg. **License**: *CC BY-SA: Attribution-ShareAlike*

- USPS mailboxes. **Authored by**: EraserGirl. **Located at**: http://commons.wikimedia.org/wiki/File:USPS_mailboxes.jpg. **License**: *CC BY: Attribution*

Public domain content

- McLarenF1. **Authored by**: Jagvar. **Located at**: http://commons.wikimedia.org/wiki/File:MclarenF1.JPG. **License**: *Public Domain: No Known Copyright*

16. Bingham 2011
17. Stephenson, E. (2012, August 1). Senators blast House leaders over Postal Service default. *Reuters*. Retrieved from: http://www.reuters.com/article/2012/08/01/us-usa-postal-default-idUSBRE8701HO20120801
18. Stephenson 2012

Choosing a Persuasive Speech Topic

"Jade Raymond" by Gamerscore Blog. CC-BY-SA.

In order to offer a persuasive speech, you must decide precisely what it is you want to talk about, to whom you will be speaking, and to what ends you hope the speech will lead. Persuasive speeches do not normally happen within a vacuum, even in a public speaking course where that might seem to be the case. In fact, most persuasive speeches serve as a response to larger circumstances—gas prices increase dramatically and drivers cannot afford to fill up their tanks; war veterans suffer from post-traumatic stress disorder (PTSD) and can find little governmental assistance for the necessary treatments; an election is forthcoming and candidates need to secure votes. These are just a few times when a persuasive speech would make sense. A driver might try to persuade their employer to embrace telecommuting as a response to the high rate of gasoline. Veterans with PTSD might stage speeches to a national audience imploring them to advocate for better mental health care for people who have fought in wars. And candidates, of course, will give many speeches during a campaign that tease out the various reasons they, and not another candidate, should be elected. Appendix A (at the end of the chapter) offers a lengthier list of possible topics for persuasive speaking, but keep in mind the advice that Burnett offers in Chapter 8 (public speaking: the virtual text) regarding topic selection. The topics in Appendix A are written as propositions that can be defended. Some are propositions of fact, others are propositions of value, and yet others are propositions of policy.

Attributions

CC licensed content, Shared previously

- Chapter 16 Choosing a Persuasive Speech Topic. **Authored by**: Sarah Stone Watt, Ph.D. and Joshua Trey Barnett. **Provided by**: Pepperdine University, Malibu, CA and Indiana University, Bloomington, IN. **Located at**: http://publicspeakingproject.org/psvirtualtext.html. **Project**: The Public Speaking Project. **License**: *CC BY-NC-ND: Attribution-NonCommercial-NoDerivatives*

- Jade Raymond - E3 2007 2. **Authored by**: Gamerscore Blog. **Located at**: http://commons.wikimedia.org/wiki/File:Jade_Ray-

Approaching Audiences

If I can get you to laugh with me, you like me better, which makes you more open to my ideas. And if I can persuade you to laugh at the particular point I make, by laughing at it you acknowledge its truth. – John Cleese

When choosing a topic for your persuasive speech, it is crucial to consider the composition of your audience. Because persuasive speeches are intended to influence or reinforce an audience's thoughts or behaviors, speakers must consider what and how the audience thinks, feels, and does. Your audience might be ambivalent about your topic, or they may be strongly opposed, in strong agreement, or somewhere along the spectrum. In persuasive speeches, it matters where they fall on this continuum. For instance, if you want to argue that abortion should be illegal and your audience is composed of pro-life advocates, your speech might seem like you are preaching to the choir. But if your audience is made up of staunch pro-choice activists, your speech would be raising a significant objection to a set of beliefs, values, attitudes, and actions the audience was already committed to.

Decaro, Adams and Jefferis offer advice for carrying out a thorough audience analysis in Chapter 5 of this book. Some questions you might ask before giving a speech include, "Who is hosting the speech?" Often this can provide a great deal of information about who will be in the audience. Audience members at a National Rifle Association gathering probably do not need to be convinced that the Second Amendment to the U.S. Constitution— the right to keep and bear arms—is worth upholding. You should also ask, "Is the audience fairly heterogeneous?" In a public speaking class, you may be able to gauge that through your interactions with your fellow classmates before you

"Photo Essay" by United States Armed Force. Public domain.

make your way to the podium; but in other settings this may not be the case. If an organization is sponsoring or has invited you to speak, this is a question that can be directed to organizational staff with access to demographic information. Some **demographics** that may be useful as you craft your speech include age, gender, sexual orientation, ethnic or cultural background, socioeconomic status, religion, and political affiliation. Each of these characteristics is known to influence a listener's beliefs, attitudes, values, and actions.

Receptive Audiences

Persuasive speakers will not generally address an audience that already fully agrees with them and is behaving in the way they would like, because that audience no longer needs to be persuaded. However, you may find yourself in situations that allow you to appeal to a **receptive audience** which already knows something about your topic and is generally supportive of, or open to, the point you are trying to make. For example, parents are generally interested in keeping their children safe. If you seek to persuade them that they should work with their kids to prevent them from being taken advantage of on social networking sites, they are likely to welcome what you have to say. Although they are

"Children Play in Push Car" **by Nils Fretwurst.** *CC-BY-SA.*

already convinced that it is important to keep their children safe, this audience may not yet be persuaded that they have the need or ability to keep their kids safe in an online environment. In order to persuade this receptive audience, you should first attempt to foster **identification** with them by highlighting things you have in common. If you are a parent you might say something like, "I have two children and one of my biggest concerns is making sure they are safe." If you are not a parent you might say, "one of the things I appreciate most about my parents is that I know they are always trying to keep me safe." With these statements, you not only relate to the audience, but also demonstrate that you share a common concern.

> If you would persuade, you must appeal to interest rather than intellect. – Benjamin Franklin

Next, offer a clear statement of purpose and tell the audience what you would like them to do in response to your message. If the audience is already likely to agree with your point, they will be looking for ways to act on it. Offer practical steps that they can take. Even if the steps must be carried out later (i.e. the parents in our example may have to wait to get home and start talking with their child about social networking habits), give them a way to respond to the message immediately and show their support. In this case you may have them write down the first thing they will say to their child, or practice saying it to the person next to them. Having them act on your message before leaving reinforces their already favorable response to what you are asking.[1]

> I swore never to be silent whenever and wherever human beings endure suffering and humiliation. We must always take sides. Neutrality helps the oppressor, never the victim. Silence encourages the tormentor, never the tormented. – Elie Wiesel

1. Beebe, S.A. & Beebe, S.J. (2003). *Public Speaking: An Audience Centered Approach* (5th ed.). Boston: Pearson.

Neutral Audiences

Most of the groups that a persuasive speaker addresses are **neutral audiences**. These audiences are not passionate about the topic or speaker, often because they do not have enough information or because they are not aware that they should be concerned. Beebe & Beebe explain that the challenge in addressing a neutral audience is to foster their interest in your proposition.[2] They offer a few tips for cultivating interest in a neutral audience. Begin by gaining their attention. To do this you might offer a story or statistic that relates the topic directly to the dominant demographic in the audience. If you are trying to convince first-year college students to avoid credit card solicitors on

"Untitled" by Petr Kratochvil. CC-0.

campus you might start with something like, "I know those t-shirts the credit card vendors are handing out are stylish and, best of all, free! But that t-shirt could cost you thousands of dollars before you even graduate." Rather than beginning with a diatribe on the evils of debt, which many of them may not yet have experienced, you relate to their desire for a free t-shirt and a common belief they are likely to share, that "free" should not translate to "expensive." If you cannot relate the topic directly to the audience, another approach is to relate the topic to someone they care about, like a family member or friend. Keep in mind that, while the receptive audience may be eager to respond immediately, the neutral audience may simply be more concerned about the topic or more inclined to consider the behavior change you are advocating.[3] In this case, consider offering resources for more information, or a few minor steps they can take when they are ready.

He who dreads hostility too much is unfit to rule. – Lucius Annaeus Seneca

Hostile Audiences

Unfortunately, some audiences may be resistant or even hostile to your persuasive speech. A **hostile audience** may take issue with your topic or with you as a speaker. In this case, your primary goal is to persuade the audience to listen to what you have to say.[4] Once they are willing to listen, then you will have the ability to change their minds in the future. Later in this chapter we will address ways that you can foster a better relationship with the audience by building your ethos. However, if the audience is opposed to your proposition, there are a few steps that you can take to encourage them to at least hear you out. If the audience is not likely to agree with your proposition, wait until later in the speech to offer it. Opening with a clear statement of purpose, which a receptive audience welcomes, will make an unreceptive audience more hostile to your goals. For example, if you begin by telling business owners that you think they should pay workers

2. (Beebe & Beebe 2003)
3. (Beebe & Beebe 2003)
4. (Beebe & Beebe 2003)

more, they are likely to think of all the reasons that will threaten their livelihood rather than listening to your message. Instead, begin by highlighting issues on which you agree. You might open with a discussion of the challenges businesses face in attempting to retain quality workers and increase productivity.

I have spent many years of my life in opposition, and I rather like the role. – Eleanor Roosevelt

Once you have identified areas of agreement, you can offer your proposition as a way of addressing your shared goals. To promote an increase in wages, you might explain that a study of more than 10,000 workers and managers in a variety of industries demonstrated that companies who pay their workers more were also more motivated to invest in new technology, enhance their management techniques, better train workers, and better deliver their services, all of which lead to higher productivity and increased profits.[5] Focusing on areas of agreement will make the audience more receptive to your proposition, but they will still hold some reservations. Acknowledge those reservations and demonstrate that you have given them ample consideration. Cite credible evidence that supports your proposition in light of those reservations. Showing that you understand and respect their opposing position is the most important step toward encouraging a hostile audience to at least hear you out.

Attributions

CC licensed content, Shared previously

- Chapter 16 Approaching Audiences. **Authored by**: Sarah Stone Watt, Ph.D. and Joshua Trey Barnett. **Provided by**: Pepperdine University, Malibu, CA and Indiana University, Bloomington, IN. **Located at**: http://publicspeakingproject.org/psvirtualtext.html. **Project**: The Public Speaking Project. **License**: *CC BY-NC-ND: Attribution-NonCommercial-NoDerivatives*
- Children play in push car. **Authored by**: Nils Fretwurst. **Located at**: http://commons.wikimedia.org/wiki/File:Children_play_in_push_car.jpg. **License**: *CC BY-SA: Attribution-ShareAlike*
- 1-1204463487cJKy. **Authored by**: Petr Kratochvil. **Located at**: https://commons.wikimedia.org/wiki/File:1-1204463487cJKy.jpg. **License**: *CC0: No Rights Reserved*

Public domain content

- Defense.gov photo essay 081112-F-6684S-757. **Provided by**: United States Air Force. **Located at**: http://commons.wikimedia.org/wiki/File:Defense.gov_photo_essay_081112-F-6684S-757.jpg. **License**: *Public Domain: No Known Copyright*

5. Applebaum, E. & Berhardt, A. (2004, December 18). Employers also benefit from a higher minimum wage. Brennan Center for Justice. Retrieved from: http://www.brennancenter.org/analysis/employers-also-benefit-higher-minimum-wage

Persuasive Strategies

Ethos

In addition to understanding how your audience feels about the topic you are addressing, you will need to take steps to help them see you as credible and interesting. The audience's perception of you as a speaker is influential in determining whether or not they will choose to accept your proposition. Aristotle called this element of the speech **ethos**, "a Greek word that is closely related to our terms *ethical* and *ethnic*."[1] He taught speakers to establish credibility with the audience by appearing to have good moral character, common sense, and concern for the audience's well-being.[2] Campbell & Huxman explain that ethos is not about conveying that you, as an individual, are a good person. It is about "mirror[ing] the characteristics idealized by [the] culture or group" (ethnic),[3] and demonstrating that you make good moral choices with regard to your relationship within the group (ethics).

"Danny Shine Speaker's Corner" by Acapeloahddub. Public domain.

While there are many things speakers can do to build their ethos throughout the speech, "assessments of ethos often reflect superficial first impressions," and these first impressions linger long after the speech has concluded.[4] This means that what you wear and how you behave, even before opening your mouth, can go far in shaping your ethos. Be sure to dress appropriately for the occasion and setting in which you speak. Also work to appear confident, but not arrogant, and be sure to maintain enthusiasm about your topic throughout the speech. Give great attention to the crafting of your opening sentences because they will set the tone for what your audience should expect of your personality as you proceed.

1. Campbell, K.K. & Huxman, S.S. (2009). *The Rhetorical Act: Thinking, Speaking, and Writing Critically*. Belmont, CA: Wadsworth.
2. Beebe, S.A. & Beebe, S.J. (2003). Public Speaking: An Audience Centered Approach (5th ed.). Boston: Pearson.
3. Campbell & Huxman 2009
4. Zarefsky, D. (2005). *Public Speaking: Strategies for Success* (Special edition for The Pennsylvania State University). Boston: Pearson.

> I covered two presidents, LBJ and Nixon, who could no longer convince, persuade, or govern, once people had decided they had no credibility; but we seem to be more tolerant now of what I think we should not tolerate. – Helen Thomas

Logos

Another way to enhance your ethos, and your chances of persuading the audience, is to use sound arguments. In a persuasive speech, the **argument** will focus on the reasons for supporting your specific purpose statement. This argumentative approach is what Aristotle referred to as **logos**, or the logical means of proving an argument.[5]

When offering an argument you begin by making an assertion that requires a logical leap based on the available evidence.[6] One of the most popular ways of understanding how this process works was developed by British philosopher Stephen Toulmin.[7] Toulmin explained that basic arguments tend to share three common elements: claim, data, and warrant. The **claim** is an assertion that you want the audience to accept. **Data** refers to the preliminary evidence on which the claim is based. For example, if I saw large gray clouds in the sky, I might make the claim that "it is going to rain today." The gray clouds (data) are linked to rain (claim) by the **warrant**, an often unstated general connection, that large gray clouds tend to produce rain. The warrant is a connector that, if stated, would likely begin with "since" or "because." In our rain example, if we explicitly stated all three elements, the argument would go something like this: There are large gray clouds in the sky today (data). Since large gray clouds tend to produce rain (warrant), it is going to rain today (claim). However, in our regular encounters with argumentation, we tend to only offer the claim and (occasionally) the warrant.

To strengthen the basic argument, you will need backing for the claim. Backing provides foundational support for the claim[8] by offering examples, statistics, testimony, or other information which further substantiates the argument. To substantiate the rain argument we have just considered, you could explain that the color of a cloud is determined by how much light the water in the cloud is reflecting. A thin cloud has tiny drops of water and ice crystals which scatter light, making it appear white. Clouds appear gray when they are filled with large water droplets which are less able to reflect light.[9]

Table 16.1: The Toulmin Model	
Basic Argument	
data	*claim*
I had a hard time finding a place to park on campus.	The school needs more parking spaces.
warrant	
If I can't find a place to park, there must be a shortage of spaces.	
Argument with Backing	
data	*claim*
Obesity is a serious problem in the U.S.	U.S. citizens should be encouraged to eat less processed foods.

5. Braet, A.C. (1992). Ethos, pathos, and logos in Aristotle's rhetoric: A reexamination. *Argumentation, 6*(3), pp. 307–320.
6. Campbell & Huxman 2009
7. Herrick, J.A. (2011). *Argumentation: Understanding and Shaping Arguments*. State College, PA: Strata Publishing.
8. Herrick 2011
9. Brill, R. (2003, July 21). Why do clouds turn gray before it rains? *Scientific American*. Retrieved from: http://www.scientificamerican.com/article/why-do-clouds-turn-gray-b/

<table>
<tr><td colspan="1">Table 16.1: The Toulmin Model</td></tr>
<tr><td>warrant
Processed foods contribute to obesity more than natural or unprocessed foods.</td></tr>
<tr><td>backing
"As a rule processed foods are more 'energy dense' than fresh foods: they contain less water and fiber but more added fat and sugar, which makes them both less filling and more fattening." (Pollan, 2007)[10]</td></tr>
</table>

Logic is the beginning of wisdom, not the end. – Leonard Nimoy

The elements that Toulmin identified (see Table 16.1) may be arranged in a variety of ways to make the most logical argument. As you reason through your argument you may proceed inductively, deductively, or causally, toward your claim. **Inductive reasoning** moves from specific examples to a more general claim. For example, if you read online reviews of a restaurant chain called Walt's Wine & Dine and you noticed that someone reported feeling sick after eating at a Walt's, and another person reported that the Walt's they visited was understaffed, and another commented that the tables in the Walt's they ate at had crumbs left on them, you might conclude (or claim) that the restaurant chain is unsanitary. To test the validity of a general claim, Beebe and Beebe encourage speakers to consider whether there are "enough specific instances to support the conclusion," whether the specific instances are typical, and whether the instances are recent.[11]

"Dining Booth" by Wayne Truong. CC-BY.

The opposite of inductive reasoning is **deductive reasoning**, moving from a general principle to a claim regarding a specific instance. In order to move from general to specific we tend to use **syllogisms**. A syllogism begins with a major (or general) premise, then moves to a minor premise, then concludes with a specific claim. For example, if you know that all dogs bark (major premise), and your neighbor has a dog (minor premise), you could then conclude that your neighbor's dog barks (specific claim). To verify the accuracy of your specific claim, you must verify the truth and applicability of the major premise. What evidence do you have that all dogs bark? Is it possible that only *most* dogs bark? Next, you must also verify the accuracy of the minor premise. If the major premise is truly generalizable, and both premises are accurate, your specific claim should also be accurate.

---

10. Pollan, M. (2007, April 22). You are what you grow. *The New York Times*. Retrieved from: http://www.nytimes.com/2007/04/22/magazine/22wwlnlede.t.html?pagewanted=all

11. Beebe & Beebe 2003

Your reasoning may also proceed causally. **Causal reasoning** examines related events to determine which one caused the other. You may begin with a cause and attempt to determine its effect. For example, when the Deepwater Horizon drilling rig exploded in the Gulf of Mexico in 2010, scientists explained that because many animals in the Gulf were nesting and reproducing at the time, the spill could wipe out "an entire generation of hundreds of species."[12] Their argument reasoned that the spill (cause) would result in species loss (effect). Two years later, the causal reasoning might be reversed. If we were seeing species loss in the Gulf (effect), we could reason that it was a result of the oil spill (cause). Both of these claims rely on the evidence available at the time. To make the first claim, sci-

"Deepwater Horizon offshore drilling unit on fire" by US Coast Guard. Public domain.

entists not only offered evidence that animals were nesting and reproducing, but they also looked at the effects of an oil spill that occurred 21 years earlier in Alaska.[13] To make the second claim, scientists could examine dead animals washing up on the coast to determine whether their deaths were caused by oil.

Pathos

While we have focused heavily on logical reasoning, we must also recognize the strong role that emotions play in the persuasive process. Aristotle called this element of the speech **pathos**. Pathos draws on the emotions, sympathies, and prejudices of the audience to appeal to their non-rational side.[14][15] Human beings are constantly in some emotional state, which means that tapping into an audience's emotions can be vital to persuading them to accept your proposition.[16]

One of the most helpful strategies in appealing to your audience's emotions is to use clear examples that illustrate your point. Illustrations can be crafted verbally, nonverbally, or visually. To offer a verbal illus-

12. Donovan, T.W. (2010, July 10). 7 Long term effects of the Gulf oil spill. *Huffington Post*. Retrieved from: http://www.huffingtonpost.com/2010/05/10/7-long-term-effects-of-th_n_562947.html#s87787title=Environmental_Damage
13. Donovan 2010
14. Beebe & Beebe 2003
15. Reike, R.D., Sillars, M.O., & Peterson, T.R. (2009). *Argumentation and Critical Decision Making* (7th ed.). Boston: Pearson.
16. Dillard, J.P. & Meijnders, A. (2002). Persuasion and the structure of affect. In J.P. Dillard & M. Pfau (Eds.), *The Persuasion Handbook: Developments in Theory and Practice* (309–328). Thousand Oaks, CA: Sage.

tration, you could tell a compelling story. For example, when fundrais-
ing for breast cancer research, Nancy Brinker, creator of Susan G.
Komen for the Cure, has plenty of compelling statistics and examples
to offer. Yet, she regularly talks about her sister, explaining:

> *Susan G. Komen fought breast cancer with her heart, body and
> soul. Throughout her diagnosis, treatments, and endless days in
> the hospital, she spent her time thinking of ways to make life bet-
> ter for other women battling breast cancer instead of worrying
> about her own situation. That concern for others continued even
> as Susan neared the end of her fight.*[17]

Brinker promised her sister that she would continue her fight against
breast cancer. This story compels donors to join her fight.

Speakers can also tap into emotions using nonverbal behaviors to
model the desired emotion for their audience. In the summer of 2012,
the U.S. House of Representatives debated holding the Attorney General in contempt for refusing to release
documents concerning a controversial gun-tracking operation. Arguing for a contempt vote, South Carolina
Representative Trey Gowdy did not simply state his claim; instead he raised his voice, slowed his pace,
and used hand motions to convey anger with what he perceived as deception on the part of the Attorney
General.[18] His use of volume, tone, pace, and hand gestures enhanced the message and built anger in his
audience.

> Speech is power: speech is to persuade, to convert, to compel. It is to bring another out of his bad
> sense into your good sense. – Ralph Waldo Emerson

In addition to verbal and nonverbal illustrations, visual imagery can enhance the emotional appeal of a
message. For example, we have all heard about the dangers of drugs, and there are multiple campaigns
that attempt to prevent people from even trying them. However, many young adults experiment with drugs
under the assumption that they are immune from the negative effects if they only use the drug recreation-
ally. To counter this assumption regarding methamphetamines, the Montana Meth project combines controversial statements with graphic images on billboards to evoke fear of the drug (see the Montana Meth
Project for some disturbing examples). Young adults may have heard repeated warnings that meth is addictive and that it has the potential to cause sores, rotten teeth, and extreme weight loss, but Montana Meth
Project's visual display is more compelling because it turns the audience's stomach, making the message
memorable. This image, combined with the slogan, "not even once," conveys the persuasive point without
the need for other forms of evidence and rational argument.

Appeals to fear, like those in the Montana Meth Project ads, have proven effective in motivating people
to change a variety of behaviors. However, speakers must be careful with their use of this emotion. Fear
appeals tend to be more effective when they appeal to a high-level fear, such as death, and they are more

17. Komen National. (n.d.). St. Louis Affiliate of Susan G. Komen for the Cure: Who We Are. Retrieved from: http://www.komenst-
louis.org/site/PageServer?pagename=whoweare_national
18. Gowdy, T. (2012). Trey Gowdy's emotional speech on Holder contempt [Video file]. Retrieved from: https://youtu.be/2bP-
G4Btwp0

effective when offered by speakers with a high level of perceived credibility.[19] Fear appeals are also more persuasive when the speaker can convince the audience they have the ability to avert the threat. If audiences doubt their ability to avoid or minimize the threat, the appeal may backfire.[20]

> I would rather try to persuade a man to go along, because once I have persuaded him, he will stick. If I scare him, he will stay just as long as he is scared, and then he is gone. – Dwight D. Eisenhower

David Brooks argues that, "emotions are not separate from reason, but they are the foundation of reason because they tell us what to value."[21] Those values are at the core of fostering a credible ethos. All of Aristotle's strategies, ethos, logos, and pathos, are interdependent. The most persuasive speakers will combine these strategies to varying degrees based on their specific purpose and audience.

Ethics of Persuasion

In addition to considering their topic and persuasive strategy, speakers must take care to ensure that their message is ethical. Persuasion is often confused with another kind of communication that has similar ends, but different methods—coercion. Like persuasion, **coercion** is a process whereby thoughts or behaviors are altered. But in coercive acts, deceptive or harmful methods propel the intended changes, not reason. Strong and Cook contrasted the two: "persuasion uses argument to compel power to give way to reason while coercion uses force to compel reason to give way to power."[22] The "force" that Strong and Cook mention frequently manifests as promises for reward or punishment, but sometimes it arises as physical or

"Speakers Corner Speaker 1987" by Deborah MacLean. Public domain.

emotional harm. Think of almost any international crime film you have seen, and you are likely to remember a scene where someone was compelled to out their compatriots by way of force. Jack Bauer, the protagonist in the American television series *24*, became an infamous character by doing whatever it took to get captured criminals to talk. Although dramatic as an example, those scenes where someone is tortured in an effort to produce evidence offer a familiar reference when thinking about coercion. To avoid coercing an audience, speakers should use logical and emotional appeals responsibly.

> The pendulum of the mind alternates between sense and nonsense, not between right and wrong.
> – Carl Jung

19. Beebe & Beebe 2003

20. Witte, K. & Allen, M. (2000). A metaanalysis of fear appeals: Implications for effective public health campaigns. *Health Education & Behavior, 27*(5), 591–615.

21. Brooks, D. (2011, November 17). TED 2001: David Brooks explains why there is no reason without emotion. *Huffington Post.* Retrieved from: http://www.huffingtonpost.com/2011/03/14/ted-david-brooks_n_835476.html

22. Strong, W. F., & Cook, J. A. (1992). *Persuasion: Strategies for public influence* (3rd ed.). Dubuque, Iowa: Kendall/Hunt Publishing.

Persuasive speakers must be careful to avoid using **fallacies** in their reasoning. Fallacies are errors in reasoning that occur when a speaker fails to use appropriate or applicable evidence for their argument. There are a wide variety of fallacies, and it is not possible to list them all here. However, speakers should watch for four common categories of fallacies: "fallacies of faulty assumption," which occur when the speaker reasons based on a problematic assumption; "fallacies directed to the person," which occur when the speaker focuses on the attributes of an individual opponent rather than the relevant arguments; "fallacies of case presentation," which occur when the speaker mischaracterizes the issue; and "fallacies of suggestion," which occur when the speaker implies or suggests an argument without fully developing it.[23] See the Table 16.2 on the following page for examples of each of these types of fallacies. To learn more about fallacies, see Chapter 6 by Russ (Critical Thinking and Reasoning), or see the supplemental handout found on the Persuasive Speaking chapter homepage.

Table 16.2: Examples of Fallacies	
Fallacies of Faulty Assumption	
Casual Fallacy	It is cloudy outside, and I feel sick. Cloudy days make me sick. The school board voted to buy new picnic tables for the lunch room. Many students were out sick the following day. The students must be upset about the picnic tables.
Bandwagon Fallacy	Everyone takes out a loan to buy a car, so you should too. None of the cool kids wear helmets when they ride bikes. You should take yours off.
Begging the Question	*The Lion King* is an excellent film because it has excellent animation. Marijuana is good for you because it is natural.
Fallacies Directed to the Person	
Ad Hominem	We should reject President Obama's healthcare legislation because it is socialism.
Poisoning the Well	Before the defense makes their closing statement, keep in mind that their client has not said one truthful word throughout the trial. My opponent is going to try to manipulate you into thinking her plan is better for the city.
Appeal to Flattery	First, I wanted to tell you that this is my favorite class. I tell all my friends how much I love it. I just think I deserve a better grade on my exam. You are such a generous person. I know you'll want to donate to this cause.
Fallacies of Case Presentation	
Non Sequitur	I don't plan to vote today because I am moving next week. You should clean your room because I am going to do the laundry.
Red Herring	I should not be fined for parking in a red zone when there are so many people out there committing real crimes like robbery and murder. War is wrong, but in times of crisis we should support the president.
Appeal to Misplaced Authority	This diet is the best one for people with my health condition. Oprah said so. I want to visit the Museum of Modern Art. My English professor says they have the best collection anywhere!
Fallacies of Suggestion	
Paralepsis	I'm not saying he cheated; he just did uncharacteristically well on that exam. If she wants to work for a crook, that's her business.
Either/Or	Either you're with us or against us. Love it or leave it.
Arrangement	I have so much to do today. I have to get my car fixed, finish a paper, take a nap, and pick my mom up from the airport. So many highly respected musicians will be there: Paul McCartney, Elton John, LMFAO, Billy Joel…

23. Herrick 2011

There are some positive steps you can take to avoid these pitfalls of persuasive speaking and ensure that you are presenting your message in the most ethical manner. We have already discussed some of these, such as offering credible evidence for your arguments and showing concern for the audience's well being. However, you should also offer a transparent goal for your speech. Even with a hostile audience, where you may wait until later in the speech to provide the specific purpose statement, you should be forthcoming about your specific purpose. In fact, be truthful with your audience throughout the speech.

It is appropriate to use fictional scenarios to demonstrate your point, but tell the audience that is what you are doing. You can accomplish this by introducing fictional examples with the phrase, "hypothetically," or "imagine," to signal that you are making it up.[24] Additionally, be sure to offer a mix of logical and emotional appeals. Blending these strategies insures that you have evidence to back up emotional claims, and that you are sensitive to the audiences' emotional reactions to your logical claims. Attending to both aspects will help you be more ethical and more persuasive.

> The most important persuasion tool you have in your entire arsenal is integrity. – Zig Ziglar

Attributions

CC licensed content, Shared previously

- Chapter 16 Persuasive Strategies. **Authored by**: Sarah Stone Watt, Ph.D. and Joshua Trey Barnett. **Provided by**: Pepperdine University, Malibu, CA and Indiana University, Bloomington, IN. **Located at**: http://publicspeakingproject.org/psvirtualtext.html. **Project**: The Public Speaking Project. **License**: *CC BY-NC-ND: Attribution-NonCommercial-NoDerivatives*
- Dining Booth. **Authored by**: Wayne Truong. **Located at**: http://commons.wikimedia.org/wiki/File:Dining_Booth.jpg. **License**: *CC BY: Attribution*
- Nancy Brinker. **Authored by**: Cliff. **Located at**: http://commons.wikimedia.org/wiki/File:Nancy_Brinker.jpg. **License**: *CC BY: Attribution*
- Speakers Corner Speaker 1987. **Authored by**: Deborah MacLean. **Located at**: http://commons.wikimedia.org/wiki/File:Speakers-Corner-Speaker-1987.jpg. **License**: *CC0: No Rights Reserved*

Public domain content

- Danny Shine Speaker's Corner. **Authored by**: Acapeloahddub. **Located at**: http://commons.wikimedia.org/wiki/File:Danny_Shine_Speaker's_Corner.JPG. **License**: *Public Domain: No Known Copyright*
- Deepwater Horizon offshore drilling unit on fire. **Provided by**: US Coast Guard. **Located at**: http://en.wikipedia.org/wiki/Wikipedia:Featured_picture_candidates/Deepwater_Horizon_fire#mediaviewer/File:Deepwater_Horizon_offshore_drilling_unit_on_fire.jpg. **License**: *Public Domain: No Known Copyright*

---

24. Beebe & Beebe 2003

Organizing Persuasive Messages

Once you have selected your topic, know who your audience is, and have settled on an end goal for your persuasive speech, you can begin drafting your speech. Outlines are organized according to the particular speech, and the following organizational patterns are used routinely for persuasive speeches.

Monroe's Motivated Sequence

Monroe's Motivated Sequence is an organizational pattern that attempts to convince the audience to respond to a need that is delineated in the speech.[1] Five separate steps characterize the Motivated Sequence organization style:

1. The *attention step* should get the audience's attention as well as describe your goals and preview the speech.

2. The *need step* should provide a description of the problem as well as the consequences that may result if the problem goes unresolved. In this step, the speaker should also alert audience members to their role in mitigating the issue.

3. The *satisfaction step* is used to outline your solutions to the problems you have previously outlined as well as deal with any objections that may arise.

4. In the *visualization step*, audience members are asked to visualize what will happen if your solutions are implemented and what will happen if they do not come to fruition. Visualizations should be rich with detail.

5. The *action appeal step* should be used to make a direct appeal for action. In this step, you should describe precisely how the audience should react to your speech and how they should carry out these actions. As the final step, you should also offer a concluding comment. See Figure 16.1 to see this method of arrangement illustrated.

---

1. Monroe, A. H. (1949). *Principles and types of speech*. Glenview, IL: Scott, Foresman and Company.

<table>
<tr><td colspan="2" align="center">Figure 16.1: Monroe's Motivated Sequence Sample Outline</td></tr>
<tr><td colspan="2">I. Attention step</td></tr>
<tr><td></td><td>A. When was the last time you saw a dog chained to a tree in a neighbor's yard, heard about a puppy mill in your town, or went into a pet store only to find dogs and cats for sale?
B. I work with the Morris County Animal Protection Group, and I would like to share some ways in which you can help prevent these travesties.
C. First, I will describe some of the major problems in Morris County, and then I will tell you how you can get involved.</td></tr>
<tr><td colspan="2">II. Need step: Many animals in Morris County are abused and neglected.</td></tr>
<tr><td></td><td>A. There are too many stray animals that are neither spayed nor neutered, resulting in an overabundance of cats and dogs.
B. These animals often cannot find enough food to survive, and the local shelter cannot accommodate such high populations.
C. The cost of local spay/neuter programs is too high for our agency to handle.</td></tr>
<tr><td colspan="2">III. Satisfaction step: Raising $1 million for the Morris County Animal Protection Agency can effectively solve these problems.</td></tr>
<tr><td></td><td>A. We could afford to spay or neuter most stray animals.
B. Obtained animals could be fed and accommodated until a home can be secured for them.
C. Additionally, we could subsidize spay/neuter costs for local citizens.</td></tr>
<tr><td colspan="2">IV. Visualization step: Imagine what we can do for our animals with this money.</td></tr>
<tr><td></td><td>A. What will it be like if we can carry out these actions?
B. What will it be like if we cannot do these things?</td></tr>
<tr><td colspan="2">V. Action appeal step: Donate to the Morris County Animal Protection Agency.</td></tr>
<tr><td></td><td>A. If you want to help protect the many struggling stray animals in Morris County, make a donation to our organization.
B. Your donation will make a real difference in the lives of our animals.
C. We cannot effect real change for the animals of our county without each and every one of you.</td></tr>
</table>

Direct Method Pattern

If your goal is to convince your audience to adopt a particular idea, you might prefer the **direct method pattern** as a way of organizing your speech. This pattern consists of a claim and a list of reasons to support it. Every piece of support in the speech directly supports the central claim you wish to make. As Jaffe points out, "It's a good pattern to use when listeners are apathetic or neutral, either mildly favoring or mildly opposing your claim."[2] The outline for a speech on vegetarianism in Figure 16.2 provides three reasons that vegetarianism provides useful health benefits for people struggling with obesity.

"Roman Rackwitz Presentation" by Romrack. CC-BY-SA.

<table>
<tr><td align="center">Figure 16.2: Direct Method Pattern Sample Outline</td></tr>
<tr><td>Proposition: Vegetarianism offers many positive health benefits for people struggling with obesity.</td></tr>
</table>

2. Jaffe, C. (2004). *Public speaking: Concepts and skills for a diverse society* (4th ed.). Belmont, CA: Wadsworth.

<table>
<tr><td colspan="1" align="center">Figure 16.2: Direct Method Pattern Sample Outline</td></tr>
<tr><td>I. Vegetarianism often reduces the amount of processed food that one eats.
II. Vegetarianism promotes a sense of reflective consumption.
III. Vegetarianism decreases the likelihood that one will contract some diseases, such as cancer and heart disease.</td></tr>
<tr><td>As you can see from this example, the statement of reasons that follows the proposition directly supports the central claim of the speech. Each reason offers another bit of evidence that vegetarianism is a good option for people struggling with obesity.</td></tr>
</table>

> History creates comprehensibility primarily by arranging facts meaningfully and only in a very limited sense by establishing strict causal connections. – Johan Huizinga

Causal Pattern

Similar to a problem-solution speech, which was covered in Chapter 8, a causal speech describes a general cause and a specific effect. In other words, a **causal pattern** first addresses some cause and then shares what effects resulted. A causal speech can be particularly effective when the speaker wants to convince their audience of the relationship between two things. With sound causal reasoning, a speech of this sort can be used to convince the audience of something they were previously opposed to believing.

As the example in Figure 16.3 illustrates, the basic components of the causal speech are the cause and the effect. Such an organizational style is useful when a speaker needs to share the results of a new program, discuss how one act led to another, or discuss the positive/negative outcomes of taking some action. Through this pattern, the speaker can convince audiences to adopt a new belief about a particular phenomenon.

<table>
<tr><td colspan="1" align="center">Figure 16.3: Causal Pattern Sample Outline</td></tr>
<tr><td>Proposition: Macintosh computers make people more creative.</td></tr>
<tr><td>I. Macintosh computers rely on a simple, intuitive interface and are sold through a marketing campaign that encourages users to "Think Different." (cause)

II. The simplicity of Macintosh computers allows people to be more creative since they are not spending their time figuring out how to use their computer. And these same consumers are socialized to "think differently" with their Macintosh computers from the moment they consider purchasing one. (effect)</td></tr>
</table>

Refutation Pattern

Sometimes an occasion will arise when your audience is already opposed to your argument. In this case, a **refutation pattern** can be engaged to persuade audience members that your side of the argument is better or more accurate. In a refutation speech, the speaker must anticipate the audience's opposition, then bring attention to the tensions between the two sides, and finally refute them using evidential support. Refutation patterns are frequently seen in debates, where speakers are fundamentally opposed to one another's arguments. Refutation generally happens through a set of four steps: (1) signaling the argument to which you are responding, (2) stating your own argument, (3) providing justification or evidence for your side of the argument, and (4) summarizing your response. An

*"Jeanette Chong-Aruldoss" **by Terence Lee.** CC-BY.*

advocate of reusing as opposed to recycling might present the argument in Figure 16.4 to respond to someone who believes recycling is the best way to individually work on environmental stewardship. As this example illustrates, a refutation speech should clearly delineate where the audience is perceived to stand on an issue, why their view is in disagreement with the speaker's, and why the audience should adopt the speaker's position. Moreover, the speaker should be sure to highlight the importance of the debate, which will clue the audience into why they should spend their time listening to a speaker who clearly disagrees with them. An example of this pattern can be found on the next page in Figure 16.4.

Figure 16.4: Sample Outline Refutation Pattern
(Imagine that the speaker is giving the speech at a recycling convention.)   **Proposition:** Reusing products is better than recycling them.
I. Although Thomas argued that recycling is the most important individual act of environmental stewardship, I would like to argue that reusing is an even better way to care for our environment. (signaling and stating)

II. Reusing has several advantages over recycling. (providing evidence)
    A. Reusing reduces consumption.
    B. Reusing extends the life of a product before it needs to be recycled.
    C. It is cheaper to reuse an item than to recycle it.

III. Given these advantages, it is more useful for people to reuse items when possible than it is to recycle them.

Neither irony nor sarcasm is argument. – Samuel Butler

Attributions

CC licensed content, Shared previously

Conclusion and Module Activities

The primary goal of persuasive speaking is to influence an audience's beliefs or behaviors so that they can make necessary or positive change. Persuasive speaking is a vital skill in all areas of life, whether it is a political candidate convincing voters to elect them, an employee convincing the boss to give them a promotion, or a sales person convincing a consumer to buy a product, individuals must understand what persuasion is and how it functions.

When formulating a persuasive speech, remember to determine the type of question you seek to answer so that you can decide whether to offer a proposition of fact, a proposition of value, or a proposition of policy. Weave the topic and the proposition together to create a compelling argument for your specific audience.

Knowing your audience can help when it comes to choosing the appropriate strategies for convincing them that you are a credible speaker. Once you have established your credibility, you can advance both logical and emotional appeals to move your audience toward the belief or behavior you hope they will adopt. As you weave these appeals together, be sure to offer the most ethical arguments by avoiding fallacies and supporting emotional appeals with relevant evidence.

"Martin Kingham, CFMEU" by pfctdayelise. CC-BY-SA.

Once you have compiled the most relevant arguments and emotional appeals for a given audience, take care to organize your message effectively. Give thought to your persuasive goals and determine whether they can be best achieved through the use of Monroe's Motivated Sequence, a direct method pattern, a causal pattern, or a refutation pattern.

The combination of a confident and credible speaker with the right organization of logical and emotional appeals can go far in swaying an audience.

It's better to get smart than to get mad. I try not to get so insulted that I will not take advantage of an opportunity to persuade people to change their minds. – John H. Johnson

Review Activities

1. Early in the chapter the prevalence of persuasion was discussed. Think of an instance in which you knew you were being persuaded. What were you being persuaded to do? Was the persuader focused on changing your beliefs, attitudes, values, or actions? How do you know?

2. Imagine you are giving a persuasive speech on _______________ [you fill in the blank]. Draft a specific purpose statement on this topic for a speech to convince. Next, draft a specific purpose statement on the same topic for a speech to actuate.

3. Draft a proposition of fact, proposition of value, and proposition of policy for one or more of the following topics:

   - Shortening class time

   - Pro-anorexia images on social networking sites

   - Airline fees

4. You have been invited to speak to administrators about increasing alumni support for the school. What steps will you take to build your ethos for this audience? What logical appeals will you make? How will you appeal to their emotions?

5. Identify the following fallacies (adapted from Labossiere, 1995):

   - If those actions were not illegal, they would not be prohibited by law.

   - Our team had a losing record until we won the last three games. I wore blue socks in the last three games. Blue socks are lucky, and if I keep wearing them, we can't lose!

   - The store Joe works at changed the dress code, requiring him to buy all new work clothes. When he went to the manager to complain, she told him that no one else voiced concern, so he must be the only one who had that problem.

   - Your roommate has invited his classmate, Annie, over to work on a project. Before Annie arrives, your roommate explains that she will probably be late because she never helps with the work and always leaves him to take care of everything.(Answers can be found on the bottom of page)

6. Imagine you are giving a speech in which you hope to convince audience members to begin retirement planning while they are still in their twenties. Which of the organizational patterns described above best fits this topic? Why? Describe its advantages over the other organization styles for the specific purpose.

Show Answer For #5

    a. begging the question

    b. causal fallacy

    c. bandwagon fallacy

    d. poisoning the well

Activities

1. Using a recent newspaper, locate an example of a proposition of fact, a proposition of value, and a proposition of policy, and underline each one. Then, see if you can locate the data, warrant, and backing for each of these claims. If you cannot locate one or more of the elements, write your own based on the information provided in the article.

2. Two organizations, Mercy For Animals (MFA) and People for the Ethical Treatment of Animals (PETA), sponsor billboard advertisements to advocate that people transition to a vegetarian diet. Examine the billboards from each organization and consider the following:

   - What logical claims are advanced by each organization's billboards?

   - Are there any logical fallacies on the billboards?

   - What emotional appeals are used on the billboards?

   - Are any of the emotional appeals unethical? If so, why?

   - Which is the more ethically persuasive campaign? Why?

Attributions

CC licensed content, Shared previously

- Chapter 16 Conclusion and Module Activities. **Authored by**: Sarah Stone Watt, Ph.D. and Joshua Trey Barnett. **Provided by**: Pepperdine University, Malibu, CA and Indiana University, Bloomington, IN. **Located at**: http://publicspeakingproject.org/psvirtualtext.html. **Project**: The Public Speaking Project. **License**: *CC BY-NC-ND: Attribution-NonCommercial-NoDerivatives*

- Martin Kingham, CFMEU. **Authored by**: pfctdayelise. **Located at**: http://commons.wikimedia.org/wiki/File:Martin_Kingham,_CFMEU.JPG. **License**: *CC BY-SA: Attribution-ShareAlike*

Glossary and References

Glossary

TERM	DEFINITION
Argument	A proposition supported by one or more reasons or pieces of evidence.
Backing	Foundational evidence which supports a claim, such as examples, statistics, or testimony.
Causal Pattern	A speech designed to explain a cause-effect relationship between two phenomena.
Causal Reasoning	The process of formulating an argument by examining related events to determine which one caused the other.
Claim	The proposition you want the audience to accept.
Coercion	A process whereby thoughts or behaviors are altered through deceptive or harmful methods.
Data	Preliminary evidence on which a claim is based.
Deductive Reasoning	The process of formulating an argument by moving from a general premise to a specific conclusion.
Demographics	Statistical information that reflects the make-up of a group, often including age, sex, ethnic or cultural background, socioeconomic status, religion, and political affiliation.
Direct Method Pattern	A speech designed to present a claim with a list of several supporting pieces of data.
Ethos	The audience's perception of a speaker's credibility and moral character.
Evaluation Criteria	A set of standards for judging the merit of a proposition.
Fallacies	Errors in reasoning that occur when a speaker fails to use appropriate or applicable evidence for their argument.
Hostile Audience	An audience that is opposed to the speaker or to the persuasive proposition.
Identification	A connection that is fostered between the speaker and their audience by highlighting shared attributes or attitudes.
Inductive Reasoning	The process of formulating an argument by moving from specific instances to a generalization.
Logos	The logical means of proving an argument.
Monroe's Motivated Sequence	An organizational pattern that attempts to convince the audience to respond to a need that is delineated in the speech through five sequential steps.
Neutral Audience	An audience that is neither open nor opposed to the persuasive proposition.
Pathos	The use of emotional appeals to persuade an audience.
Persuasion	The art of influencing or reinforcing people's beliefs, attitudes, values, or actions.

Persuasive Speeches	Speeches which aim to convince an audience to think or behave in a particular way.
Proposition of Fact	An argument that seeks to establish whether something is true or false.
Proposition of Policy	An argument that seeks to establish an appropriate course of action.
Proposition of Value	An argument that seeks to establish the relative worth of something.
Receptive Audience	An audience that is generally supportive of, or open to, the persuasive proposition.
Refutation Pattern	A speech designed to anticipate the negative response of an audience, to bring attention to the tensions between the two sides of the argument, and to explain why the audience should change their views.
Speeches to Actuate	Persuasive speeches which seek to change or motivate particular behaviors.
Speeches to Convince	Persuasive speeches which seek to establish agreement about a particular topic.
Status Quo	The current situation.
Syllogisms	Reasoning beginning with a major premise, then moving to a minor premise, before establishing a specific claim.
Warrant	The (often unstated) connection between data and claim.

References

American Civil Liberties Union (ACLU). (2012). Racial Profiling. Retrieved from: http://www.aclu.org/racial-justice/racial-profiling

Angelides, P. (2011, June 28). The real causes of the economic crisis? They're history. *The Washington Post*. Retrieved from: http://www.washingtonpost.com/opinions/the-real-causes-of-the-economic-crisis-theyre-history/2011/06/27/AG2nK4pH_stor y.html

Applebaum, E. & Berhardt, A. (2004, December 18). Employers also benefit from a higher minimum wage. *Brennan Center for Justice*. Retrieved from: http://www.brennancenter.org/content/resource/employers_also_benefit_from_a_higher_minimum_wage/

Aral, S. & Walker, D. (2012, 20 July). Identifying influential and susceptible members of social networks. *Science, 327* (6092), 337 – 341. Retrieved from: www.sciencemag.org/content/early/2012/06/20/science.1215842.short

Avlon, J. (2010, September 2). America's 9 worst demagogues. *The Daily Beast*. Retrieved from: http://www.thedailybeast.com/articles/2010/09/02/glenn-beck-and-the-history-of-americas-worst- demagogues.html

Beebe, S.A. & Beebe, S.J. (2003). *Public Speaking: An Audience Centered Approach* (5th ed.). Boston: Pearson.

Begala, P. (2012, May 28). Paul Begala: The Right hates spending, unless it pockets the cash. *The Daily Beast*. Retrieved from: http://www. thedailybeast.com/newsweek/2012/05/27/paul-begala-the-right-hates-spending-unless-it-pockets-the-cash.html

Bingham, A. (2011, July 22). Postal Service pushes to end Saturday delivery. *ABC News*. Retrieved from: http://abcnews.go.com/blogs/politics/2011/07/postal-service-pushes-to-end-saturday-delivery/

Blackman, S. (2009, September 3). Tired consumers more susceptible to advertising. *CBS Money Watch*. Retrieved from: http://www.cbsnews.com/8301-505125_162-31041103/tired-consumers-more-susceptible-to-advertising/

Braet, A.C. (1992). Ethos, pathos, and logos in Aristotle's rhetoric: A re-examination. *Argumentation, 6* (3), pp. 307-320.

Brill, R. (2003, July 21). Why do clouds turn gray before it rains? *Scientific American*. Retrieved from: http://www.scientificamerican.com/article.cfm?id=why-do-clouds-turn-gray-b

Brooks, D. (2011, November 17). TED 2001: David Brooks explains why there is no reason without emotion. *Huffington Post*. Retrieved from: http://www.huffingtonpost.com/2011/03/14/ted-david-brooks_n_835476.html

Campbell, K.K. & Huxman, S.S. (2009). *The Rhetorical Act: Thinking, Speaking, and Writing Critically*. Belmont, CA: Wadsworth.

Caplan, A. (2005). The time has come to let Terri Schiavo die: Politicians, courts must allow husband to make final decision. *NBC News*. Retrieved from: http://www.msnbc.msn.com/id/7231440/ns/health-health_care/t/time-has-come-let-terri-schiavo-die/#.UD_oVSL4LP8

Car and Driver (2011, December). 2012 10Best Cars. *Car and Driver.* Retrieved from:http://www.caranddriver.com/features/2012-10best-cars-feature

Catholic Culture. (2005). The death of Terri Schiavo. *Catholic World News*. Retrieved from: http://www.catholicculture.org/news/features/index.cfm?recnum=37860

Cerminara, K. & Goodman, K. (2012). Schiavo Timeline. Retrieved from University of Miami Ethics Program: www.miami.edu/index.php/ethics/projects/schiavo/schiavo_timeline/

DeGrazia, D. (2009). Moral vegetarianism from a very broad basis. *Journal of Moral Philosophy, 6.* Retrieved from: http://www.gwu.edu/~philosop/faculty/documents/DeGraziaMoral.pdf

Dillard, J.P. & Meijnders, A. (2002). Persuasion and the structure of affect. In J.P. Dillard & M. Pfau (Eds.), *The Persuasion Handbook: Developments in Theory and Practice* (309-328). Thousand Oaks, CA: Sage.

Donovan, T.W. (2010, July 10). 7 Long term effects of the Gulf oil spill. *Huffington Post*. Retrieved from: http://www.huffingtonpost.com/2010/05/10/7-long-term-effects-of-th_n_562947.html#s87787&title=Environmental_Damage

German, K. M., Gronbeck, B. E., Ehninger, D., & Monroe, A. H. (2004). *Principles of public speaking* (15th ed.). Boston: Pearson.

Goodstein, L. (2006, January 8). Even Pat Robertson's friends are wondering . . . *The New York Times*. Retrieved from: http://www.nytimes.com/2006/01/08/weekinreview/08goodstein.html

Gowdy, T. (2012). Trey Gowdy's emotional speech on Holder contempt [Video file]. Retrieved from: http://www.youtube.com/watch?v=2bP- G4Btwp0&feature=player_embedded#!

Herrick, J.A. (2011). *Argumentation: Understanding and Shaping Arguments*. State College, PA: Strata Publishing.

Jaffe, C. (2004). *Public speaking: Concepts and skills for a diverse society* (4th ed.). Belmont, CA: Wadsworth.

Kandel, J. (2011, July 14). Los Angeles braces for weekend of "Carmageddon." *Reuters*. Retrieved from: http://www.reuters.com/article/2011/07/14/us-carmageddon-losangeles-idUSTRE76D2D720110714

Komen National. (n.d.). St. Louis Affiliate of Susan G. Komen for the Cure: Who We Are. Retrieved from http://www.komenstlouis.org/site/PageServer?pagename=whoweare_national

Labossiere, M.C. (1995). The nizkor project. Retrieved from: www.nizkor.org/features/fallacies/

O'Hair, D., & Stewart, R. (1999). *Public speaking: Challenges and choices*. Boston: Bedford/St. Martin's.

Osborn, M., & Osborn, S. (1997). *Public speaking* (4th ed.). Boston: Houghton Mifflin Company.

Pollan, M. (2007, April 22). You are what you grow. *The New York Times*. Retrieved from: http://www.nytimes.com/2007/04/22/magazine/22wwlnlede.t.html?pagewanted=all

Reike, R.D., Sillars, M.O., & Peterson, T.R. (2009). *Argumentation and Critical Decision Making* (7th ed.). Boston: Pearson.

Rosendaal, E., Lapierre, M.A., vanReijmersdal, E.A., & Buijzen, M. (2011). Reconsidering advertising literacy as a defense against advertising effects. *Media Psychology, 14* (4), 333-354.

Stephenson, E. (2012, August 1). Senators blast House leaders over Postal Service default. *News Daily*. Retrieved from: http://www.newsdaily.com/stories/bre8701ho-us-usa-postal-default/

Story, L. (2007, January 15). Anywhere the eye can see, it's likely to see an ad. *The New York Times*. Retrieved from: http://www.nytimes.com/2007/01/15/business/media/15everywhere.html?pagewanted=all

Strong, W. F., & Cook, J. A. (1992). *Persuasion: Strategies for public influence* (3rd ed.). Dubuque, Iowa: Kendall/Hunt Publishing.

Witte, K. & Allen, M. (2000). A meta-analysis of fear appeals: Implications for effective public health campaigns. *Health Education & Behavior, 27* (5), 591-615.

Zarefsky, D. (2005). *Public Speaking: Strategies for Success* (Special edition for The Pennsylvania State University). Boston: Pearson.

photo credits

p. 2 NASUWT officer speaking by Sam Saunders http://upload.wikimedia.org/wikipedia/commons/a/a7/ NASUWT _officer_speaking_at_Bristol_public_sector_pensions_rally_in_ November_2011.jpg

p. 2 Air Pollution by US Environmental Protection Agency http://commons.wikimedia.org/wiki/File:Air-PollutionSource.jpg p. 3 California Traffic by Downtowngal http://upload.wikimedia.org/wikipedia/commons/1/1b/Interstate _10_looking_east_from_Crenshaw_Boulevard.jpg

p. 4 McLaren F1 by Jagvar http://upload.wikimedia.org/wikipedia/commons/5/53/MclarenF 1.JPG

p. 4 USPS mailboxes by Erasergirl http://commons.wikimedia.org/wiki/File:USPS_mailboxes.jpg

p. 5 Jade Raymond by Gamescore Blog http://commons.wikimedia.org/wiki/File:Jade_Raymond_-_E3_2007_2.jpg

p. 5 Audience member at USO show by .S. Air Force Master Sgt. Adam M. Stump http://commons.wikimedia.org/wiki/File:Defense.gov_photo_essay_081112-F-6684S-757.jpg

p. 6 Children at play by Nils Fretwurst http://commons.wikimedia.org/wiki/File:Children_play_in_push_car.jpg

p. 6 Credit cards by Lotus Head http://upload.wikimedia.org/wikipedia/commons/4/4f/Credit- cards.jpg

p. 7 Danny Shine by Acapeloahddub http://commons.wikimedia.org/wiki/File:Danny_Shine_Speaker%27s_Corner.JPG

p. 8 Dining booth by Wayne Truong http://commons.wikimedia.org/wiki/File:Dining_Booth.jpg

p. 9 Deepwater Horizon fire by US Coast Guard http://upload.wikimedia.org/wikipedia/commons/6/67/ Deepwater_Horizon_fire_2010-04-21.jpg

p. 9 Nancy Brinker by Nancy Brinker http://commons.wikimedia.org/wiki/File:Nancy_Brinker.jpg

p. 10 Speaker's Corner speaker by Deborah MacLean http://commons.wikimedia.org/wiki/File:Speakers-Corner- Speaker-1987.jpg

p. 12 Roman Rackwitz by Romrack http://commons.wikimedia.org/wiki/File:Roman_Rackwitz_Pres entation.jpg

p. 13 Jeanette Chong-Aruldoss by Terence Lee http://commons.wikimedia.org/wiki/File:Jeanette_Chong-Aruldoss_at_a_Reform_Party_rally,_Speakers%27_Corner,_Singapore_-_20110115.jpg

p. 14 Bonnie Franklin by Pattymooney http://commons.wikimedia.org/wiki/File:Actress_Bonnie_Franklin_Speaks_at_March_For_Women%27s_Lives_2004.jpg

p. 14 Martin_Kingham by pfctdayelise http://commons.wikimedia.org/wiki/File:Martin_Kingham,_CF MEU.JPG

Attributions

CC licensed content, Shared previously

University, Malibu, CA and Indiana University, Bloomington, IN. **Located at**: http://publicspeakingproject.org/psvirtualtext.html. **Project**: The Public Speaking Project. **License**: *CC BY-NC-ND: Attribution-NonCommercial-NoDerivatives*

Appendix A: Persuasive Speech Topic Ideas

Environmental Topics

- Citizens should try to reuse items before recycling them.

- The U.S. should ban mountaintop removal as a mode of harvesting coal.

- Contemporary climate change is human-caused.

- Governmental funding for clean energy should be increased.

- All municipalities should offer public transportation.

- The U.S. should ratify the Kyoto Protocol.

- Bottled water should undergo the same quality testing as municipal water.

- Preservation is a better environmental sustainability model than is conservation. • Hunting should be banned on all public lands.

Social Justice Topics

- The right to marry should be extended to gays and lesbians.

- Abortion should be illegal.

- State colleges should be free to attend.

- Martin Luther King, Jr. was the most influential leader of the civil rights movement

- The death penalty should be abolished.

- Convicted rapists should be sentenced to the death penalty.

- Women should receive equal pay for equal work.

- Affirmative action does not work and should be ended.

- Individuals and communities affected by environmental injustices should receive compensation.

Campus Life

- Dorm rooms should have individual thermostats.

- Professors' office hours should be held at reasonable hours, not 7 a.m. on Mondays.

- Free coffee should be provided in all classroom buildings before noon.

- Student fees at universities are too high.

- Dining halls should provide nutritional information for all meals.

- Student government leaders should host regular forums to answer questions from the general student population.

- Plagiarism should be prosecuted to the fullest extent.

Everyday Life Topics

- The legal drinking age should be lowered to 18.

- Frequent flyers should not be required to remove their shoes in airport security lines.

- Eating five meals a day is better than eating three.

- Smoking should be illegal in all public areas.

- Gmail is the best email service.

- All restaurants should offer vegan and vegetarian options or substitutes.

- Netflix and Hulu are better ways to watch movies and television shows.

- ATM fees should be outlawed.

- Proximity to religious facilities should have no bearing on alcohol sales.

Economic Topics

- Social security benefits should be guaranteed for those who pay in to the program.

- All multi-year jobs should include pension plans.

- The U.S. should spend less on wars and more on education.

- Everyone should be required to pay an equal percentage of taxes.

- A consumption tax is more just than an income tax.

- The minimum wage in the U.S. is too low.

- Multi-million dollar bonuses for corporate executives are unjust because they preclude better wages/reduced prices for others.

Quirky Topics

- Tacos are the greatest of human inventions.

- Ghosts are real.

- Short haircuts are more comfortable than long hairstyles.

- Bourbon should only be served "on the rocks."

- Traditional eyeglasses make those who wear them look smarter.

- Eating chicken with a fork should be illegal. (An actual law in Gainesville, Georgia!)

Attributions

CC licensed content, Shared previously

- Chapter 16 Appendix A. **Authored by**: Sarah Stone Watt, Ph.D. and Joshua Trey Barnett. **Provided by**: Pepperdine University Malibu, CA and Indiana University Bloomington, IN. **Located at**: http://publicspeakingproject.org/psvirtualtext.html. **Project**: The Public Speaking Project. **License**: *CC BY-NC-ND: Attribution-NonCommercial-NoDerivatives*

Chapter 12: Supporting Your Ideas

Objectives and Introduction

Supporting Your Ideas

By Sarah Stone Watt, Ph.D.
Pepperdine University, Malibu, CA

Learning Objectives

- Combine multiple forms of evidence to support your ideas.

- Differentiate between the three types of testimony, and know when to use each one.

- Navigate the library holdings and distinguish between the types of information found in each section.

- Evaluate source credibility and appropriateness for your speech.

- Explain plagiarism and implement strategies to avoid it.

- Apply chapter concepts in review questions and activities.

Introduction

> I take what I see work. I'm a strict believer in the scientific principle of believing nothing, only taking the best evidence available at the present time, interpreting it as best you can, and leaving your mind open to the fact that new evidence will appear tomorrow. – Adam Osborne

In 2010 celebrity chef Jamie Oliver won the Technology Entertainment Design (TED) Prize for his "One Wish to Change the World." In addition to a monetary award, he was given 18 minutes at the prestigious TED Conference in Long Beach, CA to discuss his wish: "Teach every child about food."[1] This chef from Essex, England, had only a short window of time to convince an American audience to change their most basic eating habits. To get them to listen he had to catch their attention and demonstrate his credibility. He managed to do both using compelling research. He began by saying, "Sadly, in the next 18 minutes . . . four Americans that are alive will be dead from the food that they eat."[2] He magnified the problem with a chart showing that many more Americans die from diet related diseases each year than die from other diseases, or even from accidents and murder. Along with the statistics, he offered testimony from people living in the "most unhealthy state in America."[3] By weaving together multiple forms of research over the course of his brief talk, Oliver crafted a compelling case for a massive shift in the way that Americans teach their children about food.

"Jamie Oliver" by Karl Grober. CC-BY.

Like Oliver, in order to give an effective speech, you will need to offer support for the ideas you present. Finding support necessitates research. Librarians have found that professors and students tend to have very different ideas regarding what it means to conduct research.[4] Professors, who regularly conduct scholarly research as part of their occupation, tend to envision a process filled with late nights in the stacks of a library.[5] Students, who regularly conduct research on where to eat or what to do as part of their weekend activities, tend to envision a less formal process that involves consulting the most popular web search results. The reality is that in order to properly support your ideas and craft a compelling speech, you will need a little of each approach, possibly combined with investigative tools with which you may be less-familiar. The wide variety of resources available for conducting research can be overwhelming. However, if you have a clear topic, recognize the purpose of your speech, and understand the audience you will be speaking to, you can limit the number of sources you will need to consult by focusing on the most relevant information.

1. Oliver, J. (2010, February). Jamie Oliver's TED Prize wish: Teach every child about food. *TED Ideas Worth Spreading.* Speech retrieved from: http://www.ted.com/talks/jamie_oliver
2. Oliver 2010
3. Oliver 2010
4. Sjoberg, L.M. & Ahlfeldt, S.L. (2010). Bridging the gap: Integrating information literacy into communication courses. *Communication Teacher, 24*(3), pp. 131–135.
5. Leckie, G.J. (1996). Desperately seeking citations: Uncovering faculty assumptions about the undergraduate research process. *The Journal of Academic Librarianship, 22*(3), p. 201–208.

Once you know the topic of the speech, you can create the specific purpose statement. This is a one sentence summary of the goal of your speech, that may begin with the phrase, "At the end of my speech, the audience will be able to…" This statement guides your research as you piece together the supporting evidence to fill out the remainder of your speech. As you work through the types of support in this chapter, continually ask yourself, "Does this evidence support the goal of my speech?" If the source offers information that contradicts your specific purpose statement, hold on to it so that you can address the contradiction with evidence for your own idea. If it does appear to support your specific pur-

"Girder Gridwork" by skycaptaintwo. CC-BY.

pose statement, the next question you will ask is "Is this evidence appropriate for my audience?" Different types of appeals and evidence are better for different audiences. The best speeches will combine multiple forms of evidence to make the most convincing case possible. This chapter will help you research your speech by combining personal and professional knowledge, library resources, and Internet searches. It will help you to evaluate the sources you find and cite them to avoid plagiarism.

Attributions

CC licensed content, Shared previously

- Chapter 7 Objectives, Outline, and Introduction. **Authored by**: Sarah Stone Watt, Ph.D.. **Provided by**: Pepperdine University, Malibu, CA. **Located at**: http://publicspeakingproject.org/psvirtualtext.html. **Project**: Public Speaking Project. **License**: *CC BY-NC-ND: Attribution-NonCommercial-NoDerivatives*

- Jamie Oliver cropped. **Authored by**: Karl Gabor. **Located at**: http://en.wikipedia.org/wiki/Jamie_Oliver#mediaviewer/File:Jamie_Oliver_(cropped).jpg. **License**: *CC BY: Attribution*

- Girder Gridwork. **Authored by**: skycaptaintwo. **Located at**: https://www.flickr.com/photos/skycaptaintwo/44554073/. **License**: *CC BY: Attribution*

Video: Using Wikipedia for Academic Research

This tutorial explains how to use Wikipedia as an exploratory tool and where it can appropriately fit in the research process.

Created by Michael Baird, Cooperative Library Instruction Project (CLIP).

- https://youtu.be/Cql_yVUYj6A

Attributions

CC licensed content, Original

- Public Speaking. **Authored by**: Christie Fierro and Brent Adrian. **Provided by**: Lumen Learning. **Located at**: http://lumenlearning.com/. **Project**: Kaleidoscope Open Course Initiative. **License**: *CC BY: Attribution*

CC licensed content, Shared previously

- Using Wikipedia for Academic Research CLIP. **Authored by**: clipinfolit. **Located at**: http://youtu.be/Cql_yVUYj6A. **License**: *CC BY-NC-SA: Attribution-NonCommercial-ShareAlike*

Personal and Professional Knowledge

Do you know the difference between education and experience? Education is when you read the fine print; experience is what you get when you don't. – Pete Seeger

Professional public speakers are generally called upon to address a topic on which they are considered an expert. You may not feel like an expert in the area of your speech at this time, but you should consider whether you have any preexisting knowledge of the topic that might assist in crafting your speech. Do not be afraid to draw on your own experience to enhance the message.

Personal Testimony

Walter Fisher argues that humans are natural storytellers. Through stories people make sense of their experiences, and they invite others to understand their lived reality as part of a community.[1] One compelling story that you can offer is your personal testimony. Although you are not a recognized authority on the topic, you can invite the audience to understand your firsthand experience. Offering your testimony within a speech provides an example of your point, and it enhances your credibility by demonstrating that you have experience regarding the topic. Additionally, personal testimony can enhance your speech by conveying your insight and emotion regarding the topic, making your speech more memorable.[2,3] For example, if you are giving a speech on the importance of hunting to the local culture, you might explain how the last buck you shot fed your family for an entire season.

Since personal testimony refers to your experience, it is easy to assume that you can offer it with little preparation. However, psychologists have found that as people tell their stories they relive the experience.[4] As you relive the experience, your tendency will be to enrich the story with detail and emotion, which is

1. Fisher, W. R. (1984). Narration as a human communication paradigm: The case of public moral argument. *Communication Monographs, 51*, pp.1–22.
2. Beebe, S.A. & Beebe, S.J. (2003). *Public speaking: An audience centered approach.* Boston, MA: Allyn and Bacon.
3. Parse, R. R. (2008). Truth for the moment: Personal testimony as evidence. *Nursing Science Quarterly, 21*(1), pp. 45–48.
4. Gladding, S.T. & Drake Wallace, M.J. (2010). The potency and power of counseling stories. *Journal of Creativity in Mental Health, 5*, pp. 15–24.

part of what makes it memorable, but this practice may also make the story too long and distract from your point. If you plan to use personal testimony in your speech, practice the story to make sure that it makes the appropriate point in the time you have.

If you do not have personal experience with the topic, you may seek out other forms of lay testimony to support your point. Lay testimony is any testimony based on witnesses' opinions or perceptions in a given case.[5] For example, if you are giving a speech about Occupy Wall Street, but you have not experienced one of their protests, you may choose to include statements from a protestor or someone who identifies with the goals of the movement.

Interviews

Lay testimony can offer insight into the past and into areas where individual sentiments are relevant, but if you are called upon to make predictions regarding the future or speak to an issue where you have little relevant experience, expert testimony may provide more convincing support.[6] Expert testimony comes from a recognized authority who has conducted extensive research on an issue. Experts regularly publish their research findings in books and journals, which we will discuss later in this chapter, but you may need more information from the expert in order to substantiate your point. For example, if you were giving a speech about how to prepare for a natural disaster, you might

"Interviews" **by Heinrich-Böll-Stiftung.** CC-BY-SA.

interview someone from the Red Cross. They could tell you what supplies might be necessary for the specific types of disasters that are likely in your region. Interviews give people the chance to expand on their published research and offer their informed perspective on the specific point you are trying to make.

> My basic approach to interviewing is to ask the basic questions that might even sound naive, or not intellectual. Sometimes when you ask the simple questions like "Who are you?" or "What do you do?" you learn the most. – Brian Lamb

If you are seeking an interview with an expert, it is best to arrange a time and place that works for them. Begin the process with a respectful phone call or email explaining who you are and why you are contacting them. Be forthcoming regarding the information you are seeking and the timeline in which you are working. Also be flexible about the format for your interview. If you can meet in person, that is often ideal because it gives you the chance to get to know the person and to ask follow up questions if necessary. A good alternative to an in person interview is a video call using a service such as Skype. These services are often free to both callers and allow you to see and hear the person that you are interviewing. If neither of

---

5. Federal Rules of Evidence. (2012). Federal Evidence Review. Retrieved from: http://federalevidence.com/rulesof-evidence#Rule701.
6. Beebe & Beebe 2003

these options will work, a phone call or email will do. Keep in mind that while an email may seem convenient to you, it will likely require much more time from the expert as they have to type every answer, and they may not be as forthcoming with information in that format.

Before the interview, write down your questions. When you talk to someone, it is easy to get caught up in what they are saying and forget to focus on the information you need. Once you begin the interview work to establish rapport with the person you are interviewing. You can foster rapport by demonstrating that you respect their viewpoint, by taking turns in your interactions, by allowing them to finish their thought without interrupting, and by giving them the freedom to use their preferred forms of expression.[7] As you ask each question, take note of their response and ask for clarification or to follow up on information you did not anticipate. If you plan to record the interview, ask for permission in advance. Even if you are given permission to record, take paper and a writing utensil along to make back-up notes in case your recording device fails. When the interview is complete, thank the person and check to see whether they would welcome further contact to follow up if necessary.

After the interview, review your notes for insight that substantiates your specific purpose statement. Look for quotes that bring together the person's expertise with their reflections on the topic you are addressing. It is likely that you will gain more knowledge from the interview than you can possibly include in a short speech. Work to synthesize the main points from the interview into a coherent statement supporting your topic. Remember to be careful about properly quoting exact phrases that the person used. Even if you paraphrase, properly cite the interview and credit the expert for all of the ideas they shared with you.

Attributions

CC licensed content, Shared previously

---

7. Lindolf, T.R. & Taylor, B.C. (2002). *Qualitative communication research methods* (3rd ed.). Thousand Oaks, CA: Sage Publications Inc.

Evans Library Resources

The most well established way of finding research to support your ideas is to use the library. However, many students see the "library and its resources as imposing and intimidating, and are anxious about how they will manage in such an environment."[1] Don't let any twinge of anxiety keep you from exploring all that the library has to offer!

When conducting research, one of your best resources is the librarian. It is their job to know all about the resources available to you, and to help you succeed in locating the material that is most relevant to your assignment. Additionally, many libraries have librarians who specialize in particular areas of research and they will be able to help you find the best resources for your specific speech topic. Ideally, you should seek some information on your topic alone before asking for their assistance. Doing some initial research independently demonstrates to the librarian that you have taken ownership of the assignment and recognize that the research is ultimately your responsibility, not theirs. They will be better equipped to help you find new information if they know where you have already looked and what you have found. Most libraries contain at least three primary resources for information: books, periodicals, and full text databases.

"Untitled" **by imelenchon.** *morgueFile.*

---

1. Leckie, G.J. (1996). Desperately seeking citations: Uncovering faculty assumptions about the undergraduate research process. *The Journal of Academic Librarianship, 22*(3), p. 201–208.

Books

Books are an excellent place to gain general knowledge. They contain comprehensive investigations of a subject in which authors can convey substantial amounts of information because they are not constrained by a strict page count. Some books are written by a single author while other books bring several scholars together in an edited collection. In both cases, you are likely to get a rich investigation of a single topic. For example, if you were giving a speech about stereotypes of black women in America, you might check out Melissa Harris-Perry's 2011 book *Sister Citizen*, because she brings together literature, theory, and political science, to offer a detailed discussion of the development of four prominent stereotypes. In the book she has enough space to offer compelling images, narratives, and social scientific evidence for the impact those stereotypes have on contemporary society.

"Untitled" by KelseyVere. morgueFile.

A library is not a luxury, but one of the necessities of life.
– Henry Ward Beecher

Most libraries make finding books easy by indexing them in an online catalog. You should be able to go to the library's website and simply search for your topic. The index will provide the titles, authors, and other publication information for each book. It will also provide a call number. The call number is like an address for the book that indicates where it can be found on the stacks in the library. Before going to the stacks, take note of the title, author, and call number. The call number is the most important element, and the title and author will serve as backup for your search if you find that the books are out of order. If you find a book that is helpful, be sure to check the shelf nearby to see if there are other promising titles on that topic. If you cannot find the book that you are looking for, consider asking the librarian to help you borrow it from another library using a process called interlibrary loan.

The length of a book can make it seem overwhelming to someone researching a brief speech. In order to streamline your research, determine what you are looking for in advance. Are you seeking general background knowledge or support for a specific idea? Use the table of contents, headings, and index to guide you to the portion of the book that is likely to have what you are looking for. You do not need to read, or even skim, the entirety of every book. It is appropriate to skim for key words and phrases that pertain to your topic. Just be sure that once you find what you are looking for, you read enough of the section around it to understand the context of the statement and ensure that the book is making the point you think it is. Take note of the point that the book is making. Careful notes will help you remember the information that you gained from each source when you get home.

In addition to the traditional stacks of books present in your library, you will also find a reference section. This section contains books that do not delve deep into any subject, but provide basic summary knowledge on a variety of topics. The reference section contains books like dictionaries, which help define unfamiliar terms; encyclopedias, which provide overviews of various subjects; abstracts, which summarize books and articles; and biographical references, which describe people and their accomplishments. Since these resources do not require extensive time to process, and they are likely to be used briefly but regularly by many visitors, the library generally will not allow you to check out reference material. Take great care in drafting notes on the information that you find, and writing down the page numbers and authors according to the style preferred in your field of study. For more information on what you will need to record see the "style guides" section of this chapter.

Periodicals

Books are comprehensive, but they can take years to get published. This means that the material in books is often at least a year old by the time of its publication date. If your speech depends on more recent information, you should turn to periodicals. Periodicals include magazines, newspapers, journals, and other publications printed at predictable intervals. These publications may appear weekly, monthly, or quarterly to update the research in a given field. Each periodical will offer a variety of articles related to a specific subject area.

"Learning Commons West is a great place for collaboration" **by clemsonunivlibrary.** *CC-BY-NC.*

When researching, it is important to understand the difference between general interest periodicals and scholarly research journals. General interest periodicals include magazines and newspapers which provide a wide array of knowledge and keep readers up to date on the news within a larger cultural context. These publications are targeted toward the general public and they often use pictures and advertising to attract attention. Examples of respected general interest publications include *The Atlantic, Women's Health, The New York Times,* and *National Geographic.*[2] These publications are intended for profit. The information in them is edited to make sure it will appeal to the audience, is well written, and consistent with the commercial goals of the publication. General interest periodicals are good for context and current events information. If you are giving a speech about the importance of military intervention in Syria, you could use a general interest periodical like the *New York Times* to discover the most recent information on the conflict.

A newspaper is a circulating library with high blood pressure. – Arthur Baer

If you are looking for more rigorous research, such as an international relations expert detailing what forms of aid are best for nations experiencing uprisings, you will need a scholarly research journal. A scholarly research journal is not for profit. It is designed to publicize the best research in a particular area. These publications are targeted toward scholars who specialize in a given subject or type of research. Examples of respected scholarly journals include *Journal of the American Medical Association, Harvard Law Review,* and *Quarterly Journal of Speech.* These journals engage in a process of peer review in which scholars send their articles to the editor and the editor has other experts in the field examine the article to determine the quality of its research, writing, and fit with the scholarly goal of the publication.

2. American Society of Magazine Editors. (2011). 2011 National Magazine Awards, Winners, and Finalists. Retrieved from: http://www.magazine.org/asme/magazine_awards/nma_winners/

Full-Text Databases

Rather than searching for a print copy of the latest periodical, many people now find articles on the computer using specialized electronic databases that contain the full text of periodicals. Most school libraries subscribe to a variety of databases which compile articles from journals within a particular specialization, industry, or field. Libraries tend to organize links to these databases on their website in two ways: (1) by the area of specialization, or (2) by the name of the database. You can use the list of specializations to identify databases that will pertain to your topic. For example, if you are interested in research on *The Simpsons,* you might go to your library's subject list, click on "Communication," and choose a database such as Communication and Mass Media Complete. Some topics will be found in databases with less obvious titles. For example, the abstractly named Lexis-Nexis database provides access to newspaper articles, legal research, and government documents. If your initial search of databases in the list of specializations is not fruitful, ask your professor or librarian for recommendations concerning the most appropriate database for your topic.

"Reading" by Moyan Brenn. CC-BY.

Full-text databases allow you access to the citations, abstracts, and articles in the journals they index. However, they sometimes limit access to the full text of articles that were published within a certain date range. If you find a title that looks promising, but is not available in the database you are searching, try the search in another database. Databases often give you the opportunity to search for articles matching your desired time period, author, publication, or key words. Some databases, such as EBSCO, allow you to specify whether you are looking for general interest or scholarly publications.

<table>
<tr><td colspan="2" align="center">Table 7.1: Follow the Citation Trail</td></tr>
<tr><td colspan="2">If you are having trouble locating information on your topic, all you need is one relevant scholarly source and then you can follow the clues to locate more information by searching backward and forward.</td></tr>
<tr><td align="center">←</td><td align="center">→</td></tr>
<tr><td>To search backward, skim the source's bibliography for earlier publications on your topic.</td><td>To search forward, use Google Scholar's "cited by" function to find more recent publications on your topic.</td></tr>
</table>

Attributions

CC licensed content, Shared previously

- Chapter 7 Library Resources. **Authored by**: Sarah Stone Watt, Ph.D.. **Provided by**: Pepperdine University, Malibu, CA. **Located at**: http://publicspeakingproject.org/psvirtualtext.html. **Project**: Public Speaking Project. **License**: *CC BY-NC-ND: Attribution-NonCommercial-NoDerivatives*

- DSC_1790_2_MorgueFile. **Authored by**: imelenchon. **Provided by**: MorgueFile. **Located at**: http://mrg.bz/RN97hE. **License**: *Other*. **License Terms**: You are allowed to copy, distribute, transmit the work and to adapt the work. Attribution is not required. You are prohibited from using this work in a stand alone manner.

- GNA9Xzuw. **Authored by**: KelseyVere. **Provided by**: MorgueFile. **Located at**: http://mrg.bz/mnFMEA. **License**: *Other*. **License Terms**: You are allowed to copy, distribute, transmit the work and to adapt the work. Attribution is not required. You are prohibited from using this work in a stand alone manner.

- Learning Commons West is a great place for colloboration.. **Authored by**: clemsonunivlibrary. **Located at**: https://flic.kr/p/dwLqBE. **License**: *CC BY-NC: Attribution-NonCommercial*

- Image of man reading newspaper. **Authored by**: Moyan Brenn. **Located at**: https://flic.kr/p/bKecSa. **License**: *CC BY: Attribution*

Internet Resources

We want Google to be the third half of your brain. – Sergey Brin

Search Engines

A search engine can be your most important resource when attempting to locate information on the Internet. Search engines allow you to type in the topic you are interested in and narrow the possible results. Some of the most popular search engines include Google, bing, Yahoo!, and Ask.[1] These sites provide a box for you to type a topic, phrase, or question, and they use software to scan their index of existing Internet content to find the sites most relevant to your search.

Each search engine uses different algorithms and techniques to locate and rank information, which may mean that the same search will yield different results depending on the search engine. Based on the algorithms it is using, the search engine will sort the results with those it determines to be most relevant appearing first. Since each site is different, you should use the one that seems most intuitive to you. However, since their ranking systems will also be different, you cannot assume that the first few sites listed in your chosen search engine are the most relevant. Always scan the first few pages of search results to find the best resource for your topic. Skimming the content of the pages returned in your search will also give you an idea of whether you have chosen the most appropriate search terms. If your search has returned results that are not relevant to your speech, you may need to adjust your search terms and try a new search.

Pay close attention to the first few sites listed in search results. Some databases allow "sponsored links" to appear before the rest of the results. If you are giving a speech about the dangers of rental cars, and you search rental car in Google, links to companies like Hotwire.com, Orbitz.com, or National Rental Car are likely to appear first in your results. These sites may or may not be relevant to your search, but they have also paid for the top spot on the list and therefore may not be the most relevant. When search engines display sponsored sites first, they typically distinguish these from the others by outlining or highlighting them in a different color. For example, while Google lists advertisements related to your search on the right-hand side of the screen, they sometimes also put a limited number of sponsored links at the top of your search results list. The only distinction between these sponsored links and the rest of the list is a subtly shaded box with a small label in the upper right indicating they are "Ads" (see Figure 7.1).

1. eBizMBA. (2012). Top 15 Most Popular Search Engines: January 2012. Retrieved from: http://www.ebizmba.com/articles/search-engines

Figure 7.1 Sponsored Websites

Google car insurance laws

Search   About 46,200,000 results (0.22 seconds)

Everything

Images

Maps

Videos

News

Shopping

More

Los Angeles, CA
Change location

Any time
Past hour
Past 24 hours
Past week
Past month
Past year
Custom range

Ads - Why these ads?

GEICO **Car Insurance** | GEICO.com
www.geico.com
You could save over $500 on **Car Insurance**. Get a free quote!

State Farm® **Car Insurance** 1 (888) 502 6012
www.statefarm.com
Switch & Save Up To $480! Get A Free Quote Online Now

Progressive **Car Insurance** | Progressive.com
www.progressive.com
Named #1 **Car Insurance** Website. Get A Free Online Quote Now

Vehicle **insurance** - Wikipedia, the free encyclopedia
en.wikipedia.org/wiki/Vehicle_insurance
The minimum coverage defined by Germany **law** for car liability **insurance** / third party personal **insurance** is 7 5 Million Euro for bodily injury (damage to people) ...
Public policies - Coverage levels - Excess - Behavior-based insurance

State-by-State Minimum **Car Insurance** Requirements
personalinsure.about.com/cs/vehicleratings/a/blautominimum.htm
State minimum insurance requirements are the **car insurance** requirements for each state, by **law**, for their residents. These minimum requirements for each state ...

"Figure 7.1" by Public Speaking Project. CC-BY-NC-ND.

Defining Search Terms

In the early stages of research it may be helpful to simply search by topic. For example, if you are interested in giving a speech about revolutions in the Middle East, you might type that topic into the database and scan the sites that come up. As you are scanning, watch for other useful terms that arise in relation to the topic and jot them down for possible use in later searches. Since people may write about the topic in different terms than you tend to think about it, paying close attention to their language will help you refine your search. Another way to approach this is to consider synonyms for your search terms before you even begin. Once you have a concrete topic and have begun to outline the arguments you want to make, you are likely to need more specific terms to find what you are looking for. In order to help with the search, you may use Boolean operators, words and symbols that illustrate the relationship between your search terms and help the search engine expand or limit your results (see Table 7.2 on the next page for examples). Although search engines regularly adjust their Boolean rules to avoid people rigging the site to show their own pages first, a few basic terms tend to be used by most search engines.[2]

Table 7.2: Boolean Operators	
OR	The word "OR" is one way to expand your search by looking for a variety of terms that may help you support your topic. For example, in a speech about higher education, you might be interested in sources discussing either colleges or universities. In this case using the term "OR" helps expand your search to include both terms, even when they appear separately.

2. BBC. (2012). What are "Boolean operators?" *WebWise: A Beginner's Guide to Using the Internet.* Retrieved from: http://www.bbc.co.uk/webwise/0/22562913

	Table 7.2: Boolean Operators
AND/+	Using the word "AND" or the "+" symbol between terms limits your search by indicating to the search engine that you are interested in the relationship between the terms and want to see pages which offer both terms together. If you are giving a speech about Hillary Rodham Clinton's work in the Senate, you might search Hilary Rodham Clinton AND Senate. This search would help you find information pertaining to her senate career rather than sites that focus on her as First Lady or Secretary of State.
NOT/-	Using the word "NOT" or the "-" symbol can also limit your search by indicating that you are not interested in a term that may often appear with your desired term. For example, if you are interested in hyenas, but want to limit out sites focused on their interactions with lions, you might search hyena -lion to eliminate all of the lion pages from your search.
" "	Quotation marks around a group of words limit the search by indicating you are looking for a specific phrase. For example, if you are looking for evidence that human behavior contributes to global warming, you might search "humans contribute to global warming," which would limit the search far beyond the simple human + global warming by specifying the point you seek to make.

When you have a well-defined area of research, it is best to start as specific as possible and then broaden your search as needed. If there is something on exactly what you want to say, you don't want to miss it wading through a sea of articles on your general topic area. To make the best use of your search engine take some time to read the help section on the site and learn how their Boolean operators work. The help section will offer additional tips to assist you in navigating the nuances of that site and executing the best possible search.

Google

You may be at least somewhat familiar with Google, the name that has become synonymous with "internet search," and called "the most used and most popular search engine."[3] You may already be adept at searching Google for a wide variety of information, but you may be less familiar with some of its specialized search engines. Three of these search engines can be particularly helpful to someone seeking to support their ideas in a speech: Google Scholar, Google Books, and Google Images.

Research is formalized curiosity. It is poking and prying with a purpose. – Zora Neale Hurston

Google Scholar

The search engines listed earlier in this chapter will help you explore a diversity of sites to find the information you are looking for. However, certain topics and certain types of speeches call for more rigorous research. This research is typically best found in the library, but Google has an added feature that makes finding scholarly sources easier. On Google Scholar you can find research that has been published in scholarly journal articles, books, theses, conference proceedings, and court opinions.

Google Scholar is not only helpful for focusing on academic research; it has a host of features that will help to refine your search to the most helpful articles. You can search generally in Google Scholar and find citations of useful articles that will help support your ideas, but you may not always find the full text of the article. You can ask Google Scholar to help you find the full text articles available in your library's databases by telling it which library you want to search. To do this, click the "scholar preferences" link next to the search button on scholar.google.com. Then scroll down to the section titled "library links," and type

3. Tajane, T. (2011). Most used search engines and total market share trend as of March 2011. TechZoom.org. Retrieved from: http://techzoom.org/most-used-search-engines-and-total-market-share-trend-as-of-march-2011/

the name of your school or library, then click "find library." When the search is complete, check the box next to the name of your library so that Google knows to include it in the search. Once you have included your library, the search results you get will have links that lead you to the articles available in your library's databases (see Figure 7.2). Clicking the links will lead you to your library databases and prompt you to log into the system as you would if you were searching on the library site itself.

Figure 7.2   A Search Result with a Library Link

[CITATION] The immediate effects of perceived speaker disorganization on speaker credibility and audience attitude change in **persuasive speaking**
EE Baker · Western Speech, 1965
Cited by 14 - Related articles - Get it @ Penn State

Full-Text @ Pepperdine Libraries

"Figure 7.2" **by Public Speaking Project.** *CC-BY-NC-ND.*

Even when you are linked to your library's databases, there may be articles in your search results that you do not have electronic access to. In that case, search your library catalog for the title of the journal in which your desired article appears to see if they carry the journal in hard copy form. If you still cannot find it, copy the citation information and use your interlibrary loan system to request a copy of the article from another library.

> I find I use the Internet more and more. It's just an invaluable tool. I do most of my research on the Net now… – Nora Roberts

In addition to enhancing your database searches, Google Scholar can also help you broaden your search in two strategic ways. First, underneath the citation for each search result, you will see a link to "related articles." If you found a particular article helpful, clicking "related articles" is one way to help you find resources that are similar. Second, as you know, researchers often look through the bibliography of a helpful source to find the articles that author used. However, when you are dealing with an older article, searching backwards in the bibliography may lead you to more outdated research. To search for more recent research, look again under the search result for the link called "cited by." Clicking the "cited by" link will give you all of the articles that have been published since, and have referred to, the article that you found. For example, if you are giving a speech on male body image you might find Paul Rozin and April Fallon's 1988 article in the Journal of Abnormal Psychology comparing opposite sex perceptions of weight helpful. However, it would be good to have more recent research. Clicking the "related articles" and "cited by" links would lead you to similar research published within the past few years.

Google Books

Just as Google Scholar can be used to enhance your research in scholarly periodicals, Google Books can be used to make your search for, and within, books more efficient. Some library catalogs offer you the ability to search for all books on a topic, whether that library has the book or not. Other libraries confine you to searching their holdings. One way to enhance your research is to search for books on Google Books and then use your library site to see if they currently have the book, or if you will need to order it through interlibrary loan. The other way that you can use Google Books is to make your skimming more effective. Earlier in this chapter you learned that you should strategically skim books for the information that you need. You can do that with Google Books by looking up the book, and then using the search bar on the left side of the screen (see Figure 7.3) to search for key words within the book. This search engine can help you identify the pages in a book where your terms appear and, with many books, give you a sample of that page to allow you to see whether the terms appear in the context you are searching for. Keep in mind that Google Books is a search engine; it is not a replacement for checking out the book in the library or buying your own copy. Google Books does not print books in their entirety, and often will omit pages surrounding a search result, so relying on the site to allow you to read enough of the book to make your argument is risky at best. Instead, use this site to help you determine which books to obtain, and which parts of those books will be most relevant to your research.

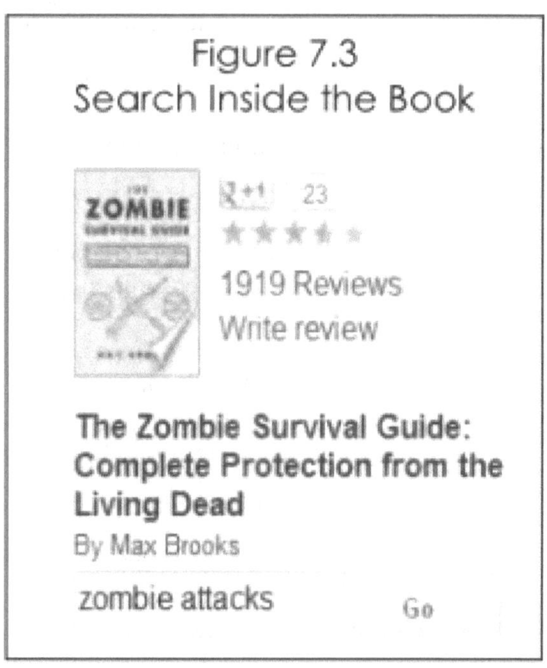

"Figure 7.3" by Public Speaking Project. CC-BY-NC-ND.

Google Images

Google Images may be useful as you seek visual aids to illustrate your point. You can search Google Images for photographs, charts, illustrations, clip art and more. For example, if you are giving a speech on the Nineteenth Amendment, you could add interest by offering a picture of the Silent Sentinel's picketing the White House. Alternatively, if you wanted to demonstrate the statistical probability of electing a woman to Congress, you could use Google Images to locate a chart displaying that information.

Since search engines match the terms you put in, it is possible that your topic could yield images containing adult content. To prevent receiving adult content, you can use the "safe search" settings (located in the option wheel in the far upper right hand corner of the menu bar) to limit your exposure to explicit images. The setting has three options:

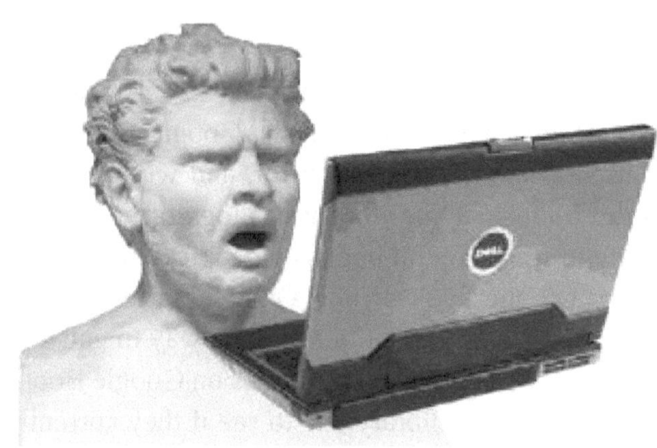

"Blog OMG!" by Mike Licht. CC-BY.

1. Strict filtering: filters sexually explicit video and images from Google Search result pages, as well as results that might link to explicit content.

2. Moderate filtering: excludes sexually explicit video and images from Google Search result pages, but does not filter results that might link to explicit content. This is the default SafeSearch setting.

3. No filtering: as you've probably figured out, turns off SafeSearch filtering completely.[4]

Remember that, as with other outside sources, you will need to offer proper source citations for every image that you use. Additionally, if you plan to post your speech to the internet or publish it more widely than your class, consider using only images that appear in the public domain so that you do not risk infringing on an artist's copyright privileges.

It is not ignorance but knowledge which is the mother of wonder. – Joseph Wood Krutch

Websites

When you use a more general search engine, such as Google or bing, you are looking for websites. Websites may be maintained by individuals, organizations, companies, or governments. These sites generally consist of a homepage, that gives an overview of the site and its purpose. From the homepage there are links to various types of information on the original site and elsewhere on the Internet. These sets of links arrange information "in an unconstrained web- like way,"[5] which opens up the possibility of making new connections

"Trading stocks on a computer" by OTA Photos. CC-BY-SA.

4. Google. (2012). SafeSearch: filter objectionable content. Google Inside Search. Retrieved from: https://support.google.com/web-search/answer/510?hl=en

5. Berners-Lee, T. & Fischeti, M. (2000). *Weaving the web: The original design and ultimate destiny of the World Wide Web.* New York, NY.: Harper Collins.

between ideas and research. It also opens up the possibility of getting lost among all of the available sources. To keep your research on track, be sure to continue asking yourself if the sources you have found support your specific purpose statement.

Most websites are created to promote the interests of their owner, so it is very important that you check to see whose website you are looking at. Generally the author or owner of the site is named near the top of the homepage, or in the copyright notice at the bottom. Knowing who the site belongs to will help you determine the quality of the information it offers. If you find the site through a search engine and are not directed to its homepage, look for a link called "home" or "about" to navigate to the page containing more information about the site itself. In addition to knowing the owner, it is important to look for the author of the material you are using. For example, an article on a reputable news site like CNN.com may come from a respected journalist, or it may be the opinion of a blogger whose post is not necessarily vetted by the company itself. Use the section of the chapter on evaluating information to determine whether the site you have found is a credible source.

When you find websites that are both useful and credible, be sure to bookmark them in your Web browser so that you can refer to them again later. Your browser may call these bookmarks "favorites" instead. To bookmark a site, you can click on the bookmarking link in your browser or, if your browser uses tabs, you can drag the tab into a toolbar near the top of the window. If you are struggling with the bookmarking process, try the command CTRL+D on your keyboard or consult the help link for your Web browser.

> Don't leave inferences to be drawn when evidence can be presented. – Richard Wright

Government Documents

Governments regularly publish large quantities of information regarding their citizens, such as census data, health reports, and crime statistics. They also compile transcripts of legislative proceedings, hearings, and speeches. Most college and university libraries maintain substantial collections of government documents. Additionally, these documents are increasingly available online. Government documents can be helpful for finding up-to-date statistics on an issue that affects the larger population. They can also be helpful in identifying strong viewpoints concerning government policies. For example, looking at the Congressional testimony regarding nuclear safety after an earthquake destroyed the Fukushima nuclear power plant in Japan in 2011 could help you make a compelling case for safety upgrades at U.S. nuclear power facilities.

> Now, whenever you read any historical document, you always evaluate it in light of the historical context. – Josh McDowell

One of the most helpful resources for searching government documents is http://fedworld.ntis.gov/. This site allows you to search Supreme Court decisions, government scientific reports, research and development reports, and other databases filled with cutting edge research. It also lists all major government agencies and their websites. Another excellent way to locate government documents is to use the Monthly Catalog of U.S. Government Publications. This index is issued every month and lists all of the documents published by the federal government, except those that are restricted or confidential. You can use the index to locate documents from Congress, the courts, or even the president. The index arranges reports alphabetically by the name of the issuing agency. The easiest way to search will be on the Government Printing Office website at catalog.gpo.gov. If you would prefer to work with hard copies of the reports, head to your library and search the subject index to find subjects related to your speech topic. Each subject will have a list of documents and their entry number. Use the entry numbers to find the title, agency, and call number of each document listed in the front of the index.[6]

"Talking on the Phone / Home Office" **by Daniel Foster.** *CC-BY-NC-SA*.

Attributions

CC licensed content, Shared previously

- Chapter 7 Internet Resources. **Authored by**: Sarah Stone Watt, Ph.D.. **Provided by**: Pepperdine University, Malibu, CA. **Located at**: http://publicspeakingproject.org/psvirtualtext.html. **Project**: Public Speaking Project. **License**: *CC BY-NC-ND: Attribution-NonCommercial-NoDerivatives*

- Blog OMG!. **Authored by**: Mike Licht. **Located at**: https://flic.kr/p/58aVnJ. **License**: *CC BY: Attribution*

- Trading stocks on a computer. **Authored by**: OTA Photos. **Located at**: https://flic.kr/p/fKu9Y3. **License**: *CC BY-SA: Attribution-ShareAlike*

- Talking on the Phone Home Office. **Authored by**: Daniel Foster. **Located at**: https://flic.kr/p/o17yj5. **License**: *CC BY-NC-SA: Attribution-NonCommercial-ShareAlike*

---

6. Zarefsky, D. (2005). *Public Speaking: Strategies for Success* (Special Ed. for The Pennsylvania State University). Boston, MA: Pearson.

Evaluating Information

The popular online encyclopedia, Wikipedia, is a great resource for general information. It is a good place to start in order to determine search terms and potentially relevant strains of thought on a given topic. However, it is not the most credible source to cite in your speech. Since anyone can update the site at any time, information may be entirely inaccurate. When using Wikipedia, look for source citations and follow the links to original source material.

The large amount of information available in your library and on the Internet can seem overwhelming. Narrow your support by evaluating the quality and credibility of each source. To determine the quality of a source, look to see whether the information provided seems comprehensive. To determine whether or not the information is comprehensive, check to see that it thoroughly covers the issue, considers competing perspectives, and cites the sources where supporting material came from.

First, check to see that your source not only discusses issues that pertain to your topic, but thoroughly explains the reasoning behind the claims it offers. Often you will already be familiar with the topic, but you will require the addition of strong reasoning to properly support your ideas. If your source cannot provide strong reasoning, it is not the best quality source. Second, determine whether the source considers competing perspectives. Debate strategists know that evidence can be found for multiple perspectives on any issue. If your source does not also recognize and consider opposing arguments, it is not the best quality source. Third, check to see that your source offers supporting data and or if it includes non-credible citations, it is not the best quality source. It is fine to use a source that is weak in one of these areas if you still find it compelling, but know that you may need to back it up with additional credible information. If the source is weak in multiple areas, do your best to avoid using it so that it does not weaken your speech.

In addition to the quality, you should examine source credibility. When evaluating credibility, focus on the sources' qualifications, the parity of their message with similar sources, and their biases. One of the most important elements of credibility is qualification. Sometimes qualifications will be linked to a person's profession. For example, if you are talking about earthquakes, you might want the expertise of a seismologist who studies earthquake waves and their effects. However, professional expertise is not the only type of credibility. If you want to discuss the feeling of experiencing a major earthquake, testimony from a survivor may be more credible than testimony from a scientist who studied the event but did not experience it. When examining credibility, check to see that the person has the training or experience appropriate to the type of information they offer. Next, check to see whether the information in your chosen source aligns with information in other sources on the issue. If your source is the only one that offers a particular perspective, and no other source corroborates that perspective, it is less likely to be credible.

> I used to sleep nude – until the earthquake. – Alyssa Milano

Additionally, check for **bias**. All sources have bias, meaning they all come from a particular perspective. You must check to see whether the perspective of the source matches your own, and whether the perspective overwhelms the ability to offer reliable information on an issue. Also check to see whether the source is affiliated with organizations that are known to hold a particularly strong opinion concerning the issue they are speaking to.

In your speech, make reference to the quality and credibility of your sources. Identifying the qualifications for a source, or explaining that their ideas have been used by many other credible sources, will enhance the strength of your speech. For example, if you are giving a speech about the benefits of sleep, citing a renowned sleep expert will strengthen your argument. If you can then explain that this person's work has been repeatedly tested and affirmed by later studies, your argument will appear even stronger. On the other hand, if you simply offer the name of your source without any explanation of who that person is, or why they ought to be believed, your argument is suspect. To offer this kind of information without disrupting the flow of your speech, you might say something like,

"Untitled" by Dmitry Ryzhkov. CC-BY-NC-SA.

> *Mary Carskadon, Director of the Chronobiology/Sleep Research Laboratory at Bradley Hospital in Rhode Island, and Professor at the Brown University School of Medicine, explains that there are several advantages to increased amounts of sleep….Her work is supported by other researchers, like Dr. Kyla Wahlstrom at the University of Minnesota whose study demonstrated that delaying school start times increased student sleep and their performance.*[1]

This sample citation bolsters credibility by offering qualifications, and identifies multiple experts who agree on this issue. You may be tempted to stop once you have found one source that supports your idea, but continuing to research and comparing the information in each source will help you better support your ideas. It will also prevent you from overlooking contradictory evidence that you need to be able to address.

Attributions

CC licensed content, Shared previously

- Chapter 7 Evaluating Information. **Authored by**: Sarah Stone Watt, Ph.D.. **Provided by**: Pepperdine University, Malibu, CA. **Located at**: http://publicspeakingproject.org/psvirtualtext.html. **Project**: Public Speaking Project. **License**: *CC BY-NC-ND: Attribution-NonCommercial-NoDerivatives*
- DSC_1199. **Authored by**: Dmitry Ryzhkov. **Located at**: https://flic.kr/p/oRLAW5. **License**: *CC BY-NC-SA: Attribution-NonCommercial-ShareAlike*

---

1. National Sleep Foundation. (2011). School start time and sleep. Retrieved from: http://sleepfoundation.org/sleep-news/school-start-time-and-sleep

Citing Sources and Avoiding Plagiarism

Style Guides

Once you have gathered the appropriate sources to support your ideas, you will need to integrate citations for those sources into your speech using a **style guide** such as those published by the Modern Language Association (MLA), American Psychological Association (APA), or The Chicago Manual of Style (CMS). These style guides help you determine the format of your citations, both within the speech and in the bibliography. Your professor will likely assign a particular style guide for you to use. However, if you are not told to use a particular style, choose the one most appropriate to your area of study. MLA style is typically used by people in the humanities, APA is typically used by social scientists, and CMS can be used in either type of writing, but is most popular with historians.[1] These style guides will help you record the places where you found support for your argument so that you can avoid plagiarism.

> Facts are stubborn things; and whatever may be our wishes, our inclinations, or the dictates of our passions, they cannot alter the state of facts and evidence. – John Adams

Plagiarism

Plagiarism is the act of presenting someone else's work or ideas as your own. Sometimes this is intentional, meaning people choose to copy from another source and make their audience think that the idea was original. Students in speech classes sometimes buy speeches from the internet, or repeat a speech written by a friend who took the class in a previous semester. These actions are cheating because the students did not do the work themselves, yet they took credit for it. Most instances of blatant cheating, such as these, are quickly caught by instructors who maintain files of work turned in previously, or who are adept at searching the Internet for content that does not appear original to the student. Consequences for this type of plagiarism are severe, and may range from failure of the course to expulsion from the school.

---

1. Miller-Cochran, S.K. & Rodrigo, R.L. (2011). *The Wadsworth guide to research*. Boston, MA: Wadsworth.

More often, plagiarism occurs by mistake when people are not aware of how to properly summarize and cite the sources from which they took information. This happens when someone incorporates words or ideas from a source and fails to properly cite the source. Even if you have handed your professor a written outline of the speech with source citations, you must also offer oral attribution for ideas that are not your own (see Table 7.3 for examples of ways to cite sources while you are speaking).

<table>
<tr><td colspan="2" align="center">**Table 7.3: Verbal Source Citations**[2345]</td></tr>
<tr><td align="center">**Proper Written Source Citation**</td><td align="center">**Proper Oral Attribution**</td></tr>
<tr><td>"Your time is limited, so don't waste it living someone else's life" (Jobs, 2005).</td><td>In his 2005 commencement address at Stanford University Steve Jobs said,"Your time is limited, so don't waste it living some else's life."</td></tr>
<tr><td>"Eat food. Not too much. Mostly plants" (Pollan, 2009, p.1).</td><td>Michael Pollan offers three basic guidelines for healthy eating in his book, *In Defense of Food*. He advises readers to "Eat food. Not too much. Mostly plants."</td></tr>
<tr><td>"The Assad regime's escalating violence in Syria is an affront to the international community, a threat to regional security, and a grave violation of human rights. . . . This group should take concrete action along three lines: provide emergency humanitarian relief, ratchet up pressure on the regime, and prepare for a democratic transition" (Clinton, 2012).</td><td>In her February 24 speech to the Friends of Syria People meeting, U.S. Secretary of State, Hillary Clinton, warned that Assad was increasing violence against the Syrian people and violating human rights. She called for international action to help the Syrian people through humanitarian assistance, political pressure, and support for a future democratic government.</td></tr>
<tr><td>"Maybe you could be a mayor or a Senator or a Supreme Court Justice, but you might not know that until you join student government or the debate team" (Obama, 2009).</td><td>In his 2009 "Back to School" speech President Obama encouraged students to participate in school activities like student government and debate in order to try out the skills necessary for a leadership position in the government.</td></tr>
</table>

Omitting the oral attribution from the speech leads the audience, who is not holding a written version, to believe that the words are your own. Be sure to offer citations and oral attributions for all material that you have taken from someone else, including paraphrases or summaries of their ideas. When in doubt, remember to "always provide oral citations for direct quotations, paraphrased material, or especially striking language, letting listeners know who said the words, where, and when."[6] Whether plagiarism is intentional or not, it is unethical and someone committing plagiarism will often be sanctioned based on their institution's code of conduct.

Attributions

2. Jobs, S. (2005, 14 June). **"You've gotta find what you love," Jobs says.** *Stanford Report.* **Retrieved from:** http://news.stanford.edu/news/2005/june15/jobs-061505.html
3. **Pollan, M. (2009).** *In defense of food: An eater's manifesto.* **New York, NY: Penguin Books.**
4. **Clinton, H. (2012, February 4). [Address]. Clinton's remarks at the Friends of Syrian People meeting, February 2012. [Transcript]. Retrieved from:** http://www.cfr.org/syria/clintons-remarks-friends-syrian-people-meeting-february-2012/p27482
5. **Obama, B. (2009, September 8). [Address]. Prepared remarks of President Barack Obama: Back to school event, Arlington, Virginia. Retrieved from:** https://www.whitehouse.gov/MediaResources/PreparedSchoolRemarks/
6. Osborn, M. & Osborn, S. (2007). *Public speaking* (custom edition for Pepperdine University). Boston, MA: Pearson.

Conclusion and Module Activities

Remember that in order to convince an audience and appear credible, you will need to offer support for each of your ideas. Gathering testimony from experienced and expert individuals will lend excitement and credibility to your speech. Combining testimony with resources from the library, such as books, periodicals, and reference material, will help you back up your ideas. Examining credible Internet resources can also enhance your speech by yielding the most up-to-date evidence for the points you hope to make. With so much information available it is possible to support almost any idea. However, you will need to take care to ensure that you offer the highest quality and most credible support. Do this by gathering a variety of sources and comparing the information to make sure the support is consistent across sources, and that you have accounted for any possible contradictory information. As you integrate the sources into your speech, remember to ask: "Does this evidence support my specific purpose statement?" and "Is this evidence appropriate for my audience?" Also, don't forget to offer written and oral attribution for each idea. Using the various resources available you will likely find more evidence than you can possibly incorporate into one speech. These questions will assist you as you refine your support and craft the most compelling speech possible.

"Tracy Price-Thompson" by Angela Elbern. Public domain.

Accuracy is the twin brother of honesty; inaccuracy, of dishonesty. – Nathaniel Hawthorne

Review Questions

1. For each of the claims below, identify the most compelling form of evidence that the speaker might offer. List as many as you can think of.

   - Photo-retouching alters our perspective on beauty.
   - The Internet is an effective protest tool.
   - Body scanners in airports are detrimental to our health.

2. You are giving a speech about the importance of legislation banning text messaging while driving. You want to offer diverse support for your argument that the legislation is necessary. What research tools would you use to find the following forms of evidence?

   - A personal narrative concerning the effects of texting while driving.
   - An academic study concerning the effects of texting while driving.
   - Existing legislation regarding cell phone use in automobiles.
   - A visual aid for your speech.

3. Checking the quality of your evidence is an important step in refining support for your argument. What are three elements that you should look for when determining source quality? Why is each element necessary?

4. You are giving a speech about bed bugs. You point out that bed bugs are a common pest that can be found almost anywhere. You have found a variety of sources for your speech including a bed bug registry website where people can report seeing bed bugs in hotels, an encyclopedia entry on bed bugs, a blog containing pictures and personal testimony about an experience with bed bugs, a scientific study on the conditions under which bed bugs thrive, and a psychological study concerning the way that people are conditioned to respond to the sight of bugs in their bed. Which of these is the most credible source to support your point? Why?

5. The following is an excerpt from John F. Kennedy's 1963 Civil Rights Address. Read the excerpt, and offer your own paraphrase of his ideas without incorporating any direct quotations from the text:

   - I hope that every American, regardless of where he lives, will stop and examine his conscience about this and other related incidents. This Nation was founded by men of many nations and backgrounds. It was founded on the principle that all men are created equal, and that the rights of every man are diminished when the rights of one man are threatened (Kennedy, 1963).

6. Imagine you are giving a speech on _______________ [fill in the blank]. Write a potential specific purpose statement. Then identify three types of research that you would integrate in order to offer balanced and compelling support for your statement.

Activities

1. Get to know your library. Use your library website to determine the name of the librarian who works with your major, or in the area of your speech topic. This activity is not designed for you to get the librarian to do your work for you, but rather for you to get to know the librarian better and make them a partner in your research process. Make an appointment with that person and interview them concerning the best way to conduct research for your speech. Take a summary of the assignment, your specific purpose statement, and at least one source that you have already found for your speech. Be sure to ask the following questions:

   • What types of sources would you advise me to focus on in my search for supporting materials?

   • What search terms are likely to yield results that are relevant to my specific purpose statement?

   • Can you offer any tips that will make searching this particular library easier?

2. Using the topics below, or your own speech topic, practice developing productive search terms. Begin by brainstorming synonyms for the topic. Then, consider other concepts that are closely related to the topic. Using those terms, conduct a preliminary search in the search engine of your choice. Skim the content on the 3-5 most promising results and highlight common terms and phrases that appear on each page. Those common terms and phrases should help you narrow your searches as you move forward with your research.

   • National Security

   • Alternative Energy

   • Economic Stability

   • Media Piracy

   • Privacy

   • Local Events

3. Using one of the topics listed in the previous activity, conduct a search on the topic using identical search terms in Google Images, Google Scholar, and Google Books. For each search, identify the source that you think would best support a speech on the topic. Cite each source using a consistent style guide (MLA, APA, or Chicago), and offer your evaluation of the sources' relevance, quality, and credibility.

4. Watch Stephen Colbert's report concerning Wikipedia or search "wikiality" if the link does not work (http://www.youtube.com/watch?v=20PlHx_JjEo). Using research that you have found on your speech topic, update the Wikipedia page for your topic. Be careful not to replicate the errors that Colbert discusses. Offer only accurate information, and cite the source where support for your entry can be found.

Attributions

- Chapter 7 Conclusion and Module Activities. **Authored by**: Sarah Stone Watt, Ph.D.. **Provided by**: Pepperdine University, Malibu, CA. **Located at**: http://publicspeakingproject.org/psvirtualtext.html. **Project**: Public Speaking Project. **License**: *CC BY-NC-ND: Attribution-NonCommercial-NoDerivatives*

Public domain content

- Tracy Price-Thompson cropped. **Authored by**: Angela Elbern. **Located at**: http://commons.wikimedia.org/wiki/File:Tracy_Price-Thompson_(cropped).jpg. **License**: *Public Domain: No Known Copyright*

Glossary and References

Glossary

TERM	DEFINITION
Bias	The predisposition toward a particular viewpoint.
Boolean Operators	Words and symbols that illustrate the relationship between search terms and help the search engine expand or limit results.
Expert Testimony	Testimony that comes from a recognized authority who has conducted extensive research on an issue.
Interlibrary Loan	The process of borrowing materials through one library that belong to another library.
Lay Testimony	Any testimony based on witnesses' opinions or perceptions in a given case.
Parity	Similarity of information across sources.
Personal Testimony	An individual's story concerning his or her lived experience, which can be used to illustrate the existence of a particular event or phenomenon.
Rapport	A cordial relationship between two or more people in which both parties convey respect and understanding for one another.
Search Engine	Software which uses algorithms to scan an index of existing Internet content for particular terms, and then ranks the results based on their relevance.
Source Credibility	Signs that a person is offering trustworthy information.
Specific Purpose Statement	A sentence summarizing the main idea, or claim, which the speech will support. It should be stated clearly toward the beginning of the speech.
Style Guide	An established set of standards for formatting written documents and citing sources for information within the document.

References

American Society of Magazine Editors. (2011). *2011 National Magazine Awards, Winners, and Finalists.* Retrieved from: http://www.magazine.org/asme/magazine_awards/nma_winners/

BBC. (2012). What are "Boolean operators?" *WebWise: A Beginner's Guide to Using the Internet.* Retrieved from: http://www.bbc.co.uk/webwise/guides/boolean-operators

Beebe, S.A. & Beebe, S.J. (2003). *Public speaking: An audience centered approach.* Boston, MA: Allyn and Bacon.

Berners-Lee, T. & Fischeti, M. (2000). Weaving the web: The original design and ultimate destiny of the World Wide Web. New York, NY.: Harper Collins.

Clinton, H. (2012, February 4). [Address]. Clinton's remarks at the Friends of Syrian People meeting, February 2012. [Transcript]. Retrieved from: http://www.cfr.org/syria/clintons-remarks-friends-syrian-people-meeting-february-2012/p27482

eBizMBA. (2012). *Top 15 Most Popular Search Engines: January 2012.* Retrieved from: http://www.ebizmba.com/articles/search-engines

Federal Rules of Evidence. (2012). *Federal Evidence Review.* Retrieved from: http://federalevidence.com/rules-of-evidence#Rule701.

Fisher, W. R. (1984). Narration as a human communication paradigm: The case of public moral argument. *Communication Monographs, 51*, pp.1-22.

Gladding, S.T. & Drake Wallace, M.J. (2010). The potency and power of counseling stories. *Journal of Creativity in Mental Health, 5*, pp. 15-24.

Google. (2012). SafeSearch: filter objectionable content. *Google Inside Search.* Retrieved from: http://support.google.com/websearch/bin/answer.py?hl=en&answer=510

Harris-Perry, M.V. (2011). *Sister Citizen: Shame, Stereotypes, and Black Women in America.* New Haven, CT: Yale University Press.

Jobs, S. (2005, 14 June). "You've gotta find what you love," Jobs says. *Stanford Report.* Retrieved from: http://news.stanford.edu/news/2005/june15/jobs-061505.html

Kennedy, J.F. (1963, 11 June). *Civil Rights Address.* Retrieved from: http://www.americanrhetoric.com/speeches/jfkcivilrights.htm

Leckie, G.J. (1996). Desperately seeking citations: Uncovering faculty assumptions about the undergraduate research process. *The Journal of Academic Librarianship, 22*(3), p. 201-208.

Lindolf, T.R. & Taylor, B.C. (2002). *Qualitative communirdcation research methods* (3 ed.). Thousand Oaks, CA: Sage Publications Inc.

Miller-Cochran, S.K. & Rodrigo, R.L. (2011). *The Wadsworth guide to research.* Boston, MA: Wadsworth.

National Sleep Foundation. (2011). *School start time and sleep.* Retrieved from: http://www.sleepfoundation.org/article/sleep-topics/school-start-time-and-sleep

Obama, B. (2009, September 8). [Address]. Prepared remarks of President Barack Obama: Back to school event, Arlington, Virginia. Retrieved from: http://www.whitehouse.gov/MediaResources/PreparedSchoolRemarks

Oliver, J. (2010, February). Jamie Oliver's TED Prize wish: Teach every child about food. *TED Ideas Worth Spreading.* Speech retrieved from: http://www.ted.com/talks/jamie_oliver.html

Osborn, M. & Osborn, S. (2007). *Public speaking* (custom edition for Pepperdine University). Boston, MA: Pearson.

Parse, R. R. (2008). Truth for the moment: Personal testimony as evidence. *Nursing Science Quarterly, 21*(1), pp. 45-48.

Pollan, M. (2009). *In defense of food: An eater's manifesto.* New York, NY: Penguin Books.

Rozin, P. & Fallon, A. (1988). Body image, attitudes to weight, and misperceptions of figure preferences of the opposite sex: A comparison of men and women in two generations. *Journal of Abnormal Psychology, 97*(3), pp. 342-345.

Sjoberg, L.M. & Ahlfeldt, S.L. (2010). Bridging the gap: Integrating information literacy into communication courses. *Communication Teacher, 24*(3), pp. 131-135.

Tajane, T. (2011). Most used search engines and total market share trend as of March 2011. *TechZoom.org.* Retrieved from: http://techzoom.org/most-used-search-engines-and-total-market-share-trend-as-of-march-2011/

Zarefsky, D. (2005). *Public Speaking: Strategies for Success* (Special Ed. for The Pennsylvania State University). Boston, MA: Pearson.

photo credits

p. 1 http://commons.wikimedia.org/wiki/File: Richard_Rouse_III_- _Game_Developers_Conference_2010_- _Day_5.jpg By Game Developers Conference 2010

p. 12 Tracey Price-Thompson http://commons.wikimedia.org/wiki/File: Tracy_Price-Thompson_%C2%B7_DF-SD- 07-44583.JPEG By Angela Elbern

Attributions

CC licensed content, Shared previously

Using Statistics

Statistics can be a powerful persuasive tool in public speaking if the speaker appropriately explains their use and significance.

Understanding Statistics

Using statistics in public speaking can be a powerful tool. It provides a quantitative, objective, and persuasive platform on which to base an argument, prove a claim, or support an idea. Before a set of statistics can be used, however, it must be made understandable by people who are not familiar with statistics. The key to the persuasive use of statistics is extracting meaning and patterns from raw data in a way that is logical and demonstrable to an audience. There are many ways to interpret statistics and data sets, not all of them valid.

Guidelines for Helping Your Audience Understand Statistics

- Use reputable sources for the statistics you present in your speech such as government websites, academic institutions and reputable research organizations and policy/research think tanks.

- Use a large enough sample size in your statistics to make sure that the statistics you are using are accurate (for example, if a survey only asked four people, then it is likely not representative of the population's viewpoint).

- Use statistics that are easily understood. Many people understand what an average is but not many people will know more complex ideas such as variation and standard deviation.

- When presenting graphs, make sure that the key points are highlighted and the graphs are not misleading as far as the values presented.

- Statistics is a topic that many people prefer to avoid, so when presenting statistical idea or even using numbers in your speech be sure to thoroughly explain what the numbers mean and use visual aids to help you explain.

Common Uses of Statistics in a Speech

Some common uses of statistics in a speech format may include:

- Results from a survey and discussion of key findings such as the mean, median, and mode of that survey.

- Comparisons of data and benchmarking results—also using averages and comparative statistics.

- Presenting findings from research, including determining which variables are statistically significant and meaningful to the results of the research. This will likely use more complicated statistics.

Common Misunderstandings of Statistics

A common misunderstanding when using statistics is "correlation does not mean causation." This means that just because two variables are related, they do not necessarily mean that one variable causes the other variable to occur. For example, consider a data set that indicates that there is a relationship between ice cream purchases over seasons versus drowning deaths over seasons. The incorrect conclusion would be to say that the increase in ice cream consumption leads to more drowning deaths, or vice versa. Therefore, when using statistics in public speaking, a speaker should always be sure that they are presenting accurate information when discussing two variables that may be related. Statistics can be used persuasively in all manners of arguments and public speaking scenarios—the key is understanding and interpreting the given data and molding that interpretation towards a convincing statement.

Communicating Statistics

Graphs, tables, and maps can be used to communicate the numbers, but then the numbers need to be put into context to make the message stick.

Introduction

Credibility makes our messages believable, and a believable message is more likely to be remembered than one that is not. But gaining credibility is not so easy. As Chip and Dan Heath note in *Made to Stick:*

If we're trying to persuade a skeptical audience to believe a new message, the reality is that we're fighting an uphill battle against a lifetime of personal learning and social relationships.

So how can we add credibility to our words? One way is to rely on statistics.

Putting Statistics into Context for Our Audiences

We are so used to resorting to statistics that we tend to bombard our audiences with too many mind-numbing numbers. As the Heaths state:

Statistics are rarely meaningful in and of themselves. Statistics will, and should, almost always be used to illustrate a relationship. It's more important for people to remember the relationship than the number.

We need to put statistics into context for our audiences. In the book, the Heaths give several good examples of others who have done this. For example, they introduce us to Geoff Ainscow, one of the leaders of the Beyond War movement in the 1980s.

Ainscow gave talks trying to raise awareness of the dangers of nuclear weapons. He wanted to show that the US and the USSR possessed weapons capable of destroying the earth several times over. But simply quoting figures of nuclear weapons stockpiles was not a way to make the message stick. So, after setting the scene, Ainscow would take a BB pellet and drop it into a steel bucket where it would make a loud noise. The pellet represented the bomb that was dropped on Hiroshima. Ainscow would then describe the devastation at Hiroshima. Next, he would take 10 pellets and drop them in the bucket where they made 10 times as much noise. They represented the nuclear firepower on a single nuclear submarine. Finally, he poured 5,000 pellets into the bucket, one for each nuclear warhead in the world. When the noise finally subsided, his audience sat in dead silence.

That is how you put statistics into context.

Using Tables, Graphs and Maps to Communicate Statistical Findings

The story of communicating your statistics does not end with putting them into context. Actually, it would be better to say that it does not begin with putting the numbers into context. In reality, the story you are telling through your evidence will probably start with the display of a table, graph, or map.

A simple table, graph, or map can explain a great deal, and so this type of direct evidence should be used where appropriate. However, if a particular part of your analysis represented by a table, graph, or map does not add to or support your argument, it should be left out.

While representing statistical information in tables, graphs, or maps can be highly effective, it is important to ensure that the information is not presented in a manner that can mislead the reader. The key to presenting effective tables, graphs, or maps is to ensure they are easy to understand and clearly linked to the message. Ensure that you provide all the necessary information required to understand what the data is showing. The table, graph, or map should be able to stand alone.

Tables, graphs, and maps should:

- relate directly to the argument;
- support statements made in the text;
- summarize relevant sections of the data analysis; and
- be clearly labelled.

Table Checklist

- Use a descriptive title for each table.
- Label every column.
- Provide a source if appropriate.
- Minimize memory load by removing unnecessary data and minimizing decimal places.
- Use clustering and patterns to highlight important relationships.
- Use white space to effect.
- Order data meaningfully (e.g., rank highest to lowest).
- Use a consistent format for each table.

Also, do not present too much data in tables. Large expanses of figures can be daunting for an audience, and can obscure your message.

Graph Checklist

- **Title**: Use a clear, descriptive title.

- **Type of graph**: Choose the appropriate graph for your message, avoid using 3D graphs as they can obscure information.

- **Axes**: Decide which variable goes on which axis, and what scale is most appropriate.

- **Legend**: If there is more than one data series displayed, always include a legend, preferably within the area of the graph.

- **Labels**: All relevant labels should be included.

- **Color/shading**: Colors can help differentiate; however, know what is appropriate for the medium you're using.

- **Data source**: Provide the source of data you've used for the graph.

- **Three-Quarters Rules**: For readability, it's generally a good rule of thumb to make the y-axis three-quarters the size of the x-axis.

Key Points

- Understanding statistics requires creating a persuasive narrative that explains the data and an adequate explanation of why a statistic is being used, what it means and its source.

- The persuasive use of statistics is one of the most powerful tools in any rational argument, especially in public presentations.

- There are many ways to interpret statistics, however a public speaker should be mindful that they are presenting a statistic in an accurate way and not misleading the audience through a misrepresentation of a statistic.

- Statistics will, and should, almost always be used to illustrate a relationship.

- Refrain from bombarding your audience with too many mind-numbing numbers.

- Before all else, the two pillars of communicating statistics are accuracy and clarity.

Terms

statistics
A systematic collection of data on measurements or observations, often related to demographic information such as population counts, incomes, population counts at different ages, etc.

mode
The value that appears the most often in a data set.

mean
For a data set, the arithmetic mean is equal to the sum of the values divided by the number of values.

median
described as the numerical value separating the higher half of a sample, a population, or a probability distribution, from the lower half.

statistics

A systematic collection of data on measurements or observations, often related to demographic information such as population counts, incomes, population counts at different ages, etc.

accuracy

Exact conformity to truth, or to a rule or model; degree of conformity of a measure to a true or standard value.

Attributions

CC licensed content, Shared previously

- Understanding Statistics. **Provided by**: Boundless. **Located at**: https://www.boundless.com/communications/textbooks/boundless-communications-textbook/supporting-your-ideas-9/using-statistics-47/understanding-statistics-193-8003/?. **License**: *CC BY-SA: Attribution-ShareAlike*

- Communicating Statistics. **Provided by**: Boundless. **Located at**: https://www.boundless.com/communications/supporting-your-ideas/using-statistics/communicating-statistics/. **License**: *CC BY-SA: Attribution-ShareAlike*

Using Testimony

Expert versus Peer Testimony

There are three types of testimonials that fall into the range of expert to peer testimony; knowing your audience leads to the best choice.

Introduction

A testimony is a statement or endorsement given by someone who has a logical connection to the topic and who is a credible source.

Testimony can be used to either clarify or prove a point, and is often used by referring to the research of experts. For example, you could quote a study conducted by an independent auditing organization that endorses your organization's ability to financially support current workforce levels.

There are three major types of testimonies, ranging from expert to peer testimony. They are:

- Expert authorities
- Celebrities and other inspirational figures
- Antiauthorities

Expert Authorities

First, we can cite expert authorities. According to Chip and Dan Heath in their book *Made to Stick*, an expert is "the kind of person whose wall is covered with framed credentials: Oliver Sacks for neuroscience, Alan Greenspan for economics [well, maybe not such a great example any longer], or Stephen Hawking for physics."

If an expert supports our position, it usually adds credibility. If we are giving a presentation on a medical issue and can find support for our position in prestigious medical reviews such as *The New England Journal of Medicine* or *The Lancet*, it would probably be a good idea to cite those authorities.

Celebrities and Other Inspirational Figures

Second, we can refer to celebrities and other inspirational figures. Take the example of Oprah Winfrey recommending a book. Her recommendations influence the book-buying habits of thousands of people. Why? Because "if Oprah likes a book, it makes us more interested in that book. We trust the recommendations of people whom we want to be like," note the Heaths.

But what if there are no "experts" or "celebrities" to be found? Well, hold on a minute. They might be closer than you think. Do you have positive feedback from satisfied customers? Is there someone on your team (including you) with certain educational background or work experience that is relevant? If so, they (or you) might be able to provide the expertise that you seek, even if they are not widely known.

Peer (Antiauthority)

Third, we can rely on what the Heaths refer to as "antiauthorities." This is also known as peer testimony, because it comes from a source that is neither expert nor celebrity, but similar status to the audience.

They cite the example of Pam Laffin, a mother of two who died at the age of 31 from emphysema-related lung failure caused by years of smoking. She appeared in several anti-tobacco commercials sponsored by the Massachusetts Department of Public Health. The commercials were difficult to watch but highly effective; Pam Laffin told a compelling story in a way that more famous people could not.

What to Consider Before Using Testimony

Before using testimony, ask:

- Is the material quoted accurately?
- Is the source biased, or perceived as biased?
- Is the source competent in the field being consulted?
- Is the information current?

In the end, your choice as to which type of testimony you use will depend on your audience.

Smokers, for example. know all of the hazards of smoking and still continue to smoke. Give them a presentation on the dangers of smoking using expert testimony and you'll probably be met with a response like, "Yeah, but it won't happen to me." Use an antiauthority like Pam Laffin, however, and the response will be totally different.

Here is a young woman who probably also thought that it wouldn't happen to her, speaking "from her grave." Smokers can relate to her. She isn't just a numerical figure. This type of testimony is quite effective when you're trying to tell people the dangers of doing something.

So get to know your audience, put yourself in their place, and choose the type or combination of evidence that will make your message stick.

How to Incorporate Expert Testimony

Expert testimony can be incorporated after introducing a point of your argument.

Introduction

Once you have found experts to support your ideas, you may wonder how to incorporate their testimony into your speech. The following will give you an idea of how to incorporate expert testimony in order to support your argument and improve your speech.

What the Body of Your Speech Should Include

The body of your speech should help you elaborate and develop your main objectives clearly by using main points, subpoints, and support for your sub points. To ensure that your speech clearly communicates with your audience, try to limit both your main points and subpoints to three or four points each;this applies to your supporting points, as well. Expert testimony is considered supporting point; it is used to support the main and subpoints of your speech.

When a claim or point is made during a speech, the audience initially may be reluctant to concede or agree to the validity of the point. Often this is because the audience does not initially accept the speaker as a trustworthy authority. By incorporating expert testimony, the speaker is able to bolster their own authority to speak on the topic.

Therefore, expert testimony is commonly introduced after a claim is made. For example, if a speech makes the claim, "Manufacturing jobs have been in decline since the 1970s," it should be followed up with expert testimony to support that claim. This testimony could take a variety of forms, such as government employment statistics or a historian who has written on a particular sector of the manufacturing industry. No matter the particular form of expert testimony, it is incorporated following a claim to defend and support that claim, thus bolstering the authority of the speaker.

Example of Incorporating Expert Testimony

Search for and watch a TED talk by Barry Schwartz, a Professor of Social Theory and Social Action at Swarthmore College and author of numerous books in the field of psychology and economics. Notice how Schwartz references expert testimony in the course of his speech to justify his point to the audience.

Schwartz begins by showing the job description of a hospital janitor, noting that the tasks do not require interaction with other people. However, Schwartz introduces the expert testimony of actual hospital janitors as a way to complicate the apparent solo nature of janitorial work. Schwartz personalizes the experts with proper names, "Mike," "Sharleene," and "Luke," and uses their testimony to demonstrate that despite the job description, janitors take social interaction to be an important part of their job.

In this instance, Schwartz incorporates the expert testimony of actual janitors as a both a foil and a support. The testimony shows that in fact janitorial work does include interaction with other people, thus foiling the initial presentation of janitorial work as solitary. In addition, Schwartz uses the testimony of these experts to show that they embody the characteristics of wisdom that Schwartz will describe in the remainder of the speech.

Key Points

- Testimonials can be obtained from expert authorities, celebrities and other inspirational figures, and antiauthorities.
- An expert is is the kind of person whose wall is covered with framed credentials.
- People trust the recommendations of people whom they want to be like.
- Antiauthorities are sources of peer testimony whose source of knowledge is firsthand experience.
- Expert testimony should be incorporated to support, defend, or explain the main point or subpoint of a speech.
- Limiting your main points, subpoints, and support points to three or four points each improves the ability for your speech to communicate with the audience.
- Noticing how professionals use the testimony of experts can provide creative examples for how to incorporate expert testimony into a speech.

Terms

peer

Somebody who is, or something that is, at a level equal (to that of something else).

antiauthority

A non-authority source.

expert

A person with extensive knowledge or ability in a given subject.

TED

Technology Entertainment Design, a series of global conferences.

Attributions

CC licensed content, Shared previously

- Expert vs. Peer Testimony. **Provided by**: Boundless. **Located at**: https://www.boundless.com/communications/supporting-your-ideas/using-testimony/expert-versus-peer-testimony/. **License**: *CC BY-SA: Attribution-ShareAlike*
- How to Incorporate Expert Testimony. **Provided by**: Boundless. **Located at**: https://www.boundless.com/communications/supporting-your-ideas/using-testimony/how-to-incorporate-expert-testimony/. **License**: *CC BY-SA: Attribution-ShareAlike*

Using Examples

Types of Examples: Brief, Extended, & Hypothetical

Brief, extended, and hypothetical examples can be used to help an audience better understand and relate to key points of a presentation.

There are many types of examples that a presenter can use to help an audience better understand a topic and the key points of a presentation. These include specific situations, problems, or stories designed to help illustrate a principle, method, or phenomenon. They are useful because they can make an abstract concept more concrete for an audience by providing a specific case. There are three main types of examples: brief, extended, and hypothetical.

Brief Examples

Brief examples are used to further illustrate a point that may not be immediately obvious to all audience members but is not so complex that is requires a more lengthy example. Brief examples can be used by the presenter as an aside or on its own. A presenter may use a brief example in a presentation on politics in explaining the Electoral College. Since many people are familiar with how the Electoral College works, the presenter may just mention that the Electoral College is based on population and a brief example of how it is used to determine an election. In this situation it would not be necessary for a presented to go into a lengthy explanation of the process of the Electoral College since many people are familiar with the process.

Extended Examples

Extended examples are used when a presenter is discussing a more complicated topic that they think their audience may be unfamiliar with. In an extended example a speaker may want to use a chart, graph, or other visual aid to help the audience understand the example. An instance in which an extended example could be used includes a presentation in which a speaker is explaining how the "time value of money" principle works in finance. Since this is a concept that people unfamiliar with finance may not immediately understand, a speaker will want to use an equation and other visual aids to further help the audience understand this principle. An extended example will likely take more time to explain than a brief example and will be about a more complex topic.

Hypothetical Examples

A hypothetical example is a fictional example that can be used when a speaker is explaining a complicated topic that makes the most sense when it is put into more realistic or relatable terms. For instance, if a presenter is discussing statistical probability, instead of explaining probability in terms of equations, it may make more sense for the presenter to make up a hypothetical example. This could be a story about a girl, Annie, picking 10 pieces of candy from a bag of 50 pieces of candy in which half are blue and half are red and then determining Annie's probability of pulling out 10 total pieces of red candy. A hypothetical example helps the audience to better visualize a topic and relate to the point of the presentation more effectively.

Communicating Examples

Examples help the audience understand the key points; they should be to the point and complement the topic.

Communicating Examples

Examples are essential to a presentation that is backed up with evidence, and it helps the audience effectively understand the message being presented. An example is a specific situation, problem, or story designed to help illustrate a principle, method or phenomenon. Examples are useful because they can help make an abstract idea more concrete for an audience by providing a specific case. Examples are most effective when they are used as a complement to a key point in the presentation and focus on the important topics of the presentation.

Using Examples to Complement Key Points

One method of effectively communicating examples is by using an example to clarify and complement a main point of a presentation. If an orator is holding a seminar about how to encourage productivity in the workplace, an example may be used that focuses on how an employee received an incentive to work harder, such as a bonus, and this improved the employee's productivity. An example like this would act as a complement and help the audience better understand how to use incentives to improve performance in the workplace.

Using Examples that are Concise and to the Point

Examples are essential to help an audience better understand a topic. However, a speaker should be careful to not overuse examples as too many examples may confuse the audience and distract them from focusing on the key points that the speaker is making.

Examples should also be concise and not drawn out so the speaker does not lose the audience's attention. Concise examples should have a big impact on audience engagement and understanding in a small amount of time.

Key Points

- Examples include specific situations, problems or stories designed to help illustrate a principle, method, or phenomenon.

- Brief examples are used to further illustrate a point that may not be immediately obvious to all audience members but is not so complex that is requires a more lengthy example.

- Extended examples are used when a presenter is discussing a more complicated topic that they think their audience may be unfamiliar with.

- A hypothetical example is a fictional example that can be used when a speaker is explaining a complicated topic that makes the most sense when it is put into more realistic or relatable terms.

- Examples are essential to a presentation that is backed up with evidence, and it helps the audience effectively understand the message being presented. An example is a specific situation, problem, or story designed to help illustrate a principle, method, or phenomenon.

- One method of effectively communicating examples is by using an example to clarify and complement a main point of a presentation.

- A speaker should be careful to not overuse examples as too many examples may confuse the audience and distract them from focusing on the key points that the speaker is making.

Terms

hypothetical
A fictional situation or proposition used to explain a complicated subject.

abstract
Difficult to understand; abstruse.

phenomenon
A fact or event considered very unusual, curious, or astonishing by those who witness it.

Attributions

CC licensed content, Shared previously

Gathering Expertise in Your Subject Area

Wikipedia

Encyclopedias represent what is known on a subject. Whereas one does not cite encyclopedias in college-level work, you should reach an understanding of what is commonly known on your subject. Encyclopedias in general, and Wikipedia specifically, will do this. If you find useful information that is cited in an article, go to that original article and read it. Then you can cite that article. Don't cite Wikipedia – learn from it. See http://www.wikipedia.org/

Google News

Search Google News for the latest news articles about your subject. See http://news.google.com/

Google Alerts

Use Google Alerts to receive news articles in your email. See https://www.google.com/alerts

US Government Resources

Search federal and state government websites. Add your state to the search to get more specific to your intended audience. See: http://www.usa.gov/

Data.gov

"The home of the U.S. Government's open data."

According to the Website: "Here you will find data, tools, and resources to conduct research, develop web and mobile applications, design data visualizations, and more." See: https://www.data.gov/

Attributions

Chapter 13: Using Language Well

Objectives and Introduction

Using Language Well

By: E. Michele Ramsey, Ph.D.
Penn State Berks, Reading, PA

Learning Objectives

After reading this chapter, you should be able to:

- Understand the power of language to define our world and our relationship to the world
- Choose language that positively impacts the ability to inform and persuade
- Choose language to create a clear and vivid message
- Use language that is ethical and accurate
- Use language to enhance his or her speaker credibility

Your purpose is to make your audience see what you saw, hear what you heard, feel what you felt. Relevant detail, couched in concrete, colorful language, is the best way to recreate the incident as it happened and to picture it for the audience.

– Dale Carnegie

The Power of Language

Imagine for a moment that you were asked to list everything that you know about the country of Italy in spite of the fact that you have never actually visited the country. What would you write? You would have to think about all that you were told about Italy throughout your life, and you would probably list first the bits of information that have been repeated to you by various people and in a variety of contexts. So, for example, you might recall that in geography class you learned particular things about Italy. You might also recall the various movies you've seen that were either supposedly set in Italy or dealt with some element of what has been deemed by the film as "Italian culture." Those movies could include *The Godfather*, *The Italian Job*, or *The DaVinci Code*. You might think about stories your Italian grandmother told you about her childhood spent in Rome or

"Venice" by MorBCN. CC-BY-NC-SA.

remember images you have seen in history books about World War II. In other words, throughout your life you have learned a lot of different things that you now assume to be true about this country called "Italy" and you've learned all of these things about Italy through language, whether it be through verbal storytelling or through your interpretation of images in a book or on a screen. Now, consider for a moment the possibility that everything you've heard about Italy has been incorrect. Since you have not ever actually been to the country and had first-hand experience with its geography and culture, for example, how would you know if what you've been told is true or not?

Language is one of the most influential and powerful aspects of our daily lives and yet very few people pay attention to it in their interpersonal and public communication. *The power of language cannot be overemphasized— language constructs, reflects, and maintains our social realities, or what we believe to be "true" with regard to the world around us.* The point of the example above is that what we "know is true" about a person, place, thing, idea, or any other aspect of our daily lives very much depends on what experiences we have had (or not), what information we have (or have not) come across, and what words people have used (or not used) when communicating about our world.

> Language is a process of free creation; its laws and principles are fixed, but the manner in which the principles of generation are used is free and infinitely varied. Even the interpretation and use of words involves a process of free creation. – Noam Chomsky

Language can also have an impact on how we feel about this reality. How we define words and how we feel about those words is highly subjective. In fact, cognitive psychologist Lera Boroditsky showed a key to a group of Spanish-speakers and to a group of German-speakers. The researchers then asked the participants to describe the key they had been shown. Because the Spanish word for "key" is gendered as feminine, Spanish speakers defined the key using words such as lovely, tiny, and magic. The German word for "key" is gendered masculine, however, and German speakers defined the key using adjectives like hard, jagged, and awkward.[1] This study suggests that the words we use to define something can have an impact on how we perceive what those words represent.

"Martin Luther King Jr" by *Dick DeMarsico. Public domain.*

Because language is such a powerful, yet unexamined, part of our lives, this chapter focuses on how language functions and how competent speakers harness the power of language. Consider the case of the Reverend Dr. Martin Luther King, Jr. Indeed, many speakers before him made the very same persuasive arguments regarding the lack of civil rights for Black Americans, yet we regularly point to the Reverend Dr. King as a preeminent speaker for the civil rights movement because he was a master of language— he employed the power of language to move his audiences in ways they had not been moved before, and we remember him for his eloquence.

Communication vs. Language

To understand the power of language, we need to differentiate between communication and language. Communication occurs when we try to transfer what is in our minds to the minds of our audience. Whether speaking to inform, persuade, or entertain, the main goal of a speaker is to effectively communicate her or his thoughts to audience members. Most chapters in this text help you determine how best to communicate information through considerations such as organizational structure, audience analysis, delivery, and the like. Language, on the other hand, is the means by which we communicate—a system of symbols we use to form messages. We learn language as a child in order to read, write, and speak. Once we have mastered enough language we can communicate with relative ease, yet growing up we rarely learn much about language choices and what they mean for our communication. We regularly hear people say, "If we just communicated more or for longer periods of time we'd better understand each other." What these types of statements reflect is our lack of understanding of the differences between communication and language. Therefore, many of us believe that when problems arise we should strive to have *more communication* between the parties. But what we need is *better communication* by focusing on language choice.

Language Creates Social Reality

Our social realities are constructed through language; and therefore, people with different experiences in, and understandings of, the world can define the same things in very different ways. Language is culturally transmitted—we learn how to define our world first from our families and then our later definitions of the world are influenced by friends and institutions such as the media, education, and religion. If we grow up in a sexist culture, we are likely to hold sexist attitudes.

Similarly, if we grow up in a culture that defines the environment as our first priority in making any deci-

---

1. Boroditsky cited in Thomas, L., Wareing, S. Singh, I., Pecci, J. S., Thornborrow, J. & Jones, J. (2003). *Language, society, and power: An introduction*, 2nd Ed. New York: Routledge. pp. 26–27.

sions, we're likely to grow with environmentally friendly attitudes. Language, then, is not neutral. As a culture, as groups of people, and as individuals, we decide what words we're going to use to define one thing or another.

> Culture is the collective programming of the mind that distinguishes the members of one category of people from another. – Geert Hofstede

For public speakers, these facts are important for three primary reasons. First, the careful use of language can make the difference between you giving a remarkable speech and one that is utterly forgettable. Second, you must remember that audience members may not share the same language for the definition of the very same ideas, realities, or even specific items. Finally, the language that you use in public (and even private) communication says something about you—about how you define and therefore perceive the world. If you are not careful with your language you may unintentionally communicate something negative about yourself simply because of a careless use of language. You should think very carefully about your audience's and your own language when you prepare to speak publicly. You can master all of the other elements in this textbook, but without an effective use of language those other mastered skills will not mean much to your audience. The suggestions in this chapter will help you communicate as effectively as possible using appropriate and expressive. You'll also learn about language to avoid so that your language leaves the audience with a positive impression of you.

The Differences Language Choices can Make

When I discuss the importance of language choice with my students, I generally begin with two different paragraphs based on a section from Reverend Jesse Jackson's "Rainbow Coalition" speech. The first paragraph I read them is a section of Reverend Jackson's speech that I have rewritten. The second paragraph is the actual text from Reverend Jackson's speech. Let's start with my version first:

> *America should dream. Choose people over building bombs. Destroy the weapons and don't hurt the people. Think about a new system of values. Think about lawyers more interested in the law than promotions. Consider doctors more interested in helping people get better than in making money. Imagine preachers and priests who will preach and not just solicit money.*

This paragraph is clear and simple. It gets the point across to the audience. But compare my version of his paragraph to Reverend Jackson's actual words:

> *Young America dream. Choose the human race over the nuclear race. Bury the weapons and don't burn the people. Dream of a new value system. Dream of lawyers more concerned about justice than a judgeship. Dream of doctors more concerned about public health than personal wealth. Dream of preachers and priests who will prophecy and not just profiteer.*

The significant difference between these two versions of the paragraph can be explained simply as the difference between carefully choosing one group of words over another group of words. My version of the speech is fine, but it is utterly forgettable. Reverend Jackson's exact wording, however, is stunning. The audience probably remembered his speech and the chills that went down their spines when they heard it long after it was over. This example, I hope, exemplifies the difference language choice can make. Using language in a way that makes you and your speech memorable, however, takes work. Few people come by this talent naturally, so give yourself plenty of time to rework your first draft to fine tune and perfect your language choice. Using some of the strategies discussed below will help you in this process.

Attributions

CC licensed content, Shared previously

- Chapter 10 Objectives, Outline, and Introduction. **Authored by**: E. Michele Ramsey, Ph.D.. **Provided by**: Penn State Berks, Reading, PA. **Located at**: http://publicspeakingproject.org/psvirtualtext.html. **Project**: The Public Speaking Project. **License**: *CC BY-NC-ND: Attribution-NonCommercial-NoDerivatives*

- Venice. **Authored by**: MorBCN. **Located at**: https://flic.kr/p/5BiQ9k. **License**: *CC BY-NC-SA: Attribution-NonCommercial-ShareAlike*

Public domain content

- Martin Luther King Jr NYWTS 6. **Authored by**: Dick DeMarsico. **Provided by**: New York World-Telegram and the Sun. **Located at**: http://commons.wikimedia.org/wiki/File:Martin_Luther_King_Jr_NYWTS_6.jpg. **License**: *Public Domain: No Known Copyright*

Constructing Clear and Vivid Messages

Use Simple Language

When asked to write a speech or a paper, many of us pull out the thesaurus (or call it up on our computer) when we want to replace a common word with one that we believe is more elevated or intellectual. There are certainly times when using a thesaurus is a good thing, but if you're pulling that big book out to turn a simple idea into one that *sounds* more complex, put it back on the shelf. Good speakers use simple language for two primary reasons.

First, audiences can sense a fake. When you turn in your term paper with words that aren't typically used by people in everyday conversation and those words are simply replacing the common words we all use, your instructor knows what you've done. Part of having strong credibility as a speaker is convincing your audience of your sincerity, both in terms of your ideas and your character. When you elevate your language simply for the sake of using big words when small words will do, audiences may perceive you as insincere, and that perception might also transfer onto your message. In addition, the audience's attention can drift to questions about your character and veracity, making it less likely that they are paying attention to your message.

Second, using a long word when a short one will do inhibits your ability to communicate clearly. Your goal as a speaker should be to be as clear as you possibly can. Using language that makes it more difficult for your audience to understand your message can negatively impact your ability to get a clear message across to your audience. If your audience can't understand your vocabulary, they can't understand your message.

A good example of a speaker whose communication was obstructed by language use is Former Secretary of State Alexander Haig. Some examples of his problematic language choice include: "careful caution," "epistemologically wise," "exacerbating restraint," "saddle

"Al Haig speaks to press 1981" **by Ronald Reagan Presidential Library. Public domain.**

myself with a statistical fence," and "definitizing an answer."[1] Chances are good that after reading these phrases over and over you still don't understand him. You can imagine how much harder it would be to understand Haig's message as it was *delivered orally*—spoken in an instant and then gone! Haig's language clouds rather than clarifies ideas, but it is easy to make sure your message gets across to the audience by avoiding big words that are not necessary.

If you're paying attention to the language strategies discussed in this chapter, you'll find that you won't need to pull out that thesaurus to impress your audience—your command of language will make that positive impression for you. In addition, when you use language that your audience expects to hear and is used to hearing you may find that the audience perceives you as more sincere than someone who uses elevated language and sounds pretentious. Remember: It is rarely the case that you should use a long word when a short one will do.

> Most of the fundamental ideas of science are essentially simple, and may, as a rule, be expressed in a language comprehensible to everyone. – Albert Einstein

Use Concrete and Precise Language

How many times a week do you say something to someone only to have them misunderstand? You believe that you were very clear and the person you were talking to thought that she understood you perfectly, and yet you both ended up with a problem we often deem "miscommunication." You said you'd "call later" and your friend got angry because you didn't. By "later" you probably meant one time frame while your friend defined that time frame very differently. Often in these cases both people are right. You *were* perfectly clear and your friend *did* understand you perfectly—so how did the miscommunication happen?

"German Shepherd" **by Magnus Bråth.** *CC-BY.*

---

1. Time.com (1981, February 23). "Haigledygook and secretaryspeak." Retrieved from http://content.time.com/time/magazine/article/0,9171,949069,00.html

"Chopper Bothy 04" by John Hudson.
CC-BY-NC-ND.

One of the primary reasons we miscommunicate is because language is an abstract phenomenon. Meanings exist in people's understandings, not the words we use. Therefore, if you're telling a story about "a dog" you could be talking about a German Shepherd while the person you're talking with is envisioning a Chihuahua. If you do not use concrete language, you risk at least sending a weaker or different message than you intended. When speaking, you want to use the concrete term "German shepherd" over the more abstract term "dog."

When you are writing your speech, look for words that you might need to define more clearly. Instead of talking about "bad weather," tell the audience that it was raining or that hail the size of golf balls was coming down. "Bad weather" means different things to different people. In discussing the aftermath of a natural disaster, rather than saying "a lot of people were affected" say, "25,000 citizens, 1 in every 5, were affected by this disaster." "A lot" means different things to different people. *Most words* mean different things to different people, so use concrete language over abstract words to better your chances of communicating your message as intended.

You also want to make sure that you're precise. Someone might call a sweater "green" while someone else calls it "teal." Even though those are just differences in perception not purposeful or mindless communication meant to be inaccurate, not being clear about exactly which color you're talking about can lead to confusion. It is best to remember to be as precise as possible when choosing words. Don't say something was "big"—tell us its weight or height, and to be sure you're communicating clearly compare that weigh or height to something we understand. So, instead of saying "The piles of garbage I saw in the local dump were really big" say "The piles of garbage I saw in the local dump weighed about 10,000 pounds, which is equivalent to the weight of the average female elephant." The more precise you are the less likely it is that your audience will misinterpret your message.

> Our business is infested with idiots who try to impress by using pretentious jargon. – David Ogilvy

Another way to avoid language that obstructs communication is to avoid the use of **jargon**. Jargon is the "specialized language of a group or profession."[2] It is appropriate to use jargon when you know that your audience understands the terms you are using. For example, if you are a computer science major and you are presenting to a group of similarly trained computer science majors, using jargon will help establish your credibility with that audience. Using terms even as basic as "RAM" and "binary code" with a general

2. Hamilton, G. (2008). Public speaking for college and career, 8th Ed. New York: McGraw-Hill.

audience, however, will likely not go over well—you risk confusing the audience rather than informing or persuading them. Even people who can use computers may not know how they work or the technical terms associated with them. So you must be careful to only use jargon when you know your audience will understand it. If you must use jargon while speaking to a general audience, be sure to define your terms and err on the side of over-clarification.

> Slang is a language that rolls up its sleeves, spits on its hands and goes to work. – Carl Sandburg

Finally, another way to avoid confusion is to avoid using slang when it is not appropriate. **Slang** is language that some people might understand but that is not considered acceptable in formal or polite conversation. Slang may be a poor choice for a speaker because some members of your audience may not be familiar with the slang term(s) you use. Slang is often based in a very specific audience, defined by age, region, subculture and the like. If you are speaking to an audience that you know will understand and respond positively, you may choose to include that language in your speech. Otherwise, do not use slang, or you may confuse and frustrate audience members and cause them to lose interest in your speech. In addition, because slang is often not considered appropriate in formal and polite conversation, using it in your speech may communicate negative ideas about you to audience members. Don't let a mindless use of slang negatively impact your audience's perception of you and your message.

"Goth" by Rama. CC-BY-SA.

Attributions

CC licensed content, Shared previously

- Chapter 10 Constructing Clear and Vivid Messages. **Authored by**: E. Michele Ramsey, Ph.D.. **Provided by**: Penn State Berks, Reading, PA. **Located at**: http://publicspeakingproject.org/psvirtualtext.html. **Project**: The Public Speaking Project. **License**: *CC BY-NC-ND: Attribution-NonCommercial-NoDerivatives*

- German Shepherd. **Authored by**: Magnus Brath. **Located at**: https://flic.kr/p/999gJ6. **License**: *CC BY: Attribution*

- Chopper Bothy 04. **Authored by**: John Hudson. **Located at**: https://flic.kr/p/78MrFu. **License**: *CC BY-NC-ND: Attribution-Non-Commercial-NoDerivatives*

- Goth. **Authored by**: Rama. **Located at**: http://commons.wikimedia.org/wiki/File:Goth_f222791.jpg. **License**: *CC BY-SA: Attribution-ShareAlike*

Public domain content

- Al Haig speaks to press 1981. **Authored by**: Ronald Reagan Presidential Library. **Provided by**: US Government. **Located at**: http://www.reagan.utexas.edu/archives/photographs/large/c1429-31.jpg. **License**: *Public Domain: No Known Copyright*

Using Stylized Language

Stylized language is language that communicates your meaning clearly, vividly and with flair. Stylized language doesn't just make you sound better; it also helps make your speeches more memorable. Speakers who are thoughtful about using language strategies in their speeches are more memorable as speakers and therefore so too are their messages more unforgettable as well.

Metaphors and Similes

One strategy that promotes vivid language is the use of metaphors. **Metaphors** are comparisons made by speaking of one thing in terms of another. **Similes** are similar to metaphors in how they function; however, similes make comparisons by using the word "like" or "as," whereas metaphors do not. The power of a metaphor is in its ability to create an image that is linked to emotion in the mind of the audience. It is one thing to talk about racial injustice, it is quite another for the Reverend Dr. Martin Luther King, Jr. to note that people have been "…battered by storms of persecution and staggered by the winds of police brutality." Throughout his "I Have a Dream" speech the Reverend Dr. King uses the metaphor of the checking account to make his point.

He notes that the crowd has come to the March on Washington to "cash a check" and claims that America has "defaulted on this promissory note" by giving "the Negro people a bad check, a check that has come back "insufficient funds." By using checking and bank account terms that most people are familiar with, the Reverend Dr. King is able to more clearly communicate what he believes has occurred. In addition, the use of this metaphor acts as a sort of "shortcut." He gets his point across very quickly by comparing the problems of civil rights to the problems of a checking account.

In the same speech the Reverend Dr. King also makes use of similes, which also compare two things but do so using "like" or "as." In discussing his goals for the Civil Rights movement in his "I Have a Dream" speech, the Reverend Dr. exclaims: "No, no we are not satisfied and we will not be satisfied until justice rolls down likewaters and righteousness like a mighty stream." Similes also help make your message clearer by using ideas that are more concrete for your audience. For example, to give the audience an idea of what a winter day looked like you could note that the "snow looked as solid as pearls." To communicate sweltering heat you could say that "the tar on the road looked like satin." A simile most of us are familiar with is the notion of the United States being "like a melting pot" with regard to its diversity. We also often note that a friend or colleague that stays out of conflicts between friends is "like Switzerland." In each of these instances similes have been used to more clearly and vividly communicate a message.

Metaphors have a way of holding the most truth in the least space. – Orson Scott Card

Alliteration

Remember challenging yourself or a friend to repeat a tongue twister "five times fast?" Perhaps it was "Sally sold seashells by the seashore" or "Peter Piper picked a peck of pickled peppers." Tongue twisters are difficult to say to say but very easy to remember. Why? Alliteration. **Alliteration** is the repetition of the initial sounds of words. Alliteration is a useful tool for helping people remember your message, and it's as simple as taking a few minutes to see if there are ways to reword your speech so that you can add some alliteration— *this* is a great time to use that thesaurus we talked about putting away early in this chapter. Look for alternative words to use that allow for alliteration in your speech. You might consider doing this especially when it comes to the points that you would like your audience to remember most.

The soul selects her own society. – Emily Dickinson

Antithesis

Antithesis allows you to use contrasting statements in order to make a rhetorical point. Perhaps the most famous example of antithesis comes from the Inaugural Address of President John F. Kennedy when he stated, "And so, my fellow Americans, ask not what your country can do for you; ask what you can do for your country." Going back to Reverend Jackson's "Rainbow Coalition" speech he notes, "I challenge them to put hope in their brains and not dope in their veins." In each of these cases, the speakers have juxtaposed two competing ideas in one statement to make an argument in order to draw the listener's attention.

You're easy on the eyes — hard on the heart. – Terri Clark

Parallel Structure and Language

Antithesis is often worded using parallel structure or language. Parallel structure is the balance of two or more similar phrases or clauses, and parallel wording is the balance of two or more similar words. The Reverend Dr. King's "I Have a Dream" speech exemplifies both strategies in action. Indeed, the section where he repeats "I Have a Dream" over and over again is an example of the use of both parallel structure and language. The use of parallel structure and language helps your audience remember without beating them over the head with repetition. If worded and delivered carefully, you can communicate a main point over and over again, as did the Reverend Dr. King, and it doesn't seem as though you are simply repeating the same phrase over and over. You are often doing just that, of course, but because you are careful with your wording (it should be powerful and creative, not pedantic) and your delivery (the correct use of pause, volumes, and other elements of delivery), the audience often perceives the repetition as dramatic and memorable. The use of parallel language and structure can also help you when you are speaking persuasively. Through the use of these strategies you can create a speech that takes your audience through a series of ideas or arguments that seem to "naturally" build to your conclusion.

Personalized Language

We're all very busy people. Perhaps you've got work, studying, classes, a job, and extracurricular activities to juggle. Because we are all so busy, one problem that speakers often face is trying to get their audience interested in their topic or motivated to care about their argument. A way to help solve this problem is through the use of language that personalizes your topic. Rather than saying, "One might argue" say "You might argue." Rather than saying "This could impact the country in ways we have not yet imagined," say "This could impact your life in ways that you have not imagined." By using language that directly connects your topic or argument to the audience you better your chances of getting your audience to listen and to be persuaded that your subject matter is serious and important to them. Using words like "us," "you," and "we" can be a subtle means of getting your audience to pay attention to your speech. Most people are most interested in things that they believe impact their lives directly—make those connections clear for your audience by using personal language.

"next10, Day1, 11.05.2010" **by NEXT Berlin.** *CC-BY.*

Attributions

CC licensed content, Shared previously

- Chapter 10 Using Stylized Language. **Authored by**: E. Michele Ramsey, Ph.D.. **Provided by**: Penn State Berks, Reading, PA. **Located at**: http://publicspeakingproject.org/psvirtualtext.html. **Project**: The Public Speaking Project. **License**: *CC BY-NC-ND: Attribution-NonCommercial-NoDerivatives*
- next10, Day1, 11.05.2010. **Authored by**: NEXT Berlin. **Located at**: https://flic.kr/p/84saJQ. **License**: *CC BY: Attribution*

The Importance of Ethical and Accurate Language

Language and Ethics

As was noted at the beginning of this chapter, language is culturally transmitted—we learn our language from those around us. For most of us this means that we may first learn language from our parents, but as we grow older, other family members, friends, educators and even the media impact our vocabularies and our choices regarding what language we use. Think about a world without language. Quite simply, we'd have no way of participating in our world without it. People constantly produce language to categorize and organize the world.

Think back to our discussion of how language influences your social reality. In my work as a mentor, I tutored a girl in elementary school who had a very difficult time saying the word "lake." I used the word "lake" as part of a homework exercise. What I had not realized was that she had never seen a lake, either in person or in a picture, or, if she had seen a lake no one had pointed to that body of water and called it a "lake." The concept of a "lake" was simply not in *her* reality. No "lakes" existed in her world. This is a key example of how the language that we learn and that we choose to use says something about our social reality.

Consider the above example another way. Let's say that my young friend had seen a lake and knew how to say the word and what the word referred to, but that she had only been privy to people who used the word negatively. If throughout her life "lakes" were discussed as "bad things" to be avoided, she would have a very different perspective on lakes than most people. Switching this example around a little helps illustrate the fact that language is not neutral. Language carries ideas, and while there is often more than one choice in terms of which word to use, often the words from which you are choosing are not equal in terms of the reality that they communicate.

Think about the difference between calling a specific place "the projects" versus calling that same place "public housing." Both phrases refer to a particular geographical space, but calling a neighborhood "the projects" as opposed to "public housing" communicates something very different, and more negative, about this neighborhood. Often students use the words that they hear more commonly used, so referring to "the projects" as opposed to "public housing" usually indicates that they have not thought enough about their word choices or thought about the impact of those choices.

> By and large, language is a tool for concealing the truth. – George Carlin

As this example points out, we have a variety of words from which to choose when constructing a message. Successful speakers recognize that in addition to choosing words that help with clarity and vividness, it is important to think about the connotations associated with one word or the other. When speakers are not careful in terms of word choice in this sense, it is possible to lose credibility with the audience and to create the perception that you are someone that perhaps you are not. If you use "the projects" instead of "public housing," audience members may view you as someone who has negative perceptions of people who live in public housing when you do not feel that way at all. Clearly, not being careful about language choices can be a costly mistake.

But what do these examples have to do with ethics? For our purposes here, there are two ways to think about communication and ethics. First, ethical communication is that which does not unfairly label one thing or another based on personal bias. So, in addition to choosing "public housing" over "the projects," an ethical speaker will choose terms that steer clear from intentional bias. For example, pro-life speakers would refrain from calling "pro-choice" people "pro-abortion" since the basic principle of the "pro-choice" position is that it is up to the person, not society, to choose whether or not an abortion is acceptable. That is a very different position than being "pro-abortion." Indeed, many pro- choice citizens would not choose abortion if faced with an unplanned pregnancy; therefore calling them "pro- abortion" does not reflect the reality of the situation; rather, it is the purposeful and unethical use of one term over the other for emotional impact. Similarly, if a pro-choice person is addressing a crowd where religious organizations are protesting against the legality of abortion, it would not be ethical for the pro-choice speaker to refer to the "anti- abortion" protestors as "religious fanatics." Simply because someone is protesting abortion on religious grounds does not make that person a "religious fanatic," and as in the first example, choosing the latter phrase is another purposeful and unethical use of one term over another for emotional impact.

> Language exerts hidden power, like the moon on the tides. – Rita Mae Brown

A second way to link communication and ethics is to remember that ethical speakers attempt to communicate reality to the best of their ability. Granted, as was noted above, each person's social reality is different, depending on background, influences, and cultural institutions, for example. But regardless of whether you think that a "lake" is a good or bad thing, lakes still exist in reality. Regardless of whether or not you think rocks are useful or not, rocks still exist. So ethical communication also means trying to define or explain your subject in terms that are as closely tied to an objective reality as is possible—it is your best attempt to communicate accurately about your topic. Sexist and heterosexist language are two types of language to be avoided by ethical speakers because each type of language does communicate inaccuracies to the audience.

Sexist and Heterosexist Language

One of the primary means by which speakers regularly communicate inaccurate information is through the use of sexist language. In spite of the fact that the Modern Language Association deemed sexist language as grammatically incorrect back in the 1970s, many people and institutions (including most colleges and universities) still regularly use sexist language in their communication.

An argument I regularly hear from students is that language has "always been sexist." This is, in fact, not true. As Dale Spender notes in her book, *Man Made Language*, until 1746 when John Kirkby formulated his "Eighty Eight Grammatical Rules," the words "they" and "their" were used in sentences for sex-indeterminable sentences.[1] Kirkby's rule number twenty-one stated that the male sex was more comprehensive than the female and thus argued that "he" was the grammatically correct way to note men *and* women in writing where mixed sexed or sex-indeterminable situations are referred to.[2] Women were not given equal access to education at this time and thus the male grammarians who filled the halls of the academy and had no incentive to disagree with Mr. Kirkby, accepted his eighty-eight rules in full.

Interestingly though, the general population was not as easily convinced. Perhaps because they were not used to identifying women as men in language or perhaps because it did not make rational sense to do so, the general public ignored rule number twenty-one. Incensed by the continued misuse of "they," male grammarians were influential in the passing of the 1850 Act of Parliament which legally asserted that "he"

---

1. Spender, D. (1990). *Man Made Language*. New York: Pandora.
2. Spender 1990

stood for "she."[3] Yes, you read correctly. Parliament passed legislation in an effort to promote the use of sexist language. And it worked! Eventually the rule was adhered to by the public and thus we have the regular and rarely challenged use of sexist language. But this use of language was not "natural" or even "normal" for many millennia.

Pretending that we haven't learned about the work of Dale Spender, let's assume that language has "always been sexist." Even if language was always sexist, that does not make the use of sexist language right. We wouldn't make a similar argument about racist language, so that argument isn't any stronger with regard to language that is sexist. It simply isn't acceptable today to use sexist language; and by learning to avoid these common mistakes, you can avoid using language that is grammatically incorrect, unethical, and problematic. See Table 10.1 for examples of sexist and non-sexist language.

Table 10.1: Comparison of Sexist and Gender-Neutral Terms	
Sexist Terms	**Gender-Neutral Terms**
Actress	Actor
Ballerina	Ballet Dancer
Businessman	Business Person
Chairman	Chairperson
Fireman	Firefighter
Fisherman	Fisher
Mailman/Postman	Mail/Letter Carrier
Male Nurse	Nurse
Policeman	Police Officer
Stewardess	Flight Attendant
Waitress	Server
He (to mean men and women)	He or She, He/She, They
Example: If a student wants to do well, he must study.	Examples: If a student wants to do well, he or she must study. If students want to do well, they must study.

Is your remarkably sexist drivel intentional, or just some horrible mistake? – Yeardley Smith

First, you should avoid the use of what is called the **generic "he" or "man,"** which is the use of terms such as "mankind" instead of "humankind" or "humanity," or the use of "man" or "he" to refer to all people. A common response from students with regard to the use of "generic he" is that the word is intended to represent men and women, therefore when it's used it is not used to be sexist. If it were really the case that people truly recognized in their minds that the term "man" includes women, then we would talk about situations in which "man has difficulty giving birth"[4] or the "impact of menstruation on man's biology." Of course, we do not say those things because they simply wouldn't make sense to us. Perhaps you can now see why the people of the 1700s and 1800s had trouble switching from non-sexist to sexist language—it defied their own common sense just as discussing how "man gets pregnant" defies yours.

3. Spender 1990
4. Spender 1990 p. 156

Second, you should avoid using **man-linked terms**, which are terms such as "fireman" or "policemen." It is appropriate to use these terms when you know that the people you are speaking about are men only, but if you do not know for sure or if you're talking about groups generally, you should avoid using these types of terms and replace them with "firefighters" and "police officers." Colleges and universities should replace "freshman" with "first-year students" and so should you. Other, non job-oriented words also suffer from this same problem. People often note that tables need to be "manned" rather than "staffed" and that items are "man-made" instead of "human made" or "hand-made."

A final common use of sexist language occurs when people use **spotlighting** when discussing the occupations of men and women. How often have you heard (or used) a phrase such as "he's a male nurse" or "that female lawyer?" When we spotlight in these ways, we are pointing out that a person is deviating from the "norm" and implying that someone's sex is relevant to a particular job. According to Peccei, in the English language there is

"Italian Soldier Olympic Games Turin 2006" by Italian Army. CC-BY.

a very strong tendency to "place the adjective expressing the most 'defining' characteristic closest to the noun."[5] Thus, as Turner points out, a phrase like the "old intelligent woman" violates our sense of "correct," not because there's anything wrong with the word order grammatically, but because it contradicts our customary way of thinking that values youth over age.[6] If you talk about a "male nurse" or a "female cop," you risk communicating to the audience that you believe the most salient aspect of a particular job is the sex of the person that normally does it, and some audience members may not appreciate that assumption on your part.

The use of sexist language is not just grammatically incorrect; its use is also linked to ethics because it communicates a reality that does not exist—it is *not accurate*. Man-linked language communicates male superiority and that there are more men than women because women are regularly erased linguistically in speech and writing. Man-linked terms and spotlighting communicate that some job activities are appropriate for men but not women and vice versa by putting focus on the sex of a person as linked to their job or activity. Finally, the use of the generic "he" or "man" communicates that men are the norm and women deviate from that norm. If all humans are called "man," what does that say about women? Sexist language can also limit what young males and females believe that they can accomplish in their lives. Ethical speakers should therefore avoid using language that communicates these sexist practices.

Speakers who choose to continue to use sexist language are not only speaking in a manner that is grammatically incorrect, they are also risking communicating negative ideas about themselves to audience members. Often the use of sexist language is because of a careless error, so be careful about language choice so that you don't accidentally communicate something about yourself that you didn't intend or that isn't true. Remember that if one person in your audience is offended by some aspect of your language use, they

5. Peccei, J. (2003). Language and age. In L. Thomas et. al., *Language, society, and power*, 2nd Ed. New York: Routledge
6. Peccei 2003

may share their opinions with others in the room. If that one person is a leader of the larger group or is someone whose opinions people care about, offending that one audience member may cause you to "lose" many other audience members as well.

Heterosexist language is language that assumes the heterosexual orientation of a person or group of people. Be careful when speaking not to use words or phrases that assume the sexual orientation of your audience members. Do not make the mistake of pointing to someone in your audience as an example and discussing that person with the assumption that she is heterosexual by saying something like, "Let's say this woman here is having trouble with her husband." When thinking of examples to use, consider using names that could ring true for heterosexuals and homosexuals alike. Instead of talking about Pat and Martha, discuss an issue involving Pat and Chris. Not only will you avoid language that assumes everyone's partner is of the opposite sex, you will also better your

"Married Gay Couple John and Jamie" by John. CC-BY-SA.

chances of persuading using your example. If the use of sex- specific names doesn't ring true with members of your audience that are homosexual, it is possible that they are not as likely to continue to listen to your example with the same level of interest. They are more likely to follow your example if they aren't confronted immediately with names that assume a heterosexual relationship. There are, of course, ethical considerations as well. Because it is likely that your entire audience is not heterosexual (and certainly they do not all hold heterosexist attitudes), using heterosexist language is another way that speakers may alienate audience members. In reality the world is not completely heterosexual and even in the unlikely case that you're speaking in a room of consisting completely of heterosexuals, many people have friends or relatives that are homosexual, so the use of heterosexist language to construct the world as if this were not the case runs counter to ethical communication.

Attributions

CC licensed content, Shared previously

- Chapter 10 The Importance of Ethical and Accurate Language. **Authored by**: E. Michele Ramsey, Ph.D.. **Provided by**: Penn State Berks, Reading, PA. **Located at**: http://publicspeakingproject.org/psvirtualtext.html. **Project**: The Public Speaking Project . **License**: *CC BY-NC-ND: Attribution-NonCommercial-NoDerivatives*

- Emerald Bay. **Authored by**: Michael. **Located at**: http://en.wikipedia.org/wiki/Lake#mediaviewer/File:Emerald_Bay.jpg. **License**: *CC BY: Attribution*

- Italian Soldier Olympic Games Turin 2006. **Provided by**: Italian Army. **Located at**: http://commons.wikimedia.org/wiki/File:Italian_Soldier_Olypmic_Games_Turin_2006.jpg. **License**: *CC BY: Attribution*

- Married Gay Couple John and Jamie. **Authored by**: John. **Located at**: http://commons.wikimedia.org/wiki/File:Married_Gay_Couple_John_and_Jamie.jpg. **License**: *CC BY-SA: Attribution-ShareAlike*

Avoiding Language Pitfalls

There are other aspects of language you should consider when thinking about how language choices impact the audience's perception of you.

Profanity

It seems obvious, but this fact bears repeating—you should **refrain from using profanity** in your speeches. One of the primary rules of all aspects of public speaking (audience analysis, delivery, topic selection, etc.) is that you should never ignore audience expectations. Audiences do not expect speakers to use profane language, and in most cases, doing so will hurt your credibility with the audience. It is true that certain audiences will not mind an occasional profane word used for effect, but unless you are speaking to a group of people with whom you are very familiar, it is difficult to know for sure whether the majority of the audience will respond positively or negatively to such language use. If you even offend one person in an audience and that person happens to be an opinion leader for other audience members, the negative impact of your language on that one person could end up having a much larger influence on the audience's perception of you.

> I wanted to cut down on the profanity, because I think I'm funnier without sayin' a lot of cuss words.
> – Chris Tucker

Exaggeration

Speakers should also be careful about exaggeration. **Hyperbole** is the use of moderate exaggeration for effect and is an acceptable and useful language strategy. What is not acceptable, however, is the use of exaggeration to an extent that you risk losing credibility. For example, while it is acceptable to note that "it snows in South Texas as often as pigs fly," it would not be acceptable to state that "It never snows in South Texas." In the first case, you are using hyperbole as a form of exaggeration meant to creatively communicate an idea. In the second case, your use of exaggeration is stating something that is not true. It is unwise to use words such as "never" and "always" when speaking. It may be the case that speakers make this mistake accidentally because they are not careful with regard to word choice. We so easily throw words like "always" and "never" around in everyday conversation that this tendency transfers onto our public speeches when we are not thinking carefully about word choice.

There are two problems with the careless use of exaggeration. First, when you use words like "always" and "never," it is not likely that the statement you are making is true—as very few things *always* or *never* happen. Therefore, audiences might mistake your careless use of language for an attempt to purposefully misrepresent the truth. Second, when you suggest that something "always" or "never" happens, you are explicitly challenging your audience members to offer up evidence that contradicts your statement. Such a challenge may serve to impact your credibility negatively with the audience, as an audience member can make you look careless and/or silly by pointing out that your "always" or "never" statement is incorrect.

Exaggeration is a blood relation to falsehood and nearly as blamable. – Hosea Ballou

Powerless Language

Finally, think about using powerful language when speaking. Because women are more likely than men to be socialized to take the feelings of others into account, women tend to use less powerful language than men.[1] Both men and women, however, can use language that communicates a lack of power. In some cases speakers use **powerless language that communicates uncertainty**. For example, a speaker might say "It seems to me that things are getting worse," or "In my estimation, things are getting worse." These phrases communicate a lack of certainty in your statements. It is likely that in the case of these speeches, the speaker is arguing that some problem is getting worse, therefore more powerful language would be acceptable. Simply state that "Things are getting worse" and don't weaken your statement with phrases that communicate uncertainty.

"Malalai Joya speaking in Finland" by AfghanKabul.

Speakers should also beware of **hedges**, **tag questions**, and **qualifiers**. Examples of hedges would include, "I thought we should," "I sort of think," or "Maybe we should." Use more powerful statements such as "We should" or "I believe." In addition, speakers should avoid the use of tag questions, which are quick questions at the end of a statement that also communicate uncertainty. People who use tag questions might end a statement with "Don't you think?" or "Don't you agree?" rather than flatly stating what they believe because it can appear to audiences that you are seeking validation for your statements. Qualifiers such as "around" or "about" make your sentences less definitive, so generally avoid using them.

Interestingly, however, there are cases when using less powerful language may be useful. While a full discussion of these instances is out of the purview of this chapter, good speakers will recognize when they should use more or less powerful language. I tell my students that there are some cases when negotiation between two or more parties is the key and that in these instances using language that communicates complete certainty might impede fruitful negotiation because other parties may incorrectly perceive you as inflexible. On the other hand, in some cases you must "win" an argument or "beat" another speaker in

1. Gamble, T. K. & Gamble, M. W. (2003). *The gender communication connection.* New York: Houghton-Mifflin.

order to even get to the negotiation table, and in those cases, the use of more powerful language may be warranted. It bears repeating that better speakers know how to use language in response to specific contexts in order to be successful, hence thinking about what contexts require more or less powerful language is always a good idea.

> There may be times when we are powerless to prevent injustice, but there must never be a time when we fail to protest. – Elie Wiesel

Incorrect Grammar

While the use of sexist or heterosexist language may imply some negative qualities about you to your audience, the use of incorrect grammar in your speech will explicitly communicate negative attributes about you quite clearly. There are four primary means by which incorrect grammar tends to make its way into speeches, including **basic error**, **mispronunciations**, **regionalisms**, and **colloquialisms**.

Basic errors occur when people make simple mistakes in grammar because of carelessness or a lack of knowledge. If you are unsure about the grammatical structure of a sentence, ask someone.

> Although spoken English doesn't obey the rules of written language, a person who doesn't know the rules thoroughly is at a great disadvantage. – Marilyn vos Savant

Practicing your speech in front of others can help you catch mistakes. Grammatical errors can also happen when speakers aren't familiar enough with their speech. If you do not know your topic well and have not given yourself an adequate amount of time for practice, you may fumble some during your speech and use incorrect grammar that you normally wouldn't use. One of the most regular critiques made of President George W. Bush is that he regularly makes grammatical errors in public. In one case President Bush stated, "Rarely is the question asked: Is our children learning?" In another instance he stated, "I have a different vision of leadership. A leadership is someone who brings people together."[2] When President Bush makes these mistakes, many people take note and it gives his detractors ammunition to critique his ability to lead. Unlike President Bush, you do not have a team of public relations specialists ready to explain away your grammatical error so you should take great care to make sure that you're prepared to speak.

"Bush delivers his second Inaugural address" by Paul Morse. Public domain.

---

2. About.com (2011). Bushisms—U.S. President proves how difficult English really is! Retrieved from. http://esl.about.com/library/weekly/aa032301a.htm

> Apparently Arnold was inspired by President Bush, who proved you can be a successful politician in this country even if English is your second language. – Conan O'Brien

In addition, you must be sure that you are pronouncing words correctly. In one instance I had a student who began discussing the philosopher Plato, except she pronounced his name "Platt-o" instead of "Play-toe." I could see students glancing at each other and rolling their eyes in response to this mistake. Indeed, it was even difficult for me to pay attention after the mistake because it was such a blatant error. Making pronunciation mistakes, especially when you're pronouncing words that the general public deems ordinary, can seriously impede your credibility. It was likely difficult for students to take this speaker's remaining comments seriously after she'd made such a big mistake. If you're unsure about how to pronounce a word, check with someone else or with the dictionary to make sure you're pronouncing it correctly. In fact, many online dictionaries such as Merriam-Webster.com and Dictionary.com now include a function that allows you to hear how the word is pronounced. And if it's a word you're not used to saying, such as a technical or medical term, practice saying it *out loud* 10-20 times a day until you're comfortable with the word. Remember that our mouths are machines and that our tongues, teeth, cheeks, lips, etc. all work together to pronounce sounds. When faced with a word that our mouths are not yet "trained" to say, it is more likely that we'll mispronounce the word or stutter some on it during a speech. But if you practice saying the word out loud several times a day leading up to your speech, you're less likely to make a mistake and your confidence will be boosted instead of hurt in the midst of your speech.

> Remember: Y'all is singular. All y'all is plural. All y'all's is plural possessive. – Kinky Friedman

Some grammar problems occur because people use regionalisms when speaking, which may pose problems for people in the audience not familiar with the terms being used. **Regionalisms** are customary words or phrases used in different geographic regions. For example, growing up in Texas I used "y'all," while my students in Pennsylvania might use "youins" or "yins" to mean a group of people. In the South, many people use the phrase "Coke" to mean any soft drink (probably because Coco-Cola is headquartered in Atlanta), while in the Northeast a "Coke" might be called a "tonic" and in other regions it might be called a "pop" or "soda pop." You must be careful when using regional terms because your audience may not interpret your message correctly if they are not familiar with the regionalism you're using. Try to find terms that are broader in their use, perhaps using "you all" or "soft drink" instead of the regional terms you may be used to using in everyday conversations.

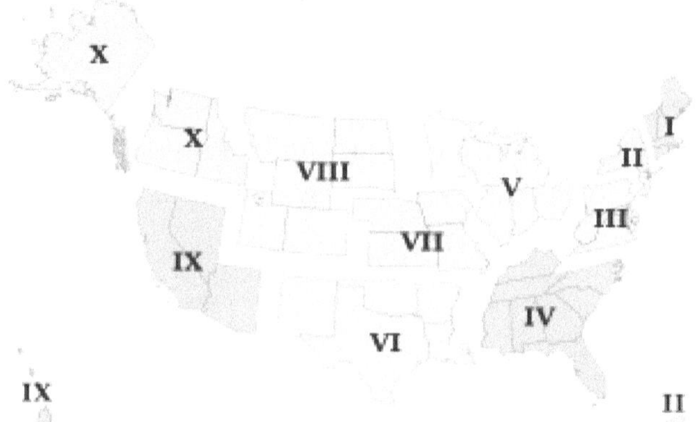

"Federal Standard Regions" by Belg4mit. Public domain.

Another grammar issue often linked to region is the use of colloquialisms. **Colloquialisms** are words or phrases used in informal speech but not typically used in formal speech. Using the word "crick" instead of "creek" is one example of a colloquialism, and in some areas "I'm getting ready to cook dinner" would be said, "I'm fixin' to make dinner." Colloquialisms can also be phrases that stem from particular regions. In some regions nice clothes are often referred to as your "Sunday best," and in some areas, when people are preparing to vacuum, they note that they are getting ready to "red up the place" (make it ready for visitors).

Like regionalisms, an audience understanding your use of colloquialisms depends on their familiarity with the language tendencies of a certain geographic area, so steering clear of their use can help you make sure that your message is understood by your audience. Another problem that regionalisms and colloquialisms have in common is that some audience members may consider their use a sign of lesser intellect because they are not considered proper grammar, so you also risk leaving a bad impression of yourself with audience members if you make these language choices for a formal presentation.

I personally think we developed language because of our deep need to complain. – Lily Tomlin

Other Language Choices to Consider

Clichés are phrases or expressions that, because of overuse, have lost their rhetorical power. Examples include sayings such as "The early bird gets the worm" or "Making a mountain out of a molehill." Phrases such as these were once powerful ways of communicating an idea, but because of overuse these phrases just don't have the impact that they once had. Using clichés in your speeches runs the risk of having two negative attributions being placed on you by audience members. First, audience members may feel that your use of a cliché communicates that you didn't take the speech seriously and/or were lazy in constructing it. Second, your audience members may perceive you as someone who is not terribly creative. Clichés area easy ways to communicate your message, but you might pay for that ease with negative feelings about you as a speaker from your audience. Try to avoid using clichés so that audiences are more likely to perceive you positively as a speaker.

Another consideration for speakers is whether or not to use **language central to the popular culture** of a time period. Whether we're talking about "groovy, man" from the 1970s or "like totally awesome" from the 1980s, or "word to your mutha" from the 1990s, the language central to the popular culture of any time period is generally something to be avoided in formal public speaking. Like slang or profanity, language stemming from popular culture can be limited in its appeal. Some audiences may not understand it, some audiences may negatively evaluate you for using language that is too informal, and other audiences will have negative preconceived notions about "the kind of people" that use such language (e.g., "hippies" in the 1970s), and they will most likely transfer those negative evaluations onto you.

Attributions

CC licensed content, Shared previously

- Chapter 10 Avoiding Language Pitfalls. **Authored by**: E. Michele Ramsey, Ph.D.. **Provided by**: Penn State Berks, Reading, PA. **Located at**: http://publicspeakingproject.org/psvirtualtext.html. **Project**: The Public Speaking Project. **License**: *CC BY-NC-ND: Attribution-NonCommercial-NoDerivatives*
- Malalai Joya speaking in Finland. **Authored by**: AfghanKabul. **Located at**: https://flic.kr/p/4avCsj. **License**: *CC BY: Attribution*

Public domain content

- USFederalRegions. **Authored by**: Belg4mit. **Located at**: http://commons.wikimedia.org/wiki/File:USFederalRegions.svg. **License**: *Public Domain: No Known Copyright*

- Bush delivers his second inaugural address. **Authored by**: Paul Morse. **Located at**: https://en.wikipedia.org/wiki/File:Bush_delivers_his_second_Inaugural_address.jpg. **License**: *Public Domain: No Known Copyright*

Conclusion, Review Questions, and Activities

This chapter has discussed a number of important aspects of language that good speakers should always consider. It is important for speakers to remember the power of language and to harness that power effectively, yet ethically. We've discussed the relationship between the language we use and the way we see the world, the importance of using language that is clear, vivid, stylized, ethical and that reflects well on you as the speaker.

The difference between choosing one word over another can be as significant as an audience member remembering your presentation or forgetting it and/or an audience turning against you and your ideas. Taking a few extra moments to add some

"Dilgo Khyentse Yangsi Rinpoche answers a young person's question…" by Wonderlane. CC-BY.

alliteration or to check for language that might offend others is time very well spent. The next time you have to write or speak about an issue, remember the importance of language and its impact on our lives—carefully consider what language will you use and how will those language choices make a difference in how your audiences defines and understands your topic.

If you talk to a man in a language he understands, that goes to his head. If you talk to him in his language, that goes to his heart. ~ Nelson Mandela

Review Questions

1. Explain the difference between communication and language.

2. Explain the relationship between language and the way that humans perceive their worlds.

3. Why should you use simple language in your speech?

4. The use of concrete and precise language in your speeches helps prevent what sorts of problems?

5. Give an example of a metaphor and explain how that metaphor functions to communicate a specific idea more clearly.

6. What is alliteration?

7. Why is personalized language important?

8. What are some examples of types of sexist language and what is the impact of those examples?

9. What are two problems associated with using exaggerated language in your speeches?

10. Explain the types of powerless language most commonly used.

11. Why shouldn't you use clichés in your speech?

12. Why is correct grammar important to good speech making?

Activities

1. Speakers should avoid the use of sexist language. Consider the sexist words and phrases listed below and think of as many replacement words as you can.

   - Bachelor's Degree
   - Bogeyman
   - Brotherhood
   - Businessman
   - Chairman
   - Forefather
   - Layman
   - Mailman
   - Manmade
   - Repairman
   - Salesman
   - Female Doctor

2. Using speeches from mlkonline.net or jfklibrary.org, choose any speech from the Reverend Dr. Martin Luther King, Jr., President John F. Kennedy, or Attorney General Robert F. Kennedy and isolate one paragraph that you believe exemplifies a careful and

effective use of language. Rewrite that paragraph as I did for my classes, using more common and less careful word choices. Compare the paragraphs to each other once you're done, noticing the difference your changes in language make.

3. Speakers should always remember that it's rarely helpful to use a long word when a short word will do and that clichés should be avoided in speeches. Look at these common clichés, reworded using language that obstructs rather than clarifies, and see if you can figure out which clichés have been rewritten.

   - A piece of pre-decimal currency conserved is coinage grossed.

   - The timely avian often acquires the extended soft-bodied invertebrate.

   - A utensil often used for writing is more prodigious than a certain long-edged weapon.

   - Let slumbering members of the canine variety remain in slumber

   - An animal of the avian variety resting on one's palm is more valuable than double that amount in one's appendage ?most often used for tactile feedback.

Attributions

CC licensed content, Shared previously

- Chapter 10 Conclusion, Review Questions, and Activities. **Authored by**: E. Michele Ramsey, Ph.D.. **Provided by**: Penn State Berks, Reading, PA. **Located at**: http://publicspeakingproject.org/psvirtualtext.html. **Project**: The Public Speaking Project. **License**: *CC BY-NC-ND: Attribution-NonCommercial-NoDerivatives*

- Dilgo Khyentse Yangsi Rinpoche answers a young person's question, monk and author Matthieu Ricard listening, Children's and Young People's Audience and Blessing, First Nations Longhouse, UBC, Vancouver BC, Lotus Speech Canada. **Authored by**: Wonderlane. **Located at**: https://flic.kr/p/8uoSqU. **License**: *CC BY: Attribution*

Glossary and References

Glossary

TERM	DEFINITION
Alliteration	The repetition of the initial sounds of words.
Antithesis	Rhetorical strategy that uses contrasting statements in order to make a rhetorical point.
Clichés	Phrases or expressions that, because of overuse, have lost their rhetorical power.
Colloquialisms	Words or phrases used in informal speech but not typically used in formal speech.
Communication	Attempts to reproduce what is in our minds in the minds of our audience.
Generic "he" or "man"	Language that uses words such as "he" or "mankind" to refer to the male and female population.
Hedges	Powerless phrases such as "I thought we should," "I sort of think," or "Maybe we should" that communicate uncertainty.
Heterosexist Language	Language that assumes the heterosexual orientation of a person or group of people.
Hyperbole	The use of moderate exaggeration for effect.
Jargon	The specialized language of a group or profession.
Language	The means by which we communicate—a system of symbols we use to form messages.
Man-linked Terms	Terms such as "fireman" or "policemen" that incorrectly identify a job as linked only to a male.
Metaphors	Comparisons made by speaking of one thing in terms of another.
Qualifiers	Powerless words such as "around" or "about" that make your sentences less definitive.
Regionalisms	Customary words or phrases used in different geographic regions.
Sexist Language	Language that unnecessarily identifies sex or linguistically erases females through the use of man- linked terms and/or the use of "he" or "man" as generics.
Similes	Comparisons made by speaking of one thing in terms of another using the word "like" or "as" to make the comparison.
Slang	Type of language that most people understand but that is not considered acceptable in formal or polite conversation.
Spotlighting	Language such as "male nurse" that suggests a person is deviating from the "normal" person who would do a particular job and implies that someone's sex is relevant to a particular job.
Tag Questions	Powerless language exemplified by ending statements with questions such as "Don't you think?" or "Don't you agree?"

References

About.com (2011). Bushisms—U.S. President proves how difficult English really is! Retrieved from. http://esl.about.com/library/weekly/aa032301a.htm

Gamble, T. K. & Gamble, M. W. (2003). *The gender communication connection*. New York: Houghton-Mifflin.

Time.com (1981, February 23). "Haigledygook and secretaryspeak." Retrieved from http://www.time.com/time/magazine/article/0,9171,949069,00.html

Hamilton, G. (2008). *Public speaking for college and career*, 8th Ed. New York: McGraw-Hill.

Jackson, J. (1984). 1984 Speech at the Democratic National Convention. San Francisco, CA: July 18. Found at http://www.americanrhetoric.com/speeches/jessejackson1984dnc.htm

King, M. L., Jr. (1963, August 28). I Have a Dream [Speech]. Washington, D.C. Retrieved from http://www.americanrhetoric.com/speeches/mlkihaveadream.htm

Peccei, J. (2003). *Language and age*. In L. Thomas et. al.,*Language, society, and power*, 2nd Ed. New York: Routledge.

Spender, D. (1990). *Man Made Language*. New York: Pandora.

Thomas, L., Wareing, S. Singh, I., Pecci, J. S., Thornborrow, J. & Jones, J. (2003). *Language, society, and power: An introduction*, 2nd Ed. New York: Routledge.

photo credits

p. 1 Rail Forum by Michigan Municipal League
http://www.flickr.com/photos/michigancommunities/5041931910/

p. 2 Rev. Martin Luther King Jr. by Dick DeMarcisco
http://commons.wikimedia.org/wiki/File:Martin_Luther_King_Jr_NYWTS_6.jpg

p. 3 Secretary of State Alexander Haig by University of Texas
http://commons.wikimedia.org/wiki/File:Al_Haig_speaks_to_press_1981.jpg

p. 4. LAMB Teal Wrap Sweater
http://www.bluefly.com/

p. 5 Goth people by Rama
http://commons.wikimedia.org/wiki/File:Goth_f222791.jpg

p. 6 Audience at Next conference by NEXT Berlin
http://www.flickr.com/photos/nextconference/4633552536/

p. 7 "Feminazi" coined by Rush Limbaugh, see
http://www.merriam-webster.com/dictionary/feminazi

p. 8 Italian Soldier by the Italian Army

http://commons.wikimedia.org/wiki/File:Italian_Soldier_Olypmic_Games_Turin_2006.jpg

p. 9 Married gay couple by John

http://commons.wikimedia.org/wiki/File:Married_Gay_Couple_John_and_Jamie.jpg

p. 10 Malalai Joya by AfghanKabul

http://www.flickr.com/photos/19712640@N05/2076699646/

p. 12 Dilgo Khyentse Yangsi Rinpoche by Wonderlane

http://www.flickr.com/photos/wonderlane/4915821372/

Attributions

CC licensed content, Shared previously

- Chapter 10 Glossary and References. **Authored by**: E. Michele Ramsey, Ph.D.. **Provided by**: Penn State Berks, Reading, PA. **Located at**: http://publicspeakingproject.org/psvirtualtext.html. **Project**: The Public Speaking Project. **License**: *CC BY-NC-ND: Attribution-NonCommercial-NoDerivatives*

Chapter 14: Ethics in Public Speaking

Objectives and Introduction

Ethics in Public Speaking

By Alyssa Millner, Ph.D., King College, Knoxville, TN
& Rachel D. Price, M.A., University of Kentucky, Lexington, KY

"Woman speaking about ending war" by Kelly Finnamore. CC-BY.

Learning Objectives

After reading this chapter, you should be able to:

- Define ethics and explain why ethics are important in public speaking.
- Differentiate between morality and ethical dilemma.
- Identify the three types of plagiarism and understand how to avoid them.
- Explain how to cite sources in written and oral speech materials.
- Develop responsible language use by avoiding hate language and using inclusive language.

- Use a speech platform to promote diversity, raise social awareness, and understand free speech.
- Employ ethical listening by readying both mind and body to avoid distractions.
- Develop patterns of ethical feedback through praise and constructive criticism.
- Apply ethical communication skills to public speaking situations.
- Apply module concepts in final questions and activities.

Maggie is helping her older sister plan for her wedding. She loves event planning and decides to give an informative speech to her classmates on "Selecting a Florist." She knows all the other women in class will adore the topic and her visual aids (an assortment of flowers and a rose for everyone to take home). As Maggie begins the speech, she creates a listener relevance link that relates mostly to the women in the class. In fact, most of the speech is directed at female listeners.

As she moves through the main points of her speech, Maggie realizes that she is running out of time and only has 1 minute left or the instructor will penalize her. During her third main point, she skips over some citations but shares the statistics of saving money on a trustworthy florist. The listeners don't notice that Maggie neglected to provide oral source citations, so she feels confident of the "expertise" she has derived. After Maggie finishes her final main point, she concludes and reminds the ladies to find her later if they have any questions about prices of quality of florists in the area.

"Wedding Bouquet" **by Ling Manh Nguyen Tran.**

When preparing for this speech, Maggie attempted an audience analysis. However, she failed to adequately involve all audience members by choosing a traditionally female topic and tailoring the language to females in the class. A second unethical decision made by Maggie was to omit oral citations, thereby failing to give credit to those who deserved it. Maggie's practices in her speech are just a few ways in which unethical public speaking can occur. The evolution of ethics is central to public speaking because it is through communication that our ideas about right and wrong or good and bad are formed.

> Ethics is knowing the difference between what you have a right to do and what is right to do. – Potter Stewart

Issues related to honesty, integrity, and morality are present in our everyday lives. We recognize the need for ethical communication when leaders make deceitful statements. For instance, we all remember President Clinton's famous quote: "I did not have sexual relations with that woman." We recognize a crafty speaker when we hear one. Ethics, however, aren't just important for presidents and other public figures. Ethical concerns arise in a variety of public speaking contexts, as this chapter portrays.

The National Communication Association (NCA) suggests that communicators should be committed to following principles of ethical communication. The NCA Credo of Ethical Communication claims that "ethical communication is fundamental to responsible thinking, decision making, and the development of relationships and communities within and across contexts, cultures, channels, and media."[1] Ethical communication also yields positive outcomes, such as truthfulness, respect, and accuracy of information. You can see that ethics is a very important part of the communication process. Likewise, it is an important part of the public speaking process.

Unethical communication can lead to poor decision-making or a lack of respect for self and others, and threaten the well-being of individuals and society. Early scholars of ethical communication, most notably Nielsen[2] and Johannesen[3] began to incorporate a discussion of ethics in all aspects of communication. These forerunners began exploring ethics in the area of public speaking. Communication experts agree that ethical communication is an important responsibility of the speaker.

Attributions

CC licensed content, Shared previously

- Chapter 3 Objectives, Outline, and Introduction. **Authored by**: Alyssa Millner and Rachel Price. **Provided by**: King College and University of Kentucky. **Located at**: http://publicspeakingproject.org/psvirtualtext.html. **Project**: Public Speaking Project. **License**: *CC BY-NC-ND: Attribution-NonCommercial-NoDerivatives*
- Wedding Bouquet. **Authored by**: Ling Manh Nguyen Tran. **Located at**: https://www.flickr.com/photos/lingdezign/3738050660/. **License**: *CC BY: Attribution*

1. National Communication Association. (1999). NCA credo for ethical communication. Retrieved from http://www.natcom.org/uploaded%20Files/About_NCA/Leadership_and_Governance/Public_Policy_Platform/PDF-PolicyPlatformNCA_Credo_for_Ethical_Communication.pdf
2. Nielsen, T. R. (1966). *Ethics of speech communication*. Indianapolis, IN: Bobbs Merrill.
3. Johannesen, R. L. (1967). *Ethics and persuasion: Selected readings*. New York: Random House.

Defining Ethics

> But I want to say one thing to the American people. I want you to listen to me. I'm going to say this again: **I did not have sexual relations with that woman**, Miss Lewinsky. I never told anybody to lie, not a single time; never. These allegations are false. And I need to go back to work for the American people. Thank you. – President Bill Clinton, 1998

Some of the early leaders in philosophy—Aristotle, Socrates, and Plato—spoke extensively about morality and ethical principles. Aristotle is frequently cited as a central figure in the development of ethics as we discuss them today in the communication discipline. Aristotle claimed that a person who had ethos, or credibility, was not only able to convey good sense and good will, but also good morals. Great philosophers have debated the merits of living well, doing good, and even communicating skillfully. Smitter describes early Greeks and Romans as teachers of public speaking; these philosophers argued that public communication is "a means of civic engagement" and ethics are "a matter of virtue." Ethics and ethical communication are not only an important part of our lives and our decision-making but also are crucial to the public speaking process. In 2011, when Representative Anthony Weiner faced accusations of sending sexually explicit photographs to a woman, he vehemently denied any wrongdoing and claimed that he had been set up. Shortly after, his denial turned to an admission and apology. This scandal called into question the ethics of Rep. Weiner, yet it was also his lack of ethical communication that exacerbated the situation.

> Moral excellence comes about as a result of habit. We become just by doing just acts, temperate by doing temperate acts, brave by doing brave acts. – Aristotle

Ethics and Ethical Standards

Morality is the process of discerning between right and wrong. Ethics involves making decisions about right and wrong within a dilemma. For example, you might claim that stealing is morally wrong. But is stealing morally wrong when a mother steals a loaf of bread to feed her four starving children? It's this scenario that requires an understanding of ethics. In a moral dilemma, we apply ethics to make choices about what is good or bad, right or wrong. Sometimes, ethical dilemmas are simple. Other times, they require complex choices, such as the decision to report your immediate boss for misrepresenting expenses or the decision to move your grandmother into a retirement community. These scenarios are more complex than simple choices between right and wrong. Instead, these examples are ethical dilemmas because two "right" choices are pitted against one another. It's good to report an unethical supervisor, but it's also good to keep your job. It's good that your grandmother feels independent, but it's also positive for her to receive extra assistance as her health deteriorates.

As public speakers, we make ethical choices when preparing and delivering a speech. We can easily be faced with a moral dilemma over what information to provide or how to accurately represent that information. Knowing the speaking setting, the audience, and our knowledge of the topic, we are able to confront ethical dilemmas with a strong moral compass. This process is made easier by our ethical standards. Ethical standards, or moral principles, are the set of rules we abide by that make us "good" people and help us choose right from wrong. The virtuous standards to which we adhere influence our ethical understanding. For instance, followers of Buddha believe that communication should be careful—good communication should exhibit restraint, responsibility, and kindness.[1]

> If you want others to be happy, practice compassion. If you want to be happy, practice compassion.
> – Dalai Lama

This stance informs one's ethical standards. In fact, Merrill (2009) explains that the holy Dalai Lama, the Buddhist spiritual leader, believes compassion is even more essential than truth. Therefore, it is justifiable to be untruthful when the deception is part of the process of caring for another. This example illustrates how one's belief system influences his or her ethical standards. These ethical standards are the guidelines we use to interpret rightness and wrongness in life, in relationships, and in public speaking. Wallace claims that "ethical standards of communication should place emphasis upon the means used to secure the end, rather than upon achieving the end itself."[2] This argument suggests that speakers must consider moral standards through every step of the speech process.

"Emerald Buddha" by WPPilot. CC-BY-SA.

"Questions of right and wrong arise whenever people communicate."[3] Once we have identified our ethical standards, we can apply these to make sure that we are communicating ethically. Ethical communication is an exchange of responsible and trustworthy messages determined by our moral principles. Ethical communication can be enacted in written, oral, and non-verbal communication. In public speaking, we use ethical standards to determine what and how to exchange messages with our audience. As you read further in this chapter, you will begin to understand the guidelines for how ethical communication should occur in the public speaking process.

Attributions

CC licensed content, Shared previously

- Chapter 3 Defining Ethics. **Authored by**: Alyssa Millner and Rachel Price. **Provided by**: King College and University of Kentucky. **Located at**: http://publicspeakingproject.org/psvirtualtext.html. **Project**: Public Speaking Project. **License**: *CC BY-NC-ND: Attribution-NonCommercial-NoDerivatives*

1. Merrill, J. C. (2009). Tenzin Gyatso, the Dalai Lama: Universal compassion. In C. Christians & J. Merrill (Eds.), *Ethical communication* (pp. 11–17). Columbia, MO: University of Missouri Press.
2. Wallace, K. (1955). An ethical basis of communication. *Speech Teacher, 4,* 1–9.
3. National Communication Association. (1999). NCA credo for ethical communication. Retrieved from http://www.natcom.org/uploadedFiles/About_NCA/Leadership_and_Governance/Public_Policy_Platform/PDF-PolicyPlatformNCA_Credo_for_Ethical_Communication.pdf

Ethical Speaking

*In January, 2012, an Australian politician, Anthony Albanese, presented a speech to the National Press Club. Several people criticized this speech, saying that he stole lines from Michael Douglas's character (the U.S. President) in the movie **The American President**. Several specific lines from Albanese's speech did seem to mirror Douglas's monologue, with only the names changed. The Liberal Party federal director, Brian Loughnane, claimed that this shows Albanese is "unoriginal and devoid of ideas." Others stated that he should be embarrassed and should apologize to the Parliament.[1]*

What do you think about Albanese's speech? Was this a simple mishap? A funny prank? Something more serious? What do you think this says about Albanese's character? His reputation as a politician? Assessing your attitudes and values toward this situation is the same as considering how ethics play a role in public speaking.

Ethical public speaking is not a one-time event. It does not just occur when you stand to give a 5-minute presentation to your classmates or co-workers. Ethical public speaking is a process. This process begins when you begin brainstorming the topic of your speech. Every time you plan to speak to an audience—whether it is at a formal speaking event or an impromptu pitch at your workplace—you have ethical responsibilities to fulfill. The two most important aspects in ethical communication include your ability to remain honest while avoiding plagiarism and to set and meet responsible speech goals.

> Integrity is telling myself the truth. And honesty is telling the truth to other people. – Spencer Johnson

Be Honest and Avoid Plagiarism

Credible public speakers are open and honest with their audiences. Honesty includes telling your audience why you're speaking (thesis statement) and what you'll address throughout your speech (preview). For instance, one example of dishonest speech is when a vacation destination offers "complimentary tours and sessions" which are really opportunities for a sales person to pitch a timeshare to unsuspecting tourists. In addition to being clear about the speech goal, honest speakers are clear with audience members when providing supporting information.

1. ABC News. (2012, January 25). Albanese accused of plagiarising Hollywood speech. Retrieved from http://www.abc.net.au/news/2012-01-25/albanese-accused-ofplagiarising-speech/3793486

One example of dishonest public communication occurs in the music industry where many cases of illegal melody lifting exist. For example, a famous Beach Boys song titled *Surfin' USA* is actually a note-for-note rendition of a 1958 Chuck Berry song. Though it may be common, the practice of not properly crediting an author for his or her work is unethical. Other examples of deceitful communication include political speeches that intentionally mislead the public. For instance, a former White House press aide, Scott McClellan, claims that President Bush misled the American people about reasons for the Iraqi war. McClellan claims that the President had manipulated sources in order to gain support for the war. Such claims can be damaging to one's reputation. Thus, responsible public speakers must actively avoid plagiarism and remain committed to honesty and integrity at all costs.

Mimi & Eunice, "Thief" by Nina Paley. CC-BY-SA.

Identify Your Sources

The first step of ethical speech preparation is to take notes as you research your speech topic. Careful notes will help you remember where you learned your information. Recalling your sources is important because it enables speaker honesty. Passing off another's work as your own or neglecting to cite the source for your information is considered **plagiarism**. This unethical act can result in several consequences, ranging from a loss in credibility to academic expulsion or job loss. Even with these potential consequences, plagiarism is unfortunately common. In a national survey, 87 percent of students claimed that their peers plagiarized from the Internet at least some of the time.[2] This statistic does not take into account whether or not the plagiarism was intentional, occurring when the writer or speaker knowingly presented information as his or her own; or unintentional, occurring when careless citing leads to information being uncredited or miscredited. However, it is important to note that being unaware of how to credit sources should not be an excuse for unintentional plagiarism. In other words, speakers are held accountable for intentional and unintentional plagiarism. The remainder of this section discusses how to ensure proper credit is given when preparing and presenting a speech.

A liar should have a good memory. – Quintilian

There are three distinct types of plagiarism—global, patchwork, and incremental plagiarism.[3] **Global plagiarism**, the most obvious form of plagiarism, transpires when a speaker presents a speech that is not his or her own work. For example, if a student finds a speech on the Internet or borrows a former speech from

2. Cruikshank, B. (2004). Plagiarism: It's Alive! *Texas Library Journal, 80*(4), 132–136.
3. Lucas, S. E. (2001). *The art of public speaking* (7th ed.). New York: McGraw-Hill.

a roommate and recites that speech verbatim, global plagiarism has occurred. Global plagiarism is the most obvious type of theft. However, other forms of plagiarism are less obvious but still represent dishonest public speaking.

If you tell the truth, you don't have to remember anything. – Mark Twain

Sometimes a student neglects to cite a source simply because she or he forgot where the idea was first learned. Shi explains that many students struggle with plagiarism because they've reviewed multiple texts and changed wording so that ideas eventually *feel* like their own. Students engage in "'patchwriting' by copying from a source text and then deleting or changing a few words and altering the sentence structures."[4] **Patchwork plagiarism** is plagiarism that occurs when one "patches" together bits and pieces from one or more sources and represents the end result as his or her own. Michael O'Neill also coined the term "paraplaging"[5] to explain how an author simply uses partial text of sources with partial original writing. An example of patchwork plagiarism is if you create a speech by pasting together parts of another speech or author's work. Read the following hypothetical scenario to get a better understanding of subtle plagiarism.

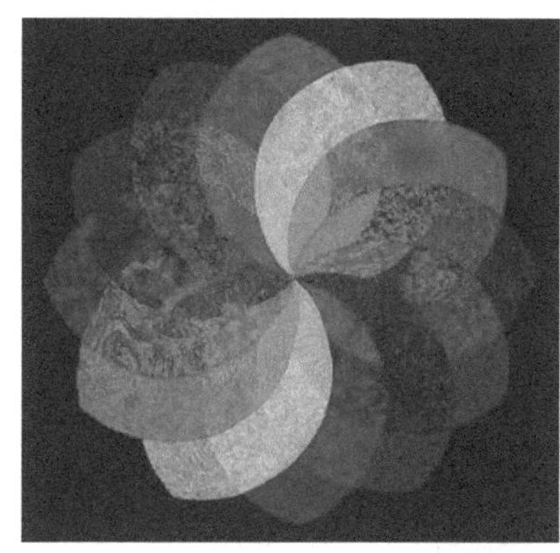

"Rainbow Dahlia quilt" by Holice E. Turnbow. CC-BY-SA.

> *Three months ago, Carley was talking to her coworkers about expanding their company's client base. Carley reported some of the ideas she'd been pondering with Stephen and Juan. The three employees shared ideas and provided constructive criticism in order to perfect each notion, and then mentioned they'd revisit the conversation over lunch sometime soon. A week later, Carley shared one of her ideas during the company's Monday morning staff meeting. Carley came up with the idea, but Stephen and Juan helped her think through some of the logistics of bringing in more clients. Her peers' input was key to making Carley's client-building idea work. When Carley pitched her idea at the company staff meeting, she didn't mention Stephen or Juan. She shared her idea with senior management and then waited for feedback.*

Did Carley behave unethically? Some would say: "No!" since she shared her own idea. Did Carley speak honestly? Perhaps not because she didn't account for how her idea took shape—*with* the help of Stephen and Juan. This scenario is an example of how complicated honesty becomes when speaking to an audience.

The third type of plagiarism is **incremental plagiarism,** or when most of the speech is the speaker's original work, but quotes or other information have been used without being cited. Incremental plagiarism can occur if, for example, you provide a statistic to support your claim, but do not provide the source for that statistic. Another example would be if a student included a direct quote from former president Ronald Reagan without letting the audience know that those were Reagan's exact words. Understanding the different types of plagiarism is the first step in ensuring that you prepare an honest speech.

4. Shi, L. (2010). Textual appropriation and citing behaviors of university undergraduates. Applied Linguistics, 31(1), 1–24.
5. O'Neill, M. T. (1980). Plagiarism: Writing Responsibly. *Business Communication Quarterly, 43*, 34–36.

<table>
<tr><td colspan="2" align="center">Table 3.1: Purdue OWL APA Guide for Citing Sources[6]</td></tr>
<tr><td align="center">Cite</td><td align="center">Don't Cite</td></tr>
<tr><td>Words or ideas presented in a magazine, book, newspaper, song, TV program, movie, Web page, computer program, letter, advertisement, or any other medium.</td><td>Writing your own lived experiences, your own observations and insights, your own thoughts, and your own conclusions about a subject.</td></tr>
<tr><td>Information you gain through interviewing or conversing with another person, face to face, over the phone, or in writing.</td><td>When you are writing up your own results obtained through lab or field experiments.</td></tr>
<tr><td>When you copy the exact words or a unique phrase.</td><td>When you use your own artwork, digital photographs, video, audio, etc.</td></tr>
<tr><td>When you reprint any diagrams, illustrations, charts, pictures, or other visual materials.</td><td>When you are using common knowledge—things like folklore, common sense observations, myths, urban legends, and historical events (but not historical documents).</td></tr>
<tr><td>When you reuse or repost any electronically available media, including images, audio, video, or other media.</td><td>When you are using generally accepted facts, e.g. pollution is bad for the environment.</td></tr>
</table>

Decide When to Cite

When speaking publicly you must orally cite all information that isn't general knowledge. For example, if your speech claims that the sun is a star, you do not have to cite that information since it's general knowledge. If your speech claims that the sun's temperature is 15.6 million Kelvin,[7] then you should cite that source aloud. Ethical speakers are not required to cite commonly known information (e.g., skin is the largest human organ; Barack Obama was elected President of the U.S. in 2008). However, any information that isn't general knowledge must be orally cited during a speech. The same is true in the text of a speech outline: cite all non-general information.

The OWL, an online writing lab at Purdue University, provides an excellent guide for when you need to cite information (see Table 3.1). Understanding when to include source material is the first step in being able to ethically cite sources. The next step in this process is to determine how to appropriately cite sources orally and in written materials.

Cite Sources Properly

You've learned the importance of citing sources. Now that you know why written and oral citations are important to the ethical process of public speaking, let's focus on *how* to cite supporting speech material. Studies show that oftentimes students do not cite a source because they're unsure of how or when to cite a reference. Shi's study describes some typical responses for why students did not cite sources, such as "I couldn't remember where I learned the information," or "I had already cited that author and didn't want the audience to think all of my information was from some outside source." Though these rationales are understandable, they are not ethical.

Understand Paraphrasing and Direct Quotations

Next, it is important to understand the process for paraphrasing and directly quoting sources in order to support your speech claims. First, what is the difference between paraphrasing and directly quoting a source? If you research and learn information from a source—the Centers for Disease Control and Prevention (CDC),

6. Stolley, K., & Brizee, A. (2011, August 24). Avoiding plagiarism. Retrieved from https://owl.english.purdue.edu/owl/resource/589/01/

7. Nine Planets. (2011). The Sun. Retrieved from http://nineplanets.org/sol.html

for instance— and then share that information in your *own* words; you don't use quotation marks; but you do credit the CDC as your source. This is known as a **paraphrase**—a sentence or string of sentences that shares learned information in your own words. A **direct quote** is any sentence or string of sentences that conveys an author's idea word-for-word. According to the APA (American Psychological Association), when writing speech content, you must include quotation marks around an author's work when you use his or her keywords, phrases, or sentences. This would be relevant for a speech outline, a handout, or a visual aid. It is also important to specify a direct quote when you are orally citing during your speech. This indicates to the audience that you are using the original author's exact words. While it is acceptable to use the phrases "begin quote" and "end quote" to indicate this to your audience, such phrases can be distracting to the audience. One way to clearly and concisely indicate a direct quote is to take a purposeful pause right before and after the quoted material. This differentiates between your words and the source material's words. See Table 3.2 for examples of how to paraphrase and directly quote an author, both in written speech materials and for an oral citation.

Table 3.2: Written and Oral Source Citations[89]		
	Written Citations	**Oral Citations**
Original Text	You cannot do a nonstop flight to the second half of life by reading lots of books about it, including this one. Grace must and will edge you forward.	Your best defense against influenza—and its possible complications—is to receive an annual vaccination. In fact, CDC recommends that everyone 6 months and older get an annual flu vaccination.
Paraphrase for Written Speech Materials	It is through the practice of showing grace that we grow and develop as individuals (Rohr, 2011).	The CDC (2008) suggests that people get a vaccination at least once a year to avoid the flu.
Direct Quote for Written Speech Materials	According to Rohr (2011), "Grace must and will edge you forward" (p. 2).	There is something you can do to avoid the flu. The CDC states that, "Your best defense against influenza—and its possible complications—is to receive an annual vaccination" (para. 6).
Oral Citation for Paraphrase	In Rohr's 2011 book, *Falling upward: A spirituality for the halves of life*, he discussed how we show grace to others which allows us to grow and develop as individuals.	According to the Centers for Disease Control and Prevention website (2008), people should get a preventative vaccination at least once a year to avoid the flu.
Oral Citation for Direct Quote	Rohr (2011), in his book *Falling upward: A spirituality for the two halves of life*, stated that [pause] "Grace must and will edge you forward" [pause].	On their website, the Centers for Disease Control and Prevention (2008) states that, [pause] "your best defense against influenza—and its possible complications—is to receive an annual vaccination" [pause].

Develop Accurate Citations

Ethical speakers share source information with the audience. On written materials, such as handouts or speech outlines, citations are handled much like they would be in any essay. In addition to written citations, oral citations provide source information to audience members who may not see your written speech. In all citations, enough information should be given so that the audience can easily find the source.

You may choose to briefly describe the author before citing him or her to lend credibility to your supporting information. Writing style guidebooks, such as APA or MLA (Modern Language Association), teach that a source's credentials are not necessary in the text of your paper. We can interpret that the same is true for providing oral citations in a speech–the author's occupation, the source website, or the journal name are

8. Rohr, R. (2011). *Falling upward: A spirituality for the two halves of life.* San Francisco, CA: JosseyBass.
9. Centers for Disease Control and Prevention. (2012). Are you at high risk for serious illness from flu? Retrieved from http://www.cdc.gov/Features/FluHighRisk/

not required but may be helpful verbal cues to explain the legitimacy of your chosen source. You should provide enough information so that an audience member can locate the source. For instance, it might be useful to describe the doctor as a leading pediatrician—after which you would state the doctor's last name, year of publication, and the quote or paraphrase. To orally paraphrase a Langer quote (see example poster in Figure 3.1), you might say to your audience:

> *I really agree with Langer (1989), who wrote in her book Mindfulness, that our world is constructed from the categories we build in our mind. I find that I interpret the world based on my initial understanding of things and have to mindfully force myself to question the categories and biases I've formally created in my head.*

Figure 3.1: Sample Poster with Key Quote[10]

[Poster Title] "We experience the world by creating categories and making distinctions among them" (Langer, 1989, p. 11).	
[Main Point 1 Content]	[Main Point 2 Content]
Image	

Note, the Langer paraphrase provides the author's last name, year of publication, and the title of the book should an audience member want to find the orally cited source.

Ethical speakers provide written, oral, *and* visual citations. Visual aids, discussed in Chapter 13, include posters, objects, models, PowerPoints, and handouts. Visual aids are used to enhance your speech message. Visual aids, just like speech content, must be displayed ethically for the audience. In other words, if you use a poster to display a famous quote, then you should cite the author on your poster (see Figure 3.1). Similarly, you should cite sources on your PowerPoint *throughout the presentation*. It is not sufficient to include a "Sources" or "References" slide at the end of your PowerPoint because that does not accurately link each author to his or her work. Instead, ethical presenters provide an author reference on the slide in which the cited content is shown (see Figure 3.2).

Speakers should also carefully select and correctly cite images displayed in their visual aid. Images should be relevant to the keywords used on your PowerPoint slide. In other words, captions are not necessary because the image can stand alone; images you display should obviously correlate with your speech content (a caption is typically used because the picture *needs* explanation). In other words, the presence of a caption typically means your image does not directly correspond with the verbal speech material. Images should support, not distract, from the verbal or visual message. Hence, there is no need for blinking, rotating, or otherwise distracting visual aids.[11] Images should be simple and relevant. All pictures should be cited, unless the presenter uses a personal, clipart, or purchased stock image. To cite an image, simply include the credit (or web link) to that picture; note, however, the font size of the link should be reduced so that it is visible to the audience without distracting from the content in your visual aid. Seeing an image link should not be distracting to audience members.

---

10. **Langer, E. J. (1989).** *Mindfulness.* **Cambridge, MA: Da Capo Press.**
11. Danoff-Burg, J. (2002). PowerPoint writing guide. Retrieved from http://eices.columbia.edu/education-training/see-u/dr/ppt_writing.html

It's also important to understand how copyright law might affect what and how you include information in your speech and on your visual aid. The fair use provision allows for copyrighted information to be shared if it is used for educational benefits, news reporting, research, and in other situations. Nolo explains, "In its most general sense, a fair use is any copying of copyrighted material done for a limited and 'transformative' purpose, such as to comment upon, criticize, or parody a copyrighted work. Such uses can be done without permission from the copyright owner."[12] In order to determine if the use of content falls under the fair use provision, there are four factors to consider:

"Question copyright" by Ttog~commonswiki. CC-BY-SA.

1. How will this be used?

2. What is to be used?

3. How much will be used?

4. What effect does this have?[13]

You can find more about these four factors at the U.S. Copyright website.

Ethical citing includes crediting authors in the text of your written speech materials, acknowledging authors aloud during your speech, and citing images and sources on your visual aid. However, ethics in public speaking encompass more than crediting source material. It's also necessary to strive for responsible speech goals.

> Ethics and equity and the principles of justice do not change with the calendar. – David Herbert Lawrence

Set Responsible Speech Goals

Jensen coined the term "rightsabilities" to explain how a communicator must balance tensions between speaker rights and responsibility to others. Ensuring that you have responsible speech goals is one way to achieve ethical communication in public speaking. There are several speech goals that support this mission. This section will focus on five goals: 1) promote diversity, 2) use inclusive language, 3) avoid hate speech, 4) raise social awareness, and 5) employ respectful free speech.

---

12. Nolo. (2010). What is fair use? Copyright and fair use, Stanford University Libraries. Retrieved from http://fairuse.stanford.edu/Copyright_and_Fair_Use_Overview/chapter9/9-a.html
13. Harper, G. K. (2007). Copyright Crash Course. Retrieved from http://copyright.lib.utexas.edu/copypol2.html

Promote Diversity

One important responsibility speakers have is fostering **diversity,** or an appreciation for differences among individuals and groups. Diversity in public speaking is important when considering both your audience and your speech content. Promoting diversity allows audience members who may be different from the speaker to feel included and can present a perspective to which audience members had not previously been exposed. Speakers may choose a speech topic that introduces a multicultural issue to the audience or can promote diversity by choosing language and visual aids that relate to and support listeners of different backgrounds. Because of the diversity present in our lives, it is necessary to consider how speakers can promote diversity.

"U.S. Air Force" by Tech. Sgt. Keith Brown. Public domain.

One simple way of promoting diversity is to use both sexes in your hypothetical examples and to include co-cultural groups when creating a hypothetical situation. For example, you can use names that represent both sexes and that also stem from different cultural backgrounds. In the story about Carley and her co-workers, her co-workers were deliberately given male names so that both sexes were represented. Ethical speakers also encourage diversity in races, socioeconomic status, and other demographics. These choices promote diversity. In addition, ethical speakers can strive to break stereotypes. For instance, if you're telling a hypothetical story about a top surgeon in the nation, why not make the specialized surgeon a female from a rural area? Or make the hypothetical secretary a man named Frank? You could also include a picture in your visual aid of the female surgeon or the male secretary at work. Ethical speakers should not assume that a nurse is female or that a firefighter is male. Sexist language can alienate your audience from your discussion.[14]

Another way that sexist language occurs in speeches is when certain statements or ideas are directed at a particular sex. For example, the "Selecting a Florist" speech described at the beginning of this chapter may be considered sexist by many audience members. Another example is the following statement, which implies only males might be interested in learning how to fix a car: "I think that fixing a car is one of the most important things you can learn how to do. Am I right, guys?" Promoting diversity is related to using inclusive language, discussed in the following sections.

> Excellence is the best deterrent to racism or sexism. – Oprah Winfrey

Use Inclusive Language

Avoiding sexist language is one way to use inclusive language. Another important way for speakers to develop responsible language is to use inclusionary pronouns and phrases. For example, novice speakers

14. Driscoll, D. L., & Brizee, A. (2010, July 13). Stereotypes and biased language. Retrieved from https://owl.english.purdue.edu/owl/resource/608/05

might tell their audience: "One way for you to get involved in the city's *Clean Community Program* is to pick up trash on your street once a month." Instead, an effective public speaker could exclaim: "One way for all of us to get involved in our local communities is by picking up trash on a regular basis." This latter statement is an example of **"we" language**—pronouns and phrases that unite the speaker to the audience. "We" language (instead of "I" or "You" language) is a simple way to build a connection between the speaker, speech content, and audience. This is especially important during a persuasive speech as "we" language establishes trust, rapport, and goodwill between the speaker and the audience. Take, for example, the following listener relevance statements in a persuasive speech about volunteering:

> ***"You" language:*** *You may say that you're too busy to volunteer, but I don't agree. I'm here to tell you that you should be volunteering in your community.*

> ***"We" language:*** *As college students, we all get busy in our daily lives and sometimes helpful acts such as volunteering aren't priorities in our schedules. Let's explore how we can be more active volunteers in our community.*

In this exchange, the "you" language sets the speaker apart from the audience and could make listeners defensive about their time and lack of volunteering. On the other hand, the "we" language connects the speaker to the audience and lets the audience know that the speaker understands and has some ideas for how to fix the problem. This promotes a feeling of inclusiveness, one of the responsible speech goals.

Avoid Hate Speech

Another key aspect of ethical speaking is to develop an awareness of spoken words and the power of words. The NCA Credo of Ethical Communication highlights the importance of this awareness: "We condemn communication that degrades individuals and humanity through distortion, intimidation, coercion, and violence, and through the expression of intolerance and hatred."[15] Words can be powerful—both in helping you achieve your speech goal and in affecting your audience in significant ways. It is essential that public speakers refrain from hate or sexist language. Hate speech, according to Verderber, Sellnow, and Verderber, "is the use of words and phrases not only to demean another person or group but also to express hatred and prejudice."[16] **Hate language** isolates a particular person or group in a derogatory manner. Michael Richards, famous for the role of Cosmo Kramer on *Seinfeld*, came under fire for his hate speech during a comedy routine in 2006. Richards used several racial epithets and directed his hate language towards African-Americans and Mexicans.[17] Richards apologized for his outbursts, but the damage to his reputation and career was irrevocable. Likewise, using hate speech in any public speaking situation can alienate your audience and take away your credibility, leading to more serious implications for your grade, your job, or other serious outcomes. It is your responsibility as the speaker to be aware of sensitive material and be able to navigate language choices to avoid offending your audience.

No matter what people tell you, words and ideas can change the world. – Robin Williams

15. National Communication Association. (1999). NCA credo for ethical communication. Retrieved from http://www.natcom.org/uploadedFiles/About_NCA/Leadership_and_Governance/Public_Policy_Platform/PDF-PolicyPlatformNCA_Credo_for_Ethical_Communication.pdf

16. Verderber, R. F., Sellnow, D. D., & Verderber, K. S. (2012). *The challenge of effective speaking* (15th ed.). Boston, MA: Wadsworth Cengage Learning.

17. Farhi, P. (2006, November 21). 'Seinfeld' comic Richards apologizes for racial rant. The Washington Post. Retrieved from http://www.washingtonpost.com/wp-dyn/content/article/2006/

Raise Social Awareness

Speakers should consider it their ethical responsibility to educate listeners by introducing ideas of racial, gender, or cultural diversity, but also by raising **social awareness**, or the recognition of important issues that affect societies. Raising social awareness is a task for ethical speakers because educating peers on important causes empowers others to make a positive change in the world. Many times when you present a speech, you have the opportunity to raise awareness about growing social issues. For example, if you're asked to present an informative speech to your classmates, you could tell them about your school's athletic tradition*or* you could discuss *Peace One Day*—a campaign that promotes a single day of worldwide cease-fire, allowing crucial food and medicine supplies to be shipped into warzone areas.[18] If your assignment is to present a persuasive speech, you could look at the assignment as an opportunity to convince your class-mates to (a) stop texting while they drive, (b) participate in a program that supports US troops by writing personal letters to deployed soldiers or (c) buy a pair of TOMS (tomsshoes.com) and find other ways to provide basic needs to impoverished families around the world. Of course, those are just a few ideas for how an informative or persuasive speech can be used to raise awareness about current social issues. It is your responsibility, as a person and speaker, to share information that provides knowledge or activates your audience toward the common good.[19]

One way to be successful in attaining your speech goal while also remaining ethical is to consider your audience's moral base. Moon identifies a principle that allows the speaker to justify his or her perspective by finding common moral ground with the audience.[20] This illustrates to the audience that you have goodwill but allows you to still use your moral base as a guide for responsible speech use. For example, even though you are a vegetarian and believe that killing animals for food is murder, you know that the majority of your audience does not feel the same way. Rather than focusing on this argument, you decide to use Moon's principle and focus on animal cruelty. By highlighting the inhumane ways that animals are raised for food, you appeal to the audience's moral frame that abusing animals is wrong—something that you and your audience can both agree upon.

"Raising John T. Williams Memorial Totem Pole" by Joe Mabel. CC-BY-SA.

If we lose love and self-respect for each other, this is how we finally die. – Maya Angelou

Employ Respectful Free Speech

We live in a nation that values freedom of speech. Of course, due to the First Amendment, you have the right and ability to voice your opinions and values to an audience. However, that freedom of speech must be balanced with your responsibility as a speaker to respect your audience. Offending or degrading the val-

18. Peace One Day. (n.d.). Introduction. Retrieved from http://www.peaceoneday.org/en/about/Introduction
19. Mill, J.S. (1987). Utilitarianism. In A. Ryan (Ed.), *Utilitarianism and other essays* (pp. 272–338). New York: Penguin Classics.
20. Moon, J. D. (1993). Theory, citizenship, and democracy. In G. E. Marcus & R. L. Hanson, *Reconsidering the democratic public* (pp. 211–222). University Park, PA: The Pennsylvania State University Press.

ues of your audience members will *not* inform or persuade them. For example, let's say you want to give a persuasive speech on why abortion is morally wrong. It's your right to voice that opinion. Nevertheless, it's important that you build your case without offending your audience members— since you don't know everyone's history or stance on the subject. Showing disturbing pictures on your visual aid may not "make your point" in the way you intended. Instead, these pictures may send audience members into an emotional tailspin (making it difficult for them to hear your persuasive points because of their own psychological noise). Freedom of speech is a beautiful American value, but ethical speakers must learn to balance their speech freedom with their obligation to respect each audience member.

Fortunately for serious minds, a bias recognized is a bias sterilized. – Benjamin Haydon

Attributions

CC licensed content, Shared previously

- Image of boy with book. **Authored by**: cybrarian77. **Located at**: https://www.flickr.com/photos/cybrarian77/6284177707/in/photostream/. **License**: *CC BY-NC: Attribution-NonCommercial*

- Chapter 3 Ethical Speaking. **Authored by**: Alyssa Millner and Rachel Price. **Provided by**: King College and University of Kentucky. **Located at**: http://publicspeakingproject.org/psvirtualtext.html. **Project**: Public Speaking Project. **License**: *CC BY-NC-ND: Attribution-NonCommercial-NoDerivatives*

- ME 109 Thief. **Authored by**: Nina Paley. **Located at**: http://commons.wikimedia.org/wiki/File:ME_109_Thief.png. **License**: *CC BY-SA: Attribution-ShareAlike*

- RainbowDhalia quilt. **Authored by**: Holice E. Turnbow. **Located at**: http://commons.wikimedia.org/wiki/File:RainbowDhalia_quilt.jpg. **License**: *CC BY-SA: Attribution-ShareAlike*

- Question copyright. **Authored by**: Stephan Baum and ttog. **Located at**: http://commons.wikimedia.org/wiki/File:Question_copyright.svg. **License**: *CC BY-SA: Attribution-ShareAlike*

- Raising John T. Williams Memorial Totem Pole 300. **Authored by**: Joe Mabel. **Located at**: http://commons.wikimedia.org/wiki/File:Raising_John_T._Williams_Memorial_Totem_Pole_300.jpg. **License**: *CC BY-SA: Attribution-ShareAlike*

Public domain content

- F-15 pilots Elmendorf. **Authored by**: Tech. Sgt. Keith Brown. **Provided by**: US Air Force. **Located at**: http://commons.wikimedia.org/wiki/File:F-15_pilots_Elmendorf.jpg. **License**: *Public Domain: No Known Copyright*

Ethical Listening

Just as you hope others are attentive to your speech, it is important to know how to listen ethically—in effort to show respect to other speakers.

> *Jordan stood to give his presentation to the class. He knew he was knowledgeable about his chosen topic, the Chicago Bears football team, and had practiced for days, but public speaking always gave him anxiety. He asked for a show of hands during his attention getter, and only a few people acknowledged him. Jordan's anxiety worsened as he continued his speech. He noticed that many of his classmates were texting on their phones. Two girls on the right side were passing a note back and forth. When Jordan received his peer critique forms, most of his classmates simply said, "Good job" without giving any explanation. One of his classmates wrote, "Bears SUCK!"*

As we can see from the example above, communicating is not a one-way street. Jordan's peers were not being ethical listeners. All individuals involved in the communication process have ethical responsibilities. An ethical communicator tries to "understand and respect other communicators before evaluating and responding to their messages."[1] As you will learn in Chapter 4, listening is an important part of the public speaking process. Thus, this chapter will also outline the ethics of ethical listening. This section explains how to improve your listening skills and how to provide ethical feedback. Hearing happens physiologically, but listening is an art. The importance of ethical listening will be discussed first.

Develop Ethical Listening Skills

The act of hearing is what our body does physically; our ear takes in sound waves. However, when we interpret (or make sense of) those sound waves, that's called **listening**. Think about the last time you gave a speech. How did the audience members act? Do you remember the people that seemed most attentive? Those audience members were displaying traits of ethical listening. An **ethical listener** is one who actively interprets shared material and analyzes the content and speaker's effectiveness. Good listeners try to display respect for the speaker. Communicating respect for the speaker occurs when the listener: a) prepares to listen and b) listens with his or her whole body.

---

1. National Communication Association. (1999). NCA credo for ethical communication. Retrieved from http://www.natcom.org/uploadedFiles/About_NCA/Leadership_and_Governance/Public_Policy_Platform/PDF-PolicyPlatformNCA_Credo_for_Ethical_Communication.pdf

One way you can prepare yourself to listen is to get rid of distractions.[2] If you've selected a seat near the radiator and find it hard to hear over the noise, you may want to move before the speaker begins. If you had a fight with your friend before work that morning, you may want to take a moment to collect your thoughts and put the argument out of your mind—so that you can prevent internal distraction during the staff meeting presentation. As a professional, you are aware of the types of things and behaviors that distract you from the speaker; it is your obligation to manage these distractions before the speaker begins.

"Bored Students" by cybrarian77. CC-BY-NC.

In order to ethically listen, it's also imperative to listen with more than just your ears—your critical mind should also be at work. According to Sellnow,[3] two other things you can do to prepare are to avoid prejudging the speaker and refrain from jumping to conclusions while the speaker is talking. Effective listening can only occur when we're actually attending to the message. Conversely, listening is interrupted when we're pre-judging the speaker, stereotyping the speaker, or making mental counterarguments to the speaker's claims. You have the right to disagree with a speaker's content, but wait until the speaker is finished and has presented his or her whole argument to draw such a conclusion.

Ethical listening doesn't just take place inside the body. In order to show your attentiveness, it is necessary to consider how your body is listening. A listening posture enhances your ability to receive information and make sense of a message.[4] An attentive listening posture includes sitting up and remaining alert, keeping eye contact with the speaker and his or her visual aid, removing distractions from your area, and taking notes when necessary. Also, if you're enjoying a particular speaker, it's helpful to provide positive nonverbal cues like head-nodding, occasional smiling, and eye-contact. These practices can aid you in successful, ethical listening. However, know that listening is sometimes only the first step in this process—many times listeners are asked to provide feedback.

> Constructive criticism is about finding something good and positive to soften the blow to the real critique of what really went on. – Paula Abdul

Provide Ethical Feedback

Ethical speakers and listeners are able to provide quality feedback to others. **Ethical feedback** is a descriptive and explanatory response to the speaker. Brownell explains that a response to a speaker should demonstrate that you have listened and considered the content and delivery of the message.[5] Responses should respect the position of the speaker while being honest about your attitudes, values, and beliefs. Praising the speaker's message or delivery can help boost his or her confidence and encourage good speaking behaviors. However, ethical feedback does not always have to be positive in nature. Constructive criticism can point out flaws of the speaker while also making suggestions. Constructive criticism acknowledges that a

2. Sellnow, D. D. (2009). Confident public speaking: COM 181 at University of Kentucky. Mason, OH: Cengage Learning.
3. Sellnow 2009
4. Jaffe, C. (2010). *Public speaking: Concepts and skills for a diverse society* (6th Ed.). Boston, MA: Wadsworth Cengage Learning.
5. Brownell, J. (2006). *Listening: Attitudes, principles and skills* (3rd Ed.). Boston, MA: Allyn & Bacon

speaker is not perfect and can improve upon the content or delivery of the message. In fact, constructive criticism is helpful in perfecting a speaker's content or speaking style. Ethical feedback always explains the listener's opinion in detail. Figure 3.3 provides examples of unethical and ethical feedback.

Figure 3.3: Unethical and Ethical Feedback	
Unethical Feedback	• I really enjoyed your speech. • Your speech lacks supportive information. • You are the worst public speaker ever.
Ethical Feedback	• I really enjoyed your speech because your topic was personally interesting to me. • Your speech lacked supportive information. You didn't cite any outside information. Instead, your only source was you. • I believe your speech was ineffective because you were clearly unprepared and made no eye contact with the audience.

As you can see from the example feedback statements (Figure 3.3), ethical feedback is always explanatory. Ethical statements *explain* why you find the speaker effective or ineffective. Another guideline for ethical feedback is to "phrase your comments as personal perceptions" by using "I" language (Sellnow, 2009, p. 94). Feedback that employs the "I" pronoun displays personal preference regarding the speech and communicates responsibility for the comments. Feedback can focus on the speaker's delivery, content, style, visual aid, or attire. Be sure to support your claims—by giving a clear explanation of your opinion—when providing feedback to a speaker. Feedback should also support ethical communication behaviors from speakers by asking for more information and pointing out relevant information.[6] It is clear that providing ethical feedback is an important part of the listening process and, thus, of the public speaking process.

> A man without ethics is a wild beast loosed upon this world. – Albert Camus

Attributions

CC licensed content, Shared previously

---

6. Jensen, J. V. (1997). *Ethical issues in the communication process.* Mahwah, NJ: Lawrence Erlbaum.

Citation Tools

About the Use of Biblio-Makers

Do not trust biblio-makers! These citation robots are only as good as their programming, development, and data inputs. Seldom do they get an APA citation completely correct. This module will assist you in learning to cite sources using APA citation style. It is, however, difficult to avoid biblio-makers as they pop-up along with databases, library guides, proper citation searches, and some instructional materials.

A working bibliography can be created using biblio-makers, and the results can later be corrected using an accurate APA 6th edition handbook or similar resources. The more popular biblio-makers are:

- Citation Machine
- EasyBib
- Cite This For Me
- Citefast
- BibMe
- Bibomatic
- KnightCite
- Landmarks Citation Machine
- OttoBit
- Researchomatic
- Zotero

Some students may have a "style sheet" provided to them by an instructor in high school or college. These style sheets are frequently good enough to use for that instructor, but seldom meet the specifications required for APA. Learning to do APA citation properly is a skill that you can use throughout your college career.

APA Resources

- Owl Purdue APA Guide
- Basics of APA Flash tutorial
- How to cite art (APA Blog)
- Identifying a scholarly source (from Olympic College)
- Citing an edition of a book (APA Blog)
- Using "et al." (APA Blog)
- Citing a Kindle text (APA Blog)
- Citing a TED talk (APA Blog)
- Citing a YouTube video (APA Blog)
- Citing a website (APA Blog)
- Citing a song (APA Blog)

Crediting Creative Commons Photographs

When you use CC Licensed works, including images from Flickr and others, it is important to attribute the work correctly where you use it, and then to make a citation for it in your References page.

When it appears in your presentation, include the creator's name and the license for the work. On the References page use this sample citation:

Author name. (Author role). (date). Title of work [Medium of work], Retrieved date of retrieval from: tiny URL. License.

> USE Tiny URL.com (http://tinyurl.com/) to input the URL for any URLs that are over one line of characters. Just visit tinyurl.com and follow the directions to get a shorter URL.

Here is a sample of a CC Licensed work cited correctly including the attribution in the image and the citation for the reference page.

Weller, D. (Photographer). (2011). Baby monkey [Photograph]. Retrieved from http://tinyurl.com/ngcnjxj. CC-BY-SA-NC.

Intellectual Property Index

Did you know that anything you create is copyrighted? According to the US Copyright Law, any creative work fixed in time and space is protected from use, adaptation, and distribution by an entity or person who doesn't own it. In this section you will learn a little bit about your intellectual property rights.

This is not intended to be legal advice. Your instructors are not lawyers. This is intended to be an overview of the concept of intellectual property as it affects you.

Readings

- What is Intellectual Property
- What is Copyright by US Copyright Office
- Uncertainty, Copyright, and Courage by ASCAP president Paul Williams

Tutorials and Films

- Copyrights and Making Films by Turner Clay (This is a two minute film that can impact what you choose to film in your own works.)
    - https://youtu.be/CuMUKxCSv0I

Open Licensing

As discussed in the intellectual property section, under Title 17 of the US Code any creative expression that is fixed in time or space is a protected work. This means no one, aside from the person or entity who owns the copyright, can distribute the material without special permission. Some people want others to use their work freely, while still retaining some control over their work.

In this section you will learn about open licensing, or instances where the copyright law is loosened by copyright holders so that works can be shared and adapted. In this section you will also learn how to find images, songs, video, and other openly licensed works for use in your own videos. Don't forget to cite/attribute the works correctly. Use the section on APA citations to find out how to do that.

Readings

- Creative Commons: What is Creative Commons?
- Wired Magazine: Creative Commons 101
- The History of Creative Commons (Wired Magazine)
- Some Rights Reserved (Wired Magazine)
- Copyright Perspectives Remix Media (Penn State)
- Free Media Sources from Penn State
- Fifteen Fantastic Sources For Free Art and Images (MOOC News and Reviews)

Tutorials

Creative Commons: Skip the Intermediaries

- https://youtu.be/4dRPMnHQLL8

Finding Creative Commons Licensed Images

- https://youtu.be/iPY9O8hOa2g

Finding Creative Commons Licensed Music

- https://youtu.be/Q1vGICHIb1c

Pictures you can legally use:

- Library of Congress Photo Galleries http://www.loc.gov/pictures/
- NIH Photo Galleries http://www.nih.gov/about/nihphotos.htm
- Creative Commons is a great source for pictures, music, video, and text people have created for sharing: http://search.creativecommons.org/

Attributions

CC licensed content, Original

- Public Speaking. **Authored by**: Christie Fierro and Brent Adrian. **Provided by**: Lumen Learning. **Located at**: http://lumenlearning.com/. **Project**: Kaleidoscope Open Course Initiative. **License**: *CC BY: Attribution*

CC licensed content, Shared previously

- Why Copyrights. **Authored by**: Duke Law. **Located at**: http://youtu.be/CuMUKxCSv0I. **License**: *CC BY: Attribution*

All rights reserved content

- Find CC Licensed Images. **Authored by**: Quill West. **Located at**: http://youtu.be/iPY9O8hOa2g. **License**: *All Rights Reserved*. **License Terms**: Standard YouTube License
- Creative Commons Get Creative. **Authored by**: saythemslow. **Located at**: https://youtu.be/4dRPMnHQLL8. **License**: *All Rights Reserved*. **License Terms**: Standard YouTube License
- Using Jamendo for CC Licensed Music. **Authored by**: Quill West. **Located at**: http://youtu.be/Q1vGICHIb1c. **License**: *All Rights Reserved*. **License Terms**: Standard YouTube License

Conclusion, Review Questions, and Activities

This chapter addresses ethics in public speaking. As ethics is an important part of our daily lives, it also plays a significant role in any public speaking situation. This chapter defines ethics and provides guidelines for practicing ethics in public speaking and listening. An ethical public speaker considers how to be honest and avoid plagiarism by taking notes during the research process, identifying sources, and deciding when it is appropriate to cite sources. Ethical public speakers also cite sources properly by understanding how to paraphrase and directly quote sources. In addition, they know how to cite in written speech materials, during oral presentations, and on visual aids.

Ethical speakers strive to achieve responsible speech goals by promoting gender, racial, and cultural diversity, using inclusive language, refraining from using hate speech, raising social awareness about important issues when possible, and understanding the balance of free speech with responsibility to audience members. Lastly, this chapter discusses ethical listening. Listening is an important part of the public speaking situation. Ethical listeners consider their responsibilities when both listening and providing feedback to speakers. Ethical listeners should prepare to listen by removing distractions, avoiding prejudging the speaker, and listen with the whole body by giving supportive nonverbal feedback to the speaker. Ethical feedback is explanatory and descriptive. Ethical feedback can include both praise and constructive criticism. With this improved understanding of how to prepare and present a speech ethically, you can accomplish the goal of ethical public speaking. Consider ethics as you learn about the public speaking process in upcoming chapters.

"Shimer College conversation with students 2010" **by Shimer College.** CC-BY.

Review Questions

1. Where did ethics originate? How are ethics used in public speaking?

2. What is plagiarism? What is the difference between global and patchwork plagiarism?

3. What is the difference between paraphrasing and directly quoting a source?

4. What free speech rights are granted to a speaker?

5. Why is raising social awareness an ethical concern when preparing a speech?

6. What are some ways to use language ethically in presentations?

7. How is listening used in the public speaking setting? What are some guidelines for being an ethical listener?

Activities

1. Think about your ethical standards. Create a list of sources from which your ethical behaviors have originated. Who or what has influenced your ethics?

2. Review the NCA Credo of Ethics. How do you interpret this credo? How can you use the principles in your public speaking?

3. Split into groups of three to five students. As a group, develop 5 example situations of unethical behavior in public speaking. Once you are finished, switch situations with a different group. Decide how you can make changes to create ethical public speaking

behavior.

4. Think about the following scenarios involving an ethical dilemma. How would you react?

   - You attend a political debate on campus. The candidate's speech contains many ideas that you don't agree with. How can you be an ethical listener during the speech?

   - You are preparing to give a speech on a topic and realize that you have lost the citation information for one of your important sources. You can't seem to find this source again. What would you do to ethically prepare for the speech?

   - When practicing your speech on influential sports figures, you realize that you refer to the audience, your co-ed classmates, quite often as "you guys." Is this ethical language use? What changes would you make?

5. When preparing for your next speech, create an ethics journal. Write down the various ethical dilemmas as you encounter them. How did you decide what to do in these situations? What was the outcome?

Attributions

CC licensed content, Shared previously

- Chapter 3 Conclusion, Review Questions, and Activities. **Authored by**: Alyssa Millner and Rachel Price. **Provided by**: King College and University of Kentucky. **Located at**: http://publicspeakingproject.org/psvirtualtext.html. **Project**: Public Speaking Project. **License**: *CC BY-NC-ND: Attribution-NonCommercial-NoDerivatives*

- Shimer College conversation with students 2010. **Authored by**: Shimer College. **Located at**: http://en.wikipedia.org/wiki/Facilitator#mediaviewer/File:Shimer_College_conversation_with_students_2010.jpg. **License**: *CC BY: Attribution*

Glossary and References

Glossary

TERM	DEFINITION
Direct Quote	A direct quote is any sentence that conveys the primary source's idea word-for-word.
Diversity	Diversity is an appreciation for differences among individuals and groups.
Ethical Feedback	Ethical feedback is descriptive and explanatory feedback for a speaker. Ethical feedback can be positive praise or constructive criticism.
Ethical Listener	A listener who actively interprets shared material and analyzes the speech content and speaker's effectiveness.
Ethical Communication	Ethical communication is an exchange of responsible and trustworthy messages determined by our moral principles.
Ethical Standards	Rules of acceptable conduct, that when followed, promote values such as trust, good behavior, fairness and/or kindness.
Ethics	Ethics is the process of determining what is good or bad, right or wrong in a moral dilemma.
Global Plagiarism	Global plagiarism is plagiarism that occurs when a speaker uses an entire work that is not his/her own.
Hate Language	Hate language is the use of words or phrases that isolate a particular person or group in a derogatory manner.
Incremental Plagiarism	Incremental plagiarism is plagiarism that occurs when most of the speech is the speaker's original work, but quotes or other information have been used without being cited.
Listening	Listening is the process of interpreting, or making sense of, sounds.
Morality	Morality is the process of discerning between right and wrong.
Paraphrase	A paraphrase is any sentence that shares learned information in the speaker's own words.
Patchwork Plagiarism	Patchwork plagiarism is plagiarism that occurs when one patches together bits and pieces from one or more sources and represents the end result as his or her own.
Plagiarism	Plagiarism is when one passes off another's work as his/her own or neglects to cite a source for his/her information.
Social Awareness	Social awareness is the recognition of important issues that affect societies.
"We" Language	"We" Language includes the use of pronouns and phrases that unite the speaker to the audience.

References

ABC News. (2012, January 25). Albanese accused of plagiarising Hollywood speech. Retrieved from http://www.abc.net.au/news/2012 -01-25/albanese-accused-of- plagiarising-speech/3793486

American Psychological Association. (2010). *Publication Manual of the American Psychological Association* (6th ed.). Washington, DC: American Psychological Association.

Aristotle. (1954). *Rhetoric* (W. Rhys Roberts, Trans.). New York: Modern Library. Brownell, J. (2006). *Listening: Attrditudes, principles and skills* (3 Ed.). Boston, MA: Allyn & Bacon.

Centers for Disease Control and Prevention. (2012). Are you at high risk for serious illness from flu? Retrieved from http://www.cdc.gov/Features/Flu HighRisk/

Cruikshank, B. (2004). Plagiarism: It's Alive! *Texas Library Journal, 80(4)*, 132-136.

Danoff-Burg, J. (2002). PowerPoint writing guide. Retrieved from http://www.columbia.edu/itc/cerc /seeu/ dr/ppt_writing.html

Driscoll, D. L., & Brizee, A. (2010, July 13). Stereotypes and biased language. Retrieved from http://owl.english.purdue.edu/owl/resource/608/05

DuPre, A. (1998). Humor and the healing arts: A multimethod analysis of humor use in health care. Mahwah, NJ: Lawrence Erlbaum Associates.

Farhi, P. (2006, November 21). 'Seinfeld' comic Richards apologizes for racial rant. *The Washington Post.* Retrieved from http://www.washingtonpost.com/wp-dyn/content/article/2006/11/21/ AR2006112100242.html

Fisher, W. R. (1984). Narration as a human communication paradigm: The case of public moral argument. *Communication Monographs, 51*, 1-22.

Harper, G. K. (2007). Copyright Crash Course. Retrieved from http://copyright.lib.utexas.edu/copy-pol2.html

Iannarino, N. T. (2011, November). Shangri-Lost in the international house of cancer: An analysis of Julia Sweeney's humorous illness narrative [PowerPoint slides]. Retrieved from author [slide adapted and used via permission of N. Iannarino].

Jaffe, C. (2010). *Public speaking: Concepts & skills for a diverse and society* (6 Ed.). Boston, MA: Wadsworth Cengage Learning.

Jensen, J. V. (1997). *Ethical issues in the communication process.* Mahwah, NJ: Lawrence Erlbaum.

Johannesen, R. L. (1967). *Ethics and persuasion: Selected readings.* New York: Random House.

Langer, E. J. (1989). *Mindfulness.* Cambridge, MA: Da Capo Press.

Lucas, S. E. (2001) . *The art of public speaking* (7th ed.). New York: McGraw-Hill.

Merrill, J. C. (2009). Tenzin Gyatso, the Dalai Lama: Universal compassion. In C. Christians & J. Merrill (Eds.), *Ethical communication* (pp. 11-17). Columbia, MO: University of Missouri Press.

Mill, J.S. (1987). Utilitarianism. In A. Ryan (Ed.), *Utilitarianism and other essays* (pp. 272-338). New York: Penguin Classics.

Moon, J. D. (1993). Theory, citizenship, and democracy. In G. E. Marcus & R. L. Hanson, *Reconsidering the democratic public* (pp. 211-222). University Park, PA: The Pennsylvania State University Press.

National Communication Association. (1999). NCA credo for ethical communication. Retrieved from http://www.natcom.org/uploaded   Files/About_NCA/Leadership_and_Governance/Public_Policy_Platform/PDF-PolicyPlatform-NCA_Credo_for_Ethical_Communication.pdf

NBC News and news services. (2011, June 16). New York Rep. Anthony Weiner resigns. Retrieved from www.msnbc.msn.com/id/43425251/ns/politics-capitol_hill/#.T-VdoJErviE.

Nielsen, T. R. (1966). *Ethics of speech communication*. Indianapolis, IN: Bobbs Merrill.

Nine Planets. (2011). *The Sun*. Retrieved from http://nineplanets.org/sol.html

Nolo. (2010). What is fair use? Copyright and fair use, Stanford University Libraries. Retrieved from http://fairuse.stanford.edu/Copyright_and_Fair_Use_Overview/chapter9/9-a.html

O'Neill, M. T. (1980). Plagiarism: Writing Responsibly. *Business Communication Quarterly, 43*, 34-36.

Peace One Day. (n.d.). *Introduction*. Retrieved from http://www.peaceoneday.org/en/about/Introduction

Pegg, B. (2000, February 15). Chuck Berry biography. Retrieved from http://departments.colgate.edu/diw/pegg/CBBiography.html

Rohr, R. (2011). Falling upward: A spirituality for the two halves of life. San Francisco, CA: Jossey-Bass.

Schouten, M. H., & Page, S. (n.d.). For Rep. Anthony Weiner, a dramatic fall via social media. *USA Today*. Retrieved July 15, 2012, from http://www.usatoday.com/news/washington/2011-06-06-Anthony-weiner-sexting-twitter_n.htm

Sellnow, D. D. (2009). Confident public speaking: COM 181 at University of Kentucky. Mason, OH: Cengage Learning.

photo credits

p.1 Occupy Bay Street by Kelly Finnamore http://commons.wikimedia.org/wiki/File:Woman_speaking_about_ending_war.jpg

p.2 President Bill Clinton Jan 26 1998 http://www.youtube.com/watch?v=VBe_guezGGc

p. 3 Thai Buddha by Lisa Schreiber

p. 4 Copy without permission by Nina Paley http://commons.wikimedia.org/wiki/File:ME_109_Thief.png

p. 5 Rainbow dahlia by Holice Turnbow http://commons.wikimedia.org/wiki/File:RainbowDhalia_quilt.jpg

p. 8 Copyrightquestion by Stephan Baum http://commons.wikimedia.org/wiki/File:Question_copyright.svg

p. 8 U.S. F15 Jet Pilots by Tech. Sgt. Keith Brown
http://commons.wikimedia.org/wiki/File:F-15_pilots_Elmendorf.jpg

p. 9 Rise above the hate by RealDealDougR
http://commons.wikimedia.org/wiki/File:Rise_Above_Hate.jpg

p. 10 Older man speaking by Joe Mabel
http://commons.wikimedia.org/wiki/File:Raising_John_T._Williams_Memorial_Totem_Pole_300.jpg

Attributions

CC licensed content, Shared previously

- Chapter 3 Glossary and References. **Authored by**: Alyssa Millner and Rachel Price. **Provided by**: King College and University of Kentucky. **Located at**: http://publicspeakingproject.org/psvirtualtext.html. **Project**: Public Speaking Project. **License**: *CC BY-NC-ND: Attribution-NonCommercial-NoDerivatives*

Chapter 15: Speaking With Confidence

Objectives and Introduction

Speaking with Confidence

By Ronald P. Grapsy, Ph.D.
Kutztown University, Kutztown, PA

Learning Objectives

After reading this chapter, you should be able to:

- Understand the nature of communicative apprehension (CA), and be in a better position to deal with your particular "brand" of CA.

- Analyze objectively the formation of your habitual frame of reference.

- Apply cognitive restructuring (CR) techniques to create a more positive frame of reference.

- Understand the importance of customized practice to become conversant in your topic.

- Create a personal preparation routine to minimize your apprehension.

Introduction

"I have to do what?"

You receive your syllabus on the first day of history class, and you see that a significant percentage of your overall grade for the semester depends upon one, ten-minute oral presentation in front of the class. The presentation is to be based on an original research project and is due in eight weeks.

You are excited to get an email after a very positive job interview. They ask you to come to a second interview prepared to answer a number of questions from a panel made up of senior management. The questions are contained in an attachment. "Please be ready to stand in the front of the room to answer," the email reads; ending with "See you next week!"

The plans are finalized: You will have dinner to meet your new fiancé's family on Saturday night—just days away. But, then you are told that your fiancé's father, a former Marine and retired police officer, will want to talk about politics and current events—and that he will likely judge what sort of person you are based on how well you can defend your ideas.

I get nervous when I don't get nervous. If I'm nervous, I know I'm going to have a good show. – Beyonce Knowles

In this chapter, you will learn about dealing with one of the most common fears in our society: the **fear of public speaking**, which is referred to as *communication apprehension* (CA). If you are one of those folks—take comfort in the fact that you are not alone! Research indicates that 20% or more of the U.S. population has a high degree of communicative apprehension[1]. CA is an isolating phenomenon; something that makes one feel alone in the struggle. This is true even as programs designed to help people overcome it—like this program and this chapter, for instance—are spreading nationwide. CA is a real phenomenon that represents a well-documented obstacle not only to academic, but also to professional success. CA can impact many diverse areas; from one's level of self-esteem (Adler, 1980) and how you are perceived by others (Dwyer & Cruz, 1998), to success in school, achieving high grade-point averages, and even landing job interview opportunities (Daly & Leth, 1976). People with higher levels of CA have demonstrated that they will avoid communicative interaction in personal and professional relationships, social situations, and importantly, classrooms. Such avoidance can result in miscommunication and misunderstanding, which only becomes compounded by further avoidance. CA left unaddressed can even lead to a negative disposition toward public interaction, which leads to a lesser degree of engagement, thus perpetuating the fear and further compounding the situation (Menzel & Carrell, 1994). The anxiety creates a vicious cycle and becomes a self-fulfilling prophecy. But it is a cycle that need not continue.

---

1. (McCroskey, 1976)

By reading this chapter, you will learn about CA; not necessarily how it develops, as that can be different in every individual, but rather about how people can deal with it effectively. You will learn how therapies employed by psychologists to help people deal with phobias can be translated into effective techniques to deal with CA. You will learn the differences between *trait-anxiety*, *state-anxiety*, and *scrutiny fear*, and how understanding the differences between them can help a person deal with their "personal brand" of CA. You will learn about how

people develop habitual frames of reference that come to define the way they approach an anticipated experience—and how anyone can employ cognitive restructuring to help change habits that are counterproductive to delivering effective presentations. Habits can be very difficult to break, but the first step is becoming aware and wanting to succeed. Going into any activity with a positive attitude is one of the basic ways of maximizing performance. CA is not something that can easily be eliminated—turned "off" as if controlled by an internal toggle switch. But it doesn't have to remain an obstacle to success either.

Effective public speaking is not simply about learning what to say, but about developing the confidence to say it. For many, it all comes down to overcoming those nerves and convincing yourself that you can actually get up there and speak! Each individual deals with CA most effectively through increased self-awareness and a willingness to work on reducing its impact. To conquer the nervousness associated with public speaking, one must identify the factors that lead to this anxiety, and then take specific steps to overcome this apprehension.

> As soon as the fear approaches near, attack and destroy it. – Chanakya

Attributions

CC licensed content, Shared previously

Classifying Communication Apprehension (CA)

CA is not the result of a single cause, and so the phenomenon itself comes in many forms. It is important for each person to recognize that their particular sort of CA (we'll call it a "personal brand") is a phenomenon that has developed uniquely through each of their lives and experiences. Just as each individual is different, so too is each case of CA. There are specific distinctions between "stage fright"—a term reserved for the common, virtually universal nervousness felt by *everyone*—and CA—which is essentially "stage fright" with a corresponding emotional trauma attached. Scholars are somewhat divided, however, on whether CA is something inherent in the individual, or if it is the result of experience. In most people, it is very likely a combination of factors.

Trait-anxiety

Some researchers (McCroskey, et al. 1976) describe CA as **trait-anxiety**, meaning that it is a type of anxiety that is aligned with an individual's personality. People who would call themselves "shy" often seek to avoid interaction with others because they are uncertain of how they will be perceived. Avoiding such judgment is generally not difficult, and so becomes a pattern of behavior. These folks, according to researchers, are likely view any chance to express themselves publicly with skepticism and hesitation. This personal tendency is what is known as trait-anxiety.

State-anxiety

Other researchers (Beatty, 1988) describe CA as **state-anxiety**, meaning that it is a type of anxiety that is derived from the external situation which individuals find themselves. While some may fear public speaking due to some personal trait or broader social anxiety, researchers have found that CA more often stems from the fear associated with scrutiny and negative evaluation. Some people may have had a negative experience in public at an early age—they forgot a line in a play, they lost a spelling bee, they did poorly when called on in front of their class—something that resulted in a bit of public embarrassment. Others may have never actually experienced that stress themselves, but may have watched friends struggle and thus empathized with them. These sorts of experiences can often lead to the formation of a state-anxiety in an individual.

Scrutiny fear

Still other researchers (Mattick et al., 1989) discuss CA as what is called a **scrutiny fear**; which stems from an activity that does not necessarily involve interacting with other people, but is simply the fear of being in a situation where one is being watched or observed, or one perceives him or herself as being watched, while undertaking an activity. When asked to categorize their own type of CA, many people will identify with this phenomenon.

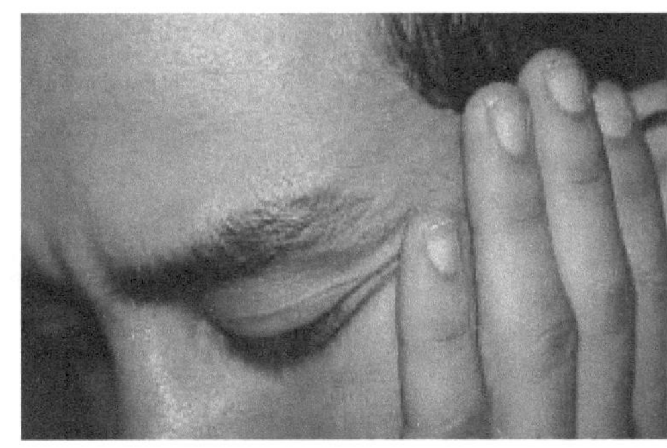

A person with their head in their hands

In order for anybody to effectively deal with CA, the first step is to consider what may be its primary cause. CA is what is known as a **resultant condition**; and those who are dealing with the challenge will recognize different intensities associated with different situations or triggers. This means that overcoming the condition requires first that you recognize, and then minimize, the cause. Each person is different, and so each case of CA is personal and unique. Trait-anxiety can be one contributing factor to CA, but is often part of a much larger condition. It is important to understand that, while the techniques discussed here would help in improving an individual's approach to public speaking opportunities, we do not claim that these techniques would work with more significant personality disorders. However, both the presence of state-anxiety, and the appearance of scrutiny fear, can be effectively addressed through the application of cognitive restructuring (CR) and careful, deliberate experience.

How little do they see what is, who frame their hasty judgments upon that which seems. – Robert Southey

Frames of Reference

Many popular movies are now based on multiple-book series like the "Harry Potter" or "Lord of the Rings" movies. If you are a fan of these book series, you know about the anticipation you felt as the next film was ready to be released—you get swept away by the memories, you look forward to seeing the characters again. Before you even enter the theatre and take your seat, you are in a very positive mood and you are looking forward to being entertained. Perhaps you are even familiar with the details of the story you are about to watch on film; and this only adds to your feelings of anticipation. Because of your previous experiences, you have developed a frame of reference toward future events. One's **frame of reference** is the context, viewpoint, or set of presuppositions or evaluative criteria within which a person's perception and thinking seem always to occur; and which constrains *selectively* the course and outcome of these activities. Once your anticipation is rewarded, this frame of reference becomes how you "approach" the release of each new film in the series—your frame of reference becomes "habitual." Evidence for this can be seen in the consistent success of the serial movies—even if critics' opinions are harsh, fans will go see the film.

Habitual Frame of Reference

Developing the habitual frame of reference with regard to public speaking usually comes from a combination of personal experiences and what has been witnessed. Formal public speaking opportunities are most prevalent within the context of formal education—thus, public presentations are generally student-oriented experiences which are strongly associated with being evaluated or judged. Because there is such a focus upon the grade that results from the assignment, there is much less focus upon the integrity of the presentation itself. Studies have even shown that the possibility of a negative experience can lead to many students to skip assignments or drop a class—even when that class is required for graduation (Pelias, 1989). Students will often worry more about their grade rather than what is contained in their presentation. Thus, the act of public speaking takes on the pressure of taking a final exam with everyone watching. It's no wonder so many students report that they are stressed out by public speaking!

Personal Frame of Reference

We can all recall a time when we've met a group of friends for lunch. Try to recall an instance when the conversation centered on the latest popular movie—and you happen to be the person in the group who saw it the night before. Was it fun? Was it worth the money? Should we go see it too? Everyone else around the table would look at you and wait to hear what you had to say. And what happened when you were faced with all these questions? Well, *probably* you focused on your favorite parts; *probably* you told the story in some sort of

organized manner; *probably* you asked your friends whether or not they wanted you to give away the ending; and *probably* you were fine with any of your friends interrupting while you were talking. In short, you *presented* to your audience. But, since the action of public presentation was not undertaken within the stressful context of a "graded assignment," but rather within the positive context of "lunch with friends," you did not feel the same level of CA as with other presentations. The action was essentially the same, but the way you approached the action was completely different—solely because you perceived of yourself engaging in a fun activity (lunch with friends), and not a stressful one (public speaking). Think about how many different experiences have prompted the formation of a habitual frame of reference in you: social events with friends, holidays with family, the weekly staff meeting at work. Consider whether the way you approach the situation has anything at all to do with the sort of experience that follows. Is there a correlation between positive mood and positive outcome? Think of all the motivational aphorisms and advice you've heard: "Think Positive!" or "Expect Success!" all of which are based on the idea that approaching an activity with a positive attitude about your potential success is the best strategy. We need to build a positive attitude about doing something we are afraid to do.

> I learned that courage was not the absence of fear, but the triumph over it. The brave man is not he who does not feel afraid, but he who conquers that fear. – Nelson Mandela

Attributions

CC licensed content, Shared previously

- Chapter 11 Frames of Reference. **Authored by**: Alyssa G. Millner, Ph.D. and Rachel D. Price, Ph.D.. **Provided by**: University of Central Arkansas, University of Arkansas at Little Rock & University of Kentucky and Southern Illinois University & University of Kentucky. **Located at**: http://publicspeakingproject.org/psvirtualtext.html. **Project**: Public Speaking Project. **License**: *CC BY-NC-ND: Attribution-NonCommercial-NoDerivatives*

- man on wire. **Authored by**: Alan. **Located at**: https://www.flickr.com/photos/image_munky/4441517406/. **License**: *CC BY-NC: Attribution-NonCommercial*

- Lunch. **Authored by**: Mark Doliner. **Located at**: https://www.flickr.com/photos/markdoliner/14146558086/. **License**: *CC BY: Attribution*

Cognitive Restructuring

Since the major difference between "presenting" to a public audience versus "presenting" to a small group of close friends involves one's attitude about the situation. Overcoming CA is as much a matter of changing one's attitude as it is developing one's skills as a speaker. A change in attitude can be fostered through a self-reflective regimen called **cognitive restructuring** (CR), which is an internal process through which individuals can deliberately adjust how they perceive an action or experience (Mattick et al., 1989).

Cognitive Restructuring is a three-step, internal process:

1. Identify objectively what you think
2. Identify any inconsistencies between perception and reality
3. Replace destructive thinking with supportive thinking

These steps are easy to understand, but perhaps may be a bit difficult to execute! The first step is to identify objectively what you are thinking as you approach a public speaking opportunity. Recall your habitual frame of reference. The first step in CR is to shine a bright light directly on it. This will be different for each student undertaking the process.

Sources of Apprehension

After years of interviewing students from my classes, the two concerns most often described are the feeling of being the center of attention—as if you are under some collective microscope with everybody's eyes on you; and the feeling that the audience is just waiting for you to make a mistake or slip up somehow—and that their disapproval will be swift, immediate, and embarrassing. Let's discuss how CR might be applied to each of these widely-held perceptions.

Impact of Apprehension

Probably the most common concern people have is being the "center of attention." When people describe this specific scrutiny fear, they use phrases like "everyone just stares at me," or "I don't like having all eyes on me." Consider for a moment what your experiences have been like when you have been a member of the audience for another speaker. Where did you look while the person spoke? Did you look at the speaker? Direct eye contact can mean different things in different cultures, but in U.S. culture, eye contact is the primary means for an audience to demonstrate that they are listening to a speaker. Nobody likes to be ignored, and most members of an audience would not want to be perceived as ignoring the speaker—that would be rude! Compare: before CR, the frame of reference reflects the idea that "everyone is staring at me"; after CR, the perception is altered to "the audience is looking at me to be supportive and polite—after all, I'm the one doing the talking."

Impact of Cognitive Restructuring	
Before Cognitive Restructuring	**After Cognitive Restructuring**
One is worried about being under scrutiny.	One recognizes that audiences look at who is speaking.
One is worried about being judged harshly.	One recognizes that audiences want success.
One is worried about making an embarrassing mistake.	One recognizes that audiences will empathize.

Another common concern is the fear of being judged harshly or making an embarrassing mistake. Go back to that memory of you as a member of the audience, but this time reflect on what sort of expectations you had at the time. Did you expect the speaker to be flawless and riveting? Did you have in mind some super-high level of performance—below which the speaker would have disappointed you? Probably you did not (unless you had the chance to watch some prominent speaker). Think back to any experiences you may have had watching another speaker struggle—perhaps a classmate during one of their presentations. Witnessing something like that can be uncomfortable. Did you feel empathy for the person struggling? Isn't it a much more pleasant experience when the speaker does well? Again, the vast majority of people empathize with the speaker when it comes to the quality of the presentation. They are willing to give the speaker a chance to say what they want to say. Thus: before CR, the frame of reference reflects the idea that "everyone is judging me harshly"; and after CR, the perception is altered to "the audience is willing to listen to what I have to say because it's a more pleasant experience for them if the speaker is successful."

Learning Confidence

Consider what comes into your mind if you are to deliver a public presentation. Are your thoughts consumed with many uncertainties. What if I make a mistake? What if they don't like what I'm talking about? What if? Try your own version of CR. Put yourself in the role of audience member and ask yourself whether your fears as a speaker are consistent with your expectations as an audience member. Remember that, just like you, the audience wants the speaker to succeed. Of course CR, unfortunately, is always easier said than done. It is a process that takes time, patience, and practice. The most important thing to remember is that you are trying CR as a means of breaking a habit, and habits are formed over periods of time, never instantaneously. The breaking of a habit, similarly, cannot be done instantaneously, but gradually, over time and with deliberate effort.

Changing your attitude is only one element in overcoming CA. The other involves improving your skills as a speaker. The presence of CA in any student brings with it the need to prepare more deliberately and more diligently. The other chapters in this book deal with the importance of preparation in all areas of public presentation. Readers should consider how the challenges involved with overcoming CA can impact the preparation process.

It usually takes me more than three weeks to prepare a good impromptu speech. – Mark Twain

Attributions

CC licensed content, Shared previously

- Chapter 11 Cognitive Restructuring. **Authored by**: Alyssa G. Millner, Ph.D. and Rachel D. Price, Ph.D.. **Provided by**: University of Central Arkansas, University of Arkansas at Little Rock & University of Kentucky and Southern Illinois University & University of Kentucky. **Located at**: http://publicspeakingproject.org/psvirtualtext.html. **Project**: Public Speaking Project. **License**: *CC BY-NC-ND: Attribution-NonCommercial-NoDerivatives*

- Tuvalu woman speaking on the climate threat her culture and nation face. **Authored by**: Takver. **Located at**: https://commons.wikimedia.org/wiki/File:Tuvalu_woman_speaking_on_the_climate_threat_her_culture_and_nation_face.jpg. **License**: *CC BY-SA: Attribution-ShareAlike*

Techniques for Building Confidence

Prepare Well

The correlation between preparation and nervousness is consistent. More practice results in less nervousness. The best, most consistent and direct way to minimize the level of nervousness you feel is through effective preparation. This is always true. Importantly, the best sort of practice is the kind that prepares you properly.

Michael Jordan was once asked the best way to learn how to shoot free throws. He said that you cannot learn to shoot free throws by walking into a gym with a ball, walking up to the line, and shooting. Instead, he described how the first step in learning to shoot free throws is to run sprints. Most importantly, his advice was to run until your body was under the same stress as it would be in a game when you needed to make those free throws—because only under those conditions would your practice become truly productive. *Only then* do you pick up the ball and shoot. And when you managed to catch your breath? All types of preparation and practice yield some benefits, but there is a significant difference between practice that is merely *helpful* and practice that is *sufficient*.

Michael Jordan at Boston Garden

There is a difference between "knowing what you are talking about," and "knowing what you are going to say." Thinking about your presentation can be helpful, but that sort of preparation will not give you a sense of what you are actually going to say. Athletes know that the best practices will re-create game conditions and test their abilities to perform in real-life scenarios. Studying a playbook? This is helpful, but not sufficient. Going over a speech in your mind? Again, it is helpful, but not sufficient.

Many students do not practice effectively, and this can result in the wrong idea that practice isn't helpful. Unfortunately, these same students usually have had little, if any, training in how one might prepare for a presentation, and so they employ the scholastic training they are most familiar with—how to write a paper. This is not the same activity as presenting, and so the lack of proper preparation only contributes to the lack of confidence. Let's look at a few elements of effective practice.

Visualize Success

Athletes and performers are often coached to visualize what they are trying to do as a way to perform correctly. Baseball players need to anticipate what they will do if the ball is hit their way so that they are ready to perform without having to make split-second choices. Football and basketball players must envision how each member of the team will move during a particular play because team success depends on speedy and flawless coordination between individuals. Dancers and divers are trained to visualize the form and positioning of their bodies as they execute their moves. Golfers are coached to visualize the flight and arc of the shot they are about to attempt. Engaging the imagination in this way can be beneficial to performance.

> I visualize things in my mind before I have to do them. It's like having a mental workshop. – Jack Youngblood

Speakers too, should visualize success. As you practice, visualize yourself presenting with confidence to a receptive audience. "See" your relaxed facial expressions and "hear" your confident vocal tone. Imagine yourself moving gracefully, complementing what you say with expressive gestures. Imagine the audience reacting appropriately—nodding appreciatively and giving thoughtful consideration to your points. Imagine the gratification of watching the audience really "get it." When you can honestly envision yourself performing at this level, you are taking an important step toward achieving that goal.

Avoid Gimmicks

Some acting coaches (and speech teachers) encourage their students to practice in front of mirrors, so that they can watch themselves perform and evaluate how they move. In acting, this can be very useful; but in speaking, it is less so. When you practice your presentation, the most important element is expressiveness. You want to become more familiar with the volume of material, the order in which you plan to present it, and the phrasing you think would be most effective to express it. Watching yourself perform in a mirror will focus your attention on your appearance first—and on what you express second. This makes using a mirror during practice a distraction from what the practice ought to achieve.

Plus, consider what you are seeing in the mirror as you practice. Obviously, it is you! But more to the point, what you see in the mirror (your reflection) will not resemble, in any way, the audience that you would see while delivering your presentation. Just as you want to visualize success in yourself as part of your preparation; you also want to visualize success in your audience—which means that you want to imagine the members of your audience reacting positively to your presentation, paying close attention and nodding their heads as you make your points.

For some reason, the myth persists that imagining your audience in their pajamas—or something similarly silly—is an effective way to make standing in front of them seem less scary. Many of my students have discussed hearing "tips" like imagining the audience wearing pink bunny-ears as a way to make them less intimidating. These sorts of gimmicks don't work! In fact, concentrating on anything other than what you are doing is distracting and not beneficial at all. Do your best to avoid such advice. Visualize success!

Breathe. Let go. And remind yourself that this very moment is the only one you know you have for sure. – Oprah Winfrey

Breathe and Release

One type of pre-presentation exercise that might be helpful is based on a therapeutic idea called **systematic de-sensitization**, which is a multi-stage regimen to help patients deal with phobias through coping mechanisms. Going through both the cognitive and behavioral aspects of systematic desensitization often requires weeks of concerted effort to overcome the body's involuntary reactions to stress. That sort of psychological therapy involves gradual exposure to what produces the anxiety, long-term self-reflection, and mental discipline. Here, we will discuss a shortened version called "**breathe and release.**" This is a short-cut relaxation technique that could be useful for nervous speakers—especially those who are concerned with the physical manifestations of nervousness, such as shaky hands or knees. The key to "breathe and release" is to understand that when nervous tension results in minor trembling, the effort of trying to keep one's hands from shaking can contribute to the whole situation—that is, trying to stop literally can make it worse! Therefore, the best approach is through relaxation.

"Breathe and Release" involves three steps:

1. Imagine the nervousness within your body. Imagine that energy bubbling inside you, like liquid being cooked.

2. Draw that energy to a high point within your body with a deep, cleansing breath. Imagine this cleansing breath to be acting like a vacuum—drawing up all of the bubbling liquid.

3. Release the energy by deliberately relaxing the entirety of your upper extremities—not just your hands, or even your hands and arms—but all the way from your fingertips to the bottom edges of your shoulder blades. Imagine how keeping any part of your upper extremities tense would result in a "kink" in the release valve, and so complete relaxation is the key to success. Remem-

ber: Relax *everything* from the fingertips to the very bottom edges of your shoulder blades.

"Breathe and Release" is something that can be done even as one walks to the front of the classroom or boardroom to begin speaking. Many speakers, especially those who are concerned about the physical manifestations of nervousness, have used this relaxation technique effectively.

> I've a grand memory for forgetting. – Robert Louis Stevenson

Minimize What You Memorize

One important hint for speech preparation involves avoiding the writing of an entirely scripted version of the presentation. Many people have the impression that writing a script of the entire speech is the necessary first step in preparation; that practicing can only happen after you are done writing the entire speech. Unfortunately, this common impression is mistaken. Remember that lunch with your friends? When you were describing the movie plot, you were being **conversant** in a prepared way. This means that you knew what you were describing, but you were not concerned with the specific words you were using. Being **conversant** is *the condition of being prepared to discuss an issue intelligently*. Fans of sports are conversant about their favorite teams. Experts are *conversant* in their fields. A well-prepared speaker is *conversant* with regard to her topic. Consider how being *conversant* in this manner allows freer, more fluid communication, with no stress associated with your ability to remember what words you wanted to use. Being conversant also gives the speaker the best chance to recognize and react to audience feedback. If you are completely focused on the integrity of scripted comments, then you will be unable to read and react to your audience in any meaningful way. Imagine how frustrating it would be for your friends at that lunch if you would not respond to any of their questions until you were finished reading a few descriptive paragraphs about the movie. They would probably just wait until you were done reading and then try to engage you in a conversation!

> If you wish to forget anything on the spot, make a note that this thing is to be remembered. – Edgar Allan Poe

Many people have had experience being in a stage play or some other type of performance that involved memorized recitation of a script. Many of us might recall moments during rehearsals when our minds would "freeze" and we might need just a quick reminder—the next word or phrase, the next few notes—to get back on track. This is because people do not memorize in units, but in phrases or chunks. The mind attaches to a rhythm—not to each individual unit, word, or note. This is why it is best to minimize what you memorize. Prepare your opening carefully so that you start smoothly. Prepare your closing comments so that you can end sharply and with style. But avoid preparing and then memorizing an entire script.

Preparing for a speech by memorizing a written script engages your mind at a different level from that of a *conversant* speaker. Concentrating on remembering words is different from paying attention to how one's audience is reacting. The pressure that arises from trying to remember the next word can be considerable, yet that pressure is entirely avoidable. The goal of public speaking should never be about loyal recreation of a script—it is about getting the appropriate response from your audience. Trying to remember an entirely scripted speech can result in the rather ironic situation of a person being able confidently and smoothly to discuss the topic in casual conversation, but still quite stressed about their ability to remember their scripted comments.

Many students forget their lines while discussing topics like their families and hometowns. Of course they knew what they were talking about, but their minds were focused on the task of remembering specific words—a task different from effective speaking. So, should you write any prepared comments at all? Yes, of course ,you should. Specifically, the feedback you should be most concerned with will happen during the body ,of the speech—when you are discussing the substance of your presentation. It is during the body of the speech when you need especially to retain the ability to adjust to how your audience reacts. Thus, memorizing your entire speech is ultimately detrimental to your ability to react to your audience. However, during the introduction and conclusion of your speech, the primary concerns are about connecting with your audience personally; which is something best assured through consistent eye contact. So, carefully preparing the introduction and the conclusion of your speech is a smart strategy—but don't make the mistake of scripting everything that you plan to say. The best rule here: Minimize what you memorize—familiarize instead!

If I don't train enough, of course I'm nervous. – Haile Gebrselassie

Practice Out Loud

Remember the very first time you tried to do anything—a game, a sport, an activity, anything at all. How good were you out of the gate? Perhaps you had talent or were gifted with a "feel" for what you were doing. But even then, didn't you get better with more experience? Nobody does anything the very best they can on their very first attempt, and everyone—even the most talented among us—will benefit from effective practice.

Speaking in public is no different from any other activity in this way. To maximize the chance that

your presentation will come out smooth and polished, you will need to hear it all the way through. By practicing out loud, from the beginning to the ending, you will be able to listen to your whole speech and properly gauge the flow of your entire presentation. Additionally, without at least one complete *out-loud practice*, there will be no way to accurately estimate the length of your speech and your preparation will remain insufficient. When dealing with CA, the last thing you want is to leave some questions unanswered in your own mind! The out-loud "dress rehearsal" is the single, most important element to your preparation. Without it, you will be delivering your presentation in full for the first time when it counts the most. Putting yourself at that sort of disadvantage isn't wise, and is easily avoided.

Consider your current method of preparing a public presentation. At some point, you will have gathered notes and information together. That represents an opportune moment for your first out-loud practice. You might even consider trying that initial practice without the benefit of any notes. Stand up; start speaking; see what comes out! Such a practice can serve as an "oral first draft" in the same vein as any written first draft of a paper, and can answer a number of questions for you:

1. Where, during your presentation, are you most—and least—conversant?

2. Where, during your presentation, are you most in need of supportive notes?

3. What do your notes need to contain?

Prepare for your public presentation by speaking and listening to yourself, rather than by writing, editing, and rewriting. Remember that when you are having a conversation, you never use the same sort of language and syntax as you do when you are writing a formal paper. Practice with the goal of becoming *conversant* in your topic, not fluent with a script.

> You can't hire someone to practice for you. – H. Jackson Brown, Jr.

Customize Your Practice

We've discussed a variety of techniques in this chapter; from the importance of out-loud practice to suggestions of when, during your preparation, you should start the out-loud practice. We've discussed Cognitive Restructuring as a means of changing your attitude about presenting in a positive way. Depending on your personal brand of CA, you may choose to implement these hints in different ways. Take a moment to reflect on what causes your CA. Do you dislike the feeling of being the center of attention? Are you more concerned with who is in the audience and what they might think of you? Or are you worried about "freezing" in front of the audience and forgetting what you wanted to say? Write some of these concerns down and put them into a priority order. If you are worried about a particular issue or problem, how might you prepare to minimize the chance of that issue arising?

Then consider your current method of preparation. Do you prepare more for a written paper than for an oral presentation? Do you have the goal of presenting a scripted message? Do you practice out loud? When, during your process, do you practice aloud? Do you practice at all *before* you begin to compose your speaking notes; or do you only practice after? Remember that dealing with CA often involves the breaking of a mental habit. It is a good idea to change what you have done previously. Be deliberate. Observe what works for your situation.

Recall what was discussed at the beginning of this chapter: CA is a condition unique to each person dealing with it. CA is the result of many varied causes—some internal and personal, some external and experiential. Dealing with anxiety may be as much dealing with your attitude as with your skills, as much a struggle with perception as with ability. Because of this, *you* are in the best position to know how to deal with your particular brand of CA. As stated earlier in the chapter: Each individual deals with CA most effectively through increased self-awareness and a willingness to take each of the steps in the entire process. After you acknowledge your reality, then you take the steps necessary to overcome apprehension. When you've read about the ways to overcome the debilitating impact of CA, the next steps in your process involve seeing what works best for you. Do not continue to prepare in exactly the same way as before. Speak more; write and revise less. Be sure to practice out-loud at least once during your preparation, in order to prepare yourself sufficiently. Reflect on your personal concerns and try Cognitive Restructuring on those concerns. Take your time. Do the work. Have confidence that your preparation will yield positive results.

Nothing in the affairs of men is worthy of great anxiety. – Plato

Attributions

CC licensed content, Shared previously

- Chapter 11 Techniques for Building Confidence. **Authored by**: Alyssa G. Millner, Ph.D. and Rachel D. Price, Ph.D.. **Provided by**: University of Central Arkansas, University of Arkansas at Little Rock & University of Kentucky and Southern Illinois University & University of Kentucky. **Located at**: http://publicspeakingproject.org/psvirtualtext.html. **Project**: Public Speaking Project. **License**: *CC BY-NC-ND: Attribution-NonCommercial-NoDerivatives*

- Kellee Santiago - Game Developers Conference 2010 - Day 1. **Authored by**: Official GDC. **Located at**: https://commons.wikimedia.org/wiki/File:Kellee_Santiago_-_Game_Developers_Conference_2010_-_Day_1.jpg. **License**: *CC BY: Attribution*

- Jordan by Lipofsky. **Authored by**: Steve Lipofsky. **Located at**: https://commons.wikimedia.org/wiki/File:Jordan_by_Lipofsky_16577.jpg. **License**: *CC BY-SA: Attribution-ShareAlike*. **License Terms**: Lipofski Basketballphoto.com

- Pitzer College Family Weekend 2015 Day 2. **Authored by**: Pitzer College. **Located at**: https://www.flickr.com/photos/pitzercollege/16637166915/. **License**: *CC BY: Attribution*

- Middle age. **Authored by**: Mu00e5ns Sandstru00f6m. **Located at**: https://commons.wikimedia.org/wiki/File:Middle_age.jpg. **License**: *CC BY: Attribution*

- NGF '08 Rita Levi-Montalcini. **Authored by**: audrey_sel. **Located at**: https://commons.wikimedia.org/wiki/File:NGF_%2708_Rita_Levi-Montalcini.jpg. **License**: *CC BY-SA: Attribution-ShareAlike*

- Chancellor giving speech. **Authored by**: University Leicester. **Located at**: https://www.flickr.com/photos/universityleicester/13289778263/. **License**: *CC BY-NC-ND: Attribution-NonCommercial-NoDerivatives*

Conclusion, Review Questions, and Activities

Conclusion

In this chapter, we've discussed *Communication Apprehension* or CA. This difficult condition can be the result of many, varied causes. Even professional researchers don't always agree on whether CA is inherent in the person, or the result of what the person experiences or perceives—with some calling it *"trait-anxiety;"* others *"state-anxiety;"* and still others classifying it as *"scrutiny fear."* The first step for any person to address this condition is self-reflection. Try to identify what has caused you to feel the way you do about public speaking. Careful introspection can result in a more productive level of self-awareness.

Whatever the root cause of CA might be for any particular individual, the first step in addressing CA is to objectively view the *habitual frame of reference* that has emerged in your mind regarding public speaking. Consider all those "what-if's" that keep cropping up in your mind and how you might begin to address them productively, rather than simply to ignore them and hope they go away. Go through the steps of *Cognitive Restructuring* or CR. Consider how many of those "what-if's" are nothing more than invented pressure that you place upon yourself.

Relaxation techniques, such as *"Breathe and Release,"* have proven to be effective for many speakers, especially those concerned with the physical manifestations of nervousness like trembling hands or shaky knees. Remember that those sorts of tremors can often be exacerbated by efforts to hold still. Don't force yourself to hold still! Relax instead.

Lastly, we discussed the most effective means to prepare—which is toward the goal of becoming *conversant* in your topic, rather than being able to recite a memorized script. By familiarizing yourself with your topic, you become better able to consider the best way to talk to your audience, rather than becoming "married to your script" and ultimately consumed with saying the words in the right order. Practicing out-loud, without a mirror to distract you, is the best way to prepare yourself.

CA is a real issue, but it need not be an obstacle to success. Take the time to become more aware of your personal brand of CA. Take positive steps to minimize its impact. Your willingness to work and your positive attitude are the keys to your success.

Believe you can and you're halfway there.- Theodore Roosevelt

Review Questions

1. What percentage of the general population is likely dealing with CA?

2. What are some of the potential issues or problems that can result from CA?

3. What are some of the different ways researchers classify CA? What are the differences between these ideas?

4. What are some of your sources of CA? Would you classify these as examples of trait-anxiety or state-anxiety?

5. How does Cognitive Restructuring work? Does it work the same for every person who tries it?

6. What does it mean to become conversant in your topic?

7. Why is memorizing a presentation a risky move? Is there any part of your presentation that should be memorized?

Activities

1. Prior to a speech, practice the following relaxation technique from Williams College (from http://wso.williams.edu/orgs/peerh/stress/relax.html):

   - Tighten the muscles in your toes. Hold for a count of 10. Relax and enjoy the sensation of release from tension.

   - Flex the muscles in your feet. Hold for a count of 10. Relax.

   - Move slowly up through your body—legs, abdomen, back, neck, face—contracting and relaxing muscles as you go.

   - Breathe deeply and slowly.

2. After your speech, evaluate the technique. Did you find that this exercise reduced your nervousness? If so, why do you think it was effective? If not, what technique do you think would have been more effective? Together with a partner or in a small group, generate a list of relaxation techniques that you currently use to relieve stress. Once you

have run out of ideas, review the list and eliminate the techniques that would not work for helping you cope with nervousness before a speech. Of the remaining ideas, select the top three that you believe would help you personally and that you would be willing to try.

3. The author of this chapter says that one of the keys to overcoming nervousness is preparation. Make a list of the barriers to your own preparation process (e.g. "I don't know how to use the library," or "I have young children at home who make demands on my time"). Having identified some of the things that make it difficult for you to prepare, now think of at least one way to overcome each obstacle you have listed. If you need to, speak with other people to get their ideas too.

Attributions

CC licensed content, Shared previously

- Chapter 11 Conclusion. **Authored by**: Alyssa G. Millner, Ph.D. and Rachel D. Price, Ph.D.. **Provided by**: University of Central Arkansas, University of Arkansas at Little Rock & University of Kentucky and Southern Illinois University & University of Kentucky. **Located at**: http://publicspeakingproject.org/psvirtualtext.html. **Project**: Public Speaking Project. **License**: *CC BY-NC-ND: Attribution-NonCommercial-NoDerivatives*

- Patrick Norton Veronica Belmont Tekzilla. **Authored by**: Tyler Howarth. **Located at**: https://commons.wikimedia.org/wiki/File:Patrick_Norton_Veronica_Belmont_Tekzilla.jpg. **License**: *CC BY: Attribution*

Glossary and References

Glossary

TERM	DEFINITION
"Breathe and Release"	This is a short-cut version of systematic de-sensitization appropriate for public speaking preparation.
Cognitive Restructuring (CR)	CR is an internal process through which individuals can deliberately adjust how they perceive an action or experience.
Communication Apprehension	CA is the anxiety resulting from fear of public speaking.
Conversant	Being conversant is the condition of being able to discuss an issue intelligently with others.
Frame of Reference	A frame of reference refers to the context, viewpoint, or set of presuppositions or of evaluative criteria within which a person's perception and thinking seem always to occur; and which constrains selectively the course and outcome of these activities.
Scrutiny Fear	Anxiety resulting from being in a situation where one is being watched or observed, or where one perceives themselves as being watched, is known as scrutiny fear. This sort of anxiety does not necessarily involve interacting with other people.
State-Anxiety	State-anxiety is derived from the external situation within which individuals find themselves.
Systematic De-sensitization	Systematic de-sensitization is a multi-stage, therapeutic regimen to help patients deal with phobias through coping mechanisms.
Trait-Anxiety	Trait-anxiety is anxiety that is aligned with, or a manifestation of, an individual's personality.

References

Adler, R. B., (1980). Integrating reticence management into the basic communication curriculum. Communication Education, 29, 215-221.

Beatty, M.J. (1988). Public speaking apprehension, decision-making errors in the selection of speech introduction strategies and adherence to strategy. Communication Education, 37, 297 – 311.

Daly, J. A. & Leth, S. A., (1976), Communication Apprehension and the Personnel Selection Decision, Paper presented at the International Communication Association Convention, Portland, OR. Dwyer, K. & Cruz, A (1998), Communication Apprehension, Personality, and Grades in the Basic Course: Are There Correlations? Communication Research Reports, 15(4), 436 – 444.

Mattick, R. P., Peters, L., & Clarke, J. C., (1989) Exposure and cognitive restructuring for social phobia: A controlled study. Behavior Therapy, 20, 3-23.

McCroskey, J. C., & Anderson, J. (1976). The relationship between communication apprehension and academic achievement among college students, Human Communication Research, 3, 73-81.

McCroskey, J. C. (1977). Oral Communication Apprehension: A summary of recent theory and research. Human Communication Research, 4, 78-96 McCroskey, J. C. (1984).

The communication apprehensive perspective. In J. A. Daly & J. C. McCroskey (Eds.), Avoiding communication: Shyness, reticence, and communication apprehension. Beverly Hills, CA: Sage Publications, Inc.

McCroskey, J. C. (1976) The Problem of Communication Apprehension in the Classroom, Paper prepared for the special edition of Communication, Journal of the Communication Association of the Pacific compiled for the C.A.P. Convention (Kobe, Japan, June 1976).

Menzel, K. E., &Carrell, L. J., (1994). The relationship between preparation and performance in public speaking, Communication Education, 43, 17-26.

Pelias, M. H. (1989). Communication apprehension in basic public speaking texts: An examination of contemporary textbooks. Communication Education, 38(1), 41- 53.

photo credits

p.   1 Rebiya   Kadeer   http://commons.wikimedia.org/wiki/File:Rebi   ya_Kadeer_Speaking_at_UN_Geneva_(3).jpg By United States Mission Geneva

p. 5 Tuvalu woman speaking http://commons.wikimedia.org/wiki/File:Tuva lu_woman_speaking_on_the_climate_threat_ her_culture_and_nation_face.jpg By Takver

p. 6 Michael Jordan http://commons.wikimedia.org/wiki/File:Jorda n_by_Lipofsky_16577.jpg By Steve Lipofsky

p. 6 Woman in wheelchair http://upload.wikimedia.org/wikipedia/commo ns/5/5a/USMC-111028-M-ZU667-58.jpg By Cpl. Andrew D. Thorburn

p. 7 Man speaking http://commons.wikimedia.org/wiki/File:Midd le_age.jpg By Måns Sandström

p.   8   98   year-old   mother   of   neuroscience   http://commons.wikimedia.org/wiki/File:NGF _%2708_Rita_Levi-Montalcini.jpg By Audrey_sel

p. 9 Kellee Santiago http://commons.wikimedia.org/wiki/File:Kelle e_Santiago_-_Game_Developers_Conference_2010_-_Day_1.jpg By Official GDC

p. 9 Two men http://commons.wikimedia.org/wiki/File:Kelle e_Santiago_-_Game_Developers_Conference _2010_-_Day_1.jpg By Official GDC

p. 10. Patrick Norton & Veronica Belmont http://commons.wikimedia.org/wiki/File:Patri ck_Norton_Veronica_Belmont_Tekzilla.jpg By Tyler Howarth

Attributions

Chapter 16: Group Presentations

Objectives and Introduction

Group Presentations

By: Jennifer F. Wood, Ph.D.
Millersville University, Millersville, PA

<table>
<tr><td>Learning Objectives</td></tr>
</table>

After reading this chapter, you should be able to:

- Identify the differences between a small group, a team, and a speaking group
- Evaluate your individual presentation skills
- Describe the four coordination elements of group presentations
- List the four common types of group presentations
- Apply chapter concepts for coordinating group communication
- Discuss techniques for coordinating a group assignment
- Plan speech organization for the intended audience
- Practice effective group delivery

Introduction

Imagine you have been assigned to a group for a project requiring a presentation at the end. "Now is the busiest time in my schedule and I do not have time to fit all these people into it," the voice in your head reminds you. Then you ask the question: "Is there ever a non-busy time for assembling a group together for a presentation?" These thoughts are a part of a group presentation assignment. The combined expertise of several individuals is becoming increasingly necessary in many **vocational** (related to a specific occupation) and **avocational** (outside a specific occupation) presentations.

Individual commitment to a group effort—that is what makes a team work, a company work, a society work, a civilization work. – Vince Lombardi

Group presentations in business may range from a business team exchanging sales data; research and development teams discussing business expansion ideas; to annual report presentations by boards of directors. Also, the government, private, and public sectors have many committees that participate in briefings, conference presentations, and other formal presentations. It is common for group presentations to be requested, created, and delivered to bring together the expertise of several people in one presentation. Thus, the task of deciding the most valuable information for audience members has become a coordination task involving several individuals. All group members are responsible for coordinating things such as themes, strong support/evidence, and different personalities and approaches in a specified time period. Coordination is defined in the dictionary as *harmonious combination or interaction, as of functions or parts*. This chapter focuses on how the group, the speech assignment, the audience, and the presentation design play a role in the harmonious combination of planning, organization, and delivery for group presentations.

A small group of thoughtful people could change the world. Indeed, it's the only thing that ever has. – Margaret Mead

Attributions

CC licensed content, Shared previously

- Chapter 18 Group Presentations Objectives, Outline, and Introduction. **Authored by**: Jennifer F. Wood, Ph.D.. **Located at**: http://publicspeakingproject.org/psvirtualtext.html. **Project**: Public Speaking Project. **License**: *CC BY-NC-ND: Attribution-Non-Commercial-NoDerivatives*

Public domain content

- US Navy 110907-N-PO203-063 Dr. Anthony Junior, left, education programs manager for the Office of Naval Research, moderates a panel discussion duri. **Authored by**: United States Navy. **Located at**: https://commons.wikimedia.org/wiki/File:US_Navy_110907-N-PO203-063_Dr._Anthony_Junior,_left,_education_programs_manager_for_the_Office_of_Naval_Research,_moderates_a_panel_discussion_duri.jpg. **License**: *Public Domain: No Known Copyright*

Communication about Group Interaction

Just say the two words separately "group" and "presentation." Note which word comes first—group (the process) and not presentation (the product). In group presentations, there is often a tendency to put the focus on "presentation." Thus, the group interaction often falls short to only include exchanging contact information and schedules before diving straight into the presentation assignment. Successful group work begins with something more than simply exchanging contact information. It begins with acknowledging the layers of "group interaction." **Small group inter-**  **action** is "the process by which three or more members of a group exchange verbal and nonverbal messages in an attempt to influence one another" (Tubbs, 1995, p. 5). Notice that the definition includes both verbal and nonverbal messages. Thus, all your individual actions and words, including silence or no response, communicate something to others. This is why group members are disappointed when other members do not attend group meetings. Their absence from the group communicates a nonverbal message.

Although "group" and "team" are often used interchangeably, the process of interaction between the two is different. Beebe & Mottet (2010) suggest that we think of groups and teams as existing on a continuum. On one end, a **small group** consists of three to fifteen people who share a common purpose, feel a sense of belonging to the group, and exert influence on each other (Beebe & Masterson, 2009). On the other end, a **team** is a coordinated group of people organized to work together to achieve a specific, common goal (Beebe & Masterson, 2009). Many—perhaps even most—vocational and avocational group members and size are determined by those who requested the group presentation. Whereas, vocational and avocational teams are guided by defined responsibilities for team members. For example, a public relations campaign team typically includes an account executive, research director, creative director, media planner and copywriter/copy editor. This chapter will not use the two terms interchangeably. It will focus on the interaction process of a group.

You may be most familiar with casual groups and social groups such as your fraternity or sorority or even your neighborhood. However, there are many types of groups formed everyday including committees, educational groups, problem-solving groups, task forces, work groups, and even virtual groups. In presentational speaking it is important to view the group as a **speaking group** , which is a collection of three or more speakers who come together to accomplish message content goals. The emphasis on "speakers" is critical because audience members come to a presentation for the speaker content and not necessarily the group's relationship. Speaking groups require all members to discuss and gain an understanding of one another's basic speaking skills related to preparation, organization, and delivery. In short, all groups require individuals to build harmony and rapport with one another but successful speaking groups are known more for their message continuity between speakers not the harmony between group members.

Group coordination is key in building message continuity. At its most basic level, group coordination focuses on **group communication**, "the process of creating meanings in the minds of others" (Tubbs, 1995, p. 186). Such coordination requires establishing shared meanings about interaction roles, the decision-making process, and conflict resolution. In short, the purpose of group coordination is to assist you in establishing a communication plan.

For many people, the mental image that forms when they hear they have been assigned to a group features some of their worst experiences or a quick private slideshow of their best group experience. Whether a negative or positive mental image, the image may be accurate of the past, but may have nothing to do with the current assignment. So when you first meet in your group, begin by coordinating an icebreaking conversation about each other's past experiences working in groups and more specifically experiences of working on previous group presentations of the *same* nature. This icebreaking conversation can play a powerful role in your group, establishing a communication plan for **cohesiveness,** or the tendency for a group to stick together and remain unified in the pursuit of its instrumental objectives (Carron, Brawley, & Widmeyer, 1998) and minimizing **social loafing**, the decreased effort of each individual member as the number of a group increases (Tubbs, 1995, p. 103). The conversation also will aid your group in a discussion concerning *what* communication vehicles and content will have priority for *this* speaking group.

> Review your work. You will find, if you are honest, that 90% of the trouble is traceable to loafing.
> – Ford Frick

Interaction Roles

Next, remember that groups are cooperative and require each member to participate in different interactions. Benne and Sheats (1948) proposed a classification of roles in three broad categories: (1) task roles, (2) group-building and maintenance roles, and (3) individual roles. Your group will need to discuss *how* they will communicate about and assign tasks related to preparation, organization and delivery (POD).

Task roles deal with a variety of logistics. Communication related to preparation include such things as guidelines for electronic information retrieval, sharing research information and visual aid content, and the scheduling of milestone appointments such as draft due dates and rehearsal times. Task roles emphasizing organization focus on script development—cohesive language, transitions, and consistent graphics. It is important that your group commits to *not* developing content independently. A group presentation is not an individual narrative. It is one master presentation. Therefore, the group must plan on how they will identify and close gaps in content and support material. Finally, task roles at the level of delivery necessitates that the group communicate about assumptions, such as every individual is familiar with presentation software like *PowerPoint* or every individual is a regular user of the videosharing website *YouTube*. Other logistical challenges associated with delivery include planning the introduction of the group, where to stand, and equipment set up.

Leadership is the capacity to translate vision into reality. – Warren G. Bennis

Table 18.1 Leaders' Responsibilities in Group Presentations	
Preparation	**Help build and maintain group communication about:** • Familiarity with the topic • Comfort level with research in this specific content area • Language and terminology barriers
Organization	**Assist members in solidifying commitments to:** • A group meeting schedule • Rehearsals • Honest status updates (establish a group atmosphere where members can indicate when they are behind; do not understand how to do something, or simply need a deadline extension)
Delivery	**Let members self-disclose about:** • What types of presentations each member has done in the past • Individual anxiety levels • Successes, failures, and no experience in group presentations in a similar setting (this may be related to different majors, topics, or modes of delivery)

In addition to task roles, group maintenance roles also play a vital role in the group's progress. Relationships within a group must be built and maintained simply because they are composed of individuals with different personalities, work styles, expertise, and availability. Your job as a group is to determine the best communication strategies for *this* speaking group. The strategies should support and enhance learning about and working with the differences. Although time restraints may limit the sophistication and quantity of your strategies, a communication plan for interaction roles should not  be skipped. The best place to start is by selecting a group leader with the most appropriate leadership style to help the group maintain credibility within the group, among the audience, in the assignment and its assessment, and during the delivery. Selection success hinges on everyone being familiar with leadership styles. Thus, all group members should be aware of three small-group leadership styles—highly directive, participatory, and negligent (Brilhart, Galanes & Adams, 2001). A *highly directive leadership style* is where a leader uses an authoritarian method of dealing with group members. The *participatory leadership style* centers around a designated leader who offers guidance, suggestions, listening, and concern for members while also showing concern for completing the task. A *negligent (or laissez-faire) leadership style* is characterized by a leader who offers little guidance or direction. The group leader may guide the communication planning by first initiating a conversation about what communication media are accessible to group members. Some group members may not have access to a smartphone, text capability or all social networking sites such as *Twitter*, *LinkedIn*, and *Facebook*; and may not have consistent access to email or the Internet. For example, it is not uncommon for a student in a class to have Internet access only during open lab or library hours. You should not assume everyone wants to use text messaging or email. Finally, keep in mind that some individual schedules or user-styles do not allow them to check email at the same daily frequency or dictate the same response style. All members should be careful not to criticize, judge or insult nonusers, limited users, and even overusers of technology. The focus of the conversation should be about commitment, that is, for *this* speaking group which communication vehicle(s) will each group member commit to using with some frequency in order to meet the group's assignment. The gathering of contact information may be accomplished within the context of this conversation. The group leader can facilitate communication about member experience in the areas of presentation planning, organization, and delivery (see Table 18.1).

Table 18.2 Group Member Responsibilities in Presentations	
Preparation	**Individually address questions such as:** • How do I prepare as an individual? • What is my experience with group work (limited, excessive, etc.)? • What is my familiarity with participatory communication modes in this setting?
Organization	**Keep the focus on yourself by asking:** • What is my knowledge related to the specific assignment? • What expertise do I have that can help the group within the time constraints?
Delivery	**Clearly think about:** • What degree of confidence do I need to develop about my own abilities? • What do I need to do to develop an interesting presentation? • What do I need to know about the audience to assess my comfort level? • What increases or decreases speech anxiety? • What do I need to do to forego a lengthy presentation and integrate simplicity? • What might I need to do in terms of dress?

Although a group leader is beneficial, each group member has a responsibility for his/her part of all interactions (refer to Table 18.2). See yourself as a co-equal partner in the group experience. Kelley (1992) suggests individuals be "skilled followers" who engage in two critical activities: (1) they are independent and critical thinkers, and (2) they actively engage in the work, rather than waiting to be told what to do.

You can contribute best by being aware of and monitoring your strengths and weakness and the effect they have on group members. You will always have to apply and modify your individual knowledge, skills, and techniques to be appropriate for the different stages of group presentations.

Further, you will need to maintain ethical relationship boundaries with group members as appropriate to your interaction roles. Thus, when interacting as a member of a new or returning group it is important to think about your familiarity with and use of participatory communication modes such as a preparedness to listen, assertiveness, clear verbal and nonverbal communication, confidence and empathy.

The great gift of human beings is that we have the power of empathy. – Meryl Streep

Decision-Making

Decision-making is not dictatorship. Plus, decision -making isn't the sole responsibility of a group leader. Decision-making is a group process of making choices among alternatives. In an individual presentation you made a lot of decisions on your own. Now it is time to come together as a group to make decisions (see Table 18.3). When you think about group coordination, decision-making is primarily about setting **protocols**—mutually agreed upon ways of interacting. As a group be very clear about how you will procedurally make decisions within *this* speaking group; and how the group will make decisions that require assimilating large amounts of information, exploring different ideas, or drawing on the many strands of experience represented among group members.

Table 18.3 Most Common Types of Decisions	
Yes/No & Focus on whether a group should do something or not:	**Either/Or:** Should we have handouts? • Should we pay for color copying?
This-or-That:	**Deciding between options:** • Should we use this inductive argument or that deductive argument? • Should we use an operational definition or a logical definition to define this concept?

Table 18.3 Most Common Types of Decisions

	Decisions put on hold until after certain decisions are met:
Contingency:	• Should we wait to determine visual aids until after we decide on how much technical language we use? • Should we wait to determine the binding for the written document until after we know how many people will attend?

The group may have to make decisions about the flow of information among members, proposed solutions, the quality of work, or even interpersonal relations among members. The goal is not to anticipate every possible decision your group may encounter. The goal is to know how *this* speaking group will make decisions. Successful principles to employ include group decisions always providing (1) a process for every group member's opinion to be heard within an explicit and articulated time period (deadlines are important); (2) a face-to-face voting method (rather than electronic); and (3) a procedure for prioritizing a set of options, ranking them, and choosing the best fit.

Table 18.4 DOs and DON'Ts of CONFLICT

DOs:	• Be open to compromise • Be willing to cooperate with others on their ideas • Be willing to discuss both strengths and weaknesses • Be willing to vote on disagreements • Avoid unpleasant or undesirable group activities
DON'Ts:	• Dominate group conversation and/or assignments • Sidetrack group meetings off the task at hand • Fail to complete agreed upon tasks • Destroy group harmony with attitudes about previous group experiences

Finally, each group member should remain flexible and learn how to accept newness, incompleteness, and how not to blame others. Thus, choose to be aware of three things. First, some decisions come in increments. Second, the amount of knowledge, understanding, and quality underlying a decision varies. Third, some things are discovered en route to the group's final outcome.

> Too many problem-solving sessions become battlegrounds where decisions are made based on power rather than intelligence. – Margaret J. Wheatley

Conflict Resolution

Perhaps the greatest interpersonal skill needed is the ability to work compatibly with others, regardless of whether or not you like them personally (Lahiff & Penrose 1997). Just because you have worked in groups before does not guarantee you have experienced all types of conflict. The conflict of ideas and conflict of feeling (personality conflict) are most common among members. The causes of conflict are many. They include incompatible personalities or value systems; competition for limited resources especially in a harsh economic climate; inadequate communication; interdependent tasks (where one person cannot complete his or her task until others have completed their work); organizational complexity and departmentalization; unreasonable or unclear policies, standards or rules; time pressure; role ambiguity; change; and inequitable treatment (Kreitner & Kinicki 1995): Foundational to successful group communication is each person's willingness to abide by some simple do's and don'ts of conflict (see Table 18.4). Successful conflict resolution also involves developing a sound negotiating strategy, which involves the overall approach you take when you exchange proposals and counterproposals with another person when discussing a settlement to a conflict (Beebe & Mottet, 2010, p. 195). By articulating a specific plan that addresses both conflict categories appropriately for this speaking group, group members gain a feel for what it will mean to balance between actively listening, doing his/her fair share, and soliciting comments throughout the process. The communication plan also may help your group reach consensus rather than engage in groupthink, which refers to a faulty sense of agreement that occurs when group members seemingly agree but they primarily want to avoid conflict (Beebe & Mottet, 2010, p. 239).

> If everyone is thinking alike, then somebody isn't thinking. – George S. Patton

Effective conflict management requires interpersonal and communication competence and draws on group members' active listening, assertiveness, empathy and clear communication skills. Keep in mind that any conflict is easier to create than resolve (deVito 1992). Overall group coordination will play a role in helping you reflect on group dynamics, plan for communication during group work, reinforce relationships, and establish a unified commitment and collaborative climate.

Attributions

CC licensed content, Shared previously

- Panel Discussion at the LCC.. **Authored by**: Alyssalevantinecenter. **Located at**: https://commons.wikimedia.org/wiki/File:Panel_Discussion_at_the_LCC..jpg. **License**: *CC BY-SA: Attribution-ShareAlike*

- Chapter 18 Group Presentations. **Authored by**: Jennifer F. Wood, Ph.D.. **Located at**: http://publicspeakingproject.org/psvirtualtext.html. **Project**: Public Speaking Project. **License**: *CC BY-NC-ND: Attribution-NonCommercial-NoDerivatives*

- actor-people-woman-speech. **Authored by**: JOSEPH. **Located at**: https://pixabay.com/en/actor-people-woman-speech-host-542726/. **License**: *CC0: No Rights Reserved*

- Microphone-active-talk-conference. **Authored by**: fill. **Located at**: https://pixabay.com/en/microphone-active-talk-conference-704255/. **License**: *CC0: No Rights Reserved*

- Group 5: Coastal Studies. **Authored by**: epeirogenic. **Located at**: https://www.flickr.com/photos/epeirogenic/3069880979/. **License**: *CC BY-NC: Attribution-NonCommercial*

- Panel Discussion Close-up, Science, Faith, and Technology. **Authored by**: David Bruce. **Located at**: https://commons.wikimedia.org/wiki/File:Panel_Discussion_Close-up,_Science,_Faith,_and_Technology.jpg. **License**: *CC BY-SA: Attribution-ShareAlike*

Preparing All Parts of the Assignment

Now it is time to think about the *what* of your presentation—the expected content. Many speaking groups are derived from an invitation to speak, and inherent in the invitation many times is a prescribed speaking assignment—or topic. In group presentations, you are working to coordinate one or two outcomes—outcomes related to the content (product outcomes) and/or outcomes related to the group skills and participation (process outcomes). Therefore, it is important to carefully review and outline the prescribed assignment of the group before you get large quantities of data, spreadsheets, interview notes and other research materials.

Types of Group Presentations

A key component of a preparation plan is the type of group presentation. Not all group presentations require a format of standing in front of an audience and presenting. According to Sprague (2005), there are four common types of group presentations.

A structured argument in which participants speak for or against a pre-announced proposition is called a very brief opening statements.

Finally, the **symposium** is a series of short speeches, usually informative, on various aspects of the same general topic. Audience questions often follow (p. 318).

These four types of presentations, along with the traditional group presentation in front an audience or on-the-job speaking, typically have pre-assigned parameters. Therefore, it is important that all group members are clear about the assignment request.

> Failure comes only when we forget our ideals and objectives and principles. – Jawaharlal Nehru

Establishing Clear Objectives

In order for the group to accurately summarize for themselves who is the audience, what is the situation/occasion, and what supporting materials need to be located and selected, the group should establish clear objectives about both *the process and the product* being assessed.

Assessment plays a central role in optimizing the quality of group interaction. Thus, it is important to be clear whether the group is being assessed on product(s) or outcome(s) only or will the processes within the group—such as equity of contribution, individual interaction with group members, and meeting deadlines—also be assessed. Kowitz and Knutson (1980) argue that three dimensions for group evaluation include (1) *informational*—dealing with the group's designated tasks; (2) *procedural*—referring to the ways in which the group coordinates its activities and communication; and (3) *interpersonal*—focusing on the relationships that exist among members while the task is being accomplished. Groups without a pre-assigned assessment rubric may use the three dimensions to effectively create a group evaluation instrument.

Table 18.5 Sample Product Assessment Guide:	
Accuracy:	• Did we edit and proofread to eliminate redundancy, grammatical, spelling and/or punctuation errors in all pieces including PowerPoint?
Approach:	• Is the tone appropriate to the purpose, audience and content?
Clarity:	• Is the central purpose clearly stated and maintained as the focal point?
Development:	• Is the material arranged in a coherent and logical sequence?
Style:	• Did we use action verbs, active voice and correct MLA or APA style?

The group should determine if the product includes both a written document and oral presentation. The written document and oral presentation format may have been pre-assigned with an expectation behind the requested informative and/or **debate**. The proposition is worded so that one side has the burden of proof, and that same side has the benefit of speaking first and last. Speakers assume an advocacy role and attempt to persuade the audience, not each other.

The **forum** is essentially a question-and-answer session. One or more experts may be questioned by a panel of other experts, journalists, and/or the audience.

A **panel** consists of a group of experts publicly discussing a topic among themselves. Individually prepared speeches, if any, are limited to persuasive content. Although the two should complement each other, the audience, message, and format for each should be clearly outlined. The group may create a product assessment guide (see Table 18.5). Additionally, each group member should uniformly write down the purpose of the assignment. You may think you can keep the purpose in your head without any problem. Yet the goal is for each member to consistently have the same outcome in front of them. This will bring your research, writing and thinking back to focus after engaging in a variety of resources or conversations.

Once the assignment has been coordinated in terms of the product and process objectives, type of presentation, and logistics, it is important for the group to clearly write down the agreed outcomes. Agreed outcomes about the product include a purpose statement that reflects an agreement with the prescribed assignment (i.e. "at the end of our group presentation the audience will be informed or persuaded about the prescribed assignment"). It also includes the key message or thesis to be developed through a ***presentation outline***, a full-sentence outline of virtually everything the speaker intends to say. The outline allows the speakers to test the structure, the logic, and persuasive appeals in the speech (DiSanza & Legge, 2012, p. 131).

> Failing to plan is planning to fail. – Alan Lakein

Logistics for Group Members

As a group, be very clear about the length of your presentation and its preparation. The length of the presentation refers to your time limit, and whether there is a question and answer period involved. Assignment preparation may or may not have a prescribed deadline. If the assignment does not have a deadline, then set one as a group. If there is a deadline, then the group begins by creating a schedule from the final deadline. As a group, create an *action timetable* explicitly listing all processes and outputs, as well as communication update points.

As a group decide the best way to leave enough time at the end to put all the pieces together and make sure everything is complete. If there is a written document, it should be completed prior to the oral presentation rather than at the same time. As a group, realize not everyone may work off a physical calendar. Thus, do not hesitate to require each member to write down all deadlines.Next, the group can strategically add meeting dates, times, and venues to the action timetable. A *meeting* is a structured conversation among a small group of people who gather to accomplish a specific task (Beebe & Mottet, 2010, p. 219). For group presentations, meetings do not always include the entire group. So a schedule of who meets with whom and when is useful for planning work and agendas. In addition, all meetings do not serve the same purpose. For example, *informational meetings* may be called simply to update all group members; *solicitation meetings* are called to solicit opinions or request guidance from group members; *group-building meetings* are designed to promote unity and cohesiveness among group members; and *problem-solving meetings* result in making decisions or recommendations by the time the meeting convenes.

Once the group is unified about the assignment objectives and time frame, it is vital to predetermine the type of note-taking required of each group member (which may vary) and the variety of information exchange. The more systematic a group is in these two areas, the more unified the process and the product. The system begins with each group member writing down the message, specific purpose, and central ideas for the group presentation. If these are still to be determined, then have each group member identify the areas of background information needed and basic information gathering. Next, simply create a general format for note-taking— whether typed or handwritten and what types of details should be included especially sources. Also with the increasing use of electronic databases be very clear on when related articles should be forwarded to group members. The email inbox flooded with PDF files is not always a welcome situation.

> True genius resides in the capacity for evaluation of uncertain, hazardous, and conflicting information. – Winston Churchill

The group should be clear on the explicit requirements for locating recent, relevant and audience-appropriate source material for the presentation. All of this leads to the foundation of clearly defining the responsibilities of each group member. All tasks should be listed, given deadlines, and assigned people. A means for tracking the progress of each task should be outlined. The group should be clear on what are individual, joint (involving more than one group member), and entire group tasks. Throughout the entire process, all group members should be supportive and helpful but should not offer to do other people's work.

Attributions

CC licensed content, Shared previously

- Chapter 18 Group Presentations. **Authored by**: Jennifer F. Wood, Ph.D.. **Located at**: http://publicspeakingproject.org/psvirtual-text.html. **Project**: Public Speaking Project. **License**: *CC BY-NC-ND: Attribution-NonCommercial-NoDerivatives*
- EMP Sound & Vision panel 01. **Authored by**: Joe Mabel. **Located at**: https://commons.wikimedia.org/wiki/File:EMP_Sound_%26_Vision_panel_01.jpg. **License**: *CC BY-SA: Attribution-ShareAlike*
- Jefferson City students educate the public about the Constitution. **Authored by**: KOMUnews. **Located at**: https://www.flickr.com/photos/komunews/15766300656/. **License**: *CC BY: Attribution*

Delivering Your Presentation as One

By completing the other three levels of coordination, the group will have decided on the key message, thoroughly researched the supporting material, developed logical conclusions, and created realistic recommendations. Therefore all that stands between you and success is the actual presentation—the vehicle that carries the facts and the ideas to your audience. Here it is important to recognize that if an assignment required both a written document and an oral presentation then be sure one effectively complements the other. Although you can reference the written document during the oral presentation, the oral presentation should be planned with the thought in mind that not everyone is given the written document. Therefore, the oral presentation may be the only content they receive. Since you will not always know who receives the written document, it is best to coordinate the presentation as if no one has the full written document, which can serve as reference tool for gaining content requiring further explanation or accessibility to detailed information. At the same time, if the entire audience is provided written material keep in mind different decision makers may be in the audience. For example, the creative director may be only interested in your creative concepts, whereas a vice president of finance may be only interested in figures.

The presentation preparation primarily focuses on your group's ability to develop a clear plan and execution of delivery. A delivery plan includes essential elements such as (1) purpose, (2) oral content, (3) dress, (4) room, (5) visuals, (6) delivery, and (7) rehearsal to ensure that the group presentation is both captivating and useful to your audience, as well as worth their time.

Purpose

Group members should keep at the forefront of their minds the answer to the question "Was the general purpose—to inform or to persuade— achieved?" As a group, practice keeping the purpose of the presentation explicit for the audience. The purpose should never become hidden during the presentation. Each group member's awareness of the purpose is important in maintaining the right kind of delivery. It is possible to have great content for a presentation and miss the entire purpose for the presentation. For example, say your group had been asked to do a presentation about *Facebook* and how it could be used  in the financial industry. You could take an informative or persuasive approach. However, if the audience—banking professionals—attends a presentation where the content is focused on *Facebook* rather than having a focus on its use in the financial industry, then the purpose was not achieved.

The delivery plan will help you evaluate if the purpose of the presentation is clearly aimed at the primary audience. In addition, the group can determine when and how clearly they are articulating the explicit purpose of the presentation. The purpose is complemented by a clear preview, the audience members' awareness of what decisions are at issue, and the audience's desire to get important information first.

Oral Content

Up to this point the majority of the group's engagement with the content has been in terms of reading and writing. It is time to orally interact with the selected content to ensure that it has been developed for *this* audience, properly structured, and clearly articulated. The delivery plan is a time to evaluate word choice, idioms, and antidotes. When working with this content, make sure that it is suited to the purpose, and that the key message is explicit so the audience remembers it well.

The introduction of group members, transitions, and internal summaries are all important elements of the delivery plan. A proper introduction of group members and content will not happen automatically. Therefore, it is important to practice it to determine if introductions fit better at the beginning of the presentation, if names need to be emphasized through the wearing of name tags, or if names are better used as a part of transition content. The use of name only may not be effective in some speaking situations. Therefore, it is important for the group to determine what a proper group member introduction includes beyond the name.

Plus, be consistent; that is, determine if everyone is using first name only or full name, do they need to know your positions, some background, or can you simply state it in a written format such as a team resume. Speech content is not useful if the audience does not accept your credibility.

> I dress to kill, but tastefully. – Freddie Mercury

Dress

As in all presentations, an awareness of your physical appearance is an important element in complementing the content of your speech. Do not hesitate to talk about and practice appropriate dress as a group. It is important to look like a group. Really consider defining a group's speaking uniform by deciding how formal or informal the dress code.

As a group, the overall question you want to be able to answer is: *Did our dress provide an accurate first impression not distracting from the content?* So what kinds of things can be distracting? The most common are colors, busy patterns, clothing that can be interpreted as seductive, and large or clinking jewelry. As a group determine what type of dress is effective in coordinating your group's credibility. It is important to take into consideration cultural, occupational and regional norms. In addition, it is important to think about branding choices. Often groups want to brand themselves for the audience. It is not necessary to mimic your audience. For example, a sales presentation to cranberry association members may entice a group to wear red. However, the cranberry association may not be the only sale your group needs to make so you will be forced to ask the question: Will each sales presentation audience determine the color we accent in dress? In short, do not let the speaking occasion brand you. Simply know what is considered professional for *this* presentation. You have spent a lot of time on preparing the content for this audience so do not detract from it.

Facilities

It is not always feasible to practice your delivery in the actual room where you will deliver your speech. However, it is extremely important that you actively plan your delivery for the room by recreating the speaking environment. If prior access to the room is not available, then you will need to do your planning by asking a series of questions of the presentation planner. Some common things to find out include the size of the room; if a projector is available and its location within the room; is there a platform and/or a stationary lectern; is there a sound system and how many microphones; where the group will be seated before being introduced; will the presentation be recorded; what is the availability of the room in advance of the presentation; and what is the number of seats and seating arrangement so the group can plan for the zone of interaction.

Visuals

The term visuals refers to both non-technology visual aids (handouts, posters, charts, etc.) and presentation technology. Visuals should not appear as though several individuals made them but rather as uniform to the group's presentation. All visuals should blend smoothly into the speech. All group members should be clear on what visuals or documents were pre-requested (so you do not eliminate them as unnecessary during rehearsal). Many times it is better to simply project or display visuals. At other times, visuals may need to be assembled in a presentation packet for all audience members. Bohn

& Jabusch (1982) suggest that there are several researched-based reasons why visual aids enhance presentations including (a) enhanced understanding—helps audience comprehend what they hear and see; (b) enhanced memory—serves as a visual reinforcement; (c) enhanced organization—visually displays your organizational strategy; (d) enhanced attention—grabs and maintains audience interest; and (e) enhanced sequencing—shows rather than describes.

Delivery

The four modes of delivery— memorized, impromptu, manuscript, and extemporaneous—are all valuable in group presentations. However, the most common mode of delivery is extemporaneous. Earlier in the chapter, developing a script was discussed. The step of transforming the script into a **delivery outline**—*an abbreviated version of the preparation outline* (DiSanza & Legge, 2012)—is a significant part of planning delivery. The ultimate goal is to figure out how the group can be confident that the entire presentation stays together and does

not just exist in pieces. The delivery outline may go as far as to stipulate vocal and gesture instructions. The delivery outline is not created to be read from, therefore, the group also should determine how speaker notes will be used. The delivery outline should be provided to every group member so everyone is familiar with the entire presentation. It is important to set up contingency plans for who will present content if someone is absent on the day of the presentation— the presenter who gets stuck in morning traffic or the professional who had a flight delay.

The key is for all group members to remain conversational in their delivery style. This may be best achieved by utilizing effective delivery strategies such as appropriate gestures, movement and posture; appropriate facial expressions including eye contact; and appropriate vocal delivery— articulation, dialect, pitch, pronunciation, rate, and volume. Group members should evaluate each other on audibility and fluency.

> One important key to success is self-confidence. An important key to self-confidence is preparation.
> – Arthur Ashe

Rehearsal

Rehearsals are for the final polishing of your presentations. It is a time to solidify logistics of how many group members are presenting, where they will stand, and the most appropriate transitions between each speaker. Group members should grow more comfortable with each other through rehearsals. A key aspect of polishing involves identifying gaps in content and gaining feedback on content (oral and visual), style, and delivery. The rehearsals are good time to refine speaker notes and to practice the time limit. The number of scheduled rehearsals is dependent on your group and the amount of preparation time provided. The most important element for the group is to adapt their rehearsal timetable based on an honest evaluation of the speaking skills represented within the group.

The only part of a group presentation that you may not be able to rehearse is responding to the *actual* audience members' questions and objections. However, you can anticipate the types of questions and practice a simple strategy of how you will respond— repeating the question, stating who from the group will respond, and answering succinctly. Four of the most common types of questions are follow-up questions; action-oriented questions focused on what would you do if; hypothetical questions focused on different scenarios; and information-seeking questions. A primary way to practice is to think of at least three questions you would like to answer, prepare the answer, and practice it during rehearsal(s).

Attributions

CC licensed content, Shared previously

- Chapter 18 Group Presentations. **Authored by**: Jennifer F. Wood, Ph.D.. **Located at**: http://publicspeakingproject.org/psvirtual-text.html. **Project**: Public Speaking Project. **License**: *CC BY-NC-ND: Attribution-NonCommercial-NoDerivatives*
- Churchill Club Top 10 Tech Trends Debate. **Authored by**: Steve Jurvetson. **Located at**: https://www.flickr.com/photos/jurvetson/5760456067/. **License**: *CC BY: Attribution*
- Presentation. **Authored by**: Marc Wathieu. **Located at**: https://www.flickr.com/photos/marcwathieu/6978659829/. **License**: *CC BY-NC-ND: Attribution-NonCommercial-NoDerivatives*

Organizing for Your Audience

In an earlier chapter, you learned about audience analysis. The analysis helps you create a profile. Organizing for your audience relates to the how the gathered content can be best arranged for them. According to Patricia Fripp (2011), a Hall of Fame keynote speaker and executive speech coach, any presentation can be intimidating but the key is to remember "your goal is to present the most valuable information possible to the members of the audience" (p. 16). Now what you think is most valuable and what the audience thinks is most valuable must be coordinated because of differences in perception (the process by which we give meaning to our experience). Therefore, organizing for your audience is focused on content, structure, packaging, and human element—not for you, not for the assignment, but for the audience. A customized plan of organization will assist your group in creating relevant messages that satisfy others' personal needs and goals (Keller, 1983).

> Act as if what you do makes a difference. It does. – William James

Content

Audience members are interested in your expertise that has been developed from solid research and preparation.

Audience members may have expectations about what foundational literature and key sources should be contained within your presentation. Therefore as a group you need to go beyond providing a variety of supporting material within your presentation to considering who will be present, levels of expertise and their expectations. In general, organizing the content should be focused on usage, knowledge levels, and objectives. First, *usage* refers to how audience members expect to use your presentational content which will help the group transform ideas into audience-centered speech points. Second, *knowledge level* means the audience's knowledge level about the topic within the audience which assists the group in developing supporting material for the entire audience. Third, the *objectives* are linked to how the content serves the audience's needs and assists the group in being intentional about helping the audience see the reason for their involvement and receive value for the time they devoted to attend. Overall, the content is coordinated in a way that keeps at the forefront who the decision makers are and what specifics they need to know, would be nice to know, and do not need to know.

Structure

Next professionally packaging a presentation for the audience deals with the structure or how you arrange points. The structure takes into consideration a strong opening, logical order, relevant key points, conciseness, and use of supplementary visual aids. In addition, the linking of points involves conversational language and the appropriate use of acronyms and technical jargon for inclusion or exclusion. The focus is geared to the perception of trustworthiness. Three strategic questions to answer include:

1. What qualities as a group will demonstrate your trustworthiness to this audience?

2. What content order needs to be achieved to give the consistent perception of fairness?

3. What content requires repeating and how should that be achieved—through comparisons, examples, illustrations, etc.?

Packaging

The packaging of successful group presentations revolves around the type of relationship with the audience, the division of time, and enthusiasm. An important dynamic of group presentations is for your group to know if audience members will be required to give an internal presentation or briefing from your presentation. As a group, know if you are packaging a one-time presentation, bidding for a long-term relationship, continuing a relationship for offering expertise, or if the presentation is tied to internal pressures to performance appraisals. Such knowledge will aid your group in developing talking points which can be re-presented with accuracy.

The type of presentation will help you divide the time for your presentation. The majority of the time is always spent on the body of the speech. A typical 30-minute speech might be divided into four minutes for the introduction, ten minutes for the body, and four minutes for the conclusion. The remainder 12 minutes is for the audience to ask questions, offer objections, or simply to become part of the discussion. It is important to leave enough time for the audience to contribute to the intellectual content. Therefore, always design group presentations with the intent not to run out of time before the audience can participate. All group presentations should have enthusiasm. Group members should be enthusiastic about the audience, message, and occasion. Planned enthusiasm should play a role in the creating the introduction, conclusion, and body of your presentations. The consistent use of enthusiasm can be planned throughout the speech outline.

Human Element

Now it is time to focus on compatibility. As a group consider what will it take to get this audience to pay attention to your presentation. Answer questions such as:

1. What can your group do to develop an introduction, transitions, and conclusions in a way to connect with this audience?

2. What types of stories are common or relatable to this audience?

3. What are the attitudes, beliefs, and values of this audience?

> What is success? I think it is a mixture of having a flair for the thing that you are doing; knowing that it is not enough, that you have got to have hard work and a certain sense of purpose. – Margaret Thatcher

Attributions

CC licensed content, Shared previously

- Chapter 18 Group Presentations. **Authored by**: Jennifer F. Wood, Ph.D.. **Located at**: http://publicspeakingproject.org/psvirtual-text.html. **Project**: Public Speaking Project. **License**: *CC BY-NC-ND: Attribution-NonCommercial-NoDerivatives*
- DMI conference. **Authored by**: Wiki4des. **Located at**: https://commons.wikimedia.org/wiki/File:DMI_conference.jpg. **License**: *CC BY: Attribution*

Conclusion, Review Questions, and Activities

Conclusion

The foundation of a group presentation is constructed from all the guidelines you use in an individual presentation coupled with additional strategies for working effectively with others. Group presentations primarily entail group communication, planning, organization, and delivery. Effective groups communicate about interaction roles, decision making, and conflict resolution. Such communication helps the group reflect on group dynamics, customize communication for *this* speaking group, and establish a unified commitment and collaborative climate.

After a group receives an invitation to speak, they begin by establishing clear objectives related to the group process and/or product. In addition, they direct their preparation by developing a unified understanding of the type of presentation, logistics, and agreed outcomes and debriefing. Preparation is foundational in guiding group research, writing, and thinking back to focus after engaging in a variety of resources or conversations.

The audience is at the core of the organizing content. A plan helps group members determine what to put in as well as leave out of the selected content. The group members work to establish group credibility and trustworthiness among their audience. In addition, the plan will assist the group in packaging for various types of *audience-centered presentations*—one-time presentations; presentations bidding for a long-term relationship; presentations continuing a relationship for offering expertise; or presentations tied to performance appraisals. The plan guides the group in determining the most compatible words, narratives, and enthusiasm to support their relevant messages.

Finally, presenting as one focuses on areas such as (1) purpose, (2) oral content, (3) dress, (4) room, (5) visuals, (6) delivery, and (7) rehearsal(s). The delivery plan allows the group to collectively be aware of their own communication and the communication of others. Also, the plan guides the group in transforming a written script or preparation outline into a delivery outline. Group members unify in elements of vocal and bodily delivery and style. However, most importantly together they identify gaps in content and gain feedback to polish oral and visual content.

Remember "delivering a dynamic presentation is not rocket science; however, it is a lot more complex than most people realize" (Fripp, 2011, p. 16).

Review Questions

1. List and explain the four coordination elements.
2. Define the three types of interaction roles.
3. Describe the difference between a group, a team, and a speaking group.
4. List and explain a characteristic of the three small-group leadership styles.
5. Define a skilled follower.
6. What are the two most common categories of conflict?
7. Describe the difference between process and product assessment.
8. What are the four common types of group presentations?
9. Define relevant messages.

Activities

1. In small groups of 3–4 people, create a presentation about a social media (*Facebook*, *Twitter*, music downloads, *LinkedIn*, photosharing, etc.) for a particular industry.
2. Describe in your journal an instance when you were both successful and unsuccessful in using participatory communication—participatory communication modes such as a pre-

> paredness to listen, assertiveness, clear verbal and nonverbal communication, confidence and empathy.
>
> 3. Before two focus groups, deliver a two-minute group presentation of a topic of your choice to a vocational audience and one to an avocational audience. Discuss the differences.

Attributions

CC licensed content, Shared previously

- Chapter 18 Group Presentations Conclusion, Review Questions, and Activities. **Authored by**: Jennifer F. Wood, Ph.D.. **Located at**: http://publicspeakingproject.org/psvirtualtext.html. **Project**: Public Speaking Project. **License**: *CC BY-NC-ND: Attribution-NonCommercial-NoDerivatives*

- Bali conference inside. **Authored by**: Oxfam International. **Located at**: https://commons.wikimedia.org/wiki/File:Bali_conference_inside.jpg. **License**: *CC BY: Attribution*

- Adam Michnik, Peter Schneider, Daniela Schwarzer, Andru00e9 Glucksmann, Ralf Fuu0308cks. **Authored by**: Heinrich-Bu00f6ll-Stiftung. **Located at**: https://www.flickr.com/photos/boellstiftung/6886589855/. **License**: *CC BY-SA: Attribution-ShareAlike*

Glossary and References

Glossary

TERM	DEFINITION
Avocational Presentations	Presentations outside of a specific occupation in which one engages.
Cohesiveness	The tendency for a group to stick together and remain unified in the pursuit of its instrumental objectives.
Debate	A structured argument in which participants speak for or against a pre-announced proposition. The proposition is worded so that one side has the burden of proof, and that same side has the benefit of speaking first and last. Speakers assume an advocacy role and attempt to persuade the audience, not each other.
Delivery Outline	An abbreviated version of the preparation outline.
Forum	Essentially a question-and-answer format. One or more experts may be questioned by a panel of other experts, journalists, and/or the audience.
Group Communication	The process of creating meanings in the minds of others.
Groupthink	A faulty sense of agreement that occurs when group members seemingly agree but they primarily want to avoid conflict.
Meeting	A structured conversation among a small group of people who gather to accomplish a specific task.
Negotiating Strategy	The overall approach you take when you exchange proposals and counterproposals with another person when discussing a settlement to a conflict.
Panel	A group of experts publicly discussing a topic among themselves. Individually prepared speeches, if any, are limited to very brief opening statements.
Preparation Outline	A full-sentence outline of virtually everything the speaker intends to say. It allows speakers to test the structure, the logic, and persuasive appeals in the speech.
Protocols	Mutually agreed upon ways of interacting.
Small Group	Consists of three to fifteen people who share a common purpose, feel a sense of belonging to the group, and exert influence on each other.
Small Group Interaction	The process by which three or more members of a group exchange verbal and nonverbal messages in an attempt to influence one another.
Social Loafing	The decreased effort of each individual member as the number of a group increases.
Speaking Group	A collection of three or more speakers who come together to accomplish pre-assigned message content goals.
Symposium	A series of short speeches, usually informative, on various aspects of the same general topic. Audience questions often follow.
Team	A coordinated group of people organized to work together to achieve a specific, common goal.
Vocational Presentations	Presentations related to a specific occupation.

References

Beebe, S.A. & Masterson, J.T. (2009). *Communicating in small groups: Principles and practices* (9th edition). Boston: Allyn & Bacon.

Beebe, S.A.& Mottet, T.P. (2010). *Business and professional communication: Principles and skills for leadership*. Boston: Allyn & Bacon.

Benne, K.D. & Sheats, P. (1948) . Functional roles of group members. *Journal of Social Issues 4*, 41-49.

Bohn, E. & Jabusch, D. (1982). The effect of four methods of instruction on the use of visual aids in speeches. *The Western Journal of Speech Communication, 46*, 253-265.

Brilhart, J.K., Galanes, G.J., & Adams, K. (2001). *Effective group discussions: Theory and practice* (10th edition). New York: McGraw-Hill.

Carron, A. V., Brawley, L. R., & Widmeyer, N. W. (1998). The measurement of cohesiveness in sports groups. In J. L. Duda (Ed.), *Advances in sport and exercise psychology measurement*. Morgantown, WV: Fitness Information Technology

deVito, J. 1992, *The interpersonal communication handbook* (6th edition). New York: Harper Collins.

Fripp. P. (2011). 9 timely tips for pre-presentation preparation. *American Salesman, 56*, 13-16.

Keller, J.M. (1983). Motivational design of instruction. In C.M. Reigeluth (Ed.), *Instructional design theories: An overview of their current status* (pp. 383-434). Hillsdale, NJ: Lawrence Erlbaum.

Kelley, R.E. (1992). *The power of followership: How to create leaders that people want to follow and followers who lead themselves*. New York: Doubleday/Currency.

Kowitz, A.C. & Knutson., T.J. (1980). *Decision making in small groups: The search for alternatives*. New York: Allyn and Bacon.

Kreitner, R. & Kinicki, A. (1995). *Organizational behaviour* (3rd edition). Chicago: Irwin.

Lahiff, J. & Penrose, J. 1997, *Business communication: Strategies and skills* (5th edition). Princeton, NJ: Prentice Hall.

Sprague, J. & Stuart D. (2005). *The speaker's handbook (7th edition)*. Belmont, CA: Thomson Wadsworth.

Tubbs, S. L. (1995). *A systematic approach to small group interaction* (5th edition). New York: McGraw-Hill, Inc.

Photo Credits

p. 1 World Diversity Leadership Summit by the United States Navy http://commons.wikimedia.org/wiki/File:US_Navy_110907-N-PO203-063_Dr.   _Anthony_Junior,_left,_education_programs_manager_for_the_Office_of_Naval_Research,_moderates_a_panel_discussion_ duri.jpg

p. 2 Panel Discussion at LCC by Alyssalevantinecenter http://commons.wikimedia.org/wiki/File:Panel_Discussion_at_the_LCC..jpg

p. 5 Science, Faith and Technology Panel Discussion by David Bruce http://commons.wikimedia.org/wiki/File:Panel_Discussion_Close-up,_Science,_Faith,_and_Technology.jpg

p. 6 EMP Sound and Vision Panel by Joe Mabel http://commons.wikimedia.org/wiki/File:EMP_Sound_%26_Vision_panel_01.jpg

p. 7 Design Management Institute Conference by Wiki4des http://commons.wikimedia.org/wiki/File:DMI_conference.jpg

p. 8 International Relief and Development Panel by Crespo Events, LLC http://commons.wikimedia.org/wiki/File:IRD_Sudan_Panel_with_Kojo_Nnamdi.jpg

p. 11 German Panel Discussion by Heinrich Boll Stiftung http://www.flickr.com/photos/boellstiftung/6886589855/in/photostream

p. 11 United Nations Conference Bali – by Oxfam International http://commons.wikimedia.org/wiki/File:Bali_conference_inside.jpg

Attributions

CC licensed content, Shared previously

Chapter 17: Speech Videos and Resources

50 Wise Speakers

50 Wise Public Speakers is a wonderful resource put together by Phil Vendetti at Clover Park Technical College in Tacoma, WA. Phil interviewed 50 prominent speakers, and his public speaking students edited the interviews and wrote transcripts for accessibility purposes.

- In the category section, you can search for speakers by genre.
- In the Questions section, you can search for topics like "overcoming stage fright."
- In the speakers section, you can search by name.

This wonderful trailer the students put together will give you an overview of the project:

- https://youtu.be/g2xuOCadUPw

Everything about the project is shared under a CC BY Open Educational License.

Here is a link to the website:
http://www.cptc.edu/fifty-wise/

Video: CC Licensed student example speeches

These students volunteered to share their speeches with a Creative Commons license.

Drew Lawson demonstrating wakeboarding – CC BY

- https://youtu.be/vvQkWjDLf4E

Joanne Eller demonstrating how to make chocolate covered strawberries filled with Grand Marnier. – CC BY NC

- https://youtu.be/qmly4i3sFS8

Heather Pederson demonstrating how to make Kimbap – CC BY NC ND

- https://youtu.be/PY4rqJnnFy0

Josh Davis demonstrating Reference Alignment – CC BY

- https://youtu.be/SVD9qChGXEg

Alexandra Kahler Informational Speech – CC By

- https://youtu.be/NjnpOe6QquI

- Josh Davis Demonstration Speech. **Authored by**: Christie Fierro. **Located at**: http://youtu.be/SVD9qChGXEg. **License**: *CC BY: Attribution*
- Alexandra Kahler Informational Speech. **Authored by**: Christie Fierro. **Located at**: http://youtu.be/NjnpOe6QquI. **License**: *CC BY: Attribution*

All rights reserved content

- Chocolate covered strawberries with Grand Marnier. **Authored by**: Joanne Moore. **Located at**: http://youtu.be/qmly4i3sFS8. **License**: *All Rights Reserved*. **License Terms**: Standard YouTube License

Video: Amy Cuddy "Your body language shapes who you are"

From TED.com: "Body language affects how others see us, but it may also change how we see ourselves. Social psychologist Amy Cuddy shows how 'power posing' — standing in a posture of confidence, even when we don't feel confident — can affect testosterone and cortisol levels in the brain, and might even have an impact on our chances for success."

This link has transcripts in multiple languages:

- https://youtu.be/Ks-_Mh1QhMc

Attributions

CC licensed content, Original

- Public Speaking. **Authored by**: Christie Fierro and Brent Adrian. **Provided by**: Lumen Learning. **Located at**: http://lumenlearning.com/. **Project**: Kaleidoscope Open Course Initiative. **License**: *CC BY: Attribution*

CC licensed content, Shared previously

- Amy Cuddy Your body language shapes who you are. **Authored by**: TED. **Located at**: http://youtu.be/Ks-_Mh1QhMc. **License**: *All Rights Reserved*. **License Terms**: Standard YouTube license

Video: Terry Moore - "How to tie your shoes"

From TED.com: "Terry Moore found out he'd been tying his shoes the wrong way his whole life. In the spirit of TED, he takes the stage to share a better way. (Historical note: This was the very first 3-minute audience talk given from the TED stage, in 2005.)"

- https://youtu.be/zAFcV7zuUDA

This link leads to the same talk with transcripts available:

http://www.ted.com/talks/terry_moore_how_to_tie_your_shoes

Video: Demonstration Speech - How to give the perfect man hug

From YouTube.com video description: "Don't get left behind, learn how to show your affection for your fellow man. Give a great man to man hug to your closest friends and family without getting that awkward feeling!"

- https://youtu.be/JUdWApwbudQ

Attributions

CC licensed content, Original

- Public Speaking. **Authored by**: Christie Fierro and Brent Adrian. **Provided by**: Lumen Learning. **Located at**: http://lumenlearning.com/. **Project**: Kaleidoscope Open Course Initiative. **License**: *CC BY: Attribution*

All rights reserved content

- How to give the perfect man hug. **Authored by**: Videojug. **Located at**: http://youtu.be/JUdWApwbudQ. **License**: *All Rights Reserved*. **License Terms**: Standard YouTube License

Video: Demonstration Speech - Easy Tube Pillow Case Tutorial

From YouTube description: "This is the easiest, cutest, quickest pillowcase you will ever make! If you are ready to move on from a generic pillowcase, try this fun and easy tutorial. Try it out to support the American Patchwork & Quilting Million Pillowcase Challenge (http://www.allpeoplequilt.com/millionpillowcases/)."

- https://youtu.be/MrYWCma9wgM

Video: Brene Brown - "The Power of Vulnerability"

From TED.com: "Brene Brown studies human connection — our ability to empathize, belong, love. In a poignant, funny talk at TEDxHouston, she shares a deep insight from her research, one that sent her on a personal quest to know herself as well as to understand humanity. A talk to share."

Follow this link for another version of the video with a transcript available: http://www.ted.com/talks/brene_brown_on_vulnerability?language=en

- https://youtu.be/iCvmsMzlF7o

Attributions

CC licensed content, Original

- Public Speaking. **Authored by**: Christie Fierro and Brent Adrian. **Provided by**: Lumen Learning. **Located at**: http://lumenlearning.com/. **Project**: Kaleidoscope Open Course Initiative. **License**: *CC BY: Attribution*

All rights reserved content

- Brene Brown The power of vulnerability. **Authored by**: TED. **Located at**: http://youtu.be/iCvmsMzlF7o. **License**: *All Rights Reserved*. **License Terms**: Standard YouTube License

Video: Elizabeth Lesser - "Take 'the other' to lunch"

From TED.com: "There's an angry divisive tension in the air that threatens to make modern politics impossible. Elizabeth Lesser explores the two sides of human nature within us (call them "the mystic" and "the warrior") that can be harnessed to elevate the way we treat each other. She shares a simple way to begin real dialogue — by going to lunch with someone who doesn't agree with you, and asking them three questions to find out what's really in their hearts."

Follow this link for the same video with transcripts available: http://www.ted.com/talks/elizabeth_lesser_take_the_other_to_lunch

- https://youtu.be/AsSd2nmoKNA

Attributions

CC licensed content, Original